O9-BTM-765

(Continued on back endsheets)

MIDDLEBURY COLLEGE

THE EGBERT STARR LIBRARY

Dictionary of Literary Biography® • Volume One Hundred Twenty

American Poets Since World War II
Third Series

Dictionary of Literary Biography® • Volume One Hundred Twenty

American Poets Since World War II
Third Series

Edited by
R. S. Gwynn
Lamar University

A Bruccoli Clark Layman Book
Gale Research Inc.
Detroit, London

MIDDLEBURY COLLEGE LIBRARY

Advisory Board for
DICTIONARY OF LITERARY BIOGRAPHY

John Baker
William Cagle
Jane Christensen
Patrick O'Connor
Peter S. Prescott

Matthew J. Bruccoli and Richard Layman, *Editorial Directors*
C. E. Frazer Clark, Jr., *Managing Editor*
Karen L. Rood, *Senior Editor*

Printed in the United States of America

Published simultaneously in the United Kingdom
by Gale Research International Limited
(An affiliated company of Gale Research Inc.)

The paper used in this publication meets the minimum requirements
of American National Standard for Information Sciences—Permanence
Paper for Printed Library Materials, ANSI Z39.48-1984. ∞™

This publication is a creative work copyrighted by Gale Research Inc. and fully protected by all applicable copyright laws, as well as by misappropriation, trade secret, unfair competition, and other applicable laws. The authors and editors of this work have added value to the underlying factual material herein through one or more of the following: unique and original selection, coordination, expression, arrangement, and classification of the information.

Gale Research Inc. will vigorously defend all
of its rights in this publication.

Copyright © 1992 by Gale Research Inc.
835 Penobscot Building
Detroit, MI 48226

All rights reserved including the right of reproduction in
whole or in part in any form.

Library of Congress Catalog Card Number 92-25459
ISBN 0-8103-7597-4

In Memoriam
Judson Jerome (1927-1991)
American Poet

Contents

Contents

Plan of the Series

. . . Almost the most prodigious asset of a country, and perhaps its most precious possession, is its native literary product—when that product is fine and noble and enduring.

Mark Twain*

The advisory board, the editors, and the publisher of the *Dictionary of Literary Biography* are joined in endorsing Mark Twain's declaration. The literature of a nation provides an inexhaustible resource of permanent worth. We intend to make literature and its creators better understood and more accessible to students and the reading public, while satisfying the standards of teachers and scholars.

To meet these requirements, *literary biography* has been construed in terms of the author's achievement. The most important thing about a writer is his writing. Accordingly, the entries in *DLB* are career biographies, tracing the development of the author's canon and the evolution of his reputation.

The purpose of *DLB* is not only to provide reliable information in a convenient format but also to place the figures in the larger perspective of literary history and to offer appraisals of their accomplishments by qualified scholars.

The publication plan for *DLB* resulted from two years of preparation. The project was proposed to Bruccoli Clark by Frederick C. Ruffner, president of the Gale Research Company, in November 1975. After specimen entries were prepared and typeset, an advisory board was formed to refine the entry format and develop the series rationale. In meetings held during 1976, the publisher, series editors, and advisory board approved the scheme for a comprehensive biographical dictionary of persons who contributed to North American literature. Editorial work on the first volume began in January 1977, and it was published in 1978. In order to make *DLB* more than a reference tool and to compile volumes

that individually have claim to status as literary history, it was decided to organize volumes by topic, period, or genre. Each of these freestanding volumes provides a biographical-bibliographical guide and overview for a particular area of literature. We are convinced that this organization—as opposed to a single alphabet method—constitutes a valuable innovation in the presentation of reference material. The volume plan necessarily requires many decisions for the placement and treatment of authors who might properly be included in two or three volumes. In some instances a major figure will be included in separate volumes, but with different entries emphasizing the aspect of his career appropriate to each volume. Ernest Hemingway, for example, is represented in *American Writers in Paris, 1920-1939* by an entry focusing on his expatriate apprenticeship; he is also in *American Novelists, 1910-1945* with an entry surveying his entire career. Each volume includes a cumulative index of the subject authors and articles. Comprehensive indexes to the entire series are planned.

With volume ten in 1982 it was decided to enlarge the scope of *DLB*. By the end of 1986 twenty-one volumes treating British literature had been published, and volumes for Commonwealth and Modern European literature were in progress. The series has been further augmented by the *DLB Yearbooks* (since 1981) which update published entries and add new entries to keep the *DLB* current with contemporary activity. There have also been *DLB Documentary Series* volumes which provide biographical and critical source materials for figures whose work is judged to have particular interest for students. One of these companion volumes is entirely devoted to Tennessee Williams.

We define literature as the *intellectual commerce of a nation:* not merely as belles lettres but as that ample and complex process by which ideas are generated, shaped, and transmitted. *DLB* entries are not limited to "creative writers" but extend to other figures who in their time and in their way influenced the mind of a people. Thus the series encompasses historians, journalists, publishers, and screenwriters. By this means

*From an unpublished section of Mark Twain's autobiography, copyright © by the Mark Twain Company

ix

readers of *DLB* may be aided to perceive literature not as cult scripture in the keeping of intellectual high priests but firmly positioned at the center of a nation's life.

DLB includes the major writers appropriate to each volume and those standing in the ranks immediately behind them. Scholarly and critical counsel has been sought in deciding which minor figures to include and how full their entries should be. Wherever possible, useful references are made to figures who do not warrant separate entries.

Each *DLB* volume has a volume editor responsible for planning the volume, selecting the figures for inclusion, and assigning the entries. Volume editors are also responsible for preparing, where appropriate, appendices surveying the major periodicals and literary and intellectual movements for their volumes, as well as lists of further readings. Work on the series as a whole is coordinated at the Bruccoli Clark Layman editorial center in Columbia, South Carolina, where the editorial staff is responsible for accuracy of the published volumes.

One feature that distinguishes *DLB* is the illustration policy—its concern with the iconography of literature. Just as an author is influenced by his surroundings, so is the reader's understanding of the author enhanced by a knowledge of his environment. Therefore *DLB* volumes include not only drawings, paintings, and photographs of authors, often depicting them at various stages in their careers, but also illustrations of their families and places where they lived. Title pages are regularly reproduced in facsimile along with dust jackets for modern authors. The dust jackets are a special feature of *DLB* because they often document better than anything else the way in which an author's work was perceived in its own time. Specimens of the writers' manuscripts are included when feasible.

Samuel Johnson rightly decreed that "The chief glory of every people arises from its authors." The purpose of the *Dictionary of Literary Biography* is to compile literary history in the surest way available to us—by accurate and comprehensive treatment of the lives and work of those who contributed to it.

The *DLB* Advisory Board

Introduction

In 1980 *DLB 5: American Poets Since World War II*, edited by Donald J. Greiner, was published in two volumes, with essays on the lives and literary careers of many poets whose birth dates ranged from 1904 to 1950. When work on the second series began in 1988, the intent was to provide essays on important poets born between 1920 and 1960. As the completed articles began to arrive, it became apparent that there would be too much material for a single volume, and thus an editorial decision was made to publish a third series as well. *DLB 105: American Poets Since World War II*, Second Series (1991), includes entries for thirty poets born before 7 December 1941. The present volume was originally planned to treat only poets born after Pearl Harbor Day. However, because it seemed imperative to include several poets of distinct achievement who have not been discussed in other volumes of the *DLB*, that date has been pushed back: the poets covered in this volume were born between the late 1920s and the mid 1950s. All of them have published at least two full-length collections and have had work included in at least one major anthology.

In *DLB Yearbook: 1986* is Ronald Baughman's essay "A Field Guide to Recent Schools of American Poetry." Following the leads of poet and anthologist Donald Hall and critic Ralph J. Mills, Jr., Baughman noted that the modernist orthodoxy that prevailed during the first half of the twentieth century met with serious challenges at the beginning of the second half: "After World War II, most American poets rebelled against the requirements for poetry established by [T. S.] Eliot and the New Criticism and instead placed emphasis on the writer's personality, the writer's self. This reversal is perhaps the single most important occurrence in the poetry of the postwar decades." Baughman's taxonomy divides American poets among eight "schools," which shared little save that their members were contemporaries and were writing in the same language: Academic poets, Concretists, Confessional poets, those of the Black Mountain School, Deep Imagists, those of the New York School, the Beat Generation, and practitioners of the New Black Aes-

thetic. While readers are referred to Baughman's essay for his comments on the most prominent members of each group, a few general statements should perhaps be made here about these groups, which seemed so vital only a couple of decades ago but are quickly fading into the pages of literary history.

First, most of the writers mentioned by Baughman are now in their twilight, having published collected editions that represent the summing up of their careers. They have won the important prizes, and a few have even served as poet laureate, a position established in 1986 and filled since that time by Robert Penn Warren, Richard Wilbur, Howard Nemerov, Mark Strand, Joseph Brodsky, and, most recently, Mona Van Duyn. Two of these senior poets, Warren and Nemerov, have died, and, while one still looks with expectations to the publication of books by Wilbur or Strand or by other major poets such as James Dickey, Gwendolyn Brooks, or Allen Ginsberg, it is not likely that they will depart significantly from their established manners and matters in any new work. Throughout the 1980s one sensed that the torch was passing to a new generation, and as we move into the 1990s the transfer of power is more or less complete.

Second, and perhaps more important, the members of the younger generation of poets covered in this volume seem reluctant to call themselves members of the existing schools identified by Baughman. It is unlikely that any contemporary poet under fifty would refer to himself or herself as a "confessionalist" or "deep imagist." Most of these poets, who were learning their craft when the schools were at their height, absorbed diverse influences in their early careers and have arrived at poetic styles that, with only a few exceptions, are not readily distinguishable from each other. A relaxed, conversational idiom; a restrained rhetoric which employs tropes only sparingly; and fairly uniform free verse lines, more often than not arranged in stanzas, characterize the work of most of the poets considered here. The poetic barricades of this generation have more often been raised along lines of gender, sexual preference, or ethnic identity than according to some aesthetic manifesto such as Ezra Pound's imagist credo. Thirty years ago it was fairly safe to say that Beat poets held certain attitudes about American society and put identifiable aesthetic principles to work in their poetry. Today one would be reluctant to make any such generalizations beyond noting, say, that female poets tend to focus more on gender-related issues than male poets do, that Native American poets frequently share some of the same mystical approaches to nature, or that gay poets seem to follow in the tradition of protest poetry. The contents of an anthology such as *Gay and Lesbian Poetry of Our Time* (1988) reveals that the rhetoric of the streets is virtually indistinguishable from that of much of our increasingly politicized and fragmented—what one critic has labeled "Balkanized"—poetry.

Still, certain poets covered in this *DLB* volume show some affinities to the schools of the older generation, and it may be useful to discuss briefly these poetic lines of descent. The Academic poets of the 1950s—Wilbur, Anthony Hecht, John Hollander—who produced a rhymed, metrical poetry of wit and linguistic precision, are often seen as the forebears of today's New Formalists—Dana Gioia, Marilyn Hacker, Brad Leithauser, Charles Martin, Mary Jo Salter, Gjertrud Schnackenberg, and Timothy Steele. While there is still no comprehensive anthology representing this group, its activities have occasioned quite a bit of critical attention and no small amount of controversy. Perhaps because they stand somewhat outside the mainstream of contemporary American poetry, the New Formalists seem to represent an orchestrated conspiracy in the eyes of some hostile critics, even though there is relatively little that connects them beyond a dedication—itself anything but hidebound—to writing metrical verse. While they have been accused, in the pages of the *AWP Chronicle*, the official organ of the Associated Writing Programs, of writing a reactionary type of "yuppie poetry," they actually represent diverse life-styles and political points of view. They have little in common as far as subject matter is concerned, and critic Robert McPhillips has pointed out that they do not share much, other than their commitment to rhyme and meter, with the Academic poets. According to McPhillips, they break with the older poets in their preference for popular forms of culture—they are after all, the Woodstock generation—and, in general, their idiom and cultural frame of reference strike the reader as somewhat less rarified than those of the Academic poets.

Concretism has remained, for the most part, a curiosity. An aesthetic that uses words as visual icons formed into interesting shapes is not likely to elicit much serious critical response. Indeed, many of the productions of the Concrete poets are perhaps more suitable for hanging than reading; e. e. cummings is the paterfamilias of the Concretists, but cummings's most enthusiastic admirers tend to forgive him his typographical experiments and instead focus on the linguistic brilliance that playfully characterizes his best poems. If the Concretists have any inheritors in the present scene, they are the poets of the so-called $L = A = N = G = U = A = G = E$ group (named after a magazine in which the work of many of them first appeared). According to critic Marjorie Perloff, the avant garde poets of the 1950s proclaimed that " 'Form is never more than an extension of content.' For the Language poet, this aphorism becomes: 'Theory is never more than the extension of practice.' " Indeed, much of the work of these poets—Susan Howe is the sole representative dealt with here—seems tailor-made for analysis by the deconstructionists, poststructuralists, and new historicists who have populated American graduate-school faculties of late.

The Confessional poets of the 1960s—Robert Lowell, Anne Sexton, Sylvia Plath, W. D. Snodgrass—remain chief influences on the poets of this generation, though the effects of novelty, in an age of "trash-talk" television, have certainly decreased poets' abilities to shock with the explicitness of personal revelations. When Lowell, scion of Boston gentility and winner of American poetry's most coveted awards, revealed, in *Life Studies* (1959), that "my mind's not right" in poems detailing family dysfunction, marital woes, alcoholism, mental illness, and psychotherapy, the reading public, perhaps feeling that such candor from a major poet was long overdue, was fascinated. Plath's suicide in 1963 caused her posthumous collection *Ariel* (1965) to be valued all the more highly by women who heard, in its most bitter moments, a cry for help that could have issued from their own lips. Sexton, the middle-class housewife who went, in less than a decade, from obscurity to the slopes of Parnassus, was a role model for a whole generation of women who came of age on the cusp of the feminist era. Some twenty years ago, in *The Confessional Poets* (1973), Robert Phillips described the typical Confessional poem, stressing its therapeutic, personal, and alienated qualities. The majority of poets in this *DLB* volume have at one time or another written poems in this vein. Indeed, the autobiographical narrative/lyric—sometimes naked, sometimes partially clad—has become a staple of these poets, especially when it deals with formerly taboo sexual topics. Bruce Weigl's "The Man Who Made Me Love Him," which describes an incident of sexual abuse perpetrated on a child, presumably the poet himself; "Kalaloch" by Carolyn Forché (discussed in *DLB 5*), with its graphic, first-person account of homosexual lovemaking; or Rita Dove's "After Reading *Mickey in the Night Kitchen* for the Third Time Before Bed," in which the poet and her daughter compare their sexual organs, are typical reflections of the extent to which contemporary poets of the mainstream (Dove is a Pulitzer Prize winner) feel free to use their most private moments for subject matter. Other poets here with ties to the Confessional tradition include Sharon Olds, Alfred Corn, T. R. Hummer, Ira Sadoff, and John Balaban, though it would be safe enough to add that almost every poet in the volume has learned from and at times imitated the type of poem popularized by Lowell, Plath, and company.

On the other hand, the Black Mountain School and the Deep Imagists have retained little direct influence. The former, named after a group of poets who studied at Black Mountain College with Charles Olsen in the 1950s, rallied around the banners of "projective verse" and various arcane theories of open form and composition by "fields." As Reed Whittemore has sarcastically remarked in his study of William Carlos Williams, if the doctor's followers, among whom the Black Mountain poets are the most prominent, had lived in the Middle Ages they would have been alchemists instead of poets. It is difficult to think of a single poet in this volume who is passionate about the metrical questions addressed by the Black Mountain poets, perhaps because open forms so completely dominate American poetry today that arguments about their validity are moot.

The Deep Imagists—Robert Bly and James Wright the most prominent—have also passed from exerting influence. They had a significant impact on young poets writing in the early 1970s, when it seemed as though a new poetic genre, an exotic hybrid of South American surrealism and Midwestern alienation amidst the not-so-alien corn, had emerged. Critic Lewis Turco dubbed it

"Blymagism" after its founder, but satire did not keep it from sweeping the graduate poetry workshops and spawning hundreds of poems that seemed to have been translated from an unidentified foreign tongue. It should be noted for the record that this sort of hallucinatory poem followed hard on the heels of the psychedelic late 1960s and was fueled by the rage of the era of Vietnam War protests; one of Bly's most typical poems of the period, "Johnson's Cabinet Watched by Ants" (1967), describes the president's military advisers as "dressed as gamboling lambs." Such self-consciously bizarre images seem passé today. Nevertheless, several contemporaries still occasionally employ surrealistic dislocations as part of their larger strategies; Reginald Gibbons, Albert Goldbarth, and C. D. Wright seem the most successful in doing so, though many others here have used these techniques.

The New York School, led by the late Frank O'Hara, Kenneth Koch, and John Ashbery, flowered in the late 1950s and early 1960s among writers who had close affinities with abstract impressionist painters, led by Jackson Pollock and Willem de Kooning. Like the Deep Imagists, the New York poets stressed subjectivity and the unconscious, but they infused their surrealism with a comic spirit much more akin to the Dadaist experiments of Paris in the 1920s than to the Bly/Wright brand of high seriousness. While Ashbery, mainly on the strength of his reputation among influential critics such as Helen Vendler, Marjorie Perloff, and Harold Bloom, remains the most fashionable poet on the contemporary scene, there are few poets here who betray his influence, unless the comic, free-associating monologues of Leon Stokesbury, Albert Goldbarth, Lisa Zeidner, and Rodney Jones are regarded as being slightly in his debt.

Similarly, the poets of the Beat Generation— Allen Ginsberg, Lawrence Ferlinghetti, Gary Snyder—seem so much the products of period and ambience (San Francisco in the mid 1950s) that their style of "hydrogen jukebox" protest poetry, to borrow a phrase from Ginsberg, is distinctly dated now. With Ginsberg, smiling in suit and tie from the pages of *Time*, having been transformed into an éminence grise of sexual and other forms of liberation, and Snyder becoming one of the chief spokesman for ecological concerns, the Beats, like so many other figures that thirty-five years ago seemed outrageous, have passed into respectability. One of the poets here gives the Beats a sly, left-handed compliment:

Dana Gioia, who was growing up in California when they were most prominent, has written, "Their unfailing verbosity and heroic self-absorption proved a constant inspiration—showing me everything I didn't want to do. One cannot overestimate the importance of negative examples at certain points in literary history when sensibilities shift." Today it is hard to imagine, given the explicit content of the heavy metal or rap lyrics that bombard one almost anywhere, that Ginsberg's *Howl* (1956) was the focus of a censorship trial when it was first published. More than any of the other groups, the Beats' program has been co-opted by franchised popular culture; ten minutes of MTV, with nuclear bombs exploding to the pulse of screaming guitars and wails of postadolescent angst, far surpasses in degree anything that might have caused the Beat poets of the 1950s to be considered dangerous sociopaths.

The last of Baughman's schools, which he labels the New Black Aesthetic, must today be expanded to include members of other minority groups—Hispanics, Orientals, Native Americans. Multiculturalism has become one of the most controversial academic issues of the era, and the spirit of affirmative action has clearly begun to influence the "politically correct" contents of anthologies and textbooks—what one conservative critic has labeled "canon to the left of them." Even the latest edition of the well-established literature text the *Norton Anthology of American Literature, Shorter Edition* contains no white male poet born since 1930. Other than Plath, the other recent poets included—Audre Lorde, Amiri Baraka, Michael Harper, Simon Ortiz, Rita Dove, Alberto Ríos, and Cathy Song—seem to have been chosen primarily as representatives of diverse ethnic groups. Readers are referred to *DLB 41: Afro-American Poets Since 1955* and *DLB 82: Chicano Writers*, First Series for entries on some of the poets from two of the most prominent minorities. Recently much attention has been paid to Native American and Oriental-American writers as well. In the present volume entries on several members of all four principal ethnic groups may be found—among them Ortiz and Dove, as well as Ai, Gerald William Barrax, Joy Harjo, Garrett Kaoru Hongo, Yusef Komunyakaa, Thylias Moss, Brenda Marie Osbey, and Marilyn Nelson Waniek. A native of India, Vikram Seth has written most of his best poetry while a resident of the United States, including *The Golden Gate* (1986), the only book of poetry in recent memory to be chosen as a selection of a major book club. As the population of the United States reflects the increasing diversity of ethnic backgrounds, it seems likely that future overviews of American poetry will also single out more and more representatives of minority cultures.

Once the schools have been discussed and their descendants identified, what remains for the many poets here who demonstrate no discernible links to their elders? If there is a main current in contemporary American poetry, it is probably indebted chiefly to the most remarkable phenomenon of all those that have helped to shape the current state of the art—the rise of the university creative-writing programs. In the mid 1960s there was only a handful of graduate programs specializing in creative writing. The current edition of *The AWP Official Guide to Writing Programs* describes over three hundred programs offering a variety of degrees from the B.A. to the Ph.D. Poet Greg Kuzma remarked in an article in *Poetry* that soon there will be a creative-writing program within safe driving distance of everyone in America. About all that is lacking is a program offering *remedial* creative writing for the functionally illiterate, but one suspects that a junior faculty member somewhere is already working up a degree plan—with himself as its tenured chief administrator.

Almost every poet in this volume has had some connection with a writing program, as student or teacher or both, and that is simply a reflection of the current economics of American poetry. Most books of verse published today include poems that have borne the scrutiny of a creative-writing class; indeed, most first books of verse are merely revised versions of theses submitted for graduate degrees. In any given year the largest portion of new books of verse is published by university presses, and the chief means of the dissemination of those books, in the absence of any real attempt to sell poetry by the chain bookstores, is the university-sponsored poetry reading, which is usually followed by an autographing session by the visiting poet. It is not hard to imagine what the effects of these market realities have been and will continue to be. For one thing, the workshop approach to poetry, with so many different hands whittling away at the original version of a poem, tends to remove vitality along with rough edges. If a poet reacts to the verdict of his peers by removing anything that gives offense to any member of the workshop, he or she may end up with a bland product, like a processed, prepackaged food, pitched to the widest possible taste but satisfying no one in particular.

The university poetry reading, where the poet must entertain a crowd largely comprised of undergraduates in search of extra-credit points, likewise has a dangerous allure. Does the poet, consciously or not, water down poems to suit a crowd that does not have a printed text to follow? Will the poet drop the mantle of the bard and instead put on the baggy pants of the stand-up comic in hopes of winning over the crowd? These are only a few of the possible effects that the writing programs may have on poetry as we enter an era when it is probable that almost every new book of poems will be produced by a poet with, at the least, an M.F.A. and that the same poet will be employed in a writing program issuing degrees to more new poets. That creative-writing programs should have become such an entrenched establishment, with a complex structure of hierarchies, career strategies, and perks, in so short a time is without precedent in the history of poetry.

The situation in 1992 is analogous to that of a century ago, when there was no consensus in either America or Great Britain about which poets, if any, were deserving of major status. The great voices of the Romantic and Victorian eras were silent, and the founders of modernism were still in knee pants. In his portentously titled critical work *The Fate of American Poetry* (1991), Jonathan Holden, who is the most eloquent apologist for the present generation, argues that the "mainstream of American poetry . . . has continued to be, whether narrative or meditative, in a realist mode that is essentially egalitarian, university-based, and middle class, and to be written in a free verse that has, by and large, vastly improved since the sixties, evolved into a flexible medley of older prosodies so rich in echoes that it bears out Eliot's famous dictum that 'No verse is ever really free.'" Whether this modest aesthetic has produced or will produce poems that will stand the test of time remains open to question. It may be that the rise to prominence of the writing programs will eventually be viewed as American poetry's quattrocento. On the other hand, the Pounds and Eliots of the first decades of the next century may see our current situation as merely a stultifying orthodoxy that can only be revitalized by open revolt. Still, if the past is any guide, of the thousands of poems produced by the members of this generation a few will survive for the delight and instruction of readers in distant places and times. *Ars longa, vita brevis.*

I am grateful to the faculty senate of Lamar University for granting a summer development leave to work on this project. Tim Summerlin, chairman of the Department of English and Foreign Languages, provided help with student assistants, office space, and computer hardware. John Idoux, executive vice-president for academic affairs, has been consistent in his support for projects of this scope, as has Kendall Blanchard, dean of the College of Arts and Sciences. Donna Buesing, Karen Holstead, and C. R. Field, Lamar students, gave editorial assistance, and Lisa Meshell and Cindy Colichia, departmental secretaries, helped with typing and other crucial tasks. As I noted in *DLB 105*, my wife, Donna, has been the first audience for the majority of my complaints and doubts. Finally, I extend my appreciation to the authors of the entries in this volume, many of whom will be recognized by readers for their distinguished articles and books on contemporary American poetry. I particularly appreciate the work of those who, owing to the long period between the submission of their original entries and the publication of the volume, agreed to update their work to cover recent publications. Both the editor and the poets whose work they examine are in their debt.

—R. S. Gwynn

Acknowledgments

This book was produced by Bruccoli Clark Layman, Inc. Karen L. Rood is senior editor for the *Dictionary of Literary Biography* series. Jack Turner was the in-house editor.

Production coordinator is James W. Hipp. Projects manager is Charles D. Brower. Photography editors are Edward Scott and Timothy C. Lundy. Layout and graphics supervisor is Penney L. Haughton. Copyediting supervisor is Bill Adams. Typesetting supervisor is Kathleen M. Flanagan. Systems manager is George F. Dodge. The production staff includes Rowena Betts, Steve Borsanyi, Teresa Chaney, Patricia Coate, Rebecca Crawford, Henry Cuningham, Margaret McGinty Cureton, Bonita Dingle, Mary Scott Dye, Denise Edwards, Sarah A. Estes, Robert Fowler, Mary Lee Goodwin, Avril E. Gregory, Ellen McCracken, Kathy Lawler Merlette, John Myrick, Pamela D. Norton, Thomas J. Pickett, Maxine K. Smalls, and Jennifer C. J. Turley.

Walter W. Ross and Dennis Lynch did library research. They were assisted by the following librarians at the Thomas Cooper Library of the University of South Carolina: Jens Holley and the interlibrary-loan staff; reference librarians Gwen Baxter, Daniel Boice, Faye Chadwell, Jo Cottingham, Cathy Eckman, Rhonda Felder, Gary Geer, Jackie Kinder, Laurie Preston, Jean Rhyne, Carol Tobin, Virginia Weathers, and Connie Widney; circulation-department head Thomas Marcil; and acquisitions-searching supervisor David Haggard.

Dictionary of Literary Biography® • Volume One Hundred Twenty

American Poets Since World War II
Third Series

Dictionary of Literary Biography

Diane Ackerman
(7 October 1948 -)

Julie Gleason Alford
Lamar University

BOOKS: *Poems*, by Ackerman, Judy Bolz, and
Nancy Steele (Ithaca, N.Y.: Stone-Marrow,
1973);
The Planets: A Cosmic Pastoral (New York: Morrow,
1976);
Wife of Light (New York: Morrow, 1978);
Twilight of the Tenderfoot: A Western Memoir (New
York: Morrow, 1980);
Lady Faustus (New York: Morrow, 1983);
On Extended Wings (New York: Atheneum, 1985);
Reverse Thunder (New York: Lumen, 1988);
A Natural History of the Senses (New York: Ran-
dom House, 1990);
Jaguar of Sweet Laughter: New and Selected Poems
(New York: Random House, 1991);
*The Moon by Whale Light, and Other Adventures
Among Bats, Crocodilians, Penguins, and
Whales* (New York: Random House, 1991).

Diane Ackerman is one of the most highly acclaimed lyric poets writing in the United States.
Her poetry displays a mastery of language, lexical precision, and a vast range of poetic forms
and voices. A passionate, disciplined writer, Ackerman creates poetry full of wit, compassion, courage, and fact; it is a poetry of wonder and celebration for the natural world and the human condition. "Ackerman is not interested in a poetry of
irony or theory or intellectual distance," notes reviewer Michael McFee. "Her poems are immediate . . . and accessible to anyone who has ever felt
anything intensely" (National Public Radio, 7 July
1991). The fusion of science and art is one feature of Ackerman's poetry that makes her distinct from her contemporaries. To those who ques-

*Diane Ackerman (photograph courtesy of the International
Poetry Forum)*

tion the appropriateness or purpose of blending
poetry with science, Ackerman replies: "Not to
write about Nature in its widest sense, because
quasars or corpuscles are not 'the proper realm
of poetry,' as a critic once said to me, is not only
irresponsible and philistine, it bankrupts the expe-

3

rience of living, it ignores much of life's fascination and variety. I'm a great fan of the Universe, which I take literally: as one. All of it interests me, and it interests me in detail" (*Contemporary Poets*, 1991). Ackerman stretches the boundaries of what poets traditionally write about, producing collections of verse that contain a rich variety of voices, moods, and subjects. Among her favorite sources of inspiration are nature, flying, astronomy, travel, and love.

Ackerman was born on 7 October 1948 in Waukegan, Illinois. Her father, Sam Fink, was a shoe salesman and later ran one of the first McDonald's restaurant franchises. Her mother, Marsha Tischler Fink, "was—and is—a seasoned world traveler." In *The Moon by Whale Light* (1991), a collection of nature essays, Ackerman reflects on her childhood years and gives a humorous account of an incident that made her realize at a young age that she had poetic tendencies. As she and three schoolmates were walking through a plum orchard, "The trees were thick with plums," and she remarked that the dark plums were "huddled like bats." Her friends instantly recoiled. "The possibility of bats didn't frighten them," Ackerman recalls. "I frightened them: the elaborate fantasies I wove . . . ; my perverse insistence on drawing trees in colors other than green; my doing *boy* things like raising turtles. . . . And now this: plums that look like bats. . . . I remember flushing with wonder at the sight of my first metaphor—the living plums: the bats."

Her fascination with the natural world continued. In college she studied science as well as literature. She began her undergraduate work in 1966 at Boston University but transferred to Pennsylvania State University the following year. She received her B.A. in English in 1970; then she entered Cornell University as a teaching assistant in 1971. At Cornell, Ackerman pursued academic studies for the next seven years, earning an M.F.A. in creative writing and an M.A. and Ph.D. in literature. She has taught writing at Cornell, Columbia, New York University, Washington University (in St. Louis, Missouri), the College of William and Mary, Ohio University and the University of Pittsburgh. At Washington University she was director of the Writer's Program from 1984 to 1986. Currently she is a staff writer for the *New Yorker* and lives in upstate New York.

Many prestigious literary awards and honors have been presented to Ackerman throughout her career. At Cornell she was awarded the Academy of American Poets Prize, Corson

French Prize, Heerman-McCalmons Playwriting Prize, and the Corson-Bishop Poetry Prize. Her other awards include the Abbie Copps Poetry Prize (1974), the *Black Warrior Review* Poetry Prize (1981), and the Pushcart Prize (1984). She has received grants from the Rockefeller Foundation and the National Endowment for the Arts. In 1985 the Academy of American Poets honored her with the Peter I. B. Lavan Award. She received the Lowell Thomas Award in 1990. Ackerman has served as poetry judge in many poetry festivals and contests, on the board of directors for the Associated Writing Programs, and on the Planetary Society Advisory Board. In 1987 Ackerman was a judge in the AWP Award Series for Creative Nonfiction. She has also participated in several poetry panels, including those of the New York Foundation for the Arts (1987) and National Endowment for the Arts (1991).

Besides being a highly acclaimed poet, Ackerman is also a prose stylist. Her four books of nonfiction have been successful and have earned lavish praise from critics. Her first nonfiction book, *Twilight of the Tenderfoot* (1980), recounts her adventures at an authentic cattle ranch in New Mexico. Not content to rely on imagination, Ackerman left the quiet self-absorption of academia to experience the life of a cowhand. Her next work of prose, *On Extended Wings* (1985), is a memoir of her experiences as a student pilot. In a review of the book, Karen Rile wrote: "Diane Ackerman is a woman of letters, not numbers. When she gets her hands on the throttle, flying exceeds metaphor; it's the whole world; and yet nothing is mundane. This isn't simply a chronicle about learning how to fly; it's a poet's notebook with wings" (*St. Louis Post-Dispatch*, 8 September 1985). *On Extended Wings* was adapted for the stage by Norma Jean Giffen in 1987. *A Natural History of the Senses* (1990) is Ackerman's third and most critically acclaimed work of prose to date. A surprise best-seller, it has since been published in sixteen countries. The paperback edition was released in 1991 by Vintage. This encyclopedia of the senses is an intriguing assortment of history, biology, anthropology, cultural fact, and folklore, woven together with poetic inspiration to celebrate the faculties of human perception. "The Senses," a five-hour PBS series based on this book, is in development. Her latest prose work, *The Moon by Whale Light*, has been highly praised.

Ackerman's nonfiction is a creative blend of journalism, science, and poetry; indeed, it is her

Woodcut by Albrecht Dürer, which serves as the frontispiece for Ackerman's first full-length book, The Planets: A Cosmic Pastoral *(1976)*

poetic vision that makes her nonfiction so successful. Adventurous and endlessly curious, she may assume different roles at different times—pilot, journalist, astronomer, horsewoman, scuba diver—but she is always a poet. Ackerman explains her writing as a form of "celebration or prayer," a way to "enquire about the world."

An obsession with astronomy led to her first full-length book of poetry, *The Planets: A Cosmic Pastoral* (1976). In this collection Ackerman travels the scenic route through the universe, as she tours the country of the Milky Way and the landscape of space. Earth's moon ("Imagine something that big being dead") and all the planets of the solar system are explored in verse. Other subjects, such as comets and Cape Canaveral, are included as well.

Poetic imagery and metaphors interweave with scientific data. The planet Venus is described as "a buxom floozy with a pink boa; / mummy, whose black / sediment dessicates within; wasp star / to Mayan Galileos; / an outpatient / wrapped in post-operative gauze; / Cleopatra in high August— / her flesh curling / in a heat mirage / light years / from Alexandria."

Then, subtly, scientific fact creeps in among the rich poetic images: "Venus quietly mutates / in her ivory tower. / Deep within that / libidinous albedo / temperatures are hot enough to boil lead / pressures / 90 times more unyielding than Earth's." Later in the poem, readers also learn that Venus's atmosphere is forty miles thick and consists of sulphuric, hydrochloric, and hydrofluoric acids.

Although *The Planets* is liberally sprinkled with astronomical terms, phrases, and facts, the science does not distract but heightens reader interest and enhances the emotional value of the poems. Ackerman has the ability to take cold scientific fact and transform it into something fresh and poetic, compelling the reader to look at a thing in an exciting new way; her poetry intrigues, teaches, and delights at the same time. The overall feeling of *The Planets* is one of wonder and fascination. In the poem "Mars" a romantic, dreamy mood is created as the speaker bids her lover to fly with her to Utopia and the highlands of Tharis (regions on Mars):

Once in a blue sun, when volcanoes
heave up grit regular as pearls,
and light runs riot, we'll watch
the sun go darker than the sky,
violet dust-tufts wheel on the horizon,
amber cloudbanks pile, and the whole
of color-crazed Mars ignite.

Critics hailed *The Planets* as an impressive debut and important work. Astronomer Carl Sagan said, "The work is scientifically accurate and even a convenient introduction to modern ideas on the planets, but much more important, it is spectacularly good poetry, clear, lyrical and soaring. . . . One of the triumphs of Ackerman's pastoral is the demonstration of how closely compatible planetary exploration and poetry, science and art really are" (*New Republic*, November 1976).

Ackerman's next two books of poetry, *Wife of Light* (1978) and *Lady Faustus* (1983), are rich and varied collections of short poems. Ackerman's range of interests appears limitless. The title *Wife of Light* is taken from a line in her poem "Period Piece," in which she begs the moon for deliverance from the depths and rages of mood caused by her menstrual cycle. Wit mingles with misery:

Cares that daily fade or lie low
hogged front-row-center in the bleachers

of my despair and there, solemn
as Kewpie dolls, began to heckle and hoot.

The last line of the poem provides the title of the book: "Moon, be merciful to your wife of light."

Nature often produces a sensual quality in Ackerman's love poems. "Driving Through Farm Country at Sunset," which is frequently anthologized, exudes this quality. At first the poem seems to be simply a tribute to nature, to "farm country," as the persona describes the sights, smells, and sounds of the rural area she is driving through: manure, cut grass, honeysuckle, washloads blowing on a line, dogwoods, a sunlit mountainside, and the samba of a dragonfly in the "puffy-lidded dusk." But images of nature are sensuously intertwined with tranquil images of domestic life to evoke a sense of longing. In the last stanza the reader becomes aware that it is a love poem:

> Clouds begin to curdle overhead. And I want
> to lie down with you in this boggy dirt,
> our legs rubbing like locusts'.
> I want you here with the scallions
> sweet in the night air, to lie down with you
> heavy in my arms, and take root.

Wife of Light displays Ackerman's tremendous range of interests and moods, and also her range of voices. Some of the voices are historical, as in the witty verse "Anne Donne to Her Husband" and the sonnet "Quixote" ("life's torpor is the blazing savanna of my loins"). Ackerman manages to turn even mathematics into poetry in "Song of π." She assumes the persona of π (pi), the mathematical symbol that represents the ratio of the circumference of a circle to its diameter. The ratio can be carried to an infinite number of decimal places—it never rounds off—and Ackerman focuses on this unusual feature: "I barrel / out past horizon's bluff, / every digit pacing like a Tennessee Walker, / unable to break even, / come round. . . ."

Lady Faustus, like *Wife of Light*, is broad in scope. Her romance with flying is one of the major sources of inspiration for the book. As a pilot, Ackerman experiences flight as a sort of rapture: "I am flight-luscious / I am kneeling on air" (from "Climbing Out"). Another pastime, scuba diving, provides inspiration for "A Fine, a Private Place." A man and woman make love underwater, "mask to mask, floating / with oceans of air between them, / she his sea-geisha / in an orange kimono / of belts and vests. . . ." The ocean is a "blue boudoir," and sunlight cuts through the water "twisting its knives into corridors of light." The same enthusiasm and sense of adventure that impel her to experience the sky and the sea also move her to explore and celebrate everyday marvels closer to home. Wild strawberries, a goddaughter, soccer, whale songs, rivers, dinosaurs, and language labs are a few of the marvels she captures in verse.

Concerning flying and scuba diving, Ackerman admits she is often drawn to pastimes that many people find frightening; however, she does not consider herself a daredevil, or even particularly daring. As she said to Jesse Green, "I'm not reckless. . . . I'd be a bad role model to younger women if I were. There are people who *like* to touch the fabric of immortality every chance they get. I'm not one. I don't take unnecessary chances. But I don't let a little bit of danger stand between me and knowledge either." She also does not pursue danger for "cheap excitation." "For me," Ackerman writes in *Extended Wings*, "it's just a case of my curiosity leading with its chin: things fascinate me whether they are dangerous or not . . . [;] there are some things you can learn about the world only from 5,000 feet above it, just as there are some things you can learn about the ocean only when you become part of its intricate fathoms."

Ackerman's innate, intense curiosity propels her into experiences that provide subject matter for her poems. Sometimes curiosity itself is the topic. One example is "Lady Faustus." In the opening lines of the poem, curiosity is expressed as a live entity, a thing barely controlled: "Devils be ready! My curiosity / stalks the outpost of its caution. . . ." The intensity of her desire to know is compared to the sun's heat: "raw heat / fitful as a cautery / I, too, on burning with a lidless flame." Later, in *On Extended Wings*, Ackerman writes that her curiosity howls "like a caged dog." This image is originally found in the closing lines of "Lady Faustus":

> A kennelled dog croons in my chest.
> I itch all over. I rage to know
> what beings like me, stymied by death
> and leached by wonder, hug those campfires
> night allows,
> aching to know the fate of us all,
> wallflowers in a waltz of stars.

Both *Wife of Light* and *Lady Faustus* were extolled by critics for their vision and poetic range: "Lyrical description is Ackerman's strong suit. Rich melodies, almost voluptuous with sound and image, her best poems and songs of celebration . . . stir and liberate all our best and kindest emotions" (*Publishers Weekly*, 29 July 1983).

Ackerman's next poetic work, published in 1988, is a long, dramatic poem, a play titled *Reverse Thunder*. She combines fact and fiction to portray the life of seventeenth-century nun Juana Inés de la Cruz, a remarkable woman and one of the best-known Spanish poets of that century. In de la Cruz, Ackerman has found a kindred spirit—a passionate, creative woman, independent in thought and action, whose raging enthusiasm for life did not allow her to conform to a conventional role. As R. W. H. Dillard writes, "This fascinating woman, as Ackerman pictures her, draws together in her life as a nun in 17th-century Mexico almost all of the conflicting and contradictory strands of life in that time; she is a nun who loves a man passionately, a believing Christian who explores the scientific view of the world, a spiritual and spirited poet who draws her inspiration from both the life of the body and of the mind. . . ." Besides being a poet, Sister Juana was also a musician, painter, and scientist. She read in several languages and taught astronomy and philosophy, which were considered profane by the church. Her library was the largest in the New World.

In the preface to *Reverse Thunder*, Ackerman writes: "Sister Juana Inés de la Cruz was an extraordinary woman who had the bad fortune to live during an era which demanded its women to be ordinary. She was a child prodigy with a gift and passion for learning at a time when education was not available to women." Such was the tragedy of Juana's life; the triumph is her poetry, which has survived the centuries to tell her story.

The philosophy in most of Ackerman's work is that the passions for life, learning, and love are intertwined and often one and the same. *Reverse Thunder* contains two themes that reflect this philosophy. The first theme involves passion for life itself. With a conviction reminiscent of Walt Whitman, she emphasizes the importance of the here and now: the joys and wonders of Earth are, at best, as sweet as heaven's. Juana says, "To know this world well, / there's Heaven in all its marvels," and "A worldly woman knows Heaven as the suburb of each day."

Another theme found in *Reverse Thunder* is the affirmation of the power of love. Juana discovers that love is greater than her passion for learning and, ultimately, her passion for life: "My world that seemed so rich before him, / once I knew him, / was not enough. / It changed from a moss that lived / only on air to an orient of petals."

This passion for life and the affirmation of love's power resonate throughout Ackerman's poetry. Both themes are aptly expressed in a poem from *The Planets*, "When You Take Me From This Good Rich Soil," which reflects the same spirited convictions of Juana Inés de la Cruz, even though Ackerman wrote this poem many years before *Reverse Thunder*. The poem acknowledges the existence of heaven, but love is recognized as the greater power: "No heaven could please me as my love / does. . . ./ When, deep in the cathedral of my ribs, / love rings like a chant, I need no heaven." Appreciation for the secular and a raging passion for life are expressed in the closing lines:

> When you take me from this good rich soil,
> and my heart rumbles like the chambers
>
> of a gun to leave life's royal sweat
> for your numb peace, I'll be dragging at Earth
> With each cell's tiny ache, so you must
> rattle my bone-house until the spirit breaks.

Ackerman's *Jaguar of Sweet Laughter: New and Selected Poems* was published in 1991. She has grown with each book, and this is her finest collection of poems to date, "a heady and generous bouquet of 15 years of Ackerman's poetry," according to McFee. In the new poems Ackerman's muse leads her from rain forest to iceberg, from her backyard to Mars, as she writes of hummingbirds, orchids, Halley's Comet, deer, contact lenses, penguins, pilots, and love. *Jaguar* is a lush collection that revels in the exotic: "Unleash me and I am an ocelot / all appetite and fur" (from "Dinner at the Waldorf ").

Highlights of the book include lyric sequences about the Amazon and Antarctica. The book ripples with adventure and sensuality: "when you kiss me, / my mouth softens into scarlet feathers— / an ibis with curved bill and small dark smile; / when you kiss me, / jaguars lope through my knees . . ." (from "Beija-Flor"). As in previous collections, Ackerman's exceptional skill with voices is demonstrated. In "St. Louis Botanical Gardens" a personified orchid, "the world's most pampered flower," describes the luxuriant existence of the orchid exhibit:

> We dine
> on the equivalent of larks' tongues

Ackerman, whose On Extended Wings *details her experiences while learning to fly a plane (photograph by Barbara Bell)*

and chocolate. We are free
from that slum of hummingbird and drizzle.
Why bother with a mosquito's
languid toilet? Why bother
with the pooled vulgarity of the rain?

In a review of *Jaguar* Donna Seaman remarked, "Ackerman frees the exotic from the familiar, finds the familiar in the exotic, the large
in the small, the personal in the vast" (*Booklist*, 1
April 1991). The corporeal is blended with the
spiritual, the modern with the primitive, as
Ackerman combines the poet's love of nature
with a scientist's understanding of nature. "We
Are Listening" is an excellent example. The "we"
refers to humankind, listening with satellites and
radios to the deep reaches of the universe, searching in "cosmic loneliness" for a sound, any
sound. Ackerman interjects the creatural to emphasize the human feeling of insignificance as
one faces the awesome silence and vastness of the
universe:

Small as tree frogs
staking out one end
of the endless swamp,
we are listening
through the longest night

we imagine, which dawns
between the life and times of stars.

The modern spiritual struggle is reflected in this
poem, as "radio telescopes / roll their heads, as if
in anguish"; humankind is affectionately referred
to as "the small bipeds / with the giant dreams."

In *Jaguar* Ackerman acknowledges in verse
a few of the poets who influenced her writing: Wallace Stevens, Sylvia Plath, and Walt Whitman.
Ackerman's lexical dexterity and precision frequently move critics to compare her to Stevens.
In "Letter to Wallace Stevens" she says that, at
nineteen, she desired Dylan Thomas's "volup-
tuousness of mind" and Stevens's "sensuous
rigor." In another poem she expresses admiration for Plath's intellect, talent, and "naturalist's
eye," but not for the pain that Plath "wore like a
shroud." Ackerman refers to Plath as "the doll of
insight we knew / to whom nearly all lady poets
write, / a morbid Santa Claus who could die on
cue." Of Plath's self-destruction Ackerman writes
these chilling lines: "You wanted to unlock the
weather system / in your cells, and one day you
did." "Walt Whitman's Birthplace" recounts a metaphysical moment in which Ackerman draws inspiration from Whitman: "in an opera athletic as

the land, / I drink from your source and swell as large as life."

Ackerman's unusual vision—the harmonious union of science and art—has made her a representative poetic voice of the twentieth century, a century in which science and technology have often separated people from nature and, thus, from themselves. In her poems, readers experience a reconnection with nature and an affirmation of life's glorious possibilities. George Garrett remarks (on the dust jacket of *Jaguar*) that "while a lot of fashionable poets have settled for a kind of whispering and mumbling in the monotonous dark, she has been making poems that can soar and sing, or talk straight and sure about interesting things, things that matter."

"Daring" is a word critics frequently apply to Ackerman and to her poetry because of her willingness to explore life and her refusal to shackle her writing to convention. Also, and perhaps more important, she has the courage to express passion and joyful exuberance for life at a time when intellectual distance and self-indulgent introspection is the vogue. In *Contempoary Poets* she states: "I try to give myself passionately, totally, to whatever I'm observing, with as much affectionate curiosity as I can muster, as a means to understanding a little better what being human is, and what it was like to have once been alive on the planet, how it felt in one's senses, passions and con-

templations. I appear to have a lot of science in my work, I suppose, but I think of myself as a Nature writer, if what we mean by Nature is, as I've said, the full sum of Creation."

Poet, journalist, and prose stylist, Ackerman is a pioneer, exploring and opening fresh realms of thought for a new generation of poets, showing them that the only boundaries are ones they set for themselves. At the end of *The Planets*, she writes:

> I return to Earth now
> as if to a previous thought,
> alien and out of place,
> like a woman who,
> waking too early each day,
> finds it dark yet
> and all the world asleep.
> But how could my clamorous heart
> lie abed, knowing all of Creation
> has been up for hours?

Interview:
Maureen Dowd, *Vogue* (September 1991): 384-388.

References:
R. W. H. Dillard, "Diane Ackerman," in *Contempoary Poets*, edited by Tracy Chevalier (Chicago & London: St. James, 1991), pp. 4-5;
Jesse Green, "Wild at Heart," *Mirabella* (September 1991): 76-78.

Ai

(21 October 1947 -   )

C. Renee Field
Lamar University

BOOKS: *Cruelty* (Boston: Houghton Mifflin, 1973);

Killing Floor (Boston: Houghton Mifflin, 1979);

Sin (Boston: Houghton Mifflin, 1986);

Fate: New Poems (Boston: Houghton Mifflin, 1991).

Collection: *Cruelty/Killing Floor* (New York: Thunder's Mouth, 1987).

SELECTED PERIODICAL PUBLICATIONS—
UNCOLLECTED:

NONFICTION

"On Being 1/2 Japanese, 1/8 Choctaw, 1/4 Black, and 1/16 Irish," *Ms.*, 6 (June 1974): 58.

POETRY

"Interview With a Policeman," *Poetry* (October-November 1987): 2-4.

Since the appearance of her first collection, *Cruelty* (1973), Ai has become a major force in contemporary poetry, pushing her chosen poetic form, the dramatic monologue, to courageous new limits. Her poetry is refreshingly simple in style, yet challenging and complex in theme and interpretation. Still growing and evolving as a skilled poet, Ai has only scratched the surface of her potential and ability.

Ai was born Florence Anthony on 21 October 1947. She did not know who her real father was until she was twenty-six years old. She was conceived during an affair Mrs. Anthony had at sixteen; when Mr. Anthony found out, he beat his wife repeatedly. Finally, after moving in with her parents, Mrs. Anthony gave birth to Florence in Albany, Texas. Of mixed ethnic heritage, Ai describes herself as "1/2 Japanese, 1/8 Choctaw, 1/4 Black, and 1/16 Irish." Ai was raised a Catholic and sent to an integrated Catholic school, where she felt an affinity toward neither the black students nor the white. Black children taunted her, calling her "nigger-jap." After trying with great difficulty to assimilate herself into the African-American culture of which she never felt a part, Ai chose instead to concentrate on the oriental facet of her ethnic heritage. She became completely devoted to "being aesthetically Japanese." Thus she took the name "Ai," which means "love" in Japanese, and earned a B.A. in oriental studies from the University of Arizona in 1969. Then she headed west to the University of California at Irvine, where she earned an M.F.A. in creative writing in 1971. To support herself while writing, Ai has worked at many jobs, including costume modeling and teaching, and has endured several periods of unemployment. Ai has lived and taught in various areas of the country, including Massachusetts, New York, and most recently Arizona State University in Tempe, where she served as visiting poet. She is married to fellow poet Lawrence Kearney.

Ai has received some critical acclaim in her short career, and it is well deserved. After *Cruelty* appeared, she received several honors, including Guggenheim and Radcliffe Fellowships in 1975 and a Massachusetts Arts and Humanities Fellowship in 1976. *Killing Floor* (1979) was named the 1978 Lamont Poetry Selection by the Academy of American Poets.

When *Cruelty* was published, Ai received a great deal of negative criticism for being too graphic, violent, and pornographic. Many literary critics seemed loath to find any redeeming qualities in the poetry's technical aspects, and even some feminist critics rejected her work because it dealt graphically with child abuse, rape, abortion, and violence against women. Later critics of *Cruelty* were kinder, but still cautious.

Cruelty is a collection of short dramatic monologues. The speakers, diverse male and female personae, play out the gritty drama of their lives in a variety of settings and situations. Ai uses direct, hard-hitting language to create vivid, yet unadorned, imagery and shockingly real scenarios. The speakers in these poems have no illusions; they do not live lives that would be considered "pretty" by the genteel standards of Middle America. These are the disenfranchised, the poor, the frightened. They survive and they endure, living

Ai circa 1991 (photograph by Nancy Fewkes)

lives of grit and resolve, knowing what they must do and doing it. This is not poetry for the faint of heart but, rather, brutally honest survival poetry. Ai quotes poet Charles Simic at the beginning of *Cruelty*: "He who cannot / grow teeth, will not survive." In "Abortion" Ai makes this survival instinct excruciatingly clear:

> Coming home, I find you still in bed,
> but when I pull back the blanket,
> I see your stomach is as flat as an iron.
> You've done it, as you warned me you would
> . . . .
> Woman, loving you no matter what you do,
> what can I say, except that I've heard
> the poor have no children, just small people
> and there is only room for one man in this house.

The flat, matter-of-fact style of writing and choice of words gives the poem its impact. The man, knowing the couple cannot afford another mouth to feed, faces the termination of pregnancy unflinchingly.

Ai sees the essentials of life as love and hate, birth and death; she strives to present these basics strongly, clearly, and honestly so there is no room for question. Using striking images and a strong sense of voice, Ai delves deep into the minds of her personae. She identifies so totally with what she sees that her poems become the voices of men, of forty-year-old prostitutes, of hitchhiker/killers, starving tenant farmers, child beaters, and corpse haulers. Because of this identification, Ai draws readers close—uncomfortably, at times—to this bare-bones way of living, of surviving. The miraculous is reduced to the trivial—not to demean it, but to bring it into the perspective of her personae. In "The Country Midwife: A Day," childbirth is reduced to an everyday occurrence through the use of simple language and simile. The midwife is helping a woman give birth: "A scraggly, red child comes out of her into my hands / like warehouse ice sliding down the chute. . . . // beneath her, a stain as orange as sunrise / spreads out over the sheet."

Birth is a recurring theme in *Cruelty*, and it is never glorified or exalted into being something it is not. In "The Unexpected" a husband is talking to his pregnant wife, who is sweeping the floor. The language is simple, yet powerfully descriptive: "woman, / pregnant walnut of flesh / waiting for birth to crack you open / with her sharp brown teeth / and force you to give up your white meat." Ai goes on to convey the distance, fear, and helplessness the man feels; he gets the dustpan and kneels down so she can sweep the dirt into it. Before she finishes, he reaches up to stroke her ankle, finding it wet: "Frightened, I stand up. / Go on, just give me the broom / and let me finish sweeping for you, / you never know who might stop by / and everything's got to be clean, clean."

Sex is another subject that is often addressed in *Cruelty*, and often it is outside the realm of "accepted social norms"; it can be violent and base. Ai's use of sex may offend some delicate sensibilities, for she presents pure sexual drive and energy with the wraps of convention stripped away. For Ai sex is a fact of life at its most basic level; her characters are unable or unwilling to love within the confines of sexual convention. In "Prostitute" readers encounter a woman who has killed her husband. She searches his pockets, finding a few coins. Then she says, "I slip your hand under my skirt / and rub it against my chili-red skin." After stimulating herself this way, the narrator puts on the man's boots and gun, and goes out to find a high-paying customer, thinking she may be worth more since she is dressed this way. In "Tired Old Whore" the persona is a prostitute who is, as the title suggests, getting old and weary. There is no illusion here, just fact, as the whore says, "Wait, I need a little help, help me, sweet thing. / Pull down your pants, / I like to see what I'm getting now, / before it gets into me." "Forty-Three-Year-Old Woman, Masturbating" is written from the point of view of a sexually unfulfilled middle-aged woman, tired of masturbation, but unable to find satisfaction or release anywhere else: "I want to kill this female hand— / its four centipede fingers. . . ." The insect imagery found in this poem helps to reduce the sexual act even more, letting readers relate to the frustration, loneliness, and smallness the woman is feeling.

Though some of the personae in these monologues are men, most are strong, capable women. Feminist critics who find Ai's poetry somehow "incorrect" should pay attention to the powerful female images. In "Before You Leave" a woman offers:

You can bite me, I won't bleed. . . .
Fill my tunnel with the howl

you keep zipped in your pants
and when it's over, don't worry, I'll stand.

These are women who can stand up for themselves, for men, and *to* their men. Even men see their strength. In "Cuba, 1962," one meets Juanita, who is "breaking the cane off at ground level, / using only her big hands." In "New Crops for a Free Man" a husband sees his wife as invincible, deadly: "One stalk of wheat no man / can pull from the ground and live to eat."

The problem that feminists encounter in Ai's poetry undoubtedly arises when "taboo" subjects are broached: child abuse, wife beating, rape. It is helpful to keep in mind that these poems are not meant to make a political statement. Ai has chosen brutal honesty and shocking truth over politics and sensibilities. The life of which Ai writes is foreign to most of us; though we are aware of it on some level, we create myths to deal with the things we do not understand. Critic Alicia Ostriker says, "Her realities—very small ones—are so intolerable that we fashion female myths to express our fear of her." Through her poetry, Ai is going about the business of debunking these myths. Her characters, Ostriker says, "live the hard life far below our myths" (*New York Times Book Review*, 17 February 1974).

In "Child Beater" Ai handles an emotional issue with detachment:

I lay the belt on a chair
and get her dinner bowl.
I hit the spoon against it, set it down
and watch her crawl to it,
pausing after each forward thrust of her legs
and when she takes her first bite,
I grab the belt and beat her across the back
until her tears, beads of salt-filled glass,
    falling,
shatter on the floor.

There are no excuses or rationalizations here, just the facts. The personae in these poems do not ask for sympathy or advocacy. They only say, "Look at me." Their lives are whole, in a sense; nature dictates their actions, the steps they must take to survive. They endure like persistent weeds in a flower bed. The narrators in *Cruelty* have sharp teeth that can tear and cut and grind. They manipulate like prostitutes, kill with resolve, and sneer at the delicate sensibilities of the genteel caste. Undoubtedly, many find the poems in this collection to be offensive because they inspire fear: fear of one's own ignorance and fear that the weeds may someday completely overtake the garden.

In *Cruelty* one of Ai's speakers says, "I've never once felt anything / that might get close. Can't you see? / The thing I want most is hard, / running toward my own teeth, / and it bites back." In *Killing Floor*, Ai's second collection of dramatic monologues, this desire is fulfilled. In *Cruelty* Ai established the importance of the essentials: birth/death, love/hate. In *Killing Floor* she goes beyond the basics to a wider vision, adopting a variety of voices and pushing her poetry toward a more universal view of the process of life and death. She achieves this shift in two ways: first, by creating diverse personae and imbuing them with a clear, unadulterated vision of real life, and second, by placing some of her narrators into historical situations, thereby enabling them to create both public and private myths.

Some of the narrators are famous or infamous public figures: Leon Trotsky, Yukio Mishima, Marilyn Monroe, Ira Hayes, Emiliano Zapata. Others are little-known or unknown characters whose situations are more vague: a German homosexual in Buchenwald, a half-mad Indian bride, a murderous fourteen-year-old boy, and others. Critic Sandra Gilbert comments, "Reading *Killing Floor* in a single sitting is like flipping through the pages of a grotesque family album full of snapshots of raging or suffering people seen from odd angles" (*Poetry*, October 1981). These concentrated snatches of pain and passion illustrate the ferocity of history, public and private. Ai's use of the public figures helps to place private struggles in a larger historical process. As Randall Albers said, "If *Cruelty* was the chronicle of little, nameless unremembered acts of inhumanity, *Killing Floor* is the chronicle of those actions played out with the full force of history's monstrous acts of cruelty resonating in the background" (*Chicago Review*, Spring 1979). The collection begins with the voice of Trotsky in the title poem, and ends with the voice of Lope de Aguirre. The vision of both men helped to form the "killing floor" upon which they were eventually sacrificed. Trotsky describes a vision of his own death:

> At noon today, I awoke from a nightmare:
> my friend Jacques ran toward me with an ax,
> as I stepped from the train in Alma-Ata.
> He was dressed in yellow satin pants and shirt.
> A marigold in winter.
> When I held out my arms to embrace him,

he raised the ax and struck me at the neck,
my head fell to one side, hanging only by skin.
A river of sighs poured from the cut.

The contrast between the gentle "marigold in winter" and "river of sighs" and the graphic description of the beheading emphasizes the antithetical nature of life. Lest readers despair, though, "The Gilded Man" shows the defiance of Aguirre, the sixteenth-century visionary who, on his single-minded quest for the public myth of the golden city of El Dorado, found his own personal myth:

> Does God think that because it rains in torrents
> I am not to go to Peru to destroy the world?
> God. The boot heel above your head is mine.
> God, say your prayers.

In "I Can't Get Started" the narrator is Ira Hayes, Iwo Jima hero turned skid-row unfortunate. Hayes, an Indian, is one of the men depicted raising the flag in the Iwo Jima memorial. In this poem, he spends Saturday night drunk in a ditch, hallucinating about a huge combat boot. Sunday morning finds him stumbling out of the ditch, shooting holes in the roof of his shack, and staring at newspaper clippings of Iwo Jima:

> I remember raising that rag
> of red, white and blue,
> afraid that if I let go, I'd live.
> The bullets never touched me.
> Nothing touches me. . . .

Hayes typifies the poet's reflections on social decay and emotional disaster, admitting, "I'm the one dirty habit / I just can't break."

Besides the historical sketches, there are also narratives that deal with the unnamed and the unknown; interestingly, of the twenty-four poems in *Killing Floor*, sixteen are told in the voices of men. Fathers, fathers-to-be, sons, young men, and male lovers all have their struggles with living and dying, and Ai has the uncanny ability to render these male experiences as realistically as she does the female ones. This ability helps to draw the poetry further from the private realm to the public. The son, for example, in "Sleep Like a Hammer" is caught up in the web of ever-increasing frustration and helplessness in the presence of his senile father: "Now you just sit, / every so often lifting your hands / as if they were holding broken glass, / and I don't know what to do, father." The poem builds

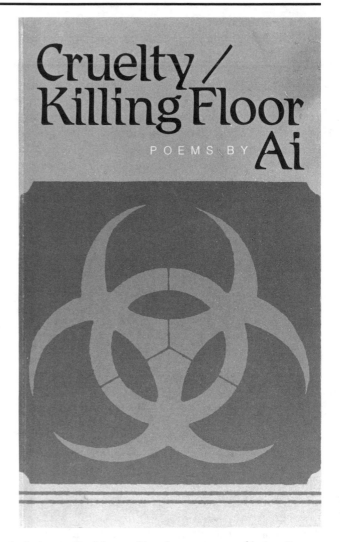

Poetry
ISBN 0-938410-38-5

$9.95 INT SERIES

"So totally does Ai identify with what she sees that all her poems become, successfully, the voices of men, 40-year-old
whores, mad hitchhiker killers, starving tenant farmers, child-
beaters, even corpse-haulers.

Not only has Ai approached new ground in exploring the human consciousness in poetry, but she is covering it in lucid style.
Like the eye of a horse she is herself lost (transformed) among
the people and events she witnesses and records."
—ALICE WALKER

"In the Bible, in the ages of exile that led to the Flood, people
used to live for hundreds of years. Ai is one of these in our own
time; so that she sees her personaes' lives and deaths synchro-
nously and says them in the same breath. She passes through
ages and characters under the skin. The Deluge, the drama, the
annihilations are for our nerves to survive."
—SANDRA McPHERSON

"She is the most talented young poet I know."
—GALWAY KINNELL

This reissue makes available Ai's first two classic collections,
including the Lamont Poetry Selection *Killing Floor*, in one volume. Her poems are crystal clear, immediately engaging and
often apocalyptic. Whether writing of Emiliano Zapata or prisoners at Buchenwald, Ai's verse is explosive and unpredictable.

Ai is also author of *Sin*, her most recent collection of poetry.

Foreword by Carolyn Forché

THUNDER'S MOUTH PRESS

93–99 Greene Street
New York, N.Y. 10012

Cover design by Loretta Li

Cover for the 1987 one-volume edition of Ai's first two books, both characterized by graphic, often grotesque subject matter

with steady control, and in its course readers learn that the father was once responsible for the death of a pregnant hound and that, when his son kicked him for his cruelty, the father lamed his son with a shovel. Finally, in the poem's dramatic climax, the son's suppressed rage breaks loose in one terrible act of self-definition:

I hear my wife yelling. . . .
But she's in another country.
There's only you. Me.
When I bring the hammer down,
your toes splay out, snap off like burned bacon.
Your lips pull back
and your tongue drifts over your teeth
and I'm moving up to your hands, shoulders, neck,
    face.
Lord, moving up.

The son is not only moving up physically, but emo-

tionally. Ai, it seems, would have people learn from their cruelties, survive, and retain their vision. As Zapata says in "Pentecost," "Dying doesn't end anything. / Get up. Swing those machetes."

While some critics accuse Ai of using the sensational to make her point, she would probably argue that the "sensational" is not really so at all, that it is simply a reaction to a numb world. In "The Kid" the speaker, a fourteen-year-old boy, massacres his family. Ai begins the poem with this line: "My sister rubs the doll's face in mud," as though giving a hint that parental abuse could somehow account for the murders. By the poem's end, though, Ai leaves only a savage, empty irony: "I'm fourteen. I'm a wind from nowhere. / I can break your heart." Any sympathy one had for the narrator at the outset is quickly dissolved in the face of grisly atrocity, but the poem still leaves one feeling as though one has been manipulated through many levels of emotion.

The symbols of blood, birth, and death dominate *Cruelty*, and the idea of the cutting edge is surely the dominant symbol in *Killing Floor*. Knives, axes, drills, pitchforks, split skulls, sliced flesh, and a jabbed sun are all present. In Ai's hands, according to Carolyn Forché, "cutting edges become instruments for penetrating and dissecting a social order which has become somehow anesthetized to human agony" (*Washington Post Book World*, 11 March 1979).

There are many similarities between *Killing Floor* and *Cruelty*: the themes of patricide, genocide, necrophilia, cannibalism, torture, and murder; the straightforward, unadorned style of language. Yet there are differences. By placing these facts of life, however unpleasant, in the light of historical perspective, Ai achieves her goal of indicting a degenerate society. Unlike *Cruelty, Killing Floor* does contain some didacticism, though in a backhanded way. Ai's moralizing is based on seeing oneself and one's environment clearly and thus creating a personal survival strategy to deal with the modern world.

The short poem "Guadalajara Cemetery" is one of the best in the collection. In it Ai shows her remarkable ability to convey a massive message in a few concise, passionate lines:

> You sort the tin paintings
> and lay your favorite in my lap.
> Then you stroke my bare feet
> as I lean against a tombstone
> . . . .
> I have never asked less.
> You, me, these withered flowers,
> so many hearts tied in a knot,
> given and taken away.

The poem conveys a common enough theme in these times, but a close look reveals the consummate skill of the poet. *Killing Floor* is filled with these moments.

Ai looks at failure and tries to create not heroes but survivors, people willing to see through illusion and distraction. This vision is epitomized in the narrator of "Ice":

> Tonight, wake me like always.
> Talk and I'll listen,
> while you lie on the pallet
> resting your arms behind your head,
> telling me about the wild rice in the marshes

and the empty .45 you call *Grace of God*
  that keeps you alive
as we slide forward, without bitterness, decade by
  decade.

If *Killing Floor* begins the transition between the personal myth and the public myth, *Sin* completes it. Published in 1986, *Sin* is another collection of dramatic monologues, and as in her previous works the personae in the poems are diverse. In *Sin* there are monologues narrated by John F. Kennedy, J. Robert Oppenheimer, Francisco Pizarro, Joseph McCarthy, and the Atlanta child murderer. There are also some unnamed narrators: a Latin-American priest, a farm woman, a Russian émigré, a *Kristallnacht* victim, a journalist covering Vietnam, and others. Ai catches her subjects, well known and otherwise, in physical and psychological crises, and she permits them neither eloquence nor redemption. They stammer through last-ditch attempts at self-justification, making excuses or explaining in a desperate kind of testimony. The title of the collection indicates some religious overtones, and, indeed, the characters seem to realize that they are damned despite their protestations. The personae in these poems value power above all else, but it seems they must be corrupted to attain it. Ai imagines a deity who is not necessarily callous and wrathful, but who allows violence and destruction to happen, especially to these power-starved people.

The monologues in *Sin* are much longer than in her two previous collections, and at times Ai seems to have trouble keeping the intensity going after two or three pages. However, the poems in *Sin* have a richness of detail and a narrative complexity not found in the other books. The bare-bones writing style of her earlier poetry has been exchanged for a more embellished style. While this slightly different style adds detail and decreases the "sensationalism" found in her earlier work, it causes her to seem less courageous and weakens some of the poems. The Kennedy monologue, which opens the collection, seems to announce its theme too blatantly, and the expressionistic, roundabout presentation never offers a character one can take seriously:

> I drove power,
> the solid gold Cadillac.
> Go ahead, frown.
> Tell me about the sin of pride
> and I'll tell you
> about the lie of forgiveness.
> It wasn't Oswald who killed me,
> it was envy.

The McCarthy monologue seems to suffer from the same problem:

> I was a wise man. . . .
> Wasn't I?
> I could already see a faint red haze
> on the horizon;
> a diamond-headed hammer
> slamming down on the White House;
> a sickle cutting through the legs
> of every man, woman and child in America.

Later in this poem, though, Ai gives a sharp, clear image of McCarthy defiling a dead Stalin. Here she uses her trademark close and cutting language to paint a vivid picture:

> The fog clears
> and I'm standing at Stalin's grave
> and he's lying in an open box.
> I get down on top of him
> and stomp him,
> till I puncture him
> and this stink rises up.

In "The Good Shepherd: Atlanta, 1981" a child murderer details his emotions and actions immediately following one of the murders: "I lift the boy's body / from the trunk / set it down, / then push it over the embankment / with my foot. / I watch it roll / down into the river / and feel I'm rolling with it." Later the murderer goes home and makes hot chocolate, cleans the blood out of the upstairs bathroom and begins to read a library book about Mythology: "Saturn, it says, / devours his children. / Yes, it's true, I know it. / An ordinary man, though, a man like me / eats and is full / Only God is never satisfied." This insight into the mind of a murderer is thought-provoking and interesting, though perhaps not totally factual. Ai again uses her skill with language: she speaks so flatly of a horrendous crime in the voice of the criminal that somehow one comes to a terrible sympathy for the murderer.

Ai cannot escape charges of some didacticism in *Sin*. "The Testimony of J. Robert Oppenheimer" ends with the depressing words, "We tear ourselves down atom by atom, / till electron and positron, / we become our own transcendent annihilation." In "The Detective" Ai recounts the horrors of Vietnam and the Cambodian "killing fields" through the eyes of a veteran suffering from posttraumatic stress disorder. Alone in his

house, he imagines the horrors of killing and death, then goes outside and gets in his car:

> I look into the back seat.
> The Twentieth Century is there,
> Wearing a necklace of grenades
> that glitters against its black skin.
> I stare, see the pins
> have all been pulled.
> "Drive," says the voice.

In *Sin* the monologues with anonymous narrators are the most successful, perhaps because readers have no preconceptions about these characters. In "The Priest's Confession" a clergyman is beset by the temptation of Rosamund, a young orphan girl in his care. At age twelve she begs to sleep in the priest's room because she is frightened. "While she slept, / she threw the covers back. Her cotton gown was wedged above her thighs. / I nearly touched her / I prayed for deliverance, but none came." The priest watches Rosamund mature, her breasts growing "in secret / like two evil thoughts." One night at confession the priest finally succumbs to his desire:

> I laid her down.
> I bent her legs this way and that.
> I pressed my face between them
> to smell "Our Lady's Roses"
> and finally, I wanted to eat them. . . .

The priest eventually hangs himself in the bell tower. The poem is rife with religious overtones, and Ai's Catholic upbringing is evident. The priest feels he is a "bead on God's own broken rosary" and speaks of the "sweet, dark Kyries" he hears. The poem is one of many that seems to indicate Ai's disillusionment with the "establishment": religion, politics, war—nothing escapes her wrath.

"The Journalist," perhaps the best poem in the collection, is spoken by a news photographer as he looks at photos he took of a Buddhist nun sacrificing herself on a street in Vietnam: "As an American, I couldn't understand / and as I stood there, / I imagined myself / moving through the crowd / to stop her, but I didn't." After the nun douses her robes with gasoline, her assistant steps forward with a match. Looking at the photographs, the journalist makes a terrible admission:

> I remember how her assistant
> spoke to the crowd,
> how no one acknowledged her,
> how we stood another two or three minutes,

till I put my hand in my pocket,
brought out the matchbook,
and threw it to the nun's side.
I stare at the last photograph—
the nun's heart that would not burn,
the assistant, her hand stretched toward me
with the matchbook in it.

Left out of the photo is the journalist striking the match and touching it to the heart. His realization of the immensity of the photo and its implications is a step on the way to becoming whole. Of himself, the narrator says: "He can't go back. He won't go back. / He never left." Through violence, then, comes self-realization. This is one of the major themes in Ai's work. She claims in "Immortality" that blood is necessary because it "sanctifies and blesses."

Ai is a poet of great skill and potential. Though one may not agree with her subject matter or her straightforward method of presentation, one can agree that she succeeds in her attempts. Her poetry is technically sound: her monologues are meticulously punctuated; her free verse is organized, disciplined, and totally devoid of the unnecessary ramblings that are sometimes found in free-verse monologues. This control helps to give her poems credibility and, as Rhoda Yerburgh says, gives Ai "an authority so absolute it looks casual" (*Library Journal*, 15 April 1986). Ai is a poet who forces one to look at the brilliance of truth, all sides of it, without shades to temper the piercing rays. She does not apologize or justify. She will continue to push the boundaries of her craft, to use force and intensity to take readers beyond what they know into the realm of the real. As David Wojahn has pointed out (in the *New York Times Book Review*, 8 June 1986), "Ai is a harrowing and courageous writer, one of the most singular voices of her generation. Though her poems adamantly refuse to console us, they cannot easily be ignored." *Fate: New Poems*, Ai's latest collection of dramatic monologues, was published in January 1991.

David Baker

(27 December 1954 -   )

Michael Burns
Southwest Missouri State University

BOOKS: *Looking Ahead* (Columbia Heights, Minn.: Mid-America, 1975);

Rivers in the Sea (Columbia Heights, Minn.: Mid-America, 1977);

Laws of the Land (Boise: Ahsahta / Boise State University, 1981);

Summer Sleep (Seattle: Owl Creek, 1984);

Haunts (Cleveland: Cleveland State University Poetry Center, 1985);

Sweet Home, Saturday Night (Fayetteville: University of Arkansas Press, 1991).

What has given David Baker his early critical success is that Baker's voice, at its best, is a combination of the voices that most readers carry with them. He can share mystery and nostalgia. But he is equally as likely to offer a glimpse of fragile selves, frightened faces staring into water or lost somewhere in the dark. His poems look forward and backward from a steady middle, however; readers tend to feel at home in them.

David Anthony Baker was born in Bangor, Maine, on 27 December 1954, to Donald and Martha Fowler Baker. David's father is a state highway department administrator and his mother a secretary. The family moved to Missouri when Baker was one, and in a 1983 interview with John Neilson and Samuel Truitt, he described growing up in a "half-Ozark, half plains, midwestern farm area." He started to write poetry as a sophomore at Central Missouri State University in Warrensburg. There Mid-America Press published two early chapbooks (what Baker calls his "first sad bastardizations of the poetic sentiment"): *Looking Ahead* in 1975 and a haiku series called *Rivers in the Sea* in 1977. Baker earned his B.S.E. in English at CMSU in 1976 and an M.A. in English in 1977. He taught high-school English in Jefferson City, Missouri, from 1977 to 1979, and during this time he married Charlotte Miller (in 1978). They were divorced in 1984. In 1987 Baker married Ann Townsend, who is also a poet.

When in 1979 Baker found that teaching high school left him little time to write, he decided to go back to school and pursue his Ph.D. He had been following the career of poet Dave Smith, and when another poet, Jim Barnes, recommended the University of Utah creative writing program, where Smith was director, Baker made up his mind. He entered the program in 1979 and finished in 1983. While a graduate student, he helped edit the literary magazine *Quarterly West*, serving as poetry editor in 1980 and 1981 and as editor or coeditor from late 1981 to 1983.

In 1981 Baker published his first full-length collection, *Laws of the Land*, with Ahsahta Press at Boise State University. The collection, with an introduction by Dave Smith, consists of thirty-two poems divided into four sections.

Part 1, "Near Deep Waters," presents what seem to be autobiographical accounts of childhood, complete with metaphorical waters that are flowing away, as well as real ponds, floods, and rivers. Sometimes the poems provide the reader with the narrator's own retrospective wisdom; at other times, they focus on less conventional wisdom and a more naturalistic vision, not always pleasant.

Part 2 gives the book its title, and the first-person speaker seems to have made it a point to determine how, as Robert Penn Warren puts it in the section's epigraph, "the world declares itself." The strength in these poems is in the way the speaker discovers his connection to, or enforced isolation from, the secret life of the natural world.

The new perspective in part 3 is a consideration of humankind's imprint on the landscape: what we leave behind, what we carry forward, and where we are "from." These poems confront loss directly; they may, in fact, pull a little too easily at the heartstrings and thus lose credibility. Baker succeeds most completely when he is least direct.

In part 4 the most ambitious of the poems is "Ephemerae." Baker uses the setting of the

David Baker

Great Salt Lake Basin for yet another meditation on humans and nature and their shifting, tenuous relationship. The poem provides an interesting final note to the book. Bringing together two phenomena of swamp life in vivid, tactile imagery, it makes one last point about how man is ultimately different: "the only animal so sickened by death, its stench, its solitude."

Critical response to *Laws of the Land* was generally positive. Smith writes in his introduction that the book is "made of poems which wed intelligence, discipline, and adventurousness." Bruce Weigl, in a spring 1982 review published in *Poet Lore*, said that, though the book is "marred . . . by the inclusion of a few weak poems which too obviously plead for the reader's sympathetic indulgence, David Baker's first book is remarkably even and consistently good." Gary Holthaus, reviewing the book for *Western American Literature* (February 1983), talked about craft, among other things: "Baker's poems are of contemporary places, but comprise a sort of journey also, the poems moving inexorably in lines long enough one sees the distances. They are filled with images that are stark and clear as the air." Barry Weller declared in *Prairie-Schooner* (Spring 1984) that "the most powerful effect of *Laws of the Land*

is cumulative" and that one of Baker's strengths is a "visionary alertness to what the ordinary surfaces of the world conceal."

While at Utah, Baker also wrote the poems accepted for publication in a chapbook, *Summer Sleep*, by Owl Creek Press in late 1982, though the book did not appear until 1984. All of the poems in this chapbook are also included in *Haunts* (1985). Baker had moved to Gambier, Ohio, in 1983 and was a visiting assistant professor of English at Kenyon College for two years. His residency qualified his manuscript for publication as part of the Ohio Poets Series at Cleveland State University Poetry Center, and *Haunts* was published in December 1985. It consists of the fourteen poems from *Summer Sleep* plus eight new ones, making it still a slender volume, typical of other books published in this series.

What Baker hopes to discover or uncover in this collection is indicated by its title. T. R. Hummer (*Western Humanities Review*, Spring 1986) has pointed out the possibilities of the word *haunts*: the common American colloquialism describes places returned to in body or in memory; the lesser-known southern ruralism, sometimes pronounced "haints," refers to people, not places, and therefore ghosts. In the best of Baker's poems in this book, readers feel the chill of recognition that accompanies the revelation of haunts—through carefully orchestrated narrative details. Often the endings of these poems open up, leaving the mystery intact but offering an understated wisdom. In the title poem, for example, the speaker has unearthed the story of a hunter who froze to death high in the mountains on the day of the speaker's birth:

> He will stay there
> finally too cold to shiver,
> relaxing, gun on lap,
> and look over the beautiful, sweeping
> emptiness the world has become,
> for all my life.

In "The Anniversary of Silence" the persona is remembering a girl who died of snakebite when she dived into the green pool of a rock quarry: "How strange to feel such loss at this small / absence. I wish I could reach out and touch her / hand where she floats, and pull her from the darkness. / I wish I heard her singing softly, safe now, saved."

A lighter poem that stands out for its social setting and sense of humor is "8-Ball at the Twilite," in which the speaker is shooting pool in a tavern: "Connie Francis may say she loves us, if we stay. / So we pass the nub of chalk between us again, / rubbing the last of it over our tips / as a new rack of balls explodes, / running hard for the far green corners." Other poems in this collection that show Baker's developing talents are "The Wrecker Driver Foresees Your Death," "Running the River Lines," and "Call Across the Years."

What goes wrong in the weakest of the pieces is either the music or the metaphor. The pentameter lines of "Hunters: the Planting," for example, seem padded with connectives and occasionally flat, as the poem tries too hard to pull together the separate images of seeds to make a central metaphor. And though it is often this poet's good fortune to draw comparisons that enrich his writing, Baker is imprecise with a few of his similes: "summer heat hangs on like a scald too deep to ignore" he writes in "Summer Sleep," and one wonders what would serve as an ignorable scald; in "Fire Watch: After You Have Gone" there is this line: "Leaves sailed in the air like ash," a comparison that seems weak and unilluminating. In "Dark Earth, 1963" Baker describes closing the cellar door with a slamming mo-

tion as if it were "the lid of a jar," a questionable image at best.

Rightfully, however, the reviews of Baker's *Haunts* praised the book's strengths and Baker's emerging talent. The blurbs on the dust jacket are worthy of mention. David Bottoms writes that Baker's "gift for language is truly impressive"; Bottoms is "struck by the courage of his vision." Though Laurence Lieberman indulges in some hyperbole (he writes that one is left "dumbfounded by Baker's matchless capacity . . ."), he speaks sensibly of Baker's tenderness and low-keyed honesty. Thomas Reiter wrote in *Quarterly West* (Spring 1986) that Baker is a poet "who deserves wide attention," and who writes poems of "direct and radiant evocation." The most insightful look into Baker's poetics is Hummer's 1986 article in *Western Humanities Review*: "*Haunts* projects a world divided along the Christian fault lines of innocence, fall from innocence, guilt, and redemption, but the axis of that pattern is skewed away from the spiritual plane of traditional Christianity into the plane of the purely human." Hummer points out that this has become a familiar strategy, and therefore a dangerous one: "There are, in fact, moments in *Haunts* when Baker comes very close to succumbing to the risk of cliché." However, Hummer also offers this appraisal of Baker's work: "I find Baker's book peculiarly convincing because the central act of this book is the miracle of resurrection: of the personal past, of the cultural past, of the history of poetry itself."

Since 1984 Baker has continued to teach writing and literature at the university level. He was Visiting Telluride Professor at Cornell University during the summer of 1985, and after leaving his temporary position at Kenyon College (where he served as an assistant editor of the *Kenyon Review*), he took a tenure-track position as an assistant professor at nearby Denison University in Granville, Ohio, where he now lives with his wife, Ann. Since the publication of *Haunts*, he has continued to write and publish, with many of his poems appearing in prestigious journals. A look at these poems shows some important differences in the new work. Baker still tells a good story, but he introduces a variety of rhetorical strategies. He also focuses more frequently on social themes, and two of the recent poems published in the *Southern Review* make use of the knowledge Baker has gained from years of playing the guitar. The guitarist in "Sweet Home, Saturday Night" (which became the title poem of Baker's 1991 book) reflects on his musical talents at one point in the poem and says that his solo was "all hype, stolen / licks, cheap fingerings, childhood / grandmother, nostalgia, you know— / all the usual moves / strung together in a dried-up stream / of self-consciousness, all / the usual moves, out of fear of sounding foolish." This poem and other recent works, such as "Dixie,"

also in the 1991 collection, provide ample evidence that Baker has dealt with any similar misgivings in his poetry.

Interview:
John Neilson and Samuel Truitt, "David Baker: An Interview," *Hika*, 44 (Winter 1983): 22-31.

John Balaban

(2 December 1943 -)

Ronald Baughman
University of South Carolina

BOOKS: *Vietnam Poems* (South Hinksey, U.K.: Carcanet, 1970);

After Our War (Pittsburgh: University of Pittsburgh Press, 1974);

Blue Mountain (Greensboro, N.C.: Unicorn, 1982);

Coming Down Again (San Diego: Harcourt Brace Jovanovich, 1985; revised edition, New York: Simon & Schuster, 1989);

The Hawk's Tale (San Diego: Harcourt Brace Jovanovich, 1988);

Vietnam: The Land We Never Knew, by Balaban and Geoffrey Clifford (San Francisco: Chronicle, 1989);

Words for My Daughter (Port Townsend, Wash.: Copper Canyon, 1991);

Remembering Heaven's Face: A Moral Witness in Vietnam (New York: Poseidon, 1991).

OTHER: *Vietnamese Folk Poetry*, edited and translated by Balaban (Greensboro, N.C.: Unicorn, 1974);

Ca Dao Vietnam: A Bilingual Anthology of Vietnamese Folk Poetry, edited and translated, with an introduction, by Balaban (Greensboro, N.C.: Unicorn, 1980).

John Balaban's central subjects and themes emanate from his moral belief in taking decisive

action to oppose human violence, particularly war. He affirmed these convictions when he became a Quaker at sixteen, while searching for an alternative to the violence he witnessed frequently in the tough, housing-project neighborhood where he was raised. Later, when drafted for military service, he sought and received permission to go to Vietnam as a civilian conscientious objector. His strong opposition to the Vietnam War and his alternative service in Vietnam provide part of the thematic framework for his poetry and prose. His voice adds the perspective of a conscientious objector to America's growing body of literature about the Vietnam War and its far-reaching effects.

Born in Philadelphia to Phillip and Alice Georgies Balaban, John Balaban attended Pennsylvania State University, earning a B.A. with highest honors in English in 1966. During his senior year he received a Woodrow Wilson Fellowship, which allowed him to study English literature at Harvard, where he received his A.M. in 1967. Balaban married Lana Flanagan, a teacher, on 27 November 1970; they have one daughter, Tally. From 1970 to 1992, Balaban taught English at Pennsylvania State University, University Park, rising in rank from instructor to professor and director of the Master of Fine Arts Program. In 1992 he was appointed professor of English and direc-

John Balaban in Hanoi, 1989

tor of the Master of Fine Arts Program at the University of Miami.

Balaban's honors and awards include the Chris Award granted by the Columbus (Ohio) Film Festival in 1969 for *Children of an Evil Hour*, a documentary film he codirected with Peter Wolff; the 1974 Lamont Prize from the Academy of American Poets for *After Our War* (1974); Fulbright lectureships in Romania for 1976-1977 and 1979; the 1978-1979 Pushcart Prize for his *Hudson Review* essay "Doing Good"; the Vaptsarov Medal from the Union of Bulgarian Writers in 1980; a National Endowment for the Arts Fellowship in translation in 1985; a 1990 National Poetry Series Book Selection for *Words for My Daughter* (1991); and the 1990 Pushcart Prize for the poem "For the Missing in Action," first published in *Ploughshares* and collected in *Words for My Daughter*.

To fulfill his alternative service during the Vietnam War, Balaban in 1967 joined Interna-

tional Voluntary Services, the largest private volunteer agency under contract to the United States Agency for International Development (USAID), and was appointed a literature and descriptive-linguistics instructor at the University of Can Tho, South Vietnam. After the university's buildings were badly damaged during the 1968 Tet Offensive, Balaban became a field representative for the Quaker and Mennonite Committee of Responsibility to Save War-Burned and War-Injured Children, a Boston-based group that offered hospital care to children.

After his alternative service was completed, Balaban returned to the United States in 1969, but Vietnam continued to draw him. In 1971 he went back and began his translations of folk poetry (published as *Vietnamese Folk Poetry* in 1974). During a 1985 trip he researched postwar changes in unified Vietnam, and in 1989 he served as a lecturer at the University of Hanoi. These activities illustrate his continuing interest in the country that becomes both a backdrop for and symbol of issues central to his work.

In the subtitle of his 1991 memoir, *Remembering Heaven's Face*, Balaban describes himself as *A Moral Witness in Vietnam*. This perspective is perhaps best exemplified by John Lacey, the protagonist of Balaban's novel *Coming Down Again* (1985). Lacey embraces a personal creed derived from Sir Philip Sidney, the sixteenth-century English "knight, poet, and Christian humanist," who wrote that "Virtuous knowledge results in human action." Merely being well-educated or knowledgeable, Balaban asserts through his protagonist, is not enough: knowledge should lead one to action. Balaban frequently denounces those who do not act; in his poem "For John Haag, Logger, Sailor, Housepainter, Poet, Professor, and Grower of Orchids" (in *Words for My Daughter*) for example, he attacks those academics who reside in "College[s] of Glooms / . . . those who speculate but never make."

The use of the first-person-plural pronoun in the title of Balaban's first major collection of poetry, *After Our War*, emphasizes that all Americans are implicated in the morass of the Vietnam War. In the initial poem, "Carcanet: After Our War," he employs classical allusions to demonstrate the corruption of contemporary figures compared to their more heroic, classical models. In the first stanza, Balaban uses a character named Hieronimo, a variation on the protagonist of Thomas Kyd's sixteenth-century revenge play *The Spanish Tragedy*, to portray a moral modern man who painfully comes to understand that "Intelligence is helplessly evil; words lie." He, like the Vietnamese people, has been betrayed and brutally wronged, particularly by four American generals on horseback who, like the biblical Four Horsemen of the Apocalypse, personify the evils of war. The reward for their brutality is a necklace—a carcanet—of spiders, a fitting reward.

A much quieter but equally intense poem, "The Guard at the Binh Thuy Bridge" dramatizes the casual disregard with which a soldier holds the power of life and death over another human being. While standing guard, this soldier "idly" watches a Vietnamese woman wash her face in the morning. To break the monotony of his duty, the soldier fixes his rifle sights on her, pauses a moment, and then casually decides not to shoot. The soldier's unthinking yet godlike dominion over whether this woman lives or dies typifies the potential for evil or good available to each soldier, though he may be unaware of the moral import of his actions.

The title of Balaban's *Blue Mountain* (1982) refers to a spiritual state rather than an actual site. Blue Mountain is associated with Mr. Blue, heaven, and "a sense of the human spirit reaching toward heaven, of that spirit being watched by heaven, where, in the Taoist-Buddhist continuum, our moral efforts are judged and weighed," as Balaban explains in his preface to *Remembering Heaven's Face*. Throughout the 1982 collection, he searches for his own personal Blue Mountain, his sense of being in harmony with a place—of being home—after Vietnam. The speaker perceives in "Crossing West Nebraska Looking for Blue Mountain" that such a site is "only as large as a thought / . . . But from its peak, one can see everything clearly." He travels the American West but feels estranged from—or at best a mere passerby to—those he meets. He listens on his CB radio to reports of shootings, knifings, and maimings, and he is reminded of his Vietnam experiences. He feels emotionally fragmented, like the dismembered body parts of American soldiers in "After Our War" that search for people to whom to attach themselves.

In the final section of *Blue Mountain* the speaker travels to Romania, the home of his ancestors, where he anticipates finding peace. But because of language and cultural barriers he discovers that he is as estranged as in Vietnam and the United States. In "All Souls Night" the speaker visits the graves of his grandparents, voicing his concern about their difficult lives as laborers but unable to connect personally with them. Balaban discovers a strong affinity with the poet Ovid, banished from Rome to ancient Romania. The two poets—one ancient, one modern—thus share a similar estrangement from their homelands and emotional isolation in the country of their exile. But when Balaban reads his own poetry at the Varna ruins, he realizes that "only poetry lasts," and with this insight he gains a qualified fulfillment of his spiritual quest.

Balaban's *Words for My Daughter* centers on the adult world passing on its legacy of brutality to children. In "For the Missing in Action," for example, Vietnamese boys discover while playing in the bombed-out, dead earth near their village, a green patch of vegetation—a dead soldier's grave—that assumes the shape of a man. The corpse ironically has given life to and assumed the characteristic of new vegetation. Rather than remaining a grotesque skeleton, the corpse has

Balaban on a boat in the Mekong River during a 1971 trip to Vietnam

produced "posies for eyes, / butterflies for buttons, a lily for a tongue." This regeneration of life, however, carries with it the suggestion that death has not been conquered, for when the villagers huddle "asleep together," they hear in their dreams "a rustly footfall / as the leaf-man rises and stumbles to them." Thus their lives are penetrated by the "rustly," stumbling, risen, but also fallen, figure of death.

In the title poem, Balaban offers a personal message to his daughter as a means of countering the adult legacy of violence. Beginning with recollections of brutality witnessed while growing up in a Philadelphia housing project, the narrator recalls vignettes from his neighborhood: an alcoholic father who beat his son; an alcoholic mother raped by a milkman; a girl with a dart in her back; and a boy nearly hanged. These scenes spur memories of a Vietnamese boy writhing in agony as the speaker tries to locate the boy's pain for American doctors, one of whom says the

boy's ears "are blown" and therefore will never hear of others' efforts to ease his pain. These scenes intensify Balaban's commitment to teach his daughter a measure of humanity: "I want you to know the worst and be free from it. / I want you to know the worst and still find good." While he attempts to teach her, he also realizes that his daughter teaches him equally important lessons: "I suspect I am here less for your protection / than you are here for mine, as if you were sent / to call me back into our helpless tribe."

Penetrating the hopeless if not evil heart of this "helpless tribe" is part of Balaban's purpose in his novel *Coming Down Again*. Set in 1974, the novel concentrates on a group of young people, most of whom have served in Vietnam as civilian volunteer workers. Two of these figures, Paul Roberts and Fay Cockburn, are captured for smuggling hashish in the jungle where Burma, Laos, and Thailand form the Golden Triangle. Imprisoned without trial, they are uncertain whether any-

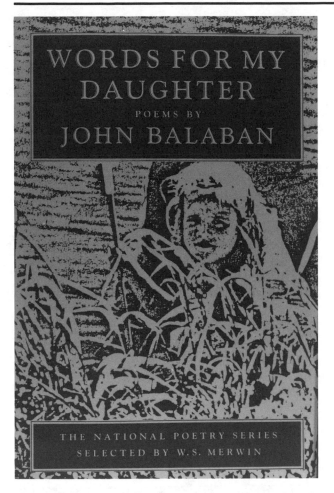

Cover for the 1991 collection. Balaban writes in the title poem: "I want you to know the worst and be free from it."

one knows of their whereabouts; the squalor of their prison life is soon paralleled by their physical and moral descent into an animal-like existence. The heart of the drug smugglers' darkness, however, is penetrated by John Lacey, the novel's protagonist, whose personal creed of moral action leads him to rescue his friends and their bisexual Vietnamese lover, Mai. With the aid of a mountain warlord, Lacey engineers a prison break. The rescue attempt occurs while a rival warlord is being entertained by prison officials. When the rival warlord's army is about to capture Lacey's group, they are granted escape by a detachment of one hundred North Vietnamese army regulars, who kill the pursuing warlord's soldiers. Balaban re-creates in miniature the Vietnam War itself, since the warring groups represent factions involved in the war. Equally as important, he again emphasizes the necessity for moral action through Lacey, though the theme is less credibly realized in the novel than it is in

Balaban's poetry and his memoir.

Balaban's most compelling and accomplished single volume about his Vietnam experiences is his memoir *Remembering Heaven's Face*, which chronicles his 1967 to 1969 service as a civilian conscientious objector as well as his later return visits to Vietnam. Balaban portrays a long list of people with whom he worked and their valiant but often thwarted attempts to provide medical, instructional, or personal aid to Vietnamese civilians; their efforts were often met with bureaucratic resistance both in the United States and in South Vietnam. The most dramatic scenes detail his attempts to provide medical care for war-wounded children. Rather than overwhelming the reader with reports of the more than a hundred thousand civilian casualties each year, Balaban tells of the agonizing experiences of a few children to convey the suffering of thousands.

As an instructor at the University of Can Tho, Balaban met a variety of Americans, including Dave Gitelson, to whom he repeatedly returns in his writing. Gitelson traveled freely among Vietnamese of various political stripes, dispensing agricultural supplies and instruction to local farmers. Gitelson's body was found one morning in a canal; he had been shot in the face at point-blank range. Balaban conjectures that Gitelson may have been killed by CIA operatives involved in the Phoenix Program because he was rumored to have compiled data about the killing of Vietnamese civilians by Americans.

Balaban's postwar return trips to Vietnam yielded not only his award-winning translations of Vietnamese folk poetry but also a new perspective on the country and all those—Vietnamese and American—inextricably bound by a shared history. In the unified country of Vietnam, he found extensive healing of both landscape and people. Such healing he views as an affirmation of the Vietnamese resolve to move beyond tragedy and into the sanity of a hopeful future. Balaban encourages all Americans, especially former soldiers, to view this transformation for themselves and in so doing help put the war behind them as part of their own healing process.

Critical assessment of Balaban's works centers on his outrage against the Vietnam War and his determination to assert personal affirmation beyond the war. Lorrie Smith has pointed out that Balaban's strong antiwar sentiments, often rendered in bitter irony, undercut heroic or romantic notions of war. Writing in the *Christian*

Science Monitor (8 October 1982), Steven Ratiner observed that Balaban combats the modern propensity for violence and alienation with an appeal to sane morality. Philip D. Beidler has noted that Balaban draws upon the modernist technique of adapting classical references to a modern context to suggest the poverty of value and meaning in contemporary life. Additionally, according to Beidler, Balaban incorporates such postmodern devices as collage and mass-media montage to give the flavor of contemporary idioms. *Remembering Heaven's Face* has received perhaps the highest critical praise. Jonathan Mirsky asserted that the war memoir is one of the best books ever written about Vietnam (*New York Review of Books*, 10 October 1991). W. D. Ehrhart's 1990 overview provides the best analysis of Balaban's desire to confront the war's issues and move beyond them. Ehrhart believes that Balaban's works manifest "a remarkable promise of hope, a refusal to forget the past and 'go on,'" "willfully oblivious to history or the lessons that ought to have been learned. . . . Balaban absorbs Vietnam and incorporates it into a powerful vision of what the world *ought* to be."

John Balaban's poetry and prose collectively form an important statement of one who is committed to clarifying, as best he can, the painful morass of the Vietnam War. His convictions about opposing the war led him to act with a moral purpose. Perhaps his most important act, however, is to inform his readers, as he does his daughter, of what he saw and did, to examine the worst possibilities, and yet, through an ongoing moral struggle, to achieve some measure of good.

References:
Philip D. Beidler, "Poets After Our War," in his *Re-Writing America: Vietnam Authors in Their Generation* (Athens & London: University of Georgia Press, 1991), pp. 145-205;

W. D. Ehrhart, "Soldier-Poets of the Vietnam War," in *America Rediscovered: Critical Essays on Literature and Film of the Vietnam War*, edited by Owen W. Gilman, Jr., and Lorrie Smith (New York & London: Garland, 1990), pp. 313-331;

Lorrie Smith, "Resistance and Revision by Vietnam War Veterans," in *Fourteen Landing Zones: Approaches to Vietnam War Literature*, edited by Philip K. Jason (Iowa City: University of Iowa Press, 1991), pp. 49-66.

Gerald William Barrax
(21 June 1933 -   )

Joyce Pettis
North Carolina State University

See also the Barrax entry in *DLB 41: Afro-American Poets Since 1955.*

BOOKS: *Another Kind of Rain* (Pittsburgh: University of Pittsburgh Press, 1970);
An Audience of One (Athens: University of Georgia Press, 1980);
The Deaths of Animals and Lesser Gods (Lexington: University Press of Kentucky, 1984);
Epigraphs (Chapel Hill, N.C.: Mud Puppy, 1990);
Leaning Against the Sun (Fayetteville: University of Arkansas Press, 1992).

SELECTED PERIODICAL PUBLICATION—
UNCOLLECTED: "The Early Poetry of Jay Wright," *Callaloo*, 6 (Fall 1983): 85-102.

Gerald William Barrax is a poet of ideas, a writer with intelligence, vision, depth, versatility, and passion. He culls the best traditions of poetry writing and makes use of traditional and original structures; his subjects span the distances between love and death, romance and reality, and drought and nourishment. Introspective postures and a voice comfortable with itself characterize his poetry as he questions, exposes, and criticizes the intricacies of a world that remains enigmatic for human beings concerned with truth and integrity.

Barrax was born on 21 June 1933 in Attalla, Alabama, to Aaron and Dorthera Hedrick Barrax, but in 1944 he moved with his parents to Pittsburgh, where he and his brother, Harold, grew up. The neighborhood of Homewood, popularized in the fiction of John Wideman, provoked Barrax to reminisce about his own growing to maturity there, but those memories in his poetry are subsumed in a broader context without specificity of locale. After service in the air force (1953-1957) he earned a B.A. in English from Duquesne University in 1963 and his M.A. from the University of Pittsburgh in 1969. Having married Geneva Catherine Lucy in 1954, he has three sons by that marriage: Dennis, Gerald,

Gerald William Barrax (photograph by Linda B. Walters)

and Joshua. The marriage ended in divorce in 1971. He had moved to North Carolina in 1969, when he became a visiting professor at North Carolina Central University in Durham. Since 1970 he has taught American literature and poetry writing at North Carolina State University. He lives in Raleigh with his second wife, Joan Dellimore Barrax, whom he married in 1971, and two daughters, Shani and Dara.

Barrax is a recognized poetry critic, as winner of the 1983 Callaloo Creative Writing Award for Non-Fiction Prose and as poetry editor

(1984-1986) of *Callaloo: A Black South Journal of Arts and Letters*. Widely recognized as an effective teacher of the craft of poetry, Barrax has conducted writing workshops in a variety of university settings, including the University of Arkansas, Wake Forest University, Washington College, University of California (Davis), and Lincoln University. In 1985 he assumed editorship of *Obsidian II: Black Literature in Review* at North Carolina State University.

Another Kind of Rain (1970), a volume in the Pitt Poetry Series and Barrax's first book, is a mature and ordered collection of forty-one poems. Some of them, such as "Letter to Cathy A," "For a Black Poet," and "Efficiency Apartment," mirror the free form and stylistic exuberance of the 1960s. Lorenzo Thomas (*Callaloo*, Fall 1985) has recognized Barrax's "For a Black Poet" as a "satirical response" to Amiri Baraka's poem "Black Art." "For a Black Poet" also satirizes superfluous rhetoric and gratuitous violence:

> BLAM! BLAM! BLAM! POW! BLAM! POW!
> RATTTTTTTAT! BLACK IS BEAUTIFUL, WHI
> TY! RAATTTTTTTAT! POW! THERE GO A
>   HON
> KIE! GIT'M, POEM! POW! BLAM! BANG!

But then he suggests that poetry has a far more profound mission than the instigation of violence: "Poetry will bring us to resurrection." Few of his poems reflect the angry stridency characteristic of black poetry of that decade. Barrax did understand and share the reasons for the anger, but its visibility in his poetry occurs only when the poem demands it, as in "Filibuster 1964": "Knowing all the ways Black men die / we hold back the impulse to laugh / when jackasses debate our existence."

Another Kind of Rain introduces many of the ideas, images, issues, and metaphors that recur in the poet's subsequent volumes: blackness, the family, male/female relationships, music, religious hypocrisy, and the juxtaposition of chance, chaos, and order are agents in the lives of human beings that engage Barrax's creativity and imagination. The arrangement of the first book, using the metaphor of weather foreshadowed in the title—forecast, drought, and rain—communicates a solid narrative coherence that is also apparent in the organization of the subsequent volumes.

Many of Barrax's poems center on the necessity, pain, and pleasure of human relationships and on their beginnings, endings, or continuance. Sons and daughters form part of his concern. In "Efficiency Apartment," for example,

the first poem in *Another Kind of Rain*, the speaker juxtaposes memories of games and living with sons with the desolation that separation from them engenders. In "Visit," from *An Audience of One* (1980), in strong direct lines, the father observes that "After eight months / I am saddened that sons can grow so tall / in the absence of their father." The fetus in the poem "The Fourth Son" was "carried / to the hospital two weeks ago / in the plastic bowl [and] proved under the / microscope to have been a perfect / boy, naturally." Barrax's first daughter's name, as he explains, in "Shani," in the same volume, means "the wonder, the surprise, the start- / ling event"; and "Dara," the poem for his other daughter, in *The Deaths of Animals and Lesser Gods* (1984), says she is "The Beautiful One, last / Child (before they close her) / Is free." The loss of his sons, dealt with in "Efficiency Apartment" and "The Fourth Son," and the gaining of his daughters are subjects that might lead some poets to sentimentality and emotional excess, but Barrax maintains the necessary distance and analytical objectivity that is characteristic of his work.

Lyrical, complex, and well-made poems involving male/female relationships form a substantial portion of Barrax's poetry. "Five-Part Invention," an ambitious poem in his first volume, is typical of his technique of situating relationships or mundane human events in a larger context through metaphor and allusion. The titles of the five parts invite the reader to visualize the formal beauty of portraits ("Nude as Cassandra," "Nude with Apple," "Nude with Flowers," "Nude with Seaweed," "Nude with Tumblers"), but the references to Cassandra, to "Juliet's deatheyed boy," and to legendary lovers (Isolde and Tristan, Helen and Paris, and Hero and Leander); the use of drowning as a metaphor; and the image of swords hanging over heads all suggest that the love is doomed and destined for catastrophe.

The first group of poems in *An Audience of One* might be read as stages in the evolution and growth of a romance. Two people are not yet lovers in "Three Meetings," where they defy nature and cause its silent wrath:

> when he kisses her shoulder the trees begin
>   humming
> in expectation and rigid happiness[.]
> . . . .
> feeling nothing from the earth
> but the vibration of voices
>   with the memory of the quick heartbeat of
>   squirrels

and honest hot sparrows and jays in their leaves
the trees begin throwing stones[.]

The maturation and consummation of the relationship, however, are described with metaphors of growth and greenery in "Without Gaudy Flowers":

> buds unfolded from our nipples,
> feathery willow began its slow growth
> . . . .
> and I was covered with peperomia
> in the crisp leaves of emerald ripple.

The setting of "Greenhouse" in *The Deaths of Animals* is not the traditional structure that simulates ideal growing conditions for plants but, paradoxically, a dark room "half buried in a hillside," where lovers nurture each other: "we discovered / That deprivation in love is hunger, is pain. . . . That was truth's light and dark: the necessity / Of pain in our world to make the joy of its / Complete reversal in each other's love." The double sestina "Geminis," a lyric poem whose intricate repetitiveness of end words might have made it merely a poetic exercise, becomes instead a tour de force that easily stands with the sestinas of Ezra Pound and W. H. Auden. *Geminis* (the twins) is cited in a headnote as being "In Egyptian and Greek mythology . . . symbolized by two goats and two children." Barrax compounds the doubling inherent in its definition with twin souls, two children, a wife and husband, and the doubling of reflection in mirrors:

> Husband, wife, friend, and lover, we have too
> Many needs to be baffled by duty
> Alone; the miracles waking in this room,
> In these speechless bodies, confound us
> More than our own abstractions, in mirrors
> That show love out growing restriction to one.

Barrax's distinctiveness in his poems about men and women in relationships emerges from the blunt reality with which he views love and need and being deprived of them. He expresses both inferred and explicit sexuality with exacting honesty, confronts the disasters that relationships may forge, and unravels the complexity inherent in certain kinds of relationships.

Music and dance, perhaps most visible in the poems about relationships, permeate Barrax's poetry. "Geminis," for example, offers the lines "I would wake empty as the wind's music,"

Cover for Barrax's 1984 book, in which he explores "truth's light and dark"

and "that music / Was your twin's lament for a lover whose love / Reaches her hands." The persona in "If She Sang" "would feel better / if she sang. / I understand song and could enter / uninvited into its world." Specifically named songs in "School Days" provide the persona a "bridge to the chasm of self-pity." The innumerable references to song and musical instruments and the use of music as image, metaphor, and symbol suggest its absolute necessity to the poet. "Cello Poem" in *Leaning Against the Sun* (1992), a poem that weds Barrax's obvious love of the cello with Walt Whitman's long prose lines, positions the music and the instrument at the center of the work to function as an extended metaphor on which Barrax sounds all of its nuances. One of his longest poems, "Cello Poem" demonstrates his skill in handling an elaborate metaphor with free form and lengthy content. His work also contains a series of numbered dance poems (in *An-*

other Kind of Rain and *An Audience of One*) in which the act of dancing becomes a complex metaphor.

One subject that appears to have occupied much of Barrax's thinking, beginning with his first volume, is the presence of a creator and the attendant concerns of life and death. Inconsistency and irrationality drive Barrax to angry questioning about the nature of the universe. Beginning with "Drought," the second poem in *Another Kind of Rain*, he suggests that drought could be "God's fine irony withholding rain" as preamble to the fire that is prophesied to destroy the earth. In "Earthlog I" and "Earthlog: Final Entry" he toys with the idea that aliens created human beings; in the former poem the diversity in human physical appearance is given by the creators "No more significance than a whim," a distraction as they "determined their destiny." In the latter poem, destiny appears to be in the hands of the created without any guidance or interference from the gods: "We let them act out / their ceremonies and rituals to us / in the name of the names they called us / . . . ashamed to be prophets and gods to fools."

Another grouping of poems discernible in Barrax's four volumes exposes hypocrisy in organized Christianity, as seen in three poems from *The Deaths of Animals*. "From a Person Sitting in Darkness" incorporates the persona's outrage at "TV evangels" and similar people who spew their potentially deadly ignorance into millions of homes, advocating violence (legally sanctioned war) and bigotry under the guise of Christianity. "In This Sign" exposes a similar use of Christianity in its chronicling of Europe's involvement in the slave trade and its justification as a means of bringing Christian religion to primitives. "Spirituals, Gospels" questions the persistence of the types of songs in the title, the paradox of singing praise to the "lord whose blood whose blood drowned our gods," but at the end of the poem Barrax cannot ignore the effect of the beauty of the music. Writing about the early poetry of Jay Wright in a 1983 essay in *Callaloo*, Barrax recognized it as unlike that of "Milton's or Eliot's, in which comforting belief in a fixed, orthodox system predominates; rather like the religious poetry of Yeats and Whitman, Wright's is questing, eclectic, dialectical. . . ." Barrax might have been identifying an affinity between himself and Wright, so distinctly is this group of Barrax's poems described by his own words.

In some of the most delightfully original of his poems, Barrax imagines the genesis of things or acts of human behavior, and, almost always, the creation occurs by chance. His sense of wry humor and his skepticism are evident in this group, as in "The Evolution" (in *An Audience of One*), told from the perspective of the first woman, who envies the reproductive ability of the animals because her coupling with man produces no young. The act of singing is named by Eve rather than "dull Adam" in "The Singer" (also in *An Audience of One*). In *The Deaths of Animals and Lesser Gods*, as the title suggests, many of the poems center on gods but from a perspective of reduction rather than mindless glory. In "The Conception of Goddeath," truth and human need are born. Men compete with Mother Nature in finding ways to destroy themselves in "Competitors." The possibility of chance being god of the universe is the insight of "More and Less": "to believe in the design of sparrows falling / we might answer with the *uncertainty* of human events, / stumbling around the nucleus of death / like electrons in unpredictable orbits." "Liberation" includes these lines:

> I could never decide which made the crueler joke
> God as male bungler
> Or God as female masochist.
> But the survivors were women.

The reader finds neither sermonizing nor blind Christian allegiance in the poems about gods and creation but, instead, tough analyses of inconsistencies and of seemingly illogical decisions.

To say that Barrax's first volume of poetry is the work of a mature poet is not to say that subsequent volumes have not shown growth, because they have. Lines have become stronger, risks with technique are evident in larger projects (such as "Cello Poem"), and the greater variety of metaphor, symbol, and subject—and their increased complexity—are assets of later volumes. In occasional poems that originate with observations about small-animal activity in the backyard while the speaker is mowing grass, Barrax has perfected the technique of finding significant acts in the mundane. This technique, however, is not limited to animal poems. Barrax often uses metaphors, symbols, and images from scientific theory, one of the methods by which his work is made intellectual and by which the everyday occurrence is made to resonate with the universal. His taut diction, an asset, nevertheless may occasionally be inaccessible to some readers, but whatever extra effort is necessary for understanding is time well invested. And Barrax has the talent of writing lines that dazzle with precision and beauty: "She touches when she talks— / must touch to smooth out syntax with her fingertips" (from "Something I Know About Her" in *An Audi-* *ence of One*); "It's all very friendly / the way the night is shrieking / joyful noise unto itself " (from "An Audience of One"). His best poems—even those based on animals, love, or music—are seldom easy but are rewardingly challenging, provocative, and memorable. Barrax is a committed and talented writer of consistently good poetry.

David Bottoms
(11 September 1949 -   )

Lynn Risser
Texas Wesleyan University

See also the Bottoms entry in *DLB Yearbook: 1983*.

BOOKS: *Jamming With the Band at the VFW* (Austell, Ga.: Burnt Hickory, 1978);
Shooting Rats at the Bibb County Dump (New York: Morrow, 1980);
In a U-Haul North of Damascus (New York: Morrow, 1983);
Under the Vulture-Tree (New York: Morrow, 1987);
Any Cold Jordan (Atlanta: Peachtree, 1987);
Easter Weekend (Boston: Houghton Mifflin, 1990).

OTHER: *The Morrow Anthology of Younger American Poets*, edited by Bottoms and Dave Smith (New York: Morrow, 1985).

David Bottoms's career has been marked by a series of critical successes. His first full-length book of poetry, *Shooting Rats At the Bibb County Dump* (1980), was chosen by Robert Penn Warren as the winner of the 1979 Walt Whitman Award from the Academy of American Poets. Bottoms has twice received the Book of the Year in Poetry Award from the Dixie Council of Authors and Journalists, first in 1983 for his second major collection, *In a U-Haul North of Damascus*, and then again in 1988 for his 1987 book *Under the Vulture-Tree*. In 1985 a group of poems from *Under the Vulture-Tree* was awarded the Levinson Prize from *Poetry* magazine. In 1988 Bottoms received several honors: an Award in Literature from the American Academy and Institute of Arts and Let-

David Bottoms (photograph by Michael Cagle)

ters, an Ingram-Merrill Award, and a fellowship

from the National Endowment for the Arts. Over one hundred of his poems have appeared in magazines such as the *Atlantic*, the *New Yorker*, *Harper's*, the *Paris Review*, the *Kenyon Review*, and the *Southern Review*, as well as in two dozen anthologies and textbooks. He is also the author of two novels, *Any Cold Jordan* (1987) and *Easter Weekend* (1990).

Bottoms's use of southern settings and characters in his work is a natural result of his background. The only child of David H. Bottoms, a funeral director, and Louise Ashe Bottoms, a registered nurse, Bottoms was born on 11 September 1949 and grew up in Canton, Georgia. He earned his B.A. in 1971 from Mercer University. On 2 February 1972 he married Margaret Lynn Bensel, whom he had met at Mercer. Bottoms attended West Georgia College, where he received an M.A. in 1973, writing his thesis on the poetry and critical theory of Henry Timrod (a poet of the Old South and Civil War). From 1974 to 1978 Bottoms taught high-school English in Douglasville, Georgia, and worked part-time in the Georgia Poets-in-the-Schools program. He began attending Florida State University in 1979 and earned a Ph.D. in creative writing in 1982. Later that year, he was hired as an assistant professor of English at Georgia State University in Atlanta, where he became an associate professor in 1987. His first marriage having ended in divorce in 1987, Bottoms married Kelly Jean Beard, an attorney from Montana, on 3 July 1989.

The subject matter in Bottoms's poetry reflects his southern experiences, but Bottoms is more than a regionalist. As David M. Cicotello notes in the *Prairie Schooner* (Spring/Summer 1981), Bottoms is one of a few poets "who, through good fortune and good inspiration, penetrate the seemingly impenetrable cloud of regional geography, culture, and poetic tradition." Underlying his descriptions of southern landscapes—from the coasts to the rivers to the ponds and homes of the small town, as well as the suburban South—is a search for collective meaning, for insight that accompanies experience. As Robert Penn Warren noted when announcing Bottoms's Walt Whitman Award, "In [Bottoms's] vision the actual world is not transformed, but illuminated." Bottoms is a realist, and his open-form poems are mostly short narratives based on concrete descriptions that are occasionally extended into simile. His most obvious poetic technique rests on sound, on subtle, internal alliteration that transforms the ordinary into the

poetic. While Bottoms describes concrete subjects realistically, often the subjects work on the level of metaphor as well. Themes are revealed in questions or are more often deduced from the response to the experience being described. David Clewell notes in the *Chowder Review* (Spring-Summer 1980) that in "a time when 'imagination' is too often synonymous only with 'invention,' [Bottoms's] narratives are refreshing reaffirmations that imagination is *recognition* as much as anything else."

In all three major books of Bottoms's poetry, as well as in his novels, there are several topics and settings that appear again and again: country-and-western music and musicians; revivals and faith healings; death by drowning; fishing and hunting; visits to cemeteries; and the relationship of the poet to his father and grandparents. These subjects give his work the color of the South. One concept that Bottoms often examines is the idea of humankind's repressed animal nature, which binds us to the natural world.

Shooting Rats at the Bibb County Dump established Bottoms as an important new voice in poetry. Both the narrative and description come from Bottoms's experiences growing up in Georgia. His New South dwells on the common people, the children as well as the adults, of the small town. Truck drivers, waitresses, honky-tonk couples, and teenagers who vandalize cemeteries or shoot rats at the dump for an evening's entertainment are the characters and voices Bottoms uses to ask the questions that give meaning to experience. Here as well are the animals and reptiles of the southern rivers, ponds, and swamps, and in his consideration of these natural elements Bottoms is at his best in presenting the relationship that binds all things.

Part 1 of *Shooting Rats at the Bibb County Dump*, "Into the Darkness We're Headed For," investigates destruction, destitution, or merely the plain drabness of life. One poem, "The Drunk Hunter," gives a concise look at a type of character often stereotyped as the southern redneck, but in Bottoms's treatment the hunter's predicament evokes the fate that awaits all people. The first section of the poem is told in the third-person-limited point of view of the drunken hunter, who gets lost while illegally hunting on posted land: "Spun on a flat rock / his whiskey bottle points out magnetic north. / All afternoon trees stagger downhill / and up along ridges above thick brush." The second section of the poem comes from the point of view of fellow hunters and ends with an ironic twist, as the hunter becomes the hunted: "Come morning they will praise his patience, / tell stories in camp of a tree stand / frozen over a creek, how *old Jack never would come back / empty-handed*. In two or three days / they will tell what found him in the deeper woods." The ending is abrupt, an ominous play on words, but the hunter has clearly, through his own weakness, become the prey. The hunter's fate is the darkness all are headed for, and the implication in "The Drunk Hunter" as well as in the other poems of part 1 is that the journey into darkness is morally justified: as the characters in part 1 destroy and desecrate, so will destruction and desecration have their own turn in the characters' lives.

In part 2, "Country and Western," Bottoms continues to look beneath the surfaces of southern characters, of men with beer guts and women with beehive hairdos. Some of the poems in this section contrast the present with the past. Examples are "A Trucker Drives Through His Lost Youth" and "Stumptown Attends the Picture Show." Other poems, such as "Jamming With the Band at the VFW" and "Writing on Napkins at the Sunshine Club," show the narrator's isolation from ordinary life in the small town. In these poems Bottoms draws from his own experiences as an amateur musician and his experiences in the honky-tonks, beer joints, and motels of life on the road. In "Writing on Napkins at the Sunshine Club," the narrator says, "What needs to be written is caught / already in Hank's lonesome wail, / the tattooed arm of the man who's all quarters, / the hollow ring and click of the tilted Red Man, / even the low belch of the brunette behind the flippers."

In part 3, "All the Animal Inside Us," Bottoms explores the world of animals: animals of the southern landscape—the catfish, the gator, and the copperhead—as well as the animal within human beings. The narrator, stimulated by alcohol, compares his brain to a small reptile in "Crawling Out at Parties," where "He takes / the gold glitter of earrings / for small yellow birds wading in shallow water, / the swish of nyloned legs for muskrats in the reeds." This affinity with the animal world is stressed repeatedly in part 3. In "The Catfish" a fish is rescued and returned to the sea, "to the current of our breathable past." In "Hunting On Sweetwater Creek" the narrator takes solace in the fact that "there is something to be said for being lost / and finding

again / a creature that crawls in the gut, / arcs the spine, curls hands inward toward claws."

In parts 4 and 5 of *Shooting Rats at the Bibb County Dump* Bottoms deals with death. In "Rubbing the Faces of Angels" a character finds that "after all this time / we are coming to judge death less critically." It is apparent, however, that in the poems that deal with the deaths of his grandmother and grandfather, the narrator cannot offer any consolation. Instead, the narrator dwells more on a strong empathy with the dying, and he concentrates on the images of death that he often expresses in the form of decaying organic objects such as fruit and flowers. In "The Orchid" he describes his dying grandmother as "white as the hospital sheet, / a pale orchid under the oxygen tent, / strange greenhouse." In "Speaking Into Darkness," a poem on the death of his grandfather, the narrator states, "I am holding no true book. / I have no orthodox dream." Amid biblical and family images, the narrator returns to the one belief that has appeared in several of his poems: "all systems shatter like dropped glass." For Bottoms the recognition and acceptance of change is an important insight into experience.

In his next two volumes Bottoms returned to many of the types of characters, settings, and themes that first appeared in *Shooting Rats at the Bibb County Dump*. In both *In a U-Haul North of Damascus* and *Under the Vulture-Tree*, however, there is more use of the first-person narrator, and there are more mature concerns in that the poet deals with life in the suburbs and with a nostalgia for his childhood. Still, Bottoms's intention to illuminate the importance of experience remains, and this intention, actualized through strong narrative and description, is the strength of his work. In the first section of *In a U-Haul North of Damascus* many of the poems illustrate the loss of vitality in the suburbs. In "Neighbors, Throwing Knives" the men practice knife throwing at animals sketched in magic marker on plywood squares. Yet, as the narrator knows, this is a parody of the real experience, and the men's animal natures seem stunted in what the narrator believes is a domesticated world "manicured by wives."

Bottoms's descriptive talents are most evident in his poems set in natural surroundings. In the southern wilderness, hunting and fishing still contain elements of danger, and Bottoms uses these settings in *In a U-Haul North of Damascus* to illustrate themes concerning the relationship of hu-

In ~~The~~ Pasture Under ~~The~~ (Round) Moon

1

~~Cradled~~ Hung between pinetops
three stars cradle the moon. Out beyond
the creek where the moss-beards of live oak
hang over the roofs of chickenhouses, the chickenwire
of a dog lot holds back the briars, and crouched
behind a ~~briar~~-trellis an old dog cries
at the great yellow roundness of the moon.

I listen from this field, this stump
I have laid my bottle on, and watch the black cattle
fold their legs, roll full-bellied on the wet ground.
The salt blocks grow around the lip of the pond
like new teeth. Wind combs the ragged Johnson weed,
ripples the skin of the water. And I think
how the moonlight falls or doesn't fall
through the window beyond the field, the pond,
the wall of trees, falls or doesn't on the bed
where you sleep. What darkness or light touches you,
touches me.

2

What might have been
is like a vague throat-pulse croaking from a cove-shade
or the gargle of bass striking frogspawn, a sound
almost clarifying, like the murmur of cicadas
from the field's edge, or the wing-purr
of bottleflies swarming over cowdung.

Or else like an image
almost solidifying, a cloud of fireflies swarming
between the poplars near the pond, one creature
almost becoming whole, molecular,
but drifting and dissolving with the quickness
of light.

Page from a revised typescript for a poem by Bottoms (by permission of David Bottoms)

mans to animals. "Kinship" is dedicated to James Dickey, who taught Bottoms to hunt with a blowgun, and this poem is a short narrative of two men who go hunting and at one point come across a water moccasin: "Startled / the mouth flowers to a white bloom, / the black stem arches." Fear of the snake drives the hunters back, but as they take their positions to hunt with the blowguns, the hunters feel "a venomous kinship / when the plane of the air is slashed by the dart / and the last of the chambered breath / exits the blowgun with something like a hiss." In the poem "Walkulla: Chasing the Gator's Eye" Bottoms again concerns himself with the human kinship to animals, a notion often forgotten in the urbanized life of the New South. Using spotlights to find gators at night, the narrator discovers the possibility of recognizing the old feelings:

> And if you approach as a part of this river, give
>   over
> to your truest self, something
> washed down like all things washed toward the
>   gulf,
> the reflector will hold above the surface of the
>   river,
> and you will see in its deep, red shining
> the reptile that moves beneath you.

The title poem of the volume is in part 5. The narrator questions his behavior in the past, his false hopes for escape from a failed life. This questioning process leads to the note of hope on which the book ends, as the narrator's journey to Damascus, Georgia, parallels Paul's journey to the biblical Damascus. The emotional self-searching in "In a U-Haul North of Damascus" is unusual in Bottoms's work, and in many ways the narrator reminds one of a modern-day southern Prufrock who asks, "What was I thinking, Lord? / That for once I'd be in the driver's seat, a firm grip / on direction?" The poem turns from thoughts of despair and escape when the smells of pine and rain remind the narrator of the hope that "the world really could be clean again." The questions that end the poem point to the change in the narrator's heart: "Could I be just another sinner who needs to be blinded / before he can see? Lord, is it possible to fall / toward grace? Could I be moved / to believe in new beginnings? Could I be moved?"

The poems in *Under the Vulture-Tree* show an increasing maturity in experience. Nonetheless, many of Bottoms's familiar themes and subjects are present. One of the poems in part 1, "Arcana

Mundi," like many of Bottoms's poems, deals with the poetic quest for insight drawn from experience. The narrator is standing outside a typical, drab small town at night, yet "Once again the heavens cast their cosmical hocus-pocus / over the oily parking lot / of Tito's Italian Restaurant." Gazing up, the narrator becomes "so entranced by the stars swelling / in the black sky, I believe they're busting / to tell me something." In the narrator's mind, stimulated by gin and the sound of blues from Blind Willie's bar, the overwhelming presence of the night sky instills the hope that ends the poem, the belief that "the great *Arcana Mundi* [secret world] might finally be revealed." This hope or quest underlies all of Bottoms's themes.

In part 2 the poem "An Old Hymn for Ian Jenkins" illustrates the importance of place. During a walking tour of New York, the narrator observes, "Southerners know / how a place can wrap you up in a dream." This idea of place carries over into the last three poems of part 2. The narrator's South is evoked by memories of a banjo musician in "Gospel Banjo: Homage to Little Roy Lewis," by a tribute to Lester Flatt in "Homage to Lester Flatt," and by the purchase of a souvenir face jug in "Face Jugs: Homage to Lanier Meaders."

Part 3 of *Under the Vulture-Tree* begins with "Awake," a descriptive poem of the stirring force of spring in a southern landscape. A kinship with animals forms the controlling thread in this section. These narrative poems describe a gar, rats, birds, and finally the vultures of the book's title. In "Under the Vulture-Tree" the narrator experiences a glimpse of the underlying ties or meaning of existence as he floats down a river and encounters a tree filled with vultures who have found a pig carcass. The pig is characterized by its "raw fleshy jowls / wrinkled and generous, like the faces of the very old / who have grown to empathize with everything." This empathy or insight is felt by the narrator as he looks back at the roost and the vultures, "calling them what I'd never called them, what they are, / those dwarfed transfiguring angels." The vultures are initially described with their red, fleshy beaks as "ugly as the human heart." But with a change of heart the narrator sees them as angels "who flock to the side of the poisoned fox, the mud turtle / crushed on the shoulder of the road, / who pray over the leaf-graves of the anonymous lost, / with mercy enough to consume us all and give us wings."

Bottoms circa 1985 (photograph by Jon Coppelman)

In part 4 the narrator looks back to his childhood and adolescence, and this return to the past leads to part 5, which contains three poems that contrast the narrator's present to his father's past. "Naval Photograph: 25 October 1942: What the Hand May Be Saying" describes an old photograph of a World War II cruiser on which a group of gunners and the narrator's father are waving to the camera. "Knowing their future," the narrator sees the waving men as the living and the dead. Those who will die as well as those who will survive "lean against the rail, / unsure who is who, and wave across the sound / toward the camera, toward us, for all of the reasons anybody waves."

"The Anniversary" is also about the narrator's father's experiences in the war; this time the poem illustrates a strange celebration of the near-fatal wound the father received during the war. Lost at sea, "forehead shattered, side pierced," the father is rescued and in a way returns from the dead. The anniversary of this event becomes for the father and for the son a lesson that "the power in the blood to terrify / is sometimes the power of love." The anniversary becomes a ritual of communion, the life of the father enabling the life of the son: "*This is your blood in remembrance of you / who died one night at sea and lived.*"

Under the Vulture-Tree reflects Bottoms's maturity as a poet. Since its publication, he has gone on to publish two novels that explore many of the themes present in his poems. He is working on another book of poetry, which is tentatively titled *Armored Hearts*. In contrast to the obscurity popular in some contemporary poetry, Bottoms's clarity of presentation remains the strongest and most engaging characteristic of his work. A large part of Bottoms's success so far has come from his use of realism as the appropriate means to heighten our appreciation of experience, for Bottoms depicts the culture of the South without the romantic, Gothic, or grotesque embellishments that have become the literary trademarks of the region. As Vernon Shetley noted, "Bottoms now stands firmly within the strain, descended from the *Lyrical Ballads* through Frost, of plain-style presentation of incidents of everyday life" (*Poetry*, May 1988).

Alfred Corn
(14 August 1943 -   )

James David Spreckels
Lamar University

See also the Corn entry in *DLB Yearbook: 1980*.

BOOKS: *All Roads at Once* (New York: Viking, 1976);
A Call in the Midst of the Crowd (New York: Viking/ Penguin, 1978);
The Various Light (New York: Viking/Penguin, 1980);
Tongues on Trees (New York: Parentheses, 1981);
The New Life (New York: Albondocani, 1983);
Navidad, St. Nicholas Avenue (New York: Albondocani, 1984);
Notes from a Child of Paradise (New York: Viking, 1984; Harmondsworth, U.K.: Penguin, 1984);
The Metamorphosis of Metaphor: Essays in Poetry and Fiction (New York: Viking, 1987);
An Xmas Murder (New York: Sea Cliff, 1987);
The West Door (New York: Viking/Penguin, 1988);
Autobiographies (New York: Viking, 1992).

OTHER: *Incarnation: Contemporary Writers on the New Testament*, edited by Corn (New York: Viking/Penguin, 1990);
"Part of His Story" [novel excerpt], *Kenyon Review*, 13 (Summer 1991): 46-58;
Marcel Proust, *L'Indifferent*, translated by Corn (New York: Sea Cliff, 1992).

Alfred Corn (photograph copyright 1984 by Thomas Victor)

Alfred Corn blends the innovative and the traditional in his poetry and has a style and tone that are unmistakable; yet, unlike other poets with highly original voices, he gives no impression of being a loner or isolated pioneer. Though Corn can express lonely anguish or metaphysical struggle, his body of poetry is, on the whole, abundant with a feeling of friendship, love, travel, nature, and the felicities of the senses and the mind. Corn owes much to such poets as Walt Whitman, Hart Crane, and Wallace Stevens, and to such contemporaries as James Merrill and John Ashbery, but his synthesis is his own. The studied openness of his style is matched by the balance of frankness and subtlety in his voice, most clearly seen in the honest, quiet manner in which he handles his homosexuality. A similar balance is evident in his approach to all his subjects and themes; Corn's style, in its free syntax, is often reminiscent of prose, while at the same time carrying all the subtlety and concentration of postmodern poetic practice. Yet the poetry of Corn also reflects the classical tradition.

Alfred Dewitt Corn was born on 14 August 1943 in Bainbridge, Georgia, to Grace Lahey Corn and Alfred Dewitt Corn (the poet has avoided the use of *junior*). Most of his upbringing was in Valdosta, Georgia. The Corns had come from England to Virginia in the 1720s, and Corn has written poetry (in *The West Door*, 1988) about a revolutionary soldier in his direct ancestry. In July 1967 Corn married Ann Rosalind Jones, whom he divorced in June 1971; this relationship supplied Corn with much material found in *Notes from a Child of Paradise* (1984).

After his high-school education in Valdosta, Corn in 1965 earned a B.A. in French at Emory University and in 1970 an M.A. in French at Columbia; during this period, his travels in Europe had a profound, cosmopolitan influence on him. In 1966 he received a Woodrow Wilson Foundation fellowship, in 1967 a Fulbright Fellowship to Paris, and in 1974 a fellowship from the Ingram Merrill Foundation. From 1968 to 1970 he was a faculty fellow at Columbia University. His travels to France, Italy, and elsewhere (1971-1977) are visible in the poetry of *All Roads at Once* (1976). Starting in 1977, he was employed in a series of visiting lectureships or associate professorships at various colleges: Yale University (1977-1979); Connecticut College (1978-1981); Columbia University (1983); City University of New York (1983-1984); the Columbia School of Arts, writing division (1985 and 1987); and Silliman College, Yale (1986). He won a Guggenheim Foundation Fellowship for 1986 to 1987. More recently Corn has held the Elliston Chair of Poetry at the University of Cincinnati, in autumn 1989, and, in the winter term of 1990, the visiting professorship of poetry at the University of California, Los Angeles. In autumn 1990 he was the resident writer at the James Thurber House at Ohio State University. He taught at the New School, Lang College, in 1991 and at the University of Tulsa in 1992. His awards include three Lamont Poetry Prizes (1987, 1988, 1989), the Roethke Prize (1989), and the John Masefield Poetry Prize (1992).

There is a strong autobiographical streak in Corn's poetry. Though it would be rash to assume the factuality of any particular detail and though he has an unquestionable gift for fiction and imaginative telescoping, his poetry books often reflect his life, especially at the period during their composition. *Notes from a Child of Paradise* and "The Outdoor Amphitheater" (in *The Various Light*, 1980) are Corn's only major works in which he recollects the past from more than a decade's distance; in the other books, the memories, when there is recollecting involved, are of recent events.

His first book, *All Roads at Once*, announces most of Corn's major themes. In this early work, written during his free-lancing and traveling from the late 1960s to mid 1970s and published the year he met J. D. McClatchy, the most immediate and also most aesthetic theme of Corn pervades—the appetite of the eye: "the feast is all for the eye," he says in "Forest." Corn's vision seems to drink in the earth, the city, the sea, and the museums. From the hungry sea in "What Sea Urchins Eat" at the beginning of *All Roads at Once* to the evocation of Charles Darwin's boat the *Beagle* in "Passages from a Voyage" at the end, appetite—physical or intellectual—is a delicate and savage disease, as in "Passages":

> thought itself may be
> A disease when one decides perversely
> And with a familiar sinking sensation
> To get to the bottom of everything. . . .

This poem and "The Bridge, Palm Sunday, 1973" are very close to the tone and spirit of Crane. Others, such as "Chinese Porcelains at the Metropolitan," with its list of lacquers like a menu, show how Corn's aesthetic preoccupations compare with Stevens's. "Dreambooks" offers a glimpse into his childhood imagination, and "Getting Past the Past" is one of his few poems about his young years in Georgia. "An Oregon Journal" is based on travels with his wife in the late 1960s. "To Bunny, Remembering Those Days" is addressed to a male lover ("our odd, problematic union, / with its neat matchings, its funny / non-congruences"), while "Marie-Claire's Spring" suggests an ethereally feminine muse. *Ethereal* is a word often used of Corn; critics commonly refer to his style as "airy." *All Roads at Once* was a great critical success, especially for a first book, garnering praise from such critics as Harold Bloom and Richard Howard.

A Call in the Midst of the Crowd (1978) was begun in New York, but about half of it was written in New Haven. The first poem, "To a Muse," invokes an elusive figure "Sometimes angel, sometimes a man" who makes the air burn "with the trace of where / You spoke." Thus Corn announces a new intensity of concern for the discovery of the timeless moment—a more elusive hunger than before. In "The Adversary" he writes:

> I wanted to take life to my lips like
> The simple water—and your hand intervenes.
>   . . . You withhold what you know, as
> Substance begins to rub away, mist from glass.

The "adversary" seems to be the gray in the crystal air: that which stands between consciousness and pure perception. Many of his poems consider the circumstances, the unusual positions or states of mind, in which perception is clearer.

The title poem of *A Call in the Midst of the Crowd* comprises more than half the book, and it is an examination of the nature of New York, a city Corn obviously views as his home, even when he is called away by a visiting professorship or residency somewhere else. With a title from Whitman and a resemblance to William Carlos Williams's *Paterson* (6 volumes, 1946-1963), in the use of extensive quotations from a wide variety of sources, the poem has a subsurface plot about the life of a young artist in New York and his relationship with a lover. There is a separation and hesitant reunion. But the poem is really about the city itself in the different seasons; the poem progresses through the year and includes passages on water, earth, fire, and air. In this respect it anticipates the more obvious influence of Dante in *Notes from a Child of Paradise*. "A Call in the Midst of the Crowd," though the causes and effects in its plot are mysterious, seems to be about the enlargement of emotion that New York City imposes on the individual, creating sometimes an unhealthy or unrealistic tumidity of feeling that affects personal relationships. But the comprehensiveness of the subject matter (the spirit of a great city) weakens the focus, and the quotes— from private letters, encyclopedias, newspapers, Whitman, Edgar Allan Poe, and Henry James— are so fascinating that they sometimes overshadow Corn's own text. Still, though critics at the time were quick to point out the imperfections, *A Call in the Midst of the Crowd* enhanced his reputation.

In 1980 Corn's third book of poems, *The Various Light*, was published. Many of the poems date from Corn's days at Connecticut College. His tendency toward greater and greater subtlety goes too far in some of the poems in this book, according to some critics, who find such pieces as "Debates" and "Songs for Five Companionable Singers" obscure. In other poems Corn's effects, however, are among his best. "A Bid" is apparently an appeal to a lover to take a more realistic view of romance. In "Repertory," "Oxygen," "The Progress of Peace," and others, the reader finds a concern for the renewal of the spirit. As seen in *Notes from a Child of Paradise*, Corn wanted to work out a metaphysic of the spirit that would give a place to the alternative conditions of love as-

sociated with homosexuality. *The Various Light* concludes with one of Corn's most engaging, accessible, and charming poems, "The Outdoor Amphitheater." A Wordsworthian account of childhood and adolescence in Georgia, the poem centers on Corn's memories of an amphitheater—the special occasions, the Easters, the summers, the adventures, the personal firsts, the choirs, plays, and beauty pageants. Corn recalls his youth lovingly, and the poem ends promising of a future that will "move on from strength to strength."

The exultation of *The Various Light*, however, is pale compared to the iridescent exhilaration of *Notes from a Child of Paradise*, Corn's best-known work to date. This long poem was composed when he returned to New York from Connecticut College and worked at Columbia; much of it was also done during the summers during that period, which he spent in Vermont. Designed as one hundred, one-page cantos divided into three parts, like the *Commedia* of Dante, *Notes* is a semi-autobiographical account of Corn's meeting, falling in love with, marrying, and living with his wife, Ann, and of his ensuing questions and conflicts about his sexuality. Interconnected with this story are passages that take their origins from Dante and passages on the northwest expedition of Meriwether Lewis and William Clark. Being set in the 1960s, *Notes* comments widely on the preoccupations and issues and popular culture of that decade. The allusiveness of the poem is wide-ranging, not only in reference to literature and nineteenth-century American scene painting but to music as well. In the radiant vision at the end, Corn expresses the peace he has sought between body and soul, between time and timelessness: *"The blossoming apple is the Tree of Heaven, / Music is the paradigm of the concord // Which took the part of the love in the first ordering."* These words are spoken at the end by the muse of the poem, a manifestation of Ann as Corn's Beatrice. The resounding conclusion has a more confident tone and less abstraction than Dante's *Paradiso*. The poem is not quite as weighted as Dante's work, however, being more in the tradition of Ludovico Ariosto, of Lord Byron's *Don Juan* (6 volumes, 1819-1824), and of James Merrill's "The Book of Ephraim" (in *Divine Comedies*, 1976). Corn's title actually derives from the French film *Les Enfants du Paradis* (1945), which had a vogue during the period about which Corn is writing.

Corn recalls with affection the wonder of being young and politically, socially, and cultur-

Emerson, "The Poet"

THE CANDLELIGHT BURGLARY

Open the vacation house after a winter's absence
which
And always some surface or hidden damage lies in wait,
~~gets~~ to confirm the adage, still not obsolete,
That nothing really ever lasts but Time itself.
This year, it took the form of a second-story man;
Amateur, a detective also amateur would judge
From simple clues: a punched-in glass pane and (power
Was off) quick recourse to a candle-end, abandoned
On the mantel first by host and then by visitor--
This marble-pale wand, guttered, with a black wire
At its core. Wouldn't anyone have thought to bring
A flashlight? Well, a stand-in was near and apropos,
Provided by the absentee. "Through all her kingdoms,   *
Nature insures herself." True, and someone has to make
An inventory: landscape with boy angling in rushing
Stream; music system, more or less new; a chiming clock;
A Federal mirror.... Portable, negotiable,
They were what attracted his quick sleights of hand.
(At least the silver knew enough to stay in hiding.)
I'm sure this place was only one of several targets;
And then, effects not used nine months a year, we can
Obviously live without, hence may not have a right to....

But look, now the hindered title, at one stroke,
Breaks free: mine--the law ~~entitles~~ --if stolen from me.
(As losses help the gambler own up to what he ~~wants~~ *lacks* ?)
In each drawer jerked open, a starry splash of marble,
Tears spilled over things taken, or rather those
Left behind for me to try to have and hold.... Imagine
The scene in eerie chiaroscuro that sprang into life
For that carpenter ant typing his way across the sill,
Who, how many nights ago, paused, antennae extended
At a blocklike grain of sugar, saw its quartz sparkle
In the glow and waver of invasive light, and then
A distant, crouching prowler, almost giant as his shadow.
A witness so marginal could hardly identify
Or think valuable what was spirited away
On the spread wings of cupidity-with-mind-made-up....
have
Nor^ followed the implications of a psyche's forcing
The issue, fear of discovery, of loss, the curious
Unconsidered spilling of light (and burning wax)
On all that's truly worth having. Worth having, that is,
When we keep, among other uninsurables, our word--
Goods possessed, for the most part, courtesy of darkness,
Which keeps things secret and doing so keeps them.

Alfred Corn

Revised typescript for a poem collected in The West Door *(by permission of Alfred Corn)*

ally active in the 1960s. But his serious purpose in *Notes*, besides creating his own poetic Bildungsroman, is to build a pragmatic synthesis of life, art, and spirit. When sections of *Notes* appeared in *Poetry* magazine in 1983 and 1984, they drew much attention. The complete, published book received great acclaim.

Throughout his career Corn has published essays and book reviews about other writers. In 1987 a book containing about half of these was published: *The Metamorphosis of Metaphor*. A note of tutorial patience runs through these witty and careful considerations of the work of other poets and of two novelists, Marcel Proust and Elizabeth Bowen. The poets covered are Crane, Stevens, Ashbery, Boris Pasternak, Andrey Bely, Eugenio Montale, Constantine Cavafy, George Barker, Robert Pinsky, Robert Lowell, Elizabeth Bishop, John Hollander, and others.

The West Door was published in 1988. Corn is known for the open form of his poems, but he is capable of closed-form poems, and *An Xmas Murder* (separately published in 1987) is a blank-verse monologue highly reminiscent of Robert Frost, and less directly of Robert Browning. In other poems in *The West Door* the deep, precise observation of nature, as in "Naskeag" and "Two Travelers on a Summer Evening," and the contemplation of history and ideas from travel, as in "From the United Provinces, 1632-1677" and "After Ireland: Five Poems," are familiar to any reader of Corn. What is new is the almost-imitative, traditional form of *An Xmas Murder*, which resembles a work by Frost silvered over with Corn's more silken style. *The West Door* also contains some of Corn's translations of famous poems by Rainer Maria Rilke, Pablo Neruda, and others. Toward the end of the book is a poem about Corn's ancestor John Peter Corn, a soldier who served under George Washington at Valley Forge. The poem concerns John's meeting and interlude with Elizabeth Hannah Parr in an apple orchard. The couple later married. *The West Door* is the first book by Corn that does not seem written by a young poet but by a man in the confidence of middle age.

Corn's *Incarnation: Contemporary Writers on the New Testament* (1990) contains essays by several modern poets, who assess the Gospels and the Epistles in a way that reaffirms their living power as literary texts and sources of insight. In assembling such a book, Corn showed his Erasmian concern for things of the spirit.

Autobiographies, published in 1992, has in common with *A Call in the Midst of the Crowd* that the first half is a collection of lyrics or shorter dramatic pieces and the other half is one long poem of major interest. Among the startling works in the first half is a dramatic monologue on Dracula, "My Neighbor, the Distinguished Count," a chilling piece about a woman who lets her neighbor have a pint of her blood at each visit. This poem and others show that Corn is approaching a New Formalist lucidity and immediacy. This quality complements his airiness with more solidity and brings him closer to mainstream American poets, such as Richard Wilbur or Anthony Hecht. Indeed, Corn's Dracula poem suggests Wilbur's often-anthologized "The Undead." Corn's "Contemporary Culture and the Letter 'K'" courts comparison to Stevens's "The Comedian as the Letter 'C.'" Corn's poem is a witty excursion through words beginning with *k*, words associated with American popular culture from the turn of the century to the age of AIDS: "Krazy Kat, Kleenex, Deborah Kerr, Korea, Koolaid, / And Jack Kennedy. . . ."

The poem "1992," which constitutes the second half of *Autobiographies*, consists of sections titled by the year in which the described experiences happened in the life of the poet. The reader is treated to a wide variety of Corn's insights on his life and times, in the mode of nonconfessional but vivid autobiography previously tried in "The Outdoor Amphitheater" and *Notes of a Child of Paradise*. As in "Contemporary Culture and the Letter 'K,'" Corn uses more references to popular culture, including rock songs, than he did in earlier poetry. Alongside the autobiographical moments are glimpses of contemporary, fictitious men and women—so realistically imagined and named and so affectingly portrayed that the reader almost suspects Corn of presenting sheer observed fact. The poem ends with short prose passages about all of the characters met in the course of 1992, but the passages all end with unfinished sentences.

Corn has also completed a novel, "Part of His Story"—a work of Proustian impressions set in London. A chapter of it has appeared in the *Kenyon Review* (Summer 1991).

Alfred Corn's place among poets of his generation and in the literature of the late twentieth century is secure, though it will be a long time before a settled view of his importance can be reached. As an artist who can be both classical and highly innovative, who writes with quiet authority and grace and, though he is in the high symbolist-modernist tradition, can nonetheless speak in resolved metaphysical, rather than in angst-ridden existential, terms (and not appear particularly Eliotian in the process); as an artist whose spiritual searchings have deep roots in tradition and at the same time have a new spirit that has no faddish or occult vulgarity, Corn is a poet set apart. But his poetry is of a type that will be influential on the work of only a few successors: Corn's approach will never have the power to carry an age, like Williams's does, for example. Corn belongs, though, in the company of the great cosmopolitan symbolists: Crane, Stevens, Merrill, and Ashbery. However, in his recent poet-ry he stands just as near modern, traditional formalists such as Wilbur, and Corn has become an even better urban realist, like Williams. Earlier Corn wrote poems that explored the spirit with a fresh relish and fed "the hunger of his eye" with landscapes, great cities, starry skies, and light. Corn continues to do the same, but the exploration of the spirit has reached some sense of home, and the hunger has lost its youthful fever but not its vigor and breadth of interest.

Reference:

Robert K. Martin, *The Homosexual Tradition in American Poetry* (Austin: University of Texas Press, 1979), pp. 208-217.

Jim Daniels

(6 June 1956 -   )

Bob Gaskin
Lamar University

BOOKS: *Factory Poems* (Alma, Mich.: Jack-in-the-Box, 1979);
On the Line (Bellingham, Wash.: Signpost, 1981);
Places/Everyone (Madison: University of Wisconsin Press, 1985);
The Long Ball (Pittsburgh: Pig-in-a-Poke, 1988);
Digger's Territory (Easthampton, Mass.: Adastra, 1989);
Punching Out (Detroit: Wayne State University Press, 1990).

OTHER: *Ten Years with the Mill Hunk Herald*, edited by Daniels and others (Albuquerque: West End, 1990).

Jim Daniels's rapidly expanding list of credits may well point to a burgeoning collective taste for rapidly moving, plain, and direct poetry such as his, a poetry remarkably clear of the usual tricks of poets. His device may be said to be a lack of device; his voice apes the voicelessness of his beneficiaries, those of the American urban working class, from which Daniels sprang and with whom he aligns himself. Daniels makes his al-legiances clear, as he told the interviewer for *Contemporary Authors* in 1987:

> Though I am currently teaching, much of my poetry focuses on the factory life in my native Detroit. My grandfather, brothers, and I have all worked in the auto industry, and that background seeps into nearly all my poems.
> I feel that there is little poetry being written about the world that I come from and the people that I care about. I try to give a voice to those who are often shut out of poetry, to explore their lives both in and out of the workplace. If nothing else, I'm trying to say that these people are important, that their lives have value and meaning.

James Raymond Daniels, currently associate professor of English at Carnegie-Mellon University, was born on 6 June 1956 in Detroit to Raymond J. and Mary Rivard Daniels. The family had third-generation roots in the automobile industry, and the poet grew up in a blue-collar suburb of "houses, factories, bowling alleys and bars," according to his autobiographical note for

Jim Daniels (photograph by Kristin Kovacic)

his chapbook *On the Line* (1981). After graduating from Alma College with his B.A. (with honors) in 1978 and earning his M.F.A. in 1980 from Bowling Green State University, where he served as lecturer for a year, Daniels moved on to Carnegie-Mellon University, beginning as writer in residence in 1981. His writing credits include winning a Devine Fellowship in poetry, selected by Galway Kinnell in 1979; the National Signpost Press chapbook contest for *On the Line* in 1980; the Wisconsin/Brittingham Prize for Poetry for *Places/Everyone* (1985), judged by C. K. Williams; a National Endowment for the Arts Creative Writing Fellowship in 1985; and Pennsylvania Council on the Arts Fellowships in Literature in 1987 and 1990. He has read his poems on the National Public Radio program "All Things Considered" and at various schools and libraries.

Factory Poems (1979) and *On the Line*, his earliest chapbooks, are devoted to factory themes and are of interest primarily in terms of how Daniels's work evolved into the fuller volumes.

His first full-length book, *Places/Everyone*, is a sequence of forty-seven poems in three sections. The first section deals with family and subjects peripherally related to factory life in and around Detroit—the bars, tools, job lines, snowstorms, and general hard times—set against an implied inventory of better days. The second section consists of the "Digger" poems, Digger being Daniels's young auto-worker persona, his poetic and proletarian alternative to John Updike's Rabbit Angstrom. The Digger persona is also featured in the limited-edition chapbook *Digger's Territory* (1989) and in *Punching Out* (1990). "Digger" in one poem was once "Daniels," "Digger" being substituted for "Daniels" in an earlier chapbook rendition of "Muscles" (*On the Line*): the foreman, Santino, shouts, "You Daniels, / carry those housings / over to the water tester"; in *Punching Out* the lines are rendered, "You, Digger, / carry the fuckin' housings over." The third section of *Places/Everyone* mixes and extends, somewhat randomly, themes suggested in the earlier two sections.

Places/Everyone attracted the favorable attention of Peter Stitt in the *New York Times Book Review* (4 May 1986), who found a similarity between the works of Daniels and Philip Levine, but with a significant difference: "whereas Mr. Levine's style is lush, Mr. Daniels's is clean." According to Stitt, Daniels takes Louis Simpson's middle-class focus for poetry past middle-class Americans to blue-collar workers. Others of course, including Walt Whitman, have looked at the plight of American workers, but few have so completely located their poetry within the dailiness of workers' lives as has Daniels. With a sometimes startling purity, he views the American class structure through hourly workers' eyes.

Julia Stein, reviewing *Places/Everyone* in the *Village Voice* (6 January 1987), said Daniels "writes theme songs—like Bruce Springsteen's—for the American working class in the '80s faced with plant closures and layoffs." Stein goes on to say that Daniels "captures, as few contemporary poets do, the sounds of North American city speech," and that his "poetry speaks to the millions of working-class people who have lost their jobs in this decade of plant closures, when whole industries have been wiped out." Daniels speaks, more often than not, in the voice of a young man nostalgic for the "glory days" of adolescence and young adulthood, a life "just wild with speed and noise" (from "Digger Can't Sleep"). The daydream is often all there is to transform the toxic present: "you think of the fork lifts at work / and their hot gassy breath / grunting up and down the greasy aisles. / You think of your wife's thick white thighs." Daniels robustly avoids any temptation to sentimentalize; rather, he tends at times to push the reader's face into the class-limited experience of blue-collar life in urban-blighted Detroit.

A remarkable aspect of Daniels's poetry is the effectiveness with which he shows the pervasive industry enmeshment that occurs in any single-industry factory town, whether it be Detroit or James Wright's Martins Ferry, Ohio. Family and friends are bonded to employment and place in ways that highly mobile professionals would not understand. Daniels projects this type of bonding by extending auto-related imagery throughout his poems, even in baseball poems and family poems. The father in "My Father Worked Late" seems so remote that "We could drive toward each other all night / and never cross the distance of those missing years." Similarly, the mother in "My Mother Walks" goes for long nightly walks into an urban-blighted danger zone:

> She walks past the crippled cars
> which line these streets, past
> the barking dogs, the whiff
> of a late barbecue
>
> past the silence of streetlights,
> the passive trees, angry bushes,
> past the names of her children
> faded in cement, counting the miles
>
> the times she's wanted to leave, walks
> away from the box with her name on it,
> walks until she's afraid enough
> to turn around.

Fears, often partially understood ones, keep people in their places.

Daniels's plainly styled visual lines give him his most distinctive effects, such as in the three-poem series "Still Lives in Detroit," which photographically presents scenes of the city in hard times, as in "#3, Behind Chatham's Supermarket": "If I could, I would watch until the earth thawed, / took in new shapes, shifted with possibility. / What could be a rat moves through the picture"; and in "#1, Rome Street":

> Chalk runs like mascara
> over the pitted cement
> fades in the rain:

> *Cindee is a Hore.*
> Who is a whore tonight?
> This cement gives back nothing.
> Scars on her knees as she reads it.

Daniels continues the recurrent automobile imagery that pervades his work in "March 17, 1972": the speaker comes upon a car wreck, sees friends dead and injured, and afterward, a "pint" in his pocket, he walks away. Daniels shifts to second person to address the reader directly—"You've probably / been there"—and then later says:

> Maybe you walked home
> a different way. Maybe
> you didn't stop to sit
> on a swing behind the grade school.
> Maybe the rain stopped
> on your night.

The lines lift this poem beyond reconstructed experience and (uncharacteristically for Daniels) into supposition, introspection, and conjecture, to a place most readers probably have been. The reader is drawn into Daniels's world of simple epiphanies, where it is enough to "stop at the first beer store / to hold a six-pack to my forehead / and rub the sweat cool / into my eyes" (as in "Getting Off Early"), or to watch at work "the ropes start shining down, / thin light through the factory windows, / the sun on its way to the time clock" (in "Factory Jungle").

One of the rare poignant touches in *Places/Everyone* comes in "Real Dancing," in which a family of losers (among others) dances on the "cement floor" of a bar: "Tonight a broken family sweeps the floor." The son, "the blond kid / with matted hair hanging in his eyes / jumps up and down off the cement floor / celebrating the empty space." But the finest touch comes in the description of the daughter and the difference between how she appears to others and how she seems to herself:

> His fat sister rolls back and forth.
> She can't jump up or bend down
> but oh she sways
> that woman inside her doing leaps
> and spins.

A lesser poet might have stooped to ridicule, but the sensitivity of Daniels's restraint in a poem set in roughness recalls Richard Hugo's expansive, if sometimes hard-boiled, sympathies.

Cover for Daniels's second full-length book, a sequence of sixty-three poems set in an automobile factory

The excellences of *Places/Everyone* are offset by a few weaknesses, such as in "Anita, A New Hire on the Line": "The first time I saw you / I wondered how you could sweat / and still be so fine." Still, such lapses barely detract from the power that drives the book, for as C. K. Williams says in the foreword, Daniels "has captured and enacted the blind and sad anguish of souls so trapped that they have ceased to know how to speak, even to themselves. . . ."

Two recent chapbooks, *The Long Ball* (1988) and *Digger's Territory*, deal, respectively, with Daniels's love of baseball and with further explorations of the Digger persona. Both works resulted from Daniels's fondness for chapbooks: "You can do things in a chapbook that you can't do in a full-length book. I like their size, I like the small presses that publish them—often the press is one individual who does it for the love of poetry."

Reviewing *Punching Out* in the *Hudson Review* (Winter 1991), Robert McDowell observed that "Daniels' compact, terse line speeds down the page with the rapidity and power of a jackhammer, rendering irrelevant the usual speculations on rhythm and meter." These comments could as justly have been said of *Places/Everyone*. *Punching Out*, Daniels's second full-length book, is a sequence of sixty-three poems set in the auto industry. The titles of the five sections of the book reveal the tone of the subject matter: "Basic Training," "Factory Stud," "The Village Idiot," "Hard Rock," and "Steel Toed Boots." More narrowly focused on the work world than *Places/Everyone*, *Punching Out* presents the auto factory in its truly proletarian, blue-collar roughness, fully drawing the reader into the quotidian, unionized limbo. To McDowell *Punching Out* is rich in "implied criticism . . . reserved for the system itself, a system that codifies human behavior and bludgeons the individual into ever more impossible roles and situations." To be sure, these are not poems that bring the reader gently to a point of cognition. A new guy on the line, along with the reader, has an eye-opening experience in the first poem in *Punching Out*, "In the Midnight Zone":

> *This your first day?* Bush asks.
> *I been here 22 fuckin' years.*
> *I was gonna work here two years.* He pauses.
> The whiskey hangs in my face.
> *Twenty-two FUCKING years*, he shouts
> above the machines' pound and hiss.
> No one looks. He throws a tube in the aisle
> to make his point.

Daniels brings with his poetry a strong perspective of class identification to add to the more familiar ones of sexual orientation, ethnicity, and gender. An important distinction is that Daniels writes *from* his identification rather than simply *about* it, as an apologist might while sanitizing subject matter for persuasive appeal. Daniels sustains a nonintrospective, limited blue-collar consciousness that is conveyed in a remarkably restricted use of metaphor, simile, and "literary" diction. His are the most nonliterary poems one is likely to read. Their plainness of style is intended to express what one would think or might feel as a worker, an inarticulate one, enmeshed in a daily milieu that shows scant patience with artifice. Consequently the work poems are laced with blue-collar sweat, cursing, sometimes cruel humor, violence, and, more rarely, joy and happiness. Still, there is a way to take all the pressure, poems such as "Timers" say:

> A man with a stopwatch stares
> at my hands, his thumb on the button.
> He is timing how long it takes me
> to take this part, put it in my machine,
> push two buttons, take it out.
>
> He is trying to eliminate my job.
> But I take a second or two
> to scratch my balls.
> *Got to allow time for that,*
> I wink at him.

It is not all one-sided: "Somebody somewhere's got a watch / on him too. Somebody's put us both here / where we can watch each other."

Throughout Daniels's poetry there is a dearth of authorial comment or use of words that might reveal what stance Daniels takes toward some of his personae's outrageous peccadilloes. The poetry is pure in this respect, apropos of characters whose cultural sustenance runs mainly to newspapers, popular magazines, rock music, and television. The only novel alluded to is Mario Puzo's *The Godfather* (1969), the only literary character Sherlock Holmes, the only magazine *Newsweek*, which the persona in "Back to the Basics," in a day full of erotic daydreams, is chided for picking up: "*That ain't no / pussy book you lookin' at ya know. / I throw it down—who wants to read / about politics anyway.*" One recognizes these scatological phrases that maintain emotional distances for what they are: cruder but no more cruel than more-practiced white-collar brush-offs.

Daniels's personae generally find antagonism the appropriate response to the mind-numbing monotony and pressure of the assembly line; frustrations are acted out through cruel humor, minor sabotage, malingering, drinking, and taking drugs on the job. The formidable Gracie in "Dishing It Out," who comes to work "chewing a few / choice words to spit at anyone / gets in her way," strikes and cuts a guard with her whiskey-laden lunch box and emerges later to the congratulations of coworkers: "She slaps us high fives / and we feel the sting." The speaker in the prose poem "But" says, "It seems like that's the only way to make a / dent—to goof things up." The robotic machine with two "idiot buttons" to punch speeds up production but deprives the worker of any sense of personal pride, other than the kind displayed by Spooner in "Fac-

tory Cool," who paints footprints on the floor and choreographs his movements so as not to get himself dirty. All this stands in stark contrast to remembrances from earlier generations, including the grandfather in the family-background poems ("My Grandfather's Tools") in *Places/Everyone*:

> He worked for Packard nearly fifty years,
> all his life his joy
> that feel of tool in hand—
> his knife, his gun, his fistful of bills—
> showing the engineers how things
> really worked.
>
> His old Packard still runs
> despite all logic. . . .

Daniels seems to achieve his best effects in the distancing made possible by such third-person treatments, and when the speaker is able to be alone, as in "After Work" (also in *Places/ Everyone*):

> You, moon, I bet you could
> fill my cheeks with wet snow
> make me forget I ever touched steel
> make me forget even
> that you
> look like a headlight
> moving toward me.

The automobile imagery is never far away, nor the need to escape it.

At their best, Daniels's poems put the reader almost shockingly close to experience. They live up to the epigraph from Celine at the beginning of *Punching Out*: "The greatest defeat, in anything, is to forget, and above all to forget what it is that has smashed you, and to let yourself be smashed without ever realizing how thoroughly devilish men can be." Daniels gives a poetic voice to auto workers, just that segment of society that would seem at the farthest remove from being themselves consumers of his poetry. Such laborers do not typically find themselves so favored by representatives of the liberating and humanizing arts, as H. L. Mencken early illustrated, speaking in *Notes on Democracy* (1926) on the eve of the Great Depression about "man on the nether levels . . . the pet and glory of democratic states": he has only "brute labor" to offer, and "even that he tries to evade." Even worse, Mencken goes on, "What is worth knowing he doesn't know and doesn't want to know; what he knows is not true." How Daniels might reply to Mencken's invective is not certain, for the class "theme song" he sings is by no means an idealizing one, including mentions of workers who wager over the size of their after-lunch defecations ("Big Shit," in *Punching Out*) and men such as the title character in "Paul Pakowski Was Here," (*Punching Out*), whose second-language ethos of thirty-eight years has distilled itself to twin phrases: "*Fuck foreman / Go slow*." But if one has only "brute labor" to offer, even that may seem to its possessor quite a lot and may be withheld in just those ways Mencken wrote about. And Daniels's characters do withhold it, at times even breaking their machines to avoid it. They are often obscene, but with an obscenity only qualitatively removed from that of club cars, closed-door board rooms, and university English departments.

Daniels refuses abstractions. He stays within the virulent anomie of factory row, showing how it is coped with daily, and he extracts a sometimes paltry meaningfulness from generally unappealing experience. This energetic, authentic poetry is drawn from truly raw materials.

Reference:
Robert McDowell, "The Wilderness Surrounds the Word," *Hudson Review* (Winter 1991): 669-677.

Rita Dove
(28 August 1952 -   )

Kirkland C. Jones
Lamar University

BOOKS: *Ten Poems* (Lisbon: Penumbra, 1977);
The Only Dark Spot in the Sky (Tempe, Ariz.: Porch, 1980);
The Yellow House on the Corner (Pittsburgh: Carnegie-Mellon University Press, 1980);
Mandolin (Athens: Ohio Review, 1982);
Museum (Pittsburgh: Carnegie-Mellon University Press, 1983);
Fifth Sunday (Lexington: University Press of Kentucky, 1985);
Thomas and Beulah (Pittsburgh: Carnegie-Mellon University Press, 1986);
The Other Side of the House (Tempe, Ariz.: Pyrocantha, 1988);
Grace Notes (New York: Norton, 1989).

Although her literary achievements are impressive, the mark that Rita Dove's literary career will reach is for the future to determine. Her poems began to appear in print as early as 1974, but until 1987, the year she won the Pulitzer Prize in poetry for *Thomas and Beulah* (1986), her name was mentioned only occasionally in college classrooms and at meetings of learned societies. Not long after she won the Pulitzer, though, her name and works began to appear in college courses and academic panels on American literature, African-American studies, and women's studies. Before Dove won the Pulitzer, Gwendolyn Brooks was the only African-American poet who had gained this coveted award.

Born in Akron, Ohio, to well-educated parents, Dove is the daughter of Ray A. Dove, the first African-American chemist to break the racial barrier in the tire-and-rubber industry. Her mother is the former Elvira Elizabeth Hord. In 1970, shortly before her eighteenth birthday, Dove was invited to the White House as a "Presidential Scholar," indicating that she had ranked among the top one hundred high-school seniors in the nation for that year. Dove earned a bachelor's degree from Miami University at Oxford, Ohio, where she enrolled as a National Achievement Scholar; in 1973 she graduated summa cum laude. During the year that followed, she studied at West Germany's Tubingen University on a Fulbright scholarship. This led to graduate studies at the University of Iowa Writers' Workshop. She went on from there to begin publishing her impressive list of poems and short sto-

Rita Dove circa 1986 (photograph by Fred Viebahn)

ries. In 1979 Dove married Fred Viebahn, a German-born novelist, and together they have a daughter, Aviva Chantal Tamu Dove-Viebahn. The family lives in Charlottesville, Virginia.

In 1974 Dove's poems began to appear in major periodicals. Critics since that time have been monitoring her progress, honoring her accomplishments, and making literary predictions about the young author's career, many of which already have materialized. After two early chapbooks, Dove's first full-length book of poems, *The Yellow House on the Corner*, was published by Carnegie-Mellon University Press in 1980. This was followed, after another chapbook, by *Museum* (1983), and in 1986 her crowning work, *Thomas and Beulah*, appeared. Since winning the Pulitzer, Dove has fulfilled some of the many requests she has received to read her works and to make other literary appearances. A high point in her career came in the fall of 1988, when she read her works and talked with students and professors at her alma mater, Miami University. While there she was reunited with her teacher, mentor, and friend, Marian Musgrave, Renaissance scholar, Germanist, and international pioneer in black studies.

Dove's concept of poetry is akin to that of such other modern American poets as Robert Frost, Langston Hughes, and Gwendolyn Brooks, especially as to rhetorical structure. Dove's readers learn that she often melds several time-tested devices to shape an original idiom. Like Alice Walker in *Good Night, Willie Lee, I'll See You in the Morning* (1979), and like Zora Neale Hurston in virtually all of her fiction, Dove bridges the gap between orality and written text.

In 1977 Dove published *Ten Poems*, the first of her chapbooks of verse. Some of these poems are set in the turbulent 1960s, with one of the poems titled "1963." Characteristically combining narrative and lyric modes, the book may be described as Dove's apprentice work, but "Adolescence II," "Adolescence III," and "The Bird Frau" reveal hints of her later strength. Included in this initial chapbook is "Upon Meeting Don L. Lee, in a Dream." Dove was inspired by such revolutionary writers as Lee and LeRoi Jones (Imamu Amiri Baraka). Both the Lee poem and "The Bird Frau" reappear in *The Yellow House on the Corner*.

In 1980 another Dove chapbook of poems, *The Only Dark Spot in the Sky*, was published. This volume also contains a couple of poems that appeared again that year in *The Yellow House*. Critics attempted to dismiss *The Yellow House* as conventional and self-serving, but some evaluators were perceptive enough to praise Dove's sparkling voice, which is as polyphonic as an African dance or chant. Admittedly *The Yellow House* is autobiographical, but as *Thomas and Beulah* revealed six years later, this autobiographical thread is the most profound source of meaning in her art. As early as her first book Dove's use of dramatic monologue and compressed narrative showed her cross-cultural perceptivity. Her keen sense of history and her well-disciplined use of rhetorical decorum set her apart; her characters and their voices move in and out of the centuries as they transcend the local and the mundane, becoming, as a result, decidedly inclusive in their view of the universe and of humanity. Moreover, Dove's allusions to the psalms and to other Old Testament verses ("Teach us to number our days," "children of angels," "some point true and unproven") provide a sense of community among the slaves, their masters, and the surrounding fields.

The poems in *The Yellow House* from which these biblical phrases are taken set forth universal themes in fresh contexts. In "Adolescence III" Dove writes of the laying on of hands and of love's ennobling effects: "I dreamed how it would happen / . . . At his touch, the scabs would fall away." Frequently in Dove's verses the healing touch of healthful mating informs the imagery.

The publication of *Mandolin*, another chapbook, came in 1982. This seven-poem sequence presents more of Dove's narrative verses that, in a few years, would function individually as segments of the opening episode of *Thomas and Beulah*, Dove's tale of her family's history. *Mandolin* shows Dove using music, musical instruments, and dance as metaphors for beauty, youth, and the power of sexuality, especially when she uses comparison to depict a dark maleness that is strong and irresistible: "with nothing to boast of but good looks and a mandolin, . . . / Heading North, . . . gold hoop / from the right ear jiggling / And a glass stud, bright blue in his left. The young ladies / saying he sure plays that tater bug like the devil!" Dove's poetry sings as she records significant events of the musician's life.

Museum, published in 1983, was Dove's most impressive work until *Thomas and Beulah*. Critical reaction to *Museum* was plentiful and frequently laudatory. This book presents a mature Dove, expert in the use of recurrent images of light and darkness. Most critics noticed these poems' polish and their author's growth since the late 1970s. In

this work the poet's voice is now sometimes meditative, sometimes clairvoyant, then at other times peering "through a glass, darkly," as if through haze or smoke. Dove's subject matter is as varied as that of *The Yellow House*, if not more so.

Dove, who has done art sketches since childhood, chose for the cover of *Museum* a self-portrait superimposed on a painting by German artist Christian Shad. This painting presents a view of two sideshow entertainers, a white male figure naked to the waist and a black woman seated below him in the posture of creative dance. Such a cover design was inspired, no doubt, by the penultimate poem in part 2 of the book, "Agosta the Winged Man and Rasha the Black Dove," a poem of seven oddly shaped stanzas, suggesting through spatial configuration the snake imagery:

> He could not leave his skin—once
> he'd painted himself a new one,
> silk green . . . turning slowly in place as the boa
> constrictor coiled counter clock wise. . . .

The poem's title is as complex and multitextured as its imagery. The appearance of the author's own last name as the last word of the title echoes the self-portraiture of the cover design and some of the poems, such as "November for Beginners," "Reading Holderlin on the Patio with the Aid of a Dictionary," "At a German Writer's Conference in Munich," "Sunday Night at Grandfather's," "My Father's Telescope," "To Bed," and "Why I Turned Vegetarian."

Although poetry is Dove's primary medium, she has also published *Fifth Sunday*, a 1985 collection of eight short stories. Like the best African-American authors, Dove has demonstrated, through this volume, her versatility, but it does not appear that she should abandon poetry in favor of the more lucrative genres, the novel and the play. Having read these prose pieces, though, Dove's readers may look forward to a novel from her, for she knows how to weave a plot. The subject matter of the stories in *Fifth Sunday* ranges from the onset of puberty and adolescent courtship—with growing awareness of the self and the selves of others—to the displacement and oddity that American blacks feel when they venture into Europe, to the flowering of womanhood and manhood in mature relationships, to sex and reproduction as life's music played on life's instruments.

Thomas and Beulah, her volume of narrative verse published in 1986, presents the saga of her

Dust jacket for Dove's sequence of forty-four narrative poems based on the experiences of her family, including her maternal grandparents, Thomas and Beulah Hord

family, depicting the generations descended from her maternal grandparents, Thomas Hord, born in Wartrace, Tennessee, and his wife Beulah, four years younger than Thomas and from the hamlet of Rockmart, Georgia. When Beulah was only two, her parents moved the family to Akron, Ohio, Dove's birthplace. Thomas, a virile young man full of wanderlust, arrived, as if by chance, in Akron in 1921. Three years later he married Beulah in a December wedding, and two years after that, Rose (Dove's aunt), their first child, was born. This verse saga steadily unfolds until it ends with Beulah's death in 1969. Only a few of the poems in this prizewinning volume had been published previously. Appropriately Dove dedicated the book to her mother, Elvira Elizabeth, in recognition of both her mother and her "mother's garden," à la Alice Walker.

Thomas and Beulah, an eighty-page volume, contains forty-four poems arranged in two parts. The first part is titled "Mandolin" and the sec-

ond part "Canary in Bloom." "Mandolin" presents twenty-three poems, and "Canary" the remaining twenty-one. At the volume's end is a "Chronology" that offers more than a little help in following Dove's mythos. The epigraph to the book's first part is this couplet from Melvin B. Tolson's *Harlem Gallery* (1965): "Black Boy, O Black Boy / is the port worth the cruise?" The quotation preceding the second part is from Anne Spencer's "Lines to a Nasturtium" (1926): "Ah, how the senses flood at my repeating, / As once in her fire-lit heart I felt the furies / Beating, beating." Both passages help the reader appreciate the permanence and depth of the love shared by Thomas and Beulah. Their love becomes a "fire" that they pass on to their children and grandchildren. They are a love-blessed pair whose marriage becomes the clan's bridge over the "troubled waters" of variance—a "viaduct," as Dove identifies it, which spans the difference between their families and which carries them all across the river that sometimes divides the sexes.

Because Thomas and Beulah have become "one flesh," one spirit, they are able to impart, carefully and lovingly, this wholeness to their progeny. As a result the clan is capable of coping with pain, guilt, despair, bereavement, and the loss of illusion, as seen in "The Event" and "Straw Hat," two poems that appear in the first sequence. "The Event" boasts of Thomas's "silver falsetto," accompanied by the mandolin of his manhood. Then, in "Straw Hat," Thomas learns that he is not perfect, that "no one was perfect." During the 1930s Thomas lent his "sweet tenor" to the "gospel choir," a kind of chorus that rocks and sways and that only the black church possesses. In "Definition in the Face of Unnamed Fury," Thomas, in shame, threatens: "I'll just / let go." And in "Gospel" the tenor from "a fortress / of animal misery" gives vent to his "sorrow and his sacrifice." Eventually overcome by an intense mixture of emotions, Thomas "lets go" and quits the gospel choir of the African Methodist Episcopal Zion Church. Dove, in *Thomas and Beulah*, harmonizes history and human experience.

Critics praised *Thomas and Beulah* and its author. Helen Vendler, in the *New York Review of Books* (23 October 1986), described Dove as one who has "planed away unnecessary matter: pure shapes, her poems exhibit the thrift that Yeats called the sign of a perfected manner." None of Dove's numerous reviewers gave this volume a negative notice, and many were lavish in their praise. Emily Grosholz, in the *Hudson Review*

(1987), wrote that "Rita Dove . . . understands the long-term intricacies of marriage, as the protagonists of her wonderful chronicle . . . testify." Critics have also described this work as wise and affectionate. Dove succeeds in treating two sides of her subject, and she warns her reader, at the bottom of the book's dedicatory page, that these poems "tell two sides of a story and are meant to be read in sequence." Dove emphasizes the separateness and the individuality of her grandparents, who dealt with hostilities and the loss of love, as well as grief at the loss of life. But through good times and bad this ancestral pair never fell out of love, maintaining their devotedness, each to the other. All critics of the book, in their own ways, have celebrated this melding of biography and lyric, one of Dove's trademarks.

Following a chapbook, *The Other Side of the House* (1988), Dove's most recent book of poems is *Grace Notes*, published in 1989. Most of the forty-eight poems in *Grace Notes* appeared previously, sometimes in varying versions, in some of the most prestigious poetry periodicals, including *Black Scholar, Boston Review, Georgia Review, Michigan Quarterly Review, Ars Poetica, Southwest Review,* and *Yale Review*. The arrangement of the poems appeals to sight, sound, and touch. Typical of Dove's manner are the first two poems, "Summit Beach" and "Silos," and the last poem, "Old Folk's Home, Jerusalem," one of her finest, a multispaced, fifteen-line poem that she has dedicated to Harry Timar. "Summit Beach" includes her earlier African maleness motif, frequently represented by images of an adult male singer who also dances to his own accompaniment or to another musician's tinkling on the xylophone or strumming on a mandolin—"masculine toys," as the poet describes them in "Silos." "Summit Beach" serves as a verse introduction to the entire volume, with "Silos" following it immediately as the first poem in the first of the book's five sequences.

The poems in this volume are shaped into groups of lines that sometimes function as one sen-

tence, which ebbs and flows across the page. Her male dancer in "Silos" impresses his woman, "the rib of the modern world," as he struts, parades, marches to a rhythm, now marcato, now staccato, now swaying with the gospel chorus. Dove's use of the color in this volume is brighter and more multifaceted than the more somber shades of *Thomas and Beulah*, ranging from yellow to orange, from red to indigo, and a favorite refrain of her male dancer reappears: "Man, she was butter just waiting to melt."

Rita Dove is not the stereotypical woman writer, nor is she simply the traditional African-American author. She appreciates the aesthetics of race and gender but does not feel the need to raise the color problem for mere color's sake. Dove writes because she enjoys creating word impressions as she wrestles with significant ideas. She defies the disabling pigeonhole or comfortable niche. Furthermore, Dove emulates what she admires in other great poets who have become her favorites: William Shakespeare, Melvin B. Tolson, Derek Walcott, Lucille Clifton, Langston Hughes, Don L. Lee, Amiri Baraka, and Anne Spencer, to name a few. Dove is not hampered by fragmentation, nor by any defensive need to justify her own experiences. Dove sets most of her verse in the past, and she handles nostalgia well. In all of her works, she presents a variety and richness of theme and structure found in fine poetry the world over.

References:

Robert McDowell, "The Assembling Vision of Rita Dove," *Callaloo*, 25 (Winter 1985): 61-70;

Arnold Rampersad, "The Poems of Rita Dove," *Callaloo*, 26 (Winter 1986): 52-60;

Lisa M. Steinman, "Dialogues Between History and Dream," *Michigan Quarterly Review*, 26 (Spring 1987): 428-438;

Peter Stitt, "Coherence Through Place in Contemporary American Poetry," *Georgia Review*, 40 (1986): 1021-1033.

Norman Dubie
(10 April 1945 -)

Christopher Baker
Lamar University

BOOKS: *The Horsehair Sofa* (Plainfield, Vt.: Goddard Journal, 1969);

Alehouse Sonnets (Pittsburgh: University of Pittsburgh Press, 1971);

Indian Summer (Iowa City: Elizabeth, 1974);

The Prayers of the North American Martyrs (Lisbon, Iowa: Penumbra, 1975);

Popham of the New Song (Port Townsend, Wash.: Graywolf, 1975);

The Illustrations (New York: Braziller, 1975);

In the Dead of the Night (Pittsburgh: University of Pittsburgh Press / London: Feffer & Simons, 1975);

A Thousand Little Things, and Other Poems (Omaha: Abattoir, 1978);

Odalisque in White (Seattle: Porch, 1978);

The City of the Olesha Fruit (Garden City, N.Y.: Doubleday, 1979);

The Everlastings (Garden City, N.Y.: Doubleday, 1980);

The Window in the Field (Copenhagen: Razorback, 1980);

Selected and New Poems (New York: Norton, 1983);

The Springhouse (New York: Norton, 1986);

Groom Falconer (New York: Norton, 1989);

Radio Sky (New York: Norton, 1991);

The Clouds of Magellan (Santa Fe, N.Mex.: Recursos, 1992).

Norman Dubie, 1989 (photograph by Jeannine Dubie)

If T. S. Eliot was correct in saying that modern poetry must embody the complexity of the era in which it is written, then Norman Dubie's poetry is assuredly modern. Yet its very complexity makes capsule definition difficult; one searches for a context or convenient tradition by which to clarify his work, but its allusiveness, historicity, realism, and narrative force combine to keep it unmistakably individual. Sally A. Lodge (*Publishers Weekly*, 16 September 1983) asserts that Dubie "is that almost unheard of phenomenon—a truly original poet—with his own vision, his own form and his own style." In an interview with James Green, Dubie states that he seeks to "challenge whatever the assumed limits of the lyric are," moving away from the frankly confessional poetry of the last generation with works whose narrators favor either retelling the stories of other voices in other rooms, or presenting scenes from a variety of compelling past histories. Though Dubie can be personal, he will often offer the experiences of poets, artists, activists, and nameless figures from history whose confrontations with the paradoxes and emotionally charged dilemmas of their own times provide mirrors for the contemporary self. Dubie is in no way limited to poetry of a historical cast, yet his ability to reify these scenes and events, vividly creating secondary worlds and selves, is an arresting feature of his work.

Norman Evans Dubie was born in Barre, Vermont, on 10 April 1945 and was one of three children. In Dubie's early childhood his father, Norman, Sr., was an insurance-claims adjuster, his mother, Doris, a registered nurse. In 1952 they moved to Manchester, New Hampshire, where, three years later, Norman Dubie, Sr., experienced a religious conversion in an orchard, which led to his entering Bangor Theological School. He then worked as a theological student at parishes in the Maine peninsula, whose landscape, along with the mountains of Vermont and New Hampshire, was an early influence on the poet. Fascinated with geology and the outdoors, the young Dubie collected rocks and crystals and for a while entertained thoughts of becoming a bush pilot in Alaska. He began writing poetry at the age of eleven; his earliest authors of interest were John Keats and D. H. Lawrence, selections he regards as "hard to reconcile" but "healthy for me." His father's first parish was a Congregational church in the mountains at Lancaster, New Hampshire; this controversial ministry was engaged in the civil-rights movement. After four years, the family returned to Manchester, where Dubie finished high school.

He had intended to enter West Point and play football, but his father, because of his opposition to the war in Vietnam, advised against it. Dubie went instead to the University of New Hampshire at Durham, where he earned A's in English and geology and failed everything else. For the next nine months he worked in construction and wrote poetry, having been rejected by the draft because of his high blood pressure. He then entered Goddard College, from which he received his B.A. in 1965. Goddard's experimental programs, gradeless classes, and excellent teachers proved a boon to the poet. He studied with Barry Goldensohn and Lorraine Goldensohn, completing his first chapbook, *The Horsehair Sofa* (1969).

He then won a teaching/writing fellowship to the Iowa Writers' Workshop, where he studied with George Starbuck, Marvin Bell, and Richard Hugo. He received his M.F.A. in 1968 and was asked to stay on as a member of the regular faculty, where he taught for four years. In 1969 he married a dancer, Francesca DiGrandis Stafford, and their daughter, Hannah, was born on 18 July 1969. This marriage ended in divorce in 1973. On Thanksgiving 1975, he married Pamela Dye Stewart, a poet and teacher.

Dubie spent a year as writer in residence at Ohio University at Athens in 1974, and a year later he accepted a post at Arizona State University as consultant in the arts, establishing the creative-writing program there, though without accepting the title of director. During 1975 he published four books of poetry; he received a Guggenheim Fellowship in 1976.

Dubie's second marriage ended in 1980, and having suffered a nervous collapse, he returned home to Lebanon, New Hampshire, to live with his parents. He went back to Arizona State in 1981 and two years later accepted a tenured full professorship. He married Jeannine Savard, a poet, on 18 June 1981. He was made Regents' Professor of English in spring 1991.

Dubie's skill at creating memorable scenes, often juxtaposing the most unlikely objects or details lends his work a tantalizing obscurity that both frustrates and rewards. There is some substance to Alan Williamson's criticism (*Poetry*, December 1980) that, in Dubie's quest to create a new world of poetic images, he runs the risk of creating "a facile and portentous symbolism," of seeming to be "a brilliant surface performer who has, finally, much less to say about history or genius than first appears." Sandra Gilbert found *In the Dead of the Night* (1975) "relentlessly, exhaustingly learned" and felt compelled to "close the book, thick-headed with fatigue" and a "feeling of sullen stupidity" (*Poetry*, August 1976). Of *The Illustrations* (1975) Lawrence Raab observed in the *American Poetry Review* (July-August 1978) that "even when most (if not all) of the facts of a given poem are clear (as, for example, in 'The Great American Novel: Winter, 1927') and the writing is sharp, controlled and engaging, the poem can seem to be talking to itself, and the reader may feel that he has blundered into the middle of a fascinating story the significance of which he can never hope to fathom." Katha Pollitt (*Nation*, 5 July 1980) likewise found his poems disturbingly disingenuous: "At once mannered and hallucinatory, histrionic and elliptic, they are surrealist costume dramas in which *something* of great urgency seems to be communicated—but with each new book it becomes harder to say what." To the charge that he is willfully and needlessly obscure, however, Dubie's response (in his interview with James Green) is to call upon readers to stretch themselves as they read contemporary poetry: "If the kind of effort we make out of natural curiosity, eavesdropping in a restaurant or on a bus, was

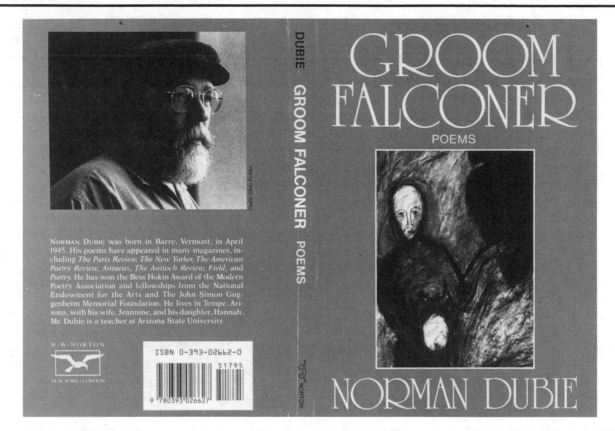

Dust jacket for Dubie's 1989 book, the second in a trilogy that also includes The Springhouse *(1986) and* Radio Sky *(1991)*

brought to the poem, we would understand the contemporary poem or the modern poem, as ordinary readers, much more readily than we do now. So, in effect, I think we are getting good poems, and I think very often we're getting reactionary or lazy readers."

Lorrie Goldensohn (*American Book Review*, December 1977) and others have noted that Dubie's work adheres to the ancient dictum that a poem is a "speaking picture." Because his technique is more often grounded in re-creating a scene than in telling a story, his visionary ability is central to his poetic intent. His narrator or protagonist will convey what was observed, sharing it with the reader as an intimate witness and thus drawing one into his poetic world. His poems focusing on painters (from *In the Dead of Night*) highlight this technique and comment on his own aesthetic as well, as in "Seurat": "Dressed and shaved, wearing / My spectacles I climb the stepladder / To my canvas; I am ascending and / That's the whole story. But / If your wife scalds her hand / I would paint / The hand red. I am honest." Dubie, like El Greco in the poem of that name, willingly confronts scenes of vivid ambiguity:

The lunatics are out of their little houses
In their yellow or orange shirts: they spin
With paper cones and triangles on their
Shaved heads. A merchant picks his nose.
You sit in the middle of this white yard.
Lost among your bits of chalk and
Soft charcoal.

Dubie's intimate, realistic observation of often dreamlike settings has drawn both praise and barbs from critics, who respect his fecundity yet sometimes find only an artistry of surfaces and provocative externals. However, in an early work, *Alehouse Sonnets* (1971), this technique has not yet reached full prominence; his mode is predominantly confessional, as he addresses fifteen-line sonnets to William Hazlitt, the Romantic essayist, who, like Dubie, was born on 10 April and was the son of a minister. The daily needs of living tend to obtrude and make the creation of poetic worlds an economic necessity: "Hazlitt, you're a critic; / you go out of town to forget the town. / I go out of life to feed a wife and daughter" ("Harvest"). Dubie comments on his experience in the company of a kindred spirit, one whose "head / is an alehouse decorated with pine boughs: an inch / of sawdust, stewed / platters of carrots and onions, and the cedar closets" ("Hazlitt at the Bench, Gravesend"). In "Organ Meats" the victory of Hazlitt's hero, Napoleon, at Austerlitz is included in a sonnet in which Dubie's social conscience is revealed: "And yes, we have new weapons: / tanks, flame-throwers, bomber squadrons, / choking gas with the odor of horseradish, the H-bomb / and our Pope's most recent encyclical on contraception." This early volume, though it suffers from a too-obvious inclusion of biographical details from Hazlitt's life and a brief sequence whose echoes of Thomas Wyatt seem thematically out of place ("Hazlitt Compareth His Heart to the Over-charged Gun"), nevertheless offers some memorable passages of deep feeling: "And in April I sat on the sand off Popham beach / and watched my father, after sermon, / as he swam in the Atlantic Ocean: wrestling / with blue seals, even the turtles loved him, / he was a happy man. That afternoon / I got my old-time religion, and I'll keep it / until the seas evaporate into empty basins" ("Our Childhood at Wem").

Two later works, *The Illustrations* and *In the Dead of the Night*, reveal the allusive style for which Dubie is best known. In his prefatory essay to *The Illustrations* Richard Howard expresses Dubie's purpose: "That you may grant this assertion—that the poem can create your experience of the world rather than that your experience must create the poem—is the risk Dubie takes, his cherished peril." Artists and historical figures are featured as characters in the book: Georg Trakl, Charles Baudelaire, Thomas Traherne, Osip Mandelstam, Helena Petrovna Blavatsky, Pieter Brueghel, the Elder; and Dubie's relationship with these who have spoken, written, and painted creates a gallery of alter egos. In poems on the death of individuals (death is a recurring theme in Dubie's later work) his tone is choric and valedictory: "Will each of us be increased by death? / With fractions as the bottom gets bigger, Mother, it / Represents less. That's the feeling I have about / This letter. I am at your request, the Czar. / And I am Nicholas" ("The Czar's Last Christmas Letter. A Barn in the Urals"). Dubie also shows an awareness of imminent threat within the mundane, as in the life of Frieda Lawrence: "And if you imagine she is being watched, then / She will never be lonely / As much later under a street lamp in London: / She nervously revolves a parasol above her, and the orbs and tassels on the parasol rise and fall, / Musical somehow / Like heavy blue buzzards

above a lame burro" ("The Red Padrona for Jose Cuevas"). Dubie's hatred of totalitarian violence emerges in "The Piano," which describes the death of the Russian royal family at the hands of the Bolsheviks: "You dance with the Czar's youngest daughter: / She's dressed in a *mikado*-yellow shirt, / There's a long strand of hair in her mouth, and / As you dance, the steps you take together / Are suggested by the bullets that are just now / Tearing at her mouth and shoulder."

A keenly perceptive narrator highlights *In the Dead of the Night* (incorporating the chapbook *Indian Summer*, 1974), where one finds frequent window imagery and acts of observation. In "Popham of the New Song: 6," "Pastor Cruickshank looks out over the lake" as he and the narrator contemplate the Nazi invasion of Poland. In "Wales" the narrator is a priest who is touched by deaths of children: "It's when the children are sick that I am most / Lost in whatever is outside the window." And in "About Infinity, and the Lenesdorf Pools" the observing is doubled, with the speaker watching a watcher:

> You are dressed all in white like the clematis
> And look down into a meadow where your father
> Is working on a watercolor of two silver trees.
> The two trees are parallel.
> He looks back at you:
> You are wishing he hadn't died making with
> His chest a sound like cows running in a stream.

The brutality of the final line reveals how often Dubie also senses violence or pain beneath the surfaces of experience. One is reminded of Joseph Conrad's artistic goal: "My task is to make you *see*." The reader is led into scenes of sinister clarity relayed by a prescient sensibility, and the reader's task—like that of the characters themselves—is not merely to watch, but to watch out.

Dubie acknowledges his realism: "I think the desire to see things with great resolution and the fact that this is a basic aspect of a narrative process brings me to realism. I think that my work does center on a kind of realism." Dubie's poems beg comparison with Robert Browning's dramatic monologues. Is a passage from "For Osip Mandelstam"—"You think her breasts are like marble with / A large blue vein standing out"— an echo from Browning's "The Bishop Orders His Tomb at St. Praxed's Church," in which a lump of lapis lazuli is "Blue as a vein o'er the Madonna's breast"? Dubie's surreal panoramas likewise at times remind one of the blasted landscape through which Childe Roland ventured. Dubie himself rejects such comparisons, pointing to Browning's fixed poetic voice: "I'm not in the Browning shade.... Robert Browning has an acquired voice through which he speaks his poems, but it's a single voice, and it's the poetic voice of Robert Browning. It does not wildly fluctuate and it does not wildly intone and it does not suffer crisis." As Phoebe Pettingell notes in a review of Dubie's *Selected and New Poems* (1983), voice is not the only distinction: "these poems, unlike Browning monodramas, do not try to capture the robust flavor of character or ideas. Instead, Dubie offers impressionistic word-paintings of significant details" (*New Leader*, 28 November 1983). Vernon Shetley has likewise seen a distinction between the two poets, but finds a critical lack: "where Browning's interest seems largely psychological, revealing nuances of character through a vivid rendering of the speaking voice, Dubie resists penetrating the minds of the historical personages he presents. One might say that Browning takes a tape recorder to the past, Dubie a camera." However, according to Shetley, "Dubie has, in his swerve from Browning, done away with just the quality that gave the earlier poet his vitality, and the loss can be felt only as a diminishment" (*New York Review of Books*, 29 April 1982).

Dubie's ability to combine unexpected details in his tableaux has led some to label his work grotesque, yet the artifacts assembled in the work acquire their own logic. According to Lodge, "His poetry asks, 'How many ways is it possible to conceive of the seemingly simple circumstances of our lives?'" His work has an epistemological urgency about it as he recombines the data of experience in unfamiliar couplings to seek the meaning within and beyond the familiar. As he says in the prologue to *In the Dead of the Night*: "Anything approaching us we try to understand, say, / Like a lamp being carried up a lane at midnight."

To be sure, his efforts are not always successful. The presumption that a significance will somehow inhere in any created scene can lead to statements that approach self-parody: "Meanwhile, my attention turns to the family / With white soup in their plates and a little prayer / Before they take the inventory. / There is a nasty theme inhabiting the potato" ("The Aster"). His attempts to clarify meaning sometimes run the risk of tautology: "There is no importance to things that have no importance" ("Indian Summer"). But as Dubie told Green, "good poets are utterly taken up with risk."

The Springhouse (1986) and *Groom Falconer* (1989) retain the three-part organization that has marked earlier collections. Dubie views this tripartite structure, as he told Green, as "sort of an *eccentric* rendering of properties that we've found traditionally in poems that argue. I'm thinking of 'turn, counter-turn, and stand,' which is the patterning of emotions and thought perhaps in my individual poems as well as my books." Both of these volumes show a movement away from his longer poems of the mid 1970s in favor of briefer lyrics with briefer titles. In *The Springhouse*, a book of dreams and violent death, he presents the imagined voices of hummingbirds that are poisoned by a clerk in Memphis; the last words of German mystic Meister Eckehart; a trolley accident in Xochimilco; and the execution of a girl in Hamburg, who was "In the last days of the war / Stripped along with six other children / And hanged in the boiler room of a post office. What she has understood / Is there are only / Two speeches the naked make well, / One is of welcome, the other farewell" ("Lamentations").

The volume takes its title from a springhouse in "The Funeral," a poem written in memory of Dubie's aunt: "It felt like the zero in brook ice. / She was my youngest aunt, the summer before / We had stood naked / While she stiffened and giggled, letting the minnows / Nibble at her toes. I was almost four— / That evening she took me to the springhouse." Later, at her funeral, "Uncle Peter, in a low voice, said / The cancer ate her like horse piss eats deep snow." Of this poem Mark Irwin observed that "the final result is a striking texture in which the beautiful is juxtaposed against, and slowly transposed into, the vulgar" (*Kenyon Review*, Winter 1988).

Dubie provides the Dantean sense of one returned from an encounter with the dead who are not dead, the past which is yet living. The telling is direct, graphic, and imagistic, as in the first eleven lines of "Archangelsk":

> The yellow goat in winter sunlight
> Is eating a birch canoe.
> The carrot fields are black.
> Snow is falling like sawdust. Joseph Stalin
> And his barber are in fine spirits
> This morning. It is the first day of Lent.
> They are laughing about a prisoner
> Who in three nights of questioning
> Confessed repeatedly
> To having painted over
> A fresh cocoon on a garden fence.

The pictorial quality of the first three lines, the stark brushstrokes of yellow and black, typify Dubie's painterly tendency, which becomes more pronounced in his poems devoted to artists such as Paul Klee, Georges Seurat, and El Greco. Typical also is his sympathy for the plight of the prisoner and the victim, despite the apparently neutral engagement of his narrator. The phrase "the first day of Lent" heightens the context of suffering, revealing Dubie's unobtrusive religious sensitivity as well. One may be tempted to agree with Calvin Bedient's judgment that "Dubie is a morally empty poet" (*Sewanee Review*, Winter 1988) because of his habit of portraying events of great pathos with a tone of simple reportage. Yet this is Dubie's narrative voice, not his personal moral stance; the graphic details of his work convey his social and individual conscience through objective correlatives that avoid the sentimentality that explicit comment would risk.

Dubie's *Groom Falconer* exhibits a fascination with the horrible that compels riveted yet perplexed attention. This volume has been greeted with what seems a critical commonplace, respect for the poet's dazzling array of unnerving imagery mingled with irritation at the lack of readily apprehensible poetic intent. While praising his "unforgettably bizarre stories imbued with individual vision," Genevieve Stuttaford remarked that "some poems strain credibility, making fantastic connections that appear to court absurdity for its own sake" (*Publishers Weekly*, 10 March 1989). Andrew Hudgins noted an absence of "that sense of passionate involvement with a literary figure," which marked *Alehouse Sonnets*, finding instead that Dubie "writes about his characters with such imagistic purity, with such an icy refusal to penetrate the surface of their actions and appearances, that they seem to exist for no other reason than to provide their creator with vivid images" (*Hudson Review*, Winter 1990).

Certainly his work here is no less recondite and demanding than in his earlier books. In the title poem the speaker visits "the insomniac / Rich child who sits naked at the window" of an asylum:

> She cuts herself for the first time, a trickle
> Of blood at the knuckle of the thumb
> Like the single red thread
> Through the lace hood and jesses
> Of the Medici falcons.
> Her concentration broken, the hand
> Loosens: *one wing, one stone.*
> The sun is seeping over the snow.

> She greets me with an acknowledgement
> One reserves for a ghost.

Dubie explained to Green that "the doctor, who is visiting this turn-of-the-century asylum, is like a groom to flights of the imagination that have gone horribly wrong in the persons of the insane. In that sense, it [the poem] is like a groom to a bird of prey, or a groom to a falcon. If you want to discuss this image in terms of my relationship to the world or to things real or imagined, you'll have to make that case for yourself."

In 1991 *Radio Sky* was published—a collection of thirty-four poems in which Dubie's focus shifts slightly to a consideration of more contemporary figures, in poems such as "Looking Up from Two Renaissance Paintings to the Massacre at Tiananmen Square," "The Diatribe of the Kite," and "Homage to Philip K. Dick" ("My visitor was at the door yesterday. / In a blue sere of a sucker suit"). The book also features a somewhat more explicit confrontation with religion: Dubie conveys no easy faith but rather grapples with the deepest of religious problems, those of suffering and evil. "Psalm XXIII" is based on the ironic contrast between the biblical poem's expression of surety and the speaker's witness to the effects of an American bombing:

> In the garden
> The water pipes gushed and froze
> Over a horse whose backside was crushed by fallen
>   bricks;
> The heated water hissed and as the horse
> Took on ice, still propped up with its forelegs,
> It stood like a feeding mantis, the awful mouth
> Open around its swollen tongue.

"A True Story of God" pits Henry David Thoreau, who thinks that "God is in nature and nature / Is in men," against the reality of a moose shot by "Humans who, while knowing they possess a soul, / Become useless." "Revelation 20:11-15" sets the death of a farm boy, drowned "While trying to swim two gray horses across the river," in the context of that New Testament passage; in "Thomas Merton and the Winter Marsh" and "Jacob Boehme Walking Outside Görlitz" readers see through the eyes of two mystics, additions to Dubie's gallery of observant narrators.

Dubie has most recently completed *The Clouds of Magellan* (1992), a collection of what he terms "heretical aphorisms" on poetry and culture. A "thirteen-part invention," the work is both an answer to and a critique of Wallace

The Apocrypha of Jacques Derrida

The ruptured underbelly of a black horse flew overhead.

Bonaparte, is what the matron said to me,

Always condescending; vulgar, slowly separating

The three syllables. And it was the last thing she said.

The engine block struck the tree. Our faces

Making brook ice of the windshield. The vaulting black horse

Now on its side in the dust. I was left

With the road, with the memory of cities burning.

Matron seemed to sleep. My nose bleeding.

I went over to inspect the huge sunflowers

That were beyond the stonewall. The sunflowers

Marched with me in Italy. They were cut down.

There was gasoline everywhere. The attendants

Will come for me. It's back to the island.

I'll study English out in the cool stucco of the shed.

I don't really believe I am the Corsican. But then

Neither did he.

The car was now burning with the tree. The black

Brook ice bursting. The horse got up and left.

A back hoof snared by intestine . . .

I was once all game leg in a fast sleigh

Passing a half-frozen cook who asked a frozen orderly,

"Is he the snow?"

　　　　　　　　　　　　　　　　　　　(no stanza break)　　　　28

Revised typescript for a poem on the founder of deconstructionist criticism, collected in Groom Falconer *(by permission of Norman Dubie)*

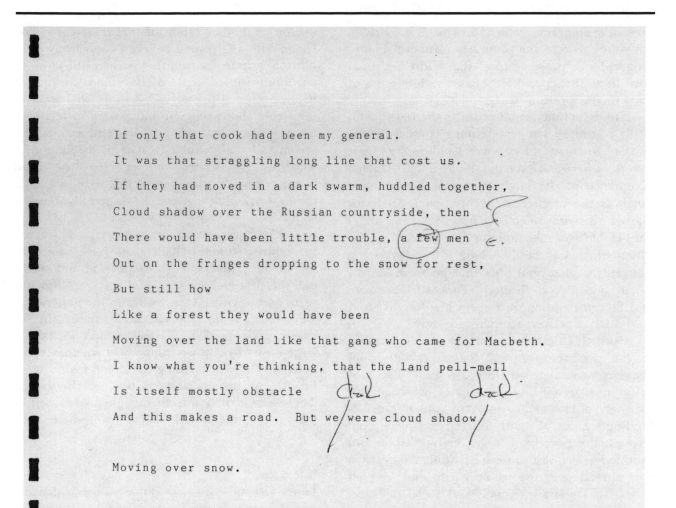

If only that cook had been my general.

It was that straggling long line that cost us.

If they had moved in a dark swarm, huddled together,

Cloud shadow over the Russian countryside, then

There would have been little trouble, a few men

Out on the fringes dropping to the snow for rest,

But still how

Like a forest they would have been

Moving over the land like that gang who came for Macbeth.

I know what you're thinking, that the land pell-mell

Is itself mostly obstacle

And this makes a road. But we were cloud shadow

Moving over snow.

29

Stevens's epigrams, which provoked it. Written for young writers, the volume is a somewhat autobiographical "prose gesture" that addresses problems in aesthetics and serves as a vade mecum of sorts for his previous work.

Idiosyncratic romanticism is the most inclusively accurate term as a defining context for the work of Norman Dubie. Lorrie Goldensohn (*American Book Review*, December 1977) noted "Dubie's acceptance of the High Romantic premise that death is the mother of beauty," and Frederick Garber (*American Poetry Review*, May-June 1982) cites Dubie's own recognition " 'of a Romantic tradition which I certainly belong to.'... Dubie is a descendant of several lines that go from Wordsworth and Byron through Thoreau, Emerson, and Stevens, adding on figures like Roethke and Berryman as they stretch our way." William Wordsworth's declaration of the poet's function in the preface to *Lyrical Ballads* (1798) could stand as a comment on Dubie's work: "In spite of difference of soil and climate, of language and manners, of laws and customs, in spite of things silently gone out of mind and things violently destroyed, the poet binds together by passion and knowledge the vast empire of human society, as it is spread over the whole earth, and over all time." In Dubie's indignation at social injustice; in his conviction that meaning inhabits facticity, yet can only be approached through the senses; in his persistent quest for that meaning, labyrinthine though it be, through permutations of character and event; in his sensitivity to landscape and his commingling of the beautiful and the damned—in all these he suggests a Blakean visionary quality as well as a Keatsian attention to perceived reality. His statements on his poetics recall John Keats's declarations on the truth of the imagination and the value of negative capability. Dubie said to Green, "I believe whatever my lyric/narrative strategies are, they want to be close to an uninterrupted sense of the mind working in its own original privacy.... I think all I want to say freely about religion and poetry in terms of my own life is that the experience of making the poem, as I said, involves a state of meditation in which we're very alert and yet lost to the world in many respects. But out of this state magically comes work that we can be especially pleased with."

The challenges Dubie's poetry poses for the reader arise from the challenge he has set for himself: to mediate between the physical and spiritual, the past and present, and the seen and unseen; and to engage the reader in the experience that results from this volatile synthesis. In his words, a "large dose of realism, and we take a large dose of realism in this world whether we're watching CNN or crossing the street, invites us to project, to invent, and to become the other. There's an invitation to the imaginative as well as the real, and I would like to meet them both equally."

Interview:

James Green, "Norman Dubie: *Groom Falconer*," *American Poetry Review* (November/December 1989): 28-31.

References:

Frederick Garber, "On Dubie and Seidel," *American Poetry Review*, 11 (May-June 1982): 44-47;

Richard Howard, Introduction to Dubie's *The Illustrations* (New York: Braziller, 1977), pp. vii-x.

Tess Gallagher

(21 July 1943 -   )

De Villo Sloan
Wells College

BOOKS: *Stepping Outside* (Lisbon, Iowa: Penumbra, 1974);

Instructions to the Double (Port Townsend, Wash.: Graywolf, 1976);

Under Stars (Port Townsend, Wash.: Graywolf, 1978);

Portable Kisses (Seattle: Sea Pen, 1978);

On Your Own (Port Townsend, Wash.: Graywolf, 1978);

Willingly (Port Townsend, Wash.: Graywolf, 1984);

Dostoevsky: A Screenplay, by Gallagher and Raymond Carver (Santa Barbara: Capra, 1985);

The Lover of Horses (New York: Harper & Row, 1986);

A Concert of Tenses (Ann Arbor: University of Michigan Press, 1986);

Amplitude: New and Selected Poems (Saint Paul: Graywolf, 1987).

The publication of Tess Gallagher's early poems coincided with a ground swell of feminist awareness and the birth of a new feminist literature in the United States. In addition to chronicling the emergence of a feminine identity, Gallagher's poems also move beyond gender in their exploration of what it means to be human.

Tess Bond Gallagher was born in Port Angeles, Washington, on 21 July 1943, and was the oldest of the five children of Leslie O. and Georgia Marie Morris Bond. During her childhood, Tess's father worked first as a logger and then as a longshoreman. As a child, she helped her father with logging and later did farm work on the small ranch her family owned. References to the natural beauty of Washington State and childhood memories, such as salmon fishing with her father in the Straits of Juan de Fuca, appear consistently throughout her poetic work. From age sixteen she worked as a reporter for the *Port Angeles Daily News*.

Intending to become a journalist, she attended the University of Washington; but a poetry-writing class with faculty member Theodore

Tess Gallagher circa 1987 (photograph by Penelope Moffat)

Roethke shifted her interests. Her first poems, written for Roethke's class, concerned her father and explored her origins. She did not complete her course work in four years, leaving the university to marry Lawrence Gallagher, a sculptor, in June 1963. The dissolution of her marriage in 1968 sparked new poems, many of which are in her first full-length collection, *Instructions to the Double* (1976).

Gallagher received her B.A. in English from the University of Washington in 1968 and her M.A. from the same institution in 1970, then attended the University of Iowa's Writers Workshop, graduating with an M.F.A. in 1974. She has since had a distinguished career as a writer and teacher. She has taught at Saint Lawrence University (1974-1975); Kirkland College (1975-1977); the University of Montana (1977-1978); the University of Arizona, Tucson (1979-1980); and Syracuse University (1980-present). She was the recipient of a Creative Artist Public Service Grant from the New York State Arts Council (1976); the Elliston Award (1976); National Endowment for the Arts grants (1976 and 1981); a Guggenheim Fellowship (1978-1979); two Governor's Awards for Poetry from the state of Washington; and the Chancellor's Citation from Syracuse University. In May 1973 Gallagher married Michael Burkard, a poet; they divorced in 1977. In 1979 she began living with Raymond Carver, a writer and teacher, whom she married shortly before his death in 1988.

Tess Gallagher's most influential collection, *Instructions to the Double*, documents a woman's identity in transition. In the four sections of the book, Gallagher explores the roles that her traditional, working-class upbringing offers; rejects those roles with some ambivalence; explores alternatives that the literary tradition offers; and finally accepts her identity as a poet.

The poems in *Instructions to the Double* fall into two distinct categories. Those in the first, dominant in the first half of the book, are influenced by the confessional school and, notably, by Gallagher's mentor, Roethke. Thematically they explore memories from childhood to early adulthood that mark crucial moments of transition in her development. These poems are inclined toward naturalism in description and make use of narrative techniques, although Gallagher's personal style, which synthesizes several contemporary modes, is obvious throughout all the poems. Ultimately, confessional poetry is Gallagher's major influence. The second category of poem has as its subject the relationship between language and self. These poems are decidedly abstract and influenced by surrealism and postmodernism as practiced by Robert Bly.

Two notable poems from *Instructions to the Double* derived from the confessional school are "Breasts" and "Black Money." In "Breasts" Gallagher recounts the discovery of womanhood, disillusionment with that role, and acceptance of herself as a woman. The first stanza describes the moment when she first recognizes sexual difference. Playing with her brothers as a child she becomes aware of her breasts: "Swart nubbins, I no-

ticed you then, / my mother shaking a gritty rag from the porch / to get my shirt on this minute." The speaker is pulled from her brisk childhood play and relegated to the less equal role of young woman: "Brothers, / that was the parting of our ways, for then / you got me down by something else than flesh."

In the second stanza of "Breasts," Gallagher expresses disillusionment with her role as a woman by describing three shattered relationships with men. These short vignettes signify unrequited love, violence, and betrayal. The speaker, by the third stanza, concludes that the notions of romantic love between men and women are a sad deception; however, she also accepts responsibility for her own actions and transcends her previous feeling of victimization. Using her breasts as a vehicle for self-reflection, she says: "But I have hurt you as certainly / with cold sorrowing as anyone, / have come the long way / over broken ground to this softness." In the final lines, she recognizes that her own resourcefulness has allowed her to survive even "when heaven was a luckless dream."

"Black Money" draws on Gallagher's childhood in Washington and begins her poetic exploration of the complex relationship between father and daughter. Although this theme is presented autobiographically, it clearly has universal resonance. By describing her father's working conditions, Gallagher causes the poem also to exist on a sociopolitical level that seems to portray the economic and social constraints that enslave humans. This poem also employs surrealistic techniques.

In the first stanza her father returns home from a day of brutal physical labor. He encounters his children, "a cloud of swallows about him," and his wife, "her back the wall he fights most." After establishing the dismal emotional and physical terrain, the second stanza shifts to the sleeping family. In their dreams, they travel through the industrial and spiritual wasteland of their waking lives. They float "past banks and businesses, / the used car lots, liquor store, the swings in the park."

By the third stanza they penetrate to the core of these dreams, which is a mill burning in the night, and "Then like a whip / the sun across the bed, windows high with mountains." At this point Gallagher discards the third-person point of view and becomes a child again, hearing her father as he "snorts, splashes in the bathroom" and prepares for the routine to begin again.

The fourth stanza describes him departing, "coffee bottle tucked into his armpit," after he has taken the "black money" from his pockets, "shoveled from the sulphur pyramids heaped in the distance / like yellow gold." "Black Money" portrays the family as the living dead, victims of a vast exploitive economic system, their father selling his soul for tainted money. This image of the past represents, for Gallagher, the mental and physical American landscape, a landscape she longs to escape.

The book's title poem, "Instructions to the Double," chronicles the emergence of Gallagher's identity as a poet and liberation from the constraints of her past. This birth is an ordeal, and she employs the techniques of postmodernism, surrealism, and the concept of Carl G. Jung's shadow figure to express the struggle.

In the first stanza Gallagher instructs her double, a manifestation of her new identity, which has not yet been born, to go forth: "Take up / this face, these daily rounds / with a cabbage under each arm / convincing the multitudes / that a well-made-anything / could save them." As the poem unfolds, "a well-made-anything" is a reference to poetry. The second stanza concerns her womanhood: her abandonment of the confining roles that have been placed on her since childhood, and the acceptance of womanhood, including sexuality: "Walk / into some bars alone / with a slit in your skirt." Men will call her many names:—"virgin, whore, daughter, adulteress, lover"—because she has become the embodiment of literary womanhood, but, with self-understanding, all the old names lose significance. Her instructions are to approach the living world of poetry, the "temple of the poets, not / the one like a run-down country club, but the one on fire / with so much it wants / to be done with." This new poetry will be her task, not inside the patriarchal academic tradition, which the fourth stanza disclaims. She is well aware of the risks that the end of the poem describes: "It's a dangerous mission. You / could die out there. You / could live forever."

Gallagher's second full-length collection, *Under Stars* (1978), is a continuation of her journey of self-discovery. Whereas *Instructions to the Double* is an essentially inward-looking book concerned with the formation of a woman's identity, *Under Stars* is concerned with woman's identity as defined by place and intimate relationships with others. The book is divided into two sections:

"The Ireland Poems" and "Start Again Somewhere."

The lyrics in "The Ireland Poems" vacillate between naturalistic descriptions of both the Irish landscape and conditions in contemporary Ireland, specifically "Disappearances in the Guarded Sector" and "Sligo Footraces," and poems that incorporate the rich Irish literary tradition, such as "The Ballad of Ballymote." In many of these poems Gallagher's writing functions as a camera lens, capturing scenes and events from a perspective that gives them increased significance. In other places, a mature voice appears eager to reveal the joys and problems of independence.

Ireland is, for Gallagher, a paradox. She can explore the land of her ancestors and measure herself in an environment that is clearly alien to her. In the most successful poems in this section, landscape, characters, and narrative voice coalesce to function as allegory. "Women's Tug of War at Lough Arrow" is a near-perfect lyric. In the first stanza, using an objective, third-person point of view, she describes a group of women engaged in a tug of war. She imagines the women are on a boat: "and leaning like boatmen rowing into / the damp earth they pull / to themselves." This image immediately establishes a sense of unity among the women. The rope becomes another connective thread to establish their sisterhood.

At the beginning of the second stanza, Gallagher writes: "The steady rain has made girls of them, / their hair in ringlets. . . ." The water image has been sustained, extended to become an image of rebirth and innocence. They continue to struggle "to the cries / of husbands and children, until the rope / runs slack, runs free. . . ." Through this simple game, the women have suddenly found themselves as a distinct group with its own identity. Letting go of the rope creates an incredible release of tension: the structure of oppositions in the game (and in life) is broken, and the women, already returned to a state of innocence by the rain, fall into each other's arms.

The poems in the second section of *Under Stars*, "Start Again Somewhere," continue Gallagher's tendency toward a more narrative, confessional poetry that moves away from the linguistic experimentation with postmodernism in *Instructions to the Double*. One notable exception to this departure is the final poem, "Your Letter is Being Written Without You." The poems in "Start Again Somewhere" are not wedded to geo-

Cover for the 1987 collection that includes Gallagher's choice of poems from her previous books, plus new poems based on memories of travel, family life, and her relationship with the late Raymond Carver

graphic location, and, although thematically uneven, they consistently return to the subject of time, and form the beginning of a penetrating self-examination of her relationships with male figures that serves as the basis of Gallagher's later poems.

The ground-breaking "3 A.M. Kitchen: My Father Talking" marks an important shift in Gallagher's poetic style. Stripping away the layers of metaphor that have accumulated in her work since *Instructions to the Double*, she attempts to communicate experience directly without the influence of a complex poetic language. "3 A.M. Kitchen: My Father Talking" is presented as a transcription in verse of her father telling a story in his own language without interjection or comment by the poet. This poem marks the beginning of Gallagher's full compassion, reaching out

and understanding the pains and joys of another's experience.

In her third full-length volume, *Willingly* (1984), Gallagher, having been profoundly changed by experiences since the publication of *Under Stars*, emerges as a mature individual and poet. *Willingly* is expansive in scope and breadth. A book in which her vision exceeds all her previous writing, it is concerned with establishing a compassionate, humane, and meaningful way of living in a world where traditional moral systems, based on religion, have been abandoned. *Willingly* is also concerned with establishing a poetic discourse that effectively communicates with the reader. This project transcends issues of gender that preoccupy her in the earlier works.

The experience at the core of *Willingly* is her father's death. This event had such a profound impact on Gallagher's poetic development that the three sections of the book can be read as an extended elegy. The second section contains poems describing his life and death, including "3 A.M. Kitchen: My Father Speaking," given new meaning in a different context. The most significant and ambitious poems in *Willingly* are sustained narratives written in a lucid, stripped-down verse that is seen beginning to emerge in *Under Stars*. These new, narrative poems show the influence of Carver (to whom the volume is dedicated). They also indicate Gallagher's new willingness to accept her past. By acknowledging the power of common speech (from her working-class upbringing) and lucid description (from her training as a journalist), she is accepting the past she once vehemently rejected.

In the first section of *Willingly*, Gallagher confronts the problem of finding a moral system for living in a world where traditional systems have been discarded. "Linoleum," a seventy-five-line lyric divided into three stanzas, is Gallagher's greatest accomplishment in writing a sustained, primarily rhetorical poem. The first stanza contrasts the mundane act of having her car washed with the transcendent beliefs found in both Buddhist and Christian teachings. Gallagher acknowledges the need for a moral way of living that gives life meaning: "In the carwash, / thinking of yogis under a tree / plucking hair by hair the head / of an initiate, I feel at least / elsewhere those able for holiness— / its signs and rigors— are at work." She cannot reconcile her present way of life with those philosophies.

The second stanza finds her at the county library reading Buddhist texts in order to understand the values these systems represent. Finally she constructs a list of values she admires: "forbearance, indulgence, / straightforwardness, purity / veracity, restraint, freedom from / attachment to anything, poverty / and chastity." By returning to the past and combining its wisdom with her experience, she is able to construct a list of values she can personally admire and hope to live by. This stanza indicates her belief that a synthesis of the wisdom of the past with knowledge gained from individual experience can result in a moral system for living.

In the third stanza Gallagher returns to the mundane world with her newly gained insights. On a trip to the supermarket, she listens to the news, which includes the story of a child nailed into a broom closet by the parents for twenty-four hours. This story causes her to reflect: "I feel a longing / for religion, for doctrine swift / as a broom to keep the path / clear." At home she attempts to reconcile her values with the world she lives in: "Overwhelmed by the loneliness / of the saints, I take up my broom / and begin where I stand, / with linoleum." Living with one's beliefs first requires knowledge of the world as it is. Then one must take action and live one's beliefs in the world. The product is an integrated, moral personality. The act of sweeping is the first important step in this new moral existence.

Another significant achievement in *Willingly* is the autobiographical narrative poem "Boat Ride." This sixteen-stanza poem chronicles a fishing trip Gallagher took with her father. In this poem she is finally able to understand her father, confront his death, and practice her newly gained understanding of morality. Written in finely crafted free verse, "Boat Ride" uses a narrative structure, fictional devices, and common language to create an important American elegy.

The first three stanzas connect Gallagher's girlhood memories of fishing with her father to the present excursion. Accompanying him and her is a man identified throughout the poem only as a "friend." "Boat Ride" is rich with symbolic possibilities, including Christian imagery such as the Trinity, baptism, and fishing.

The fourth stanza describes her father: "His mind / in the no-thought of guiding the boat." Observing him, Gallagher begins to gain insight into his personality. This study of her father is broken by deep self-reflection. From the water, she observes the distant coast, seeing the land where she grew up from a distance: "Port of the An-

gels, / the angels turning on kitchen lights, / wood smoke stumbling among scattered hemlock, / burning up questions, the angels telling / their children to get up, planning the future / that is one day long." These lines echo the childhood memories in "Black Money." In the contemplative space provided by the fishing trip, Gallagher explores her past and its relationship to the person she has become.

Fishing is described in stanzas 9-12. They catch no salmon and are plagued by dogfish they do not want. Gallagher watches her father as he catches a dogfish: "My father grabs the line, yanks / the fish toward the knife, slashes twice, / gashing the throat and underbelly so / the blood spills over his hand." From viewing this incident, she becomes aware of her father's anger and underlying frustration with life, and she reaches a stage of empathic understanding that she has not previously been able to achieve. In stanzas 13 and 14 her father tells stories about his past, about quitting jobs where he was exploited, the loss of his youth and freedom, and the sacrifices involved in raising a family. Gallagher hears these old stories with new appreciation for her father.

In stanza 15 readers are told, "It is the last fishing trip / I will have with my father." Then, in a memory sequence, Gallagher recounts his final illness. In the final stanza, after experiencing the joy of the fishing and the agony of his death, she writes, "It is good then, / to eat salmon on the water, to bait the hook. . . ." She learns the lesson of living and dying from her father, "who, / in the last of himself, cannot put together, / that meaning, and need not, but yields in thought, / so peacefully to the stubborn brightness of / light and water: we are awake with him / as if we lay asleep."

Amplitude (1987) includes selected poems from all Gallagher's previous major collections. The "New Poems" in the final section mark a movement following the trend established in *Willingly* toward narrative and common language. The poems consist of travelogues, family memories, and lyrics that describe her relationship with Carver, whose losing battle with illness and death in 1988 moved Gallagher as much as her father's death. If there is any unifying factor in this eclectic mix of new poems in *Amplitude*, it is their consistent emphasis on morality. Many of them can best be described as didactic.

"That Kind of Thing" is a narrative poem of seven stanzas written during a trip to Bahia, Brazil, in 1984. The first stanza establishes the setting—a luxury hotel room where Gallagher and Carver are visited by an information officer from the American Consulate of Salvador, the capital of Bahia province. Gallagher is uneasy in the hotel and says to her companion, before the arrival of the officer, " 'I feel like we've / walked straight into a bank / where they keep people.' " She is genuinely revolted by the intrusion of the officer, "in a khaki shirt so tight on him / the buttons ripple open when he / sits down, revealing little jets of / flesh and chest hair." The poem overflows with sarcasm and irony, elements that are relatively rare in Gallagher's work.

In the second and third stanzas, the officer describes the danger of thievery the pair will encounter, telling them not to wear jewelry. He recounts the story of a woman who came to his office with her throat ripped open after a robber had grabbed her necklace. Another story concerns a bandit who held a tourist at gunpoint and attempted to suck a stubborn gold wedding band from his victim's finger. By the way the officer tells these stories, he is revealed as a cold, bored bureaucrat who has no concern for or interest in the country and only wishes to go home to the sterile, but what he perceives to be superior, culture of the United States: "He's got a year to go in Salvador, / one of those places, he wants us to know, not / on the top of anyone's assignment list. . . ."

The officer continues to announce his opinions in the fourth and fifth stanzas, expressing his lack of sympathy for striking university professors and their students. He tells anecdotes about his Japanese wife, whose only function in life, it appears, is to cook. Throughout these stanzas a tone of anger is brewing beneath the surface of the poem. The object of Gallagher's anger becomes increasingly clear: the smug, complacent world the officer represents, a world that, by adopting a stance of moral superiority, takes no responsibility for human suffering. The information officer talks as if he had once been a revolutionary, "But he's gone on to more dignified / pursuits as befits a man who represents / a government whose banks have bankrolled debts / so colossal its bankers would have to / confiscate whole countries / to turn this thing around."

The final three stanzas detail his slow departure. He has read Carver's fiction but finds it "too depressing." Bitterly ironic, "That Kind of Thing" is a didactic, political poem. Highly accomplished in narrative technique and very clear in meaning, it is far removed from the poems in *Instructions to the Double*.

In contrast to the political didacticism in *Amplitude*, there are intensely moving, personal poems that speak of a different kind of morality. "Bonfire" is a wrenching, stream-of-consciousness lyric about Carver's final illness. To contain the flood of emotion inherent in such a task, Gallagher resorts to a highly variable line that ranges anywhere from three to more than fifteen syllables in length and wanders across the page in homage to Charles Olson's projective verse. "Bonfire" seems always on the verge of collapse, barely held together with associative images that combine beauty and pain: a giant bird-wing butterfly being shot down with a shotgun in the Pacific; lovers exchanging embraces in the night so intensely that their identities become intertwined; and, finally, ice-skating while holding a fragile violin.

In the second half of the poem, Gallagher selects the violin as a metaphor for her relationship with Carver. Once in Quebec on a dare, she explains, she skated with a friend's violin. Putting the fragile beauty of the violin ahead of herself, she stayed on her feet and returned the instrument. That image becomes intertwined with a scene in which a doctor announces that his patient has an incurable disease. Gallagher learns the primacy of love even in the face of death. Through the experience of suffering, she learns truth: the greatest human courage is putting another ahead of yourself, and that transcendence of self is the supreme challenge of living: "It wasn't for music / you came to me, but / for daring—mine / and yours."

Tess Gallagher's poetry is primarily concerned with self; but in the poetic tradition of Walt Whitman, she discovers a transcendent self whose paradoxical salvation is through love of others. In her work, readers see the ever-growing dynamics of human experience.

Interview:
Nicholas O'Connell, *At the Field's End: Interviews with Twenty Pacific Northwest Writers* (Seattle: Madoran, 1987), pp. 154-177.

Reginald Gibbons

(7 January 1947 -   )

Chris Willerton
Abilene Christian University

BOOKS: *Roofs Voices Roads* (Princeton, N.J.: Quarterly Review of Literature, 1979);
The Ruined Motel (Boston: Houghton Mifflin, 1981);
Saints (New York: Persea, 1986);
Maybe It Was So (Chicago: University of Chicago Press, 1991);
William Goyen: A Study of the Short Fiction (Boston: Twayne, 1991);
Five Pears or Peaches (Seattle: Broken Moon, 1991).

MOTION PICTURES: *The American Literature Series*, includes 13 scripts by Gibbons, Films for the Humanities, 1977-1978.

OTHER: *Selected Poems of Luis Cernuda*, edited and translated, with an introduction, by Gibbons (Berkeley & London: University of California Press, 1977 [i.e., 1978]);
The Poet's Work: 29 Masters of 20th Century Poetry on the Origins and Practice of Their Art, edited by Gibbons (Boston: Houghton Mifflin, 1979); republished as *The Poet's Work: 29 Poets on the Origin and Practice of Their Art* (Chicago: University of Chicago Press, 1989);
Guillén on Guillén: The Poetry and the Poet, translated by Gibbons and Anthony L. Geist (Princeton, N.J.: Princeton University Press, 1979);
Jorge Guillén, *Fuera del Mundo*, translated by Gibbons (Trenton, N.J.: Eleutherian Printers, 1981);
William Goyen, *New Work and Work in Progress*, edited by Gibbons (Winston-Salem, N.C.: Palaemon, 1983);
Criticism in the University, edited by Gibbons and Gerald Graff (Evanston, Ill.: Northwestern University Press, 1985);
Goyen, *Had I a Hundred Mouths: New and Selected Stories, 1947-1983*, edited by Gibbons (New York: Potter, 1985);
TQ 20: Twenty Years of the Best Contemporary Writing and Art from TriQuarterly Mazazine, edited by Gibbons and Susan Hahn (Evanston, Ill.: Northwestern University Press, 1985);
The Writer in Our World, edited, with a preface, by Gibbons (Boston & New York: Atlantic Monthly, 1986);
"Some Gifts," in *The Ways We Live Now: Contemporary Short Fiction from The Ontario Review*, edited by Raymond J. Smith (Princeton, N.J.: Ontario Review Press, 1986);
"Political Poetry and the Example of Ernesto Cardenal," in *Politics and Poetic Value*, edited by Robert von Hallberg (Chicago: University of Chicago Press, 1987);
From South Africa: New Writing, Photographs and Art, edited by Gibbons, David Bunn, Jane Taylor, and Sterling Plumpp (Chicago: University of Chicago Press, 1988);
"Mr. Walsh's Mare," in *New Growth*, edited by Lyman Grant (San Antonio: Corona, 1989);
Fiction of the Eighties: A Decade of Stories from TriQuarterly, edited by Gibbons and Hahn (Evanston, Ill.: TriQuarterly, 1990);
Thomas McGrath: Life and the Poem, edited by Gibbons and Terrence Des Pres (Champaign: University of Illinois Press, 1991).

SELECTED PERIODICAL PUBLICATIONS—
UNCOLLECTED: "William Goyen: Reflections of a Rhapsodic Writer," *Texas Humanist*, 6 (January-February 1984): 37-42;
"Poetic Form and the Translator," *Critical Inquiry*, 11 (June 1985): 654-671;
"Poetry and Self-Making," *TriQuarterly*, 75 (Spring/Summer 1989): 98-118.

Reginald Gibbons's poetry comes out of the same sensibility as his criticism, translation, editing, and teaching. As a critic and promoter of literature Gibbons labors to connect poetry with the rest of culture, and American writers with the rest of the world. As a poet he strives for the range and sensitivity he praises in great writers: "the largeness of the writer's response to worlds both large and small, to experiences both mate-

Dust jacket for Gibbons's second book, which includes two long poems about traveling

rial and spiritual, to realms both contemporary and imagined" (preface to *The Writer in Our World*, 1986).

These ambitions have brought him a busy career. He has participated in readings, lectures, and residencies at universities across North America and in England, Mexico, and Venezuela. Besides encouraging writers and readers through his editorship of the journal *TriQuarterly*, he has served the Associated Writing Programs on its board of directors (1984-1987) and as vice-president (1985-1986) and treasurer (1986-1987). He organized the 1984 *TriQuarterly* symposium "The Writer in Our World," which explored the relation between the artist and society. The range of his political concern for the "citizen-artist" informs his preface to the resulting 1986 collection of speeches. This preference for action as opposed to words alone is clear, too, in his essay in *Politics and Poetic Value* (1988).

Gibbons's cosmopolitan view of poetry accounts for the international range of his 1979 anthology *The Poet's Work* and of *TriQuarterly*, which he has edited since 1981, producing special issues on Spain, Poland, and South Africa, as well as on Chicago. The breadth of his taste enriches his own poetry, for which he has won major prizes and Guggenheim and National Endowment for the Arts fellowships. Gibbons's work in translating has reinforced the craft and the love of language that distinguish his own poetry collections. His principal themes—separation, the past, making one's identity, and the uses of art—owe some of their universality to his wide reading. The variety of settings in his poems—from Texas to Chicago to Spain to Greece—show his travels as well as his readings. The best result of Gibbons's long study of literature is his belief that art must serve, clarify, nourish, and comfort. His own poems have grown steadily toward that ideal.

Gibbons was born in Houston on 7 January 1947 to William Reginald Gibbons and Elizabeth Lubowski Gibbons. His father's parents lived in Mississippi; his mother's parents had emigrated from Poland. The young Gibbons discovered his love of Spanish as he studied it in public school. When he left Houston for the Ivy League, his academic training broadened him steadily. At Princeton he won the Morris Croll Prize in Poetry and attained Phi Beta Kappa, graduating in 1969 with an A.B. in Spanish and Portuguese. He married Virginia Harris on 8 June 1968.

While a student at Princeton, Gibbons began the ten years of writing that culminated in *Roofs Voices Roads* (1979). His first publication came in 1969 (four poems in the anthology *Story 69*). With a Woodrow Wilson Fellowship and later a Ford Foundation Fellowship, he went to Stanford, completing his M.A. in English and creative writing in 1971. After a year in Spain as a Fulbright fellow (1971-1972), he returned to Stanford, completing his Ph.D. in comparative literature in 1974. His area of specialization was "Poetry from 1850 to the Present in Romance Languages and English." His dissertation, under Donald Davie, was *Selected Poems of Luis Cernuda* (published in 1978). Gibbons's professional career showed the same energy as his preparation for it (even though, in his biographical sketch for *Roofs Voices Roads*, Gibbons dismissed his early employment as "irregular and ordinary"). After graduating from Stanford, he taught Spanish at Rutgers (1975-1976) and creative writing at Princeton (1976-1980). He won a *Denver Quarterly* Translation Award in 1977. *Roofs Voices Roads* won the *Quarterly Review of Literature* Poetry Prize in 1979.

The settings and allusions in *Roofs Voices Roads* reflect not only Gibbons's coming to terms with his heritage and with romantic love but also his Fulbright travels and his intense academic training. In his afterword to the collection, Gibbons assists his reader by identifying settings (from New York to the Gulf of Mexico to California to Greece to northern Spain) and persons in the poems (including Zen master Mu Chi and flautist William Kinkaid).

Reading the collection as autobiography would be a mistake, though. The five sections of the book are five suites on the theme of separation. But not all the nostalgia and dismay come out of Gibbons's private life; some is cultivated. In his afterword he points out "not only a nostalgia for known places, and a longing to see certain persons, but also a kind of loneliness that is not a reaction to absence but itself an appetite. A wishing-for—not *who-is-not-here*, but *who-is-not*. A wish for one who is not, who never was. So in thinking of grandparents, and of others, I have sometimes had to create figures in order to miss them. This habit, however innocent, may disable one's relationships with the living; nevertheless it seems a fruitful stratagem of desire, when imagination finds this appetite in its path." In *Saints* (1986) this stratagem comes to fruition in a rich set of dramatic monologues.

Section 1 of *Roofs Voices Roads*, which features a man troubled about his beloved, is the only one where the style resembles confessional poetry—an influence hard to avoid for any student of poetry in the 1960s. In "Dusk" the speaker blames gold miners for leaving bedrock exposed, lamenting his own tendency to "bare too much / in the attempt to attract love." At the end of the poem, he cries, "What a relief to see the fire of loneliness / there too, breaking // from another man's heart!" In most of the poems, fortunately, images rather than outbursts carry the theme. In "Half Asleep at Midnight, Upstairs, on the Coast, in a Storm," the speaker, isolated from his wife by her sleeping, thinks helplessly of the "chaos" around him—the storm outside and the drinking, dice-shooting, and careening of billiard balls in the game room downstairs.

Section 2 gives the most attention to European settings and characters. Whereas the first section had stressed psychological separation, this stresses separation by time, language, and nation. In "The Years" time separates the speaker from his grandmother and her youth as he muses over her 1901 Russian/English dictionary, bought when she emigrated. In "The Sleighbells Fade" he ponders how, in 1890, time separated his grandfather from knowledge of the death he would meet twelve thousand miles to the west. Several poems focus on the speaker as a foreigner. In "Teos" he feels separated by centuries from those who built the Greek temple at Teos. Indeed, as he gazes on ruins left to the wind and the wasps, he feels time sundering humankind from all pleasure, work, and worship. "The Foreigner (1)" epitomizes the section. Paths the speaker had hiked in Vermont, Switzerland, and Texas were mental as well as physical, and the one that has brought him to Madrid, standing on a balcony amid the natives' indifference, runs "inward," too.

Section 3 features more exotic "foreigners" and introduces the theme of language. In "The Liberian Freighter" an American and a native woman loading the ship communicate with glances as he wonders whether and how to communicate with words. "Glyphs" describes Spanish poet César Vallejo's struggles to write ("I want to write, but I feel I'm a beast; / to wear laurel wreaths, but I stew like an onion") and the impossibility of translating fully his *Poemas Humanos*—"Leaps, sobs, spite, heart, heritage— / these catch in the screen and can't come through." "The Red

Tree" is a myth of the ultimate foreigner, Madroño, a tree who became a man.

Sections 4 and 5 of the book treat the final form of separation: separation from the destiny one might have embraced, from the self one might have been. Death is the main destroyer of possibilities in section four, which includes two elegies on friends, a monologue by a traffic victim, a poem on archaeologists opening an Egyptian tomb, and one on future archaeologists viewing humankind's collective tomb. Such hope as there is in section four is not in a heaven ("The Life Everlasting" dismisses any wish for one) but in self-making through art. In "The Foreigner" he "longs for the book / whose pages will be mirrors." Section 5 focuses less on death than on society, which numbs or even abuses individuals. "In the Chips" shows the speaker imagining the potential selves now lost in the past—the bookstore clerk, the oil worker, the savings-and-loan officer, and others that he chose not to be. In "Welfare" readers see poverty and bureaucracy ("armed terriers who bark / Next Please") crushing the selves that the welfare clients might have become: "No one called us to act when we were ready, / now there is no more desire." To be satisfied in life, one must reject perfectionism and cherish individuality, which means cherishing the "flaw" that is "the glyph of some spirited form." An essay Gibbons published ten years later, "Poetry and Self-Making" (*TriQuarterly*, Spring/Summer 1989) complements these poems, explaining how the poet's own individuality is realized in crafting poems.

Gibbons's second book of poems, *The Ruined Motel* (1981), was published after he had taught a year at Columbia (1980-1981) and moved to his present post as editor of *TriQuarterly* at Northwestern. Gibbons's second collection surpasses the first in range and cohesiveness. The focus is not the fact of separation but coming to terms with it.

The first and last sections are single poems about tourists. Unlike the melancholy "foreigners" of *Roofs Voices Roads*, these travelers have self-possession and joy. The speaker in "In the Kingdom," walking the English countryside with his wife, helps a lamb extricate its head from a fence. Although they are foreigners, they enjoy "a happy solitude that year" living in a village. In the last poem, "At the Temple of Asklepios on Kos," the poet and his sunburned countrymen are thirsty after hiking to the ruin. Refreshed after they find water, they start up a staircase, and he has an epiphany: "I made / the connec-

tion: my work is to make, / to make speech whole, to heal." The first poem mentions a stream named "Healeyes," and the final poem is set at the temple of healing.

The second section, "At Latitude Thirty," comprises eleven poems on the speaker's growing up. Gibbons's family is the main source. Latitude 30 runs just north of his boyhood home of Houston and just south of the Mississippi border (his grandparents' home was near Jackson). Readers see boy's-eye vignettes of the father rising at 5:00 A.M. ("The Days"), the mother sitting at the hospital with her dying sister ("We Say"), and kids tormenting their tongue-tied classmate as they wait for the school bus ("Today"). The poem "At Latitude Thirty" resembles a snapshot album: the speaker and his brother as kids playing with horned toads; the speaker, grown up, breaking through Mississippi brush with his father to see his father's old home place; the speaker returning after years to a homecoming dinner (he is detached and half embarrassed yet moved by love). Section 2 of the book is tough minded in its reminiscence, conveying an adult's complex understanding of events that during childhood seemed either simple or beyond understanding. In "The Letter," for example, the speaker muses on being put out of the family car with the three other children when their bickering became intolerable. "When the car comes back, the ten-year-old boy— / the oldest—talky, thin, vain, wanting / too soon to reason and argue, will look in / at the startled man and woman, / the three children, and turn away, / a stranger of thirty, unable to speak." Although the speaker seems to have had a kind family and no more grief than usual, he needs reconciliation to the past, and he finds it through imagination: "This is none of this true. / What was true was less // and worse, what is true now / is still unfinished and will // come, like a whipping, too late // yet with a kind of love" ("At Latitude Thirty").

The third section of the collection is the poem "This Morning," a meditation begun when the speaker "loosened / my grip on yesterday and let it go." Weaving in and out of memory, he accepts the inevitability of losing love and friends and family. Death ("The plummet-speed I will / ride down someday") may or may not bring him to "another power." Thus, ripeness is all. He has released yesterday so he can open his hands to the loved ones in his future, knowing that he will fail them in some way: "Come afterward, then, strength; / come, touch that will break like foam /

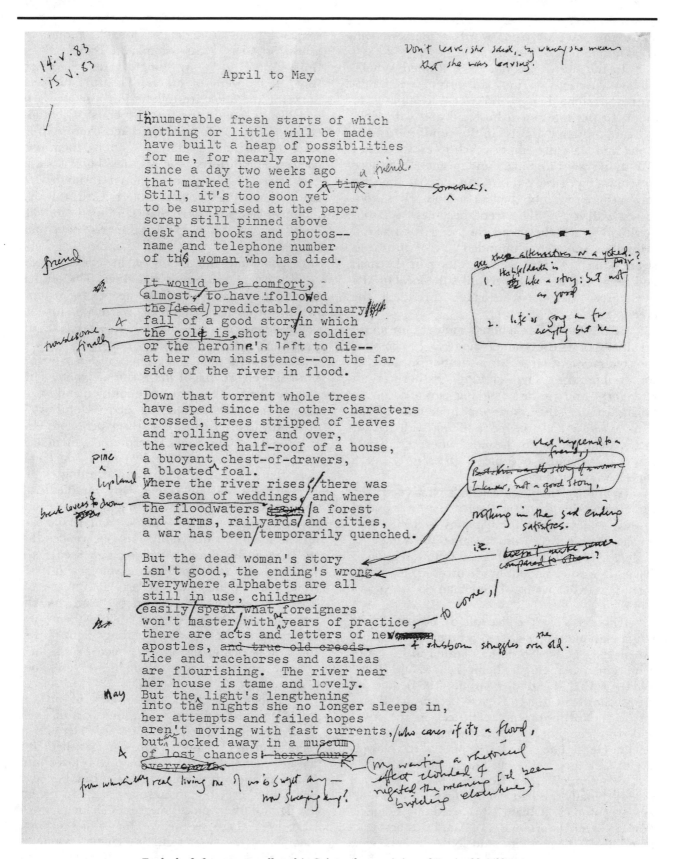

Early draft for a poem collected in Saints *(by permission of Reginald Gibbons)*

above the wave of pain; words / someone will speak unbidden to soothe / all loss. . . ."

In the fourth section, "The Ruined Motel," Gibbons presents various misfortunes and failures and some better and worse responses to them. In the title poem husband and wife seem to hear "unhappy ghosts" in the rundown seaside motel and walk the empty beach to escape them: "We didn't want to make / any mistakes but those we could say were ours. // But in that time we stayed there / we took the loss into ourselves, / obsessed with it. . . ." The scene becomes "a lesson-book" in which they read the need for realism. "Hope" is something pounded out of the "cold clean skulls" of giant whelks rolling in the surf, and religion is isolated and futile (the local fundamentalists' "fierce / conviction shredding the creeds").

If the family is Gibbons's emblem for an individual's past, the ruined motel is his emblem for civilization at large: an institution meant only for temporary stays—shifting gatherings of strangers—and always sinking toward decay. Small wonder, then, that the final note of the book is existential, the poet hiking with friends to the dead temple of healing, where he discovers that he must become a priest—"to make speech whole, to heal."

Winning Houghton Mifflin's New Poetry Series competition with *The Ruined Motel* was one of several achievements for Gibbons in 1981, since it was the year he also became the editor of *TriQuarterly* and a Bread Loaf fellow. His marriage, however, ended in divorce in 1982. He then married Cornelia M. Spelman on 18 August 1983.

Gibbons's next collection of poems, *Saints*, was a National Poetry Series winner in 1985. Between 1981 and 1986 he had added to his list of achievements a Guggenheim Fellowship (1983-1984), a CCLM Editor's Grant (1984), and an NEA Fellowship (1984). He had become a full professor at Northwestern, an officer in the AWP, and was coeditor of *Criticism in the University* (1985). He had been a visiting poet at the University of Chicago (1983) and taught his first stint in the Warren Wilson College MFA program (1984). Finally, he had begun his service as literary executor to William Goyen, editing a collection of Goyen's stories (1985). Amid this hectic activity, the Guggenheim and NEA grants gave Gibbons time to complete *Saints*.

The term *saints* gets a fresh definition in Gibbons's book, starting with the prefatory comic sonnet listing "St. Pete, St. Joe, St. Cloud, St. Louis, St. Clair, / Sts. Mom and Dad /. . . / St. Crazy Snake, / St. Washington and St. Enola Gay," and dozens of others. The first nineteen poems in the book are followed by a sequence titled "Saints." As in the first two books, Gibbons's characters are both threatened and comforted by twists of fortune, by family, and by their own choices. The difference in his third book is a new complexity of viewpoint, realized through dramatic monologues. What readers learn, through multiple viewpoints, is that sainthood, in Gibbons's empiricist universe, is existential, not supernatural.

This time the family poems describe the speaker's wife and young daughter. The tenderness of these poems is all the deeper for its tang of fear (from his daughter's "warm well-lit dollhouse where no one is tired or weak and the wind can't get in," he glances out the window to a jobless young man going house-to-house with a snow shovel). Poems of the fortunate young family are mixed with poems of separation and loss—about a man whose son has died ("Her Love"), about divorce ("Eating"), Turkish prisoners executed in war ("The Eager Interpreter"), mental illness ("The Vanishing Point"), and a concentration camp ("Dutch Thursday Mornings"). In "Elsewhere Children" a bag lady huddles in a doorway on an icy day, squinting at a young man who tries to sweet-talk a young woman. In the banter, he mentions his young son; she replies that she has a daughter. Watching the scene, the speaker longs to keep his own young child safe from a harsh life. But his last look at the old woman confirms his helplessness: "And she who was once somebody's darling / blinks them away and gone in the between-buildings light, / they could be her children, she was once // someone's, but she can't look after them, / we can't look after our own."

Despite this final helplessness of all humans, several characters in the first part of *Saints* make gestures of consolation. In "Her Love" there is no replacing the son who has died. But the grieving father has a woman who loves him: "So when she offers him what / she can, her love, he takes it / greedily, thankfully, glad." In the latter part of the book, however, Gibbons's world lacks even these gestures. The ironies echoing among the ten poems in the "Saints" sequence are harsh. A monologue by an abused wife is followed by a mail-order evangelist's form letter hawking a "Blessed Faith Handkerchief." In the

Dust jacket for Gibbons's 1986 collection, in which he presents sainthood as human and existential

third poem the recipient of the letter grieves for a young woman he had known from girlhood, now dead from a car accident. In the fourth a man's musing on his brother's suicide is interspersed with echoes of the Faith Handkerchief letter—"*Someone has hurt me,*" "*I have a personal need in my life.*" Next comes a chain letter promising "GOOD LUCK" to the recipient who will "THIRST IN THE LORD WITH ALL YOUR HEART" and send the letter on "TO YOUR FRIENDS / PEOPLE AND AXQUAINTANCIES."

The sixth poem is a preacher's lambasting of his new congregation, the seventh a Texas-dialect description of a neighbor's impulsive shooting of a biker. Disaster lurks like the "snarling dog" of the raucous eighth poem, and kindness can be wasted, as in the ninth. Religion ought to ennoble but is only another arena for selfishness and failure. "Saints" brings to mind the determinism of Theodore Dreiser, John Steinbeck, and other literary naturalists but not the cynicism of Friedrich Nietzsche. Gibbons's monologues in "Saints" are all by victims or distressed observers. But if virtues are defined by their absence, at least they are defined. Gibbons's "New Preacher" never mentions faith or hope—in fact, never mentions God—but he still treats charity as a moral imperative. In its moral framework as well as its de-

terminism, *Saints* harks back to *The Grapes of Wrath* (1939). Acts of kindness are precious though seldom rewarded, and in an unfair universe they are all that keep people from despair.

Gibbons's fourth collection of poems, *Maybe It Was So* (1991), offers more multiple viewpoints on the mysteries of good and bad fortune. Nearly half the poems in the first section appropriate viewpoints and idioms from foreign authors Gibbons admires. For example, two poems are subtitled "after Eugenio Montale" and another "after Osip Mandel'shtam." Another is noted as an "homage to Nadezhda Mandestaum." All the poems in this section valorize human beings over the abstractions of government, art, and philosophy: "Another [person] is looking for meat scraps and orange rinds in the mud. / How can I write about the Infinite after that?" ("One of César Vallejo's Human Poems").

The second section, the centerpiece of *Maybe It Was So*, is the long poem "From a Paper Boat," which won the 1991 John Masefield Award from the Poetry Society of America. The speaker in this rich monologue is a Chinese man who, having lost his family, lives on his boat and wanders the river. The poem imitates in its stanzas and frequent end-stops the three-to-five-line classical poetry written by Tu Fu (who provides the epigraph) and others. Gibbons's poem's variety, length, and poignancy make it his finest monologue to date. In the speaker's longing for his wife and sons, the poem is Gibbons's best realization of the "stratagem" proposed in the afterword to *Roofs* thirteen years earlier—"to create figures in order to miss them." But by taking on the poetic idiom as well as the experience of a character, Gibbons achieves something completely new—"a metaphorical translation," he calls it in a letter, "something like a translation of a (Chinese) poem that never actually existed"—more than writing a poem "after Tu Fu" or following Ezra Pound's imitating of Oriental verse. "From a Paper Boat" has anachronisms that dislodge the reader from the T'ang Dynasty. The line "The Emperor awarded me a year's living" begins the poem, but, later, readers watch the square of the capital city where "defiant students in their faded caps / Stood thick as the grain before the harvest," recalling the Beijing massacre of 1989. The poem mixes shopping malls, supermarkets, automobiles, and trains into the premodern, pre-Communist landscape. Because Gibbons rejects a merely historical sense of reality, the poem reverberates between eras and cultures. Fusing everything is the speaker, by turns remorseful, wry, and resolute. In his reminiscences and his travels, the speaker is a great-hearted survivor in an unpredictable life.

The third section of *Maybe It Was So* shows other victims of fortune, including an elderly miner whose sons are trapped by an explosion and a Vietnam veteran who still sees bodies in the jungle. But some survivors are more fortunate—sturdy gypsy children in Madrid, for instance, and the captain and first mate whose freighter has made it through icebergs. Most fortunate are those who have been overlooked by disaster and know it: the young father adoring his wife and daughter, aware that "the luckless" and "the loveless" will never know their happiness; and the hiker near Devon who thinks of the bombers and the burning in the past of a peaceful village and hears "praise of courage and pity" in the very squawking of the starlings.

Gibbons's *Five Pears or Peaches* (1991) is an intriguing collection of prose poems. He succeeded in the occasional short prose form in *Saints*, but *Five Pears* is his first full excursion in it. Not really stories—despite the publisher's labeling—the pieces in *Five Pears* gain by their brevity (one to four pages) and suggestiveness. As Gibbons remarks in a letter, they "have the same emotional

curve I try to achieve in my narrative poems, but the unit of composition, and of the rhythm of language, is the sentence instead of the line." Eschewing the full plotting of stories and the heavily metaphorical language of some prose poetry, these pieces take their power from situation, image, and understatement.

The title piece and five others had already appeared in *Saints*. There they join various poems as arguments for caution and compassion. The new context of *Five Pears* strengthens their implications of the uncanniness of life. The title piece still argues that family happiness is fragile: as the speaker lifts his sleeping daughter, the span of her little shoulders is like "five pears or peaches, it might be, dreaming in a delicate basket." "Friday Snow" still honors the jobless young man who offers to shovel snow. But "Vanishing Point," with the young man "crazy and half-blind" who sketches in the subway, has even more powerful strangeness than it did in *Saints*, now being set next to "Arms," where an armless mannequin becomes the Venus de Milo in a dusty Chicago shop window.

Several of the new pieces are uncanny. In "Proserpine at Home" Gibbons imagines the humid, grimy house in the underworld where Proserpine lives with Pluto half of each year. "Three Persons on a Crow" describes a mother, father, and son riding the back of a giant crow into some legend. These images are easy to use as emblems of real lives—but that is not the point. Gibbons wants readers to be struck not with the aptness or strangeness of the images but with the strangeness of life itself. "Courthouse" describes a young child who can only use stories and drawings to testify about being sexually molested. Besides outrage at the child's mistreatment, the poem conveys a wonderment that the court system and even human communication have so little of the solidity and truthfulness that we attribute to them. The poems "He" and "She" include phrases and activities connected with male and female stereotypes. These lists are not only funny but enlightening, making unreal the social roles that so many people assume to be solid and natural. In the final poem, "All-Out Effort," the speaker is surprised by joy as he reminisces in a rocking chair at the end of a day's cleaning: "But I'm wading and flying now, I'm off, I'm headed into a place of ago, the radio's getting fainter, a little wind of time is starting to whip my pants legs and sleeves and make my eyes smart. Let the tears come! This rocker is gathering some speed. I'm going back, I'm going to rescue all of it!"

Gibbons's accomplishments as a writer, editor, translator, and promoter of literature are impressive, and he can expect to accomplish more. He is working on new poetry and fiction, and he continues as Goyen's literary executor, preparing more of Goyen's work for posthumous publication.

Interviews:
"The Poet's Voice: An Interview with Reginald Gibbons," *Chicago Literary Review*, 93, no. 24 (1983): 22, 23, 26;
"Reginald Gibbons" [recording], *New Letters On the Air*, University of Missouri—Kansas City, 1986.

Margaret Gibson

(17 February 1944 -   )

Ann Townsend
Denison University

BOOKS: *The Duel* (Hollins, Va.: Tinker, 1966);
Lunes (Washington, D.C.: Some of Us, 1973);
On the Cutting Edge (Willimantic, Conn.: Curbstone, 1976);
Signs (Baton Rouge: Louisiana State University Press, 1979);
Long Walks in the Afternoon (Baton Rouge & London: Louisiana State University Press, 1982);
Memories of the Future: The Daybooks of Tina Modotti (Baton Rouge: Louisiana State University Press, 1986);
Out in the Open (Baton Rouge: Louisiana State University Press, 1989).

OTHER: *Landscape and Distance: Contemporary Poets From Virginia*, edited by Gibson and Richard McCann (Charlottesville: University Press of Virginia, 1975).

Margaret Gibson's poems are profoundly moral. She explores the human condition as it is rooted in the land and in social relationships. Influenced by Zen and Christian teachings, her poems show her to be meditative, curious, concerned, and loving.

Gibson was born in Philadelphia to John and Mattie Ferguson, and was raised in Richmond, Virginia. In 1966 she received her B.A. from Hollins College and a year later earned her M.A. from the University of Virginia. She married Ross Gibson on 27 August 1966; they were divorced in May 1974. On 27 December 1975 she married the poet David McKain; they live in Preston, Connecticut, with the two children from his previous marriage, Joshua and Megan. Since 1967 Gibson has taught English at various institutions, among them George Mason University, the University of Connecticut, Phillips Academy in Andover, and Virginia Commonwealth University.

In her first full-length book, *Signs* (1979), Gibson introduces the themes and subjects of the poetics to which she remains true through her most recent volume, *Out in the Open* (1989). Gibson has a reverence for the energy found within the natural world. Her intellectual openness (an ability to accommodate various schools of contemplation, from Christian to Buddhist) is paired with a penetrating eye, a talent for watching. Though *Signs* is a hesitant record of these tendencies and does not always display the technical and emotional sureness of Gibson's more recent work, it is an early indicator of what is to follow.

The poem "Signs: A Progress of the Soul" is an extended meditation on seasonal changes, both exterior and interior to the speaker. Though the speaker, gardening barefoot, feels "a

Margaret Gibson (photograph by Jim Holzworth)

tickle of roots in my feet, / an impulse to be the reaching downward / tap of the seed," she knows, too, the unavoidable "Dark, dark, dark. / There's always that blind / spot in the eye, part of the field / I look at, can't see." Gibson's awareness of this "blind spot" (a term she often uses, urging herself to look for what lies beyond immediate sensation) makes her, according to Dave Smith, "not an imagist but a celebrator; she intends to derive from the natural world a philosophy of feeling."

The four sections of *Signs* mark the passage of the year. But the poems surpass their orderly arrangement: rooted in Gibson's devotion to nature, they explore the various and rich manifestations of human love—of the body, of family, and, importantly, of the as-yet unborn and the already dead. The search for self-understanding is seen in "Lives in Translation": "As I study the lines of my body, its deft / histories, its one name, I'm drawn / near other lives." *Signs* reveals both the power that comes from describing these lives and the terror of being the one described, peeling away the layers of the self.

Long Walks in the Afternoon, the Lamont Poetry Selection of the Academy of American Poets for 1982, opens with epigrams from Saint Augustine and Franz Kafka. Kafka's words are instructive, both for this book and for Gibson's work in general: "You do not even have to leave your room. Remain sitting at your table and listen. Do not even listen, simply wait. Do not even wait, be still and solitary. The world will freely offer itself to you to be unmasked, it has no choice, it will roll in ecstasy at your feet." Such stillness leads to visionary revelation, a wisdom the earth offers.

Structured in three orderly sections, *Long Walks in the Afternoon* moves from private confession, to public exposure of political cruelties, to a series of (ostensibly private) elegies, which gain authority from their proximity to the preceding group of poems. The first section links the work of poetry to elemental tasks of the hand, like gardening and carving, the "arts of dust and milk, larder / and closet" (from "The Inheritance"). In "Invisible Work" the speaker reclaims and praises domestic tasks that go unrecorded:

> Each poem I try to set right what last winter
> tracking prints through snow I found:
> a clean fled space
> abruptly there
> tracks vanished
> as if complicity of hawk or wind had swept
> up everything . . .
>
> a miracle
> though some would call it common
> as a table spread white
> with cloth.

In "Ice Storm" Gibson marshals her passion for the abandoned and invisible: "Someone somewhere / must be homeless, dark, and drifting / to madness with all this glitter. . . . The pines list, steep and grave. / I want to say *gravid*." There is an ambivalence about the pleasure taken in language while human tragedy continues to inhabit her mind.

The self-reflective tone of the first section gives way in the second section to a more reportorial account of public violence. Peter Stitt finds that "Death is the central fact of life in these poems. . . . Coming to terms with death means, for this writer, coming to terms as well with life. . . ." Gibson feels responsible for the stories she tells, and she denies an easy solution to the violence she reports. In "Fasting 6 Days" the speaker abstains from food while keeping the hunger and misery of a political prisoner in Chile in mind. In the process, her senses and her sympathy sharpen. "Burning the Root" takes the speaker through a more explicitly sensuous episode, a moment seemingly free of violence, until the end: the roots of a tree burning in the lovers' fireplace send smoke into the room, "a curl of contempt / in the wind, not unlike the smoke of a cigarette / held to a bound woman's nipple."

The ten poems of the third section are called elegies but mourn "no one." Their subject is absence, a refusal of desire, and the stillness and acceptance called for in the book's opening epigraph by Kafka. "October Elegy" delves into the regions of emptiness the speaker both fears and desires. Stitt sees that the poem depicts, in the character called "no one," "not a deceased friend, but an absence, purely an imagined spiritual possibility, something deeply longed for but which has never possessed existence." Of "no one" Gibson says,

> if I were able to forget you, or find you, I might learn
> to enter the cup I am washing, door I am closing, word
> I am opening with careful incision, lover or child embracing—
> > and fall toward that moment fire
> > cracks
> from common stones, a sunrise in evening.

To "wake once, if a split-second only, / and live" is the poem's effort. This existential self-reckoning colors the whole of *Long Walks in the Afternoon*, which has an organic shapeliness, a progressive understanding that moves out of isolation into the world of pain and light.

In *Memories of the Future: The Daybooks of Tina Modotti* (1986 winner of the Melville Cane Award of the Poetry Society of America) Gibson departs from the confessional lyrics of her first two volumes to enter the consciousness of another woman. These biographical poems trace the life of Tina Modotti (1896-1942), an Italian-born actress who appeared in Erich von Stroheim's silent film *Greed* (1924). In a fictive journal, Gibson records the final year of the woman who became a political activist, photographer, nurse, and revolutionary in Mexico and Spain. The project grew, in part, out of Gibson's involvement with the Puerto Rican community in New London, Connecticut, where she worked for tenants' rights in the housing projects there. She says in the preface to *Memories of the Future*: "as

Dust jacket for the collection in which Gibson includes elegies for a character she calls "no one"

my interest in Modotti and my feelings for this community fed each other I came to know that I would write about Tina Modotti, this woman who had learned to live single-mindedly, who through a series of dramatic historical and radical personal transformations had lived according to her vision and in accord with principles that put her on the side of the poor and the oppressed."

Gibson also continues to be fascinated by the question of physical and spiritual sterility. Like the speaker in "Unborn Child Elegy" (from *Long Walks in the Afternoon*), Modotti is unable to bear children, which affects both the way the world perceives her and how she defines herself and her own work. Even before she finds her life's work in Mexico, recording the faces and landscapes of working men and women, Gibson's Modotti (in "Doctrines of Glass and Wood") knows her future will be somehow singular:

> Of me alone, Papa asked—
> Who are you? What have you done? What more can you give? For whom are you poor enough?—

until the questions had dignity, and my life,
which was to answer in work, had a chance
at dignity, might build something new.

The repetition of these questions from volume to volume in Gibson's work (they are spoken in "Catechism Elegy" in *Long Walks in the Afternoon* as ritual questions to meditate upon) indicates their central position in her ethos. In the absence of children, the women in these poems seek work that serves both a social and an artistic function. For Modotti, and for Gibson, that work constitutes identity. By journey's end Modotti emerges as one who has lived—as woman, lover, activist, and exile—a life of integrity.

Gibson's *Out in the Open* is her most accomplished book. The volume received the praise of Philip Booth, who remarked that nowhere "do the poems superimpose mere poetry upon the language their making demands; if there are flaws, they are the flaws of imperfect humanity, never the flaws of a poet who fakes language to prove emotion." Still wanting to peel away the layers of self, still wishing for absolute answers, Gibson allows that in "the long journey to be other than I am, / I have struggled and not got far" (from "A Ripple of Deer, A Metamorphosis of Bear, A Metaphor of Mountains"). The speaker of these poems is more relaxed about the journey, observing her surroundings with clarity and not a little humor (as in "Garlic"), and occasionally obtaining that moment of awareness she often longs for, as in "Doing Nothing":

> I watch my hands learn
> their way past each
> edge, each horizon,
> lightly, touching
> until between each berry
> there is such space
> I no longer have to hold
> back, let go, or grasp.

Out in the Open also includes a series of poems for a loved one's death ("Keeping Still," "In Here," "Last Rites, Recurring Dream," and "Out in the Open"). Gibson's "heart is not quiet"; she has not found a faith that will provide solace for every absence, every death: "How can anyone stunned by the night's consolation of stars / dare say, 'I have not seen what I want'— / and yet, I say it" (from "Keeping Still"). Confronted, in the title poem, with the recurring "blind spot" in the eye, that "black hole we stood at the edge of," the speaker realizes once again that the signs and signals of disaster are the "patterns, blind in time, we learn to see."

The poems in *Out in the Open*, as in all of Gibson's poetry, are characterized by a double impulse: the need to probe the dark side of the human condition, its deaths and "blind spots," and the drive to find peaceful resolution in nature's immutable strength and loving relationships. This tension creates a delicate balance by which the speaker, in "Beginner's Mind," can know herself and the objects around her through a simultaneously self-doubting and innocent exploration. A cobalt-blue glass, an object out of childhood, lifted high in sunlight, reveals this: "Suddenly I hold everything / I know, myself most of all, / in question."

References:

Philip Booth, "Loners Whose Voices Move," *Georgia Review*, 42 (Spring 1989): 161-178;

Dave Smith, "One Man's Music," in his *Local Assays: On Contemporary American Poetry* (Urbana: University of Illinois Press, 1985), pp. 39-54;

Peter Stitt, "Words, Book Words, What Are You?," *Georgia Review*, 37 (Summer 1983): 428-438.

Sandra M. Gilbert

(27 December 1936 -)

Wendy Barker
University of Texas at San Antonio

BOOKS: *Acts of Attention: The Poems of D. H. Lawrence* (Ithaca, N.Y. & London: Cornell University Press, 1972; revised and enlarged edition, Carbondale: Southern Illinois University Press, 1990);

In The Fourth World (University: University of Alabama Press, 1979);

The Madwoman in the Attic: The Woman Writer and the Nineteenth-Century Literary Imagination, by Gilbert and Susan Gubar (New Haven & London: Yale University Press, 1979 [i.e., 1980]);

The Summer Kitchen (Woodside, Cal.: Heyeck, 1983);

Emily's Bread (New York: Norton, 1984);

Blood Pressure (New York: Norton, 1988);

No Man's Land: The Place of the Woman Writer in the Twentieth Century, 2 volumes, by Gilbert and Gubar (New Haven: Yale University Press, 1988, 1989).

OTHER: *Shakespeare's Sisters: Feminist Essays on Women Poets*, edited by Gilbert and Susan Gubar (Bloomington & London: Indiana University Press, 1979);

Kate Chopin's The Awakening, and Selected Stories, selected, with an introduction, by Gilbert (New York: Penguin, 1984);

The Norton Anthology of Literature by Women: The Tradition in English, edited by Gilbert and Gubar (New York: Norton, 1985);

The Female Imagination and the Modernist Aesthetic, edited by Gilbert and Gubar (New York: Gordon & Breach, 1987).

As a girl, Sandra M. Gilbert would ask her mother, a schoolteacher who frequently took courses in psychology, to tell her about the "cases" she was studying. Fascinated even in childhood by the stories of people's lives, fears, and desires, Gilbert has gone on to become, along with co-author and coeditor Susan Gubar, a pioneer in uncovering the stories women have told about their own lives. As Laura Shapiro put it (in *Ms.*,

January 1986), the names Gilbert and Gubar are destined to become "campus shorthand all over the country." Together, Gilbert and Gubar are greatly responsible not only for establishing the academic respectability of the study of literature by women but also for redefining the canon of literature. Through such influential critical works as *Shakespeare's Sisters* (1979), *The Madwoman in the Attic* (1980), and *No Man's Land: The Place of the Woman Writer in the Twentieth Century* (2 volumes, 1988, 1989), Gilbert and Gubar have been pivotal forces in redefining and revising notions about the relationships between women's lives and the stories they tell, and the two have also been instrumental in developing cultural awareness of the relationships between gender and genre, between sex and art.

Gilbert has published four volumes of poetry, three of them full-length collections and one a chapbook. The subjects of these volumes parallel Gilbert's critical work in uncovering fascinating "cases," stories of women's lives—including her own.

Sandra Mortola Gilbert, an only child, was born in Brooklyn on 27 December 1936. Shortly after her birth, her parents moved to Queens, where she spent her first five years, and then relocated again, this time in Jackson Heights. Gilbert's mother, born Angela Caruso outside Palermo, Sicily, immigrated with her family to New York when she was six and grew up in the Italian part of Brooklyn. Gilbert's father, Alexis Joseph Mortola, was born in Paris; his mother, who was Russian, and his father, who was from Nice, moved to Manhattan when Alexis was two.

Alexis Mortola was a civil engineer in Queens, and Angela Mortola taught grammar school. Beginning with the third grade, Gilbert attended PS 69, where her mother taught and where Gilbert was taunted for being a teacher's pet and, worse, a teacher's daughter. After having spent her first two years of school happily and anonymously in a little private school, Gilbert found PS 69 a nightmare. The only way she

Sandra M. Gilbert and Susan Gubar, whose Madwoman in the Attic *has been a model for other feminist critics (photograph by Terence McCarthy)*

was able to separate herself from being identified with her teacher/mother was to rebel and become a troublemaker. High school, fortunately, was different. Always precocious, Gilbert was twelve years old when she entered Hunter College High School for intellectually gifted girls. Released from the pressure of being a teacher's daughter, she developed friendships with other similarly gifted girls from widely diverse backgrounds all across New York City. She worked on the school literary magazine, the *Argus*, and among her companions were such future writers as Diane di Prima and Audre Lorde.

Friendships that nurtured intellectual and literary talents continued to flourish in college. Although Gilbert had hoped to attend Radcliffe, she received a state scholarship to Cornell, her father's alma mater. The early 1950s were exciting years to be at Cornell: Harold Bloom and Toni Morrison had just graduated; Thomas Pynchon,

Larry Lipking, Nina Baym, and Robert Scholes were students at that time, as were Gilbert's close friends Joanna Russ, Dory Gilbert, and Ronald Sukenik. Gilbert worked on the campus literary magazine, the *Cornell Writer*. Since her freshman year, the graduate student Elliot Gilbert had fascinated her; they married on 1 December 1957, the year she received her B.A. with high honors in English. In 1961 she earned her M.A. in English from New York University, and in 1968 she received her Ph.D. from Columbia. She taught as an assistant professor of English at California State University at Hayward from 1968 to 1971; at Indiana University as an associate professor from 1973 to 1975; at the University of California at Davis from 1975 to 1985; at Princeton from 1985 to 1989; and since 1989 again at Davis, where she is a professor of English. She has received the Charity Randall Award from the International Poetry Foundation and the Eunice

Tietjens Memorial Prize from *Poetry*, as well as a Guggenheim Fellowship and a Rockefeller Foundations Humanities Fellowship. In 1986 she was named (along with Susan Gubar) *Ms.* Woman of the Year.

One of Gilbert's earliest honors influenced the direction of her writing. The summer after Gilbert graduated from Cornell, before she married, she was a member of the prestigious College Board of *Mademoiselle*. In the novel *The Bell Jar* (1963) Sylvia Plath writes about her own experiences serving on this select board of college girls (four years before Gilbert did). Chosen for their writing talents, the girls spent their summer choosing clothes and cosmetics, as well as trying to please Managing Editor Cyrilly Abels, who, according to Gilbert, was a wonderful woman but frightening: "she was so serious, so severe, so scrupulous." It was only much later, in the 1970s, when Gilbert was an associate professor, author of *Acts of Attention: The Poems of D. H. Lawrence* (1972), and mother of three children (Roger, Kathy, and Susanna), that she began to realize what was so centrally disturbing about her experience at *Mademoiselle*. After reading Plath's novel, Gilbert said, "There was no strategy for understanding" both her own summer at the magazine and the frightening experiences of the novel. Gilbert "only knew to get sick about it."

Of course, Gilbert, together with Gubar and other pioneers of feminist theory, has now provided a "strategy for understanding" *The Bell Jar*. Plath's tale of an intelligent, talented, ambitious, and social young woman who attempts suicide was highly autobiographical; nevertheless, it was also the story of many young women in the 1950s, and it was therefore Gilbert's story, too, but only to a point. For in a sense it became the primary "case" Gilbert took on as her own to learn, understand, and then explain to the world: the story of the particular conflicts experienced by women writers. Such conflicts are not only subjects for Gilbert's scholarly writing but also for her poetry. The three full-length books of Gilbert's poems chronicle her story.

Gilbert's first volume of poetry, *In the Fourth World*, which won the AWP Poetry Series Prize in 1979, opens with a poem based on a crisis: "Getting Fired, or 'Not Being Retained.'" Darkly humorous, this poem is not the only one that includes an element of fear; Richard Eberhart says in his introduction to the book that "the actual world is threatened repeatedly by dark forces behind appearances." Images of black books, suitcases, and scarves seem to swim through these poems like sharks underwater, forces only vaguely seen but whose danger is acutely felt. The letter in the poem "Getting Fired," which surrealistically turns into a sinister secret agent, causes all the books in the house to become "black paperbacks." Similarly the intruder in "3 A.M." loads "his stacks of black / suitcases into our heads." In "Bad News" the unwanted message "steals out of a bureau drawer / like a black scarf that nobody notices." Throughout Gilbert's first collection something not yet understood, something unnamed and terrifying, is relentlessly moving in.

Yet this same darkness is also transformative. In the section titled "The Dream Work," "The Grandmother Dream" describes the speaker's Sicilian grandmother:

I see her black hair gleam like tar as
she draws from her small black midwife's bag
her midwife tools; heavy silver instruments
polished like doorknobs, polished—misshapen, peculiar—
like the knobs of an invisible door.

From the darkness comes the female ancestor's "silver instruments" that will allow a safe passage for new life. Paradoxically this kind of darkness is both terrifying and potentially redeeming. Although in Gilbert's first collection the forces of darkness are not yet seen clearly enough to be identified or named, it is clear that from these dark suitcases, these ominous black-covered paperbacks, and especially from the grandmother's bag, a new—although at first frightening—energy is moving into the "house" of the poet, preparing the way for a new birth, a new awareness, perhaps what Emily Dickinson metaphorically called "the different dawn." In Gilbert's poem titled "Dawn" those who are sleeping, toward morning, "sink deeper into themselves: / darkness blooms on the inside of their skulls / like new fur."

By the time Gilbert's second full-length volume of poetry, *Emily's Bread* (1984), was published, the darkness has bloomed. It is as if all the dark places are opened to the light. The contents of these secret places may cause anger, even rage, but now that they are no longer hidden, no longer vague, black nightmarish fears in the night, they are invigorating, energizing; as poet Marge Piercy might say, they can be "of use." *Emily's Bread* opens with the poem "For the Muses." There are no vague black shapes, but one finds the tools for birthing and also the means for creating art. The speaker's aunts offer her a gift of light, which spills out of their old "rosewood wardrobe."

The magical "immigrant aunts" of this poem are based in part on Gilbert's Aunt Frances, who lived in a traditional Brooklyn brownstone, very different from Gilbert's parents' home in a WASP neighborhood of Queens. At Aunt Frances's house the young poet could participate as traditional Italian dishes were prepared and consumed, and could join the lively arguments and activities of her Italian-speaking cousins. It seemed that everyone spoke noisily and easily; Gilbert's mother remembered Sicily, but did not want to talk about it. Aunt Frances and her family talked about everything.

Just as "For the Muses" is a tribute to Aunt Frances, so are other poems in *Emily's Bread* tributes to the real stories behind the gloss of ladies' magazine pages and the old "prettified" versions of women's lives. One of the most powerful poems in the collection is "Daphne," in which Gilbert juxtaposes the earlier version of the myth with her own poetic revision. In Gilbert's poem Daphne is, to quote from Dickinson, "Adequate— Erect":

> At first, astonished, how she must have
> clattered, hissed, seethed
>
> in her new language. . . .
> . . . .
>
> Swaying, sucking, leaning
> into that hidden body,
> at last she learned
>
> the truth of the dark eating
> that goes on forever,
>   under the ground.

This Daphne is not frozen forever as the property of Apollo; she learns secrets he can never imagine.

In the concluding poem, "The Emily Dickinson Black Cake Walk," Gilbert pays tribute in culinary terms to Dickinson, foremother for so many women poets:

> I tunnel among your grains of darkness
> fierce as a mouse; your riches
> are all my purpose, your currants and death's eye raisins

wrinkling and thickening blackness,
and the single almond of light she buried
somewhere under layers of shadow. . . .

In *Emily's Bread* this "single almond of light" spills over the pages. Just as the mixture of currants and "death's eye raisins," flour, eggs, and the single almond combine to make the cake, so does Gilbert in this collection fuse the stories of writers such as Dickinson and Emily Brontë, of mythological characters such as Daphne and Psyche, and of her relatives and friends. All these stories, or "cases," become in effect one story, just as, in the poem "Anna La Noia," the poet says of "the sister I never had": "At noon in the simmering vineyard / we embraced, / we became one woman."

Gilbert's *Blood Pressure* (1988) begins with a series of poems based on Hans Christian Andersen's *The Snow Queen* (1844). Gilbert examines with wry humor "The Love Sickness" in her poem of that name:

> the damned old nausea
> of desire, the ague that shakes the last right angle
> of reason from your bones
> and turns the world to stupid
> metaphors for passion.

No one else has written more honestly and humorously about female desire, especially that desire for the unattainable male "prince" who, like the "lover, the kind physician" in the "The Cure," "declines. / Polite but cold. Explains he's allergic to your skin. / Implies you have a noxious odor." Even when "you toss your curls like a cheerleader in Houston, / show him your eyelids,"

> He says never, he says
> forget it, he looks at your bones the way a logger
> looks at redwoods: he wants to chop you down, only
> he wonders which way you'll fall.

In the title poem, the speaker wonders at the fierce energy of the literal blood:

> How it pounds in you, how it
> urges through you, how it asserts
> its power like a tide of electrons
>
> flashing through your veins, shocking your fingertips,
> exhausting the iron gates of your heart.
> *Alive, always alive,* it hisses,

crackling like the lightning snake that splits
the sky at evening, *alive*, a black rain
lashing the hollows of your body. . . .

Part of this "black rain" that lashes the body has
to do with the subtleties of human relationships.
Other poems in the book, such as "Singles, or,
Never Eat Standing Up" and "Reproduction,"
muse on the difficulties produced by the multiplicity of choices of available life-styles, choices that,
Gilbert suggests, cannot always be made with
clear insight or awareness. In "But I Don't Love
Him" she meditates on the tragic aspects of long-
term marriages in which love seems to be long
gone. At the end, she calls out to Aphrodite, goddess of love, insisting, "I want to learn / what you
bring. . . ."

   In a sense this entire volume is an attempt
to learn what Aphrodite can bring. Although Gilbert, in the third section of *Blood Pressure*, might
seem to be sidestepping the difficulties of this over-
riding question about the nature of love, actually
the section titled *The Summer Kitchen* (separately
published in 1983) provides the materials necessary to answer the plea to Aphrodite. The poems
trace the birth of love, the places, the homes, and
the people who first showed Gilbert the possibilities for love. Aunt Frances's summery kitchen is
described "when the Brooklyn garden / boiled
with blossom"; the 1948 "New Year's Eve" in
Brooklyn, just after "the War was over," is remembered with the poet's cousins who "wore Carmen
Miranda / dresses: their ruffles leaping like wind-
blown leaves" and who, as they danced the samba
with "men in their twenties," "did mysterious
hops and skips, swaying to South American rat-
tles." There are poems to Gilbert's first love, who
is called "Old Friend, dead one," with whom she
can inhabit a new planet, where "we bicycle
faster than the speed of light. / In our extragalac-
tic language / there are no words for love or
death."

   The sense that love may be something beyond language is explored further in one of the
poems in the final section. In a love poem to her
husband of many years, Elliot, Gilbert writes:

Your beard begins to get gray,
but not your eyebrows.
We're stuck in the thick of it, we smile wryly,
we fatten, we grow dumb.

Once in a while
I have to hang on to your hand.
I cannot imagine who else
we might have become.

In "Rain/Insomnia/North Coast" the husband
and wife of the poem finally sleep, "lapse into
moisture":

It's gray outside, and misty.
The tongues of silence are growing like kelp.
All night they lick our windows, all night
the drowned house
creeps through the fields toward the sea.

After all these years the married couple have become one: "Talking to you is as embarrassing as
talking / to myself." This love needs no language:
it merges with the sea; it is a love of children, kitch-
ens, and "Making love like adolescents on the
sly." (Tragically, Elliot Gilbert died in February
1991.)

   In the final poem, "2085," Gilbert describes
herself walking with a seventeen-year-old girl, a Sicilian relative. "My sentences won't help you," Gilbert says,

     the road unfolds and shines ahead
like the history neither of us understands.

It turns you
toward the sea, toward
the inarticulate Aegean.

These poems explore the elements of love, the
pressures of the blood that drive all people—
those forces that work far below and beyond language. Yet Gilbert explores these issues with a
style of language that is wise and often funny.
Kevin Clark has understandably praised Gilbert's
"unconventional and alluring voice," her "happily direct and . . . gently ironic" female idiom, so
different from "the cerebrally elegiac tone of so
many contemporary poets" (*Iowa Review*, Spring
1992). As Bruce Bennett commented in the *New
York Times Book Review* (12 March 1989), Gilbert
not only knows love "when she sees it" but she
also "helps others to know it too."

References:
Richard Eberhart, Introduction to Gilbert's *In
   The Fourth World* (University: University of Al-
   abama Press, 1979);
Laura Shapiro, "Women of the Year: Sandra Gil-
   bert and Susan Gubar, Editors, 'The Norton
   Anthology of Literature by Women,' " *Ms.*
   (January 1986): 59-62 +.

Dana Gioia

(24 December 1950 -   )

Lewis Turco
State University of New York at Oswego

BOOKS: *Two Poems* (New York: Bowery, 1982); translated into Italian as *Two Poems / Due Poesie* (Verona, Italy: Ampersand, 1987);
Daily Horoscope (Iowa City: Windhover, 1982; enlarged edition, Saint Paul: Graywolf, 1986; Calstock, U.K.: Peterloo, 1991);
Letter to the Bahamas (Omaha: Abattoir, 1983);
Summer (West Chester, Pa.: Aralia, 1983);
Journeys in Sunlight (Cottondale, Ala.: Ex Ophidia, 1986);
Words for Music (Tuscaloosa, Ala.: Parallel, 1987);
Planting a Sequoia (West Chester, Pa.: Aralia, 1991);
The Gods of Winter (Saint Paul: Graywolf, 1991; Calstock, U.K.: Peterloo, 1991).

OTHER: *Sequoia: Twentieth Anniversary Issue: Poetry, 1956-1976*, edited by Gioia and others (Stanford, Cal.: Associated Students of Stanford University, 1976);
Weldon Kees, *The Ceremony & Other Stories*, edited by Gioia (Port Townsend, Wash.: Graywolf, 1984);
Poems from Italy, edited by Gioia and William Jay Smith (Saint Paul: New Rivers, 1985);
"Lives of the Great Composers" [poem] and "A Tune in the Back of My Head" [essay], in *Ecstatic Occasions, Expedient Forms*, edited by David Lehman (New York: Macmillan, 1987);
Mottetti, Poems of Love: The Motets of Eugenio Montale, translated, with an introduction, by Gioia (Saint Paul: Graywolf, 1990);
New Italian Poets, edited by Gioia and Michael Palma (Brownsville, Oreg.: Story Line Press, 1991).

SELECTED PERIODICAL PUBLICATIONS—
UNCOLLECTED: "Poetry and the Fine Presses," *Hudson Review*, 35 (Autumn 1982): 483-498;
"Business and Poetry," *Hudson Review*, 36 (Spring 1983): 147-171;

Dana Gioia

"The Barrier of a Common Language: British Poetry in the Eighties," *Hudson Review*, 37 (Spring 1984): 5, 7-20;
"Studying with Miss Bishop," *New Yorker*, 62 (15 September 1986): 90, 92-98, 101;
"Picketing the Zeitgeist Picket," by Gioia, Lewis Turco, and others, *American Book Review*, 8 (November-December 1986): 3, 23;
"Notes on the New Formalism," *Hudson Review*, 40 (Autumn 1987): 395-408;
"The Difficult Case of Howard Moss," *Antioch Review*, 45 (Winter 1987): 98-109;
"The Poet in an Age of Prose," *Verse*, 7 (Winter 1990): 9-15;

"Can Poetry Matter?," *Atlantic*, 267 (May 1991):
   94-98, 100, 102-106.

   Bruce Bawer (*Connoisseur*, March 1989) notes
that Dana Gioia

> is . . . one of several younger poets—dubbed
> "The New Formalists"—who are challenging the
> poetry-world status quo in significant, possibly
> even historic, ways. Some of his more vociferous
> critics would have one believe that he is out to
> eradicate free verse, repeal the modernist revolu-
> tion, and inaugurate an era of philistine poetics.
> It is more nearly correct to say that, unlike many
> younger poets these days, Gioia includes [tradi-
> tional] form among his options and is capable of
> using it very effectively.

   Michael Dana Gioia was born in Hawthorne, California, a working-class suburb of Los
Angeles, on 24 December 1950. He was the
first of the four surviving children of Michael
Gioia, a cabdriver and shoe-store owner, and
Dorothy Ortiz Gioia, a telephone operator.
Dana's mother, of Mexican descent, was born in
Hawthorne. His father had moved to Los Angeles from Detroit with his immigrant family during the Depression. The Gioia family was a
tightly knit Sicilian clan; over a dozen relations
lived in two adjacent triplex apartments, presided
over by Dana's paternal grandfather. Since many
older family members knew little English, the
young Gioia grew up hearing their Italian dialect
spoken as commonly as English. This early bilingual world may account for Gioia's subsequent interest in foreign languages. He has learned
Latin, French, and German, as well as standard
Italian, and has published translations of poets as
diverse as Eugenio Montale and Nina Cassian.
   Gioia attended local Catholic schools and,
after winning a scholarship to Stanford University, became the first member of his family to attend college. He originally planned to study
music, but his interests soon shifted to literature.
He reviewed books and music for the *Stanford
Daily* and became editor of *Sequoia*, the campus literary magazine. In 1973 he earned his B.A. with
high honors in English, having won the department's prize for the best senior essay, a study of
Edgar Allan Poe's fiction. He entered the master's program in comparative literature at Harvard University, where he eventually studied with
Robert Fitzgerald and Elizabeth Bishop and received his M.A. in 1975.

   His time at Harvard confirmed Gioia's vocation as a poet, but it also filled him with doubt
that academia was the best place for him to develop as a writer. "For me at least," he told David
Lehman in a 1990 interview for *Business Month*,
"the university wasn't the best place to write poetry. I was shocked that people who spent their
whole lives studying literature could look at it as
fodder for thematics and theory instead of something that affects your life." After completing the
course work for a Ph.D., Gioia left Harvard to
enter Stanford Business School. There he met
Mary Hiecke, whom he married on 23 February
1980. After completing his master's degree in business administration in 1977, Gioia took a position
at the General Foods Corporation in White
Plains, New York. Resolved to keep his business
and literary lives separate, Gioia told none of his
fellow workers that he was also a writer. "I liked
the privacy that gave me," he told Lehman. But
eventually his growing literary reputation made
this cover impossible to maintain. Gioia worked
for General Foods for fifteen years in a variety of
positions, eventually becoming a vice-president.
In 1992 he left business to become a full-time
writer.
   Gioia has always retained his interest in poetry and has written a great deal of criticism for
some of the most respected journals in the
United States. Gioia says, "During my two years
at Stanford Business School I wrote at least one literary review every two weeks. I also reviewed occasionally for journals such as the *San Francisco Review of Books*. In effect I taught myself to be a
professional critic. That's the old fashioned way,
I guess, of learning to write in public. By the
time I left Stanford for New York in 1977 I was
a seasoned reviewer." Gioia thus became one of
those rare poets who establish critical reputations
before they publish a collection of poetry.
   In his critical essays Gioia has consistently
proved one of the most knowledgeable contemporary proponents of metrical verse; his response
to Diane Wakoski's attack on formal poetry, "The
New Conservatism in American Poetry" (*American
Book Review*, May-June 1986), was one of five published under the overall title "Picketing the Zeitgeist Picket" in the November-December 1986
issue of the same periodical. Additionally, Gioia
contributed a long poem, "The Homecoming," to
a special issue of *Crosscurrents* titled "Expansionist
Poetry: The New Formalism and the New Narrative," published early in 1989, and his 1987 *Hudson Review* essay, "Notes on the New Formalism,"

was listed in the bibliography. ("The Homecoming" is collected in *The Gods of Winter*, 1991.)

Dana Gioia's first full-length collection of poems, *Daily Horoscope*, was published in 1986; the title sequence had appeared separately as a chapbook in 1982. In 1983 Gioia published *Summer*, another chapbook of poetry. *Words for Music* (1987), also issued in a limited edition from a small press, contains poems that he had excluded from *Daily Horoscope* because he "knew critics would find them too formal." Gioia's second full-length collection of poems is *The Gods of Winter*. British editions of both full-length collections and *Planting a Sequoia*, a limited edition of six poems reprinted from *The Gods of Winter*, were also published in 1991. Since 1976 Gioia has also published other chapbooks and a collection of translations of Eugenio Montale's poems, has edited several books and anthologies, and is completing work on two projects: a collection of his reviews and critical essays, and an edition of the poems of Weldon Kees.

Greg Kuzma, in a 1988 review of *Daily Horoscope* titled "Dana Gioia and the Poetry of Money" (*Northwest Review*), specifically and personally attacked Gioia, comparing his first book with that of Donald Justice, published twenty-six years earlier: "Gioia's use of form does not seem traditional in this way. It is almost as if the concealing of meter and rhyme is Gioia's singular purpose. True, at times meter and rhyme clang and scan too neatly and emphatically and what one gets is verse." Proceeding from the assumption that Justice's "way" is the only way to use traditional forms, Kuzma sets up a straw man and then sets fire to it. Typical of his strategy is the attempt to cite a stanza from Gioia's "Cruising with the Beachboys" as representing what Kuzma considers the poet's lack of metrical variety:

> Some nights I drove down to the beach to park
> And walk along the railings of the pier.
> The water down below was cold and dark,
> The waves monotonous against the shore.
> The darkness and the mist, the midnight sea,
> The flickering lights reflected from the city—
> A perfect setting for a boy like me,
> The Cecil B. DeMille of my self-pity.

But there are many rhythmic variations Gioia has worked into the poem; there is nothing "neat and emphatic" about Gioia's meters; they do not "jingle," though they do scan as iambic pentameter lines. Gioia is saying, "The water down below was cold and dark, / The waves *monotonous*

against the shore" [emphasis added]. The meter imitates the motion of the waves, but even so the line itself is not monotonous. Gioia resolves the problem of how to write a poem whose subject is sentimentality and nostalgia, without allowing the poem itself to sink into banality.

While it cannot be denied that both Gioia's work and sympathies are formal, he is not hidebound. His work appears in most of the "New Formalist" anthologies, including Lehman's *Ecstatic Occasions, Expedient Forms* (1987), which contains a poem and an explanation by each contributor of how he or she came to use or develop the structure of the poem. Gioia's contribution is "Lives of the Great Composers"; his comment is titled "A Tune in the Back of My Head." Far from being doctrinaire about "traditional form," Gioia reveals an interest in formal innovation:

> The musical effect I missed most in poetry was counterpoint, so it is not surprising that for years I fantasized about writing a fugue, the most fascinating of all contrapuntal forms, in verse. I say fantasize because for years it remained only that—a seductive daydream. I could imagine a poem where variations on a single theme would tumble down the page in elaborate counterpoint, but I had no practical notion of how to write it. The one example I knew of, Paul Celan's magnificent "Todesfuge," was too unique and lofty a model to provide any specific help, though its existence proved that the form could be approximated in verse.

Gioia thus conducted an experiment in prosody. Searching for a new form, he developed an original one for "Lives of the Great Composers," which is also in *Daily Horoscope*; in a note in that book Gioia says, "This poem is cast as a verbal fugue in a form suggested by a poem of Weldon Kees's." The Kees poem to which Gioia refers is titled "Round." Kees, who died in 1955, was a short-story writer (whose book of fiction Gioia edited in 1984), journalist, painter, filmmaker, jazz pianist and composer, and, in poetry, a formal experimentalist. The subject of Gioia's fugal poem is itself music:

> On rainy nights the ghost of Mendelssohn
> brought melodies for Schumann to compose.
> "Such harmony is in immortal souls . . .
> We cannot hear it."

Gioia's title poem "Daily Horoscope" is dedicated to the poet and translator Fitzgerald, with whom Gioia studied. It begins with an epigraph from Dante's *Inferno* praising the "master" and his beautiful style. The narrative perspective of the quotation is second person, "you," and this viewpoint is maintained throughout the poem, as is the premise of the *Inferno*—that the speaker is describing a tour of the underworld. Like the *Inferno*, "Daily Horoscope" is divided into cantos—six of them in this case, all quite short—each titled from its first line: "Today Will Be ... ," "Nothing Is Lost . . . ," "Do Not Expect . . . ," "Beware of Things in Duplicate . . . ," "The Stars Now Rearrange Themselves . . . ," and "News Will Arrive from Far Away. . . ." The cantos themselves are subdivided into strophes, which are also verse paragraphs. When a paragraph begins in midline, it is also stepped down, as in strophe 3 of canto 1:

> These walls, these streets,
> this day can never be your home, and yet,
> there is no other world where you could live,
> and so you will accept it.
>
>   Just as others,
> waking to sunlight and the sound of leaves,
> accept the morning as their own, and walk
> without surprise, through orchards crossed by
>   streams,
> where swift, cold water is running over stone.

Gioia's handling of the blank-verse mode is skillful throughout. The prosody is normative accentual-syllabics, and the meter is generally iambic pentameter, though a few lines are longer—hexameter—and several are tetrameter or, on occasion, as short as trimeter. The poem does not contain complex figures of speech. The primary tropes are descriptions, but there is a subdued central metaphor—that death is the ordinary world without focus: "Beyond your window, something like a wind / is filling in the emptiness of air. / Vast, hungry, and invisible, it sweeps / the morning clean of memories, then disappears." There are rhetorical tropes that give the poem a tone of admonition, as though these descriptions own something of the nature of commands, as in the beginning of the third canto:

> Do not expect that if your book falls open
> to a certain page, that any phrase
> you read will make a difference today,
> or that the voices you might overhear
> when the wind moves through the yellow-green
> and golden tent of autumn, speak to you.

The prevailing mood in this portrait of the underworld is bleakly sorrowful. Of course, the main subject is death. The schemes Gioia employs to depict his landscapes, including the inner weathers of the speaker, are inclusive; as the poem progresses, the poet adds increments of detail. Canto 3 continues:

> Things ripen or go dry. Light plays on the
> dark surface of the lake. Each afternoon
> your shadow walks beside you on the wall,
> and the days stay long and heavy underneath
> the distant rumor of the harvest.

The abstraction, death, is made extraordinarily concrete. Nevertheless, the underworld depicted is not the religious vision of Dante; instead, it is an existential vision of both the real world and the world of the afterlife. Gioia's theme is that death is at best nothing more than the empty memory of life, and the memory resides in the minds of those left behind, not in that of the deceased.

Gioia's emotional range, then, is wide, extending from the memorial to the humorous, but his forte is the elegiac. *The Gods of Winter* is a dark volume dedicated to the memory of his first son, Michael, who died in infancy. (The Gioias have another son, Theodore.) Published simultaneously in America and Great Britain, the book significantly broadened Gioia's readership. Before then Gioia had been virtually unknown as a poet in England. The volume, however, was chosen as the main selection of the influential British Poetry Book Society, an honor almost never given to American poets. The resulting publicity plus the book-club sales caused the British edition to go into an immediate second printing.

British reviewers were generally laudatory. Poet Carol Ann Duffy in the *Guardian* praised Gioia's poems on time, memory, and loss, "which are all the more moving for their quiet integrity." In the *Oxford Times* Andrew Swarbrick agreed with critics who saw similarities between Gioia's work and Philip Larkin's. "Gioia," Swarbrick wrote, "has the same rather melancholic reflectiveness, and his poems move between narrative and observation with something of Larkin's thoughtful probing." Meanwhile, in America reviewers also viewed the book favorably. In a review titled "Poetry Formal and Free" (*Sewanee Review*, Fall 1991), Christopher Clausen declared that "New Formalism" was an inadequate and confusing term when applied to Gioia's poetry, since *The Gods of Winter* contains equally excellent poems in both free and formal

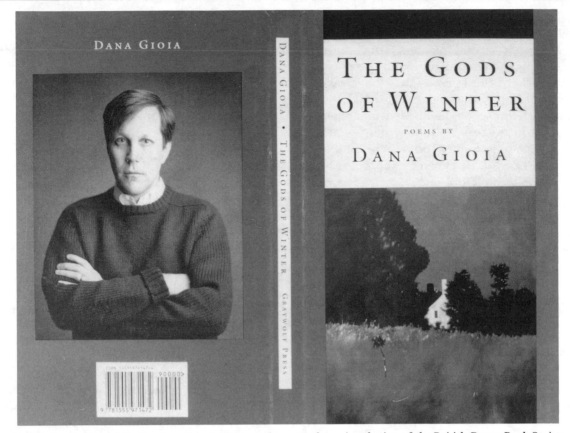

Dust jacket for one of the few American books ever chosen as the main selection of the British Poetry Book Society

verse. In the *Christian Science Monitor* Thomas D'Evelyn explored Gioia's thematics, noting that "Gioia's personae—which include visionaries, curmudgeons, and killers—often involve family roles: nephew, father, brother. His best poems confirm family responsibilities."

Typical of the collection in many ways is "Night Watch," which has the epigraph "For my uncle, Theodore Ortiz, November, 1955." Ortiz is a crewman aboard a freighter that "pulls away from the coast of China, / the last lights of Asia disappearing in the fog." Behind him is most of his life:

> For now you know that mainland best from dreams.
> Your dead mother turning toward you slowly,
> always on the edge of words, yet always
> silent as the suffering madonna of a shrine.
> Or your father pounding his fist against the wall.

"There are so many ways to waste a life," Gioia also says in the poem; "Why choose between these icons of unhappiness" when one can more profitably spend one's hours reading upon "the undisguised illusion of the sea . . . ?"

> Breathe in that dark and tangible air, for in a few
>   weeks

you will be dead, burned beyond recognition,
left as a headstone in the unfamiliar earth
with no one to ask, neither wife nor children,
why your thin ashes have been buried here
and not scattered on the shifting grey Pacific.

The uncle becomes an unquiet spirit—not unquiet as a phantom might be but, rather, as a memory is. Here again is the theme of "Daily Horoscope," except that this voyage into the underworld cannot be made, for the soul of the mariner is doubly land-bound, locked in both "the unfamilar earth" and in the contemplation of the speaker.

The title poem, "The Gods of Winter," takes a cold look at reality: "Storm on storm, snow on drifting snowfall, / . . . March squanders its wealth." The speaker of the poem says, "The world is annihilated and remade / with only us as witnesses." But the poem is a conceit, an extended metaphor. Readers understand that the true subject is Michael, the Gioias' firstborn son, who fell victim to sudden infant death syndrome:

> Briefest of joys, our life together,
> this brittle flower twisting toward the light

even as it dies, no more permanent
for being perfect. Time will melt away
triumphant winter, and even your touch
prove the unpossessable jewel of ice.
. . . .
                                    . . . But if
the light confides how one still winter must
arrive without us, then our eternity
is only this white storm, the whisper
of your breath, the deities of this quiet night.

This poem and the next in the book, "Planting a Sequoia," conclude the first section. In the latter poem the speaker is performing a ritual; he and his brothers are planting a tree, one known for its hardiness and longevity: "Digging this hole, laying you into it, carefully packing the soil." It seems at first that the tree itself is being addressed by the narrator, but the sequoia is primarily a sign of something else:

In Sicily a father plants a tree to celebrate his first
    son's birth—
An olive or a fig tree—a sign that the earth has one
    more life to bear.

This particular planting, however, is not exactly such a ritual.

But today we kneel in the cold planting you, our na-
    tive giant,
Defying the practical custom of our fathers,
Wrapping in your roots a lock of hair, a piece of an
    infant's birth cord,
All that remains above earth of a first-born son,
A few stray atoms brought back to the elements.

Poetry is here performing one of its primal functions: the easing of pain, laying to rest the griefs that constitute the human condition on earth. But in that burying/planting also resides something that will outlast the merely individual:

And when our family is no more, all of his unborn
    brothers dead,
Every niece and nephew scattered, the house torn
    down,
His mother's beauty ashes in the air,
I want you to stand among strangers, all young and
    ephemeral to you,
Silently keeping the secret of your birth.

"Counting the Children" is a narrative, spoken by an accountant who must take inventory of the estate of a deceased eccentric woman who col-

lected dolls by night, rummaging through trash barrels. This intriguing situation becomes the foundation for a philosophical reverie on the subject of the souls of children. The narrative carries the ruminations of the narrator to a satisfying and believable conclusion, one that is simultaneously sad and joyous as he watches over his own sleeping daughter:

I stood confused beside my daughter's bed
Surprised to find the room around me dim.

Then glancing at the bookshelf in the corner,
I saw she'd lined her dolls up in a row.
Three little girls were sitting in the dark.

Their sharp glass eyes surveyed me with contempt.
They recognized me only as a rival,
The one whose world would keep no place for
    them.

I felt like holding them tight in my arms,
Promising I would never let them go,
But they would trust no promises of mine.

I feared that if I touched one, it would scream.

In an essay published in the *Atlantic* in May 1991, "Can Poetry Matter?," Gioia charged that "American poetry now belongs to a subculture. No longer part of the mainstream of artistic and intellectual life, it has become the specialized occupation of a relatively small and isolated group." Despite the facts that more poetry books are generated in the United States than ever before, that many "little" magazines and academic journals exist to publish contemporary poetry, and that many college and university faculty positions are filled by poets—teaching thousands of students who would be poets themselves—Gioia persuasively argues that "Little of the frenetic activity . . . [thus generated] ever reaches" beyond this hermetically sealed literary universe. "As a class poets are not without cultural status. Like priests in a town of agnostics, they still command a certain residual prestige. But as individual artists they are almost invisible." In less than six months this essay generated over four hundred letters to the *Atlantic* and an enormous amount of discussion, including a dozen newspaper and magazine articles in the United States and the British Isles.

Perhaps Gioia is an unusual young poet in a more important way than the articles on him in the business journals and some of the literary journals would indicate. It is not of particular note for the long run that he is not an academic in an age of academic poets. Rather, Gioia is unusual because, unlike many of those poets who teach, he knows precisely what he is doing in his poetry and shows it through a masterful handling of the various levels of his poems. Unlike many of his academic peers, he is able to articulate his theory and practice in intelligent and constructive criticism, nearly a lost art among contemporary poets.

Interview:
David Lehman, "Room for Rhyme," *Business Month* (March 1990).

References:
Bruce Bawer, "The Poet in the Gray Flannel

Suit," *Connoisseur* (March 1989): 108-112;
Robert McPhillips, "Reading the New Formalists," *Sewanee Review*, 97 (Winter 1989): 73-96;
Fleming Meeks, "Free To Be Creative," *Forbes*, 141 (21 March 1988): 170-172;
Mary Anne Ostrom, "Of Rhyme and Reason," *Manhattan, Inc.* (October 1986);
Robert Richman, "Impatient Faith," *New Criterion* (February 1987);
Lewis Turco, "Neoformalism in Contemporary American Poetry," in his *The Public Poet, Five Lectures on the Art and Craft of Poetry* (Ashland, Ohio: Ashland Poetry Press, 1991), pp. 39-56.

Albert Goldbarth
(31 January 1948 -)

David Starkey
Francis Marion College

BOOKS: *Under Cover* (Crete, Nebr.: Best Cellar, 1973);
Coprolites (Saint Paul: New Rivers, 1973);
Opticks (New York: Seven Woods, 1974);
Jan. 31 (New York: Doubleday, 1974);
Keeping (Ithaca, N.Y.: Ithaca House, 1975);
A Year of Happy (Raleigh: North Carolina Review Press, 1976);
Comings Back (New York: Doubleday, 1976);
Curve: Overlapping Narratives (Saint Paul: New Rivers, 1976);
Different Fleshes (Geneva, N.Y.: Hobart & William Smith Colleges Press, 1979);
Ink, Blood, Semen (Cleveland: Bits, 1980);
The Smuggler's Handbook (Wollaston, Mass.: Chowder Chapbooks, 1980);
Who Gathered and Whispered Behind Me (Seattle: L'Epervier, 1981);
Eurekas (Memphis: Raccoon, 1981);
Faith (Saint Paul: New Rivers, 1981);
Goldbarth's Book of Occult Phenomena (Des Moines: Blue Buildings, 1982);

Original Light: New & Selected Poems, 1973-1983 (Princeton, N.J.: Ontario Review Press, 1983);
Arts & Sciences (Princeton, N.J.: Ontario Review Press, 1986);
Popular Culture (Columbus: Ohio State University Press, 1990);
A Sympathy of Souls (Minneapolis: Coffee House, 1990);
Delft (Maryville, Mo.: Green Tower, 1990);
Heaven and Earth: A Cosmology (Athens: University of Georgia Press, 1991).

OTHER: *Every Pleasure: The "Seneca Review" Long Poem Anthology*, edited by Goldbarth (Geneva, N.Y.: Hobart & William Smith Colleges Press, 1979);
Kenyon Review, special "impure forms" issue (Spring 1990), edited by Goldbarth.

Ambitious, eloquent, and erudite, Albert Goldbarth has produced in less than twenty years a body of work that has had an undeniable im-

Albert Goldbarth

pact on contemporary American poetry. As much as any other living poet, Goldbarth has tested the limits of what a poem can do and be. As Michael Heffernan noted in the *Midwest Quarterly* (Winter 1975), "Albert Goldbarth has extended his range perhaps broader than any other poet of the mid-seventies and, in doing so, has taught himself more tricks than most mature poets could use by the end of the century." Incredibly prolific, Goldbarth has been both derided and praised for his copious output. Writing in the same issue of the *Midwest Quarterly,* Dave Smith said, "It has been suggested that a tourist in, say, Vladivostok, picking up the local literary magazine, would find a story by [Joyce Carol] Oates and a poem by Goldbarth." Perhaps because of his relentless energy, Goldbarth has also been an important figure in the development of the long poem.

Albert Goldbarth was born on 31 January 1948 and raised in Chicago, Illinois. His father, Irving, was an underwriter for an insurance company, and his mother, Fannie Seligman Goldbarth, worked as a secretary. Goldbarth graduated with a B.A. from the University of Illinois, Chicago Circle campus, in 1969 and received his

M.F.A. from the University of Iowa in 1971. From 1971 to 1972, he taught at Elgin Community College in the Chicago area. During that time Goldbarth also worked as a coordinator of the Traveling Writers Workshop for Chicago-area public schools.

In 1973 he returned to school and completed a year's worth of classes toward his Ph.D. in creative writing at the University of Utah. With the *Poetry Northwest* Theodore Roethke Prize, a chapbook, and two books of poetry to his credit, Goldbarth left Utah early for brief stints as an assistant professor at Cornell and Syracuse Universities before accepting a position as professor of creative writing at the University of Texas at Austin, where he remained from 1977 to 1987. In 1987 he joined the English department at Wichita State as Distinguished Professor of Humanities.

Goldbarth's facility with language and his amazing variety and range of learning are apparent in his first full-length book, *Coprolites* (1973). Coprolites are fossilized human feces, and the book focuses on, among other things, the literal and figurative dirt that human beings leave behind. Archaeology is a dominant trope in this book; Goldbarth digs into matters that were "deep buried" and asks, "what rite / was this?" In his desire to uncover and include as much as possible in every poem, Goldbarth obviously shares an affinity with Walt Whitman. But unlike Whitman, Goldbarth is not concerned so much with present-day America as he is with the whole of human history. In fact one of the most fascinating sections of *Coprolites,* "Interstices," juxtaposes dramatic monologues by historical figures who are disparate in time. The "dialogue" between Joan of Arc and William Harvey is particularly provocative.

Coprolites received, on the whole, favorable notices. Dillon Johnston in *Shenandoah* (Winter 1975) compared Goldbarth to Robert Browning, "not only because Goldbarth adapts his monologue form but also because the modern poet's dense texture, his chiaroscuro of grotesque images alternating with flaring insights, and the long, energetic, alliterative lines, all suggest that Victorian model." Heffernan, in his *Midwest Quarterly* review (Winter 1975), remarks that Goldbarth's poetry is "full of play, the free play of an exhilarated and exhilarating imagination— child's play of the most truly serious kind. . . ." Goldbarth had overcome the most difficult obstacle for any new poet: he had attracted attention.

Opticks (1974), Goldbarth's second full-length book, comprises a long poem that examines the nature of glass and the nature of perception. The seven sections alternate between what Goldbarth calls "subjective explorations" of the subject and dramatic monologues that narrate a fanciful account of the invention of glass and of the fate of two characters who are involved in the creation and preservation of a piece of medieval stained glass known as the Eshcol Window. This window becomes an important metaphor because, as Goldbarth explains, "Everything's in it. That's *everything.*"

Although Dave Oliphant (*Margins,* December 1974) praised *Opticks* as linguistically "delicious, with "language as beautiful as that of *Lear,*" Dave Smith (*Midwest Quarterly,* Winter 1975) complained that "Immaturity translates to selfishness in *Opticks.*" Goldbarth is obviously aware of the inadequacies of his own poetry. In what became a familiar gesture, Goldbarth pokes fun at himself when he comes closest to grandiloquence. The book ends with a mock book review by the author:

In "Opticks" Goldbarth has created a truly experimental poem. His radical style consists of never using one word when three can be substituted, of never trusting his own language or the reader's perceptiveness enough to settle for a single exemplification, of never considering subtlety if a blackjack is available. And sometimes he drives all the way across town in order to get that blackjack.

In spite of whatever faults he may have found in himself, Goldbarth was rewarded for his efforts when his next book, *Jan. 31* (1974), was nominated for a National Book Award. In the long title poem he meditates on natural and historical cycles. One of its central metaphors, weather, is especially appropriate for a Goldbarth poem since he is so concerned with the way the world is simultaneously, and paradoxically, mutable and stable. Critic Jonathon Katz, while admiring Goldbarth's erudition, lamented in the *Midwest Quarterly* (Winter 1975) that "The poems in *Jan. 31* are largely repetitive in mood," a complaint that some later readers would also voice.

Goldbarth received an NEA Fellowship in creative writing for 1974-1975 and continued his astonishing productivity. However, two small-press books, *Keeping* (1975) and *A Year of Happy* (1976), received relatively little critical attention. Despite his continued and often successful experiments with montagelike effects in extended narratives, these books may likely have suffered from the fact that there was simply too much poetry available from Goldbarth.

Nevertheless, the abundance of ideas and the virtuosity of language in *Comings Back* (1976) could not be ignored. Victor Contoski observed in *Prairie Schooner* (Winter 1977-1978) that Goldbarth seems "less interested in 'Art' than in ideas, in intellectual excitement." The poet, he notes, "gives the impression of not being able to write fast enough to keep up with the flow of his thoughts." There is, indeed, an incredible energy in *Comings Back.* Goldbarth's ability to *invent* on any subject is manifest throughout the book. From the silly (a theme and variations on peanut butter and tuna fish in "The Pocket Song") to the grotesque (his song on the "sweet-reeking, celebratory, beneficent / canon of coprophilia") to the sublime (a disquisition on the "rotundity of time" in "Kaddish: The Whole Picture"), Goldbarth ranges widely, his imagination inflamed.

This long book, 141 pages, is infused with Goldbarth's need to tell stories, to talk through chaos into harmony. As he acknowledges in "Narrative Continuity," he has always wanted to write a novel, but his mind is too easily led astray by ideas that would seem spurious to most people:

> [I] have no knack
> for narrative continuity, a Bedouin or thieving politi-
>   cian
> always bouncing off the wrong mote
> of Brownian motion, and a tangent
> to my life becomes my life, as an amoeba's sticking
> a trifle of itself out into the ecosphere
> becomes the amoeba. I'm speaking
> of locomotion in unicellular creatures
> now, in the middle of what
> was to be a love poem, see?

Yet Goldbarth cannot throw things away. He is an inveterate saver and savorer of whatever comes his way, unable to toss out even the "Refrains/Remains/Reminders" that form the final section of *Comings Back*.

Goldbarth's achievement in the long poem was recognized when he was invited to edit *Every Pleasure: The "Seneca Review" Long Poem Anthology* (1979); and his next full-length book, *Different Fleshes* (1979), he called a "novel/poem." The fragmented story examines the life of a Texas transvestite, Vander Clyde, who went to Paris in the 1930s and became famous as Barbette, a high-wire walker who performed stunts dressed in elaborate women's costumes. *Different Fleshes* borrows from an assortment of texts and touches on the lives of several characters, including the outlaw Sam Bass, who frequently robbed banks dressed as a woman, as well as many of the literati of Paris between the wars. The poem moves rapidly in time and place, in typical Goldbarthian fashion: "Hemingway walked home. 'Home?' Yes. It / was 1923, Monet looked up. It was 1878. And / he was a man on the Seine. . . ." Michael King wrote in the *American Poetry Review* (March-April 1980) that the poem "is a mask as elaborate and artificial as the extravagant cosmetics of Barbette," that, like the writers of the period, Goldbarth is "engaged in constructing a mask which [will], by covering his everyday skin, reveal a richer and more profound, because created, body." Barbette's story, despite its farcical aspects, is poignant. In his thwarted quest for happiness, the hero may be Goldbarth's vision of a late-twentieth-century Everyman. "Everybody with a heart," Goldbarth writes, "was looking for a skin."

Different Fleshes was followed by another flurry of publishing activity, including *The Smuggler's Handbook* in 1980 and *Eurekas* in 1981.

Along with these pamphlets, Goldbarth put out a full-length collection, *Who Gathered and Whispered Behind Me* (1981), which consists of three long poems. Writing in the *Northwest Review* (Winter 1982), John Addiego compares Goldbarth's technique with that of the painter Marc Chagall, whose "anti-intellectual, whimsical, dream-centered visions have a similar montage effect as the overlapping series of voices, quotes and points of view in Goldbarth's poem[s]." In fact he takes the title of the book from a quote of Chagall's:

> [the] poor hands of my parents and of others and
> still others, with their mute lips and their closed
>   eyes,
> who gathered and whispered behind me, would
> direct me as if they also wished
> to take part in my life.

And the longest poem, "The Window Is an Almanac," dwells upon the influence Goldbarth's family, especially his grandmother, has had on him.

This exploration of family themes becomes even more extensive in his next full-length book, *Faith* (1981). The collection is divided into two long sections with a coda at the end. The first section, "A Dozen Roses *of the Same Family*," includes poems about Goldbarth's grandparents, parents, and sister. In one of the most affectionate poems in the book, "35,000 Feet—The Lanterns," Goldbarth imagines his grandfather, who was a coal seller, and his grandmother, a fish seller, making love:

> —Grandpa could smell her three
> landings down, and had learned the odor
> of kipper and perch as arousing. Six
> days a week they were both too tired but
> on Saturday, the piscine unscrubbably
> in her still, they'd tangle the one good
> set of sheets as if the world were
> Poland again, that first night ever.

This poem is also interesting for the glimpse it provides into Goldbarth's sources of inspiration: between teaching classes, the speaker reads eagerly in a library book about fish that live at the bottom of the ocean—"170 species of the / lantern fish alone"—discovering metaphors on every page.

The second section of *Faith*, "Chai, *Books of Belief*," finds Goldbarth, a nonpracticing Jew, examining his Jewish heritage. "This is the nature of prayer," he writes, "the fact it can't, the fact it can't, the fact it can't / and the faith it can anyway." Though not conventionally religious, Goldbarth nevertheless religiously celebrates the mystery of the cosmos. *Faith* was not heavily reviewed—by this time a new book by Goldbarth could hardly be seen as a literary event—but the volume remains one of his most moving and most controlled efforts.

In 1983 Goldbarth published *Original Light: New & Selected Poems, 1973-1983*. In ten years he had written more pages of poetry than many novelists had written pages of fiction. Not surprisingly, the critical response was extensive and varied. Robert Cording wrote in *Carolina Quarterly* (Winter 1984), "[Goldbarth] has that rare gift of seeing metaphor in almost any event, of discovering a poem in the most unlikely places." Cording claimed that "*Original Light* contains ten years of work which both deserves careful attention, and which will repay that attention tenfold." Other critics, however, were less laudatory. William Logan warned in *Poetry* (November 1984), "Goldbarth's huge output is of course suspect in a time that legislates spareness." And Diane Wakoski scolded in the *American Book Review* (May-June 1984) that "Such a collection invites a retrospective view of the poet's career, as well as a comparison with other poets who are the history of any century." In Wakoski's opinion, Goldbarth did not yet deserve such a retrospective comparison.

Nevertheless, publishing his selected poems might have been an essential move in Goldbarth's career. In *Original Light* he was able to sort through and order ideas that had recurred throughout his work. The book is divided into three sections: "Distances," "A Sanguinary," and "Chronologues." Themes that had obsessed him— the cyclical nature of time, the power of memory, the metaphorical significance of science in everyday lives, and the surprising amount of truth contained in apparent mistakes—all are rearranged and reexamined in *Original Light*. "Oh, sure, there's rich / perfect glass: that's lucidity," Goldbarth writes in "The Errors," "but here, these chips of cheap sheeting of ours: / how the light, when we tilt right, goes rainbow in the flaws."

In the three years before his next book was published, Goldbarth was awarded a Guggenheim Fellowship and taught as a visiting writer at universities throughout the country. Also in the mid 1980s Goldbarth's work began to be consistently featured in important anthologies such as *The Harvard Book of Contemporary Poetry* and *Ameri-*

Cover for Goldbarth's 1991 book, which won a National Book Critics Circle Award for Poetry

can Literature Since 1945, and was awarded several Pushcart Prizes. Increasingly, this man, who in many ways fits the general public's idea of the "mad poet," was being accepted by academia as a major American writer.

Arts & Sciences (1986) is unmistakably a book by Albert Goldbarth. In *Poetry* (April 1987) David Shapiro characterized Goldbarth's work as "maximalist." His poetry, Shapiro wrote, "offers an aureate antidote [to the reigning 'principles of restraint']. This is what anthropologists might call 'thick description' of our lives, a density and repleteness of particulars that avoids the conventional and aspires toward constant transgression." Indeed, if it is possible, *Arts & Sciences* seems even more densely packed with images and wider ranging in its references than his earlier books. The lines are longer, and the speed with which he shifts from one idea to another is regularly emphasized by stanza breaks that occur in midsentence, as in this passage from the longest poem in the book, "Cathay":

> I was universe-stuff of a certain amalgam and density.
> To me, I was eager, sensitive, hesitant, foolish, loony to enter
> her sexual wigwam. Then she answered the door in her
>
> sari and bing cherry caste-mark. You see? The
> answer is: 1)3)5)7)9) . . . as "fact." It is in *my* world,
> anyway. To the "Indios," Columbus and his men arrived
> "from the sky," on creatures with massive, white wings. . . .

The three sections—"Some Science," "Some Art," and "Some People"—cover familiar terrain, but they do so energetically. Goldbarth never tires of celebrating *everything:* "We / can never sing praises too many. Of even a rhizome, a protein, / one bulbette of roe."

Over three years passed before the publication of Goldbarth's *Popular Culture* (1990), winner of the Ohio State University Press Award for 1989. Like so many of his books, *Popular Culture* is a sequence of loosely related poems. The narrator's father has died, and the event leads him to examine the myriad aspects of the culture in which he lives. In "The Multiverse," for instance, he sees parallels between the characters in science-fiction novels and the people in his neighborhood who, with their "rosefoliate secrets," are just as bizarre. An anonymous review of the book in *Publisher's Weekly* (6 October 1989) noted, "Trenchant observations abound in these long serial poems, though Goldbarth's run-on sentences and nonchronological time sequences can appear convoluted, and some poems may stymie the reader with madcap philosophizing." As usual, Goldbarth manages to blend bits of esoteric learning with all manner of kitsch—from comic-book characters and flea-market throwaways to television shows and "Aluminum Siding Queens."

Readers of Goldbarth's poetry may occasionally feel that the genre is too prone to compression to allow for his natural expansiveness, and *A Sympathy of Souls* (1990) proves that there are new avenues open to Goldbarth in prose. As does all of his work, this essay collection attempts to fuse apparently unrelated ideas and images in an effort to make sense of the world. "It's not that we lie," he writes in "After Yitzl." "It's that we make the truth."

In his chapbook *Delft* (1990) Goldbarth again argues that even the smallest creature is part of one design, which, as Ralph Waldo Emerson described it in "The American Scholar," "unites and animates the farthest pinnacle and the lowest trench." The ostensible subject of Goldbarth's "essay-poem" is fleas, but these insects, which once symbolized the limit of the finite universe, are in fact only a point of departure for an extended meditation on the interrelationship of time and space.

Heaven and Earth: A Cosmology (1991), winner of a National Book Critics Circle Award, returns to a familiar theme—the poet's confrontation with the unsettling void posited by science: "Maybe a God, // even a God of terrible vengeance, is less frightening / than floating through physics," Goldbarth writes in "Reality Organization." On balance, though, the book is far from gloomy. Though physics can "make a rose a wasteland," the speaker will "set one, simply and with faith / in its cohesion," at the bedside of his hospitalized mother.

As long as Goldbarth remains able, he will undoubtedly continue to write, and, if his most recent work is any indication, he will do so with great vigor and insight. Like Whitman—his most obvious forebear—Albert Goldbarth has an insatiable appetite for the physical and the spiritual, and he has created a poetry that is, as Whitman believed it should be, "bold, modern, and all-surrounding and cosmical."

Jorie Graham
(9 May 1951 -   )

Peyton Brien
University of Toronto

BOOKS: *Hybrids of Plants and of Ghosts* (Princeton, N.J. & Guildford, U.K.: Princeton University Press, 1980);
Erosion (Princeton, N.J. & Guildford, U.K.: Princeton University Press, 1983);
The End of Beauty (New York: Ecco, 1987);
Region of Unlikeness (New York: Ecco, 1991).

OTHER: *The Best American Poetry 1990*, edited by Graham and David Lehman (New York: Scribners, 1991).

In a 1992 interview with Thomas Gardner, Jorie Graham told him, "I feel like I'm writing as part of a group of poets—historically—who are potentially at the end of the medium itself as a vital part of their culture—unless they do something to help it reconnect itself to mystery and power." Of those poets who are at the forefront of this effort to revitalize and redefine American poetry, Graham and her own writing must be counted among the most mysterious and powerful. She is a composer of deeply searching and skillfully wrought poems that emerge from her firsthand, academic experience of art, literature, history, and religious thought. They are grounded in her concerns with philosophy, society, and the metaphysical aspects of being.

While Graham's work is expressly written for others to read and consider, her verse reminds one of Robert Bly's comment that "The poem is a dance written for some being in the other world." As she also commented to Gardner, "Poetry is an extraordinary medium for spiritual undertaking." This statement does not mean that her poetry is overbalanced by qualities of the ethereal, as such. It does suggest, though, the extent to which her own perceptions and style have been influenced by what in Zen teaching is called *yugen*—the sensation of the ineffable. One of her major motivations in writing, she has said, is to attain this spiritual level not only for herself but to bring the reader to it as well.

Jorie Graham, 1985 (photograph by Bill Pepper)

Critical responses to Graham have been largely favorable, if also, on occasion, puzzled. There are, of course, detractors, yet even the most severe of these, such as J. D. McClatchy in the 26 July 1987 *New York Times Book Review*, still must admit that "many of the poems stand out starkly against the flat landscape of much American poetry. . . . Ms. Graham writes with a metaphysical flair and emotional power."

Graham's understanding of the world could be said to have a deep anthropological sense to it. She does not write of closed, synchronic, ending-dependent systems—moments frozen in time; reality, as expressed in her poetry, is a diachronic passage of events, one of ever-shifting and weaving patterns.

Jorie Graham was born in New York City on 9 May 1951 to Curtis Bill and Beverly Stoll Pepper, who had met in Italy and married in France.

Beverly Pepper returned to her home in the United States to give birth to Jorie, and after three months they returned to Europe. The child grew up first in the south of France and then in different parts of Italy. Much of this early childhood, she says, was spent playing in the churches of Rome and looking at the paintings there, experiencing their images from both aesthetic and religious viewpoints.

Graham's creativity and much of the direction in her poetry stem from the influence of her parents. Her mother was a painter who took up sculpting and was well known in the European art world. Some of Graham's earliest memories are of the regular time spent with her mother in her art studio, playing and observing the parent's creative endeavors. Graham's father's primary interests were religion and theology. He was a serious student of the history of art and is an authority on the history of the Catholic church. This combination of the secular and the theological, derived from her parents, with both involved in the aesthetic perspective, played a substantial role in the formation of her own artistic searching.

Graham was educated in the French system which, she commented in an interview with Ann Snodgrass, "predisposes one to generalization and abstraction." Her earliest postsecondary education was at the Sorbonne in Paris. While there (as dramatically described in "Hiding Place," a poem in *Region of Unlikeness*, 1991) she was involved in the student uprisings of 1968. A year later she returned to the United States, and in 1973 she received her B.F.A. from New York University. She was awarded an M.F.A. by the University of Iowa in 1978.

Graham began her academic career as an assistant professor of English at Murray State University in Kentucky in 1978. From fall 1979 to spring 1982 she taught at Humboldt State University in Arcata, California. The 1982-1983 school year was a busy one and saw her employed not only as a workshop instructor at Columbia University but as a teacher at the Radcliffe Institute and the Writer's Community of New York City. Since 1983 she has been a professor of English and workshop instructor at the University of Iowa. In that same year she married James Galvin. They have a daughter, Emily, born in 1984.

Graham was encouraged in her pursuit of a literary career by the nearly immediate embrace given her work by the publishers of magazines and journals, including the *American Poetry Review, Iowa Review, New England Review, Georgia Re-*view, and the *New Yorker*. Her success in regularly being published in periodicals is reflected also in the assistance given her by the literary community in bringing her book publications to press and otherwise aiding and maintaining her writing career. Publication of *Hybrids of Plants and of Ghosts* (1980) was aided by a grant from the Paul Mellon Fund of the Princeton University Press. The Whitney Darrow Publication Reserve of Princeton University Press aided her in bringing *Erosion* (1983) to press. (Both of these publications were part of the Princeton Series of Contemporary Poets.) Graham was aided in publishing *The End of Beauty* (1987) by grants from both the Guggenheim Foundation and the National Endowment for the Arts. A grant from the Whiting Foundation is given special credit for assistance in bringing *Region of Unlikeness* to press.

In addition she has been honored since the beginning of her career with such awards as the American Academy of Poets Prize from the University of Iowa (1977); three Pushcart Prizes (1980, 1981, and 1982); and the American Poetry Review Prize in 1982. She was the cover feature for the *American Poetry Review* in both 1982 and 1987. Her most recent awards have been the Lavan Award from the Academy of American Poets (1991) and the Academy and Institute of Arts and Letters' Morton Zabel Award (1992).

Graham told Snodgrass, "Those poets I most admire are often those whose difficulty of style forces the reader to participate actively in the reading of the poem." The first poet whose complete works she read was William Butler Yeats, and it was in response to the ontological and moral questions posed through his poetry that her own experiments in composing verse began. Beyond this, she has suggested that it is between Wallace Stevens and T. S. Eliot that the central definitions of her own concerns may be found. Reading Graham, then, one might consider the doctrine of impersonality of statement in Eliot's modernist school, and the quotation from Stevens that "The poem must resist the intelligence almost successfully." Graham feels the language of Stevens so forcefully, she has said, that it is sometimes almost a problem.

A strong influence from John Milton is also present in Graham's work, with his emphasis on religious experience grounded in the body. She was also influenced by John Berryman and Emily Dickinson. Graham has mentioned her sensitivity over the fact that only one of the poets she claims as a strong influence is a woman; however,

Graham says she finds it difficult to concentrate on any of them as being especially or primarily female or male. When asked once if she believed there was such a thing as, quoting Gertrude Stein, "a female imagination," she commented that this was not so in her experience, but that there was only "great imagination and imagination that faints at the threshold."

Graham did not begin seriously writing poetry until her mid twenties. At that time it was mostly a form of journal keeping for her. Her earliest publications began appearing in periodicals in 1977. The result, by 1980, was *Hybrids of Plants and of Ghosts.*

The title is derived from Friedrich Nietzsche's characterization of human beings. Much of Graham's motivation and ambition in writing poetry is suggested in the title of the poem that opens *Hybrids of Plants and of Ghosts:* "The Way Things Work." Further evidence of her searching nature is seen in other titles from the book: "On Why I Would Betray You," "Mirrors," followed immediately by "Self-Portrait," and later "How Morning Glories Could Bloom at Dusk," "The Nature of Evidence," "The Afterlife," and so on. Literary and artistic interests have compelled Graham throughout her career, and some of these can be seen in poems about Paul Eluard, Voltaire, Paul Cézanne, and Mark Rothko.

Graham's formal strategies in the book are relatively simple and well designed to enhance the intellectual searching of a neophyte poet. Most of the poems are short, extending to no more than twenty or thirty lines. Some are written in series of couplets, and others are composed as series of three- , four- , and six-line stanzas. Others have only one stanza. Strict metrical formats seem rarely to be among Graham's concerns.

Many of her poems show a gentle sense about the ironies of life—such as "Ambergris," which among its topics explores the role of squids in the creation of perfume, and "Cross-Stitch," which utilizes a lost, noisy cricket to make its point.

Referring to Graham's "mixture of wisdom and discord, desire and faith," Margaret Gibson (*Library Journal,* 15 May 1980) noted further that "Weighted towards mind and observation, these are distanced poems, whose difficult language catches and moves us with its beauty." These comments allude directly to an element of Graham seen in almost every poem and which continues in later volumes: her concern with moral experience. This is not to imply that the poems take a moralistic or dogmatic tone. Her fascination is with the idea that all people experience life from a moral perspective and come to very different philosophical conclusions.

As Helen Vendler suggested in the *New York Times Book Review* (17 July 1983), "Graham's pictorial surface is sometimes alive with movement, at other times contemplative and still." In either of these cases, Graham has, in *Erosion,* an increased awareness of the purpose of each individual poem. *Erosion* was seen by most reviewers as an advance from the poems of *Hybrids of Plants and of Ghosts,* as a less "diffuse" work than the former. Some, such as William Logan in the *Times Literary Supplement* (10 June 1983), thought that the new poems lack "the energy and wild images" of earlier poems, but he felt this lack was alleviated through greater precision and calmness in her verses. Often reviewers seemed uncertain of exactly what to think of her. Writing in the *Library Journal* (1 May 1983), Ray Olsen complained of "too many vagrant ruminative rambles," while allowing that some poems, especially those deriving from Graham's experience of Italy and art, were measured, "tensely focused works."

Graham herself, in her interview with Snodgrass, said that "*Erosion* seems to me a book about accountability, and accountability seems to me a very American obsession." Suggested here again is her continuing preoccupation with moral experience. Exhibited also in many of the individual poems of *Erosion* is a remarkable ability to consider a topic from two perspectives—both theoretically and "on-the-ground."

In a searching, if too-brief, article about Graham in *Georgia Review* (Winter 1983), Peter Stitt looked upon her exploration of reality as resolving itself "into a contest between the attractions of Platonism—which prefers a world of ideal forms, of ideas, of timeless perfection—and the tenets of realism—which prefers the physical universe *despite,* or perhaps because of, its limitations." After examining the title poem and "Plato," Stitt concluded that, while "strongly attracted by the Platonic vision," Graham's sympathies in the end "lie on the anti-Platonic side. . . ."

Fullest witness to Stitt's conclusion is seen in the last poem in *Erosion,* "The Sense of an Ending." The poem looks at the options of both "paradise" and this current world, where "human / souls are in a frenzy / to be born. . . ." It sides with reality over any envisioned paradise: "no matter / how short or broken" are human lives, "No matter / the hundred kinds of burn, the thousand kinds / of rot—no matter / the terrible insufficiencies of matter . . . ," these must be understood as inevitably and infinitely preferable to ideal worlds existing only in individual imaginations.

Graham's formative years in Europe and her studies there of paintings in galleries and churches are manifested more in the subject matter of *Erosion* than in her previous volume: included are poems about the paintings or personalities of Masaccio, Gustav Klimt, Piero della Francesca, Francisco José de Goya, and Luca Signorelli. She continues to acknowledge her literary influences as well, with pieces honoring John Keats and John Berryman. Yet equally as important are the poems about the more immediate concerns of life—"Wanting a Child," "The Daffodil," "I Watched a Snake," "Making a Living," and "Love" among them. As Vendler commented, "The attempt to find all the stops, to range through the gamut of possibility, makes Miss Graham a poet of landscape and memory as well as a poet of art."

The vital role Graham is playing in the development and definition of postmodernist poetry has often been alluded to. Examining a couple of her uncollected poems, Jonathan Holden refers to one of them, "For Hope," as "an example of the discursive conversation poem at its best." As he utilizes her poem for an extended analysis of this specific writing mode, he especially praises her composition of "the relationship between speaker and reader." Reviewers have commented on the abstract quality in many of Graham's poems. Holden concentrates on "Jackpot" for its use of abstract images and calls it "a beautiful realistic deployment of the abstract image technique," where, in some cases, a word's range of reference can be "simply endless." In some instances the precision with which she is able to place a word renders it with simultaneously "both an abstract and a concrete meaning." He repeatedly praises the emotional complexity and "urbanity" of Graham's usages.

The culmination implied in the title of *The End of Beauty* is, as Graham states early in the poem "The Lovers," "the present." It is this present moment that "the vista fed into. What it wants to grow out of, creeping, / succulent. . . ." There may be a philosophical dilemma for Graham, though, in her search for non-ending-dependent truths, wherein death need not be seen as "the mother of beauty." Beauty, in

Graham's terms, is what has happened up until this very moment—that which people have generated, what has been created around them, and how they choose to perceive all this. The future is less than tenuous: it is a hypothesis that never, in actuality, comes to pass.

One criticism leveled against Graham's experiments with form in this volume may not be entirely deserved. Graham's formal experiment was perhaps devised in the effort to overcome a Western tendency toward ending-dependent writing and reading styles. The complaint against her is with the long strings of numbered but very short stanzas, many of one line only, which characterize several of the poems in *The End of Beauty*. Possibly some of these critics, including McClatchy, are too easily distracted. A number is like a word—only a concept. Yet unlike what one does with the words of a poem, one need not pause at each new number to consider it before moving on. This format, then, is one of Graham's efforts to resolve the challenge she has set for herself to defeat the illusion, generated partly through historicity, that there is a moment in life where everything comes to an end and something else begins. There are no precise stops. Her problem then is analogous to a painter's need, given the inevitability of limited space, to carry his subject beyond the tyranny of the frame, the painting's borders.

One example of such a poem is "Pollock and Canvas." The tendency is inherent within Jackson Pollock's work to force one viewing it to go beyond notice of the borders—by taking the viewer more deeply within the material presented. Working with words and paper rather than paint and canvas, Graham has attempted to meet her challenge through using the format described to render at first the appearance of constant stops. Yet these are not really "stops," because the segments contained do not necessarily reveal complete moments or thoughts, only fragments. Graham hopes the reader will eventually be forced to cease thinking so much about an end, or artificially creating one—be it an end of thought, end of verse, end of sentence, end of poem, or end of beauty.

Thus the mythic dimension that often characterizes Graham's poetry also becomes more noticeable. In *The End of Beauty* her language has been freed up as well. Vendler, in a *New Yorker* review dated 27 July 1987, compares elements of Graham's style to that of Percy Bysshe Shelley and praises her "exultant or sardonic or ecstatic

Cover for Graham's 1987 book, which prompted favorable comparisons between Graham's figurative language and that of Percy Bysshe Shelley

cascades of language." There may be some appropriateness as well in Jessica Greenbaum's observations in a 5 September 1987 review in the *Nation*. She finds Graham both "astonishing and bewildering" and "probably rarely accessible to most of us." But this may depend, of course, on whether one is willing to read a poem more than once, and how deeply.

Graham seems to be responding to such critiques in her introduction to *The Best American Poetry 1990*, where she comments that "to comprehend poetry one must, after all, practice by reading it." Because her professional life includes teaching other poets, a full examination of her work should include at least some review of what she has written philosophically, aside from her verse. Of all such writings, Graham has been most satisfied with her anthology introduction. In the process of her exploration and summation of the state of contemporary American poetry, including a concerted defense of its strategies and motivations, she also details much of her political

and aesthetic approaches to writing and reading poetry, as well as expressing the spirit and moral passion that guide her.

The political presence behind her poetry is manifest in her comment that "poetry clearly undertakes a critique of materialist values . . ." for these must be seen through in order to discover deeper and more resonant values. Yet the process poetry must undertake for this critique may be challenging "because much of it [poetry] attempts to render aspects of experience that occur outside the provinces of logic and reason." The dilemma, that is, lies in poetry's merging of "irrational procedures with the rational nature of language."

On the moral and perhaps ultimate purpose of poetry, she writes: "Each poem is, in the end, an act of the mind that tries—via precision of seeing, thinking, and feeling—to clean the language of its current lies, to make it capable of connecting us to the world. . . ." She is extremely critical of poets who seem to make no effort in this capacity, writing instead "the poetry of the mere self . . . a voice that expands not to the size of a soul but to the size of an ego."

As Graham explained to Gardner, "For me each book [of mine] is a critique of the previous [one by me]." This may in part suggest that in *Region of Unlikeness* she has pronounced her experimentation with numbered stanzas to be of limited success only, for this strategy does not appear in her 1991 collection. The average length of poems has again increased, a trait that has been marked since her first book. She is certainly aware that there may be a few obscurities or idiosyncrasies in some poems, for she includes two pages of explanatory endnotes. At the beginning of the book are ten quotations from theologians, philosophers, and the Bible (including several from Saint Augustine's *Confessions,* from which comes the title phrase, "region of unlikeness").

While there is little reason to doubt that Graham will scale to even greater heights in her poetry, *Region of Unlikeness* shows her as having already arrived at a certain kind of artistic pinnacle. She writes with a degree of confidence that in itself reveals the level of experimentation in many of her earlier poems—including some of her finer ones—as she searched for the devices through which her personal and spiritual quest could be best developed and expressed in writing. For example, her concept of the tenuousness or fluidity, even the fearfulness, of identity is expressed in "The Tree of Knowledge":

When I reached for your hand in there,

when I ran my hand into your hand,
  it was to get that other sense of flesh,
where touch is the way to disappear,
  the old dream of an underneath,
is it still there?

Equally effective is "The Holy Shroud," with her abstract metaphor that draws together a thornberry bush in the dead of winter, the great flock of birds drawn to it, and the Shroud of Turin. Yet another compelling poem is "Chaos," where Eve is considered in the moment of her creation, when she is awake but has not been released from the body of Adam. It is not necessar-

ily a religious poem so much as an exploration of the mystery of existence.

In 1991, at a poetry reading for the Eighth Annual Presidential Lecture at the University of Iowa, Graham spoke of "the erosion of language in our culture for some time now." Elsewhere, she has referred to "a genuine revival of poetic ambition" (in her introduction to *The Best American Poetry 1990*). There is no contradiction here. Shortly after this (in her anthology introduction) she adds that "all these poems seem deeply political to me." At the very time that language, the most essential tool human culture has for connecting itself to the world, is waning, the artistic world of poetry renews itself, in order to fulfill its "bedrock role" and "clean the language of its current lies"—the foremost of which must be the banishment of thought through the "attempted destruction" of the use and comprehension of language.

Jorie Graham is sincerely concerned and deeply fearful about such matters and unwilling to assume some cultural process will work its way through without her. She has committed herself to an artistic role in salvaging a world in which there can once again be, quoting Lawrence Ferlinghetti, "a rebirth of wonder." She is not yet in her mid forties, but she has already seen more of her work in print and achieved more honors than many poets hope to accomplish in a lifetime. The dynamic energy and skill with which she has carried her role in the world of poetry make it more than likely that, at the conclusion of her career, its results—which most visibly include her poetry but, because of her teaching, go far beyond this—will be seen and felt for generations to come. She is among the most important poets in North American literature today.

Interviews:
Ann Snodgrass, "Interview: Jorie Graham," *Quarterly West* (Tenth Anniversary Issue);
Thomas Gardner, "An Interview with Jorie Graham," *Denver Quarterly* (forthcoming 1992).

Reference:
Jonathan Holden, *Style and Authenticity in Post-Modern Poetry* (Columbia: University of Missouri Press, 1986), pp. 40-44, 64-67.

Marilyn Hacker
(27 November 1942 -   )

Felicia Mitchell
Emory and Henry College

BOOKS: *The Terrible Children* (New York: Privately printed, 1967);

Highway Sandwiches, by Hacker, Thomas M. Disch, and Charles Platt (N.p.: Privately printed, 1970);

Presentation Piece (New York: Viking, 1974);

Separations (New York: Knopf, 1976);

Taking Notice (New York: Knopf, 1980);

Assumptions (New York: Knopf, 1985);

Love, Death, and the Changing of the Seasons (New York: Arbor House, 1986; London: Onlywomen, 1986);

Going Back to the River (New York: Random House, 1990);

The Hang-Glider's Daughter: New and Selected Poems (London: Onlywomen, 1990).

RECORDINGS: *The Poetry and Voice of Marilyn Hacker,* Caedmon, 1976;

Treasury of American Jewish Poets Reading Their Poems, edited by Paul Kresh, Spoken Arts Recordings, 1979;

Marilyn Hacker, University of Missouri, New Letters, 1979.

OTHER: *Quark,* 4 volumes, edited by Hacker and Samuel R. Delany (New York: Paperback Library, 1970-1971);

Woman Poet: The East, edited by Hacker (Reno: Women in Literature, 1982);

Ploughshares, special issue, 15 (Winter 1989-1990), edited by Hacker.

Marilyn Hacker (photograph by Robert Turney)

Marilyn Hacker fits into the contemporary poetry scene because of her unusual critical perspective, which bridges the traditional and the feminist. In a literary era in which women are purportedly confronting the patriarchal tradition and showing how singularly distinctive women's writing is, Hacker has insisted and shown that the traditional poetic forms are as much women's as they are men's—even if men were acclaimed and published more frequently in the past. As a feminist in her own terms, she is simply follow-

ing in the footsteps of Marie de France and Christine de Pisan, reclaiming the language. "The language that we use," she said in her interview with Karla Hammond, "was as much created and invented by women as by men." In extending the tradition, Hacker has achieved distinction for following her apprenticeship through to mastery of form and especially for wedding contemporary diction to traditional forms.

Hacker's life also reflects her individuality and tendency to defy categories of definition. The child of Jewish immigrants Albert Abraham Hacker (a business consultant) and Hilda Rosengarten Hacker (a teacher), she was born on 27

November 1942 and grew up in the Bronx, leaving the Bronx School of Science at the age of fifteen. She went on to New York University, where she took five and a half years to complete a B.A., during which time she spent a year as a full-time student of painting at the Art Students' League and traveled alone in Mexico for four months. She received her B.A. in 1964. This period was also marked by her 22 August 1961 marriage to black, gay novelist Samuel R. Delany, with whom she edited *Quark: A Quarterly of Speculative Fiction* from 1969 to 1971 (collected in four volumes, 1970-1971). Married for thirteen years, permanently separated in December 1974, and divorced in 1980, the couple spent their time apart and together in a nontraditional marriage in New York, San Francisco, and later London. Making her living as an antiquarian book dealer in London from 1971 to 1976, Hacker—philosophically estranged from the United States during the Vietnam War—felt at home. Her daughter, Iva Alyxander Hacker-Delany, was born there in 1974. Hacker has publicly identified herself as a lesbian since the late 1970s and has lived with Karyn London since 1986.

Before returning to live in the United States in 1976, Hacker established herself on the literary scene, gaining respect in both mainstream and feminist circles. After an impressive record of journal publications, Hacker was recognized by a New York Poetry Center Discovery Award in 1973. Widely published in journals from *Ms.* and *Calys* to *Poetry, Grand Street,* and the *Paris Review,* Hacker has been the recipient of fellowships from George Washington University (Jenny McKean Moore Fellowship, 1976-1977), the Guggenheim Foundation (1980-1981), the National Endowment for the Arts, and the Ingram Merrill Foundation (both 1985). Her first full-length book *Presentation Piece* (1974), chosen (prepublication) as a Lamont Poetry Selection in 1973, won the National Book Award in 1975.

Since the publication of *Separations* (1976), Hacker, then a single mother in New York, has held a variety of university teaching positions. In 1990, for example, she was a visiting professor at the State University of New York at Binghamton. She has also been active as an editor of literary journals, including the *Little Magazine,* and the feminist literary magazine *13th Moon,* of which she was editor from 1982 through 1985 and for which she received a Coordinating Council of Literary Magazines Fellowship in 1984. She edited a regional anthology of northeastern women poets,

published in 1982, and a special issue of *Ploughshares* (Winter 1989-1990), which focused on literary, gender, and racial diversity in contemporary American poetry. She has also published reviews and critical articles on contemporary poetry. In June 1990 she was appointed editor of the *Kenyon Review;* she is one of the half-dozen American editors who refused NEA fellowships containing the controversial "obscenity" restriction.

Since 1978 Hacker has recrossed the Atlantic frequently, returning not to England but to France. The people of Paris and the landscapes of the southern French countryside have been increasingly present in her books since *Taking Notice* (1980). She has kept a small permanent residence in Paris since 1984 and currently divides her time between Paris, New York, and Kenyon College in Gambier, Ohio.

Hacker's poetry is feminist in its themes as it reveals how the personal is political. She writes about the process of self-discovery through observing the self, persona, or alter ego in generally urban settings and experiencing different facets of various relationships with lovers, her daughter, and her mother. Hacker's poetry is as much about language as it is about life: Ben Howard noted this quality in his review of *Presentation Piece,* which foreshadowed many concerns that she would develop and air later. He said that Hacker was "attempting to formulate . . . a language of instinct and feeling—of a woman's bodily awareness—and to express the body's longings" (*Poetry,* April 1975). Hacker's intention is to fuse tradition with a modern woman's psyche, played against the context of city streets and personal memories, and the result is distinctive verse, which relies on mythology, history, and fairy tales—especially from Hans Christian Andersen—for images and symbols that make the personal seem less so. To write her poems, however educated an imagination she has, Hacker relies ultimately on her own life for her subjects and nuances of feeling. Thus the poems are autobiographical without being confessional or self-absorbed.

Presentation Piece, because of its awards, was widely reviewed, and it firmly established Hacker's reputation as a technically acute writer, capable of mixing tightly structured free verse and traditional forms, including sonnets, villanelles, and sestinas. Unfortunately this book also prompted the beginning of critical descriptions such as "willful," "self-conscious," and even "strained," which would set a standard for comparison that would

Dust jacket for Hacker's 1986 novel in verse, which traces the course of a lesbian relationship

follow Hacker in reviews of later collections. But no one doubted that this was a poet with a real talent, even though a few critics remarked that the poems seemed at times to be too technically contrived. Howard first noted a tone of "incipient despair," too, which reviewers would find in *Separations*, though it wanes in *Taking Notice*. The poems in *Presentation Piece* contain Hacker's perennial topics—love, separation, and alienation—but what is most indicative of her contribution to contemporary poetry is the way she talks about these subjects. She forces the reader to consider different perspectives with poems such as "Elektra on Third Avenue," which juxtaposes the classical heroine with a contemporary urban scene described with the vernacular set in sonnet form:

I know you know I think your mouth is sweet
as anything exhibited for sale,
fresh coffee cake or boys fresh out of jail,
which tender hint of incest brings me near
to ordering more coffee or more beer.

Hacker's equating of life and language is seen in "Iceplants: Army Beach":

There is a poem in touching
or not touching. The poem
defines the tension between skin and skin,
increasing, decreasing, rhythmically
changing the space it defines.

This stanza is Hacker's way of saying, as she also does in the often-quoted "Untoward Occurrence at Embassy Poetry Reading," that her subjects choose her and not vice versa. Form grows out of what she has to say and helps to hold it. The images of the body, the harsh and honest sounds and words of common language, which are held by the form, and the sense of humor ensuring that disappointment never seems like despair constitute Hacker's mark.

Because *Separations* was published a year after Hacker won the National Book Award and received so many reviews, it met with a slightly biased reception, which led Hayden Carruth (*New York Times Book Review*, 8 August 1976) to insinuate that Hacker was riding on the recent glory, that the poems were the ones that may have been sifted out of the previous collection. A fairer assessment came from Stanley Plumly when *Taking Notice*, her next book, was published, and he noted that the first three seem to be a trilogy (*Washington Post Book World*, 2 November 1980). While still playful with her language and attitude, Hacker also deals with the topic of separation via death, distance, and abandonment in *Separations*. A tone of what reviewers termed disappointment, or what feminists might call just being realistic, was also noted. But her use of traditional form continued to provoke some reviewers, though not the readers who have helped Hacker to build a solid reputation. Reviewer Robert Holland's remarks illustrate the general critical stance: "All of this technical skill is in the service of a dark, somewhat sordid urban vision which is sometimes lightened, but more often further darkened, by love" (*Poetry*, February 1977). Holland's comment, however, says more about his school of criticism than it does about Hacker. William H. Pritchard (*Hudson Review*, Autumn 1976) noted Hacker's potential and addressed the feminist undertones. He analyzed the way in which personal history, poetic tradition, and modern times interact to create Hacker's verse. "Somewhere in a Turret" exemplifies this interaction:

Somewhere in a turret in time,
castled and catacombed in but

still on a tan street that
ends with a blue-and-white gingerbread house,
those rooms are still filled
with our pictures and books. On the sill
our black-and-white cat hums after a fly.
It is getting light. When we come in,
no one will ask you to leave, no one will send me
    away.

This softer tone foreshadows the poems in her next collection.

While reviewers were still too often counting the exact number of sonnets in Hacker's repertoire in *Taking Notice*, as well as calling one's attention to a pantoum and two canzones, they in general acknowledged that this collection showed that Hacker was growing in both intellect and soulfulness. Since several poems in this collection pertain to the emerging mother-daughter relationship and to a satisfying lesbian relationship, it would seem that Hacker was mellowing. As she grew in self-awareness through the writing of poems, the poems in turn grew richer and less arcane. Her tone softened, even hinted at joy. The highest praise for this collection came from Marilyn Krysl, who suggested that while the publication of this volume was "a significant event in the women's movement," the poems were "not so much about women as about living . . ." (*Frontiers*, Fall 1980). Reviews seemed to suggest that the breadth of Hacker's vision was increasing as her experiences gave her more depth of emotion and that her blend of formal structure and informal speech seemed less contrived and more natural.

The final section, twenty-five sonnets on the progress of a love affair between two women, laid the groundwork for *Love, Death, and the Changing of the Seasons* (1986) and also established Hacker as a passionate yet disciplined person who wrote best within the framework of the Petrarchan sonnet. Connecting the pieces of her life, the sonnets rely more on personal yet accessible imagery and less on classical references; the voice is conversational, intimate: "My child wants dolls, a tutu, that girls' world made / pretty and facile. Sometimes. Sometimes I / want you around uncomplicatedly." The connection in this sonnet between her daughter's innocence in wanting girls' things and her innocence as a new lover testing the waters shows that Hacker can use images from her personal life as easily as from mythology.

In her interview with Hammond, Hacker was adamant in stating, "I'm very uncomfortable with terms like 'bisexual' and 'androgynous.' They affirm, by implication, that certain qualities of mind or body are essentially female and that other qualities are essentially male, that there has to be a combination of the two in this special creature, the artist." This view of her sexuality is evident in *Assumptions* (1985). The poem "Graffitti in the Gare Saint-Manqué" is, as critic Reg Saner described it, witty and rueful, a "self-amused inventory of loneliness" (*Denver Quarterly*, Summer 1985):

Would it have saved Simone Weil's life to be
another Jewish Lesbian in France?

It isn't sex I mean. Sex doesn't save
anyone, except, sometimes, from boredom
(and the underpaid under-class of whoredom
is often bored at work).

Other questioning poems in this collection thus address the narrator's varying roles as mother, lover, daughter, feminist, lesbian, and Jew as she continues to search for her identity, not because she is "lost" but because life is a process of self-discovery. Kathleen Aguero notes that the book is "about bonds between women, about the intimate and sometimes painful ties between mothers and daughters and lovers, the more relaxed and nurturing ties of friendship, and the invigorating act of claiming ties with women from the past" (*Women's Review*, September 1985). Because of the interrelatedness of the concerns, Carole S. Oles commented that "the whole volume reads like a single poem" (*Nation*, 27 April 1985). Reviewers were seeing less of an annoying self-absorption, which they felt had led to opaque lines and allusions, and were commenting on Hacker's graceful introspection. J. D. McClatchy (*New York Times Book Review*, 26 May 1985) commented, "She is our latter-day Byron, and has made out of herself a personification of style in her formal verse and the witty fictiveness of her ideas. She dredges her romantic impulses with irony; however raw her subject, her tone is knowing and her technique has a tempering effect." With their readings of *Assumptions* critics were beginning to see what Hacker wanted to do with her fusion of traditional forms and feminist subject matter. Sandra M. Gilbert said, "What's wonderful—literally wonder-ful—about Hacker's new book is the way in which it challenges some of our most deep-rooted assumptions, most especially the assumption that (as some of the advocates of 'Feminitude' whom she attacks have ar-

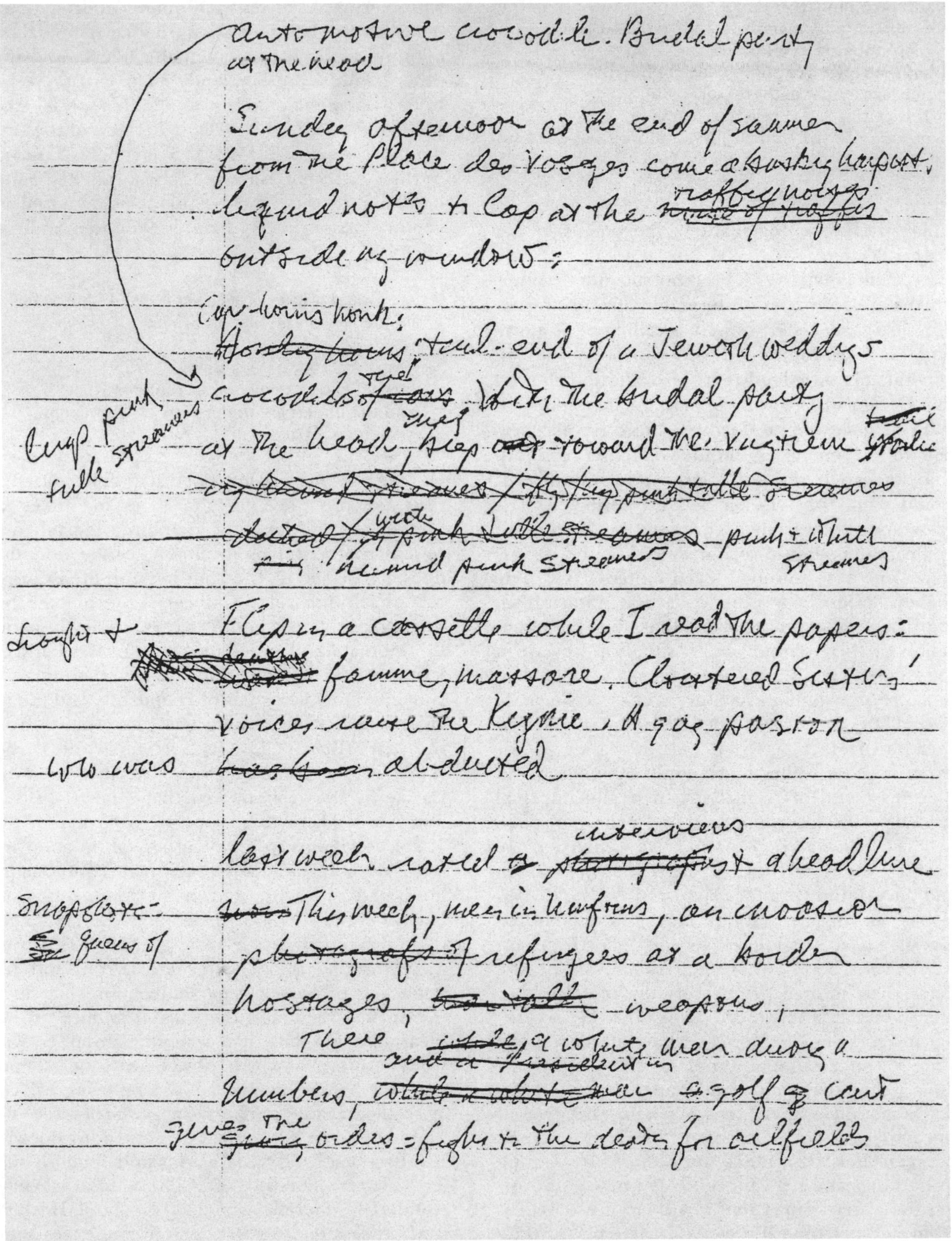
automotive crocodile. Bridal party
at the head

Sunday afternoon at the end of summer
from the Place des Vosges come a husky harpist,
liquid notes + Cop at the raffling noises
outside my window:

Car-horns honk:
~~Honking horns~~ tail-end of a Jewish wedding's
crocodile of ~~cars~~ with the bridal party
at the head, they step ~~out~~ toward the rue
~~streamers~~
~~pink tulle streamers~~ pink + white streamers
around pink streamers

long pink tulle streamers

Flips in a cassette while I read the papers:
famine, massacre. Cloistered Sisters'
voices raise the Kyrie. A gay pastor
who was ~~has been~~ abducted

last week rated ~~photographs~~ interviews + a headline
This week, men in keffiyehs, an incursion
~~photographs~~ of refugees at a border
hostages, weapons,
There's a white man among
numbers, a golf cart
gives the orders: fight to the death for oilfields

Snapshots:
queens of

Draft for a poem (by permission of Marilyn Hacker)

gued) if you're a sexual radical, you have to be an aesthetic radical" (*Poetry*, December 1985).

After the earlier interconnected poems, a volume that was best read as a whole long poem, *Love, Death, and the Changing of the Seasons*—called a novel in verse—seemed inevitable. This book, which relies on Hacker's most acclaimed form, the sonnet, traces one relationship. Although it was widely reviewed, Maria Margaronis (*Nation*, 27 December 1986) observed that the book did not receive as much public acclaim as it deserved because of the lesbian nature of the central relationship. Margaronis also reminded readers of Hacker's ability to write about love generally, though the focus is on women: "Everything that is in love has found its perfect shape here: longing and grief; jokes and tenderness; food, shopping, jealousy and sex." Though the affair fails, Hacker's intent is to reveal herself, not the failure. Mark Jarman (*Hudson Review*, Summer 1987) suggested that Hacker's achievement is in her revelation:

> First, I want to make you come in my hand
> while I watch you and kiss you, and if you cry,
> I'll drink your tears while, with my whole hand, I
> hold your drenched loveliness contracting. . . .

Adrian Oktenberg (*Women's Review*, March 1987) applauded both the narrative and the "high art," commenting on Hacker's ties to William Shakespeare: "Like Shakespeare, she plunges into the thick of life and love." Carol Muske (*New York Times Book Review*, 13 June 1987) summed up her reaction with this sentence: "She's colloquial, lyrical, uncouth, old-fashioned, and fun." Hacker has achieved with this collection, it seems, the fusion of form and content that, in its more developmental form, sometimes so distracted reviewers in earlier poems.

Judith Barrington, however, did not see Hacker's formalism as purely traditional: "When those who are marginal turn to traditional forms, they stand in a different relationship to the literary history which has birthed and nurtured those forms" (*Women's Review*, July 1990). Calling Hacker a radical formalist, Barrington sees her work in perspective and suggests that technique overshadows content only rarely in Hacker's early work and not at all in *Going Back to the River* (1990), the volume before *The Hang-Glider's Daughter: New and Selected Poems* (1990). The poems in *Going Back to the River* again fuse formal structure with Hacker's personal tone and subject mat-

ter, and again address ties to places, people, partner, daughter, and writing. The contemplative title poem, in one section, has the poet addressing herself:

> What do I tell myself when I open and
> write in the notebook keeping me company?
>   Don't stay indoors tomorrow morning.
>   Do the week's shopping at Sunday market.
>
> Go to the river, take what it offers you.
> When you were young, it guarded and promised
>   you
>   that you would follow other rivers
>   oceans away from a landlocked childhood.

Along with the distances (from childhood, from the Hudson, from her lover) the narrator mentions, readers see the stability of everyday rituals helping to lend identity.

Whereas Hacker's early quest for identity through her poetry was distinguished at times by a tone of vulnerability or disappointment, however buffered by Hacker's wry wit and occasional humor, her vision has further mellowed, and one can see in the poetry a reflection of the growth of the woman. It is ironic, and intentional, that the title *Love, Death, and the Changing of the Seasons* hearkens back to the earlier "Untoward Occurrence at Embassy Poetry Reading":

>   My poetry
> is what it is. Graves, yes, said love, death
> and the changing of the seasons
> were the unique, the primordial subjects.
> I'd like to talk about that. One subjects
> oneself to art, not necessarily pleased
> to be a colander for myths.

From the early, sometimes self-conscious exercises to the later work, Hacker has emerged as a poet who confronts both literary tradition and feminist revisions of the tradition. Both belittled and praised for her allegiance to standard poetic forms, she has followed her voice. Despite her radical feminism, however, her poetry has eluded some mainstream feminist critics, who find little or nothing to say about Hacker as they write their history of today's poetry. But Hacker's poems suggest that she eschews the critics. As Krysl observed in her review of *Taking Notice*, after noting Hacker's technical acuity, "Probably the other most important characteristic she possesses . . . is a discerning eye for the truth, however unpleasant, however against the grain, however out of vogue." While meriting generally positive comments, this independent poet has also provoked some reviewers, who admire her use of form but find her choice of subject matter too arcane, indelicate, or harsh. Rising above this type of criticism, and meriting more and more consistently positive remarks, Hacker has continued to write, to be widely published and widely anthologized—in, for example, the second edition of *The Norton Anthology of Modern Poetry* (1988).

Interviews:

An Interview with Marilyn Hacker [recording], Washington, D.C., Feminist Radio Network, 197-?;

Karla Hammond, "An Interview with Marilyn Hacker," *Frontiers: A Journal of Women's Studies*, 5 (Fall 1980): 22-27.

Rachel Hadas
(8 November 1948 -   )

Robert McPhillips
Iona College

BOOKS: *Starting from Troy* (Boston: Godine, 1975);

Slow Transparency (Middletown, Conn.: Wesleyan University Press, 1983);

Form, Cycle, Infinity: Landscape Imagery in the Poetry of Robert Frost and George Seferis (Lewisburg, Pa.: Bucknell University Press / London & Toronto: Associated University Presses, 1985);

A Son from Sleep (Middletown, Conn.: Wesleyan University Press, 1987);

Pass It On (Princeton, N.J.: Princeton University Press, 1989);

Living in Time (New Brunswick, N.J.: Rutgers University Press, 1990);

Unending Dialogue: Voices from an AIDS Poetry Workshop, by Hadas and others (Boston & London: Faber & Faber, 1991);

Mirrors of Astonishment (New Brunswick, N.J.: Rutgers University Press, 1992).

OTHER: Stephanos Xenos, *Trelles (Follies)*, translated, with an afterword, by Hadas (Athens, Greece: Privately published, 1978);

Saturday's Women, edited by Hadas, Charlotte Mandell, and Maxine Silverman (Upper Montclair, N.J.: Saturday, 1982);

Alan Ansen, *Contact Highs: Selected Poems, 1957-1987*, includes an afterword, "Fructifying a Cycle," by Hadas (Elmwood Park, Ill.: Dalkey Archive, 1989).

SELECTED PERIODICAL PUBLICATIONS—
UNCOLLECTED: "A Reading of *The Sacrifice of Abraham*," *Byzantine and Modern Greek Studies*, 6 (1980): 43-59;

"Enjoying the Funeral: Constantine Caryotakis," *Grand Street*, 3 (Autumn 1983): 153-160;

"Upon Foreign Verse: Translation and Tradition," *Translation Review*, 11 (1983): 31-36;

"The Mystic Vision of James Merrill," *Religion and Literature*, 16 (Autumn 1984): 85-92;

"Spleen à la Grecque: Karyotakis and Baudelaire," *Journal of Modern Greek Studies*, 3 (May 1985): 21-27;

"Morose Confusion," *Kenyon Review*, new series 13 (Spring 1991): 149-153;

"The Ark of What Has Been: Elegiac Thoughts on Poetry," *AWP Chronicle*, 23 (May 1991): 1, 7-12;

"Visiting Schools," *Partisan Review*, 58 (Fall 1991): 713-716.

Rachel Hadas, a poet, translator, essayist, critic, and professor of literature, grew up in an environment on the Upper West Side of Manhattan contiguous to Columbia University and connected with the generation of New York intellectuals that largely dominated the American literary

Rachel Hadas

and political scene from the 1930s through the 1960s and continues to be influential three decades hence. Yet Hadas experienced an unusual journey from Radcliffe and Harvard in the 1960s to her emergence in the 1980s, with five published books of poetry (some mixed with prose), as perhaps the most prolific poet among the New Formalists—a categorization about which she has expressed, like most of the poets connected with the movement, a decided ambivalence in essays in both the *Kenyon Review* and *AWP Chronicle*. Instead of proceeding directly to graduate school to study either classics or creative writing, Hadas spent much of her twenties married to a Greek, living with him on the island of Samos, running an olive-oil press, and being tried for and acquitted of arson in connection with the press's mysterious destruction.

Rachel Chamberlayne Hadas was born on 8 November 1948 in New York City and was the daughter of Moses Hadas, a Columbia University classical scholar and professor, and Elizabeth

Chamberlayne Hadas, Moses's second wife—a former student of his and later a teacher of Latin at the Spence School in Manhattan. Rachel attended the Riverdale Country Day School in the Bronx, where she began her study of Latin. Though her father was to die when Rachel was seventeen, she read Latin texts with him while she was in high school, and he was to become a considerable posthumous influence on her work, as can be seen in her 1989 collection, *Pass It On,* about the various forms in which one generation influences another. Her father also taught her the Greek alphabet, which facilitated her study of that language when she matriculated at Radcliffe College in fall 1965. Hadas majored in classics and was elected to Phi Beta Kappa during her junior year. At Harvard she took her only poetry-writing course as an undergraduate with Robert Fitzgerald, the poet and classicist who taught such other poets as Robert B. Shaw, Katha Pollitt, Brad Leithauser, Mary Jo Salter, and Dana Gioia. Hadas was the poetry editor of the *Harvard Advocate* during her senior year (1968-1969).

After graduating magna cum laude with a B.A., Hadas made her first extended visit to Greece in fall 1969 under the auspices of an Isobel M. Briggs Travelling Fellowship. With the assistance of a letter of recommendation from John Hollander, a former student of her father's at Columbia, Hadas made the acquaintance of such American poets in Athens as James Merrill, Chester Kallman (at whose home Hadas met W. H. Auden), and Alan Ansen. It was through Ansen, a homosexual poet whose mentors were Auden and William S. Burroughs, that Hadas met her first husband, Stavros Kondylis, a houseguest of Ansen's whom she married in November 1970. As recounted in her essay, "Mornings in Ormos," included in *Living in Time* (1990), these three constituted an unusual love triangle: both Ansen and Hadas were in love with Stavros, a blond "Greek peasant who had, as they say, finished fourth grade"; and Hadas was attracted to both—to Ansen primarily as a paternal mentor, to Stavros by desire. "And Stavros—did he love us both? Or was he just innocently, or not so innocently, enamored of being in love?" These are questions Hadas is unable to answer. Both men proposed to Hadas—Ansen with the goals both to have a child and to return as a "respectable" figure to the expatriate American community in Venice, "the city which he said had expelled him in the wake of a homosexual scandal"—but she chose the young Greek, with whom she returned to the United States for a while before taking up residence on the Greek isle of Samos from 1971 to 1975.

This residence in Greece forms the background and subject matter for most of the poems of two apprentice volumes—her chapbook *Starting from Troy* (1975) and the book-length *Slow Transparency* (1983). Despite the rich emotional background and the vividly beautiful landscape that ground these poems, as well as Hadas's obvious intelligence and her technical proficiency with a variety of meters and verse forms, neither volume is fully successful in exploiting these resources. Amid many dazzling shards of Aegean imagery and pleasingly musical phrases, the reader remains somewhat uncertain about the point of many of these poems. The literary references are often oblique, primarily to classical literature, as would befit her landscape, but to English and continental literature as well. Her frequent use of foreign words in her poems—particularly Greek ones—can also create a barrier for a contemporary audience unlikely to share Hadas's training in classical languages and comparative literature.

Happily, this does not apply to all of the earlier poems in these two volumes. "Sappho, Keats," in *Starting from Troy*, is one of her more successful and appealing "literary" poems:

> The girls in Lesbos have dark eyes
> And scorn to play their natural role.
> Flowers don't photosynthesize
> On beach and field there, blooming damp
> And rich in moonlight. Mushroom-pale
> They must have been, but Sappho saw
> What flowers blossomed at her feet.

A similarly effective literary poem from Hadas's first volume is "Daughters and Others," an examination of literary women—Zelda Fitzgerald, Lucia Joyce, and Sylvia Plath—who defined their identities against those of their successful fathers or husbands. Given the relationship with her own father, Hadas feels an affinity toward these women even as she criticizes them sarcastically:

> What stern, indulgent wraith will be on hand
> to scold and slap and kiss you afterwards?
> They buried father, but he's not dead.
> He's watching us all.

These final two lines, attributed to Lucia Joyce, the Irish novelist's mad daughter, serve as an ele-

giac refrain throughout the poem, undercutting its sarcasm and making it a moving tribute to Hadas's own father. It is a refrain that will reverberate throughout her subsequent poetry.

Memories—of dead fathers, of landscapes inhabited, and of books read—become a central theme in *Slow Transparency*, a focus also seen in her more recent work. In the rather obscure but melodious title of this volume's third section—"Locked in an Aorist Amber"—Hadas refers to the ability to freeze time, preserve it as in amber.

Slow Transparency is dedicated to George Edwards, Hadas's second husband, a composer and professor of music at Columbia University, whom she married on 22 July 1978, shortly after her divorce from Stavros. Between the publication of her first book in 1975 and her second in 1983, Hadas studied at the writing workshop at Johns Hopkins, from which she received her M.A. in poetry in 1977. Among her fellow student-poets there were Tom Sleigh, Molly Peacock, and Phillis Levin. She went on to the doctoral program in comparative literature at Princeton University, where, under the guidance of Robert Fagles and Edmund Keeley, she wrote her dissertation on Robert Frost and George Seferis. A revised version of this dissertation, *Form, Cycle, Infinity: Landscape Imagery in the Poetry of Robert Frost and George Seferis,* was published in 1985. She received her Ph.D. in 1982. Since 1981 she has taught at Rutgers University—Newark, where she is currently an associate professor of English. She lives on the Upper West Side of Manhattan and, during the summer, in St. Johnsbury, Vermont.

Hadas's third poetry collection, *A Son from Sleep,* published in 1987, is dedicated to her son, Jonathan, born on 4 February 1984, and he is the subject of many of the poems in this volume. Indeed, as motherhood and domesticity have become more central to Hadas's work, her poetry has become notably more accessible linguistically and more emotionally direct and engaging than her sophisticated but often opaque apprentice work. Still, in this transitional volume—its first few poems return to Greece for their setting—Hadas has not fully come into her own as a poet. In addition to introducing such domestic subject matter as breast-feeding, this book is notable for two long poems written in numbered sections; such poems become increasingly characteristic in Hadas's subsequent books. The better of the two long poems is "That Walk Away as One: A Marriage Brood," a ten-part meditation on marriage, inspired by a random comment—"*Married? some-*

how you don't / look married." The poem concludes its largely free-verse "brood" upon being married with these lines:

> This walking arm in arm in harmony
> having come from separate directions—
> this is marriage too. It looks so easy
> and is perhaps so easy and is not.
> It always is a gift.
> It gives a form to life
> perhaps invisibly. I don't look married.

Another theme that emerges in *A Son from Sleep,* in "The Cistern," is the connection between the intellectual nourishment Hadas still receives from memories of her late father and the physical nourishment she provides for her son through her body. This theme receives its most powerful development in Hadas's fourth volume of poems, *Pass It On.* This volume, her strongest collection of poems to date, fully consolidates the potential only sporadically on view in her earlier books. Not only is it a completely unified volume focused on the various ways life and knowledge are passed down from generation to generation— from parents to children, from teachers to students, from books in general, and through the writing of poems—it also makes clear that Hadas's greatest strengths as a poet are less apparent in individual lyrics than they are in the larger units of poetic sequences and in full-length books.

Pass It On is divided into three sections, the first a seasonal cycle recounting a sabbatical year, partly spent in her family's summer home in Vermont, partly in Manhattan. The poems in this section—as in the other two—are extended lyrics that, taken as a whole, constitute a meditative narrative more coherent than those in *A Son from Sleep.* Hadas's return to conventional meter and rhyme add to the increased clarity and verbal richness. The third poem, "Fix It (Winter)," comprises seven numbered sections, in a variety of meters and stanzaic forms, from unrhymed, loosely iambic pentameter couplets, to rhymed trimeter quatrains and pentameter tercets. It juxtaposes a broken string of the speaker's agates with her son's demands upon his mother to "fix" the world, in the double sense of putting what is broken (a balloon or the moon) back together and in stabilizing the world through language:

> I lean my ladder on
> the beautiful, the flawed

Dust jacket for Hadas's 1990 book, which includes "The Dream Machine," a poem that has been compared to William Wordsworth's Prelude *and Samuel Taylor Coleridge's conversation poems because of Hadas's speculations on psychology, art, and metaphysics*

> handiwork of God
> and turn to spy my son
>
> busy way down there
> patching a balloon,
> filling in the moon.
> The whole world needs repair.

Perhaps the most effective poem in the first sequence, however, is its penultimate one, "Hortus Conclusus (Spring)," which recounts, primarily in rhymed couplets, the narrator's morning stroll with a friend through upper Manhattan, "Each [with her] bestrollered son / (Jonathan at two, Sam at one)."

The poems in the second, untitled section focus less on mortality than on passing down tradition from generation to generation, in this case literary tradition. Hadas shows she has inherited her father's professorial role, teaching Homer, Sophocles, and Emily Dickinson to her students.

Yet the finest poem in this section, "Teacher between Terms," is not about teaching any particular text but instead about the emotions of a professor when she is not teaching. Assuring a hypothetical class in revery between terms that "I'm [not] here to bore you," she argues,

> If from my fragile perch I seem ridiculous,
> remember that my task's to give a clue,
> some clue you can remember, to a past
> you never knew, spectacular and vast,
> and also to a future that I pray
> we'll live to taste. Life's not one dull day.

This poem is one of Hadas's most sustained individual lyrics.

The final section of *Pass It On* is similar to the first, this time recounting a summer in Vermont, specifically "Our son's first summer here." Hadas is better at dramatizing the domestic details of motherhood than in *A Son from Sleep,* as in these lines from "Three Silences": "Of all the times when not to speak is best, / mother's and infant's is the easiest, / the milky mouth still warm against her breast." In general, the more Hadas relies on strict meter and rhyme, the more controlled and effective her poems.

In 1990 Hadas won an award in literature from the American Academy and Institute of Arts and Letters. That same year, her *Living in Time* was published. This volume marks an innovative expansion from *Pass It On* while taking up many of the same themes. A long meditative poem on the poetic imagination, among other things—teaching, reading, mothering—forms the central "panel" of a literary triptych, whose first and third panels show her meditating on the same subjects in prose. The central panel, "The Dream Machine," is Hadas's version of William Wordsworth's *The Prelude* (1850). Among contemporary poems, the one it most brings to mind is Alfred Corn's book-length *Notes from a Child of Paradise* (1984). Corn, in his review of *Living in Time* (*Poetry,* December 1991), considered it "a reckonable beginning, *mutatis mutandis,* to her own *biographica literaria,*" and he wrote the most extensive discussion of "The Dream Machine," likening it to Samuel Taylor Coleridge's "conversation poems," rather than to Wordsworth's work, "where the author postulates a readership interested in psychological, aesthetic, and metaphysical speculation." Much of Hadas's own speculation, as Corn noted, is brought about by her son's persistent questions about the nature of reality, dreams, and language (as in *Pass It On*). Many

of the themes of "The Dream Machine" coalesce in the thirteenth section, "Our Need for Stories": "as we old hands need reminding, / stories, whether true or not, are hints, / clues, sources, charts to an unknown domain."

"The Dream Machine" concludes on a strong note in its final section, "The Way We Live Now." This title is the same as that of a Susan Sontag short story on AIDS, and the section opens with the narrator listening to Sontag read the story about a group of friends drawn to the room of a friend dying of AIDS. The friends are unable adequately to verbalize an understanding either of AIDS or of their sense of loss. Hadas has, in fact, run a poetry workshop for People with AIDS (PWA) at Manhattan's Gay Men's Health Crisis (GMHC) since the spring of 1988, with the exception of the 1988-1989 academic year, during which she had a Guggenheim Fellowship. Listening to Sontag's story reminds Hadas of her own difficulty in dealing with the imminent death of one of her students: "Alas, the task of making up a story / and telling it to someone close to death / proves not to be an easy one. . . ."

"Elegy Variations" is one of the strongest of Hadas's sixteen poems growing out of her GMHC experience; these poems, along with her prose commentary, make up a major portion (section 3) of *Unending Dialogue: Voices from an AIDS Poetry Workshop* (1991). The first section is "The Lights Must Never Go Out," her essay that begins with a meditation on the "endless acronyms" associated with AIDS. The middle section contains forty-five poems by members of the workshop. However, the success of such a poem as "Elegy Variations" aside—nicely controlled and poised—does not fully salvage the volume. Hadas's recycling of earlier material, as well as images and lines in her own poems from those of her students, may well test the patience of readers of her previous volumes. One senses, too, in this volume, as in her first few, that Hadas has not yet mastered this new material and has perhaps published it too hastily. Yet the bitter irony this observation drives home is that Hadas—as she proves herself aware in "The Way We Live Now"—will have time to polish her perceptions and poems, a luxury unshared by her HIV-infected students.

Indeed, despite her facility with meter and fixed forms, one senses that Hadas has not fully achieved closure in her work; her six books read like a poem in the process of being written, just as readers experience, through them, her life in the process of being lived. Those who have read *Pass It On* and *Living in Time,* in particular, will look forward to the continuation of the poem that is her life in her subsequent work, including her next collection of poetry, *Mirrors of Astonishment* (1992). These poems—including "Genealogy," a long meditation on her father as teacher, which appeared in the fall 1990 issue of *Verse* (devoted to the New Formalism)—return to her thematic preoccupations, particularly "passing it on," both through the body and literature, and the question of time and mortality. Hadas has also recently completed a translation of Seneca's *Oedipus* and almost completed a book of translations of Charles Baudelaire's poetry.

Both her craft and her intelligence promise that she will continue to engage an audience. However, in his discussion of Hadas's moving among several genres—from prose to lengthy meditative verse to shorter, self-contained lyrics in *Living in Time*—Corn perceptively observed that, while these lyrics, in context, constitute "a finished, glazed ware," they "probably wouldn't carry so far if taken in isolation." The most interesting aesthetic question that Rachel Hadas poses at this point in her career is whether she will remain content to write a continuous, absorbing, albeit sometimes vexingly repetitious poetry, or whether she will work more rigorously at polishing her lyrics. One would feel more certain about her ultimate permanence as a poet if she selected the latter path, though Hadas's talent is obviously substantial.

Reference:
Christopher Benfey, "From the Greek," *Parnassus: Poetry in Review,* 16 (Summer 1991): 405-415.

Joy Harjo

(9 May 1951 -   )

C. Renee Field
Lamar University

BOOKS: *The Last Song* (Las Cruces, N.M.: Puerto Del Sol, 1975);

What Moon Drove Me to This? (New York: Reed, 1979);

She Had Some Horses, edited by Brenda Peterson (New York: Thunder's Mouth, 1983);

Secrets from the Center of the World, by Harjo and Stephen Strom (Tucson: Sun Tracks / University of Arizona Press, 1989);

In Mad Love and War (Middletown, Conn.: Wesleyan University Press, 1990).

RECORDING: *Furious Light*, Washington, D.C., Watershed, 1986.

To read the poetry of Joy Harjo is to hear the voice of the earth, to see the landscape of time and timelessness, and, most important, to get a glimpse of people who struggle to understand, to know themselves, and to survive. As Harjo has continued to refine her craft, her poems have become visions, answers to age-old questions, keys to understanding the complex nature of twentieth-century American life, and guides to the past and the future.

The daughter of Allen W. and Wynema Baker Foster, Joy Harjo was born in Tulsa, Oklahoma, and is an enrolled member of the Creek tribe; when she was sixteen, she moved to the Southwest to attend the Institute of American Indian Arts. She graduated from the University of New Mexico with a B.A. in poetry in 1976. She received her M.F.A. in creative writing from the University of Iowa in 1978, after which she taught for a few years at the Institute of American Indian Arts, Arizona State University, and the University of Colorado, before joining the English faculty at the University of New Mexico in 1990. She has two children: Phil and Rainy Dawn.

Harjo has published five books of poetry; in addition, though, she is accomplished in several other areas. She has many screenwriting credits, including teleplays, public service announcements, and public broadcasting/educational televi-

sion work. In 1986 the tape *Furious Light* was released, consisting of Harjo reading selected poems backed by musical accompaniment. Harjo has also edited several literary journals, including the *High Plains Literary Review*, and is currently a contributing editor for *Tyuonyi* and *Contact II*.

Frequently anthologized, Harjo's work is reaching a broader audience every year, helped in part by her extensive travels to do readings, workshops, and literary festivals. She is the recipient of several awards, including the American Book Award from the Before Columbus Foundation, the Poetry Society of America's William Carlos Williams Award, and the American Indian Distinguished Achievement Award, as well as other grants and fellowships, including a National Endowment for the Arts Fellowship in 1978.

Harjo is very active in her profession, having served on several advisory panels, including the Native American Public Broadcasting Consortium Board of Directors, the New Mexico Arts Commission, and an NEA literature policy panel, among others. She has extensive teaching experience at the postsecondary level and is currently a full professor at the University of New Mexico. She has been writer in residence at several institutions, including the University of Montana and the State University of New York at Stony Brook. Harjo has also been very active in the Artists-in-the-Schools programs. One of Harjo's other passions is music, especially the tenor sax and flute, and she currently plays in a rock band, a big band, and a jazz band.

Harjo is at work on several projects, including a collection of poetic prose called "The Field of Miracles" and an anthology of native women's writing in the Americas titled "Reinventing the Enemy's Language." She has had a children's book, "The Good Luck Cat," accepted for publication by Harcourt Brace Jovanovich. Much like the characters in her poems, Harjo's poetry is always evolving, always moving, and becoming more universal over time. Harjo is a Native American, and while it is not advisable to lock any author into

Joy Harjo (photograph by Robyn Stoutenburg)

an ethnic box, her heritage does figure, either directly or indirectly, in her poetry. Being an American Indian carries with it a dual perception of the world, and much of Harjo's poetry deals with the often tenuous relationship between that which is "American" and that which is "Indian." Native American symbols and ideas are important to Harjo, but she writes of these in relation to the larger world they inhabit. Many of Harjo's poems are set in cities, airports, and bars, where the "traditional" Indian ways run head-on into the white establishment, often with devastating results, always with a profound truth coming out of the encounter. The desire for harmony and balance is a distinct undercurrent in Harjo's poetry, as she skillfully creates sense out of apparent chaos.

Harjo's first collection of poetry was a nine-poem chapbook called *The Last Song*. It was published in 1975, and most of the poems are set in ei-

ther Oklahoma or New Mexico. The poems are often linked to the landscape and to the idea of survival, and though the poems have a definite modern feel, their roots in the red-dirt country of Oklahoma are obvious. Harjo lived in Oklahoma for several years and remembers the red earth vividly; as she told Geary Hobson: "When I was a little kid in Oklahoma, I would get up before everyone else and go outside to a place of rich, dark earth next to the foundation of the house. I would dig piles of earth with a stick, smell it, form it. It had sound. Maybe that's where I learned to write poetry" (*The Remembered Earth*, 1979). Though Harjo no longer lives in Oklahoma, she retains ties to it, familial and otherwise, which are clear in the title poem "The Last Song":

it is the only way
i know how to breathe
an ancient chant

that my mother knew
came out of history
woven from wet grass
in her womb
and I know no other way
than to surround my voice
with the summer songs of crickets
in this moist south night air

oklahoma will be the last song
i'll ever sing.

The red soil is the source of the ancient songs, of history. Hobson points out that most of Harjo's poetry does not focus specifically on her Creek heritage and speculates that the lines "oklahoma will be the last song / i'll ever sing" may be a "promise of the theme Harjo will turn to in time." In any case, Harjo's deep connection with and understanding of the land are established in her first volume.

Also established in *The Last Song* is the previously mentioned balance between contemporary American life and ancient tribal truths, as articulated in "3AM":

in the albuquerque airport
trying to find a flight
to old oraibi, third mesa
TWA
            is the only desk open
bright lights outline new york
                        chicago
and the attendant doesn't know
that third mesa
is part of the center
of the world
and who are we
just two indians
at three in the morning
trying to find a way back[.]

Harjo keeps her origins close to her, and they inspire her, whether or not they appear in the poetry. Her Creek ancestors helped lead the resistance during the time of President Andrew Jackson's removal of the Creeks from Alabama to Oklahoma.

Harjo's second published work and first full-length collection is *What Moon Drove Me to This?* (1979). All of the poems from the earlier chapbook appear, as well as many new ones. With this collection, Harjo continued to refine her ability to find and voice the deep spiritual truths underneath everyday experiences, especially for the Native American. Often these truths are revealed

through bitter anger and irony, as in "Blackbirds":

The United States Army says
it knows how to kill
a million blackbirds.

Blackbird lives are easy—
bones and black feathers
scatter in the wind
over Kentucky.
(A blue sky stained with feathers and blood.)

But the United States Army
doesn't know
that every blackbird has a thousand lives.

Harjo has the ability to look beneath the surface and then to articulate this vision. Her native tradition provides her a storehouse of images on which to draw, and her poetry is filled with the perception of woman as earth, people as horses, and wind as mother. This fusion of myth and tradition gives Harjo a rich source for her figurative language and her readers a deep and clear look straight into the center of existence. In this poetry, everything has its own identity and connection to the larger web of life.

In Harjo's poetry a harmonious balance is achieved through the careful juxtaposition of past and present, of mythic and mundane. In "For Two Hundred Years" this relationship is clear:

You were drunk that time
Over at the powwow grounds
Dust and Spit
Flew from the corners of your mouth.
. . . .
Chino said it was time to go
But you wanted to stay 200 years
With one afternoon.

Harjo is also good at articulating the experiences of the individual, especially of women. In "Fire," the ideas of female harmony and balance come through clear and strong:

look at me
i am not a separate woman
i am a continuance
of blue sky
i am the throat
of the sandia mountains[.]

In Harjo's 1979 book readers are also introduced to Noni Daylight, an alter ego, a personality who can move with ease among the mythic, the concrete, the past, the present, and the future. Noni began as a real-life friend whose name Harjo could not use in the poem. Readers first meet Noni as she attempts suicide, then they travel with her on many journeys, including one to the Grand Canyon, in "Origin":

> Noni Daylight . . . drove west
> into the shiny side of the earth. . . .
> Noni heard
> that the Hopi say the Grand Canyon
> is the birthplace of their people. . . .

In "Evidence" Noni takes the speaker for a ride in which they drive off into a great unknown. The narrator's desire to get out of this layer of life is united with Noni's ability to take her to a different level. In Noni's world the boundaries of time and space mean nothing.

Another frequently occurring image in Harjo's poetry is the moon. It becomes something of a private symbol for her and appears often in her early poems as lover, guide, light, and woman. In "Going Toward Pojoaque, A December Full Moon/72," the moon is spirit, predator, and revealer:

> it is a winter ghost
> hunter
> for old bones in the snow
> the full moon
> was so bright
> I could see the bones
> in my hands.

In "Looking Back," the full moon is, as the speaker says, "a good excuse for anything." By following the moon, the speaker ends up driving ninety miles an hour "into its yellow shoulder / not even looking back." The moon is a guide, a beacon to higher meaning and experience, or as critic Jim Ruppert calls it, an entrance into "mythic space."

Harjo's next volume of work, *She Had Some Horses*, was published in 1983 and is, at this writing, in its eighth printing. In this collection Harjo synthesizes many of the ideas and images established in her earlier work into a well-defined whole. The thrust is freedom and empowerment, mainly accomplished through self-knowledge and the letting go of fear. The book has a circular structure, for which Harjo credits editor Brenda Peterson. The book opens with "Call it Fear":

> There is this edge where shadows
> and bones of some of us walk
> > > backwards
> Talk backwards. There is this edge
> call it an ocean of fear in the dark. Or
> name it with other songs.

Once the fear is named, it can be dealt with, and it is, in the poems that follow. The volume is full of poems that name fears, claim power, and thus increase the chances of surviving a world of paradox and polarity. The polarity of life in the modern world sits in direct opposition to the Native American concept of harmony and balance. In "For Alva Benson, and for Those Who Have Learned to Speak," the ideas of the cyclical nature of birth, death, and life are articulated:

> And we go on, keep giving birth and watch
> ourselves die, over and over.
> And the ground spinning beneath us
> goes on talking.

The idea of survival is central to Harjo's work, both survival of the individual and of Native Americans as a people. In "The Woman Hanging from the Thirteenth Floor Window," an Indian woman hangs from a window ledge, contemplating suicide. Harjo makes the experience universal—the woman hanging there could be Anywoman. As readers near the end of the poem, they can imagine themselves hanging there, weighing options:

> The woman hangs from the 13th floor window crying for
> the lost beauty of her own life. She sees the
> sun falling west over the grey plane of Chicago.
> She thinks she remembers listening to her own life
> > break loose, as she falls from the 13th floor
> window on the east side of Chicago, or as she
> climbs back up to herself again.

Horses also figure prominently in Harjo's work, becoming another symbol. This volume is filled with horses: prehistoric horses, and black horses, blue horses, running horses, drowning horses, and ice horses. The title poem, "She Had Some Horses," is one of Harjo's most anthologized and recognized works. It is a beautiful, chantlike poem, and, upon hearing Harjo read the poem, one becomes entranced:

> She had horses who danced in their mothers' arms.
> She had horses who thought they were the sun and

their bodies shone and burned like stars.
She had horses who waltzed nightly on the
     moon....
She had horses who liked Creek Stomp Dance
     songs.
She had horses who cried in their beer....
She had horses who said they weren't afraid.
She had horses who lied.

Harjo says this is the one poem about which she is asked most often, yet it is the one about which she has "the least to say." The horses are representative, she says, of "different aspects of probably any person...." The horses are spirits, neither male nor female, and, through them, clear truths can be articulated.

She Had Some Horses is dedicated to Meridel LeSeur, a writer Harjo credits as "having a lot of influence on me in terms of being a woman who speaks as a woman.... She kept to her particular viewpoint ... and has often been criticized for it" (interview with Joseph Bruchac, Spring 1985). Harjo's women are strong, no matter what their situation. They may not have the answers, but they have within them the power to find them. Even the woman hanging from the window ledge is not weak. Harjo told Brucac: "I think they reach an androgynous kind of spirit where they are very strong people. They're very strong people, and yet to be strong does not mean to be male, to be strong does not mean to lose femininity, which is what the dominant culture has taught. They're human beings ... it's time to break the stereotypes."

She Had Some Horses ends where it began. In "I Give You Back," Harjo releases the fear that she articulated in the first poem. The ritual, chantlike nature of the poem acts as a kind of exorcism of fear, and the poem goes beyond the letting go of fear to taking power over it:

I release you ...
I take myself back, fear.
You are not my shadow any longer.
I won't hold you in my hands.

In 1989 Joy Harjo collaborated with Stephen Strom on the critically acclaimed *Secrets from the Center of the World*. Strom's photographs of Navajo country, the Four Corners area, are accompanied by Harjo's prose poetry. Critic Luci Tapahanso calls it "a powerful combination ... rare beauty all at once: songs of birth, love, history, and the land—which is our life" (dust jacket). Harjo's work is very much earth-

centered: "My house is the red earth; it could be the center of the world." It goes beyond mere description of the land, past the boundaries of space and time to higher truths. Eventually, the poetry and the land become one, true to the cyclic, harmonious nature of Native American thought: "This land is a poem of ochre and burnt sand I could never write, unless paper were the sacrament of the sky, and ink the broken line of wild horses staggering the horizon several miles away."

The leap from *She Had Some Horses* to *In Mad Love and War* (1990) is a long one. The poems in the latter are rich and varied, drawing on many different areas. Harjo's Native American voice is still present: images such as deer, laughing birds, the "language of lizards and storms," trickster crows, and rabbits inhabit the pages. But Harjo moves beyond these symbols and traditions, detailing lives and deaths of dreamers, who failed because of circumstances or violence: "the man from Jemez" huddled in a blanket in the snow who mistakes the narrator for his daughter ("Autograph"); civil-rights activist Jacqueline Peters hanged by the Klan in an olive tree ("Strange Fruit"). One of the most moving poems in the book is "For Anna Mae Pictou Aquash, Whose Spirit is Present Here and in the Dappled Stars...." Aquash was a young Micmac woman, an active American Indian Movement member who was murdered for her work:

Anna Mae,
          everything and nothing changes.
You are the shimmering young woman
          who found her voice
when you were warned to be silent....
          (It was the women who told me) and we
     understood
                              wordlessly
          the ripe meaning of your murder.

Harjo's narrators are strong and insightful. In "Javelina" the speaker stands squarely as "one born of a blood who wrestled the whites for freedom, and I have since lived dangerously in a diminished system." Reviewer Leslie Ullman calls Harjo "a storyteller whose stories resurrect memory, myth, and private struggles that have been overlooked and who thus restores vitality to the culture at large" (*Kenyon Review*, Spring 1991). These storytelling skills are honed and heightened by Harjo's sensitivity to the natural order and balance of the world and to the history, past and recent, which has violated that order. The rest of the title of the "Aquash" poem reads: "for we remember the story and tell it again so that we may all live."

This sensitivity carries over into other issues. There are several poems in the "Wars" section that deal with Nicaragua, including "Resurrection": "I have no damned words to make violence fit neatly / like wrapped packages / of meat to contain us safely."

Some critics chide Harjo for being too "politically correct," of carrying a banner for too many causes, and, at first reading, that may seem true. However, Harjo writes of war, peace, native concerns, economics, crime, poverty, love, hate, revolution, and death—all universal themes and all of concern to a Native American woman living in the late twentieth century. She does not tell her reader how to feel but simply tells the truth she sees. Harjo's poetry is not so much about "correctness" as it is about continuance and survival.

Besides social concerns, much of Harjo's poetry contains music imagery, probably because of her growing interest in and connection to jazz. Billie Holiday, John Coltrane, Charlie "Bird" Parker, Nat King Cole, and Aretha Franklin are all featured, and the poems in which they appear exude a smoky, erotic quality, like a saxophone riff. Besides the musical references Harjo also includes tributes to the tradition from which she comes: there are poems dedicated to June Jordan and Richard Hugo, two poets who have influenced her work.

Harjo is sometimes unfairly criticized for placing too much emphasis on the "prose" part of her prose poetry. She is a skilled wordsmith, though, as proven by some of the figurative language found in her 1990 volume. In "Climbing the Streets of Worcester, Mass," "houses lean forward on thin hips," and in a brilliant passage from "We Encounter Nat King Cole," Harjo's ability to use figurative language is showcased:

Yesterday I turned north on Greasewood
the long way home and was shocked to see a double
rainbow

two stepping across the valley.
Suddenly there were twin gods
bending over to plant something like
themselves in the wet earth.

In "Nine Lives," "Cicadas climb out of the carcasses their voices made, into their wings of fragile promises to glide over the wet grass."

Joy Harjo has a powerful voice and a clear vision. Her poetry moves in and out of the realms of dream and reality, hope and despair, and survival and extinction, pulling together the diverse strands into a harmonious, balanced whole, as in "Eagle Poem," from *In Mad Love and War*:

> knowing we are truly blessed
> because we
> were born, and die soon within a
> True circle of motion,
> Like eagle rounding out the morning inside us.
> We pray that it may be done
> In beauty.
> In beauty.

Interviews:

Joseph Bruchac, "Interview With Joy Harjo," *North Dakota Quarterly*, 30 (Spring 1985): 220-234;

Laura Coltelli, *Winged Words: American Indian Writers Speak* (Lincoln: University of Nebraska Press, 1990), pp. 55-68.

References:

Geary Hobson, ed., *The Remembered Earth: An Anthology of Contemporary Native American Literature* (Albuquerque: Red Earth, 1979);

Jim Ruppert, "Paula Gunn Allen and Joy Harjo: Closing the Distance Between Personal and Mythic Space," *American Indian Quarterly*, 7 (Spring 1983): 27-40;

Patricia Clark Smith, "Earthly Relations, Carnal Knowledge," in *The Desert Is No Lady: Southwestern Landscapes in Women's Writing and Art*, edited by Vera Norwood and Janice Monk, (New Haven: Yale University Press, 1987), pp. 174-196.

William Hathaway

(18 December 1944 -)

Gary Pacernick
Wright State University

BOOKS: *True Confessions and False Romances* (Ithaca, N.Y.: Ithaca House, 1972);

A Wilderness of Monkeys (Ithaca, N.Y.: Ithaca House, 1975);

The Gymnast of Inertia (Baton Rouge: Louisiana State University Press, 1982);

Fish, Flesh, & Fowl (Baton Rouge: Louisiana State University Press, 1985);

Looking into the Heart of Light (Orlando: University of Central Florida Press, 1988).

SELECTED PERIODICAL PUBLICATION—
UNCOLLECTED: "True and Phony Woe: A Self-Education," *Reaper*, 17 (1987): 1-23.

In an autobiographical essay in the *Reaper* (1987), William Hathaway writes: "The most important influence (?) on my life, my thinking and writing, has been alcoholism. I was drunk from age fifteen to thirty-three, experiencing much difficulty and failure. The interesting paradox is that drunks yearn for spirit that is anaesthetized by alcohol but when the spirit is reinvigorated through sobriety the rational mind is freed to expand in ever-widening possibilities." What he suggests is that even in his recent books, where alcoholism has not been a major preoccupation, it has still served as an influence on his approach to life and poetry, which has changed from being passionately confessional and romantic to being more searching, intellectual, and humanistic.

The key to Hathaway's significance is the constant growth in range and energy of his voice and vision. Among his peers he stands out as fiercely independent. While he has written mostly in free verse, he repeatedly turned to metrical forms and light verse long before these modes became fashionable once again. In addition he mixes tragedy and comedy to satirize and criticize himself, other poets, academia, and various other targets. This blending of tones and modes, along with his recent change to a more serious, wide-ranging satire, make him distinctive and may account for his high standing among his fel-

William Hathaway and his dog

low poets, such as Albert Goldbarth and Norman Dubie, who have highly praised *Looking into the Heart of Light* (1988), with Dubie calling him "a great American poet."

Hathaway was born in Madison, Wisconsin, to Baxter L. (a professor) and Sherry Kitchen Hathaway (an art-gallery owner), whose other children are Hannah and James. William Hathaway was married on 28 February 1966 to Dixie Blaszek (a store manager), and they have three children: Jesse, Nathaniel, and Susanne. The marriage ended in divorce in 1989.

Hathaway grew up in Ithaca, New York, where his father taught at Cornell University. The young poet attended American College in Paris, Cornell, the University of Montana (B.A., 1967), and the University of Iowa (M.F.A., 1969). He taught at Louisiana State University in Baton Rouge from 1970 to 1983. At LSU he directed the creative-writing program, hosted a PBS radio program, and was active in regional literary affairs. He resigned that position to move back to New York state in 1983 and has held a visiting associate professor position at Union College in Schenectady, New York, since 1984.

Hathaway's first book, *True Confessions and False Romances* (1972), contains many of the subjects, concerns, and techniques that have remained with him. Most striking is the open, confessional statement of the endangered, defiant self, long suffering from alcoholism, that refuses to take others' advice to be practical and not cause turmoil, as in "Practical Pig":

And every time I look in a mirror,
like right now, at my drunk and
tear-stained face I know what I am.
I'm practical. Practical pig.
And I always feel a little triumphant.

At that time Hathaway could rationalize his alcoholism as part of "the celebration of the non-rational" that the poet must affirm to be true to his art. His mentor, Richard Hugo, encouraged him with the axiom "Quest for a self is fundamental to poetry." Hugo valued "emotional honesty" above all, and he, too, suffered from alcoholism. So, despite troubles and torments, Hathaway could feel that there was a purpose, almost a badge of honor, in his manic alcoholic vision. ("Like Huck Finn, he *knew* he was damned, but *felt* righteous," Hathaway said of Hugo in his *Reaper* essay.) Hathaway basked in the encouragement of his mentor, whom he perceived as "my father or something," in "For Dick Hugo." After all, many of the famous poets of that time— Robert Lowell, John Berryman, Theodore Roethke, Sylvia Plath, Anne Sexton, and others—wrote openly about alcoholism, madness, and suicide.

Beyond this confessional preoccupation, there is Hathaway's iconoclastic attitude toward life and death, tied in with his personal predicament but extending to others. "After a Memorial Service" is addressed to the deceased. The narrator hates the funeral service because the poems and eulogies are false, "but we didn't believe that shit either." It would be far more interesting if

the soul of the dead could "sing" like birds or "travel" like wind. The satirist who sees through the facades of others as well as of himself finds increasing solace in nature, as Hathaway's later poems reveal.

His second book, *A Wilderness of Monkeys* (1975), continues in the confessional mode along with some notable poems in formal verse, such as the sonnet "Lawnmowing" and "Sugar-Teat Villanelle," and some satirical glances at his southern surroundings, such as "Baton Rouge Newspaper Vendors" and "Homesick Yankee." There are also poems about family life, tinged with bitterness and disillusionment. In "All the Pains and All the Pleasures," the narrator takes stock of his domestic life (children, paperbacks, paintings, furniture, his "bloated soul") and begins to cry because he is sorry for "everyone who is not me." The husband of "It Was Nothing and Better Then" looks back to a more callow, sensuous love as he stumbles home in a drunken stupor. This lonely, desperate man drinks to escape loneliness and despair. Everything, including love, was "better then," and now "What is gone still sings in a creaking hinge / my wife's mouth and the drumming rain."

In "X's" readers again find the drunken, defiant bad boy of "Practical Pig." He gets drunk watching television, takes care of neither himself nor the house, and is shunned by "nice people" and girls who "leer" at him and call him "creepy." Yet there is a modest affirmation, for he moves with pleasure when the sun warms him as he sleeps in his chair. It is too late, though, to be saved by his wife's love (as seen in the poem "Love Cancer"), for as "Hospital Song" suggests, only medical treatment can help the desperate narrator, whose "liver sings a little song."

The Gymnast of Inertia (1982) represents a breakthrough for Hathaway. The direct expression of strong feelings through a mixture of seriousness and wit, and in various metrical and free-verse forms, is used to dramatize a variety of experience far beyond the poet's own and yet reflecting his insights and beliefs. One of the most memorable of these poems is the first one in the volume, "For the Soul of Karl Wallenda." Instead of focusing on himself, Hathaway shares his response to a tragic public event, Wallenda's fall from the high wire. But the poem is also about each artist's desperate quest for beauty. Unlike Lawrence Ferlinghetti's "charleychaplin man" (in "Constantly Risking Absurdity"), who stays aloft and keeps his balance by trying to "perceive taut truth" step-by-step while waiting to catch beauty in her "death-defying leap," Wallenda falls, and the narrator laments: "Listen, I hate this stern truth: / there is no art in falling, the beauty / is to stay." Like Robert Frost, his true mentor in this book and his next, Hathaway is able to create a clear but subtle extended metaphor. In addition he speaks to the reader in a sagelike voice and thus offers instruction as well as delight. His vision is rendered in the convincing picture of the experience. But despite his artistic control and moral overview, Hathaway's narrator is tense, skeptical, even depressed, like the persona in the first two books, and echoing John Keats at the poem's conclusion: "I'm half in love with your easeful sleep."

The volume is filled with strange, fascinating poems, such as "Sleeping in Church," a funny, iconoclastic portrait of churchgoing. A moving elegy for Edgar Allan Poe, "The Beginning of Myth," vividly depicts a topsy-turvy drunken vision:

> A reptile becoming a bird groans
> in the trees. A purple tongue hangs
> from the fish's mouth and its bright
> blood drips to beetles in palmetto.

"Dentistry" is a particularly impressive example of wit, ingenuity, and dexterity. Hathaway captures many nuances of the dentist's drilling craft in an ingenious, mock-heroic manner. In "Dear Wordsworth" a young student writes an ironic letter to that bard: "I / think it would be romantic to have a French / girlfriend and a dopefiend for a best friend."

One of the most serious poems in the book, "The Initiation," describes the tense drama of a sadistic initiation ritual. While Hathaway emphasizes many realistic scenic details, the overall effect suggests the Crucifixion:

> And when the hidden
> ice was jammed against his back
> his scream was animal and pure as
> Love. We held his limp body like a lamb.

"The American Poet—'But Since It Came to Good . . .'" is another compelling dramatization. The central character is a Frost-like poet, who "awoke alone / in the midst of his life, in a dark wood," and who "wished Dante's hell was real." While he is a well-known, meticulous craftsman, he reacts with indifference to the death of a neighbor who falls while working on a roof, and the

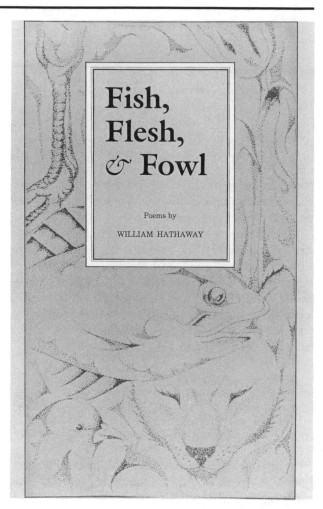

Dust jacket for Hathaway's 1985 collection, which includes nature poems and meditations on such subjects as sound and color

poet goes on to express hate toward everyone but Richard Nixon. The narrator speculates that hell's circles still exist as well as sin, despite attempts to cover them up.

"Halzelden, 1979" is a confessional poem raised to a high level of eloquence and a significance beyond the poet's personal circumstances. Again, the poem can be read as having a moral. It echoes the style and meaning of Frost's "Reluctance," from *A Boy's Will* (1913), which speaks of the need to "accept the end / of a love or a season." The recovering alcoholic in Hathaway's poem is hiking through Minnesota woods and learns humility from the earth, for the way is "To bend to a season's pleasure" and to "submit to the sober light."

Although there is less surface drama in *Fish, Flesh, & Fowl* (1985), Hathaway finds his way in nature. In "Late and Early Geese" he writes of geese as "ragged checkmarks" with "a stately V for victory strut." In "Carp" Hathaway creates a painterly portrait of canoeing and tells of fishing for carp as a boy, but the poem turns sour at the end. The narrator remembers wanting to kill his neighbor the doctor for speaking foolishly about carp and questioning the boy's romantic view of nature.

According to Hathaway human beings cause trouble when they denigrate nature. In "Horse Sense" the narrator remembers when he was overcome by the sensuous beauty of horses: "I was drunk of the whiff of their / sweat, on the rhythmic turmoil of muscle / and hoof." However, in part 2 when the narrator takes his children fishing, they are assaulted by heat and insects, and horses terrify them. The poem includes a degrading scene: the "old nags / hooked to tourist buggies" on Bourbon Street. Finally the narrator recalls his father as a boy seated on a horse while reading classics. Pure nature, romantic nature, exists only in dreams and in memories.

Besides other descriptive nature poems, such as "Peckerwoods" and "Cedar Waxwings in Ligustrum Lucidum," there are several highly unusual and original poems, including "Speaking of Sounds" and "The Physics of Yellow." The former is a catalogue of fascinating sounds, all of which occur on a very subtle frequency: "Dreamsounds, perhaps variations of the buried bloodbeat." When the poet speaks of pressing a finger against the lidded eye "so inner suns / glare forth," he imagines this produces "memory of light, our final terror." In the midst of these deep sounds and imaginings, he comes to intuitive knowledge of the spirit.

In "The Physics of Yellow" Hathaway offers an ingenious, scientific meditation on yellow. Everything becomes yellow ("Smoke, beer, piss, and pine sol") and reminiscent of a bubble: "Someday I will be nothing, like the space / where a bubble was. But everywhere will be / my stain." This poem reveals Hathaway's ability to see deeply into nature and write in a meditative style evoking Wallace Stevens.

In *Looking into the Heart of Light* Hathaway turns away from the successes of his earlier books to write a new kind of poetry from a new rational and discursive perspective. Or at least this is true of the two long poems "When I Consider" and "Timor Mortis: Sermo," which dominate the

volume near the beginning and at the end. Ostensibly he wrestles with pedagogical matters and shares his frustrations as a teacher and a poet, but he also seems to criticize implicitly the modern American tradition in favor of a tradition rooted in his heroes: John Milton, Horace, and Dante. Hathaway had, after all, warned in his poem "The American Poet" that "there are still circles in our modern / diagram of hell and a spot where each can wail." But the implications are not rendered narratively and dramatically as in the best poems of the two previous books. Instead, in the two ambitious cornerstone poems of his 1988 book, Hathaway meditates and pontificates in a form that resembles verse lectures or sermons.

Some of the shorter poems suggest a personal crisis and may well point to his marital problems and eventual divorce. In "Negative Incapability" the tension between lovers is enacted in his wry, witty version of the Adam and Eve story. In Adam's voice, this monologue shows that even in paradise there is trouble because, as Adam tells Eve, "you loved you the best."

In "Impatience" the tone and texture of the narrator's voice is direct and bitter, as in some of Hathaway's earlier confessional poems:

> I curse at the first squall of light
> that fell on the glistening slime
> of my birth. I keep a face calm
> and hard as a potato but my heart
> rejoices for the fact of death.

In addition to the reversion to the earlier confessional style, there is the added element of sin that surfaces in the later poems and is explicitly expressed in "Inflation." The message of that poem seems to be that no modern techniques of psychotherapy can eradicate "our secret sins."

William Hathaway may well be in tune with the New Formalists. Beyond fashion, he always utilized traditional forms, and he has not been afraid to moralize. He is very much at the center of his poems, confessing his consternation and rage at the human predicament. And he continues to challenge himself and his readers, who have come to view him as one of the most skilled, serious, and independent of living American poets.

Conrad Hilberry

(1 March 1928 -   )

Jonathan Holden
Kansas State University

BOOKS: *Encounter on Burrows Hill* (Athens: Ohio
University Press, 1968 [i.e., 1969]);
Struggle and Promise: A Future for Colleges, by
Hilberry and Morris Keeton (New York:
McGraw-Hill, 1969);
Rust (Athens: Ohio University Press, 1974);
Man in the Attic (Cleveland: Bits, 1980);
House Marks (Mount Horeb, Wis.: Perishable
Press, 1980);
The Moon Seen as a Slice of Pineapple (Athens: Uni-
versity of Georgia Press, 1984);
Jacob's Dancing Tune (Mount Horeb, Wis.: Perish-
able Press, 1986);
Luke Karamazov (Detroit: Wayne State University
Press, 1987);
The Lagoon (N.p.: MellanBerry, 1990);
Sorting the Smoke: New and Selected Poems (Iowa
City: University of Iowa Press, 1990).

OTHER: *The Poems of John Collop*, edited, with an
introduction, by Hilberry (Madison: Univer-
sity of Wisconsin Press, 1962 [i.e., 1961]);
The Third Coast: Contemporary Michigan Poetry, ed-
ited by Hilberry, Herbert Scott, and James
Tipton (Detroit: Wayne State University
Press, 1976);
*Contemporary Michigan Poetry: Poems from the Third
Coast*, edited by Hilberry, Scott, and Michael
Delp (Detroit: Wayne State University Press,
1988).

Wallace Stevens wrote that the poet's "role
is to help people to live their lives. He has im-
mensely to do with giving life whatever savor it
possesses." Stevens might have been describing
the poetry of Conrad Hilberry, a poetry forged,
like Stevens's, as a way of adding "savor" to a scru-
pulously ordered, carefully observed life spent
mostly in the Midwest, a life of teaching, reading,
and domestic continuity, a life in which nothing
spectacular happened. Hilberry has led a life of
conscious modesty and has a distrust of personality.

Conrad Hilberry

Conrad Arthur Hilberry was born on 1
March 1928 in Melrose Park, Illinois, and grew
up in Ferndale, Michigan, a suburb of Detroit.
He was the son of Clarence (a teacher who became president of Wayne State University) and
Ruth Haase Hilberry. Clarence Hilberry's father
was a Methodist minister in northern Ohio who
often moved with his family.

According to Conrad Hilberry, to avoid
such disruption, "my father spent his whole career at Wayne University in Detroit, coming there
as an instructor in 1931 and retiring as president
in 1965. We lived in the same house all the years

I was growing up. . . . I have sometimes felt that my childhood was so reasonable, so steady that it supplied me with no experiences, no character."

From 1946 to 1949 the young Hilberry attended Oberlin College, earning a B.A. in English. In his sophomore year he spent the summer in Mexico with the American Friends Service Committee. From then on Mexico was to figure in Hilberry's life and poetry in significant ways.

While at the University of Wisconsin doing graduate work, he met Marion Bailey, an English teacher who had also worked in Mexico with the Quakers. They married almost immediately (on 21 April 1951), and while they were still in Madison, they had two daughters, Katharine and Marilyn. Hilberry earned his M.S. in English in 1951 and his Ph.D. in 1954. At DePauw he taught English from 1954 to 1961, and he and Marion had a third daughter, Jane. On the way to Zaragosa, Spain, where he had a Fulbright appointment, the Hilberrys were in a railroad accident, and Katharine was killed. She was nine years old. The Hilberrys moved to Kalamazoo, Michigan, the following year and had another daughter, Ann. Since 1962 Conrad Hilberry has taught at Kalamazoo College.

About his life as a poet, Hilberry recalls his father's woodworking shop and says, "Almost everyone I know is handy at some craft. But I've always been clumsy enough so that the effort seems out of proportion to the results. But with words I'm all right—awkward and silent in conversation but OK on paper. It was this impulse, to build something out of words, that first attracted me to poems." Hilberry's earliest influences were Philip Larkin, Richard Wilbur, and Alfred North Whitehead:

Whitehead offers an alternative to our ordinary, atomistic, Newtonian notion of how the world is constituted . . . the basic units of which the world is made up are not particles of matter but instants of time, minute happenings. He called these moments *actual occasions*. Each occasion comprehends, takes into itself, the occasions that have gone before it. It brings together the past, momentarily, into a new whole. And each occasion yearns forward toward succeeding occasions, in which it will have its place. . . . The present is, in fact, composed of the past, and it is one of the elements of the future. Causation occurs, instant by instant everywhere. Also this scheme puts great emphasis on the creative surge of time, in

every moment creating a new world that did not exist a moment before. . . .

In Hilberry's speech "Life in a Flux of Form," honoring the Whitehead Center at the University of Redlands on the occasion of the seventy-fifth anniversary of the university (February 1983), he included the poem "Stop Action," an explicitly Whiteheadean poem "that tries to imagine what one of these actual occasions might be like":

Slowly as in an underwater dance
the shortstop dips to take the ball
on a low hop, swings back his arm, balancing
without thought, all muscles intending
the diagonal to the first baseman's glove.

As the ball leaves his hand, the action stops—
and, watching, we feel a curious poignancy,
a catch in the throat. It is not this play
only. Whenever the sweet drive is stopped
and held, our breath wells up like the rush

of sadness or longing we sometimes feel
without remembering the cause of it.
The absolute moment gathers the surge
and muscle of the past, complete,
yet hurling itself forward—arrested
here between its birth and perishing.

This poem is, like most fully achieved lyric poems, about the elusiveness of experience itself, the elusiveness of beauty. The poem is both a rediscovery and a dramatization of the aesthetics implicit in Whitehead's ontology. Hilberry makes this ontology come alive by presenting "actual occasions" in terms of human value. His notions of value are similar to those of Stevens. It is the elusiveness of lives that gives them their actual value, or, as Stevens put it in "Sunday Morning," "Death is the mother of beauty." Conversely, stasis is the death of beauty. In *Man in the Attic* (1980) Hilberry's poem "The Happy Man" "describes a man who thought he could perfect his life":

He used to believe that happiness
must lie in the perfection of a few

choice goods. But now perfection pales.
Does nature like an envious governor
lay a surtax on the happy man
diminishing his pleasure year by year?

He feels his satisfaction growing tired
even as he admires his favorites,

7/19/81

Mexico: Explosions at 4:00 a.m.

I am afraid in this dark country, where everything
                                                    the fat leaves
                                                    of ferns
where things well up from underneath: oil
lava,   ferns that grew as large
        resentment [and desire] pressed   from the leaves of   as desire
from old lake bed & the prehistoric ferns that grew   prehistoric ferns
from   old compulsions. I am afraid   the ferns of   desire contracted to the spines of cactus.

at the corners of walled streets, afraid where the way   read
                                      austere unlighted   the mountains.
empties into the perfect night bare need of cactus
                    am   for my daughter absent somewhere in the
& stone. I have been afraid when my daughter was late   night.

But this is not fear, exactly. [as the explosions roll   but a familiar emptiness. as when
     four   sadness.
in from the rim of the mountains] Black. Black.
In the tall trees to the west, egrets stir & honk, and
dogs across the valley curse in their sleep. Black.
Are they executing Maximillian again? [that foppish
foreigner] The blasts are too deliberate to be a
celebration or a shoot-out in the hills.
They are truths detonated in our foreign dreams:
let x be what is given. [what is broken in the earth]   underground
Black. If only these were skyrockets spreading
streamers on the sky before the solid shock,
if a crowd could all cry oooh together as the
light fountained & fell; if only there were light—

Draft for one of Hilberry's many poems set in Mexico; the final version was collected in The Moon Seen as a Slice of Pineapple *(by permission of Conrad Hilberry).*

the bronze chrysanthemums along the walk
that bloom as solid as the heads of nails.

Of Hilberry's poetry collections, the most fully realized is *Man in the Attic*, reprinted in *The Moon Seen as a Slice of Pineapple* (1984), which also contains Hilberry's "Mexican Poems." Mexico has figured in his life and art in ways similar to Key West in the poetry of Stevens. In "The Frog" Hilberry describes the allure of the expatriate life-style:

> Here I become
> absurd, an embarrassment—too tall, too pink,
> missing the jokes, getting the sexes wrong.
> The customs police found my cache of words
> and confiscated it; I took a deep breath
> at the border, blew it out, and was no one,
> a foreign body with a limp. And yet
> I keep returning. There's something to it,
> this emptiness. . . .

It was in *Rust* (1974), however, where Hilberry discovered the metaphor that became the dominant metaphor of his best poetry: reading. In "A Thin Song for a Girl" he watches a daughter learning to read: "Your eyes / worry with words / And the curl of / Numbers, fearing / A wrong turn. . . ." But, like Stevens in "The Man on the Dump," Hilberry worries about the degree to which one's ability to read interferes with his ability to perceive the world freshly:

> I wish I could say
> Unlearn them—
> The world's skin
> Is unlettered
> And *n* is no
> Count.

Similarly, in "Wise Man" he writes: "Creation, then, is the only axiom—and it declines to spell itself across / the sky in Roman letters."

In "Sorting the Smoke," one of the new poems (and the title poem) in Hilberry's *New and Selected Poems* (1990), his theme of language-about-language becomes more explicit and insistent. In

"Five Poems from Crete," for example, the first section, "Heraclitus' Bird," includes these lines: "Heraclitus' / ostrich, being made of / words, still flaps / its curious wings. . . ." In "Flora," Hilberry declares:

> Thin-petalled poppies
> blue kalva silvestris,
> purple orchids on
> a straight stem,
> . . . .
> these, too, are words
> of a sort, something
> between us and the rock.

In "Tertium Quid in a Trench Coat," Hilberry invokes Stevens's favorite categories:

> Subject and object, imagination
> and reality—these opposites
> account for everything. But who's
> this tertium quid, carrying
> papers from both countries,
> hanging around harbors and landing
> fields, betraying secrets both ways?

Hilberry remains, as Stevens was, at heart a philosophical poet, his oeuvre consisting largely of a type of poetry that is meditative rather than dramatic; like the vintage poetry of Wilbur, it is also metaphysical, a poetry of wit and formal elegance, employing extended metaphors in order to test their conclusions. All these qualities might be epitomized by "Headlights" (from *Man in the Attic*), a sonnet oddly similar, in its premise, to Stevens's "The Idea of Order at Key West." "Headlights," among the chores it takes on, comprehends self-consciously a Whiteheadean ontology:

> She stops at a turnout, cuts the ignition,
> and walks a few yards into the spongy woods,
>
> where dark clings like cobwebs. Now, if she knows,
> it is not knowledge of luminous paint edging
> the road. She guesses the night's dip and strike.
> She hears the roar of her own body, creating
> itself, instant by instant, as the trees grow
> and steam and sing themselves into fact.

Edward Hirsch
(20 January 1950 -   )

Nancy Eimers
Western Michigan University

BOOKS: *For the Sleepwalkers* (New York: Knopf, 1981);
Wild Gratitude (New York: Knopf, 1986);
The Night Parade (New York: Knopf, 1989).

OTHER: "Birds-of-Paradise: A Memoir," in *The Pushcart Prize*, volume 13 (1988);
"My Grandfather's Poems," in *Contemporary American Poet-Critics*, edited by James McCorkle (Detroit: Wayne State University Press, 1989).

SELECTED PERIODICAL PUBLICATIONS—
UNCOLLECTED: "A War Between the Orders: Yeats's Fiction and the Transcendental Moment," *Novel*, 17 (Fall 1983): 52-66;
"Wisdom and Power: Yeats and the Commonwealth of Faery," *Yeats-Eliot Review*, 8, no. 1 (1986): 22-40;
"Guide for the Perplexed: The Poetry of Gerald Stern," *Poetry East*, 26 (Fall 1988): 52-67.

For Edward Hirsch the night is not merely the stretch of time to be endured by the restless insomniac—a character that recurs throughout his poems. It is also imagination's twists and turns; knowledge of history; memory; and the desire, despite all odds, to survive. In his poetry Hirsch celebrates the capacity to live, gladly, in this night.

Edward Mark Hirsch was born on 20 January 1950 to Kurt and Irma Ginsburg Hirsch in Chicago. He and his two sisters, Arlene and Nancy, grew up in Chicago and in Skokie, a suburb. Hirsch received a B.A. from Grinnell College in 1972 and was then awarded a Watson Traveling Fellowship (1972-1973). He received his Ph.D. in folklore in 1979 at the University of Pennsylvania. On 29 May 1977 Hirsch and Janet Landay were married; their son, Gabriel David Landay Hirsch, was born in 1988. Hirsch has taught in the Poetry in the Schools Programs in New York and Pennsylvania (1976-1978), at Wayne State University (1978-1985), and, since

Edward Hirsch

1985, in the Creative Writing Program at the University of Houston. He has been the recipient of many awards and grants, including an Amy Lowell Traveling Fellowship (1978), an Ingram Merrill Foundation Award (1978), a National Endowment for the Arts Creative Writing Fellowship (1982), a Guggenheim Fellowship in Poetry (1985-1986), and the prestigious Rome Prize (1988), for which he was nominated by Robert Penn Warren. Hirsch is a prolific writer of poetry and prose: widely published and frequently anthologized, he is the author of three books of poetry as well as various scholarly and critical articles on W. B. Yeats (the subject of his dissertation) and on contemporary poetry.

Hirsch's first book, *For the Sleepwalkers*, published in 1981, received the Lavan Younger Poets Award from the Academy of American Poets and the Delmore Schwartz Memorial Award from

New York University. The volume won the attention of critics for the energy, even exuberance, of its voice and for its technique and promise. The excess that sometimes occurs is at worst his most interesting mistake, at best one of his most singular accomplishments. These poems explore the mysteries of imagination, insomnia, art, life, survival, and loss.

The voice in these poems is deceptively childlike: whimsical, a little raucous, always insistent, yet capable of a deeply troubled astonishment over the details of everyday life. "I want to say something wonderful," Hirsch announces in the title poem. His admiration for the sleepwalkers' vulnerability and willingness to take emotional risks has a child's ebullience: "I love the way that sleepwalkers are willing / to step out of their bodies." The role of the poet, he writes in "Cocks," is "to astonish, yes, and to offend"—for in a world that believes in the law of natural selection, it is the poet who proclaims that "the weak survive!" Hirsch frequently uses imperatives: "Call it the sun"; "Wake up and listen." But there is something so pleading about the demands that their effect is less bossy than strenuously inviting, as if the speaker is involving the reader in his own urgency and longing: "we have to drink the stupifying cup of darkness / and wake up to ourselves, nourished and surprised."

Hirsch celebrates the fact that, despite catastrophe, "we manage, we survive / so that losing itself becomes a kind of song, our song." He does not, however, gloss over the pain of this process. Through a series of images suggesting heaviness, he conveys "the inconsolable burden that is ours": a factory worker describes her tired body as "too heavy for clothes" and the summer heat as a "heavy tongue" that "repeats / its one heavy syllable"; poets, children, and soldiers are "weighted down" by "our dead planets"—those terrors rehearsed on sleepless nights.

In a book that often alludes to sleep, insomnia becomes a metaphor for the restless imagination. Those unable to sleep are forced to explore some darker realm, not merely of the nighttime world but of personality. Part of this journey involves confrontation with things that, waking, people try hard not to think about:

> And all night
>
> you're left sitting at a desk
> frightened, thinking of the skull
>
> under the smooth skin. . . .

Thus "the old wars with sleep" become the old, difficult strivings within the self. Hirsch even imagines a community of insomniacs who "know about the black trenches of moonlight on the ceiling" and for whom, nightly, consciousness is "the darkest mirror" that "extends inwards / for at least a thousand years."

Yet despite their introspection, these poems are not merely personal. As Peter Stitt observed, "Hirsch's is not a solipsistic art—these poems of wonder and consolation are not dedicated to his own precious soul, but comment on the world, lovely and rapacious by turns, that we all inhabit." Many are spoken by or addressed to fictional characters—waitress, shop girl, garbageman, acrobat—or to artists and poets.

Many of the poems in this volume concern the role and the obsessions of the artist. Hirsch is fascinated by the ways artists perceive their existence: César Vallejo, who sees a woman's face in a muskrat; Arthur Rimbaud, to whom sexuality is "stray pigs chasing / the dogs"; and Henri Matisse, who sees dancers as "colorful wild beasts." For the artists in these poems, desire is detail: the colors and shapes that haunt the dance and the subway.

The poems in *For the Sleepwalkers* are often characterized by their insistent use of metaphor. One metaphor succeeds or is transformed into another at a rapid-fire pace; these metaphors are whimsical, even fantastic in nature.

In "Transfigured Night, Come Down to Me Slowly," pears are "a cluster of green fists" that shine "like enormous / gray moths, or a string of tiny lamps." While occasionally this method becomes, in critic Hugh Seidman's words, "a seductive inventive excess" (*New York Times Review of Books*, 13 September 1981), for the most part it generates the passion and the visionary quality of these poems. With each metaphor it is as if, to quote from another poem, "The veils are lifting from our windows." Metaphor is offered as consolation, for "these imaginings make it possible / To survive, to endure the hard light."

Hirsch is clearly interested in the form and shape of his poems, and his stanza patterns are usually regular and symmetrical. He is praised for his success with the sestina—his use of this form in such poems as "At Kresge's Diner" and "Nightsong: Ferris Wheel by the Sea" allows him, as William Harmon pointed out, "both intimacy and control." Other poems, in particular "Cocks" and "Gerard de Nerval: Fairy Tale for a Whore," employ a sestinalike repetition that creates and maintains Hirsch's characteristic intensity of voice and subject matter.

His second volume, *Wild Gratitude* (1986), won the National Book Critics Circle Award and the Texas Institute of Letters award for poetry. Hirsch wrote this book during his time at Wayne State in Detroit. The epigraph from W. H. Auden, with its "affirming flame," accurately characterizes the general stance in these poems: while Hirsch, like Auden, acknowledges and laments "negation and despair," his second book is also a celebration not merely of survival but of the intense desire to survive. As in *For the Sleepwalkers*, he writes about insomnia, art, life, and victimization; however, these poems are more overtly political and autobiographical. Critics comparing it with *For the Sleepwalkers* have generally praised *Wild Gratitude* for its greater control and maturity of technique and subject matter.

One notices throughout these poems a longing for transcendence and escape from the waking world. Imagining the "pallbearers of sleep," the speaker explains, "I need their help to fly out of myself." As in *For the Sleepwalkers*, consciousness becomes a burden: the sleepless speaker "can't lift the enormous weight / Of this enormous night from my shoulders"; the patient, overworked horse pulling a carriage of tourists waits "for the intolerable burden of its life to stop." However, in these poems, just what it is that makes consciousness burdensome is more clearly identified. It is awareness of boredom, it is homelessness, it is a friend's early death, it is living with Nazi atrocities—and the desire to escape these things is expressed as a yearning for weightlessness or ascension. If escape or transcendence is possible, it occurs only in sleep—at best elusive— or in death. In "Paul Celan" the smoke that rises from the city's smokestack is transformed by the artist's memory and imagination: first, to the smoke pouring out of the trains taking victims (including his parents) to Nazi death camps; second, to "two ghosts billowing from a huge oven."

Yet, as David Wojahn suggested in the *New York Times Book Review* (8 June 1986), "even though his poems usually begin as troubled meditations on human suffering they end in celebration." The poem about the Polish Home for the Aged, for example, ends with acceptance, affirmation, and the memory of a mother's lesson:

One day the light will be as thick as a pail
Of fresh milk, but the pail will seem heavy.

You won't know if you can lift it anymore,
But lift it anyway. Drink the day slowly.

Hirsch celebrates those who "drink the day slowly" despite their own pain and fear. The poem "Leningrad" ends with a tough image of violence and survival: "slowly we touched a sharp razor to our necks / And scraped away the useless blue skin / And the dead flesh. Somehow we survived."

Some of the poems in Hirsch's second collection deal more directly with autobiographical material than those in his first. He remembers his first love in a theater in Skokie, the breakup of his parents, and the deaths of his grandparents. "Omen," an elegy for Dennis Turner, a friend who died young, is more sparse and direct in its presentation of details than most of Hirsch's earlier poems: "I can't stop thinking about my closest friend / Suffering from cancer in a small, airless ward / In a hospital downtown." Even some of his poems about artists are informed by the personal: observation of his own cat Zooey is what brings home to him the "wild gratitude" in Christopher Smart's meditations.

In "Edward Hopper and the House by the Railroad (1925)," the whimsical and adjectival excesses that sometimes occur in *For the Sleepwalkers* have vanished. Reviewer Liam Rector wrote that "*Wild Gratitude* is a remarkable maturing and has a cohesive sense of restraint in its baroque effusiveness" (*Hudson Review*, Winter 1986-1987). In "Edward Hopper," Hirsch's urgent voice, whimsical imagery, interest in art and artists, and his love for personification all come to fruition. The house by the railroad is very human: "strange, gawky," wearing "the expression / Of someone being stared at," "ashamed of itself," while the artist is presented as more a way of painting than an individual: "relentless," "brutal as sunlight." Then Hirsch allows the personification to transform the artist from distanced accuser, "believing the house must have done something horrible," to a being more humanly vulnerable, even as the house is: "the house begins to suspect / That the man, too, is desolate, desolate / And even ashamed." The last stanza echoes the language of the first one, predicting that all the artist's paintings of houses, storefronts, and cafeteria windows will bear the look that is peculiarly human, peculiarly American: the look of "someone who is about to be left alone / Again, and can no longer stand it." What this personification and repetition ultimately accomplish is not a visionary transformation of suffering into something more bearable and inanimate but a return to the burden of human consciousness at its breaking point. *Wild Gratitude* earned Hirsch high praise from Robert Penn Warren, who said in a letter to the publisher (Knopf), "the best poems here are unsurpassed in our time."

The Night Parade, Hirsch's third book of poetry, was published in 1989. Its title, taken from a poem in *Wild Gratitude*, underscores both a certain thematic continuity in the volumes and a shift in focus from insomnia to its more personal causes—that troubling procession of images from "a world we call the past, / As if it could tell us who we are now." Written while Hirsch was teaching in Houston, these narrative poems approach a past in which public and private events are intermingled: the rebuilt urban landscape of Chicago, where Hirsch's parents and family lived, becomes background and source of the family stories of departures, separations, and betrayals.

If the poems in *The Night Parade* are, as the poet claims, "memorandums of my affection," then affections are pulled in conflicting directions, toward old and new. Part of this tension is public. In his poems about the great Chicago fire—"For the New World," "When Skyscrapers Were Invented in Chicago," and "American Apocalypse"—fire is both destructive and creative. No longer itself an affirming flame, it wreaks havoc on the rural—the barns, cow cribs, and stables—as well as the urban (Opera House, Post Office, Water Works) and leaves only a scorched rubble in its wake. Because of fire's undiscriminating fury, the past is obliterated, but the future is also newly possible; men and women are "young and free / Of history at last," free to be about the business of creating "a city that aspired upward toward the sky."

In fact, the imagery of building—with a peculiarly American architecture—is an important part of the collective argument of these poems. The expanse of Illinois prairie represents both limitless emptiness and possibility. Hirsch says of the aftermath of the fire:

> There is something American in the moment, something
> Dark and innocent about our faith in a future rising
> On the prairie, immense and open-hearted, the skeleton
> Construction of skyscrapers just around the corner. . . .

And though such architecture is later to be replaced by a paradoxical yearning for the past, the "houses, American houses, were growing on the prairie." The emptiness has been filled. Like the rubble left by the 1871 fire, memory has a way of surviving in fragments, and so one pieces together "these details rescued from the flames."

In a series of family poems, Hirsch explores not so much the literal events of the past as the ways they are remembered for "the past, too, is under revision, / Changing as we change, the way our sufferings / Are converted into reasons we can understand." Early criticism has not been in agreement about how well Hirsch deals with the material of autobiography and family history. While Pat Monaghan (*Booklist*, January-April 1989) praises Hirsch's "sure sense of the line between emotion and sentimentality," Helen Vendler takes him to task for "being familially prosaic" (*New York Review of Books*, 6 August 1989). While admiring "Infertility" for its "quiet, believable quality," she sees in other personal family poems an inventorylike quality that renders them unbelievable.

In "Infertility"—a poem about being unable to have children—Hirsch mourns the interruption in the flow of family history. The possibility and excitement contained in spaces "unfenced and wild"—the southwestern desert, the prairie—is seen in this poem as a barrenness, "the shape of nothing / Being born." This is the volume's darkest personal statement.

Few of these poems possess the visionary exuberance that marked, in particular, the poems in *For the Sleepwalkers*. Instead of nourishment and surprise, "the stupifying cup of darkness" leaves, at best, a mingling of "disappointment and joy." If, as Hirsch says in the poem "Incandescence at Dusk," "There is fire in everything, / shining and hidden," then it is the fire of sunset reminding people of mortality, and there is no transcending mortal existence:

> I don't believe in ultimate things.
> I don't believe in the inextinguishable light
> of the other world.
> I don't believe that we will be lifted up
> and transfixed by radiance.
> One incandescent dusky world is all there is.

In *The Night Parade* images of rising are either limited to material accumulation—skyscrapers that rise into the sky, for example—or they are frustrated: the "faint wingbeats" of the grandfather's poems are ineffectual, unhappy; hearts will be carried "On invisible wings / And then set down in an empty field." The promise that "Someday we will let them go again, like kites" seems tenuous—as if the spirit is willing, but the flesh is very weak. The recurring image of rain operates as a kind of consolation in these poems—a rain that falls after fire, soothing and eerily beautiful.

Other poems in the volume deal with night, terror, and death in both public and private situations. "Skywriting" is another elegy for Turner; "Execution" is for Hirsch's deceased high-school football coach; "Birds of Paradise" is for his mother-in-law. In each of these poems mourning an individual, however, death is terrible precisely because it is so impersonal, its fury "machine-like," "perfect." In his larger portraits of suffering—which Vendler has criticized for their generality and reliance on anaphora—he deals with the plague (with an implied parallel to the AIDS crisis) and with the personal destruction caused by the Chicago fire. The poignance lies perhaps not in the long descriptions of suffering and wreckage but in the prosaic lament—stated once and implied throughout—that "we were not meant to live in paradise."

The stylistic and formal techniques of *The Night Parade* are unlike those of Hirsch's first two volumes and perhaps represent a transitional period in his work. In many poems Hirsch abandons the regular, blocky stanza in favor of a more airy play with dropped lines reminiscent of some of the poems of Charles Wright. This form seems particularly effective in "Incandescence at Dusk" and "Infertility."

From fairly early in his career, Hirsch has been regarded as one of the most promising young American poets. His work has earned him the serious attention of such poets and critics as W. S. Merwin, Warren, Stitt, Vendler, and Gerald Stern. His poetry has remained basically affirmative, and affirmation has gradually been less informed by a pleading exuberance and more by a calm sorrow and acceptance. One misses some of the quirkiness of his early, fast-paced metaphors, but poems such as "Edward Hopper," "My Father's Back," "Incandescence at Dusk," and "Infertility" show Hirsch doing some of his best work. The stylistic shifts in *The Night Parade* may suggest that he has more surprises in store. Always a prolific writer, Hirsch is certain to produce a substantial and distinguished canon of work in the years to come.

References:

William Harmon, "A Poetry Odyssey," *Sewanee Review*, 91 (Summer 1983): 457-473;

Peter Stitt, "The Objective Mode in Contemporary Lyric Poetry," *Georgia Review*, 36 (Summer 1982): 438-448.

Garrett Kaoru Hongo
(30 May 1951 -   )

Barbara Drake
Linfield College

BOOKS: *The Buddha Bandits Down Highway 99*, by Hongo, Alan Chong Lau, and Lawson Fusao Inada (Mountain View, Cal.: Buddhahead, 1978);

Yellow Light (Middletown, Conn.: Wesleyan University Press, 1982);

The River of Heaven (New York: Knopf, 1988).

PLAY PRODUCTION: *Nisei Bar & Grill*, Seattle, Ethnic Cultural Center, June 1976.

SELECTED PERIODICAL PUBLICATION—
UNCOLLECTED: "In Search of the Silent Zero," *Greenfield Review* (Spring 1977): 74-76.

Garrett Kaoru Hongo is an important voice in post-World War II Asian-American literature. He was awarded the 1987 Lamont Poetry Prize by the Academy of American Poets for *The River of Heaven* (published the following year). However, even though ethnic considerations are constant elements in his work, he is also regarded as a mainstream American poet who speaks for an idealistic generation intent on learning, understanding, and possibly correcting the mistakes of recent history.

Hongo's work is strongly narrative, and he is at his best when telling stories—his own or stories that have been pieced together from bits of family anecdote, written and oral histories, and speculation. There is sometimes a sense of outrage in his work, as in the long poem "Stepchild" in *Yellow Light* (1982). "Stepchild" describes various painful chapters in the history of Japanese-Americans, including the World War II relocation, the mistreatment of immigrant laborers, and the horrors of Hiroshima. In other poems, however, he is more apt to use humor and joy to persuade the reader. In the uncollected poem "In Search of the Silent Zero," published in a special "Asian-American Writers" issue of the *Greenfield Review* (Spring 1977), he uses comic absurdity to make his point. He depicts himself as a

Garrett Kaoru Hongo

sinister Japanese character in an old war movie, then says, "You have always wondered how / I speak your language so well. / I am one of you. / Have always been. / I will escape from this movie, / and, in another generation, / wear Levi's, Pendleton, Addidas, / and pass unnoticed near military installations." Other poems overflow with sensuous pleasure and enthusiasm. It is a pleasure expressed in love of family; in catalogues of exotic flowers, foods, or landscapes; and in travel, as well as in his love of baseball or in memories of growing up in California.

Hongo was born on 30 May 1951 in Volcano, Hawaii, to parents of Japanese ancestry: Albert Kazuyoshi Hongo, an electrician, and Louise Tomiko Kubota Hongo. When he was six, the family moved to Los Angeles, and later to Gardena, California, where he attended a high school that was "one-third Japanese, one-third white and Chicano, and one-third black," a mixture that sensitized the young Hongo early in life to questions of history and ethnic background. After graduation from high school he attended Pomona College, where he graduated with honors (B.A., 1973) and was awarded a Thomas J. Watson Fellowship (1973-1974) to spend a year writing in Japan. He then entered the University of Michigan as a graduate student in Japanese language and literature, but after a year of studies, during which he won the university's Hopwood Poetry Prize (1975), he changed direction and moved to Seattle, where he worked as poet in residence for the Seattle Arts Commission and was founding director of the Asian Exclusion Act, a locally based theater group.

Hongo explains his motivation for this move largely in terms of his identification with the West Coast and his interest in other Asian-American writers such as Frank Chin and Lawson Inada, who were making significant contributions to literature. In Seattle, Hongo staged Chin's play *The Year of the Dragon* and other works, including his own *Nisei Bar & Grill*. He feels that *Nisei Bar & Grill* was important more for its spirit than for its script, but the experience helped develop his feeling for cultural history and the ethnic connection so central to his poetry. After his work in Seattle, Hongo continued his graduate education at the University of California, Irvine, where he received his M.F.A. in 1980 and then continued graduate studies for another two years.

He has taught at the University of Washington; the University of California, Irvine; and the University of Missouri, where he was poetry editor of the *Missouri Review*. In 1989 he was appointed director of the Creative Writing Program at the University of Oregon in Eugene, an appointment that began in January 1990. On 15 May 1982 he married Cynthia Anne Thiessen, a violinist and musicologist, and they have two sons: Alexander and Hudson. Hongo has been the recipient of the Discovery/*The Nation* award, two NEA fellowships, the Lamont Poetry Prize, and a Guggenheim Fellowship.

In 1978, with two other Asian-American writers, Alan Chong Lau and Lawson Fusao Inada, Hongo published a collection of poems, *The Bud-*

dha Bandits Down Highway 99, an early effort to assert his identity as a poet in connection with other writers with a common ancestry and engaged in related discoveries. Highway 99, the old route connecting the inland cities of the West Coast of the United States, represents the geographical connectedness of the three poets as well as being a jazzy, twentieth-century symbol of movement and vitality, reminiscent of works by the Beat authors. The motif of travel or migration is important throughout Hongo's work, and the motif is made manifest in rich images of landscape, whether it is the landscape of modern-day Los Angeles or "the Hongo Store near the summit of Kilauea Crater on the Big Island of Hawaii."

Hongo's section of *The Buddha Bandits Down Highway 99*, titled "Cruising 99," begins with "A Porphyry of Elements," in which he identifies his personal history in relation to everything from the geology of the Sierras "to the internal combustion engine," "from the death of the last grizzly" and "floods of the Sacramento" to "this aggregate of experiences." There are echoes of Walt Whitman as Hongo celebrates his connectedness to nature, geography, and history. "Cruising in the Greater Vehicle / A Jam Session," "Body & Fender / Body & Soul," "Confession Of The Highway / The Hermit Speaks," and five other poems by Hongo in the 1978 book also make up a section of his first full-length collection, *Yellow Light*, which shows his scope expanding dramatically as he experiments with different voices and points of view.

The title poem depicts an anonymous woman coming home from work through a multiethnic Los Angeles neighborhood, "passing gangs of schoolboys playing war, / Japs against Japs, Chicanos chalking sidewalks / with the holy double-yoked crosses of hopscotch, / and the Korean grocer's wife out for a stroll / around this neighborhood of Hawaiian apartments." Hongo imagines the landscape as it would have been in the spring, filled with flowers and delicate expectation, "But this is October, and Los Angeles / seethes like a billboard under twilight." The woman, carrying her groceries, climbs "two flights of flagstone / stairs to 201-B." The poem ends: "The moon then, cruising from behind / a screen of eucalyptus across the street, / covers everything, everything in sight, / in a heavy light like yellow onions." The effect of the poem is poignant but ambiguous, sensuous and appealing; the foreboding beauty of the landscape is

G/12

J. goku

Sometimes I think, I'll go look for them
and not, this once, to borrow money
or to ask them to invest, support me
~~in an interesting scheme to~~
in a scheme ~~to~~ make wealth and leisure.

I don't much think I'll look for them,
try to get them to come in on a scheme —
export custom Mustangs to Japan

I've gone it alone pretty much, ever since
I left Hilo for good by troop ship to Japan
and then, by cargo plane, to these snowfields
          in Korea.
~~I never talked much after that~~

~~It must have been for good that I left~~

I [must have always] wanted to go it alone
ever since I~~t~~ left Hilo that morning
on the troop ship bound for Korea
and the skirmishes and the hordes of dead
and the taunting shouts of *Hey Pineapple!*
rising from the trenches ~~from~~ the scattered members
of our island platoon announcing
          they were still alive.
I remember ~~walking~~ stumbling over foxholes
and the half-corpses of dead G.I.s —
guys like "Itchy" and the Capt., Miwwa
    and "Kewpie" Kozai —
~~There were three of us holding on to each other~~
at the end there were only three of us;
~~holding~~
me, the Medic using a rifle for a crutch,
and the other two hanging on like crabs
grabbing at the ~~frayed~~
       head and tail of the bait.

Page from a draft for a poem collected in The River of Heaven *(by permission of Garrett Kaoru Hongo)*

brought together finally in an earthy image of yellow onions, instead of the "Wisteria" and "orange butterflies" of spring. "Yellow Light" sets the mood for what follows in the book. Other poems deal with Hongo's father, who works the "swing shift at Lears" and puts his hope in betting on horses; Hongo's brother, whom he remembers "When we were younger . . . / . . . in the garage / with his guitar, an amplifer / the size of a shoe box, practicing / for the priesthood, preaching the blues"; and other members of the family.

In *Yellow Light* Hongo explores the roots of his creative impulse. The poetry has a persistent narrative element: in "What For" he writes, "I lived for stories about the war / my grandfather told over *hana* cards"; and "I lived for songs my grandmother sang / stirring curry into a thick stew." Hongo's desire to be a writer is largely an impulse of love. Witnessing his father's pain, he says: "I wanted to become a doctor of pure magic, / to string a necklace of sweet words / fragrant as pine needles and plumeria."

Hongo writes about his journey to Japan and his attempts to reclaim his ethnic heritage; then, in "Roots," he expresses a sense of reconciliation. After traveling in Japan, "When I came back to California, / to the foothills stubbled with wild oat / and the valleys ragged with house tracts, / I appreciated the joy of street slang and jive, / . . . / and sensed I had come to own my face / in whatever state or prefecture, / in whatever place." This joy, however, is bittersweet. Older family members resist his need to know about the unhappiness of the past: "It's not talked about / Not shared. / Something stopped the telling. / Someone pulled out the tongues / of every Nisei / raped by the felons / of Relocation." To repair the omissions, he includes quotations from oral histories, a list of books dealing with Asian-American experience, fragments of recollection from older relatives, imagined scenes and characters, and images from his own past, out of which he creates a collage that makes a whole of the fragments.

The final poem in the book uses the persona of a musician-gardener who "learned / how to grow the bamboo / in ditches next to the fields," and then, from bits of found and stolen materials, he fashions the bamboo into flutes. During the war the flute maker is suspected of sabotage. He burns his flutes and then is interned in the relocation. After the war, an old man, he finds solace at last in sitting in the "thicket / of memory," where he can "shape full-throated songs / out of wind, out of bamboo, / out of a voice / that only whispers." The character is in some sense an alter ego for the poet, also a maker of songs out of found, borrowed, and created materials. The poem may remind readers that, although Hongo's parents, residents of Hawaii, were not relocated during World War II, his grandfather was seized by the FBI and interned as a "potential saboteur," simply because of his prominence in the Japanese-American community. A *Los Angeles Times* article (19 March 1987) describes Hongo's belief that "All Japanese-Americans were victimized by the relocation in one way or another, . . . and all Americans suffered from the government's action."

In *The River of Heaven* Hongo continues to combine personal memory with cultural history and narrative. The bitterness of "Stepchild" has gone out of these poems, even when he moves into the persona of a tragic character, as in "Pinoy at the Coming World," the story of a plantation worker who moves up into a position as storekeeper but then loses everything that really matters to him, or in "Jigoku: On the Glamour of Self-Hate," the story of a former soldier turned gambler and street tough. The way in which these characters speak for themselves and achieve dramatic reality reminds one of the writer's early work in theater.

In "Cloud-Catch" Hongo puts together bits and pieces of the family story and says, "And that's about all I do, / piecing the lives together, / getting the stories folks will tell me, / dust in the gleam of light / swirled with a cupped hand, / finding a few words. / They're not enough though, / no matter how sweet or bitter."

Since the publication of *The River of Heaven* Garrett Kaoru Hongo has been writing memoirs, documentary essays, and natural history, as well as poetry. In fall 1989 he was the subject of a program in Bill Moyers's PBS series *The Power of the Word*.

Interview:

Warren Nishimoto, "Interview with Writer Garrett Hongo, Oral History and Literature," *Oral History Recorder* (Hawaii, Summer 1986): 2-4.

Susan Howe
(10 June 1937 -)

Jane Hoogestraat
Southwest Missouri State University

BOOKS: *Hinge Picture* (Cherry Valley, N.Y.: Cherry Valley/Telephone Books, 1974);

Chanting at the Crystal Sea (Boston: Fire Exit/ Corbett, 1975);

The Western Borders (Willits, Cal.: Tuumba, 1976);

Secret History of the Dividing Line (New York: Telephone Books, 1978);

Cabbage Gardens (Chicago: Fathom, 1979);

Deep in a Forest of Herods (New Haven, Conn.: Pharos, 1979);

The Liberties (Guilford, Conn.: Loon, 1980);

Pythagorean Silence (New York: Montemora Foundation, 1982);

Defenestration of Prague (New York: Kulchur Foundation, 1983);

My Emily Dickinson (Berkeley, Cal.: North Atlantic, 1985);

Articulation of Sound Forms in Time (Windsor, Vt.: Awede, 1987);

A Bibliography of the King's Book, or, Eikon Basilike (Providence, R.I.: Paradigm, 1989);

The Europe of Trusts: Selected Poems (Los Angeles: Sun & Moon, 1990);

Singularities (Middletown, Conn.: Wesleyan University Press / Hanover, N.H.: University Press of New England, 1990);

Silence Wager Stories (Providence, R.I.: Paradigm, 1992);

The Nonconformist's Memorial (New York: New Directions, forthcoming 1993);

The Birth-Mark: Expression and the Wilderness (Middletown, Conn.: Wesleyan University Press, forthcoming 1993).

In a prologue to *The Europe of Trusts* (1990) Howe writes of her desire to speak for those who have been silenced by history: "I wish I could tenderly lift from the dark side of history, voices that are anonymous, slighted—inarticulate." Her poetry attests to the difficulty of the process of representing, of recovering by an act of the imagination, the speech of those left out and left homeless by official documents, often including the official documents of academic literary canons.

Howe employs both formal and discursive practices that call into question the binary structures of language and even the adequacy of language. She makes extraordinary demands on a reader by using fragmentary syntax and by deliberately disregarding the poetic and linguistic conventions that readers depend on to find their way through poems. But she expands the range of who can be included in the poetic landscape, and she makes a place in that landscape where readers might simultaneously learn to mourn the lost people of history. She also helps readers begin, however haltingly, to recover the sense of the sacred that still haunts the language of the twentieth century.

Howe has made the transition from publishing only with very small presses in limited editions to publishing with larger, mainstream presses. The recentness of this transition attests both to the difficult, even marginal quality of her work and to the fact that there is a sufficient dissatisfaction among readers of American poetry with the typical "workshop" poem. The alternative that Howe poses has been characterized by Linda M. Reinfeld as "the refusal of that cocky American greeting (good morning, good morning) so many of us as readers of American literature have grown to count on. The sound forms here articulated are sometimes more like gurgles than greetings: such things happen. The trail can disappear."

Howe was born on 10 June 1937 to Irish-American parents in Boston and she remains acutely conscious of the time into which she was born, indicating (in the prologue to *The Europe of Trusts*) her awareness of the scale of historical events underway in 1937 and continuing through her childhood in the 1940s: "This is my historical consciousness. I have no choice in it." Her poetry shows the influence of that history filtered through, among other things, her earlier career in the visual arts and her wide reading, particularly in literary theory and history. Howe was educated as a painter at the Boston Museum School

Susan Howe (photograph by Janet Chalmers)

of Fine Arts and had work in several group shows in New York City; she moved gradually from painting toward poetry via collage and performance pieces. Since 1991 she has served as a professor of English at the State University of New York at Buffalo.

From the start, Howe has focused on recasting fragments from sacred texts and other mythological or ancient sources to call attention to the strangeness of certain fragments and stories—to the violence contained in them, to the people obviously omitted, and to the haunting quality of these stories that still keeps them sacred. Rachel Blau DuPlessis explains that Howe "does spiritual and metaphysical work yet without the authoritarian or prophetic claims that often accompany this practice." But Howe does something else as well: she acknowledges that people need ancient texts, classical philosophy, and mythology even if there is much that is flawed—binary, authoritarian, and destructively patriarchal—in this work.

In *Hinge Picture* (1974), for example, Howe writes of an almost primeval author who is both a source of fear and a source of hope because of what is contained in his texts:

> a hermit strode the hush beyond
> has pushed off from our honey voices

> to a litter of shells become cavern
> . . . .
> I have been so afraid of him
> when he sits there
> a hope among insipid legends
> a ray of light across the darkest age[.]

This process of a cautiously hopeful and treacherous recovery shows up again when Howe turns the account of the Tower of Babel from Hebrew scriptures into something other than tragedy:

> fictive hanging babel all
> the tongue of Universe of wild
> dazzled by imperial majesty of
> God and imitating zodiac rejec
> t the joy the persian triumphs[.]

Howe returns again and again in her early poetry to imagining the origin of language, as if to suggest that, if one could mark this point, one could somehow begin to undo all that language has done wrong, or could at least begin to understand how language is implicated in what has gone wrong. But this inquiry is not at all despairing, because the moment when gesture crosses over into language is for Howe a joyous occasion, one celebrated by both the human and the natural world:

> Under ice I say gesture and my people cross over
> Singing in tongue as of the open once . . . .
> Deliver us back to the wide world's oldest song
> when mother a fairy woman same root as Finn
> pinion on the clean fin clear clear wave[.]

While Howe's word play on *Finn* points in more than one direction, it includes an allusion to Fionnuala, a mythological woman who was turned into a swan and condemned to the water until Christian missionaries came to Ireland. As such, *Finn* takes on ancient, pre-Christian connotations of a world before institutionalized Christianity; imagining that world places readers one step closer to imagining a world before language.

Secret History of the Dividing Line (1978) continues a similar theme, so that the dividing line includes the line between the gestures of the body and more formal, symbolic language:

> In its first dumb form
> language was gesture
> technique of travelling over sea ice
> silent. . . .

The dividing line also refers to binary thinking and rigid or oppressive classification; it may also refer to the lines that divide language and silence as well as to the line that divides language and nature.

With *A Bibliography of the King's Book, or, Eikon Basilike* (1989) Howe continues her inquiry into the nature and construction of authority in language; *Eikon Basilike*, as Howe explains in her introduction, was a collection of prayers, essays, and other writings that circulated after the death of Charles I of England and which, while originally attributed to the king, turned out to be a forgery. Howe notes of the *Eikon Basilike*, "The absent center is the ghost of a king." Her rendering of the book touches on what it can possibly mean to claim that a king can rule by virtue of legitimate authority, what it can mean to claim legitimate authorship, and, finally, what claim a forgery, ghostwritten in the name of a king, can make to truth.

What is most striking, however, are the passages in Howe's book that invoke religious authority. For example, an epigraph on the first page (printed at an angle on a page where other text is printed upside-down or overlapping) reads:

Cover for Howe's largest collection of poems (1990), which includes The Liberties *(1980), her series of poems on the relationship between Hester (Stella) Johnson and Jonathan Swift*

"Oh Lord / oh Lord / different from / Laws / zeal"; later in the book, printed in standard lineation, readers find: "Opening words of *Patriarcha* / Sentences in characters / Judges and ghostly fathers." Layered throughout *Eikon Basilike* there is more than a hint that there is also something subversively feminine both in the original *Eikon* and in the interpretative processes Howe uses to reclaim the book. Howe invokes "Archaic Arachne Ariadne" and then continues, "She is gone she sends her memory." She also plays with the attribution of the *Eikon:* while John Gauden stepped forward to claim authorship during the Restoration, in Howe's account we hear of "Mrs Gauden's Nar- / rative / attributed in Primitive / times to Jesus Christ / his Apostles and other / papers Regicides took."

Singularities (1990) includes *Articulation of Sound Forms in Time* (1987), which contains an imaginative historical account based loosely on the journal of Puritan minister Hope Atherton, who wandered on the fringes of a battle between American settlers and Native Americans. The remainder of *Singularities* is a larger meditation on what seems to have gone wrong with the American voice and point of view from almost the first step on the shores. The long poems "Thorow" and "Scattering as a Behavior Toward Risk" are also in *Singularities*. "Thorow" comprises an extended meditation on what Howe terms the "Elegiac Western Imagination," which she filters through a particularly American landscape. "Thorow" succeeds by combining Howe's ambitious philosophical and historical reflections with a sense of play and a sense of concrete particulars, both of which prevent the poem from being either grandiose or ponderous:

> The Source of Snow
> the nearness of Poetry
> The Captain of Indians
> the cause of Liberty
> Mortal particulars
> whose shatter we are
> A sort of border life
> A single group of trees[.]

The Europe of Trusts, Howe's most extensive collection to date, includes *Defenestration of Prague* (1983), *Pythagorean Silence* (1982), and *The Liberties* (1980). The *Defenestration of Prague*, arguably the most inaccessible of Howe's works, refers to a specific historical event in 1617, when Calvinist rebels threw Catholic officials out of windows in Prague, thereby beginning the Thirty Years' War; in the context of Howe's book, this event is superimposed on Irish history to create a dense historical structure including battles and ballads. In *Pythagorean Silence* Howe's renderings of history are more accessible, and there seem to be more strands of narrative that, while fractured, may allude to Howe's Buffalo childhood and her early memories of Pearl Harbor and of her father—the partial subject of the poems—who died in 1967. As elsewhere in Howe's work, there is a connection between war and the forms of language that make war possible. Howe argues that this connection can be recovered: "weaving fables and faces War / doings of the war // manoeuvering between points / between / any two points."

The Liberties, the most important of Howe's works to date, continues her ongoing interrogation of language in the particular context of making room for the feminine in language, for both the historical experience of women and the ways in which language might be inflected as feminine. Howe's concern continues to be, as she noted in her interview with Tom Beckett, with "members of the silent faction—the feminine. They *were* and somewhere they still are. Traces are here. Outside the central disciplines of Economy, Anthropology, and Historiography is a gap in causal sequence. A knowing excluded from knowing." The particular example Howe selects in *The Liberties* centers on the story of Hester Johnson, whom Jonathan Swift referred to as "Stella." At Swift's encouragement both Stella and her companion Rebecca Dingley moved to Ireland to become lifelong companions of Swift.

The finest example of Howe's re-creation of Stella's story is in a dramatic section near the end of *The Liberties* entitled "God's Spies." The main characters are Stella, Cordelia (from William Shakespeare's *King Lear*), and the ghost of Swift. That Swift appears only as a ghost reinforces the reversal: Stella's language becomes the primary focus. The play opens with an exchange over language between Stella and Cordelia: "Her heart was in her throat—(Stella) Her words—(Cordelia) —were unintelligible (Stella)." Later, Cordelia speaks more: "In history people are all dead. / The plot *was* this—the fantasy *was* this— / Her spirit flew in feathers." Stella and Cordelia then speak together: "Space—room—gate—lid— / noise—ruin—heart—breast—years—family / souvenir—wedding ring—whatsoever— / clear as day—." Words are being used like talismans here, like magical chants that might recall the human experiences they mark. The words mark the experiences that have been denied to both Stella and Cordelia (including "years," "family," "wedding ring," and others), and they also mark, however fragmentarily, the experiences that have not been denied ("space," "room," "heart," and so on). What follows is a celebration of language encoded as feminine:

love	tongue	milk	pasture	words
bare	arm	cause	cube	words

Whatever other functions these words serve, they celebrate the feminine and the margins of language. This celebration continues in the cryptic ending of *The Liberties*: "Tear pages from a calendar / scatter them into sunshine and snow."

Howe's work is not incomprehensible and does not preclude interpretation. While it can be difficult and arcane, it does not seem less accessible than the late works of Wallace Stevens,

H. D.'s *Trilogy,* or the work of Ezra Pound or Marianne Moore. There is ample precedent for the highly learned, allusive poetry in Howe's canon. There is less precedent for Howe's effort to think through to the end (borrowing insights from poststructuralism) the dual problem of, on the one hand, being trapped in binary logic and language, and, on the other hand, discovering so little space for representations of either the feminine or women in that logic and language. The philosophical weight of these issues does not deter Howe's willingness to play with language, her sense of humor and of history, or her eye for the fragments of joy that can be recovered. Howe continues to be a productive writer: a chapbook, *Silence Wager Stories,* was published in 1992; a new book of poems (*The Nonconformist's Memorial*) and a collection of essays (*The Birth-Mark: Expression and the Wilderness*) are set for 1993 publication. Her work is not idle word play: the trails that have disappeared can appear again.

Interviews:
Tom Beckett, *"The Difficulties* Interview," *Difficulties,* 3, no. 2 (1989): 17-27;

Janet Ruth Fallon, "Speaking with Susan Howe," *Difficulties,* 3, no. 2 (1989): 28-42;
Edward Foster, "Interview with Susan Howe," *Talisman,* 4 (Spring 1990): 14-38.

Bibliography:
"Susan Howe: Contributions Toward a Bibliography," *Talisman,* 4 (Spring 1990): 119-122.

References:
Tom Beckett, ed., *Difficulties,* special Howe issue, 3, no. 2 (1989);
Rachel Blau DuPlessis, " 'Whowe': On Susan Howe," in her *The Pink Guitar: Writing as Feminist Practice* (New York: Routledge, Chapman & Hall, 1990), pp. 123-139;
Marjorie Perloff, "Canon and Loaded Gun: Feminist Poetics and the Avant-Garde," *Stanford Literature Review,* 4 (Spring 1987): 23-46;
Perloff, " 'Collision or Collusion with History': The Narrative Lyric of Susan Howe," *Contemporary Literature,* 30 (Winter 1989): 518-533;
Linda M. Reinfeld, "Susan Howe: Prisms," in her "Writing as Rescue: Language/Lyric/Poetry," Ph.D. dissertation, State University of New York at Buffalo, 1988, pp. 168-213.

Andrew Hudgins
(22 April 1951 -)

Clay Reynolds

BOOKS: *Saints and Strangers* (Boston: Houghton Mifflin, 1985);

After the Lost War (Boston: Houghton Mifflin, 1988);

The Never-Ending (Boston: Houghton Mifflin, 1991).

SELECTED PERIODICAL PUBLICATIONS—
UNCOLLECTED:

FICTION

"In Summer Heat," *Chariton Review* (Fall 1979): 21-25;

"To the Funeral," *Southern Review*, 19 (Autumn 1983): 899-906;

"There's No Telling," *Sequoia*, 29 (Winter 1985): 71-79;

"The Yellow House," *Missouri Review*, 9 (1986): 13-19.

NONFICTION

"*Paterson* and Its Discontents," *Arizona Quarterly*, 35 (Spring 1979): 25-41;

" 'I Am Fleeing Double': Duality and Dialectic in *The Dream Songs*," *Missouri Review*, 4 (Winter 1980-1981): 93-110;

" 'The Burn Has Settled In': A Reading of Adrienne Rich's *Diving Into the Wreck*," *Texas Review*, 2 (Spring 1981): 49-65;

" 'How Will the Heart Endure': Robert Lowell on Jonathan Edwards," *South Atlantic Quarterly*, 80 (Autumn 1981): 429-440;

"*Leaves of Grass* from the Perspective of Modern Epic Practice," *Midwest Quarterly*, 23 (Summer 1982): 380-390;

"Walt Whitman and the South," *Southern Literary Journal*, 15 (Fall 1982): 91-100;

"Landscape and Movement in *The Scarlet Letter*," *South Dakota Review*, 19 (Winter 1982): 5-17;

" 'The Real Life and the Buried Life': Louise Glück's *Descending Figure*," *Vanderbilt Poetry Review* (Spring 1983): 28-39;

" 'My Only Swerving': Sentimentality in Contemporary Poetry," *Syracuse Scholar*, 5 (Spring 1984): 5-14;

"An Interview with Donald Justice," *Sequoia*, 28 (Autumn 1984): 18-28;

" 'One and Zero Walk Off Together': Dualism in Galway Kinnell's *The Book of Nightmares*," *American Poetry*, 3 (Fall 1985): 56-71;

"Risk in Contemporary Poetry," *New England Review*, 8 (Summer 1986): 526-553;

"Contemporary Poetry: Four Anthologies," *Missouri Review*, 12, no. 1 (1989): 197-216.

Andrew Hudgins attracted the attention of the Pulitzer Prize Committee with his first volume. He writes in a more traditional mode than the open-form, free-verse style of many contemporary poets, and he reflects in his work a sensitivity to and identification with the Deep South. In the case of Hudgins's *Saints and Strangers* (1985) and *After the Lost War* (1988), the almost unanimous reaction of critics and readers is that Hudgins speaks with an original voice that expresses his southern identity and fundamentally American persona. His verse will have an impact on the way modern poetry is conceived and on the role modern poetry plays in contemporary letters.

Born on 22 April 1951 in Killeen, Texas, to Andrew L. and Roberta Rodgers Hudgins, the young Hudgins hardly had an opportunity to find regional roots anywhere. At the time of his birth, his father, who had completed service in the U.S. Navy during World War II and then graduated from West Point, was a career air force officer. The family moved from Fort Hood, where the senior Hudgins was stationed when Andrew was born, to New Mexico, England, Ohio, North Carolina, Southern California, and France. Their final destination was Montgomery, Alabama.

Hudgins's adolescent years played a part in his development as a poet sensitive to the South. From 1966 until 1969 he attended Sidney Lanier High School in Montgomery; the football team's name was the Poets. Hudgins completed his B.A. in English and earned a teaching certificate in 1974 at Huntingdon College, which was close to his home, thus allowing him to commute by bicycle and to hold down various part-time jobs. He then taught sixth grade for a year in a school

Andrew Hudgins (photograph by David Riund)

situated between two housing projects. He married Olivia Hardy in 1974.

After an unsuccessful application for admission to the University of Iowa, he enrolled at the University of Alabama and received his M.A. in English in 1976. His thesis was "Tom Jones and the Monomyth," and he was named dean's scholar. He and his wife then relocated to Syracuse, where he studied two years toward a Ph.D in English while Olivia earned a law degree. Although he won a creative-writing fellowship and received the Delmore Schwartz Award for Creative Writing, he did not complete his Ph.D. They left Syracuse and returned to Alabama, where he taught at Auburn University at Montgomery, a junior-college campus, and held odd jobs until his divorce from Olivia. He was accepted into the Writers Workshop at Iowa, where he received his M.F.A. in 1983. From 1984 to 1985 he worked as a lecturer in creative writing at Baylor University. In the summer of 1985 he was named John Atherton Fellow in poetry at the Bread Loaf Writers' Conference. Since 1985 he has been teaching at the University of Cincinnati, where he is an associate professor. He remarried in 1992.

In addition to being named runner-up for the 1986 Pulitzer Prize in poetry for *Saints and Strangers*, Hudgins has also received awards from the Great Lakes College Association, the Society of Midland Authors, the Texas Institute of Letters, and the Alabama Library Association. Hudgins was named to membership in the Texas Institute of Letters (1988) and has received grants from the National Endowment for the Arts (1986) and the Ingram Merrill Foundation (1987). He also won the Witter Bynner Award of the American Academy and Institute of Arts and Letters for 1988. Hudgins has augmented his two published volumes with scholarly articles, review essays, short stories, and poetry publications in over thirty different periodicals including the *American Poetry Review*, the *New Yorker*, and *Poetry*.

Saints and Strangers attracted qualified but generally complimentary reviews when it appeared. Most critics agree with Mark Jarman, who noted in the *Hudson Review* (Summer 1986) that Hudgins's poetic narratives are "state of the art"; but more would acknowledge that Robert B. Shaw's comment in *Poetry* (April 1986) is also on target: "I do not envy Hudgins the problems he faces in finding an audience. The people who would understand his preoccupations best are likely to read revivalist tracts rather than poetry; Yuppies, on the other hand, won't have a clue as to what lies behind all his extravagant morbidity." From the outset it was clear that Hudgins's poetry was outside the mainstream of his contemporaries' verse.

Morbidity, death, and grim images of horror all combine with what Shaw called "a lack of condescension" in Hudgins's treatment of fundamentalist religion. Virtually every reviewer noted that there are considerably more "saints" than "strangers" in the poetic portraits, but most of Hudgins's saints are ironic angels at best, and the best of those are sometimes pathetically mad. His themes are perhaps best summarized by Louie Skipper in *Prairie Schooner* (Fall 1986): Hudgins's world "is a Biblical reversal: Luke before Genesis, before Daniel, the Light of the world coming into the eternal darkness until the Light is no more and the darkness is made man, and man names the darkness within him, calling it the world." Indeed, Hudgins's collection of personae—drunk drivers, female convicts, murdered girls, and minor biblical figures—suggests a sense of the grotesque that is also seen in the work of the southern Gothic poets he admires.

Hudgins appreciates many southern poets, Robert Penn Warren, for example, although Hudgins claims he hates to be called a "Southern Gothic Poet" by reviewers and critics: "I don't believe there is a Southern Gothic. It just seems like things I've seen all my life." Robert Lowell and Louise Glück are particular favorites of his, but he also cites T. S. Eliot and William Carlos Williams as poets whose work has especially inspired him from time to time. The "rhythmic religious poems" of John Donne also are indirect influences on him, as is the work of John Berryman and other poets. But Hudgins does not believe his poetry is directly connected to any one or even several of these other writers, and, apart from obvious analogies between his work and that of Robert Browning or Ezra Pound—also masters of the dramatic monologue—critics seldom draw comparisons between Hudgins's work and that of other poets. More often, the names of Flannery O'Connor and William Faulkner are evoked when Hudgins's stark, macabre, and grotesque images are discussed.

The bulk of Hudgins's poetry is composed in blank verse, and his favorite devices are dramatic monologue and descriptive, narrative portraits of single individuals cast against the back-

drop of some bizarre event. His occasional rhyme or caesura emphasizes his narrative point, and he is fond of "tag" lines that bring the thesis of a poem home to the reader in one stark statement. He rarely uses the interrogative, and his syntax generally follows compound or complex forms. Images and metaphors are often drawn from nature, and many of his poems are pastoral in tone and setting. A favorite subtheme is the juxtaposition of man-made structures and creations with natural phenomena.

An example of his technique is "Mary Magdalene's Left Foot," a poem occasioned by a picture in "*Newsweek* or *Time*":

> The news is littered with the bodies of women
> —whores, some—who have returned to minerals,
> a pile of iron and zinc and calcium
> that wouldn't even fill a shoe. We glimpse
> of Mary Magdalene a golden whole
> that never ached for flesh or grew hair coarse
> enough to scrub mud from a traveler's foot.

With this observation Hudgins draws the reader away from the commonplace depiction of statues, icons, and relics and drives his point home as he explores the emotions beneath the hard, man-made images of Mary Magdalene:

> But gold is meretricious flattery
> for the whore who washed Christ's feet with tears,
> who rubbed sweet oil into his sores, then kissed
> each suppurating wound that swelled his flesh,
> knowing that it was God's clear flesh beneath
> its human dying. And that is more than you or I
> will ever know of where we place our lips.

The effect of such verse is stunning, as it creates a tactile relationship between the reader and the subject of the poem, a relationship that is disturbing.

Characters with familiar names appear throughout *Saints and Strangers*, including Saint Francis, John James Audubon, Zelda Fitzgerald, and various biblical figures. At the center of many poems is the relationship between real behavior and religious conviction, and as grotesque image is piled on horrid scene, the reader is tempted to think of the world of Carson McCullers or Erskine Caldwell.

But more important than assessing the images and poetic phrasings Hudgins uses is the question of the power of his verse to accomplish something literary, something artistic that is often missing from much contemporary poetry. In al-

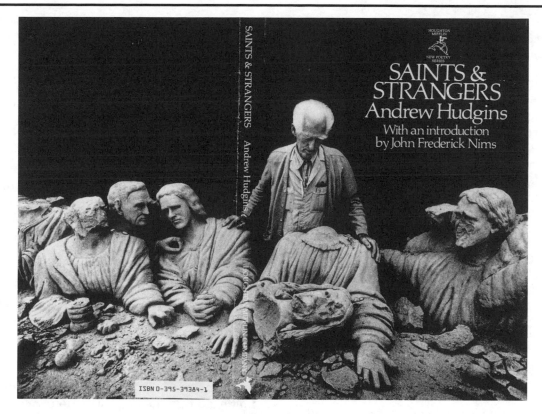

Dust jacket for Hudgins's first book, which was short-listed for a Pulitzer Prize in 1986

most every poem in the volume, Hudgins uses his verse to penetrate the images—statues, photographs, paintings, news stories—of individuals to whom real things happen or have happened and to excite the reader's imagination. This common device for Hudgins emerges more significantly in *After the Lost War*. But it is in the strikingly macabre and the horrifyingly commonplace that Hudgins's power is best revealed. In "Claims," for example, he opens the poem with a comment that is designed to chill the reader's thoughts and at the same time awaken curiosity about the morbid:

> It's boys who find the bodies in the woods
> and mostly boys who put them there.
> At cowboys and Indians—a murder game—
> they found two naked, dead, and rotting girls
> covered with leaves and brush—not even dirt.

As with so many of Hudgins's poems, the speaker then draws connections between the real incident at hand and his insecurities and doubts, and the result is often traumatic:

> When they came to ask me what I knew
> I didn't know a thing, but wanted to so bad

I had to watch my tongue for fear
that I'd invent a clue to help them out. . . .

From such inward musings Hudgins extends the meaning and closes the verse with a metaphysical observation:

> The girls . . . are turning into nothing.
> At dawn their eyes struggle for more darkness,
> at night their lost breath tangles in the breeze,
> and somewhere deeper in the labyrinth of days
> there's the sound of an opening being opened.

Hudgins's most common themes in *Saints and Strangers* center on fundamentalist religion. Ranging from "One of Solomon's Concubines, Dying, Exults in Her Virginity" to "Returning Home to Babylon" to "Awaiting Winter Visitors: Jonathan Edwards, 1749," he explores the people behind the images who have themselves become virtual icons of faith. For example, Edwards contemplates the failure of "The Great Awakening" to restore Calvinist Puritanism to its former glory:

> Beneath a tired December sky
> we looked for a descending light
> to radiate from New England shores
> to the almost mythic cusp of Asia.

Instead, the signs would not form
a prophecy. Attendance fell;
the fervor would not hold its bloom.

The fourth and final section comprises an eight-part poem from which the volume takes its title. Hudgins manages to combine his southern vision and voice with his religious theme as he examines the life of an itinerant preacher from the point of view of the minister's daughter, Marie:

One night two hunters, drunk, came in the tent.
They fired their guns and stood there stupidly
as Daddy left the pulpit, stalked toward them,
and slapped them each across the mouth. He split
one's upper lip.
                    They beat him like a dog.

Hudgins then defines his theme for the entire volume: "They got three years suspended sentence each / and Daddy got another tale of how / Christians are saints and strangers in the world." Marie's insights into the compassion of her father lead the reader to penetrate yet another image.

In *After the Lost War* Hudgins turns from a collection of tortured individuals, dark scenes, and religious themes to focus on a single figure, the poet Sidney Lanier; Hudgins follows Lanier's life through one of the most horrible series of events any man could face: war and the knowledge of his own, impending death. Once more, Hudgins penetrates history and biography to reveal a deeper meaning, a truer self.

After the Lost War did not receive the enthusiastic response excited by *Saints and Strangers*. Writing for *Poetry* in October 1988, Paul Breslin found the work "metronomical" and complained that Hudgins failed adequately to mesh his form and content into something that could "transcend its technical difficulties" and deliver "the epic amplitude it promises." R. S. Gwynn, in a long essay in *Shenandoah* (Summer 1989), noted: "Read purely as a fiction, *After the Lost War* is as compelling as a novel in its narrative flow, and the poet's lines are often moving." But Gwynn went on to complain that Hudgins's "violent imagery" is so completely antithetical both to the historical Lanier's sensibilities as well as to the poet's verse that it offends the nature and the art of poetic, narrative biography.

This complaint seems to be the most frequent against this long poem, particularly by those who are defenders/admirers of Lanier's reputation and poetry; however, Gwynn also noted that the reader sometimes wishes that the "long-

dead poet [would] arise and make truer use of the materials he found close at hand." Gwynn believes that Hudgins's attempt to "raise Lanier in our esteem" fails to rouse sympathies either for the historical figure or for the fictional character Hudgins creates. Gwynn regards the poem as "a damning critique of the Romantic stance in general and Lanier's poetics in particular, . . . the ironic history of a poet's utter failure to come to terms with his experience."

Other critics tend to agree that, regardless of the wisdom of Hudgins's choice of Lanier as a character of focus, the contemporary poet's work far outstrips his subject's importance and, possibly, Lanier's talent as well. Writing for *Library Journal* (January 1988), Fred Muratori concluded: "Free of the sentimentality and archaisms too often present in Lanier's own poems, these deft tetrameter lines may well outlast the ones that inspired them." R. F. Clayton, on the other hand, asserted that the other critics are wrong about Hudgins's relationship to Lanier. Although Clayton does not believe the book lives up to "the power and grandeur of its vision," he wrote that it would make "excellent collateral reading" for students of Lanier's poetry (*Choice*, May 1988).

It may be, however, that these critics have missed an essential point about Hudgins's verse that is not clearly revealed until one compares this second volume to the first. In *Saints and Strangers* Hudgins chose more or less fictional characters to speak through his iambic lines. When the personae were real, they were often drawn from Bible stories or, more commonly, they were inaccessible in terms of their personalities, their inner thoughts being masked by their publications or actions as public figures. In the case of Lanier, however, Hudgins settled on a nineteenth-century poet whose sensibilities were revealed directly through his poetry and whose life and work have become intertwined as his poetry continues to be read and studied.

"I thought of changing the name of the character," Hudgins states in response to comments that his poem does not bear a direct correspondence to Lanier or Lanier's biography. "But I had been calling him Sidney for ten years or so, and I just kept him as he was." Hudgins does not find Lanier's verse inspiring or evocative in any particular way that would connect to his own. He points out that the true focus of the book is the Civil War—its effect on those southerners who experienced it, who felt its loss—and the use of

Lanier's fading life as a metaphor for a defeated South seems appropriate.

Even so, Lanier's poetry provides a special meaning to *After the Lost War*. Although Hudgins does not try to emulate Lanier's verse, he does borrow recurrent themes and manages to weave them into the story of a young man of special talent whose life is shattered by the combined forces of war and disease but whose worldview is informed by his special ability to sense the power of verse as an interpreter of the meaning of nature and of the fundamental elements of the human spirit.

Although it is possibly fair to characterize Lanier as an artist who was born too late to be a romantic or transcendentalist and too early to be a realist or naturalist, Hudgins demonstrates that a poet does not have to reach classical or even iconoclastic literary heights to have a lasting and perhaps ironic effect on his reader even long after the poet is dead. The Lanier persona illustrates this point in near self-parody: "There's one thing you can say about a skunk: / it actually smells better as it rots"; but such grim irony, expressed near the end of the monologue when Lanier is trying to come to terms with his failure as a poet, in no way negates the respect and even love Hudgins demonstrates for his subject.

Thus, *After the Lost War* is not merely a poetic biography of Lanier; in fact, Hudgins does not pretend to tell the story of Lanier's life; nor are these monologues supposed to represent poetry that Lanier might have written either in content or form. Rather, Hudgins uses the same technique he employed in *Saints and Strangers* to penetrate the biographical facade of the actual figure and to trace the ramblings of the poetic mind as well as the development of the poetic sensibility, the forming of his soul, as it were. Beginning with the most significant events of Lanier's life—while he was a soldier in the Civil War—and concluding with the imminent arrival of his death from consumption, Hudgins permits Lanier's thoughts and feelings to emerge as loosely connected, disorderly events, all of which find their common theme in Lanier's role as a southerner in a defeated land, as an artist whose celebrations of nature become more and more ironic as his life slips away from him.

After the Lost War begins with a picture of Lanier as a child. "Child on the Marsh" recalls the terror he experienced when he found himself lost, wandering aimlessly through the grass, fighting panic as he sought some landmark that would lead him home. This opening poem serves a dual purpose: it sets a motif in motion for the entire narrative—a child, or childlike spirit lost in a world that bewilders and frightens in the suddenness with which familiarity can change to horrible, inevitable strangeness; it additionally establishes a cycle of "marsh" poems that provide a quadripartite view of a particular landscape, each of the four visits made at a different time in Lanier's life.

"A Soldier on the Marsh" shows Lanier on leave, revisiting the place where he had been lost before, and finding there not the terror he remembered but rather the recollections of pain from bee stings and, ironically, from his mother's whipping him for tricking his brother into touching a live insect. In "A Father on the Marsh" Lanier slaughters a turtle to demonstrate to his sons the art of making soup from the reptile. Only after he has killed the turtle and begun to prepare it for the fire does he pause to ask himself about the significance of his actions. In observing his boys' reactions, he understands that his recollections of being lost and of playing with bees and birds have had much less impact on him than this grotesque experiment will have on his own sons: "*What have I done to my boys?*" he asks himself in horror.

In all the "marsh" poems mystery, pain, and fear blend with the bucolic pleasure Lanier finds in the marsh's wild grass and streams. Hudgins mines this conflict to the fullest, making the marsh itself a sort of touchstone for Lanier's other conflicts, a place to confront them metaphorically and to deal with them as best he can.

"A Christian on the Marsh" completes the cycle and finds Lanier near the end of his life, when the inevitability of his untimely death rests heavily upon him. Recalling themes in his first volume, Hudgins offers a metaphysical reflection:

I've heard a preacher say the dead,
in heaven, watch our every move.
It's dumb. But I think I believe it.
You'd think they'd find a better way
to waste eternity.

Although Hudgins's Lanier laments "how everything I say becomes / a symbol of mortality," he seeks to find in the marsh, the landscape that has become for him a microcosm of all that has meaning in life and nature, an answer. But as he moves through the saw grass and watches the marsh creatures, he is unable to arrive at satisfactory conclusions. The final prospect of Hudgins's

Dust jacket for Hudgins's sequence of narrative poems based on the life of poet Sidney Lanier, whose experience as a Confederate soldier is the focus of the book

a wounded squirrel, carefully nursing the animal until it dies, its jaw shot away by shrapnel:

> I edged up slowly, murmuring "Clifford, Cliff,"
> as you might talk to calm a skittery mare,
> and then I helped him kill and bury all
> the wounded squirrels he'd gathered from the field.
> It seemed a game we might have played as boys.
> We didn't bury them all at once, with lime,
> the way they do on burial detail,
> but scooped a dozen, tiny, separate graves.
> When we were done he fell across the graves
> and sobbed as though they'd been his unborn sons.

This scene starkly contrasts with "Burial Detail," which finds the character Lanier looking into a mass grave and commenting:

> The bodies in dawn light, were simply forms;
> the landscape seemed abstract, unreal.
> It didn't look like corpses, trees or sky,
> but shapes on shapes against a field of gray.

Almost all the war scenes, however graphic and gruesome, leave the reader wondering how anyone could retain poetic sensitivity after witnessing anything so inhumane and barbaric. Yet Hudgins permits the narrator's sense of irony to distance him from the facts of the horror around him. Yet the most significant passages in Hudgins's narrative are those that indicate the overwhelming and lasting scars left on the poet by his role as a private soldier:

> But I see clear in memory
> what I ignored back then: the dull
> inhuman thud of lead on flesh,
> the buckling of a shot man's knees,
> the outward fling of arms, and the
> short arc a head inscribes before
> it hits the ground. . . .

Even such direct references have less impact on the reader than the indirect discoveries the persona makes about his own nature when he examines it in light of his combat experiences. Further, such revelations point again to Hudgins's consistent technique of showing the inner nature, the truer self of his poetic subject.

Aside from the war themes and the images of nature that run throughout the narrative, humor also plays a part in the narrator's makeup. A barnyard joke about a randy rooster is countered a bit later with an extended anecdote about skunks; and once again Hudgins allows the humor to soften the blow of a more stun-

fictional persona, therefore, is to seek the meaning of his life in his own being, not in idle symbols. In this subtle shift toward existential conclusions at the close of the character Lanier's life, Hudgins reveals the fundamental meaning behind the poet Lanier's formative, transcendental ideas.

Aside from the marsh—the image of which recurs as a counterpoint to other themes such as the clover and corn plants—the most pervasive connecting thread is Lanier's war experience, his personal role as a soldier, prisoner, and southerner. Hudgins introduces the reader to Lanier's reactions to battle in the first section of the book: images of campfire revelry contrast sharply with a frantic search Lanier undertakes to find his brother Clifford, who, he fears, is dead; the search ends when Lanier finds him standing over

ning point, to distance the reader from the grim subject at hand, Lanier's imminent death. Even as the persona, feeble and coughing blood, remembers "The Cult of the Lost Cause" and contemplates his past as a soldier, Hudgins keeps irony close to the surface to offset bitterness: "boys who had conjugated Latin verbs / were conjugated likewise into death, / which is, I guess, the future perfect tense." Additionally, bizarre scenes such as in "Postcards of the Hanging" and in the canto of the title poem that deals with "flaming birds"—buzzards set on fire by sailors and then released to race across the night sky—bring home to the reader the wide swing of extremes in the persona's experience and explain much of the shaping of his sensitivity to life and art.

In the "flaming birds" sequence, the thesis of this exploration of Lanier's life is summed up. As the buzzards are doused with kerosene and released, he remarks that they look like "burnt-out stars," and even though he recognizes that "For them it must be hideous," he cannot help but draw a particular lesson from the spectacle:

> with the younger generation of the South
> after the lost war, pretty much
> the whole of life has been not dying.
> And that is why, I think, for me
> it is a comfort just to see
> the deathbird fly so prettily.

This poem underscores the point that Hudgins is making about the almost hopeless spirit of the South that flamed so brightly and so hideously in death as it tried to escape a personal and regional history that continues to haunt it like the vision of the burning buzzards over the Alabama River and like Lanier's own brightly flaming life, scarred as it was by war, as it gradually lost its brilliance and died.

Throughout the narrative, Hudgins's poetry flows with the ease of a gentle conversation but never strays far away from metaphoric originality: "Because the flute's a woodland instrument, / I felt incongruous in the desert quiet. / But soon my playing built a decent forest," he writes of Lanier's experience in the nearly treeless plains near San Antonio. And even when dealing with the most grotesque and macabre scenes, Hudgins offers metaphors and similes to manage that encapsulation of thought that is the essence of good poetry. In "Rapprochement with Death," for example, the metaphor "My life is balanced on my lungs / the way an anvil rests upon an

egg" illuminates the personality of the poet Hudgins is characterizing.

This volume of poetry, then, is far more than a narrative account of the life of Sidney Lanier. As in *Saints and Strangers* Hudgins has achieved two of the most difficult tasks of modern letters: he has managed to capture and characterize the persona of an actual historical personage, not by showing the reader life as Lanier saw it but rather life as Lanier felt it; second, Hudgins has written verse of such high quality that it stands alone as praiseworthy, even if it has little to do with the poetry penned by Lanier. The poems of *After the Lost War* read with an intensity that may be a better testimony to Lanier's experience than anything he himself was capable of writing. The book was awarded the Poets' Prize for 1988.

Hudgins's *The Never-Ending* (1991), winner of the Texas Institute of Letters Poetry Award, demonstrates many of the same elements of excellence that characterized the earlier collections. For one thing, Hudgins's metrical analysis of human behavior once again shocks as often as it soothes. From the opening poem, "How Shall We Sing the Lord's Song in a Strange Land," which mentions a racist lynching, to the quiet, somber reflections of vandalism and the ravages of time and memory in "New Headstones at the Shelby Springs Confederate Cemetery," Hudgins evokes the pain of startlingly cogent revelations.

Often Hudgins's personae's observations are more realistic because of their commonplace settings. "Heat Lightning in a Time of Drought," for example, opens with a frightening scene:

> My neighbor, drunk, stood on his lawn and yelled,
> *Want some! Want some!* He bellowed it as cops
> cuffed him, shoved him in their back seat—*Want Some!*—
> and drove away. Now I lie here awake,
> not by choice, listening to the crickets' high
> electric trill, urgent with lust. Heat lightning flashes.

Just as often, Hudgins evokes a startling image in the middle or at the end of poems to shock the reader into an awareness of the significance of the apparently insignificant elements of life. It is a technique he uses to advantage in all his poetry, and somehow he manages to keep it fresh and stunning each time.

In about half the poems of the volume, Hudgins takes on a theme that characterizes *Saints and Strangers*, the relationship of great works of art to those who observe them and, as if for the first time, begin to analyze their subjects. In this new volume he centers his poetic examination on images of Christ in paintings, sculptures, hymns, and popular stories. His treatment of Jesus is not theological; rather, he attempts to deal with the human nature of the man who is so often depicted in art forms. Often, the observer is a child or someone who studies for the first time the man behind the God who had to deal with the pain and ignorance of an ungrateful creation.

Throughout the volume there is much food for philosophical reflection on the eternal nature of life's ironies, but what makes this collection of poetry most effective is Hudgins's cunning wit and sensibility to how people think. He evokes an intensity in his study of how people react to experience, and in doing so, moves a giant step closer to establishing himself as one of the major poetic voices in America today.

In an unfinished, in-progress volume, "The Unpromised Land," Hudgins's poetry begins to take a turn to more traditional subjects, although his penchant for horrific images and carefully controlled metrical lines is still in evidence. Although there are monologues in this new book, the pattern of using verse to shatter the outer images of characters, well known and unknown, shifts more to the commonplace happenings of life: women hanging wash; husbands and wives; and suburban neighbors. Nevertheless, Paul Gauguin, Sandro Botticelli, Christ, and the Magi appear as well.

The poetry of Andrew Hudgins is significant as much because of his ability to control his verse and to present his poetic vision in closed form as because of his choices of and approaches toward his subject matter. In the manner of the greatest of poets, Hudgins has demonstrated that the proper study of poetry is humankind, not effusive outpourings of emotion born out of boredom and the desire to say something in an odd, elliptical manner. Hudgins's poetry fulfills the purposes of poetry as outlined by William Wordsworth and Samuel Taylor Coleridge and carried forth by the best of twentieth-century writers. His poetry illuminates, illustrates, and fulfills the imagination, freeing it to wonder further about the subjects he chooses.

References:

R. S. Gwynn, "Looking for Sidney," *Shenandoah*, 39 (Summer 1989): 57-67;

Clay Reynolds, "Crossing the Line of Poetic Biography: Andrew Hudgins' Narrative of the Life of Sidney Lanier," *Journal of the American Studies Association of Texas*, 20 (October 1989): 27-40.

T. R. Hummer
(7 August 1950 -   )

Roger D. Jones
Southwest Texas State University

BOOKS: *Translation of Light* (Stillwater, Okla.: Cedar Creek, 1976);
The Angelic Orders (Baton Rouge & London: Louisiana State University Press, 1982);
The Passion of the Right-Angled Man (Urbana: University of Illinois Press, 1984);
Lower-Class Heresy (Urbana: University of Illinois Press, 1987);
The 18,000-Ton Olympic Dream (New York: Quill/ Morrow, 1990).

OTHER: *The Imagination as Glory: Essays on the Poetry of James Dickey,* edited by Hummer and Bruce Weigl (Urbana: University of Illinois Press, 1984);
Corrinne Hales, *Underground,* introduction by Hummer (Boise: Ahsahta, 1986).

SELECTED PERIODICAL PUBLICATIONS—
UNCOLLECTED: "Merwin and Roethke: Two Voices and the Technique of Nonsense," *Western Humanities Review,* 33 (Winter 1979);
"Robert Penn Warren: *Audubon* and the Moral Center," *Southern Review,* 16 (Fall 1980);
"Revising the Poetry Wars: Louis Simpson's Assault on the Poetic," *Kenyon Review,* 6 (Summer 1984);
"The Heroics of Clarity: On Dave Smith," *Kenyon Review* (Spring 1986);
"The Thousand Variations of One Song: The Influence of James Dickey," *James Dickey Newsletter* (Fall 1986);
"Bluegrass Wasteland" [poem], *Georgia Review* (Spring 1987).

In an interview with Phil Paradis, T. R. Hummer referred to his poems as "acts of attention" and called his predominant poetic concern—passion—a "way to make connection" with the world. With the publication of his first five books of poetry, Hummer has established himself—alongside such figures as Nathaniel Hawthorne, William Faulkner, and, more recently, Robert Penn Warren, James Dickey, and Dave Smith—as

T. R. Hummer circa 1985 (photograph by Marion Hummer)

a writer of the self, concerned with individuality, self-knowledge, and, by extension, the moral and psychological growth of the human race.

Born on 7 August 1950 to Charles (a postman and farmer) and Marion Slocum Hummer, Terry Randolph Hummer grew up in Noxobee County in rural eastern Mississippi not far from the area made famous by Faulkner. Hummer earned his B.A. and M.A. in English (1972, 1974) from the University of Southern Mississippi, where he studied under fiction writer Gordon Weaver, and earned his Ph.D. (1980) at the University of Utah, where he studied with poet and fellow southerner Dave Smith. Hummer has taught at Utah, Oklahoma State, and Kenyon College (where he briefly edited the *Kenyon Review*) and is currently teaching at Middlebury College, where he edits the *New England Review*. He has also served as visiting professor at Exeter College in England and as writer in residence at the University of California, Irvine. Hummer has received a fellowship from the National Endowment for the Arts (1987) and in 1983 was a Bread Loaf fellow.

Hummer's first collection, *Translation of Light* (1976), attracted little critical notice, though Henry Dalton (*Southern Literary Review*, Fall/Winter 1976) credited the poems as "deeply felt . . . often impressive, yet . . . uneven." The title reflects Hummer's recurring emphases on light imagery and on the role of the individual's perception in the process of making sense of the world. Though several poems in the volume are included in later collections, the book suggests a writer still seeking his own voice and poetic identity. "A poetry this young is still looking for itself," Dalton wrote. "There are times when the subject seems to overwhelm the poem, resulting in loss of clarity, or overwriting."

By the time of Hummer's second collection, *The Angelic Orders* (1982), Hummer's studies under Smith at Utah had yielded a more concrete, clear, confident poetic voice. Reviewer David Baker cites the collection as "generous-hearted, energetic, revelatory" and calls the book "a sort of poetic *Bildungsroman*, tracing the maturation of a single speaker who stays with us most of the volume." Baker writes that the volume's predominant theme is "passion—sexual awakening and involvement [as well as] the irresistible grace of the passionate moment that allows us to rise beyond the daily lives" (*New England Review*, Spring 1983). The book's title, taken from Rainer Maria Rilke's first Duino elegy, suggests an emphasis on a visionary, spiritual realm within the empirical world. Hummer, who with poet Bruce Weigl coedited a collection of essays on James Dickey (1984), repeats Dickey's poetic impulse toward a more just and shimmering order of reality.

Though heavily narrative, many of the poems in *The Angelic Orders* take the form of epiphanies, in which a speaker is brought suddenly in contact with evidence of this higher order, which sometimes evokes terror in him and sometimes approaches that realm the Romantics referred to as the "sublime." In "What Shines in Winter Burns," for example, a boy on a school bus sees a frozen man beside the road, his "right hand frozen to the whiskey bottle . . . and his frozen dead

eyes open / Staring up at me, answering, *Boy, you will never / Understand love until you lay your hand / Where mine is now. Touch me. This is the body, I know.*" In "The Man Who Beat the Game at Johnny's Truck Stop," a rejected lover brings his fist down through a pinball machine's glass, where "the cowgirl's breasts / Lit up, one red, one green." Later the speaker says:

We wrapped his [hands]
In napkins, and he sat a long time
Not talking, not minding the dark
Blot the bound fingers left
On the table, not listening
When we told him again and again
He had a home.

"There is one world," Hummer writes in "Inland Hurricane: A Love Poem," "but it moves relentlessly." Throughout the five sections of the book, Hummer's speakers try to locate themselves, through passionate perception, in the midst of this tornadic flux, a feature particularly pronounced in the last section, which deals specifically with the speaker's sexual awakening and with relationships between men and women. In "Cement," "Sunrise: Passion: A Dream of Horses," "How Far I Walked This Morning with the Deer to Find You," and "A Refusal To Mourn the Death of the World by Fire," Hummer depicts romantic love as tense, delicate, and easily destroyed. Perhaps the best of such depictions is the book's finest piece, "Where You Go When She Sleeps," whose speaker looks down at the golden hair of the woman sleeping in his lap and thinks of "the boy you heard of once who fell / Into a silo full of oats, the silo emptying from below . . . / the boy . . . / gone already, down in a gold sea, spun deep in the heart of the silo."

In *The Passion of the Right-Angled Man* (1984), which poet-critic Corrinne Hales referred to as a "brave and uncompromising book (*New Jersey Poetry Journal*, 1985), Hummer focuses directly on sexuality, passion, and those features of the world William Wordsworth called the "dark inscrutable workmanship of nature." "With astonishing clarity of vision," Hales noted, "Hummer explores the consequences of passion—what it means to become aware of the awful disparity between *want* and *is*."

Heavily indebted to Wordsworth's poetry, these poems echo Warren's question in *Audubon* (1969): "what is man but his passion?" In the book's opening poem, "Coming Back, False

Cover for Hummer's 1987 collection, which includes skeptical poems on the uncertainties of beliefs and memories

Dawn," with its echoes of Wordsworth's "Tintern Abbey" (1798), Hummer's speaker walks alone on a road where earlier he had seen a vision of a woman's face and thought, "Passion is everything." "Say it was time and place / And a man unhinged by love. Say it was circumstance," Hummer writes. "I'll believe anything." With its dark, brooding setting and almost mystical tone, the poem—like many in his 1984 collection—does not state overtly so much as intimate the mysterious inner complexities of passionate emotion and perception that enable the speaker to "make contact" with an inner order in the midst of the intense velocity of circumstance.

In "Love Song" a bar musician witnesses a knife fight between two men over a woman. In "The Oracle of the Lonely Man in Stillwater, Oklahoma," the speaker, in a bar, watches "some man's beautiful daughter" place her hands "on the leg of a boy who might be / Me, grown suddenly young / And stupid with the unexplainable rising / Of passion in a public place." Similar moments are expressed in "The Beating," "Because

You Will Not Let Me Say I Will Love You Forever," "Any Time, What May Hit You," "Traps," and "First Love: When It Falls." In the title poem, "The Passion of the Right-Angled Man," a drunken, lovesick man who has accepted a dare climbs up a television tower while a radio in a car below "plays a song / About honky-tonks and passion, about some poor fool in love / With somebody gone." "Too high for that busted heart," the man wishes only that "someone he doesn't believe in anymore" will "let some lonely woman miles away turn her TV on / And see him . . . grown / Whole on the screen, alive in the height of his passion, / Over the air and there for her, ninety degrees from the ground." Throughout these poems, Hummer advances the implicit argument that, in the face of the world's irrationality, the saving moment is the moment of passionate involvement—tense, shattering, and often revelatory to the point of vision.

Like Warren and Dickey (who are stylistic as well as thematic influences), Hummer also seeks logic in a world where sporadic violence always constitutes the darker and more painful antithesis to love. In "Circumstance: The Vanishing" the speaker comforts a couple whose stillborn infant "Turned sharp in its dark world of body // The blood-rope twisted wrong." In "A Kindness" the speaker watches a dog killing an egret, and reflects that "God's mercy, it is high / And lonely as an angel, set white / On the long grave of its shadow."

Ultimately *The Passion of the Right-Angled Man* is a book about knowledge, a lyrical record of spiritual questing, and an exploration of how one may act in a world where so much lies outside logic, and where the individual must accept the consequences of action, regardless of how much knowledge is available. Caught in what Warren has called the "blind ruck of events," Hummer's speakers slog valiantly on, yearning for whatever grace or vision can illuminate time and indicate sound judgment. The volume attracted much favorable critical response: Michael J. Bugeja, for example, cited the work as a "modern masterpiece" (*Quarterly West*, Fall/Winter, 1984-1985). It marked Hummer's complete arrival in the populous contemporary poetry landscape, and it established indisputably both Hummer's technical/stylistic prowess and his distinct themes.

Lower-Class Heresy (1987) extends many of the themes of *The Passion of the Right-Angled Man*, yet also takes deliberate issue with many of Hummer's earlier approaches and conclusions. *Lower-Class Heresy* can be seen, among other things, as a penetrating survey of the spiritual and psychic landscape of the baby boom generation. Hummer came of age in the 1960s, when people questioned virtually all dogma and institutionalized practice as means for social and political oppression, and ultimately replaced faith with romantic love and sexuality.

Lower-Class Heresy is a book about faith, knowledge, action, and the possibilities of belief. Moreover, Hummer studies the role of faith in human action, taking as his main texts not the works of British Romanticism, but the writings of the American transcendentalists, the spiritual forerunners of the 1960s. Whereas in his 1984 volume Hummer explored the meanings of passion, in his 1987 book he sorts through the implications of *dogma*—any belief that has hardened into social convention—and *heresy*, any deviation from that convention. Hummer explores both public and private dogma. Though he continues (as in "The Second Story," "Domestic," "Legal Limit," "Convention: An Alternative," and others) to write of sexuality and passion, he is as much interested in the way humans base their actions on metaphysical, religious, or psychological grounds, which often turn out to be misguided, empty, inadequate, or groundless.

In "The Unpoetic," for example, Hummer turns naturalist to take issue with Ralph Waldo Emerson, who talked to the Rhodora "the way I would to a woman.... / He thought the flower symbolized the soul." Such poems in this collection as "Heresies Overheard," "Course of Empire, *North America 1985*," and "The Afterworld," among others, deal similarly with belief, and the difficulties of belief in a world where so little can be known. "In Shock" presents the speaker confronting an urban environment: "Sometimes I feel this way. I want to love / Everything.... I want to say / 42nd St. is a sudden avenue into memory, // But it would be a lie." Over and over Hummer chronicles how speakers and characters build their belief on uncertain grounds, then watch in helpless disillusionment as those grounds, and that belief, erode. Everything ultimately becomes suspect, even memory itself.

Hummer refers to his characters as "subscendentalists," a pun he coined to refer to the twentieth century's preoccupation with the unconscious—the "Undersoul"—and with the prevailing Dionysian energies. Ultimately Hummer narrows his focus to the folly of thought in America, where "something turns good people into fools." Two poems in particular act as showcase pieces for Hummer's indictment. In "Dogma: Pigmeat and Whiskey," a poem in loose terza rima, Hummer's speaker describes an invalid grandfather at "the last of the great reunions." The old man demands as his right the chance to oversee the pig roast, where the speaker—a boy—has been allowed, despite family tradition. Stubbornly the old man clings to an erroneous version of his life, insisting that his father had been killed by Yankees in the Civil War, while in truth, as the speaker tells us, "he died in a prison camp of typhus." But the family's capitulation to the old man's story becomes its capitulation to myth, and Hummer paints a powerful indictment of the irrational, stubborn southern tendency to cling to tradition long after it outlives its reasons.

In its potent, relentless insight into the complexities of American thought, *Lower-Class Heresy* solidly places Hummer in the lineage of American doubters that has included Mark Twain, Theodore Dreiser, Faulkner, and others. Moreover the book demonstrates Hummer's growth from the narrative poems of his early career to a longer, denser, more complex and sophisticated form that weaves history, philosophy, literature, and culture into a relatively seamless whole. Hummer continued developing this style in "Bluegrass Wasteland," a thirty-page poem that first appeared in spring 1987 in the *Georgia Review* and then as the most important poem and the last of three sections in Hummer's 1990 collection *The 18,000-Ton Olympic Dream*.

Though resistant to easy categorization, "Bluegrass Wasteland" could perhaps best be described as a philosophical poetic treatise in which Hummer enters the ongoing poetic dialogue of the structuralists, deconstructionists, objectivists, and others concerning the relationship between language and reality. Hummer focuses on a handful of situations on an Ohioan winter night—a couple having an affair, a local bluegrass band performing at a bar, the speaker's memories of his Louisiana boyhood, and the uneventful lives of local townspeople. He contrasts these to the way the mind—"the voice"—frames it all through language. Though much of what happens in the town is commonplace, falling into "cliché, the fossil history of the heart," Hummer explores how "the voice" helps determine the meaning of events, "the fractured vision / Of the human world, which isolates everything you do." He writes:

if we knew what to call
Nature beyond that self-fulfilling and -defeating
                                                    name,
We would have a language so pure it would require
No mind to contain it, no voice to speak it,
                                                    nobody
To breathe it out of its own air into its own air.

Language clearly either exists or does not exist
Without us. The way you think about it
Is a matter of pure faith, maybe, but the answer
                                                    you choose
Determines everything.

The poem moves toward familiar Hummer terrain: the couple make love clandestinely in *the passionate illusion . . . the reality of consequence,* where the couple makes contact with the "inarticulate mystery of every human life." While language has transported people into this scene, and into the lives of other people as well, Hummer implies that language—"the voice that owns everything"—has its limits.

Cinematic in technique, "Bluegrass Wasteland" is also the logical extension of the general discursive direction Hummer's work has taken throughout his career, developing its main ideas in deliberate fashion. Unfortunately the poem is marred by the few recurring weaknesses Hummer's work has shown over the years—tedious, pedantic murkiness and occasional overwriting that seems, at times, almost pompous. Yet, clearly, the poem takes its greatest risk in its sheer ambition, and for a poem that tackles such obviously large and ambitious metaphysical concerns, it is surprisingly successful and can be seen as a modern counterpart to Walt Whitman's "Song of Myself" (1855) in America's long philosophical poetic dialogue.

In the title poem of *The 18,000-Ton Olympic Dream* (which comprises the first section of the book), Hummer continues to mine the ground of American thought, contrasting American culture to British and European culture through the metaphor of the *Olympic Dream,* a tanker that sank in 1987 in the Mediterranean roughly at the same time that the "Irangate" scandal became public. Weaving these events, and the American decline they imply, into his own meditations on being an American in a distant country, "one son of a bitch / In a universe at the mercy of sons of bitches / With bodyguards or mandates / Or Presidential Bibles, or Truth half baked / Like a bastard file in [Robert] MacFarlane's sickeningly sweet / Key-shaped cake," Hummer creates a poem expressive not only of America's declining importance in world affairs as the century nears its end but also of the negative political implications of the Ronald Reagan era, and the bewilderment Americans themselves face as they approach the limits of the national mythos.

The disillusionment of this poem carries into the book's middle section as well, which comprises shorter poems set in various real or imagined locations in America. Unlike Whitman, however, in whose nineteenth-century view America was bustling with supreme promise (and whose long lines Hummer sometimes employs), he sees the country as a wasteland sprawling with disillusioned people, empty lives, and exhausted hopes: "a dream of lost words / We are living through, // The story that goes on being / Mumbled behind the thick, / Old-fashioned plaster of the walls / Of a mind we all share." Moreover, in such poems as "Courtly Love," "Poem in the Shape of a Saxophone," "The August Possessions," and "Decorum," even love and sexual passion—celebrated in Hummer's earlier work—become openly suspect. "This is what men and women do to each other," he writes in "Poem in the Shape of a Saxophone": "make / Breathy worlds and expect each other to live there, / Beautifully improvised." As in "Bluegrass Wasteland," love and sexuality, in the context of the general exhaustion of human lives, become sad, though momentarily appealing, antidotes to the overall monotony and the "unconscious reality that doesn't give a damn / What any mind thinks it means." Thus, throughout *The 18,000-Ton Olympic Dream,* Hummer extends the questioning he began in *Lower-Class Heresy* and incorporates disillusionment fully into the texture of American life and the search for meaning.

Critic Sidney Burris has written that Hummer's work is "truly an American poetry" (*Sewanee Review,* October 1985). Though the future direction of Hummer's work remains to be seen, his recent works indicate that he will continue wading into the stream of American thought. He had already traveled an impressive distance in that stream before his fortieth birthday. In his skillful blend of narrative and lyrical impulses, in his emphasis on passion and "acts of attention," in his literate exploration of the implications of both romantic and realist strains in American and British literature, Hummer has come in a short time to the forefront as one of his generation's most talented poets, as well as one of its most insightful voices of conscience.

Interview:

Phil Paradis, "Poetry: Connecting with the World: An Interview with T. R. Hummer," *Cimarron Review,* 71 (April 1985): 53-61.

Reference:

Michael J. Bugeja, "The Poetry of Passion: Proclamation for T. R. Hummer," *Quarterly West,* 19 (Fall/Winter 1984-1985): 67-74.

Mark Jarman

(5 June 1952 -   )

Richard Flynn
Georgia Southern University

BOOKS: *Tonight Is the Night of the Prom* (Pittsburgh: Three Rivers, 1974);
North Sea (Cleveland, Ohio: Cleveland State University Poetry Center, 1978);
The Rote Walker (Pittsburgh: Carnegie-Mellon University Press, 1981);
Far and Away (Pittsburgh: Carnegie-Mellon University Press, 1985);
The Black Riviera (Middletown, Conn.: Wesleyan University Press, 1990);
Iris (Brownsville, Oreg.: Story Line, 1992);
The Past from the Air (West Chester, Pa.: Aralia, 1992).

OTHER: "Robinson, Frost, and Jeffers and the New Narrative Poetry," in *Expansive Poetry: Essays on the New Narrative & the New Formalism,* edited by Frederick Feirstein (Santa Cruz, Cal.: Story Line, 1989);
"Poetry and Religion," in *Poetry After Modernism,* edited by Robert McDowell (Brownsville, Oreg.: Story Line, 1991).

One of the founders of the New Narrative movement in contemporary poetry, Mark Jarman recovers lost storytelling traditions in a poetry that is grounded in specific places (California, Scotland, and rural Kentucky) and specific times (particularly his childhood and adolescence in the 1950s and 1960s). With partner Robert McDowell, Jarman was the cofounder of the *Reaper,* the primary organ of the New Narrative move-

Mark Jarman (photograph by Amy Jarman)

ment. Jarman has often advanced highly polemical arguments for narrative poetry as an antidote to what he sees as exhausted lyric and meditative modes of contemporary verse. But his collections of poems are more convincing arguments for narrative, demonstrating a growing facility with all aspects of the art. However strident the *Reaper* pronouncements may have been at times, Jarman's poetry is not strictly narrative but combines narrative, lyric, meditative, and dramatic elements with increasing skill.

Born in Mount Sterling, Kentucky, on 5 June 1952, to Donald and Bo Dee Jarman, Mark Jarman is the eldest of three children. His father was attending the College of the Bible (now the Lexington Theological Seminary) when Mark was born, and a year later the family moved to Santa Maria, California, where the Reverend Mr. Jarman served the First Christian Church. When Mark was six, the family moved to Kirkcaldy, Fife, Scotland, where his father was pastor at the St. Clair Street Church of Christ as part of the U.S. Christian Church (Disciples of Christ) Fraternal Aid to British Churches. In 1961 the family moved to Redondo Beach, California, where the elder Jarman was the minister for the South Bay Christian Church. Mark Jarman's childhood, divided between Scotland and California, became the primary subject of his first full-length collection, *North Sea* (1978); the struggles with religious faith that he experienced as the son of a minister and grandson of an evangelist are also important subjects, particularly in *The Rote Walker* (1981); likewise Jarman's adolescence in Redondo Beach provided inspiration for some of his mature poems, such as "The Supremes" and "Cavafy in Redondo," from *Far and Away* (1985), and the title poem of *The Black Riviera* (1990).

Though Jarman was only twenty-six when *North Sea* was published, he had already distinguished himself as a poet. At the University of California, Santa Cruz, he studied with Raymond Carver and the poet George Hitchcock, editor and publisher of the influential little magazine *kayak*. By 1974, when Jarman received his B.A. in English literature with highest honors, he had also received the Joseph Henry Jackson Award for poetry from the San Francisco Foundation and had published an impressive chapbook, *Tonight Is the Night of the Prom* (1974). At Santa Cruz he also met McDowell, with whom he was to found the *Reaper* in 1981, and Amy Kane, whom he married on 28 December 1974.

From 1974 to 1976 Jarman attended the Iowa Writers' Workshop as a teaching/writing fellow, studying under Marvin Bell, Donald Justice, Sandra McPherson, Stanley Plumly, and Charles Wright and earning his M.F.A. in poetry. Jarman then taught at Indiana State University, Evansville (now the University of Southern Indiana) from 1976 to 1978, the University of California, Irvine, as a visiting lecturer (1979-1980), and Murray State University, Murray, Kentucky (1980-1983), before settling at Vanderbilt University, where he is a professor of English. In addition to his teaching and editing, Jarman has also received three National Endowment for the Arts grants in poetry and a 1991 Guggenheim Fellowship in poetry. He lives in Nashville, Tennessee, with his wife and their two daughters, Claire Marie and Zoë Anne.

The chapbook *Tonight Is the Night of the Prom* explores the material of Jarman's California adolescence. Although Jarman was barely past adolescence when he wrote the poems, they are remarkably accomplished; indeed, many of them were published as early as 1972 in magazines such as *kayak*, *Antaeus*, and *Poetry*. At once elegiac and tough-minded, the poems explore an adolescence lived on a "strip of sand littered with strange, / intolerable acts—trash cans aflame, / perversions coming on the tide like grunion" ("Elegy for Redondo Beach"). The speaker laments the loss of this seamy landscape now that the "city fathers" have "lined the Esplanade with lamps / to flood the beach with decency." If this apprentice work seems of a piece with the fashionable surrealism of the 1970s, the surrealism is suited to the material—the landscape of southern California mirrors the furtiveness of teenage sexuality, and many of the poems distinguish themselves from run-of-the-mill verse by their early indications of Jarman's gift for narrative.

Jarman returns to California and adolescence in the poems of his later collections. But first he turns to his childhood in *North Sea*, particularly to the years his family spent in the linoleum-factory town of Kirkcaldy in Scotland. The volume consists primarily of shorter lyrics, and some of them seem unnecessarily hermetic. Jarman seems to have deliberately abridged his narrative, perhaps because of his Iowa experience. But some of the poems show the benefit of his apprenticeship, succeeding beyond the poems in the 1974 chapbook. In "My Parents Have Come Home Laughing," the speaker's parents return from a feast for Robert Burns; their ribaldry about haggis and Burns's "Nine Inch Will Please a Lady," which might well have been the whole substance for the younger Jarman, gives way to his tender recollection of a somehow comforting primal scene:

> the strength to keep laughing breaks
> In a sigh. I hear, as their tired ribs
> Press together . . .
> And hear also a weeping from both of them
> That seems not to be pain, and it comforts me.

A longer meditation on the family history and the family name, titled "History," concerns the child's (and the adult's) need to make a name for himself. The poem culminates in a prose meditation about the "logic" of "a child who believed his name could be magical." The child's logic, Jarman says, "is also his selfishness": "I wanted my name to have a meaning of utmost secrecy. I did not want ever to mistake my identity for the one my family gave me."

There are other moving poems about family life in *North Sea*, such as "The Crossing," and the love poem "Lullaby for Amy." The latter poem's refrain, "The earth is a wave that will not set us down," later serves as the epigraph to Jarman's watershed collection, *Far and Away*. The increasing maturity and the unsentimental tenderness of the finest poems in *North Sea* more than make up for the occasional emaciated lyric that mars it.

The Rote Walker combines the best strategies of the previous collections and represents a further advance in Jarman's poetic growth. The subject matter is fraught with conflict, examining his rejection of rote faith in order to find poetic faith, more sacred because it is more hard won. The book is framed by poetic musings about the secular folk song "Greensleeves" and the Christmas carol with the same tune, "What Child Is This?" In the poem "Greensleeves" the speaker, fooling around on a piano, recalls only the melody of the song of the same name:

> A scrap of melody,
> it is the one piece
> I ever played well; my heart
> is still in it, too.
> It is possibly this
> that I mean. So much meant
> to be lost is saved.

In "Does the Whale Diminish?" the speaker

questions his father's rejection of the drunk, the wife beater, the bigot, and the one who "was merely suspicious." But rather than chide his father, the speaker recognizes that "all of us" are "suspect," that there is some essential truth in the father's view of him as an "ungrateful son / . . . lost in impossible poems." The speaker empathizes with the father's difficulty in deciding. Similarly, the title poem inverts the Sermon on the Mount ("Blessed the first to recite their assignments / for they shall be first to forget"; "The meek do not want it") but ends echoing T. S. Eliot's *Four Quartets* (1943): "The end of the task / is to forget the task." As critic Peter Makuck says, "Buried in his No he [Jarman] has found a Yes."

In addition to the primary theme of the poet's struggle with the faith of his forebears, *The Rote Walker* also contains accomplished poems that are harbingers of Jarman's recent work. In "Los Angeles" Jarman returns to his southern California adolescence but with the distance of maturity and a moral stance that was undeveloped in his apprentice work. The speaker, a "preacher's kid," recalls an adolescence devoted to fast cars and "girls with flammable skin," but he realizes he has rendered the city and his past "out of reach":

> the city like a model
> of our past, under glass.
> At times, we kneel before it,
> worshipping our lives there.
> At times, we hover over, knowing,
> helpless, looking on.

Far and Away returns again to the lost landscapes of Jarman's adolescence and represents a breakthrough in his method and techniques. On the dust jacket, Jarman characterizes the poems as "experiments with narration and the reconstruction of experience. Today the part of L.A. where I was a teenager bears little resemblance to what it was then. And yet my backward look isn't altogether nostalgic. I have no desire to return to the past, only to recover some lost people and places." Indeed, the best poems in the volume eschew the nostalgia common to lyric remembrances of things past; Jarman both trusts the compelling subjects of his narratives and paradoxically maintains a moral distance from those subjects. Invoking the great poet of memory, in "Cavafy in Redondo" Jarman notes that "Our ruins

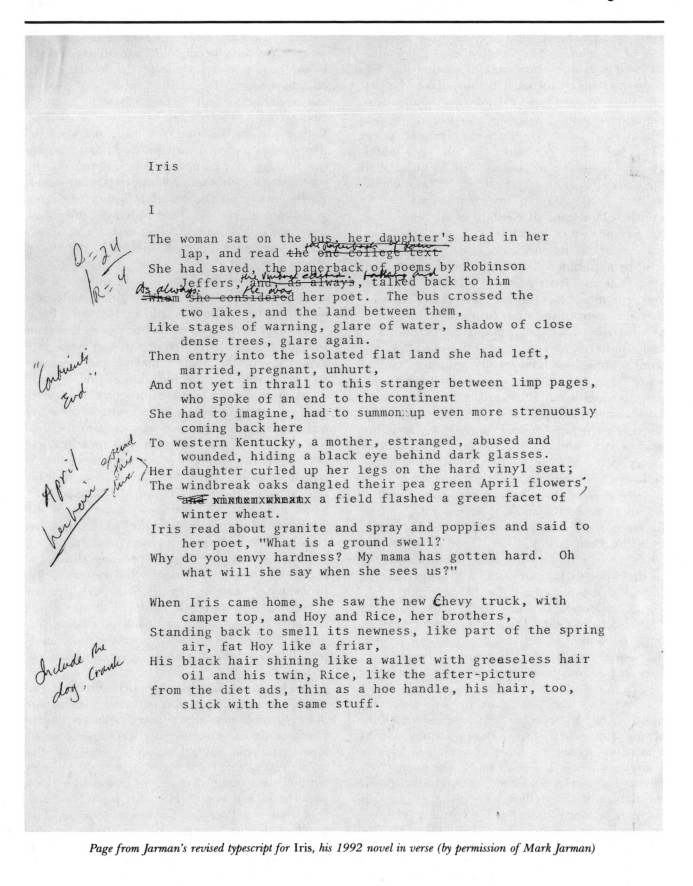

Iris

I

The woman sat on the bus, her daughter's head in her
    lap, and read ~~the one college text~~
She had saved, the paperback of poems by Robinson
    Jeffers, ~~and, as always,~~ talked back to him
~~Whom she considered~~ her poet. The bus crossed the
    two lakes, and the land between them,
Like stages of warning, glare of water, shadow of close
    dense trees, glare again.
Then entry into the isolated flat land she had left,
    married, pregnant, unhurt,
And not yet in thrall to this stranger between limp pages,
    who spoke of an end to the continent
She had to imagine, had to summon up even more strenuously
    coming back here
To western Kentucky, a mother, estranged, abused and
    wounded, hiding a black eye behind dark glasses.
Her daughter curled up her legs on the hard vinyl seat;
The windbreak oaks dangled their pea green April flowers,
    ~~and~~ a field flashed a green facet of
    winter wheat.
Iris read about granite and spray and poppies and said to
    her poet, "What is a ground swell?
Why do you envy hardness? My mama has gotten hard. Oh
    what will she say when she sees us?"

When Iris came home, she saw the new Chevy truck, with
    camper top, and Hoy and Rice, her brothers,
Standing back to smell its newness, like part of the spring
    air, fat Hoy like a friar,
His black hair shining like a wallet with greaseless hair
    oil and his twin, Rice, like the after-picture
from the diet ads, thin as a hoe handle, his hair, too,
    slick with the same stuff.

Page from Jarman's revised typescript for Iris, *his 1992 novel in verse (by permission of Mark Jarman)*

run back to memory," and he recognizes "the magnet of nostalgia." The speaker of the poem refuses to give in to sentimentality, noting that, like the remembered teenager on the make, the past can often "flatter, listen / cajole, make little whining endearments, / plodding ritualistically among landmarks." Similarly, the widely praised poem "The Supremes" compares the speaker's nostalgia for his "innocent" teenage lust, as he watched the black singers on a "portable T.V." at the now-defunct "Ball's Market," to his nostalgia for the vanished landscape of coastal Los Angeles. From the perspective of an adult on an airplane "leaving . . . for points north and east," the landscape (and by implication the early Supremes) can "still look frail and frozen / full of simple sweetness and repetition." But this is only a trick of perspective: the truth of the story belies the falsifications of nostalgia. The speaker and his friends who had huddled around the television "in wet trunks, shivering" were really ignorant "tanned white boys, / wiping sugar and salt from [their] mouths / and leaning forward to feel their song." Furthermore, the poems imply, sentimental nostalgia is a tempting though untenable stance, but neither is it "acceptable / to cough with cold or shiver with irony / at your own home / or at the amusement of your family" ("Far and Away").

In *Far and Away* Jarman returns to some of his most powerful subject matter with a new-found poetic distance, and the extended narratives "A Daily Glory" and "Lost in a Dream" cover new ground in terms of poetic technique. In these poems Jarman works with longer lines, a change that is important for his later poetry. In *The Black Riviera* two poems, "The Mystic" and "The Death of God," employ lines reminiscent of those of Robinson Jeffers, about whom Jarman has written, and Jeffers becomes a central presence in Jarman's book-length narrative poem *Iris* (1992).

Whereas the poems in *Far and Away* are narrative experiments, *The Black Riviera* (cowinner of the 1991 Poets' Prize) shows Jarman in full command of his narrative powers. As Andrew Hudgins notes in his jacket blurb, the poems "tell fascinating stories and meditate passionately on the nature of storytelling." Even the poems that concern Jarman's southern California past operate in a larger historical context. In one of the finest, "The Shrine and the Burning Wheel," the speaker witnesses "a gang of boys" setting fire to a bicycle tire in the parking lot of a Quick Stop. This scene of meaningless violence occasions a

meditation on art, transcendence, and history, in which Edna St. Vincent Millay, assorted Shriners, Edgar Bergen and Charlie McCarthy, Janis Joplin, and the Boy Scout Expo all figure in the speaker's recognition that "Transcendence is not / Going back / To feel the texture of the past." Rather it involves a "poetry of heaven and earth" that meshes personal with public history, despite the feelings of meaninglessness inherent in the postmodern condition. Although Jarman values family history, in the broader historic and geographic contexts of these poems, "the black box / Recorded with the last message of childhood" threatens to become "gibberish" ("Between Flights").

Like the muffled stories of adults that the child in "Story Hour" hears through the walls, personal histories alone are "full of lacunae / Fragments in a burning hand written / On less than water—air." The child's feeling that he is the sole audience—that he holds a magical power—gives way in maturity to the recognition that "I have no such power." The true power of stories, as the final poem in the book suggests, involves the active making of one's own narratives in the context of history and of the world. The speaker's nostalgic reminiscence about a long-ago story must finally give way to the present—a moment with his daughters in an imperfect world where a blue-white flower grows, incongruously, next to the "Sanitary Sewer." Though the story of "Miss Urquhart's Tiara" exerts a powerful influence on the speaker, his daughters' "pressing close" enables him "to close the book" and return to the problematic present. *The Black Riviera* demonstrates not only Jarman's masterful command of narrative technique but also his sophisticated understanding of the ways in which narrative masters and commands human beings and human histories.

The lengthening of the poetic line and the relative lengthening of the narrative pace in *The Black Riviera* (there are seventeen poems in a fifty-four-page volume) anticipate Jarman's *Iris*. In long, Jeffers-like lines, this novel in verse tells the story of its title character. Iris, a young mother in rural western Kentucky, has an obsession with "a paperback of poems, / The only book from college that she'd saved, Robinson Jeffers." The poem charts over twenty years in Iris's often unhappy, yet heroic life in terms of her lifelong argument with Jeffers's "inhumanism." The poem reaches its climax when Iris, along with her hitch-hiker companion Nora, finally makes her belated pilgrimage to Tor House. Late in the poem, Iris recapitulates her story to Nora:

> You'd think with
>   all the death in it, my life
> Would be a tragedy. But I've kept my real life a
>   secret—reading Jeffers
> And trying to imagine him imagining someone like
>   me. It's when he says
> He has been saved from human illusion and foolish-
>   ness and passion and wants to be like rock
> That I miss something. I think I have been stead-
>   fast, but what does rock feel?

Deciding that she likes Jeffers best when she feels his wife's human presence in the poetry, Iris ends up rejecting the tragic view that so tempted Jeffers. Discovering the "secret lodge[d] with her," that Tor House and even Jeffers's Hawk Tower were built for human reasons, Iris enters "The house where pain and pleasure had turned to poetry and stone, and a family had been happy." By mastering her own narrative (indeed by reinventing it), Iris manages to transcend the potential tragedy of her life by rejecting the "hardness" of her favorite poet. *Iris* is an ambitious nar-rative that should do much to enhance Jarman's already secure reputation.

Jarman's accomplishment is remarkable for a poet of forty. Especially in his recent work, he engages both the personal and the public in increasingly fruitful ways. Though David Wojahn, among others, has taken some New Narrative poets to task for failing to create stories of "deep delight," it is clear that he finds Jarman an exception. Whether, as Wojahn states in his jacket blurb for *The Black Riviera*, Jarman "can win back for poetry many of the readers it has lost in recent years" remains to be seen. But in terms of expanding the range of technique and subject matter in contemporary poetry, Mark Jarman is an innovator and one of the finest contemporary narrative poets.

References:

Peter Makuck, "Sensing the Supreme, Working the Self's Heavy Soil," *Tar River Poetry*, 22 (Fall 1982): 44-53;

David Wojahn, "Without a Deep Delight: Neo-Narrative Poetry and Its Problems," *Denver Quarterly*, 23 (Winter/Spring 1989): 181-202.

Denis Johnson

(1 July 1949 -   )

Joe Nordgren
Lamar University

BOOKS: *The Man Among the Seals* (Iowa City: Stone Wall, 1969);

Inner Weather (Port Townsend, Wash.: Graywolf, 1976);

The Incognito Lounge, and Other Poems (New York: Random House, 1982);

Angels (New York: Knopf, 1983);

Fiskadoro (New York: Knopf, 1985);

The Stars at Noon (New York: Knopf, 1986);

The Veil (New York: Knopf, 1987);

Resuscitation of a Hanged Man (New York: Farrar, Straus & Giroux, 1991).

Described by an anonymous reviewer for *Esquire* (December 1985) as "a writer who slips smoothly from poetry to the novel and back again," Denis Johnson has produced a significant body of work since he began publishing in the late 1960s. His poetry is distinguished by its stylistic vitality and emotional honesty, indicating his intense engagement with language and experience. Forgiveness and surviving memories and mistakes of the past are his dominant themes, since it is impossible to live, in his words, as a "fallen person."

Johnson was born on 1 July 1949 in Munich, Germany, the older of the two sons of Vera Childress Johnson and Alfred Nair Johnson. As a consequence of his father's working for the United States Information Agency, Johnson had an international upbringing until he was in his mid teens. "I had an ideal childhood in Tokyo," he recounts in an interview with Lynda Hull and David Wojahn. "I was surrounded by all these tiny and beautiful people who were never threatening to kids and who really loved children. Then I had the ideal adolescent experience in Manila," he goes on to say, "where there was no drinking age and everything was steamy and sexy. The universe of the tropics is just like what is going on inside the adolescent boy. So it was great." The imprint of these years often appears in his writing: "I knew my father's assignment could be changed at any time. . . . I think this gave me the impression that life was similarly transient and un-

Denis Johnson (photograph copyright Jerry Bauer)

predictable . . . and that attitude certainly comes out in my poetry."

Following residence in Manila, his family returned to the United States, and Johnson enrolled at T. C. Williams High School in Alexandria, Virginia, from which he graduated in 1967. His interest in becoming a writer prompted him to attend the University of Iowa. Remarkably, *The Man Among the Seals* (1969), his first book of poetry, was published when he was nineteen. After completing his B.A. in English in 1971, he then drifted in and out of the Iowa Writers Workshop until receiving his M.F.A. in 1974. Johnson credits poet and teacher Marvin Bell for encouraging him. From Iowa City he moved to the industrial confines of Evanston, Illinois, and commuted north to Chicago, where he taught at Lake Forest College. Discovering he lacked the temperament for academe, he left after a year for the Pacific Northwest, working odd jobs in and around Seattle, Tacoma, and Gig Harbor.

For the better part of 1978 and 1979 Johnson took a hiatus from writing while rescuing himself from drug and alcohol addiction. Though not a confessionalist in the strictest sense of the term, he has continued to draw on the "drama of failure and resurrection" that he associates with this time. "To go on living and to understand the past," he emphasizes, "is like taking up another life. It is like waking up after your death and being able to look back and understand." This belief is a recurring motif in several of his most challenging poems.

In striking contrast to his time in the Northwest, from 1979 to 1981 Johnson lived in Phoenix (a mythic coincidence) and taught in the medium-security section of the Arizona State Prison. The effect of working there, including his trying out the sensory deprivation tanks, convinced him that people too often compromise their freedom and live as though they have been confined, by not giving themselves permission to do the things they want to do. He determined not to turn the key on himself in this way.

In 1981 Johnson was awarded a fellowship to the Fine Arts Work Center in Provincetown, Massachusetts, where he became intrigued by the type of "seeing" that was particular to the visual artists he met. He concedes, "The freedom that artists allow themselves affected me more greatly than actually looking at the paintings." While at the center he likewise kindled an interest in becoming a better student of the impulses that drive his own work. Acknowledging the influence the visual arts have had on his writing, he included poems in *The Veil* (1987) that pay tribute to Sam Messer ("Red Darkness"), Edward Hopper ("All-Night Diners"), and James Hampton ("The Throne of the Third Heaven of Nations Millennium General Assembly"). Finding Cape Cod to his liking, Johnson settled in Wellfleet, and between 1981 and 1986 he published his third book of poetry, *The Incognito Lounge, and Other Poems* (1982), and his first three novels, *Angels* (1983), *Fiskadoro* (1985), and *The Stars at Noon* (1986), establishing himself in critic Gary Krist's estimation "as one of the most serious and provocative writers of his generation" (*New Republic*, 3 June 1991).

From Wellfleet, Johnson moved to a ranch in Gualala, California, in the southwest corner of Mendocino County, not far from the Pacific Ocean. He left California in 1989, preferring to be surrounded by the Kanishu National Forest in the northern tip of Idaho. In the early months of 1991 Johnson went to Saudi Arabia on assignment for *Esquire* to render his impressions of the Gulf War. His fourth novel, *Resuscitation of a Hanged Man*, was published in the summer of 1991, and he has completed a collection of short stories whose working title is "Jesus' Son."

Never one to falsify emotions, Johnson is an uncompromising and demanding writer. In addition to *The Incognito Lounge* being selected for the National Poetry Series in 1982 and his being the recipient of the American Institute of Arts and Letters' Sue Kaufman Award for Fiction for his novel *Angels*, he has received grants from the Arizona Arts Commission, the Massachusetts Arts Council, the John Guggenheim Foundation, and the National Endowment for the Arts.

With few exceptions, Johnson experiments with an array of open forms in the thirty-two poems of *The Man Among the Seals*. Not to be confined by the rules of traditional punctuation and time-honored poetic structures, he refutes capitalization, uses run-on lines and unconventional enjambment, and varies stanza length from one to fifteen lines, relying on his readers to find for themselves his poems' rhythmic flow.

Though he writes about and uses the voices of people of all ages, in one way or another many of his early poems involve loss or being trapped in no-win situations. In "The Woman at the Slot Machine," for example, an aging widow is seeking "any victory." As the revolving symbols of the machine click into place, she momentarily wins back her family, when the sound of a bell "sang like a beautiful daughter" or when her husband, bedridden with a broken leg, would ring for her to come upstairs and listen with him to Jack Benny's playing the violin on the radio. Her gamble to recapture the past is futile; there is only the desperate "plunging down / of the handle" as she tries to get a grip on her sorrow.

In "Checking the Traps" a despondent husband attempts to appease his wife by strategically placing several mousetraps around their kitchen. Thinking himself a victim of her "pregnancy trap," he stays up late and listens to the mice foraging for scraps, nudging ever closer to their demise. After a restless night, he is distressed by what he finds:

one mouse's head is barely
in the trap, one eye probing

toward the ceiling where i could tell him
there is nothing.
the other mouse is flung willing under the iron
bar. i wonder, were they
married? was she pregnant? they are
going out together,
in the garbage this morning. it was
morning when we were married.
it has been morning

for a long time.

Yet not all of these poems languish in life's inequities. In "The Man Among the Seals" the speaker, observant of the way people interact with animals, witnesses an amazing event. By day in the park the seals scrape among the rocks above their pool that is littered with trashy food tossed by curious onlookers. In the early morning before dawn, however, they dive with a natural grace and dignity that they will not display during the day to the anxious crowd. Curiously, one night while hidden in "an audience of trees," the speaker watches a man strip to his underwear and jump into the pool. If the man is drunk or a "staggerer on land," the speaker guesses, "perhaps he hopes to move cleanly, / like a seal, through water." On the other hand, if he is sober, he might be trying "to assume / the clumsiness of the seals." Askance in diving into his own thoughts, the speaker knows the man will return time and again,

to watch his seals as they rise
above the rocks to pluck the floating

bits of food, as they slide through
the air over the trees, the
ferris wheel grown

stationary with shame, the tiny
unfamiliar bodies jerking
under balloons through the lighted park.

Free to rise above their "land-locked captors," the seals "float" into a moment of magical realism. An anonymous reviewer for the *Virginia Quarterly* (1971) summarized the poems: "Denis Johnson finds moments of psychological nakedness, moments when the devious corners of our minds are illumined, and presents them in an imaginative and gracefully colloquial way."

Johnson's second book, *Inner Weather* (1976), is a slender collection of fifteen poems, and Johnson forgoes some of his stylistic experimentation: through internal punctuation he more fully directs the rhythm of his poems. By doing so, his poetic structure more consistently complements his poems' sense and themes. He brings attention to this strategy in the closing stanza of "Falling." The persona, an aspiring poet who writes at night during his off hours, has just been fired and is submerged in "an aquarium of debt." William Shakespeare and John Milton have taught him that poetry can be "fathered in any intensity of light, and light / in all thicknesses of darkness." He resolves that there "are descents more final, less graceful / than this plummeting / from employment."

In all but two poems, "Prayer: That We May be Given This Day the Usual Business" and "Looking Out of the Window Poem," the emotional climate is turning or has turned desolate. An exhausted husband quietly, yet ceremoniously, tries to welcome the arrival of dusk in "An Evening With the Evening." Soon, however, there is "total blackness," and then "it is the end, / which is only himself, going / home to his wife and children, / turning and trying to walk away from the darkness / that precedes him, darkness of which he is the center." Along the gutter-lined streets in "Winter," people lug the "baggage / and garbage of their humanness" while being "dragged by the legs upstream / like poor stooges sunk to drowning / for a living." In "Commuting" passengers hold their "lives up in [their] arms like the victims / of solitary, terrible accidents." Contrary to what the optimists have told him about "great poems" filling the emptiness that threatens in "There Are Trains Which Will Not Be Missed," the speaker declares that it "is death which continues / over these chasms and these / distances deliberately like a train."

These illustrations are not meant to indicate that Johnson is a trafficker in the quotidian. Rather, while dramatizing daily events and searching for ways to allow his subjects to project themselves, he accounts for the less than perfect, the less than dazzling aspects of life that people gloss over so as to avoid blame or guilt. Johnson faces himself squarely in this collection, including poems about divorce ("Working Outside at Night"), the scalding "noon" of a guilt-laden insomnia ("An Inner Weather"), and the silent "bearing of wreckage" for what has been lost ("Employment in the Small Bookstore").

Mark Strand selected *The Incognito Lounge, and Other Poems*, Johnson's third collection, for the National Poetry Series in 1982. As quoted on the dust jacket, David St. John finds that the

Johnson with his dog (photograph copyright 1991 by Robert Miller)

poems "speak—with passion and wit—for every hushed or broken voice in America's cities of night." Johnson's most persistent theme is that "survival is salvation." As critic Peter Stitt notes, "The characters who people these poems are drawn from the streets, the diners, the lounges, and especially the buses of America. They possess neither money nor college diplomas, have no status and not much dignity. They are people we might condescend to, if Johnson did not handle them so well, handle them in a way that reveals the love he has for them." Johnson admits, "The person who really can't say anything for himself is often the one who fascinates me." But there is a spiritual dimension underscoring his giving of a voice to those "who cannot articulate for themselves their suffering, their sense of bewilderment, their moments of emotional extremity, or celebration." Johnson explains: "What I'm talking about when I portray the insides of bars is an experience of hell—a place where everybody is in it for himself and there isn't any escape.... But there can be a miraculous rescue from that place,

and the place we're rescued to is purgatory, heaven, a place where things begin to have meaning and people can reach out to each other, where events start to make some kind of sense."

Bereft of family and friends, some of Johnson's characters are invaded by a solitude that approximates death. In "Vespers" the speaker, having lost his lover, says: "The towels rot and disgust me on this damp / peninsula where they invented mist / and drug abuse and taught the light to fade." For him, "Things get pretty radical in the dark: / the sailboats on the inlet sail away; / the provinces of actuality / crawl on the sea." "In a Light of Other Lives" presents a flashing red ambulance light awakening a man in his empty room:

> All night long I can betray myself in the honky-
> tonk
> of terror and delight, I can throw away my faith,
> go loose in the spectacular fandango
> of emergencies that strum the heart
> with neon, but I can't
> understand anything.

The male persona in "On the Olympic Peninsula" also is afflicted by a lack of understanding as he goes looking for his girl in a trendy lesbian bar, where he believes she is being seduced by "sinister embraces" in a place "where the men / stink like murdered sea animals." His jealousy and homophobia darken his impression of life as he becomes

an image of blood
graven amid peace and wine,
a strange one,
claustrophobic and heart-stopped among
garden parks through which boys
jog perspiring in their red basketball
shorts and in which toddlers
in blue parkas on toy horses rock themselves,
already stupefied, toward oblivion.

The nine segments of "The Incognito Lounge" (perhaps echoing Dante's *Inferno*) make up a frightening—at times surreal—descent into the refuse of fallen lives. It is late afternoon in a "trashy" city in Arizona where "questions of happiness" are "about as unobtrusive as a storm of meteors." People seem more anemic than alive: "The manager lady of this / apartment dwelling has a face / like a baseball"; "I go everywhere," the speaker attests, "with my eyes closed and / two eyeballs painted on my face"; there is a woman living "across the court with no face at all." People out shopping as a way of changing the "face" of boredom, "carry their hearts toward the bluffs / of counters like thoughtless purchases." Of the bars, "Only the Incognito Lounge is open. . . . at the center of the world," where the nameless come to dilute their grief with cheap liquor. How forbidding is this place? In the closing segment Johnson tells his readers of a bus that "wafts like a dirigible toward suburbia / over a continent of saloons, over the robot desert that now turns / purple and comes slowly through the dust."

In many poems, including "Night," "White, White Collars," "Passengers," "The Confession of St. Jim-Ralph," and "Now," finding a way to stand within the light being shed by the past on present events is crucial to Johnson's vision of "failure and redemption." From an existential viewpoint, his characters are defined by the choices they make. They can either be victims trapped in the wreckage of previous defeats, or they can learn that "waking is / birth, a life / is many lives." As his "resurrected one" tells the speaker in "The White Fires of Venus," " 'You will recover / or die,' " for it is "cold inside the body

that is not the body, / lonesome behind the face / that is certainly not the face / of the person one meant to become." After drugs, alcohol, deceit, reckless betrayal, and running life "past the edge," forgiving the self can be the most demanding of miracles.

Surviving is no guarantee of safety, and in *The Veil* Johnson is still concerned with the hard progress of extending the self into experience. The book combines ambitious lyric, dramatic, and narrative techniques; critic Paul Jenkins describes *The Veil* as "daring, frequently disarming, sometimes beautiful, and always on edge." To Paul Breslin, "The best poems . . . more than compensate for the others," and he is drawn to "the common ground between poet and reader" on which Johnson succeeds in describing the "mute, inarticulate sense of the strangeness of being, persisting just below the surface of everyday life, recognized in glimpses by 'ordinary' people as well as by poets."

The details Johnson presents in *The Veil* can be distressing. A young cripple dreams that he is being chased by wolves through the snow, only to awaken and discover he cannot move his legs. Having followed "desire" through a museum of primitive art, a "spinster" aches for the sensual touch and smell of a "human night." An insomniac monk lives out the "terror" of "being just one person" having "one chance, one set of days." Someone sitting alone in an "all-night diner" admits that the loss of a loved one "can make the tragedy of a whole age insignificant." For the most part, Johnson allows his people to tell about their own lives, accentuating the harrowing fear of emotional isolation.

Isolation can be self-imposed, a fact about which the speaker is aware in the title poem:

When the tide lay under the clouds
of an afternoon and gave them back to themselves
oilier a little and filled with anonymous boats,
I used to sit and drink at the very edge of it,
where light passed through the liquids in the
      glasses
and threw itself on the white drapes
of the tables, resting there like clarity
itself, you might think,
right where you could put a hand to it.

With the meaning of life at the speaker's fingertips, each impression, each sound, each gesture is charged with an inescapable meaning that defies words. As one drink leads to the next,

in this originating
brightness you might see
somebody putting a napkin against his lips
or placing a blazing credit card on a plastic
   tray
and you'd know. You would know goddamn it. And
   never be able to say.

According to Johnson, "the poem is about the *illusion* of having had that crucial experience . . . that suddenly everything is fraught with meaning. The feeling is very common if you're spending an afternoon in a cocktail lounge . . . but it's an illusion." The "illusion" is the "veil."

Isolation and loneliness dominate the sonnets titled "Red Darkness," too. As the headnote to the sequence indicates, the sonnets were written when Johnson was at the Fine Arts Work Center and served as the accompanying text for a group of paintings by Messer on display at the Hudson D. Walker Gallery in February 1982. A painting by Messer, *Loneliness causes cracks in the walls of madness*, was selected for the dust jacket of *The Veil*.

Though several fine individual sonnets appear in Johnson's previous collections, "Red Darkness" is more intricate. The nine sonnets interconnect in a loose narrative whose theme is repeated as the opening line of the first and last poems in the group: "Endeavor is that of seeking to be understood." Driven by unbearable loneliness, the speaker wants more than anything to convey his feelings to a woman he loves (it could be the wife from whom he is separated), but who is presently involved with another man. His guttural longing is manifest in the third sonnet:

I wish I had a way
Of telling you my heart is broken without calling
   on
Exactly those words, but when I marshall the terms
of my situation I see only two neon skulls
And one broken heart.

"Red darkness" is symbolic of the deepest type of suffering, a kind of lonely insanity that causes him to project the catastrophe of his inner life onto the world around him. As in the fifth sonnet, he never expected to be conscious of

Feelings in which all the plant life have been
   killed,
Darkness in which the suffering is turning red,
Money on which the faces are so lonely
. . . .
A network of feelings, darkness, and money, a web

Of plant life and suffering and faces
Where everything is killed and red and lonely.

While the narrator is sweating it out in a red hotel room, the past keeps repeating itself like a nightmare. If he could script an ending, he would change his fate without having "to suffer any change." As in other poems, the psychological consequences are as they should be. Change, Johnson affirms, is never achieved by a wishful dry snap of the fingers. Suffering change, and learning from that suffering, are necessary for survival.

The final poem in the volume, "The Throne of the Third Heaven of the Nation's Millennium General Assembly," is a sojourn into the artistic process. Johnson mentions that while he was at Provincetown someone gave him a pamphlet from the Smithsonian Institution about *The Throne* created by James Hampton. A janitor for the General Services Administration in Washington, D.C., Hampton, "at the behest of certain heavenly voices," built *The Throne* out of scavenged debris from the streets around where he worked and lived. The project became an obsession. Hampton spent fourteen years building it, and when Johnson saw the piece in the early 1980s, it took up an entire room at the Museum of American Art. Though "insane and visionary," Johnson adds, "it is the closest thing I can think of, in terms of an artistic experience, to an absolute act of faith."

Though the poem begins as a dream within a dream, the speaker (undoubtedly Johnson himself) later recounts driving home with a friend from Key West to Massachusetts, making two important stops along the way: the first at Elloree, South Carolina, and the second at the National Museum of American Art in Washington, D.C., in order to see *The Throne*. Early on, when the speaker awakens from his dream about the "miserable" conditions in D.C. that compelled Hampton toward his "vision," the car's headlights are shining on the small rural town of Elloree, where Hampton was born in 1909. To the speaker's amazement, no one in the town knows either of Hampton or of his work. Next, at the National Museum of American Art, he is overwhelmed by the "rushing-together parts" of *The Throne*, feeling an immediate friendship and identity with Hampton, who was also moved toward creation by living amid "the spilled and broken people and hearts" that litter the streets like bits of glass. "If you stand / In the world," as did Hampton, "you'll go out of your mind," Johnson warns.

Back in Massachusetts, the speaker describes a photograph of Hampton standing in front of a blackboard, completely lost in the intricacy of his plans for *The Throne*. This frozen image leads to several powerful elegiac lines:

> The streetcorner men, the shaken
>   earthlings—
> It's easy to imagine his hands
> When looking at their hands
> Of leather, loving on the necks
> Of jugs, sweetly touching the dice and bad checks,
> And to see in everything a making
> Just like his, an unhinged
> Deity in an empty garage
> Dying alone in some small consolation.

Yet, from "the trash of government buildings," from "jelly glasses," "upholstery tacks," "cardboard," "kraft paper," and "desk blotters," an astonishing vision was brought to life. The poem's closing "Revelation" (an unambiguous religious allusion) proclaims that if people can give up the specter of waiting for the arrival of a better place and time and use their creative energies "here and now" to build monuments born of compassion and hope, then there is no need "to fear."

In Johnson's poetry readers enter the imagery of dreams, rejoice in moments of unconditional love and forgiveness, and absorb the shocks of fear, loneliness, and entrapment. His poetic risks italicize W. S. Merwin's belief that "The encouragement of poetry is a labor and a privilege like that of living" ("Notes for a Preface," in *Regions of Memory*, 1987).

Interview:

Lynda Hull and David Wojahn, "The Kind of Light I'm Seeing: An Interview with Denis Johnson," *Ironwood*, 13 (1985): 31-44.

References:

Paul Breslin, "The Simple Separate Person and the Word En-Masse," *Poetry*, 143 (October 1988): 30-47;

Paul Jenkins, "American Poetry," *Massachusetts Review*, 29 (Spring 1988): 97-135;

Peter Stitt, "A Remarkable Diversity," *Georgia Review*, 36 (Winter 1982): 911-922.

Rodney Jones

(11 February 1950 -)

Tim Summerlin
Lamar University

BOOKS: *The Story They Told Us of Light* (University: University of Alabama Press, 1980);
The Unborn (Boston: Atlantic Monthly, 1985);
Transparent Gestures (Boston: Houghton Mifflin, 1989).

Rodney Jones is one of America's most distinguished younger poets. His three volumes of verse have demonstrated growing mastery of his medium. Peer recognition has come in the form of the Lavan Award in Poetry from the Academy of American Poets (1986), a Guggenheim Fellowship (1988), the Jean Stein Prize in poetry from the American Academy and Institute of Arts and Letters (1989), and the National Book Critics Circle Award (1990).

Jones was born on 11 February 1950, to Lavon and Wilda Owens Jones in Falkville, Alabama. The young Jones was reared in rural northern Alabama in an environment combining agrarian and urban cultures. His father was first a farmer then an employee in a plant that manufactured metal tubes. Both parents encouraged their children's ambition and interests. For Rodney, those ambitions were diverse: as a boy he aspired, variously, to be a professional athlete, a United States senator, and a Dickensian novelist. He had found his true craft, however, by his late teens.

Jones received his B.A. in English from the University of Alabama in 1971 and his M.F.A. in poetry from the University of North Carolina at Greensboro in 1973. He taught poetry in the public schools of Tennessee, Alabama, and Virginia from 1974 to 1978. Since then he has been on the faculties of Virginia Intermont College (1978-1984) and Southern Illinois University at Carbondale (starting in 1984). Jones has a daughter (Alexis) by his first wife (Virginia Kremza, whom he married in 1972) and a son (Samuel) by his present wife, Gloria Nixon de Zepeda Jones, a native of El Salvador whom he married on 21 June 1981. He has become more active as a public reader of his work since receiving his re-

Rodney Jones circa 1985 (photograph by Gloria Jones)

cent awards and has found that his current teaching schedule allows him to concentrate more on creative work. Jones considers his influences to be numerous; he cites Rainer Rilke, Pablo Neruda, T. S. Eliot, C. K. Williams, and James Wright among the most important.

Jones's first published volume, *The Story They Told Us of Light* (1980), is the work of his twenties. Its overarching theme is the function of the imagination, developed in familiar antinomies of past and present, light and darkness, order and disorder, grace and despair. In the first section of the book, personal memory is a particularly strong element, offering images of the land, of awakening urges, and of a fundamentalist ethos. At times, as in "Blue Hair" or "Looking Natural," the voice has the callow tone of a sensitive soul caught in a brutal world. The best poems rise above this self-consciousness, however, as they attempt to "translate" the memories of childhood into imaginative experience. As Jones concludes in "The Error of Translation," "each thing has its language, / if only we knew how to read it." "Going Ahead, Looking Back" expresses a notion common to his poems: psychic progress is dependent on finding the language to articulate the past. The short lyric "O Wordsworth" is comic in tone, but there can be no doubt of Jones's essentially Wordsworthian reverence for critical "spots of time."

Rural Alabama, not surprisingly, figures prominently both as literal landscape and as metaphor. Jones savors the concreteness of the earth as he does the sharp angles of remembered experience. In "Chain Saw" he uses the forest to convey the confused tangle of experience that the wordsmith must enter, saw in hand, to cut and shape in order to "know, if only for a while / There is grace on the earth."

Memory is a form of "inventing mercy," then, for Jones, and he does not ignore the fact that much retrieval from memory and imagination is "Debris" ("a day of wobbly passes thrown at our feet") or "Loose Ends" from the motley wear of life. That most familiar of post-Romantic poetic themes, the power of imagination and the validity of its vision, appears in the majority of the poems in Jones's first book, and it continues to be present in the two that have followed.

The power of the past is no less strong in Jones's second volume, *The Unborn* (1985). Readers encounter the sights, smells, and conversations of the poet's southern roots. His recollections are in surer terms, and the poems suggest a more complex pilgrimage than that in the earlier volume. The forms are more varied, and Jones frequently employs a longer, essentially iambic line in some of the most memorable of the poems. The line proves capable of conveying both a comparatively flat conversational tone and a more oracular, heightened rhetoric.

"Remembering Fire" realizes the method of memory, moving against the current of time "toward the unborn," like a film run backward. Jones is specifically recalling the destruction of his home through fire, but more generally he is reminding readers of that incorrigible human resistance to "that universal cataract of death," as Robert Frost called it in "West-Running Brook," the swerving of consciousness in opposition to entropy. Ironically that death-resisting consciousness is drawn to decay and oblivion as well as to health and vitality. In "The Neckties" the speaker is aware that his Whitmanesque urge to peel away the respectability of his father's ties and clean nails is in part a longing for death, and he smells the "odor of death in the odor of the sea."

But humor is also present in *The Unborn*. The self-deprecating humor of "A History of Speech" is directed toward the compulsive speaker, whose contributions to "this inflation / in the currency of language" create misunderstanding with his girlfriend and an unfriendly bigot. The speaker's rueful apology ("At my luckiest, I'm only saying the grace / the hungry endure because they're polite") cannot erase the sense of his delight in and commitment to that speech.

The poems of *The Unborn* provide readers with a sharper image of the person who is engaged in such reflections than did Jones's previous book. As before, he employs family incidents and memories from childhood as dramatic contexts for his poems, but his command of what the incident can mean is more confident, as in the playing off of private against public reality in "For Those Who Miss the Important Parts" or the blend of sympathy and estrangement in "Sweep." Poems such as "The Magic Cloak" (concerning his daughter, Alexis) and "The Laundromat at the Bay Station" (alluding to a desperate time of life after marital separation) show that there is more adult history to counter recollections of the past. The latter poem is one of the thematic keys to the volume:

> Most of the customers I don't remember, but I
>   can't forget
> the divorcees in tight black stretch pants, cautiously
>   sorting
>   their lace panties, talking too loud
> and pulling their stringy, cotton-headed kids out of
>   the garbage pails.

The graphic portrayal of the seedy locale evokes a scene and a condition being recalled by the speaker, who is fiercely determined to maintain his stake in the "vulnerability" of such persons. "I don't want a new life spun clean of its dirt and chaos," he insists. This preference for the maculate reality of existence is expressed in many forms.

Without sentimentalizing, Jones offers several poems that explore the animal in humans. By contrast, abstract visions of life, such as those in the student papers that the speaker contemplates in "Some Futures," leave him dismayed. As in his first volume, Jones expects to find deliverance only by embracing and translating a concrete world.

Memory, Jones asserts, "shines most repeating the commonplace," and, as before, his most characteristic poetry emerges from the imagination's work on memory. Perhaps the most consciously literary piece in *The Unborn* is "Imagination," Jones's commentary on John Keats's "Ode to a Nightingale," the 1819 fusion of heightened sensation, oblivion, and celebration of the visionary world. In Jones's reverie, memories of observing the sudden flight of ducks on a canoe trip with his wife merge with the present sound of her voice on the telephone, a Beethoven sonata, and the numbing effects of bourbon. Jones backs away from asserting any comprehensive aesthetic ("Now I don't know any more than the ducks if imagination saves or betrays us"), but there is no mistaking the significance of his question:

> What good is my life unless I save that bird, unless
>   I let that river enter me now
> as the sun enters through the venetian blind, laying
>   down a keyboard of shadow and light,
> and the slow composition of Beethoven breaks; one
>   crystal at a time?

For Jones, problematic as it may be, the organizing act of imagination is Wallace Stevens's "necessary angel," and the act of poetry the central act of life.

Jones, who organized his poems in the first two volumes into untitled sections of general thematic integrity, gave titles to the groupings in *Transparent Gestures* (1989). His categories are "Who Runs the Country" (character sketches); "The Kitchen Gods" (personal, familial meditations); "Academic Subjects" (intellectual views of life); and "The Weepers" (occasions for grief). Each of these categories has its counterparts in the earlier works by Jones, and there are formal similarities as well. However, his comment that he has attempted to move to "more embracing

forms" and to poetic structures employing a variety of forms in his later work, is also true. *Transparent Gestures* offers new modes, new voices.

"Winter Retreat" satirizes the impeccable but denatured social values of academics who are gathered to discuss "the instruction of the disabled, the deprived, / the poor, who do not score well in entrance tests." Jones's manipulation of personal memory in "Dangers" permits a somewhat different voice to emerge, one less obviously that of his familiar persona and closer to the dramatic monologue. The same can be said of "My Manhood," where the experience and emotions related are a statement of a universal urge to dominate. In "Mimosa," in which Jones explores a sentimental side that he paradoxically affirms but does not trust, the lilting anapests suit the occasion: "Among many lovely and cheap, that perfume still haunts, / and a ballad wisdom I thought I had left comes back, / but I still do not know whether to trust in the mimosa." Jones is a poet sensitive to form, sound, rhythm, syntactic balance, and contrast, although he does not often employ conventional poetic forms. His creed that "the form somehow has to bend to intuition" expresses the view of one steeped in traditional values yet not a traditionalist.

Not surprisingly, *Transparent Gestures* is also rich in meditations on the human need to mediate experience through imagination. Jones is impatient with the detached intellect. In the satiric ode "Pure Mathematics" he confesses his inability to grasp abstract theory ("crabs comprehending opera") and relishes a concrete world where theory is realized as fact, where pure mathematics becomes a published rate of exchange:

> The dollar went
> Down on its knees and prayed to the Allah of the
>   Saudis
>   and the Buddha of the Japanese
> To rise changed into millions of lire. . . .

Similarly a visit to the Smithsonian space exhibit excites a distrust in the distantly cosmic ("That scalpel held / to the autopsy of God is no bow to rub the music of the spheres"). By contrast, in "Academic Subjects," as Jones reflects on abstract history and human existence, he offers what could well serve as the motto for all his meditations:

> Awakenings, enlightenments, I have
>   thought of as vast cities, unoccupied.
> The place of poetry is darker, and the unremitting
>   test of love and poetry

Plies its single-minded questions: What, if anything, will last?

He is still trying to discern "the grace on the earth," to remember that "each thing has its language / if only we knew how to read it."

Jones can be both sardonic and caring. The section entitled "The Weepers" is rich in both voices, and the poem of that name manages both to blast the absurd sentimentality of much sorrow and also to affirm its power. This view of grief is reminiscent of the imaginative balancing of antinomies (spirit and flesh, word and silence, past and present) that is so characteristic of his work.

Jones's decade of poetic progress has revealed both growth and continuity, and the 1990s may find an even greater emphasis on new directions. He is presently well into his next volume of verse, which, he promises, will be very different from what has preceded it. He is working with poems in at least four types of voices, which he describes as "direct narrative," "post-modernist playful," "settled and intellectual," and "crazy-romantic." Rodney Jones has already created a poetry both various and authoritative, on which he can confidently build.

Jane Kenyon
(23 May 1947 -   )

Robin M. Latimer
Lamar University

BOOKS: *From Room to Room* (Cambridge, Mass.: James, 1978);
The Boat of Quiet Hours (Saint Paul: Graywolf, 1986);
Let Evening Come (Saint Paul: Graywolf, 1990).

TRANSLATION: *Twenty Poems of Anna Akhmatova*, translated by Kenyon and Vera Dunham (Saint Paul: Eighties/Ally 1985).

Jane Kenyon epitomizes many poets of the 1970s and 1980s: a feminist of sorts; an academic brought up through the ranks of little-magazine publication, followed by contracts with the independent presses. Her residence in New Hampshire and her marriage to well-known poet and editor Donald Hall have been major influences on her work.

Born in Ann Arbor, Michigan, on 23 May 1947, Kenyon attended the University of Michigan, earning her B.A. in 1970 and her M.A. in 1972. That same year, she married Hall (on 17 April). She has won several awards, including fellowships from the National Endowment for the Arts (1981) and the New Hampshire Commission on the Arts (1984).

Her first book, *From Room to Room* (1978), is the poetic diary of a honeymoon, in which a young wife explores the spaces between her and her husband, and her new and former homes. Several poems concern short spates of the husband's absence; "The First Eight Days of the Beard" explores the gender gap; and a furtive poem, "Cleaning the Closet," shows the wife finding a dusty suit her husband has not worn since his father's funeral and turning to see her husband watching, whereupon she "fumble[s] to put the suit / back where it was." This last line of the poem tells the story of the book. There is no "back where it was" for either husband or wife.

The overlay of the new on the old continues as the main character progresses through her first anniversary, chronicled in "Year Day," revamping room after room of her new home. As she does so, she encounters the emblems, both universal and personal, of her female lineage, a grandmother's tablecloth here, an heirloom thimble there. And Kenyon's young wife is alert to these emblems, perceiving them with a new feminist consciousness. So it is that, when she finds one of her gray hairs floating in the mop water,

Jane Kenyon with her cat at Eagle Pond Farm in Danbury, New Hampshire

she feels akin to those who have scrubbed the floor before her, feels her life "added to theirs."

This squarely narrative book dates itself. It is replete with back-to-quilting feminism, and the fact that it manages to sidestep all of its potential triteness lies in Kenyon's craft—her haikulike precision in rendering an effect and her clear regard for smooth sound.

It is redeemed as well by what has been called "quiet violence." Kenyon's violence is leashed, and thus more alarming. In "The Socks" one finds the wife folding her husband's socks into "tight dark fists," for example. The anger expressed is a woman's, more specifically a twentieth-century woman's, insofar as it expresses the conflict of a woman who has been trained to desire security but who is also very aware of its costs, the sacrificing of individuality and sensitivity. Clearer examples of this anger might be found in a poem in which the wife inures herself to the fact that she has crushed a pet cat beneath the wheels of her car. Her method is to focus on what color to repaint the house. In another poem she uses the vacuum cleaner's drone to block the noise of a man's felling of the eighty-

year-old oak, the branches of which menace the house.

In *From Room to Room* Kenyon asserts her connection to the New England poetic tradition less in her fairly standard rendering of that setting than in her vocal style. She is, in fact, frequently compared to Robert Frost and Emily Dickinson, though such comparisons should be viewed as more evocative than exact. And one can hear some Anne Sexton in Kenyon's poetry, too, especially in "Starting Therapy," where the wife's repressed conflicts appear in a neurotic dream: a brain, "hovering over" a porch, "won't come in and . . . won't go away." Critics of this book hailed its simplicity but also mentioned Kenyon's thematic complexities and her masterful craftsmanship.

Kenyon closed *From Room to Room* with translations of six of Anna Akhmatova's poems; clearly the two poets share concerns—for example, desire as reflected in the natural world—as well as musicality and economical imagery. Kenyon's follow-up to her first book was *Twenty Poems of Anna Akhmatova* (1985), which appears to be Kenyon's contribution to a feminist revision of the literary canon as well as a set of finger exercises in the economical poetic style Kenyon prefers. But her merits as a translator have yet to come under real scrutiny; most reviewers have read the translation without much reference to the original.

In *The Boat of Quiet Hours* (1986) Kenyon continues to employ a clear narrative framework for the poems, though a more flexible one than that of *From Room to Room*. According to reviewer Marianne Boruch, the poems in Kenyon's 1986 book read "like entries in a day book, patient commentary on things worth gathering" (*American Poetry Review*, March 1987). The themes of the first book persist as well. An eloquent short piece on an heirloom gravy boat, for example, recounts the speaker's grief in observing "a hard, brown / drop of gravy still / on the porcelain lip." And the wife's understanding of love has taken on new dimensions, as in "Song":

> How lucky we are
> to be holding hands on a porch
> in the country. But even this
> is not the joy that trembles
> under every leaf and tongue.

These two examples also reveal Kenyon's range, her keen alertness to the concrete world, and her ability also to render the abstract.

Brother was allowed to ride
off by himself on his bike.
He'd be gone for hours, come
back with things : a stick
embraced by a cocoon, a puff
ball, owl pellets -- bits of
undigested bone and fur -- , and
pieces of moss that seemed   [could be]   [might have been]

to be the tongues of preposterous   the tongue of a preposterous
  green men,   green man
          , but went , instead,
into a bottle to make a terrarium.
          learning and freedom

appeared to be his domain ;   as he mounted and named the bone
and I brooded on that, introspe-   on a piece of poster board.
I fell into a long reverie,
speechless.,

Early draft for "A Boy Goes into the World" (by permission of Jane Kenyon)

The Boat of Quiet Hours is more concerned with literary tradition than *From Room to Room*. Allusions—to John Keats's *Endymion* (1818), William Shakespeare's *Hamlet*, the Bible, and the plays of Anton Chekhov—abound. And one anonymous critic (*Women's Review of Books*, July 1987) observed that the persona of these poems has clearly become a New Englander as evidenced, for example, in the lines "How long winter has lasted—like a Mahler / symphony, or an hour in the dentist's chair."

The reviewers of *The Boat of Quiet Hours* were unanimous that, within her select boundaries, Kenyon is formidable. But she was criticized for failing to flirt with excess, as if, having toed the tightrope above a host of similar poetry, she should attempt a somersault or two.

The title of Kenyon's *Let Evening Come* (1990) is perhaps a response to the critics, a resigned imperative, asserting security: the collection reads, in fact, like a continuation of *The Boat of Quiet Hours*, formatted still to the chores and routines of the same contemplative but disciplined speaker, one who, upon hearing news of a loved one's recurring cancer, retains the capacity to "snap the blue leash onto the D-ring / of the dog's collar," to attend to "that part of life / [which] is intact." Dog-walking is alarmingly recurrent in this collection of close to sixty poems, a repetition that may bring accusations of mundanity

and manipulativeness. However, that Kenyon dares use this simple image of coping, of the mind strolling with itself as it waits for what the speaker dreads, is somehow affirming.

Keats, alluded to in *The Boat of Quiet Hours*, is a character in Kenyon's 1990 collection, evoked, in the speaker's knowledgeable reconstruction of his last days, in various reposes. This reference to Keats is refreshing on the part of Kenyon because it clarifies her awareness that she is subject, as was he, to the criticism that she is a poet's poet. She baits this criticism in her poems in which the speaker registers alarm at or resistance to public places, events, the uneducated, and the unwashed, opting for the privileged retreat to "the sound of pages turning, and coals shifting."

As one has come to expect, Kenyon's craft in sound and image is consummate. The poems, pointedly arranged so as not to concentrate linked themes and subjects, invite a slow, unaggressive reading, one that recapitulates the rhythms of water, leaf, and wind—despite all the clamor for something more stimulating. Faith and meaning, Kenyon urges, as in all of her works, lie in a rhythm so constant one might view it as cliché.

Yusef Komunyakaa

(29 April 1947 -   )

Kirkland C. Jones
Lamar University

BOOKS: *Dedications and Other Darkhorses* (Laramie, Wyo.: R.M.C.A.J., 1977);
Lost in the Bonewheel Factory (New York: Lynx House, 1979);
Copacetic (Middletown, Conn.: Wesleyan University Press, 1983);
I Apologize for the Eyes in My Head (Middletown, Conn.: Wesleyan University Press, 1986);
Dien Cai Dau (Middletown, Conn.: Wesleyan University Press, 1988).

Yusef Komunyakaa began publishing his poetry during the turbulent 1960s, a period that included what has been called the Second New Negro Movement, suggesting the fervor that characterized the Harlem Renaissance. His early verse appeared in such periodicals as *Black American Literature Forum*, the *Beloit Poetry Journal*, *Chameleon*, *Colorado Quarterly*, *Free Lance*, and *Poetry Now*. Some of his Vietnam verse has been collected in *Carrying the Darkness*, an anthology edited by W. D. Ehrhart, and in *The Morrow Anthology of Younger American Poets*. Most of his poems that were published in journals are reprinted, some in altered versions, in his first full-length book, *Lost in the Bonewheel Factory* (1979).

Born in Bogalusa, Louisiana, on 29 April 1947, Yusef Komunyakaa attended public school there, graduating from Central High School in 1965. Immediately thereafter he entered the U.S. Army, doing a tour in Vietnam, for which he earned the Bronze Star and during which he served as correspondent for and editor of the *Southern Cross*. After returning to the States, Komunyakaa entered the University of Colorado, where he earned his B.A. in 1975; he then attended Colorado State University and received his M.A. in 1979. He earned an M.F.A. in creative writing at the University of California, Irvine, in 1980.

Komunyakaa taught English at the Lakefront Campus of the University of New Orleans, and for a brief period he taught poetry for grades three through six in the public schools of

Yusef Komunyakaa (photograph by Mandy Sayer)

New Orleans. He has received several grants from learned societies and is an associate professor of arts and sciences at Indiana University at Bloomington, where he has taught since 1985. During the academic year 1989-1990 he held the Ruth Lilly Professorship, an endowed chair. Each year he reads his poems at colleges, universities, and museums in the United States and abroad. He has also lived briefly in Australia, Saint Thomas, Puerto Rico, and Japan.

The headings of the six sequences of *Lost in the Bonewheel Factory*—"Intermission," "Rituals and Rides," "Sideshows," "Testimonies," "Passions," and "Family Skeletons"—indicate the range of Komunyakaa's subject matter. In these sequences, as also seen in his subsequent volumes, he is absorbed in the pathos of the human experience, but he insists all the while that the reader accept and cope with hard reality, for only then can the beauty that lies within the human spirit come forth. The ability to see life's bareness and coldness is addressed in the first poem of his 1979 book, "Looking a Mad Dog Dead in the Eyes," a title that becomes a metaphor for life in the South of his youth, one of Komunyakaa's favorite and most fruitful themes:

> Perception
> can kill you.
> It can force you to crawl
> on God's great damn stone floor
> & scrape your knees to the bone,
> in love with the smooth round ass
> of death. . . .

In this poem he invokes images of the Crucifixion, describing Christ as a "young man with a nail in his foot" and "a thorn through his tongue." In other poems in this volume Komunyakaa also uses biblical images. The reader discovers the root-and-vine imagery of the medieval mystic alongside Judeo-Christian metaphors, such as "Jacob and the Nocturnal Angel," a phrase in the poem "Following Floor Plans." Repeatedly stone and rock images surface, and the landscape of life is "granite-colored."

A pretty woman's face becomes, again and again, a mirror reflecting humanity's nakedness, and the bones left by death's decay are not able to come to life again the way the biblical "dry bones of Ezekiel's vision will live." The human tongue is evil: like the Valley of Jehosophat, it is a sign and agent of sin, death, disease, the mortality that bespeaks God's judgment upon humanity's evil heart. The tongue becomes the "many-headed biblical beast / embracing a mad, pretty woman / in her sleek black get-up." Like frail, hungry sparrows, the human spirit in this valley of death "begs for whatever it needs." Repeatedly in the volume the reader sees a deformity of the skeleton, symbolizing the moral and physical grotesqueness of the poet's created world. In "Sitting in a Rocking Chair at the Window, Going Blind" Komunyakaa shapes the lines on the page to form the *s* curve of "a woman's dance . . . in a dark world." Beauty is tomorrow's "sack of bones," and no matter how much the dancer denies death and death's message, "what we deny comes full-swing around again," for "Everything

isn't ha-ha in this valley." In the Valley of Death that is human existence there is no place for daydreaming, for to do so is to blind oneself to the truth as the poet sees it.

Komunyakaa's second book-length collection, *Copacetic* (1983), presents jazz poems and blues poems in the manner of Langston Hughes and Amiri Baraka. The poems in *Copacetic*, like many of the poems Komunyakaa is writing for a forthcoming volume he is calling "Magic City," hearken back to his boyhood and early manhood. These poems examine folk ideas, beliefs, sayings, and songs, and the terminology of blues and jazz. Typical are "Blackmail Blues," which is the first poem in the book, and "Mojo," the title poem of the second and final sequence. Other poems that reflect the book's central themes include "Fake Leads," "The Way the Cards Fall," "Faith Healer," "April Fool's Day," "Jumping Bad Blues," "Woman, I Got the Blues," "Street Cool Clara," and "Blues Chant Hoodoo Revival." The familiar mirror imagery of his first book is repeated in his use of the words *mirror* and *reflection*. Settings are decidedly southern: "piney woods" and "cottonmouth country." The reader encounters the bloodhounds and "freight train hopper" of Richard Wright's fiction, elements that provide a narrative quality even to Komunyakaa's lyrical poems. Such phrases as "milkweed & blackberries," "the rope dangling from / a limb of white oak," and "rope and blood," and references to crickets (cicadas) and cornfields call forth the atmosphere of Jean Toomer's *Cane* (1923).

In the mode of Gwendolyn Brooks's poem "We Real Cool," but minus its staccato, Komunyakaa has penned "Jumping Bad Blues," which also echoes T. S. Eliot's "Love Song of J. Alfred Prufrock":

> I've played cool,
> hung out with the hardest
> bargains, but never copped a plea.
> . . . .
> I've fondled my life in back rooms,
> called Jim Crow out of his mansion
> in Waycross, Georgia, & taught
> him a lesson he'll never forget.

For its candor and subtle restraint, and for its appeal to audiences everywhere, "More Girl Than Boy" is the strongest poem in the volume:

> You'll always be my friend.
> Is that clear, Robert Lee?
> . . . .

You taught me a heavy love
for jazz, how words can hurt
more than a quick jab.
Something there's no word for
saved us from the streets.

Komunyakaa captures the rareness of a platonic love that outlasts frustration and disappointment.

I Apologize for the Eyes in My Head (1986) is a book of contrasts etched in verse. The mood changes from light and breezy to deeply sorrowful. From lost love in the city to loved ones and friends lost to the evils of slavery and Jim Crowism in the Deep South, Komunyakaa continues his fascination with ghosts reflected in life's looking glasses, with images of skeletons, and with other symbols of mortality and life's fragility. He experiments with longer poems, such as "Dreambook Bestiary" and "1984." There are hints of the Vietnam verse of his book that followed this one; but these war scenes are not as particularized. These are scenes that can happen anywhere that "combat boots" and corpses are found: Iwo Jima, Seoul, or Saigon. Nostalgia pervades the work—the persona recalls some pretty, nameless girl; revisits his home in Bogalusa; and leaves his heart with some absent lover in a distant city. Komunyakaa implies that life is a "mirage," and the unsuspecting lover is always surprised, it seems, by death: "he knows how death waits / in us like a light switch" ("The Thorn Merchant"); "Pretty Boy throws a kiss / to death, a paradoxical star in each eye. Naturally / he's surprised when he stumbles / & snags his suit coat on an ice pick" ("The Thorn Merchant's Right-Hand Man").

Komunyakaa employs metaphors that imply difficult transitions, or the inability to adapt to change and loss. The lover sometimes is forced to straddle a continent with one foot in the piney woods and the other in New York City. Or the lover spans "an empty / space [that] defines itself like a stone's weight," as he adjusts to the loss of love while aimlessly searching for a new love to fill the void, as in "The Heart's Graveyard Shift."

Equally powerful is "Landscape for the Disappeared," set in a centuries-old cypress swamp in Louisiana. In a manner reminiscent of the Louisiana cane fields of Toomer and similar to the elegiac tone of James Weldon Johnson's verse sermon "Go Down Death" (1927), Komunyakaa recites this litany for his dead ancestors who have

Yusef Komunyakaa (photograph by Carolyne Wright)

succumbed, long before the speaker was born, to the unhealthful Louisiana climate.

Lo & Behold. Yes, peat bogs
in Louisiana. The dead
stumble home like swamp fog,
our lost uncles and granddaddies
come back to us almost healed.

The power of a collective experience is transmitted through a culture centuries old and deeply mysterious.

Komunyakaa's Vietnam poems rank with the best on that subject. He focuses on the mental horrors of war—the anguish shared by the soldiers, those left at home to keep watch, and other observers, participants, objectors, who are all part of the "psychological terrain," as he has termed it, "that makes us all victims" and rages behind the eyes long after the actual fighting has ceased. *Dien Cai Dau*, his first book fully dedicated to this theme, was published in 1988. Its title, military slang for *crazy*, suggests his reliance on surrealistic imagery to chronicle the Vietnam experience. These poems emphasize the mental warfare that the American soldiers waged along with their physical struggles. This type of warfare was so intense and so bizarre that it requires an abnormally strong response that cannot rely entirely on aesthetic distancing, but this is not to imply that there is any absence of poetic conventions. Each of these brief poems chronicles an aspect of Komunyakaa's wartime experience. He uses imagery from nature to describe the acts of war, which are superimposed on a bleak landscape: "The moon cuts through / night trees like a circular saw / white hot." In another poem "Sunlight / presses down for an answer." At other times soldiers fade into their surroundings for cover, as suggested in the opening poem, "Camouflaging the Chimera":

> We tied branches to our helmets.
> We painted our faces & rifles
> with mud from a riverbank,
>
> blades of grass hung from the pockets
> of our tiger suits. We wove
> ourselves into the terrain,
> content to be a hummingbird's target.

There are tunnels, manholes, the odors of dampness, and the ghostlike feelings of pitch darkness. The only sights are seen through the scope "of your M-16," and "men breathe like a wave of cicadas." The "smoke-colored" Vietcong creep against the landscapes like vultures, leaving in their wake scarring memories that even nature cannot heal.

Komunyakaa tries through comparative devices to make order of a war that has no moral clarity. Through these techniques the personas in the poems remain simultaneously inside and outside the experience. These poems, all in the present tense, fix the fleeting images like mountings in a zoology lab—under glass. The war, then, becomes both the reader's illusion and the author's mental creation, seen most clearly in such compositions as "Roll Call" and "Seeing in the Dark."

As powerful as the opening poem is the closing one, "Facing It," which is a description of a visit to the Vietnam War Memorial in Washington, D.C.:

> My black face fades,
> hiding inside the black granite.
> I said I wouldn't,
> dammit: No tears,
> I'm alone. I'm flesh.
> . . . .
> Brushstrokes flash, a red bird's
> wings cutting across my stare.
> The sky. A plane in the sky.
> A white vet's image floats
> Closer to me, then his pale eyes
> look through mine. I'm a window.
> He's lost his right arm
> inside the stone. In the black mirror
> a woman's trying to erase names:
> No, she's brushing a boy's hair.

Reminiscent of the genealogical sequence in Rita Dove's prize-winning volume *Thomas and Beulah* (1986) is Komunyakaa's preoccupation with relatives and family backgrounds in his forthcoming book "Magic City." Some of the poems have appeared in journals, but the majority will be new. In "Mismatched Shoes" he writes, "my grandfather came from Trinidad / Smuggled in like a sack of papaya / On a banana boat, to a preacher's / Bowl of gumbo & jambalaya to jazz," and in "Cousins" Komunyakaa asks the poignant question, "Where did the wordless / Moans come from in the dark / Rooms between hunger / & panic?"

Yusef Komunyakaa has come of age, not only as a Southern-American or African-American bard, but as a world-class poet who is careful to restrain the emotions and moods he creates, without overdoing ethnicity of any kind. In his Vietnam verse he keeps before the world what it meant and still means to be American, black, and a soldier, and what the painful inequities of this combination add up to. His poetry is as rhythmic and fluid as his speaking voice, and just as mellow and introspective.

Sydney Lea

(22 December 1942 -   )

Norman German
Southeastern Louisiana University

BOOKS: *Searching the Drowned Man* (Urbana & London: University of Illinois Press, 1980);

Gothic to Fantastic: Readings in Supernatural Fiction (New York: Arno, 1980);

The Floating Candles (Urbana & London: University of Illinois Press, 1982);

No Sign (Athens: University of Georgia Press, 1987);

A Place in Mind (New York: Scribners, 1989);

Prayer for the Little City (New York: Collier / Toronto: Collier Macmillan, 1991);

The Blainville Testament (Brownsville, Oreg.: Story Line, 1992).

OTHER: *Richard Eberhart: A Celebration*, edited by Lea, M. Robin Barone, and Jay Parini (Hanover, N.H.: Kenyon Hill, 1980);

The Bread Loaf Anthology of Contemporary American Poetry, edited by Lea, Parini, and Robert Pack (Hanover, N.H.: University Press of New England, 1985);

The Burdens of Formality: Essays on the Poetry of Anthony Hecht, edited by Lea (Athens & London: University of Georgia Press, 1989).

SELECTED PERIODICAL PUBLICATIONS—
UNCOLLECTED: "Reconsideration: The Poetry of Richmond Lattimore," *New Republic*, 176 (30 April 1977): 37-39;

"Wordsworth and His 'Michael': The Pastor Passes," *English Literary History*, 45 (1978): 55-68;

"From Sublime to Rigamarole: Relations of Frost to Wordsworth," *Studies in Romanticism*, 19 (Spring 1980): 83-108;

"On 'The Feud,'" *Kansas Quarterly*, 15, no. 4 (1983): 97-103;

"Eighty Percenters: Reflections on Grouse and Grouse Dogs," *Gray's Sporting Journal* (Fall 1986): 121-129.

Sydney Lea (photograph copyright John Karol)

Sydney Lea—poet, critic, novelist, editor, essayist, and teacher—in 1977 founded the *New England Review*, sponsored by Middlebury College, as a forum for little-known writers. Though works by Anthony Hecht and Robert Penn Warren have appeared in its pages, 98 percent of the contents come from unsolicited material. Lea's own poetry displays a relaxed formalism that avoids the T-square and metronomic effects of his forebears, the strictured New Critics.

Born of moderately affluent Episcopal parents in a Philadelphia suburb (Chestnut Hill), Lea counts his uncle's farm near Ambler, Pennsylvania, as his spiritual home. The oldest of the five children of Sydney L. W. Lea (a business-man) and Jane Jordan Lea, Sydney Lea, Jr., attended the private, all-male Chestnut Hill Academy. His brother Mahlon's death in 1980 at age thirty-five, of a brain aneurysm, continues to influence his writing. Lea earned his B.A. (1964), M.A. (1968), and Ph.D. (1972) from Yale, where he played pool and hockey, and, though given to carousing, he belonged to an intellectual fraternity. He wrote stories and poems but avoided the campus literary crowd. Now he includes writers as diverse as T. R. Hummer, Mark Jarman, Jorie Graham, and Anthony Hecht among his literary advisers and confidants. Lea has taught at Dartmouth (1970-1979) and Middlebury (since 1979) and has won Rockefeller and Guggenheim fellowships. He has two children, Creston and Erika, from a sixteen-year marriage with Carola Bradford (which ended in divorce); and three, Amico Jordan, Catherine Margaret, and Sydney Portia, by his second wife, Margaret Robin Barone, a lawyer he married on 9 July 1983. A self-described "borderliner"—an outdoorsman with his head full of books, a litterateur connected to the outdoors—Lea is both a catch-and-release fisherman and a respectful hunter. He expresses impatience with the antihunting lobby, some of whom seem not to mind "the ski resorts that kill more wildlife than all the hunters in five states." Lea, a "Deepwoods Christian," is a Congregationalist deacon, though committed to religious tolerance.

Reading Lea, one gets the impression of two poets with antipodal concerns collaborating under a pseudonym. While his frustration with the distorting effects of language casts him as a semiotician trapped in a poet's body, his childlike capacity for wonder betrays him as a Wordsworthian mystic. Lea's subjects include natural objects, moods, and processes, and, increasingly, the family. His themes involve undercut expectations, nature's grandeur and indifference, and language's inability to capture the essence of objects. As a critic, Lea believes contemporary poetry has alienated readers by jettisoning much that would make it "more widely accessible—attention to plot, characters, history, politics, racial or social relations." Holding forth William Wordsworth and Robert Frost as models, Lea suggests corrective "narrative values" even in first-person lyrics, in which the "I" should show character. For over a decade *NER/BLQ* has sponsored an annual narrative poetry competition in order to promote such values.

Family, place, and a connecting language—the central concerns running through all of Lea's writings—emerge in *Searching the Drowned Man* (1980), wherein the many elegies and poems with dedicatees testify to Lea's affections. Lea's chronic philosophical malaise is prefigured in the opening, title poem, which, like many of Lea's poems, was generated by an actual incident. The speaker has joined a search party, hoping for some ultimate communication from a dead man:

> Whatever I'd thought,
> it wasn't this
> declarativeness, a face that looked
> engaged by plainest ideas: Now where
> did I leave my jacket,
> shoes?

Throughout the volume, Lea's personae must revise their a priori notions in the face of intractable reality.

Another of Lea's favored ploys in *Searching* is to focus on an insular "he" in a situation where the modes of transportation are emblematic of a self in transition, as in "Night Trip across the Chesapeake and After" or "Recalling the Horseman Billy Farrell from an Airplane in Vermont." Reminiscent of Wallace Stevens's "Sunday Morning," Lea's "The Bus to Schenectady" shows a traveler who has a tarnished epiphany as urban clutter and clatter "compose themselves, as in a miracle":

> His thoughts come down
> to this: No god in nature but as if in nature,
> not to him revealed in full for now.

Other echoes of Stevens, notably from his "The Snowman" and "How to Live. What to Do," appear in the first part of Lea's "Drooge's Barn":

> Look if you like
> through the roof beams;
> but don't compare them to ribs.
> . . . .
> Stones in the cellar,
> boards on the floor, are stones and boards,
> not crying, not refusing to cry.

Warning against the fraudulence of figurative language, the poem becomes a call to confront natural objects unbuffered by the interpretive intrusiveness of words.

In *Searching* Lea views nature both as intrinsically tropological ("jonquils bobbing / with simile") and as deceitful: if nature is "a sign, / [it has]

nothing to signify." Still, as "Incantation against Revelation" implies, nature's plenitude compensates for her treachery. Feeling that the inclination to attach larger significance to events is at best presumptuous, Lea crafts his poems to admit that words and rituals enrich what spare meaning exists, but that they are no more than fictions, though nonetheless necessary fictions. The voice in *Searching* feels its way toward, but never quite achieves, the ability to sit in the midst of doubt without reaching for explanations.

Stronger in its craft, variety, and confidence, *The Floating Candles* (1982) communicates Lea's maturer, darker vision, especially manifested in a Melvillian perception of white as symbolizing malevolent emptiness. A controlling idea in the volume is that words, stars, and people, nearly devoid of significance in isolation, generate meaning as they constellate with their kind in binding patterns. Thus, Orion's appearance on the cover does double duty in pointing to the themes of hunting and of meaningful, though often superstitious, configurations imposed by humans on the natural world.

With a syntactic interpretation of life, Lea's opening lines indicate a continued concern with the influence of language on perception: *"Why, like a sentence that qualifies itself / to forestall the inevitable period, did I want your dying / protracted?"* (from "Dirge for My Brother: Dawn to Dawn"). The often somber Lea takes a lighthearted detour in "Bernie's Quick-Shave," which closes the first section. Managing both humor and pathos, the placid meditation on lonely barbers in the hairy 1960s praises the courage of these "for whom some central thing has vanished." Even their older patrons, now bald, are truant.

Almost as an antidote, a more accessible blank-verse narrative follows the coldly impressionistic poems that dominate the first section. Concerning revenge and counterrevenge, "The Feud" begins when the Walker family leaves a pile of "deer guts cooking in the sun" on the narrator's lawn. Via slashed tires, bashed mailboxes, and poisoned hogs, the rustic philosopher learns the danger of judging another's behavior by one's own beliefs and observes how choice becomes fate: "Maybe fate is notions // that you might have left alone, but took instead." Ultimately he determines that doubt is the only certainty. The feud culminates in a child's death, possibly by arson: "Do I know what led to what // or who's to blame? This time I'll let it go. / No man can find revenge for a thing like this."

Dust jacket for Lea's 1991 book. The title poem spiritually links a group of ice-fishing huts to Bethlehem.

An appendix to the periodical publication of the poem in the *Kansas Quarterly* is "On 'The Feud,'" Lea's "meta-narrative" that reveals the poem as philosophical, poetic, and personal allegory. The feud participants are "moral bullies . . . who so confuse their own ethical and perceptual categories with actuality that they feel suited to pass righteous judgment on others' moralities and perceptions." Lea's essay further suggests that lyric poets are often moral absolutists cut from the same cloth as the antagonists in the feud, yet staking out moral territory robs a person of the poetic capacity to project himself compassionately into another's situation. The narrator of "The Feud" is thus "anti-poetic precisely in his inability to enter another mode of imagination. . . ." Last, Lea discloses the "coded meaning" of the poem as involving what he learned from his brother's being struck down in the middle of his life's journey—that petty contentions mean nothing after death. In its didactic effect, Lea's personal "stroke of domestic disaster" is analogous to the lesson by fire in the poem.

The poems after "The Feud" rescind the programmatic aesthetic distance running through much of Lea's early work (and, by extension, much of twentieth-century poetry) and invite the reader to share the indited emotions. To this end, even dogs figure prominently in *Candles:* as objects and subjects of devotion, as mimetic of their masters, and as human caricatures. "The Lesson" and "Instructions: The Dog" parallel child rearing and bird-dog training: "When he's a pup, / just let him go."

In several poems death is objectively correlated to "the white of winter." As a Frostian symbolist, Lea sees death in deer tracks filling with water; as semiotician, he reads it in "ink going white." Against such vacuity, humans construct dams of meaning with family rites that arrange the participants in meaningful relationships, much as stars form constellations of extended meaning.

In *Candles* Lea refines the elegiac voice unveiled in *Searching:* from the opening "Dirge for My Brother" to "The New Year: 1980," a closing lament on the loss of people, places, and times. This ending shows not so much an expansion as a concentration of his signature themes: language, place, and binding superstitions.

The title of Lea's *No Sign* (1987) portends despair, but the book affirms a faith in "what is," as the final poem confirms. Lea seems amazed that the world may require neither belief nor action but only "to be here now," as "The Dream of Sickness" puts it. There is a discernible technical shift, too, in Lea's reliance less on self-conscious figurative uses and more on unadorned, though sometimes windy, narratives.

The poem "Fall" signals his movement away from a tone of gloomy bewilderment. Irritable questioning gives way to a pacific drift; despair gives way to wonder—even at loss:

> We're good at this thing we do,
> but for each bird that falls,
> three get by us and go
> wherever the things that get by us go.
>
> To the realm of baby shoe and milk tooth;
> kingdom of traduced early vow. . . .

The first section continues with improvisations on time: "Telescope" speculates about what one would see through an instrument that allowed a view into the past; "The Light Going Down" projects what it would be like to live backward from

death, growing younger and approaching a prebirth eternity. Lea's melancholic disposition, however, expunges the joy of his pleasure domes. "Telescope" concludes, "But all these moments are fixed forever, / and such a lens no more effective / than memory, no more corrective."

In *No Sign* Lea is more interested in capturing moods than corralling meaning, as "High Wind" and "Sereno" attest. In the latter, good ducks out of the hunter's range provoke this meditation on equanimity: "My blood flows easier with age, the rage to question // Faltering. Like useless thoughts, the trash-birds strafe my blind." Though more busily peopled, the poems in *No Sign* exude a convincing serenity that bears witness to a Christian influence missing from his early books. Lea, however, is best when brooding, as in "Reckoning," a discourse on the inadequacy of numbers to quantify experience:

> Minus twenty-five outside. Second
> month, third day. Inside my child it's one
> hundred and three. For five straight nights this
> nameless thing (or things) has wandered in
> my girl at will. . . .
>   I remember
> hearing of a child who crashed through ice
> while skating our Unami River,
> the father or mother only one
> field away, which was one too many. . . .

The last poem in the volume, and perhaps Lea's best poem to date, is an "Annual Report" to his "very perfect wife." Down this calendar of twelve irregular sonnets, a "worm" tropes its way. After the initial fourteen-liner, set in May, month of "our son's late birth," June, in a thirteen-line sequence, breeds the worm (of despair, self-pity, and lust) that corrupts the year's otherwise harmonious round. In July the speaker plants an archetypal apple tree. September draws forth "the child's opposing teeth, with which he bled / your tender breasts." April completes "the year's full circle":

> cased blossoms bursting from the apple tree,
> the prostrate dog now grass, one son a man,
> a daughter who like you grows beautiful,
> an infant who has found a way to stand,
> the worm entombed as if beneath a mountain. . . .

Such sure formal accomplishment forecasts the direction of *Prayer for the Little City* (1991) and *The Blainville Testament* (1992). Lea, however, disavows the designation *neoformalist*, perhaps because he views *formalism* as a superlative beyond qualification, or because adherence to any final ideology would be inimical to his ongoing experimentation with form.

Despite a few Italian detours, *Prayer* continues Lea's fascination with New England terrain and characters. What is new is that Lea often imbues his settings with Christian meanings. Even the structure of the book—three sections of poems, many composed in tercets—uses Christian numerology. The dominant tone is wistfulness for people, places, and times that have passed, are passing, or will pass.

In the opening, title poem, the "little city" is a village of ice-fishing shacks on a pond. Subtly, then overtly, the village is compared to Christ's birthplace as evoked in the carol "O, Little Town of Bethlehem." Subconsciously the gruff fishermen seek a more accurate and intimate communion between themselves than the jokes and friendly curses that commonly bond them together. They posture "as if in prayer for a novel fish, or a novel way / by which to address some thing they're feeling. . . ." Throughout the book, the persona in the poems moves in earthly and spiritual worlds interwoven so tightly as to seem more a unified world than opposing realities. The first section, "Six Sundays Toward a Seventh," gives specific Lenten applications to biblical passages. Section 2, "Manifest," chronicles pedestrian but nonetheless wonderful revelations. In "At the Flyfisher's Shack," arguably the best poem in the volume, the persona looks for hints to an old man's character among the quaint marvels of his flytying detritus. What the speaker comes up with are contradictory revelations: "Was this man good? Like us he was and wasn't." Several poems in section 3, "Museum," make use of Lea's knowledge of Italy and its language. "Over Brogno" is noteworthy, too, for its line breaks and stanza patterns that imitate the persona's desire and subsequent climb "to rise above all," as if

> the higher powers
>   are something one has
>   to seek in a higher order.

Ultimately, as the poems seem collectively to say, the persona learns from his uphill journey, as Frost writes in "Birches" (1916), that "earth's the

right place for love." So Lea's speaker is drawn back down

> to cottage and shack,
>   to human traffic,
>   where souls move close to ground.

The title poem of *The Blainville Testament* dramatizes many of Lea's concerns, especially focusing on people's judgmental nature and their tendency to pin a moral tale on every plain-donkey occurrence. At the heart of the parable is a tragicomic story: while on the pressing task of reporting a young friend's imperilment (a dead cow has fallen on him in the grave intended for the animal), an eighty-year-old man gets sidetracked by nature's beauty, thereby contributing to the youth's death.

Throughout the book, the world is depicted as a "runic narrative" that "begs translation," as the narrator of "The Blainville Testament" says. As in his previous verse, Lea capitalizes on his knowledge of New England landscapes. Throughout *Blainville*, Lea employs, again in the words of the narrator of the title poem, "a language brightly eloquent of place."

In "Spite: Her Tale," an epistemological exploration, Lea enlists "a twisty beech" to reify the insidious convolutions of revenge. The speaker, after losing her sight and her husband, relocates her integral self by means of a tree:

> And once I fitted out the shape again,
> then I could see the farm; and once I saw
> the farm, the cows or steers or calves, whatever,
> then I felt I knew where I belonged
> in all this universe. . . .

When her son and daughter-in-law—spitefully, she thinks—cut down the beech, the narrator cultivates her slow revenge. Unwittingly voicing an ambiguous truth, she says she "knew that tree / as well as my own soul. . . ." The poem closes with the woman rocking in the night, relishing the fact that her descendants consummate her passive retribution by playing out their dead-end lives in weekend dance halls filled with lights that blind and music that deafens.

Whatever brand of Christianity Lea professes, his poetic vision in *Blainville* waxes pantheistic. His personal philosophy, though, seems expansive enough to contain any apparent contradiction in views. In fact, one of the virtues of Lea's poetry, both early and late, is the way it camouflages polemical tensions and offers its wisdom plainly, as in the words of Billy Fields, in "The Blainville Testament": "If heaven's worth the breath the preachers use, / it'll be just like your life was at its best."

Lea's determination to express in his poetry an immanent and transcendent presence carries into his first novel. Evoking the ambience of Ernest Hemingway's "Big Two-Hearted River" (1925), *A Place in Mind* (1989) commemorates male friendship, a river, and a time. Set in 1961, the novel is about the aging Brant Healey, a man who thinks the one constant in his life is a place, the McLean River, but who discovers other constants: a man, his lifelong fishing buddy Louis McLean; and a woman, Anna Graves, with whom he had a brief affair in 1921. The tragedy in the novel is not the disappearance of salmon on the

McLean, nor the loss of the wilderness soon to be only a place in mind, nor Louis's son's death by explosion, nor even Louis's own death by heart failure, but "a memory of something never to be caught and held and known" that becomes idealized with time. Speaking of women and fish, Brant says, "The ones that escape have a famous way of growing in memory." Woven into the sometimes confusing skein of flashbacks is Brant's curious tendency to diagram life as a literary plot and to impose on it a satisfactory denouement.

Sydney Lea's early interest in narrative verse has led to a belated calling as a novelist, and his autobiographical impulse has caused him to develop an avocation as a personal essayist. Currently he is putting the final touches on "Cranks" (a novel) and a collection of essays on hunting, fishing, and dog training.

Brad Leithauser
(27 February 1953 -)

Robert Darling
Keuka College

BOOKS: *Hundreds of Fireflies* (New York: Knopf, 1982);

Equal Distance (New York: Knopf, 1985; New York & London: Penguin, 1990);

A Seaside Mountain (New York: Sarabande, 1985);

Cats of the Temple (New York: Knopf, 1986);

Between Leaps: Poems 1972-1985 (Oxford & New York: Oxford University Press, 1987);

Hence (New York: Knopf, 1989; New York & London: Penguin, 1990);

The Mail from Anywhere (New York: Knopf, 1990).

SELECTED PERIODICAL PUBLICATIONS—
UNCOLLECTED: "Metrical Illiteracy," *New Criterion,* 1 (January 1983): 41-46;

"The Confinement of Free Verse," *New Criterion,* 5 (May 1987): 4-14.

Brad Leithauser has been one of the most fortunate of the younger poets grouped under the general title of New Formalists. Even preced-

ing the publication of his first book, *Hundreds of Fireflies* (1982), he had been published in several of the leading journals that print poetry and had been the recipient of numerous awards. However, he has also paid the price of early acclaim, as even critics friendly to his poetics have grown impatient to see him fulfill his full potential.

Leithauser was born on 27 February 1953 in Detroit and is the son of Harold Edward Leithauser (a lawyer) and Gladys Garner Leithauser (a children's writer and college professor). After secondary school in the Detroit area, Leithauser graduated from Harvard University with a B.A. in English in 1975 and a J.D. in 1980. While an undergraduate, he was awarded the Academy of American Poets Prize at Harvard in 1973 and 1975, and the Lloyd McKim Garrison Prize for poems in 1974 and 1975. He married fellow poet Mary Jo Salter on 2 August 1980, and they set off for a three-year residence at the Kyoto Comparative Law Center in Kyoto,

Brad Leithauser (photograph by Jerry Bauer)

Japan. He was also awarded an Amy Lowell Traveling Scholarship in 1981 and a Guggenheim Fellowship in 1982. The Leithausers have two daughters, Emily and Hilary.

Hundreds of Fireflies was accorded an unusual amount of critical attention for any book of poetry, let alone a premier performance. Most reviewers for the major periodicals were enthusiastic, several of them hailing the arrival of an important new poet. In the *New York Review of Books* (23 September 1982) Helen Vendler termed mildness "Leithauser's chief personal form of stylization" and added approvingly, "Mild poets are rare." Vendler also claimed that each of Leithauser's poems "repays rereading; most have a shapeliness of evolution that pleases all by itself...." Robert B. Shaw simply remarked of the book, "Reading it made me happy" (*Poetry*, December 1982).

But there were also some reservations expressed. Jay Parini, while saying that the "poems rush like water down hill, lucently fresh" and praising the work for avoiding both surrealism and unconvincing metaphors, does sound a warning, writing that some of Leithauser's poems "read like exercises in descriptive poetry and have less imaginative pressure than one expects in serious work ..." (*New Republic*, 14 April 1982). The poems do seem to make smaller claims than does typical lyric poetry. The technical execution

seemed, to many critics, to outdistance the actual substance of the poems.

But Sven Birkirts had a counterclaim against such criticism. Writing in the *New Boston Review* (June 1982), he held that "We have been schooled to approach poetry in a certain way, taught to extract content, a message.... [Leithauser's] lines embody the perceptual experience, *are* that experience; they hug their content and will not give it up. The poems are not about anything. Their meaning consists of the progress of the eye across the texture of the page...." This style of poetry is seen in terms of absolute music or the visual arts. But language takes its power from the fact that it is both denotative and connotative.

It is questionable if a poem such as "An Expanded Want Ad" delivers much more than its title; the observations are certainly sound, though such lines as "a few screens are torn and various / uninvited types may flutter through, / some of them to bite you" leave a bit to be desired both in content and in craft. About halfway through the poem a shack is mentioned "where two loggers outbraved the bitter / sting of a Michigan winter," and the reader senses the possibility of the coming of the real core of the poem in the human adventure of their "whittled lives," but instead the speaker describes a copse of birch. Very often in *Hundreds of Fireflies* description seems its own end. There are some poems in the volume, such as "Giant Tortoise," "Duckweed," and "Along Lake Michigan," in which physical description leads to something akin to philosophical observation, but these are the exception to the rule.

Nevertheless, *Hundreds of Fireflies* was an impressive debut, and it was greeted with a surprising succession of awards. The book was nominated for a National Book Critics Circle award, and Leithauser received a Lavan Younger Poets Award from the Academy of American Poets in 1983. Most impressively he was awarded a MacArthur Fellowship for the years 1983 to 1987, one of the most lucrative literary awards available and one usually reserved for artists who are better established.

All this attention did not ingratiate Leithauser with those who did not share his traditional poetic aesthetics, and he further aligned himself with the New Formalists in his criticism, detailing his position in the *New Criterion* of January 1983. Writing of the diffuse poetic climate, Leithauser noted that there are "hundreds and hundreds of bad poets saying, 'There are hun-

dreds of bad poets out there,' " and then he offered an even more damning view of the poetic
scene: "A great many well-known poets simply
have not worked in form and could not successfully if they tried.... Formlessness ... may,
then, actually be kept alive by conservatism in its
most basic sense—conservation of the self, the
preservation of one's reputation in the poetry
scene." These sentiments may be substantially
true, but they did little to curry favor in journals
such as the *American Poetry Review,* among others.

Upon returning from Japan, Leithauser
worked as visiting writer at Amherst College for
the 1984-1985 academic year and published a
novel, *Equal Distance,* in 1985. The book received
mixed reviews. Ruth Doan MacDougall found
Equal Distance filled with the weaknesses of a first
novel but liked its "great good humor" (*Christian
Science Monitor*, 21 January 1985). Writing in *Com-
monweal* (8 March 1985), Robert Jones claimed
that Leithauser "spends more time saying things
beautifully than thinking about what he says"
and asserted that the author "risks nothing."

Leithauser also published a chapbook of
poems, *A Seaside Mountain*, in 1985; the grouping
was included the following year in his second full-
length book of poetry, *Cats of the Temple*. This
1986 collection also seemed more like a promising first book than the work of a maturing poet,
and therein lay the problem for critics who had reviewed *Hundreds of Fireflies* favorably. Some reviewers praised Leithauser's technical facility but
found the poems emotionally arid. Vendler
sensed too much of Marianne Moore's influence:
"the poem begins to seem a form of ventriloquism" (*New York Review of Books,* 23 October
1986), though Vendler's review was generally favorable. D. J. Enright made a particularly cogent
observation in the *New Republic* (27 October
1986) when he too addressed the problem of emotional involvement in Leithauser's poetry: "Nature in Leithauser's verse might be more engaging than it is if men and women were a little
more to the fore. In 'At Greg's' a lot of things
are around—books, maps, a hash pipe, an empty
donut box, dental floss—but not Greg.... There
is rather more of human interest, or interest in
the human, in Leithauser's first book...." While
Cats of the Temple garnered a generally friendly reception, reviews tended to echo Calvin Bedient's
reservation that Leithauser is "formally careful,
but he generates only a modest emotional hum
... still practicing his scales" (*Sewanee Review*, Winter 1988).

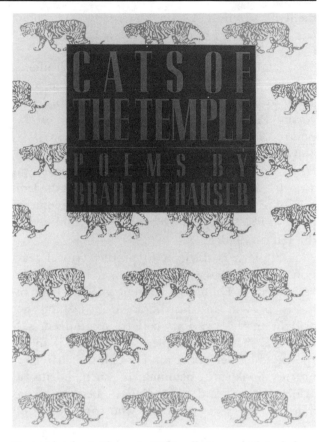

*Dust jacket for Leithauser's 1986 collection, which includes a
group of poems about Japan, where he and his wife lived
from 1980 to 1983*

Leithauser seems to have anticipated this reaction: in the "Author's Note" he writes, "Oblig-
ing readers will greet this book as a sequel to my
first, *Hundreds of Fireflies*." Once again it is natural description that dominates, but, unlike *Hundreds of Fireflies*, a major section of the 1986 book
features observations of Japan. The Japanese setting is one that seems in many ways ideal for
Leithauser's subtle, unostentatious gift; the poem
"In Minako Wada's House," for example, is simply an appreciation of a Japanese residence:

> Just to
> Wake in the night inside this nest,
> Late, the street asleep (day done,
> Day not yet begun), is what
> Perhaps she loves best.

The poem offers no great philosophical insight,
but the simple treatment and quiet craft do seem
to mirror the general tone of Japanese spareness.
But in many of the poems concerning natural observation too often the flatness may produce
more of a shoulder shrug than a feeling of involve-

ment or admiration from the reader. The book was nevertheless nominated for a National Book Critics Circle award.

Leithauser spent the 1987-1988 academic year as a lecturer at Mount Holyoke College, a position to which he returned in 1990. Oxford University Press published a British edition of his poetry, *Between Leaps: Poems 1972-1985,* in 1987, and Knopf published Leithauser's second novel, *Hence,* in 1989. That same year, Leithauser was awarded a Fulbright Fellowship to teach at the University of Iceland in Reykjavík. A new volume of poetry, *The Mail from Anywhere,* was published in the fall of 1990.

While it is difficult to predict critical reaction, *The Mail from Anywhere* seems to be a clear development in Leithauser's poetic growth. Humanity is present in this book in a fashion not evident in the previous collections; indeed, section 3 is titled "A Peopled World," as if in response to earlier criticism. Though the characters in the book are fictional, in such poems as "Uncle Grant" and "The Caller" Leithauser has managed to create personae who come to life on

the page as none of his previous characters did, even when he wrote of himself. "Old Bachelor Brother," the final poem in the collection, is superb, seemingly destined to become an anthology piece. The brother, a "flanking member of the groom's large party," watches the bridal party come down the aisle, the familiar women suddenly transformed, "approaching him / in all their passionate anonymity." Even Leithauser's descriptive nature pieces have, on the whole, more depth than does his earlier work. "Two Grotesques" in particular has more of a sense of the malevolence of the natural world. *The Mail from Anywhere* achieves some of the potential promised by *Hundreds of Fireflies* and is clearly his best collection to date.

Leithauser's craft is highly polished, though sometimes his syllabics appeal only to the eye, the ear hearing only prose. One can discern from his critical writings a keen and probing intelligence, but this intelligence may seem too little evident in his poetry. Regardless, Leithauser is an exceptional talent, and if he continues to develop, his should be a rewarding career to follow.

Larry Levis

(30 September 1946 -   )

Steven M. Wilson
Southwest Texas State University

BOOKS: *Wrecking Crew* (Pittsburgh: University of
  Pittsburgh Press / London: Snyder, 1972);
The Rain's Witness (N.p.: Southwick, 1975);
The Afterlife (Iowa City: University of Iowa Press,
  1977);
The Leopard's Mouth Is Dry and Cold Inside, by
  Levis and Marcia Southwick (St. Louis: Gen-
  tile, 1980);
The Dollmaker's Ghost (New York: Dutton, 1981);
Sensationalism (Iowa City: Corycian, 1982);
Winter Stars (Pittsburgh: University of Pittsburgh
  Press, 1985);
The Widening Spell of the Leaves (Pittsburgh: Univer-
  sity of Pittsburgh Press, 1991).

OTHER: "Some Notes on the Gazer Within," in
  Field Guide to Contemporary Poetry and Poetics,
  edited by Stuart Friebert and David Young
  (New York: Longman, 1980), pp. 102-123.

SELECTED PERIODICAL PUBLICATION—
UNCOLLECTED: "War as Parable and War as
  Fact: Herbert and Forché," *American Poetry
  Review*, 12 (January/February 1983): 6-12.

A persistent complaint about the American
poetry of the 1970s and 1980s is that the writers
(often academics) became almost exclusively concerned with themselves and the symbolic possibilities of their lives, writing in first person and creating metaphorical systems so reliant upon personal intuition or events that they shut out most
readers. Critics often point to such a tendency as
a major reason for the public's turn away from contemporary poetry. Larry Levis unfortunately
came to symbolize for many critics the self-
referential writer pampered by the academic
ivory tower and spending his writing career in endless exploration of himself. He has been awarded
important prizes, including the International Poetry Forum United States Award (1971), a Lamont
Poetry prize (1976), a National Poetry Series
Award (1981), and a National Endowment for
the Arts Fellowship (1973); his work has ap-

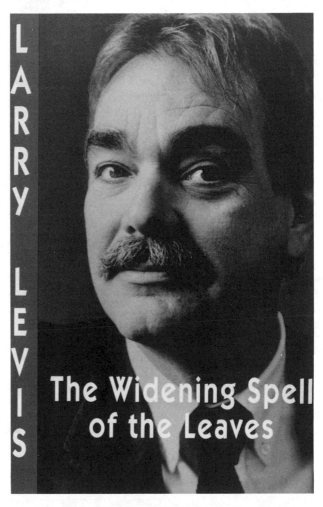

Cover for Levis's 1991 book, the third collection of his poetry
to be published by the University of Pittsburgh Press

peared in the *American Poetry Review*, *Field*, *Poetry*,
the *Antioch Review*, the *New Yorker*, and *Ploughshares*, among others. Even so, many see such acco-
lades and recognition as evidence that Levis is
only receiving praise from other like-minded
poets and academics in positions of influence.

Critic Eric Torgersen asserts that Levis is
merely repeating the method he sees around
him: "This pride-in-pose can be seen as a measure of inflation. . . . Levis is a falling off from

[Galway] Kinnell, [James] Wright, [Philip] Levine, whose similar professions of wretchedness went against their early training and did not, at first, come easily. For anyone of Levis' generation, such professions are a response learned from these masters, and don't cost much. This is a tired poetry that cannot carry us much farther." Even Jeff Schiff, who praises Levis's work, at one point says that the poetry affords the reader "a view of some masturbatory relationship the poet has with himself " (*Southwest Review*, Summer 1983). Of course, as is the case with any categorization, this use of Levis as evidence of the deterioration of American poetry is partly correct and partly incorrect. As Levis has progressed and has drawn more heavily from his experiences, his work has taken on greater depth and eloquence, so that in later books many poems are self-referential but are also moving, insightful meditations on living. Levis uses his life, but also looks outside himself and beyond the events he remembers to find connections with broader truths. Thus he is an important figure in contemporary American poetry, both as a highly decorated practitioner of a style and philosophy many see as the dominant method of poetry in recent decades and as a writer who considers, with at times artistic brilliance, the issues involved in being human and being American.

Born in Fresno on 30 September 1946 to William Kent Levis and Carol Mayo Levis, Larry Patrick Levis grew up among migrant farm workers in his parents' vineyard. Life on the farm, the struggles of the workers, and living in a rural community are subjects to which Levis returns again and again in his books for inspiration, imagery, and revelations.

He graduated from California State University, Fresno, in 1968 with a B.A. Levis then attended Syracuse University on a Ward Fellowship. From this period in his life Levis also gathered material for poetry, working as a janitor in a steel mill, where he met people who were tough, at times violent, and often crude. One can find several poems in *Wrecking Crew* (1972) and *The Afterlife* (1977) that draw directly on these encounters that, for Levis, symbolize the inherent cruelty of American society.

After receiving his M.A. from Syracuse in 1970, Levis became a lecturer at California State University, Los Angeles, for two years before receiving a fellowship at the University of Iowa, where he earned his Ph.D. in 1974. Since then he has taught at the University of Missouri (dur-

ing which time he found sources for poetry in the landscape of the plains, which to him was a metaphor for death and the passing of time) and, since the mid 1980s, in the writing program of the University of Utah. Levis has been married twice: to Barbara Campbell in 1969; and on 8 March 1975 to poet Marcia Southwick, with whom he has one son, Nicholas.

Levis's first book, *Wrecking Crew*, includes poems on war, rape, discrimination, death, and wasted lives. However, little of the book suggests solutions to the troubles; the book is more an existentialist's litany of America's cruelty. An anonymous reviewer in *Choice* (October 1972) argued that Levis separates himself from his subjects and their pain by "seeing violence through multiple layers of repulsion and recoil." So *Wrecking Crew*, while presenting a narrator who is clearly disturbed and disheartened by the world around him, at the same time illustrates a speaker resigned to cynical stoicism, a narrator who can with little emotion describe a sexual assault in "For the Country" and conclude that "I will say nothing, anymore, of / my country / . . . I will close my eyes, / . . . and that is the end of it." Levis approaches his subjects, then, with a careful detachment. He describes the book as "overtly political," and he does deal with the major concerns of his day, but his decision to "witness" leaves the reader ultimately disappointed by what could be seen as artistic cowardice.

Additionally, unlike later works, the *Wrecking Crew* poems are short—often very short—relying on calculated understatement and the connecting of concretely described images (a sort of exhausted imagism), often explained by the use of simile: "Once I thought my mouth was a scar / that disappeared / like spittle being wiped off a plate" ("The Magician at His Own Revival"). Peter Dollard (*Library Journal*, 15 December 1971) said *Wrecking Crew* "displays a sophisticated control of tone and imagery," but it is more likely that the final assessment will agree with Jascha Kessler (*Poetry*, February 1973): "*Wrecking Crew* is not exactly what I'd call finished work." Although Levis maintains the stance in his later work of an observer searching events and objects for meaning, his style after *Wrecking Crew* becomes freer, including longer poems, longer lines, and a trust in allowing intuition an explicit role. Perhaps the final failure of *Wrecking Crew*, then, is that he had not yet found the technique that best suited his poetic philosophy.

The Afterlife is evidence of a maturing writer. Behind the poems of this collection is someone who has begun to trust the leaps of logic and imagery provided by his intuition, and a reader is better able to follow the narrator of each poem as he struggles to find meanings in a chaotic world.

Once again most of the poems are written in first person and call upon specific events from Levis's life—his childhood in California, life in a small town, and marriage—and for some, such intrusions of the personal serve only to construct a wall between reader and poem, although Schiff argues that the idiosyncratic systems of reference and metaphor are realistic recountings of the poet's wrestling with death, the passing of time, and the search for meaning through poetry (*Southwest Review*, Summer 1980). In his personal exploration of past, symbol, and psychology, Levis naturally includes some details and leaps of logic that another person might not understand. Such a technique owes a clear debt to Robert Bly's valuing of intuition; however, it raises the question of what the purpose of poetry is. Is it to recount a personal exploration through a personal set of symbols, or to communicate with other, and different, people? Many poets of the 1970s, including Levis, decided on the former purpose. Still, because *The Afterlife* preserves many of the excursions of the imagination intact, most of the poems *do* communicate the issues and concerns with which Levis is dealing.

The Afterlife is divided into three sections. In the first are poems concerned with the passing of time and its effect on the narrator. In general the speaker of the poems is keenly aware of his surroundings and uses that sensitivity to discover reasons for death or lost youth, since, as Levis says in the first poem of the collection, "Rhododendrons," the belief in life after death no longer exists:

> Beneath the trees
> a young couple sits talking
> about the afterlife,
> where no one, I think, is
> whittling toys for the stillborn.
> I laugh,
>
> but I don't know.
> Maybe the whole world is absent minded
> or floating.

By the end of this first section of *The Afterlife*, the poet/narrator decides to believe in and explore

Cover for Levis's first book, a collection of poems on cruelty and violence that he has characterized as "overtly political"

an afterlife of a different sort: the spirit of the past as it remains in the physical world.

Thus, in section 2 Levis includes poems about finding patterns or messages in nature: "Inventing the Toucan," "The Map," and "The Invention of Maps." In each of these poems speakers work through the maze of the physical, following their imagination. Levis's conclusion, however, is not one of reconciliation and hope. The final poem of section 2 is "In Captivity," a refutation of the Romantic notion that a study of the natural world and its cycles will calm troubled souls:

> We'll turn slowly, flowers
>
> In the mouths of drowned cattle.
> In a dawn of burned fields,
> The sun disappoints you,
> And the blight you begin to remember
> Is me.

People are trapped in time, trapped by nature. Even the poet becomes a "blight," because he can only remind others of the same reality.

What finally brings the excursion of *The Afterlife* into question is the last section of the book: one long, twelve-part poem entitled *The Rain's Witness* (separately published in 1975). It is not necessarily a bad poem, and there are moments of moving insight and effective use of image, but the poem is merely another way to say what was said, and said more believably, in the first two sections. By the end of the poem, Levis is questioning whether it is even worthwhile to write his poems. Nothing matters or makes any difference, and his friends "are all tired of reading." A reviewer for *Choice* (February 1978) called the exercise "poetic gadflying." Perhaps this is not far from the truth. In the essay "Some Notes on the Gazer Within" (1980) Levis recounts his work on the poem: "I was, throughout, relatively untroubled about what the poem might mean to anyone, or what it should mean. . . . I was anyone forgetting himself inside a task: the only thing I tried to do in the poem concerned craft. I tried to break a rule in each section—do something I'd never done before." Experimentation is part of a writer's exploration and refining of his art, but it brings the sincerity of *The Afterlife* into question. How many of the metaphors are mere experiments?

In the end, then, *The Afterlife* is at times enjoyable, but taken as a whole it is disappointing philosophically and annoying technically, which makes Levis's later poetry an unexpected pleasure, as he moves beyond experimentation into an artistry and insight of the best kind.

Ralph Waldo Emerson argued that the human soul naturally strives to find examples of abstract ideas in the physical world. For him, this tendency suggested an important purpose of nature: through careful observance of nature one begins to discover a unity among all things and eventually comes to understand God. Although Levis never seems to accept the notion of a supreme being, he does begin to place importance in the relationship between the human spirit and the physical world. In his first books the poetry reflected a denial of meaning or value in anything. But beginning with *The Leopard's Mouth Is Dry and Cold Inside* (1980), there is a gradual shift toward considering symbolism and seeing the search for similarities between man and nature as a necessary, sustaining element.

The Leopard's Mouth is a small collection of prose poems: seven by Levis and seven by his wife, Marcia. Levis's contribution to the book, written while he lived and worked in Missouri, uses the plains as a symbolic background. In each poem there is a sense of openness; emptiness; the constant presence of wind; and endless, distant horizons. The people in these poems live and speak from the center of this vastness, the flat landscape serving as an enormous stage for the daily events of life.

The works in *The Leopard's Mouth* still arise from the same somber outlook on life contained in earlier poetry by Levis; the lot of humanity remains cold and depressing. However, there is a hint here that Levis has begun to value the task of the poet: the ordering of symbols, the digging beneath surfaces for meanings. In "Schoolhouse," for example, a young narrator comes to understand that things may be more than they appear: "Each day I would look up at my teacher and imagine her secret life, her dress with the orchid print and the brittle, 78 records she would play, afternoons, drinking brandy and trying to get into the mood, while she looked out at the bleak, charmed sky." What interests the narrator is not the reality of this woman, but her substance—what might be below the surface. The image of life is not an uplifting one, but these interpretations reveal something about the narrator, and, indirectly, something of Levis's character. The sky—nature—is "charmed" because people are able to use it to see reflections of human life, leading to a clearer understanding of themselves.

In *The Leopard's Mouth* are the beginnings of an important feature of Levis's work: he uses his poetry and imagination to reach into other people's lives and find symbols there. At the same time, though, he continues his search for a better understanding of himself, because his imagination creates the details and metaphors within his characterizations. The value Levis discovers in poetry, then, seems to be its ability to illustrate the similarities of all people. *The Leopard's Mouth* contains the first hints that Levis wants his poetry to help despairing human beings find others who understand. He has become a romanticist in spite of himself.

In *The Dollmaker's Ghost* (1981), the winner of the National Poetry Series competition, there is evidence that Levis, though still troubled by the hardship of existence, has come to view life as something of great importance. According to Schiff, the book "seems to be a portent of self-health." Levis uses his experiences more in this book than in any of his previous work, but the images are effective and integrated into a symbolic whole. There is a moving clarity of vision in *The Dollmaker's Ghost*, and Levis's technical abilities have matured, resulting in a volume that contains his best writing to that point.

The Dollmaker's Ghost concerns the attempt to discover why the physical world reminds people of the past and of the dead. In part 1 Levis shows how certain places or things cause him to remember vividly people and events from long ago. But Levis argues that the physical world has no importance or meaning in and of itself (in "The Cocoon," "Wasps," and "The Future of Hands"). For Levis, objects have no spirit of their own, so he is led to consider why they remind people so often of spirituality.

To that end, Levis gathers several poems in part 2 that use physical detail to reveal and revive the substance of people's lives. Additionally he discovers an ability to construct lives for people based purely upon their appearance, their surroundings, and his own poetic insight. Peter Stitt (*Georgia Review*, Fall 1981) says "pathetic projection" is the projection of one's feelings onto a stranger. Stitt believes that such an approach is an inherent part of Levis's character: "it seems in his hands not to be a technique at all, but an indication of how he actually perceives the world." In *The Dollmaker's Ghost* Levis seems to believe that the spirits of the dead survive in and become a part of the physical world. Thus when Levis senses something about a person's life, it is not so much his imagination providing symbolic details as it is the subject's spirit speaking to Levis through nature.

Part 3 of *The Dollmaker's Ghost* deals with the ways in which people confront death and with their transformation from corporeal into spiritual beings. This section begins with a poem entitled "Words for the Axe":

> Whoever it is that holds me, my one friend,
> Is only a flowing of blood:
> And blood spreads like branches in summer,
> The leaves shading a house where the people
> Sleep, and the birds keep their distance
> From other birds, and it is the world.
>
> It *is* the world. . . .

This affirmation of life is surprising from a poet who before was so doggedly nihilistic.

Based upon this affirmation, Levis considers the deaths of important literary figures such as Anna Akhmatova, Zbigniew Herbert, and Federico García Lorca, all of whom, like Levis,

wrote poems about oppression. For each, death was a transformation into pure spirit, but this spirit remains a part of the world and speaks through nature in symbols. For example, in "For Miguel Hernandez in His Sleep and in His Sickness: Spring, 1942, Madrid," Levis, speaking to Hernandez's spirit, says:

> And without breath,
> You would become the street:
> You would become these goats braying,
> The scrape of soldiers,
> A girl's laugh inside a bar. . . .
> I could visit you years from now
> In these bricks and these black shops and even
>
> In this shattered glass that no one cleans up,
> That shines in the sun. . . .

Levis reaches the conclusion that the afterlife is an existence without pain; however, in part 4 he indicates that it is also an existence of emptiness, of looking back at lost life. In this last section Levis presents the lives of spirits: they wander the physical world watching and listening to people who cry out in fear of death and the passing of time. It is a fear they understand too well, because death has taken what the spirits love and desire most: their lives. Thus, by the end of this section, Levis has shown that it is their spirits that lead people to fear death so intensely. Listening to the soul causes one to detest an existence that ends inevitably in death, even while one fears losing that existence. People may become consumed by fear and waste life in endless search for meaning and reason. *The Dollmaker's Ghost*, then, is finally a call to enjoy life, even if doing so is a kind of ignorant bliss. In "Blue Stones" (dedicated to Levis's son, Nicholas), the poet decides that he will not tell his son just how painful and hopeless he believes life to be:

> Let me be the stranger you won't notice,
> And when you turn and enter a bar full of young
>   men
> And women, and your laughter rises,
> Like the stones of a path up a mountain,
> To say that no one has died,
> I promise I will not follow.

Written in the voice of Levis's spirit after he has died, "Blue Stones" is an acceptance of life and an indictment of those, such as Levis, who have spent their lives governed by the death-fueled sadness of their spirits.

Winter Stars (1985) continues Levis's exploration of issues that have concerned him throughout his career: death, the power of nature to trigger memories, the ability of the poet to sense and describe the substance dwelling within the physical world. In this book, however, Levis has called upon his philosophies to aid him in a personal confrontation with tragedy. Readers learn early in *Winter Stars* that his father has died, and much of the book is an examination of how one comes to terms with great personal loss.

The first section shows how adolescence is a time of looking toward the future. He describes his youth in his father's vineyard, recalling events that led him to see the inherent pain in life (in "The Poet at Seventeen," "Adolescence," and "The Cry"). For Levis, the transformation from youth to adulthood is made when one begins looking back at the past. Life, then, is built upon sadness for what is gone and what is no longer possible. An adult knows that pain and death are inevitable.

It is in section 2 of *Winter Stars*, "Elegies," that readers learn of Levis's father's death. As in *The Dollmaker's Ghost*, Levis describes life beyond death as the existence of the spirit in the physical world. Thus nature serves both to sustain the dead father and to sustain Levis's memory of him. In "Childhood Ideogram," for example, Levis discusses how symbols absorb the essence of what they symbolize, since they can re-create experiences and sensations completely in one's imagination. When Levis sees snow and the coming of winter, he is naturally led to thoughts of his father: "Outside, it's snowing, cold, & a New Year. / The trees & streets are turning white. / I always thought he would come back like this." As Levis does in previous poems, he suggests that such memories are comforting and painful at the same time; it is clear that this paradox is, for Levis, a central dilemma of human existence.

So, too, is the need for human companionship when one is faced with the death of a loved one, as Levis shows in section 3 of *Winter Stars*, "Let Nothing Dismay." Why do people seek other people at times of death, knowing that they, too, will die? As Levis says in "In the City of Light," "My father died, & I was still in love." Levis sees love as a desire for lasting companionship, but such a desire is the stuff of childhood, for adults know that nothing lasts. Permanence, Levis says, only comes through death, when people become memories and can change no more.

The remainder of *Winter Stars* shows symbol and personal memory giving insight into the human condition. In poems such as "The Assimilation of the Gypsies" and *Sensationalism* (separately published in 1982), Levis uses the physical world as a way of igniting poetic insight. He is looking for human truth. Poems, then, are the products of one voice trying to communicate this truth to others. In "Those Graves in Rome" he writes:

> I stood here with my two oldest friends.
> I thought, then, that the three of us would be
> Indissoluble at the end. And also that
> We would all die, of course. And not die.

What he grasps, grappling with his father's death, the death of John Keats, and all death, is that poetry may look squarely at the truth—including sadness, pain, and oblivion—and, by saying that truth, recapture the days of youth, when life seemed to go on and on. Poetry does so, Levis believes, by enlisting the power of memory. *Winter Stars*, even though it concerns the death of Levis's father, is finally an affirmation of the ability of the poet and his art to rejuvenate the soul.

The Widening Spell of the Leaves (1991) is a journey through moments from the poet's life that have taken on symbolic or personal importance, and that lead him through a sometimes dizzying maze of images and meanings as he explores the uses of intuition and personal history in reaching an understanding and acceptance of human existence. "Oaxaca, 1983," for example, employs long, Whitmanesque lines and relies on the personal association of ideas and events, including Central American violence, making love, the Kent State tragedy, and peep shows. Much of *The Widening Spell of the Leaves* takes the reader on similar excursions, though the enlivening leaps of imagery one finds in Levis's earlier work are rare. There are, in fact, troubling stock phrases and predictable details; in "Slow Child with a Book of Birds" Levis writes:

>   Coleridge at
> The rail of a ship sailing back
> From Malta . . .
> . . . .
> Watching as two sailors from America
> Tortured a pelican on deck by tossing
> Scraps to it, then flailed it with sticks
> When it tried to eat. . . . Coleridge
> Saw the world to come.

Still, even if the book is disappointing stylistically, the poems further Levis's ongoing desire to capture and halt time—to stop change, if only for five seconds, and he draws more freely from the details of his past than before. The memories he recalls are often painful—lost youth, his parents' separation—but he believes that stopping the passage of time would yield true value: one moment would be *the* moment. He writes that people "cling to a belief in the Self, which memorizes, which is nothing." Levis is again struggling to know what truly matters in life—to draw truth from "the unremarkable." From the beginning of his career, this struggle has involved the continual, honest confrontation with the maze of the world for the recovery of the human soul.

Interview:

Leslie Kelen, "After the Obsession With Some Beloved Figure: An Interview with Larry Levis," *Antioch Review*, 48 (Summer 1990): 284-299.

References:

Stanley Plumly, "Two: Image and Emblem," *American Poetry Review*, 7 (May/June 1978): 21-32;

Jeff Schiff, "Poetry as a Psychology of Ritual," *Southwest Review*, 65 (Summer 1980): 332-335;

Schiff, "A Rose for the Lover," *Southwest Review*, 68 (Summer 1983): 291-294;

Eric Torgersen, "Inflation and Poetry," *American Poetry Review*, 12 (July/August 1983): 7-13.

William Logan

(16 November 1950 -   )

Richard Flynn
Georgia Southern University

BOOKS: *Dream of Dying* (Port Townsend, Wash.: Graywolf, 1980);

Sad-Faced Men (Boston: Godine, 1982);

Moorhen (Omaha: Abattoir, 1984);

Difficulty (Edinburgh: Salamander, 1984; Boston: Godine, 1985);

Sullen Weedy Lakes (Boston: Godine, 1988).

An April 1981 *Life* magazine feature on eleven poets, with photographs by Annie Leibowitz, pictured William Logan lying on a sleeping bag in a sparsely furnished apartment. The accompanying text proclaimed that, although "early in college, Logan's love was rock 'n' roll," he was pursuing "more literary" interests; he is quoted as saying, "I was thrilled by *The Waste Land*." Of a piece with the fashion-magazine mentality of the spread (with a bare-chested Robert Penn Warren and with Tess Gallagher shown as Lady Godiva on horseback), there is little in the photograph or text that suggests the erudite formality of Logan's poetry.

Born in Boston to William Donald Logan, Jr. (a salesman with Alcoa, and later the general manager of Allan Marine, the director of gas marketing at Con Edison, and a real-estate broker), and Nancy Damon Logan (also a real-estate broker), the young Logan was raised in Braintree and Westport, Massachusetts; Pittsburgh; and Huntington, New York, where he graduated from high school in 1968. He received his bachelor's degree from Yale in 1972 and his M.F.A. from Iowa in 1975. Since 1974 he has lived with the poet Debora Greger.

Since 1975, Logan's poems and reviews have appeared regularly in major magazines and newspapers, such as the *New Yorker, Poetry*, the *New York Times*, the *Washington Post*, and the *Paris Review*. He has received grants from the Ingram Merrill Foundation and the National Endowment for the Arts, and has won an Amy Lowell Traveling Scholarship, the 1988 Citation for Excellence in Reviewing from the National Book Critics Circle, and the Lavan Younger Poets Award from the Academy of American Poets. Since 1983 he

William Logan (photograph by Deborah Brackenbury)

has taught in the Creative Writing Program of the University of Florida, where he is currently associate professor of English and director of creative writing.

Logan spent four years in England over the course of the 1980s, and his poetry often seems more British than American. Even when he deals with highly personal subjects, he is reticent and allusive. His poetry is composed, for the most part, in tightly formal structures that often seem as constricting as they are potentially expansive and invigorating. Both his admirers and his detractors characterize his poetry as "impersonal." Simon Rae, writing in *TLS*, said, "William Logan's poetry is cerebral, abstract, and elusive. Its tone is fastidious, at times clinical, and its prevailing mood is sombre" (14 December 1984). Praising Logan's first full-length collection, *Sad-Faced Men* (1982), Richard Howard in the *Nation* almost succeeded in burying it. Although he lauded the "expert, lowering poems" as "the poems in Prospero's drowned book," he criticized Logan's poetry for its unrelenting severity—"its figures [are] drastic in their closure, their abeyance from sealed realm to realm; its measures slack with exhaustion, a tension literally beyond bearing; its vocabu-

lary chastened. . . . " Howard praised the poems individually as "enigmatic and resonant" but concluded that the collection as a whole is "more likely to foreclose than to mystify" (20 March 1982).

Logan's poems seem antinarrative, a quality that may, as Howard suggested, rescue them from sentimentality but one that also leaves them open to the charge of willful obscurantism. Logan's distrust of narrative is made explicit in one of the best poems from *Sad-Faced Men*, "The Man on the Bed," in which he describes his grandfather's use of anecdote to persuade "Midwest housewives to buy / His merchandise":

> My grandfather was no honest man,
> For honesty is of little use when a man,
> By profession, sells kitchen gadgets
> To people who will be hard-pressed recalling
> The reason for their purchase.

Recognizable narrative, any good yarn, is seen by the poet to be only the tool of con men or traveling salesmen. Indirectly the poem is a sort of *ars poetica*, a reason for Logan's rejection of mainstream, anecdotal poetry. Narrative, the poem argues, is the stuff of deception.

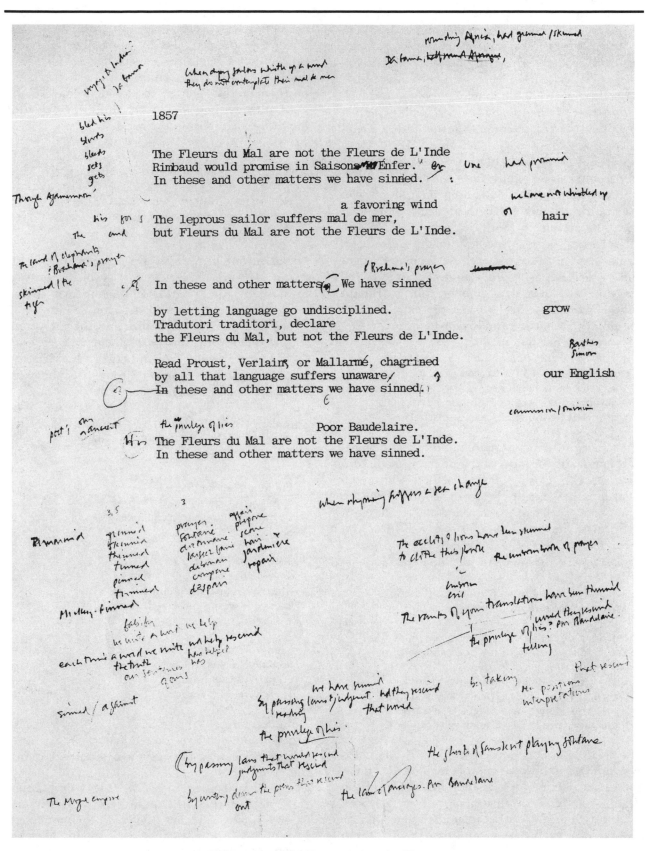

Draft for Logan's "1857" (by permission of William Logan)

Recognizing that this stance might lead him to "write things into extinction," Logan grapples with this problem in his second book-length volume, *Difficulty* (1984). Critic Stephen Romer recognized the power of the long title poem, acknowledging that "Logan's linguistic difficulty finds a purpose, in trying to come to terms with a terminated love affair" (*New Statesman*, 18 January 1985). However, none of the reviewers of *Difficulty* seemed to recognize the central crisis, which concerns the couple's "phantom daughter," who has been lost either through abortion or miscarriage. In section 5, with its echoes of W. D. Snodgrass's "Heart's Needle" (in the 1959 book of that name), the speaker, having envied a man who "wrestl[ed] with his daughter," rejects the image of the lover in a photograph as "Design without speech, a face starved of text, / it does not promise what it cannot deliver," and he decides to burn her letters,

> clumsy dissections of a passion's reach.
> Your once familiar blue
> scrawl became a scroll of ash, more true
> where pictures alone are honest teachers.

The image of the phantom daughter, kept deliberately enigmatic for most of the poem, is made concrete in the closing lines, before which the speaker lashes out at the lover, saying that "ten years ago" she had deceived him "each night with words you never wanted to say, / words you never meant." But the speaker's need to blame the lost lover is tempered with understanding:

> I understand that now. I understand the love
> That twists us into lives we never meant.
>
> One long night, before you were pregnant,
> You held a wet cloth to my head and hour
> after hour whispered love into my ear.
> I know better what those whispers meant.
> Or tell myself I know. The clock has stopped,
> whose hour comes by accident. The carpet's
> in the attic. You're never coming back.

The speaker indicts himself for his unwillingness to acknowledge his own complicity in the termination of the pregnancy and the termination of the affair, and this self-indictment proves far more powerful than the rather condescending indictment of the grandfather/salesman in "The Man on the Bed."

The problems of narrativity and reflexivity in language are also taken up in *Difficulty*. "Arca-

num" bears an ironic epigraph from René Descartes ("as soon as I see the word *arcanum* in any proposition I begin to suspect it"), which introduces a poem that lampoons the jargon of poststructuralist literary criticism, while at the same time paying homage to the importance of the poststructuralists' discoveries:

> Writing cannot
> comprehend the lineaments of message.
>
> Deaf to its own urgings, it outraces
> presence, arriving before beginning,
> always already the father of itself.

Logan, having provided a "proposition" titled "Arcanum," invites readers to cast suspicion on that proposition (the poem), which in turn invites them to suspect their own suspicion.

The multilayered ironies and the important subject matter of the best poems in *Difficulty* show Logan's poetic growth between his first and second volumes. However, some of the less-ambitious poems signal the direction Logan's work takes in *Sullen Weedy Lakes* (1988). "The Shootist" (from *Difficulty*) is a ballad presumably spoken by John Hinckley as played by John Wayne:

> I'm in a hotel waiting,
> watching a man on t.v.
> I can see him on three channels
> but he can't see me.
>
> Tomorrow I'll take a stroll
> down by his hotel
> where he'll be talking and talking
> like a guy with a car to sell.
> . . . .
>
> I have no mother or father,
> no daughter and no son,
> no past and no future,
> but I have a little gun.

Admittedly this doggerel is chilling, but it is also occasional and overly dependent on topicality—British reviewers, for instance, seemed to miss the point.

A similar poem in *Sullen Weedy Lakes*, "Political Song," elicited the praise of Sven Birkerts (*Boston Review*, October 1988), who commended Logan for "Audenizing" poetry again; likewise, David Lehman calls *Sullen Weedy Lakes* "vivaciously Audenesque" (*Washington Post Book World*, 28 August 1988). Both critics assume that such

"Audenization" is a virtue—hardly a foregone conclusion. Randall Jarrell, a great admirer of the early work of W. H. Auden, said of Auden's work after the 1930s, "a poet has turned into a sack of reflexes" (*Kipling, Auden & Co.*, 1980). To his credit, Logan, in his poem "Auden," seems fully aware of this decline. Yet all too often in *Sullen Weedy Lakes*, Logan succumbs to what Jarrell (again speaking of Auden) calls "dreary facetiousness that would embarrass a radio comedian."

Though *Sullen Weedy Lakes* offers welcome relief from the almost unrelieved darkness of his earlier books, one hopes that Logan has not abandoned grappling with the difficulties of human relationships and language. When Logan writes about more personal concerns, as in "Debora Sleeping," his characteristic wit seems more honest than it does in poems such as "To the Honor-able Committee," which is merely witty. In "Debora Sleeping" he ironizes the neoclassical rhetoric that mars some other poems in the volume:

Sleep's our disease, the heart's adagio.
We wallow in its sty, refuse to leave
the rundown precinct of its raveled sleeve,
the only ease bodies so close can know.

Or so I thought.

William Logan is currently completing a new volume of poems, "Vain Empires," and has collected his essays on contemporary poetry in a volume he says is "tentatively and recklessly titled" "All the Rage: Prose on Poetry, 1976-1990." He is an accomplished, engaging, and idiosyncratic poet and critic.

Susan Ludvigson

(13 February 1942 -   )

Gwendolyn Whitehead
Lamar University

BOOKS: *Step Carefully in Night Grass*, as Susan L. Bartels (Winston-Salem, N.C.: Blair, 1974);
The Wisconsin Women (Tempe, Ariz.: Inland Boat/Porch, 1980);
Northern Lights (Baton Rouge & London: Louisiana State University Press, 1981);
The Swimmer (Baton Rouge: Louisiana State University Press, 1984);
Defining the Holy (Emory, Va.: Iron Mountain, 1986);
The Beautiful Noon of No Shadow (Baton Rouge: Louisiana State University Press, 1986);
To Find the Gold (Baton Rouge: Louisiana State University Press, 1990).

A relatively little-known contemporary poet, Susan Ludvigson has generally found a warm and generous audience with critics. She has been commended for her minimalism, her ability to avoid sentimentality when dealing with sentimen-tal subjects, and her skill with both closed and open forms. Particularly in her later volumes, Ludvigson deals with several pervasive themes. Memories from childhood are an important part of her work as is the inner working of the female mind. While Ludvigson's poetic voice is not stridently feminist, she captures well the essence of feminine nature from childhood to maturity. Ludvigson is also able to bring characters to life in her poems. Humor, often offbeat humor, also plays a role in her poetry.

Susan Ludvigson was born in Rice Lake, Wisconsin, on 13 February 1942. She is the oldest of the four children of Howard C. and Mabel Helgeland Ludvigson. The poet's father owned two restaurants in Rice Lake, but when she was ten, he was unable to maintain the leases on his buildings, so he pursued other kinds of business. The thought of poverty frightened her: "I think the earlier sense of privilege perhaps gave me a

Susan Ludvigson (photograph by Laura Ely)

certain confidence about the future and my own possibilities in the world, while the fear of real poverty may have awakened, if I didn't have it before, the empathy I hope is one of the strengths of my poetry."

On 20 February 1961 Ludvigson married her high-school sweetheart, David Bartels. In September 1961, their son, Joel David, was born. She and Bartels were both enrolled as undergraduates at the University of Wisconsin in River Falls, where she studied English and psychology. She earned her B.A. with honors in 1965. After graduation the Bartels family moved to Ann Arbor, Michigan, where Bartels did graduate work and Ludvigson taught in a junior high school. From Ann Arbor, they moved to Charlotte, North Carolina. Ludvigson joined a group of women who were writing and attempting to publish literature of all kinds. Her first book of poetry, *Step Carefully in Night Grass* (1974) was written during this time. She received her M.A. in English from the University of North Carolina at Charlotte in 1973. From 1974 to 1976 she did further graduate work at the University of South Carolina, studying with James Dickey. Since 1975 Ludvigson has taught English at Winthrop College in Rock Hill, South Carolina.

In October 1988, having divorced Bartels (in 1974), she married novelist Scott Ely, who also teaches at Winthrop. They try to divide their time between residences in Rock Hill and the south of France.

Ludvigson has held fellowships from the Virginia Center for the Creative Arts (1979 and 1981), MacDowell Colony (1979-1980), North Carolina Arts Council (1987), and the Witter Bynner Foundation (1986-1987). In 1983 a Guggenheim Fellowship was awarded to her. The following year the *Virginia Quarterly Review* gave her the Emily Clark Balch Award. Ludvigson has also been the recipient of National Endowment for the Arts Fellowships, most recently for 1984-1985, just prior to the publication of *Defining the Holy* (1986) and *The Beautiful Noon of No Shadow* (also 1986). She has also held a Fulbright Fellowship, on which she visited Yugoslavia (1984-1985).

Step Carefully in Night Grass was published under her married name, Susan L. Bartels. Compared to Ludvigson's later work, this first book of poetry lacks maturity. Many of the poems are short, cryptic verses that often leave the reader guessing about the poet's intent. Despite Ludvigson's wish that everyone would forget about

Step Carefully in Night Grass, there are flashes of the later Ludvigson in the poems in the volume.

The title comes from the initial poem, "Contrasts." The first stanza describes various kinds of death that crawl "from under these familiar rocks." Among those mentioned are copperheads, rattlers, and spiders. The stanza ends, "We step carefully in night grass / never barefoot."

Even in this early, rather uneven volume, one of the her recurring themes can be seen: the life of a woman. In "Woman" Ludvigson presents a modern Eve as temptress and destroyer, using nuclear weapons. The woman of this poem has no need to be reborn; she says, "I am immune to dying fully. // I am the eternal witch / offering Snow White the apple." The poem ends ominously: "If I offer you a dish of mushrooms / think of me gathering them in a garden / hair falling to sweep the ground / as I bend to pluck them from the moss / beneath an apple tree. // Remember who I am."

Ludvigson's *Northern Lights* (1981) seems to be highly personal without being overly confessional. The volume is divided into three parts, a manner of division that Ludvigson has employed in all of her book-length works. In the first section, Ludvigson writes mostly of memories of childhood. Even at this stage of development, however, the strength of the female can be seen.

Ludvigson uses memory as a means of attempting to understand the present, as in "Little Women," where she writes of little girls playing dress-up, learning "to handle anything— / husbands who stepped in / just long enough / to sample the cookies, / gardens that washed away / in the first spring storm, / and babies crying." At other times the girls dream of growing up to be missionaries or astronauts. In the end, however, all, including the speaker, who has earlier proclaimed her refusal to marry and have children, once again put on their mothers' clothes and resume their dress rehearsal of their later lives. In *Style and Authenticity in Postmodern Poetry* (1986) Jonathan Holden writes that "Little Women" is "a good example of the fully achieved, narrative, free-verse conversation poem." Tone of voice, according to Holden, is what distinguishes such a work. Many of Ludvigson's poems fit this category.

"Search Party" is headed by a note: "It is believed that a dermoid, a tumor made up of skin tissue, sometimes having hair and teeth, may be the remnant of a woman's undeveloped twin." When the speaker of the poem undergoes surgery to remove one of these dermoid cysts, the surgical team is described as a team of explorers setting out to discover a long-buried personality within the body of the patient: "When they come out, victorious, / the foreman reports, / she was there, all right, / curled like any victim / into herself, barely recognizable / after all these years."

The second section of *Northern Lights* explores isolated moments in the lives of thirteen different women; it was originally published as the chapbook *The Wisconsin Women* (1980). The poems are based on Michael Lesy's *Wisconsin Death Trip* (1973), which contains a series of news clippings and photographs from the *Badger State Banner*, a turn-of-the-century, small-town newspaper. While critics have commented on *The Wisconsin Women* poems as good examples of Ludvigson's treatment of dramatic monologues, these poems also correspond to Holden's definition of conversation poems. The women of this section are grotesque characters, much like those found in the work of Flannery O'Connor. In the *Columbia* (South Carolina) *State* (29 November 1981) William Starr quoted Ludvigson: "The most human qualities are what I care about, even though it's the crazy people I'm drawn to. In my real life I seem to be something of a magnet for the crazies. I guess that's because I see even and especially in exaggerated forms the common denominator of such people."

Frequently introduced by excerpts from the *Badger State Banner*, the poems in *The Wisconsin Women* section are about just such people. Ludvigson, almost in the manner of Edgar Lee Masters in his "Spoon River" poems, gives ordinary women (and sometimes not-so-ordinary women) a chance to offer a defense of themselves. In "Victoria," for example, Ludvigson imagines the letter Victoria Hanna might have mailed to a neighbor—a letter that was allegedly "of the filthiest description." From the headnote, the reader knows that Victoria was jailed for the writing and mailing of this letter. In the poem, the reader finds that Lars Anderson, the husband of the recipient of the letter, habitually peeps through Victoria's windows as she undresses. Knowing of his presence, Victoria puts on a show for Lars night after night. The whole episode comes to its conclusion with the letter and Victoria's arrest, after Victoria has tired of Mrs. Anderson's smugness and has let her know of her husband's actions.

Part 3 of *Northern Lights* concerns modern women. In "A Romance" a woman in mid life attempts to come to terms with her body. The speaker opens the poem by saying, "My legs are dreaming / of a new life." She pushes the muscles of the legs to their limits of endurance with exercise and ballet. In the middle of the poem the speaker remarks: "These are legs / I cried for at thirteen, / sitting in the bathtub, / asking God please to make them / just *average*. How I hated them, / skinny as pine, disdaining their length, their whiteness." Years later she can enjoy her legs as they are: "Now, at mid-life, the body / learns to love itself."

In addition to legs, Ludvigson also examines the importance of other parts of a woman's body and, in one case, of a man's body: in "Some Uses of Art" the speaker devotes herself to a photographic study of "your shoulder, / the smallest lines on your wrist, / one muscular thigh." Once the exquisiteness of each part has been isolated, the body will come together again, "The leg will straighten / and shake itself loose, / the tongue moisten, the chest, that silvery field, / sigh as I take you in."

In the penultimate poem, Ludvigson presents what might be the strongest of any of her themes. Entitled "Things We Can't Prepare For," the poem catalogues just such things, including, in the last stanza, "A fear that your life is narrowing / to the town, the street you'll choose / next, a dark house where love / will be a small vacation, a month / at most when you'll neglect the yard."

In her next volume, *The Swimmer* (1984), Ludvigson again faces something difficult to prepare for—the death of close friends. Grief and the attempts to cope with it are the overwhelming themes. The book's dedication informs the reader that the grief is not hypothetical. Three friends are dead, and the book documents Ludvigson's reactions to the losses. Divided into three parts, "Grief," "Escape," and "Crossing," the book leads readers through the maze of sorrow.

Ludvigson uses water as a recurring symbol throughout the volume. In the *Columbia State* (28 October 1984) Idris McElveen wrote that the swimmer was a "heroic figure . . . who has found in the natural, physical acts of swimming and floating pleasurable means of sustaining oneself above the psychic depth of grief and that all-too-human failure to understand." In twenty short lines Ludvigson describes grief as the passage from winter to spring. Just as a late snowfall

dashes the hopes for spring and rebirth, grief can sneak in just when one thinks recovery is certain. Hope goes "white / and silent again."

"Trying to Come to Terms" is probably the pivotal poem in the "Grief" section, perhaps in the entire volume. Written in terza rima, the poem shows that Ludvigson is capable of handling a very rigid form without the form ruling the poem: "In the mountain retreat where birch / and maple absorb the night sounds / of animals, of human grief," the speaker tries to put the events of the outer world into a perspective she can understand. Mid poem, Ludvigson comes to the heart of the work—the three friends stricken and dying with cancer. While trying to distance herself, while trying to come to terms, the speaker finds that she is deeply affected: "I put on sterile gloves / and mask, tell myself this has nothing / to do with me. Then, shaken with fear, shove // the bouquets aside and admit it: Breathing / is precious as any dream of the future."

Escape is the controlling theme and metaphor of the second section of *The Swimmer*. From the woman in "My Advice" who seeks to flee from the image of herself that is held by others, to the title character in "Man Arrested in Hacking Death Tells Police He Mistook Mother-in-Law for Raccoon," to Cleopatra, the characters in this section all seek an escape from their lives and things that have gone wrong.

In "The Man Who Brought the Gypsy Moth," Leopold Trouvelot seeks a mental deliverance. He has secured a physical escape, having left Boston for France. His dreams, however, are still tormented by the havoc-wreaking moths he unintentionally loosed on America: "In my nightmares, / oak leaves turn in an instant to excrement."

In part 3, "Crossing," water becomes the most dominant symbol. Ludvigson has used snow early on as the symbol of grief; she uses water as the symbol for the escape from grief. In "The Crossing," the first poem in the section, Ludvigson writes of a journey on the "bridge of night." To make it across this bridge, one must trust completely the guiding voice at one's back. One must also be able to envision the journey's end—"a huge four-postered bed, layers of quilts," and the decreasing murmur of the voice of the guide.

The title of the poem "Swimming" also refers to the ebbing of grief. To the speaker, the water offers an invitation, inviting one to "drift beneath the surface / like reflected clouds / in a

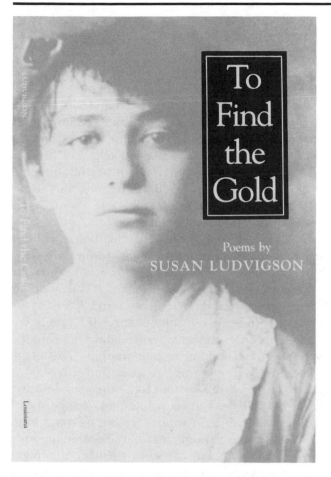

Dust jacket for Ludvigson's 1990 book, which includes "The Gold She Finds: On the Life of Camille Claudel, Sculptor," a long poem that Ludvigson considers her best

quick wind." One is not invited to drift forever, though. "The cool splash of voices / at the pool's edge" must be accepted in exchange for "the desire to stay down." Life beckons one from the darkness of grief.

In the last poem, the title poem of the book, the reader meets the swimmer: "Imagine yourself a strong swimmer." The strong swimmer can make it through to the end, or "there might be no end to it, just water / darkening into night, then slowly / restoring itself to blue." The reader recognizes the swimmer as the speaker of the poems, the one who has passed through the various stages of grief.

In 1986 Ludvigson's second chapbook, *Defining the Holy*, was published, and, compared to her other work, the poems seem a little out of character. Written at about the same time as the poems in *The Beautiful Noon of No Shadow*, these poems deal with Ludvigson's trip to Yugoslavia, documenting the journey and a love affair begun there. Ludvigson says the poems, including some

on artist Edvard Munch, did not fit with the works in *The Beautiful Noon of No Shadow*; consequently they were published separately. The Munch poems were reprinted in her 1990 volume, *To Find the Gold*. The poems chronicling the love affair especially mark this chapbook as disparate from most of Ludvigson's canon. While she does not shy away from personal topics, these poems possibly come closer to revealing her true self than any others.

Ludvigson received much praise for *The Beautiful Noon of No Shadow*. Fred Chappell, for example, called her a "beautifully accomplished poet" (*Raleigh News and Observer*, April 1987). Instead of a dominating theme or symbol for each of the three parts of the book, this book is dominated by the symbol of light. Written during a time when she was traveling throughout Europe, the poems depict the world she observes.

Ludvigson begins the book with "The Turning," which introduces the light that infuses the rest of the poems: "again and again / your eye lights on the names / that tell you / what you're heading toward, / as if flares had just been lit. . . ." Ludvigson pulls the reader into the main body of the work with "In the Absence of Angels." She juxtaposes light and dark, speaking of those who must identify morning "by the relative lightness of gray," and finally asking "how can we learn to be who we are / in the beautiful noon of no shadow?"

"Sunday in November" is the first of the poems to refer to Ludvigson's travels. Written in the voice of an eyewitness, the poem is about rather strange goings-on at Normandy beach. A Japanese film crew builds a sand replica of the Gaudi Cathedral in Barcelona, then proceeds to film its destruction by the tide. After the sea ultimately triumphs, the crew packs its gear, and the onlookers "return to their houses / behind the banks and the bunkers."

"Point of Disappearances" also has a geographical reference, but the theme is universal. Described in *Poetry* (January 1988) as "a triumph of empathy and technique," the poem describes a young man's suicide attempt in the Paris Metro. The speaker thinks of what it would be like to be eighteen or nineteen again, remembering a body that "could go days / without sleep." She also recalls how terribly wounding a harsh word or indifferent smile could be at that age. Remembering her own feelings of despair leads to a comment on the many teenagers pursuing suicide as a manner of problem solving. Finally the speaker comes to her own son, and one can sense her anxiety for him when she writes: "I see my son lift // his head to examine his awkward presence / in a hall of mirrors. He locates / on a shimmering surface his point of disappearance."

"From the Beginning" concludes *The Beautiful Noon of No Shadow*. While many of the earlier poems discuss the need for finding the self, this poem deals with the losing of the self for love. Ludvigson writes that love makes people ready to "fling // away what we've worked for hardest, / the creation of ourselves—those children we've taught to walk / alone on narrow bridges / solve problems of addition." Once the shock of losing the self has passed, lovers decide that this was the way it was meant to be from the beginning.

In March 1990 Ludvigson's *To Find the Gold* was published. It includes her longest poem, a dramatic monologue supposedly spoken by Camille Claudel, one-time mistress of Auguste Rodin and sculptor in her own right. Ludvigson considers "The Gold She Finds: On the Life of Camille Claudel, Sculptor," to be her strongest poem so far. It contains a series of pieces, many of them in the form of letters, about Claudel, from her childhood to the end of her life. The work as a whole describes the process of disintegration, both artistic and personal, suffered by Claudel in her subjugation to Rodin. The first two parts deal with Claudel's childhood as she discovers the powers of art. The third part, "The Meeting, 1884," describes her first meeting with Rodin. In "Note to Rodin after *Sea Foam*, 1884" Claudel's voice seems to have matured: "You discovered / something quiet in me, and made it grow, / . . . / I am no longer / that country girl with talent, / but a woman whose joy has found / its voice in marble."

Rodin promises Claudel he will leave his wife, Rose, and marry her instead. Claudel's art becomes secondary to her love of Rodin, for whom she keeps waiting. She is torn by her desire for Rodin and her desire to get on with her life and her art. In " 'La Demoiselle Elue,' 1890" she says: "why does that potbellied old man / keep my

soul? He's like a cancer that creates a gorgeous fever, / all the while gnawing away at the heart / of everything." Claudel continues to try for independence from Rodin, but finds it difficult. Her sanity suffers, and subsequently she is locked away in an asylum. Claudel's family keeps her imprisoned even when she appears to be improving from her breakdown. In "From the Asylum de Montdevergues, 1938" Claudel tells her brother how he has been deluded about her insanity and says, "You tell me / God has mercy on the afflicted, / God is good, etc. Let's talk about God, / who lets an innocent woman rot."

The second section of the book features poems on several subjects, some of which are autobiographical. "After Thirty Octobers" sends the speaker traveling back in time: "This weather brings back Sundays / after church," when she was fifteen years old. She pictures the family engaged in different activities—reading the funnies, cooking, and talking to one another. The poem ends with a merging of past and present as Ludvigson writes, "Through the window we watch / tall field grass ripple and change, bend deep / and white in wind. I go out to stand in it, / as under the darkening sky, it's become ocean."

In viewing her career as a whole, one might easily agree with Ludvigson's own assessment: *To Find the Gold*, and the Claudel poem in particular, is probably her strongest work. However, each of her volumes is good within its own scope and is a significant contribution to contemporary poetry.

Interview:

Gayle R. Swanson and William B. Thesing, *Conversations with South Carolina Poets* (Winston-Salem, N.C.: Blair, 1986), pp. 99-117.

Reference:

Jonathan Holden, *Style and Authenticity in Postmodern Poetry* (Columbia: University of Missouri Press, 1986), pp. 34-38.

Charles Martin
(25 June 1942 -   )

Richard Moore
New England Conservatory of Music

BOOKS: *Room for Error* (Athens: University of
Georgia Press, 1978);
Passages from Friday (Omaha: Abattoir, 1983);
Steal the Bacon (Baltimore: Johns Hopkins University Press, 1987);
Fulvio Testa (New York: Bernard Gallery, 1990).

OTHER: *The Poems of Catullus*, translated by Martin (Omaha: Abattoir, 1979; revised edition, Baltimore: Johns Hopkins University Press, 1990);
"Poetry's Place," *Parnassus: Poetry in Review* (Spring/Summer 1982): 254-263.

Charles Martin is known among his fellow
poets and seems soon to be recognized more
widely as a writer of wit, lyrical delicacy, and compelling form, who has developed an artistic language with which he can deal with fundamental
questions in American life. The distinguished record of his publications and the honors he has
won attest to his growing reputation.

He was born on 25 June 1942 in the Bronx
and has lived in New York all his life, as did his father, Charles Justus Martin, of Protestant German descent, and his mother, Kathleen McCormack Martin, an Irish Catholic. Martin was
educated in Catholic schools and has degrees in
English from Fordham University (A.B., 1964)
and the State University of New York at Buffalo
(M.A., 1965; Ph.D., 1967). Upon completion of
his graduate work, he returned to New York City
and taught at Notre Dame College of Staten
Island (1968-1970) and, starting in 1970, at
Queensborough College, where he is now an associate professor. He has also occasionally taught
courses in the Johns Hopkins Writing Seminars
in Baltimore. In 1965 he married Leslie Barnett;
they have a son, Gregory, and a daughter, Emily.

In the late 1960s and early 1970s Martin
began to meet with considerable success, placing
his poems in well-known literary magazines. *Poetry*, for example, under the editorship of the classically educated and formalist-minded Daryl

Hine, published thirteen of the poems collected
in *Room for Error* (1978).

A good place to get a sense of Martin's
method and style in his first book is the opening
stanza in "The Rest of the Robber Barons":

Opening up one's dog-eared Tennyson
Or battered Arnold, one is led to dream
Of barren beaches, of a flamboyant, blood-red sun
Smeared messily against an asphalt sky
Beneath which no one picnics: all is all in doubt,
One follows the tide with one's eyes. The tide is History,
Or Culture, and it's clearly going out.
One follows the tide. One essays a scream.

Caught up in the apparently arbitrary, almost surrealistic associations, one hardly notices
the elaborate rhyme scheme (abacdcdb), which is
precisely kept for the rest of the poem, and the
subtly varied meter. The effect—one might call it
"irony of treatment"—is complex. The elaborate
forms of Alfred, Lord Tennyson and Matthew Arnold are being used mockingly. Yet on another
level the lines imply that these particular Victorians at least did sense the modern world coming,
for the metaphor of the receding "tide" as "History, / Or Culture" is a clear echo of the metaphor of the tide as religious belief in Arnold's
"Dover Beach" (1849). The epithets "dog-eared"
and "battered" suggest a similar ambiguity: do
they mean that time has made the books unrecognizable and, symbolically, useless—or that it has
kept them well-used and current? Coupled with
this complexity, which suggests a more confused
and advanced stage of the doubt that agonized Arnold in "Dover Beach" and Tennyson in his *In Memoriam* (1850), there are words such as *messily* in
line 4 and *essays* in line 8 that project a cool reserve and chilly detachment in the face of catastrophe. The situation merits "a scream," but screaming, after all, requires effort. And the speaker, as
his last verb implies, is too learned, too politely academic, to do anything vulgar like screaming. He
cannot make the effort because he has used all

Charles Martin (photograph copyright 1987 by Hazel Hankin)

his energy in merely understanding. He is like "the best" in William Butler Yeats's pronouncement in "The Second Coming" who "lack all conviction, while the worst / Are full of passionate intensity."

But the tone of disdain, ultimately implying self-congratulation, discernible in Yeats's lines is absent in Martin's. There is no pride or confidence of understanding, rather a sense of mockery of one's own impotence under "an asphalt sky / Beneath which no one picnics"—where even horror is belittled, a gesture that deftly finesses the hysteria that tends to plague poems of this kind.

From the beginning Martin has been committed to ambitious projects that combine bookish parody with personal experience and social concern. One senses a search for the quirky, the odd point of view. Thus, "Four for Theodore Roethke," a poem in ironic celebration of the married life, becomes a precise parody of Roethke's well-known marriage poem "Four for Sir John Davies," and central to *Room for Error* are two other sequences intricately related to literary antecedents.

The first of these, "Institutional Life," is a series of twelve regular sonnets with quasi-surreal settings suggestive of a mental hospital and Franz Kafka's fictive bureaucracies. It is also an outrageous, funny parody of Homer's *Odyssey*. Given the opportunity of playing the hero and killing the suitors, Martin's Odysseus turns and runs, with "devouring / Legend . . . anxious for remains" in hot pursuit. "So many murders, armed robberies and rapes— / Your men *were* swine," Circe ("Kirke") tells him.

At times the sequence has a "pop" carnival atmosphere, which is also very characteristic of Martin—as in the description of a motion picture reversed for comic effect in sonnet 5: "Flapping like wings the dated pages fly / Swarming back onto their calendar." The original meaning of *satire* was "a dish of mixed ingredients," and once the reader's initial confusion settles, the elements of Martin's mixture work well together.

The other principal sequence is "Calvus in Ruins," purporting to be the literary remains of Gaius Calvus, a close friend of Catullus; actually it is almost entirely Martin's composition, for

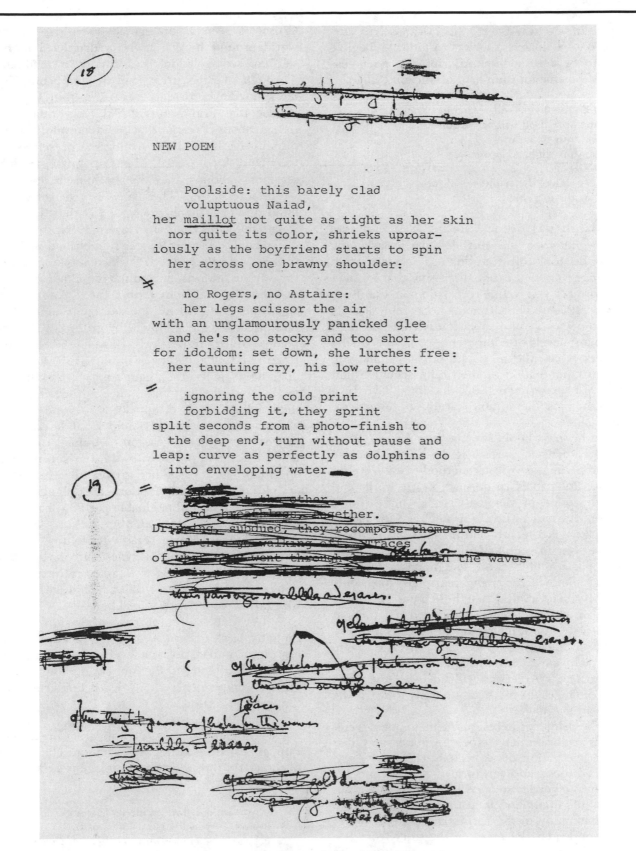

Draft for a poem (by permission of Charles Martin)

only a line or two by the historical Calvus survives. With scholarly asterisks to indicate illegible portions of a ruined manuscript, the poem expresses the splendid nihilism of ancient Rome:

> soon no one living will remember Caesar,
> but memory itself will be forgotten
> before your name is   *   *   *
>   your slightest gesture;
> *   *   *   *   *   *   *   *
> *   *   like the crumbs of flowers
> on a madman's chin   *   *   *

Martin was deeply affected by the classics courses he took in Buffalo—particularly the course he took on Catullus—as is clear from *Room for Error*, so it is not surprising that his next large project was a full translation of Catullus's poems (1979). The Roman poet had already been so copiously and so variously translated and at so many levels of competence, that one at first wonders what Martin could possibly add. But with his combination of metrical fascination and modernist experimentation, he may have produced the most memorable Catullus of his generation.

In his next book, *Passages from Friday* (1983), Martin returns to parody in his most elaborate and compelling use of that method to date. He retells the Robinson Crusoe story in the words and from the point of view of Crusoe's man Friday. First Martin had to invent a language for Friday to speak: seventeenth-century, archaic, broken English—but in regular iambic quatrains. Teaching English as a Second Language at Queensborough College for many years has apparently given Martin an abiding delight in the ways the language can be fractured and misused. He hints at this autobiographical element in *Passages from Friday* by prefacing the volume with the poem "E.S.L.," in which his foreign students are destined to learn American culture with the same sadly comic results as their attempts to learn the American language.

The primary interest in the main poem is cultural as well. Daniel Defoe's original story had been a celebration of western European energy, resourcefulness, and technical ingenuity, and for the knowing reader steeped in the new capitalism of the Enlightenment, it justifies the subjugation and exploitation of the "primitive" peoples represented by Friday. By retelling the story from Friday's point of view, Martin turns the values of the original story upside down, obliterates its certainties, and produces some excellent comedy.

Crusoe is seen as an egotist insensitive to the world around him, a bully, a drunkard in his self-imposed isolation, and finally, a madman. Through Martin's great skill in conducting Friday's narrative, readers see in it things about Crusoe that Friday has missed; yet Friday sees things about Crusoe that readers might have missed—his insensitivity to magical presences on the island, for instance. Then, of course, readers see things about Friday that he himself does not see or want to see. The many-layered ironies remind one of a much greater book than Defoe's: Jonathan Swift's *Gulliver's Travels* (1726).

Passages from Friday was republished in Martin's *Steal the Bacon* (1987), which was nominated for various awards, including the Pulitzer Prize and the National Book Critics Circle Award. *Passages from Friday* forms the center of the collection, preceded and followed by groups of shorter poems, titled respectively "From the Nesting Place" and "Landscape without History." The opening set, as its title suggests, emphasizes the domestic and the intimate: mice wondering why their fellows keep disappearing beyond a wall where a trap waits; a Neanderthal burial site, with its surprising revelation of human care and tenderness, juxtaposed with Martin's son making an "Eden" in a Frigidaire carton furnished with an old blanket, whose odors are "imaginary / Friends from an unimaginable past; / Warmed by his warmth. . . . " In another poem, "Speech Against Stone," Martin again shows how he can draw profound human themes out of the most commonplace situations, as he realizes the implications of painting over "a wall brilliant with childish graffiti" with "institutional beige."

The final section returns to the troubled perceptions, so clear in *Room for Error*, of human cruelty on the public, political level and of the threatened violent end of life on earth. The public cruelty complements the private tenderness of the opening section.

The last poem, "Making Faces," is a sequence of eight sonnets, describing a "Bread and Puppet" carnival-parade in Vermont. The fusion of the world with the carnival image is striking:

> The world has drawn beside us now and soon
> Will pass us by as the clouds pass us by
> Overhead. The clouds move at their own pace
> And so to us they hardly seem to move,
> Those ghostly, gray-white oxen of the sky
> Drawing the world through realms of empty space.

The end of the world is described with carnival images of death and of driving death away by making faces (which are like poems). Finally come the people who clean up the carnival: the Garbageman and last of all the Washerwoman, who carries a sign, ending the poem and the book, as James Joyce ended *Ulysses* (1922), with the single word "YES."

Martin has plans for future poetry projects. Judging by what he has already produced—its technique, ambition, and inspiration—important things are to be expected.

Heather Ross Miller
(15 September 1939 -   )

Marcella Thompson
University of Arkansas

BOOKS: *The Edge of the Woods* (New York: Atheneum, 1964);

Tenants of the House (New York: Harcourt, Brace & World, 1966);

The Wind Southerly (New York: Harcourt, Brace & World, 1967);

Gone A Hundred Miles (New York: Harcourt, Brace & World, 1968);

Horse, Horse, Tyger, Tyger (Charlotte, N.C.: Red Clay, 1973);

A Spiritual Divorce and Other Stories (Winston-Salem, N.C.: Blair, 1974);

Confessions of a Champeen Fire Baton Twirler (Raleigh: North Carolina Review Press, 1976);

Adam's First Wife (Davidson, N.C.: Briarpatch, 1983);

Hard Evidence (Columbia: University of Missouri Press, 1990);

La jupe espagnol, translated (into French) by Michel Gresset (Perpignan, France: Mare Nostrum, 1990).

SELECTED PERIODICAL PUBLICATION—
UNCOLLECTED: "Thoughts on Poesy," *Kentucky Poetry Review* (Summer 1990): 11.

Heather Ross Miller's poetic voice and subject matter are unusual: Greek myths and fairy tales grow darker and more magical in the isolation of the North Carolina piney woods. Characters from Christian mythology and classical literature are transported to the stark reality of an aluminum-smelting town. The world of nature, beautiful and innocent one minute, turns ruth-

Heather Ross Miller in 1990 (photograph by Chris Boese)

less and deadly the next. The clarity of Miller's poetry is enhanced by her mastery of language and sound. Poet James Whitehead says of her poetry, "Her lines are as rhythmically and phonically elegant as those of anyone writing today." She has the voice of a southern woman struggling with the people and things she loves—to have them, to keep them, and not destroy them—and ultimately dealing with her feelings about them. Of her poetry, Miller says, "What are we doing here? Poems don't have answers to such arrogant questions. What poems do have are ways to get through the day, sitting and listening, sometimes telling a story, staying alive. Whatever, angry or calm, full of joy or bitterness, it is the energy, the voice, and the living through that matters" (*Kentucky Poetry Review*, Summer 1990). Miller's poetry is perhaps not fashionable, but her distinctive style and voice have in recent years attracted an ever-increasing audience of readers and critics.

Heather Ross Miller was born on 15 September 1939 in Albemarle, North Carolina, as the only child of Fred E. and Geneva Smith Ross. Her father's family was frequently referred to as "The Writing Rosses": Fred Ross, himself a novelist and news editor, won the Houghton Mifflin Literary Fellowship in 1951; his brother James published novels and short stories; his sister Jean, a short-story writer, married poet Donald Justice; his sister Eleanor, a distinguished poet, married writer Peter Taylor. Immersed in contemporary fiction and poetry, classics, and storytelling from her earliest memories, Miller gave little thought to her family's place in the literary world: "They were just my family. I thought all families told stories and read the kind of stuff I read." She began writing at the age of six, with the publication of a neighborhood newspaper. "It was a back alley rag," Miller says, "a chronicle of whose cat had died, who had run off with whom, all the important gossip of the neighborhood." She wrote poetry in high school, then short stories and poetry in college.

Miller graduated magna cum laude as a Phi Beta Kappa from the Woman's College of the University of North Carolina at Greensboro (B.A., 1961). Randall Jarrell, a friend of the family for many years, became her teacher and mentor at Greensboro, and he had a profound effect on her poetry in the years to come. In her second year at Greensboro, she met Clyde Miller, who worked for the North Carolina Division of State Parks. They were married on Valentine's Day 1960. In September 1961, while a full-time student, Miller gave birth to her first child, Melissa. Jarrell helped with Miller's mastery of poetic style and technique, and the wilderness of North Carolina served as the stage for much of her best writing.

Upon graduation, Miller was awarded a Woodrow Wilson Fellowship to attend the University of North Carolina at Chapel Hill. After one semester, her husband was named park superintendent at the remote Singletary Lake State Park, and she left the university to live in a four-thousand-acre wilderness. In 1963 her second child, Kirk, was born. For the next thirteen years Miller wrote, and her husband's struggle to bring order to the wilderness, to maintain the delicate balance between civilization and the wild, became the underlying metaphor for her fiction and poetry.

While living in the park, she published three novels and one book of poetry and completed her M.F.A. at the University of North Carolina at Greensboro. Among her awards are three fellowships from the National Endowment for the Arts, the North Carolina Award for Literature, and the Blaine R. Hall Award in Poetry. Her academic career has included faculty positions at Pfeiffer College in North Carolina and the University of Arkansas, where she has taught creative writing since 1983.

While Miller's poetry is autobiographical in terms of place, the intensity and distinctive voice come from a powerful ability to connect consciousness and emotions to other people and to objects in the natural world. This combination of the autobiographical and the subjective gives rise to metaphors and images that are sometimes dazzling, sometimes brutal, but always uncompromising in their originality and honesty.

The Wind Southerly (1967) was a critical success and firmly established her mastery of technique. More important, it established the thematic arena that has remained consistent throughout her work—marriage, family, nature, and the dreams of childhood carried to adulthood. The narrative poems are dramatic and scenic, informed by classical mythology, fairy tales, and literature.

While the metaphor and imagery of these early poems hint at the dark nature and possible ambiguity of life, her later poetry peels away the facade and posits an acceptance of that darkness and ambiguity as a fact of spiritual existence. While the perceived consequences of isolation are a common thread in the early poems, the reality of isolation becomes the common thread in her later poems.

In "Night Horses" (from *The Wind Southerly*) a young wife sits in front of the fire with her husband and muses on her wedding, her children safely in bed, her husband as a child, the comfort and safety of her fire, and her life:

> *How many years you've existed without me.*
> In just five seasons of my time,
> A wedding, two children, a fireside in the night.

While the poem is obviously set in the isolation of the state park, that isolation is romantic, idyllic, a fairy tale come true.

In *Hard Evidence* (1990), the romance of isolation becomes a dark reality, and the wife in "Pregnant" is alone in the park, her husband "gone off" to tag bears or fish. The fairy tale is not of happily-ever-after, but of "a poor old fairy tale girl / locked up to spin pure straw to gold":

> You knew I was pregnant
> You knew I could dream dumb straw
> to gold and cut my fingers, bleed.

She pleads with her husband to come back soon and:

> Find this dark dream genuine,
> the best my blood could spin,
> real children.

In "The Fairest One of All" Miller takes the metaphor a step further and imagines an isolation taken to its darkest conclusion: "You hit me, I hit the baby, the baby hit the dog." The young woman is once again alone—with shabby furniture and a dog—but in this poem she can no longer conjure up a fairy-tale ending. She can only regress to a childhood lost ("I want Baby to go to sleep so I can play Girl"), as if by going back she might make it come out right the next time.

Clyde Miller died in March 1991. In "Camera Obscura, The Last Morning," from the forthcoming collection "Friends and Assassins" (University of Missouri Press), the wife is older now, alone again, but the isolation is of a different kind:

> *I'll die*
> *in this bed,* you said
> and I believe you meant this way:
> a hard driving breath
> slips off, contracts your dark pupil
> to an accurate bull's-eye
> privately, secretly,

> the blue aperture widens
> *one more!*
> and you're gone.

Miller's poetry reflects her strong emotional ties to the natural world, and as her poetry matured, she came to an acceptance of the duplicity of nature. There is no sentimental merging of humankind with nature. The relationship is more like an armed truce, with skirmishes that can go either way. In "Snow Prison" (in *The Wind Southerly*) winter is a lyrical magical time with "places of wide snow wind / Earth and sky curl in an infinite blue ball." There is no dark edge to this winter, only the beauty of a snow-clad wilderness. In "The Park" (from *Hard Evidence*), the wilderness takes on another aspect: "It is not for everyone. / Snakes, alligators, and bears. . . . " A man is lost when he hikes off a winter trail and falls down the Cape Fear bluffs. He follows a creek in a futile search for help. After three days park officials in a state helicopter find him on a back fire trail and hover over him, "scaring him so he howled like a dumb old dog, / wallowing the snow, throwing it, / showing us his teeth." The helicopter sets down, the man is put on a stretcher.

> He had a broken arm, two broken ribs,
> and only when we calmed him,
> warmed him to his pain again,
> did he know us.

Humankind has almost lost this skirmish, yet it is clear from the elegant, distant voice of the poem that such struggles are to be expected rather than feared.

The poem "Delight" (in "Friends and Assassins") is about a man who tries to transplant (female) meat-eating plants from the Carolina bogs to his garden. He fails each time and becomes obsessed with his need to make them live:

> What did it take, you raged,
> to make these things live with you,
> lie down and love you
> tenderly, tenderly
> tongue to tongue
> so sweet and so murderous?

It is a daring poem that speaks of the futility of attempts to reorder nature and of the seemingly inherent danger of the female of the species.

In the same collection "Inventory" describes roses from the hot house, "Their scent cool and sweet as dirt / cold even, almost shocking. . . . "

Later the roses open and the petals shatter. The rose at its peak is beautiful—and dying: *"This is how to die. Spread wide open, / celebrate!"* Just as winter in Miller's nature is sometimes sad, sometimes beautiful, death holds a beauty of its own.

Much of the energy and emotion of Miller's poetry comes when her small-town characters are transported to a world of myth and fairy tale, or when mythical characters are set down in the wilderness or in a modern-day family. The mythology often becomes entwined with dreams—dreams of the future, dreams of a different future. A young girl in "Marsh King's Daughter" (in *The Wind Southerly*) dreams of being a king's daughter and going to find her lover. Her dreams are filled with childish fantasies of her lover and a long, magical journey to find him.

"Seventh Grades" (in "Friends and Assassins") re-creates such dreams, but the dream of love is tempered by age, by a life lived. Young girls are sitting in the grass chaining clover: "We said we'd have it all, / bridesmaids, babies, / hot abundant nectars. . . . " The speaker understands that dreams come from childhood's flowering period, understands the innocence and perhaps the frivolity of such innocence, and calls her generation "unlucky three-leafed":

> each one an unwed
> troublesome weed
> of a girl
> growing April through October,
> chaining clover, easy as cattle
> in good pasture.

What Miller promises in her early poems is delivered in her later work. The young girl has lived through life and survived—with an acceptance of life, without the repudiation so common in women's poetry.

The mark of a good writer is to make one see the world in a new way. The mark of a great writer is to make one see the world in a way never before even imagined. Miller consistently brings readers the first and frequently brings the latter. Best known in her early years as a fiction writer, Miller's recent books have reestablished her reputation and importance among American poets.

Robert Morgan

(3 October 1944 -)

Roger D. Jones
Southwest Texas State University

BOOKS: *Zirconia Poems* (Northwood Narrows, N.H.: Lillabulero, 1969);

Red Owl (New York: Norton, 1972);

Land Diving (Baton Rouge: Louisiana State University Press, 1976);

Trunk & Thicket (Fort Collins, Colo.: L'Epervier, 1978);

Groundwork (Frankfort, Ky.: Gnomon, 1979);

Bronze Age (N.p.: Iron Mountain, 1981);

At the Edge of the Orchard Country (Middletown, Conn.: Wesleyan University Press, 1987);

The Blue Valleys (Atlanta: Peachtree, 1989);

Sigodlin (Middletown, Conn.: Wesleyan University Press, 1990);

Watershed (Atlanta: Peachtree, 1990);

Green River: New and Selected Poems (Middletown, Conn.: Wesleyan University Press, 1991).

SELECTED PERIODICAL PUBLICATIONS—
UNCOLLECTED: "Biographical Note," *Small Farm*, 3 (March 1976): 40-43;

"Notes on the Verse Line," *Epoch*, 29 (Winter 1980): 207-209.

Born and raised in the rural Appalachian region of western North Carolina, Robert Morgan is not only one of the most talented and distinct spokesmen for that particular area, its people, and its culture but also one of the most prolific, technically accomplished, and consistently interesting poets in contemporary American writing. He is a regionalist in the widest sense of the term, drawing, as many writers have done, on the specific culture and energies of his region as an alternative response both to the breakdown of traditional social, religious, and moral systems in Western culture and to the various solutions to that breakdown that poets and writers have proposed.

Morgan was born on 3 October 1944 in Hendersonville, North Carolina, to Clyde R. (a farmer) and Fannie Levi Morgan. He earned his B.A. in English from the University of North Carolina at Chapel Hill in 1965 and his M.F.A in

1968 from the University of North Carolina at Greensboro, where he studied with poet and fiction writer Fred Chappell. After teaching during the 1968-1969 school year at Salem College, Morgan worked as a self-employed writer, farmer, and housepainter for two years. He then took a position as a lecturer at Cornell University, became an assistant professor in 1973, and has taught at Cornell since then. Morgan has received several awards and recognitions, including a Guggenheim Fellowship, four National Endowment for the Arts Fellowships, a New York Foundation for the Arts Fellowship, the Eunice Tietjens Prize from *Poetry* magazine (1979), and the First Fiction Award from the American Academy of Arts and Letters for his short-story collection, *The Blue Valleys* (1989). On 6 August 1965 he married Nancy Bullock, and they have two sons and a daughter.

Morgan has said that his poems usually begin with a specific object, which he tries to look at as closely and clearly as possible. Critic Louis Bourne has written that "metaphor for Morgan is finally the key to meaning in his poems. Many that on first sight seem to be but brilliant imagist exercises in which he selects a particular material for imaginative recreation only attain their full significance when the gap between two ideas or objects is appreciated." One of the earliest assessments of Morgan's work came from writer and fellow North Carolinian Fred Chappell, who described the "background" of Morgan's work as consisting of "the enormous and imperious operations of nature, of a society of poor, narrow and proudly embittered people, and of fundamentalist religion. This landscape is, in short, contemporary southern Appalachia, which Morgan sometimes widens out as a simile for earlier American history." Morgan's descriptions of his native region, and his upbringing there, frequently depict the primitiveness of the area. For example, he has mentioned that electricity did not arrive in the area until the late 1940s, and that, before Morgan reached eight, his "father had neither car

Robert Morgan (photograph by Susan Snead)

nor pickup and we hauled corn out of the field with the horse and wagon, and used them to gather creek rock for our new house" (*Small Farm*, March 1976).

Morgan grew up near Zirconia, North Carolina, an area with mines of zircon and other minerals. "All over our property," Morgan explained, "there are pits and depressions where my ancestors dug for zircons or explored for lead, or mica, or gold. The tiny stream below our barn called Kimble Branch yields a trace of gold and during the Civil War it was panned repeatedly." The imagery of mining—of exploring the native soil for everything of value therein—recurs in Morgan's work and is widened to become a metaphor of the quest for identity and meaning from the physical and psychic grounds of one's own formation. Trained initially in science and mathematics, Morgan brings to this search a scientist's objectivity. Rather than sentimentalizing the native soil, the ancestors who lived there, and his own memory, Morgan sifts through them with curious, though fond, detachment, as if searching for the spiritual ore within the culture itself.

One important feature of that culture that also appears repeatedly in Morgan's work is fundamentalist religion. Morgan's mother and father were Southern Baptist and Pentecostal Holiness

adherents, respectively, and Morgan has described how his father "often took part in the services of various splinter groups, in private homes, shouting and speaking in tongues." In his interview in *The Post-Confessionals* (1989) Morgan likened the process of glossolalia to the act of poetic composition: since "so much of the power of poetry comes from that particular fusion of unconscious, memory, dream with consciousness . . . it takes both the control of consciousness and the rush from the unconscious to write good poetry." Despite its drawbacks, he also recognizes that fundamentalism provides the people of the area a vital source of psychic life and gives the culture much of its distinction in a time when most local or geographically defined cultures are vanishing.

The blend of Appalachian culture and the unconscious is perhaps the most distinct characteristic of Morgan's early work. The poems in his first two books, *Zirconia Poems* (1969) and *Red Owl* (1972), are also marked by his use of the "deep image" techniques of such poets as Robert Bly and James Wright. "From a Cliff," in *Zirconia Poems*, exemplifies these early pieces:

Looking down through electric chairs of space.
Distance, a hot dry mouth, opens,
draws me to its roots

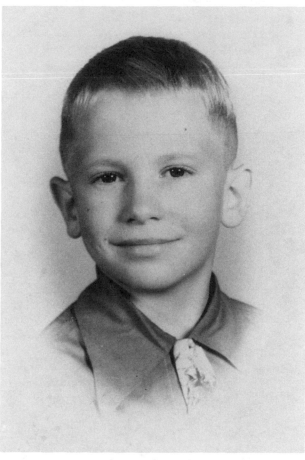

of frost. Winds the clock inside that yells, Jump,
crush the arms of gravity.

Such pieces as "High Country," "Close," and
"Awakening," also in *Zirconia Poems*, repeat these
techniques, while others, such as "Water Tanks,"
"Night Rain," and "Truck Driver," exhibit the clarity and objectivity that would become staple features of Morgan's more mature work. One gets
the sense, reading through the *Zirconia Poems*, of
a young writer in the laboratory of craft, picking
up each technique, testing it for its effect and its
potential uses. But as Morgan's later work would
prove, the self-consciousness necessary to write
"deep image" poetry is ill-suited to a mind like
his, which works best when receiving external images and placing them, through metaphor, into a
context that requires much less ego-interference.

Zirconia Poems received a moderate amount
of critical response for a first book. Critic William Harmon, for example, criticized the Bly-like
poems, insisting that "while they show his customary virtues of clarity and originality of vision,
they lapse into perfunctory verse expressing
perfunctory feelings." Sherer James, on the other
hand, applauded the collection, asserting that
"the poems here place him [Morgan] in the vanguard of the fruitful revolution going on in American poetry today. . . . Morgan is good" (*Virginia
Quarterly Review*, 1970).

In *Red Owl*, which critic Guy Owen (*Southern
Poetry Review*, Spring 1973) called "one of the
freshest collections of poems I have read in
years," Morgan continued perfecting the techniques established in *Zirconia Poems*. Like the
poems in that volume, the pieces in *Red Owl* are
short—few exceeding twenty lines—and are built
from the juxtaposition of disparate, distinct, and
often semisurreal images. However, there is a concentrated attention on the natural world, and the
profound nonhuman features of its various operations. In "Exhaustion," for example (Morgan
often employs one-word titles), he suggests the
minor place human death actually occupies in
the larger operations of nature:

> The earth is our only bed, the deep
> couch from which we cannot fall. Suddenly
> this need to lie down.
> The flesh will flow out in currents of decay,
> a ditch where the weeds find dark treasure.

The poems in *Red Owl* also contain a notable absence of the first-person voice. The emphasis is
on observation, keen study of the object at hand,

Morgan in 1952

and the subsequent flow of images that the object
triggers.

Morgan's 1976 collection, *Land Diving*, represents an important breakthrough in his career. A
rich collection full of poems about relatives, southern legends, and the local landscape, the volume
marks Morgan's turn toward a much more literal, studious, and fully developed poem and
away from the crystalline poems of his early
work. There is more of a dramatic, human
subtext beneath the poems. The balance of inner
and outer worlds goes on, but in the more focused form of the specific metaphor. In "Pumpkin," for example, after a short description of the
field in fall, Morgan compares the ripe pumpkins to "huge beacons" that "shine through /
like planets submerged and rising." In "Squirrel,
Shadow" Morgan compares the squirrel with an
old man who "walks through fields / overturning
rocks and boards / looking for an entrance. . . . /
The sun focuses directly at his face / harvesting / itself and trailing off, / throws heavy gangplanks
across the hill." As critic Peter Stitt notes, the
book is divided into three sections—the first con-

Si—godlin

When old carpenters would talk of buildings
out of plumb or out of square, they always
said they were anti-sigodlin, as though
si-godlin meant upright and square, at proper
angles as all structures should be, true to
spirit level and plumbline, erect away from
the very center of the earth, solid
and joined firm, orthogonal and right,
no sloping or queasy joints, no slouching
rafters or sills. A man made as he was unoly,
the heavy joists and studs perfectly yoked
and showing the dimensions themselves, each
mated pair of timber to embody
and enact the center of space in its
real extensions, the verticals to be
the virtual pith of gravity, horizontal
aligned with the surface of the earth at
its local tangent. And when they sifted
and nailed or pegged in place, downright
and upstanding, strung up and down and level flat
as water, established the coordinates
thereon of their place in creation's
history, in a word learned perhaps from
masons who heard it in masonic rites
loaned from ancient rosicrucians who had
derived the term from Greek mysteries'
love of fertile geometries to denote
assurtrot only of joining done right.
the power whose center is everywhere.

6/22/86

Page from a draft for the title poem in Sigodlin *(by permission of Robert Morgan)*

taining "a detailed, personal, anecdotal portrayal of the region," the second containing "poems which lovingly and accurately describe scenes, objects and events from nature and from country life," and the third containing poems "concerned with specific things" but "unified neither by time nor by place" (*Ohio Review*, Summer 1978).

In poems such as "Face," "Going Barefoot," "Horseshoe," "Rose Tree," and others, Morgan creates sharp, affectionate pictures of his region and its culture, and most critics applauded the book. Marvin Bell praised Morgan for his range of diction and for his "fierce stance and . . . relentless method" (*Poetry*, October 1978). Stitt, on the other hand, praised numerous pieces but ultimately found the work disorganized, and he criticized Morgan for belonging to the "Southern Profuse Moveable Fact'ry of Country Po'try." Nonetheless, with *Land Diving* Morgan fully arrived at the specific methods and subjects that have carried through his work to date.

He sharpened this style of poetry in his next two collections, *Trunk & Thicket* (1978) and *Groundwork* (1979). In the former, Morgan explores fully the intricacies of the natural world and its harmony with the Appalachian people. The book comprises three sections: the title section; a prose essay titled "Homecoming"; and a long poem, "Mockingbird." The long, segmented title poem, "Trunk and Thicket," is part family history and part exploration of an art and sense of identity created by one's relationship with a region and its history (an exploration Morgan advances in the middle essay). Drawing together language, nature, and poetry, Morgan calls for "a powerful enjambment / like a stream carried on and over / its rocks, sometimes pausing / in deep pools and then darting / in a channel . . . but always / careering, always arriving / and leaving at once, always on / its way."

He puts these ideas into practice in "Mockingbird," which Harmon called "one of the most remarkable poems in American literature." In construction and execution "Mockingbird" resembles the longer poems of Morgan's Cornell colleague A. R. Ammons, as well as the stream-of-consciousness writing in Theodore Roethke's "Lost Son" poems. The poem asks the question "What does the world say?" "Morgan has arranged a spillway of words," Harmon explains, "that . . . sound like a mockingbird." Moving through bursts of expressive description, and a wide range of diction and geography, "Mockingbird" represents one of postwar American

poetry's most ambitious attempts to create a direct bridge between human and nonhuman language. Unfortunately, despite outstanding passages, the poems in *Trunk & Thicket* lapse too often into prose and journal-like entries broken into lines. Taken as a whole, it constitutes what is perhaps Morgan's weakest collection.

Morgan grouped the poems in *Groundwork* thematically and according to subject matter into a tightly unified whole. The result is a book that ranks as Morgan's finest to date and one of the best collections of contemporary southern literature. With such titles as "Slop Bucket," "Huckleberries," "Reuben's Cabin," "Appalachian Trail," "The Flying Snake," and "Smokehouse Dirt," he weaves together past and present, mythic and real time, and human and natural into a resonant, fully realized body of work.

The book marks Morgan's technical maturation: though most of the poems are in free verse, Morgan experiments with stanzaic and metrical forms, and he combines a distinct poetic voice with so clear a sense of line—the "powerful enjambment"—that critic Alice Fulton would later write, "no poet today has a better ear" (*Poetry*, January 1988). "My first principle of versification was, make something happen in every line," Morgan says in "Notes on the Verse Line" (*Epoch*, Winter 1980). "Line-length is a way of speeding or slowing the poem's current . . . one of our most effective ways of measuring out the delivery of idea, image, perceptual energy." In "Death Crown," for example (which, like "Bricking the Church" and "Baptism of Fire," renews Morgan's interest in primitive Christian lore as a subject), he describes how, when "one especially worthy lay dying," the feathers in the victim's pillow would

knit themselves into a crown
that those attending felt in perfect
fit around the honored head.
The feathered band they took to be
certain sign of another crown,
the saints and elders of the church,
the Deep Water Baptists said.

Morgan combines, in these lines, an expert sense of line breaks with an ear that takes the basic trochaic-tetrameter measure and varies it with iambic lines ("The feathered band they took to be") and other variations that create a rich, musical texture beneath Morgan's plainspoken colloquial diction.

The poems in *Groundwork* meander affectionately through the history and lore of Morgan's region. In "Mountain Bride" he recaptures the Eden myth with an often-told legend of a groom being bitten by snakes on his wedding night. In "Plankroad" Morgan traces the history of settlers in the region through the image of the wooden road on which they traveled. In "Bricking the Church" the local citizens' decision to brick the church, in "a crust the same dull red // as clay in nearby gullies," illustrates how, "as its doctrines soften," the church "puts on a hard shell / for weathering this world." Morgan includes poems about his relatives, thus exploring not only the larger mythic texture of the area but his own roots there as well, implicitly illustrating the thesis advanced by such writers as Wendell Berry and Gary Snyder that identity and spirituality begin when one locates one's roots in a specific place with its natural energies.

In his recent work Morgan has continued both the subjects and the quality of his work in the 1970s. In his 1987 collection, *At the Edge of the Orchard Country* (which includes some poems first collected in a limited-edition, 1981 volume titled *Bronze Age*), Morgan focuses more on relatives and people than on the natural world. As critic P. H. Liotta points out, the book's three sections move from a historical perspective ("Horace Kephart," "Passenger Pigeons," "Looking Homeward," and "Halley's Comet") to minute observations, often from childhood ("Radio," "The Gift of Tongues," and "Uncle Robert"), to observations of family. Though Morgan does include close observations of nature as well ("Dead Dog on the Highway," "Manure Pile," and "Brownian Motion"), he puts equal emphasis on the qualities of people that enable them to survive and endure hardship. "Lost Colony," for example, describes the fate of the famed old North Carolina settlement. Morgan includes poems about specific relatives: his uncle in "Uncle Robert"; a "stocky hoojer" cousin in "Man and Machine," who, on a tractor, became "a man inspired"; his father in "Sunday Toilet," who "raked / a waterbucket full of lime" and "flung comets and smoking hands / on the walls of the hogpen."

A series of short, imagistic pieces, such as "Radio," "Ancient," "Brownian Motion," and others, illustrate Morgan's command of the lyric form. In "Lightning Bug," which makes use of the traditional lyric device of the apostrophe, he writes:

> You are winnowed
> through the hanging gardens of night.
> Your noctilucent syllables
> sing in the millenium of
> the southern night with star-talking
> dew. . . .

As critics often point out, the particular value of the lyric mode is its ability to stop time, expand the single moment, and contemplate the specific. The specific, luminous objects Morgan studies form a counterpoint to the lives of the local populace, which he defines largely in terms of hard work and endurance. As Fulton argues, in Morgan's world "holiness pervades the tiniest as well as the dirtiest mote." Critics generally lauded *At the Edge of the Orchard Country*, and its quality prompted Liotta to ask, "why is Robert Morgan the most unknown poet in America?"

Throughout his career, Morgan has crafted his work toward an increasingly musical, lyrical precision. His most recent poems indicate that he will continue this lyrical vibrancy. The poems of *Sigodlin* (1990) and *Green River: New and Selected Poems* (1991) continue the themes and subjects that have marked his career and illustrate the continuing sharp clarity of ear that has brought Morgan success and esteem among contemporaries. In such poems as "Hayfield," "Writing Spider," and "Moving the Bees," he presents clear, crisp portraits of Appalachian culture, though such poems as "Vietnam War Memorial," "Time's Feast," and "Middle Sea" are more universal meditations. In all of these it is Morgan's "focused recognition" (as he has termed it) that predominates.

Morgan has rendered a prodigious, consistent body of outstanding work in a short while. His poetry provides proof that spiritual and metaphysical moorings are to be found first, and most powerfully, in the ground itself. Modernist and postmodernist writers from Thomas Hardy to Wendell Berry have traced the spiritual incoherence that occurs with dispossession, fragmentation, and the erroneous faith in technological control of nature. "The theory of agrarianism is that the culture of the soil is the best and most sensitive of vocations," John Crowe Ransom wrote in *I'll Take My Stand* (1930). Morgan's poetry, according to Sherer James, is an attempt to continue restoring such a "culture of the soil" and is ample illustration of his belief in "the ultimate metaphor, that everything is, in some fantastic way, the same thing."

Interviews:

Suzanne Booker, "A Conversation with Robert Morgan," *Carolina Quarterly*, 37 (Spring 1985): 13-22;

Stan Sanvel Rubin and William Heyen, "The Rush of Language: A Conversation with Robert Morgan," in *The Post-Confessionals*, edited by Rubin, Earl G. Ingersoll, and Judith Kitchen (Rutherford, N.J.: Fairleigh Dickinson University Press / London & Toronto: Associated University Presses, 1989), pp. 196-209.

Bibliography:

Stuart Wright, "Robert Morgan: A Bibliographical Chronicle, 1963-1981," *Bulletin of Bibliography*, 39 (September 1982): 121-131.

References:

Louis Bourne, "On Metaphor and Its Use in the Poetry of Robert Morgan," *Small Farm*, 3 (March 1976): 63-77;

Fred Chappell, "A Prospect Newly Necessary," *Small Farm*, 3 (March 1976): 49-53;

William Harmon, "Robert Morgan's Pelagian Georgics: Twelve Essays," *Parnassus*, 9 (Fall/Winter 1981): 5-30;

P. H. Liotta, "Pieces of the Morgenland: The Recent Achievements in Robert Morgan's Poetry," *Southern Literary Journal*, 22 (Fall 1989): 32-40;

J. B. Merod, "Robert Morgan's 'Wisdom-Lighted Islands,'" *Small Farm*, 3 (March 1976): 54-62;

Robert Schultz, "Recovering Pieces of the Morgenland," *Virginia Quarterly Review*, 64 (Winter 1988): 176-188.

Thylias Moss

(27 February 1954 -   )

Gerri Bates
Howard University

BOOKS: *Hosiery Seams on a Bowlegged Woman* (Cleveland: Cleveland State University Poetry Center, 1983);
Pyramid of Bone (Charlottesville: University Press of Virginia, 1989);
At Redbones (Cleveland: Cleveland State University Poetry Center, 1990);
Rainbow Remnants in Rock Bottom Ghetto Sky (New York: Persea, 1991).

Since the publication of Thylias Moss's first book of poetry in 1983, her reputation has soared. As a poet who emerged a generation after the poets of the turbulent 1960s, Moss produces poetry that is nevertheless indicative of this political period in that her work is sometimes caustic, social, and moral, but she also breaks away from the antiestablishment protests and develops a fresh richness in her poetry with sensitivity, delicacy, and humanism. What emerges as a result of her ability to be an observer are poetic expressions that are vivid, accurate, and distinctive. She also achieves through her poetry a tonal quality that progresses from anger to joy, a quality that finally accomplishes in her fourth book of poetry what she terms "control." She weaves themes of freedom and mother-daughter relationships into her work. Although Moss's poetry is not strictly autobiographical, it does reveal a panorama of what she has seen and heard. She is a copious recorder of others' realities as well as her own. The result is introspective narrative poetry and the articulation of deep-seated emotion and thoughts.

Born into a stable, working-class environment in Cleveland, Ohio, on 27 February 1954, Thylias Rebecca Brasier Moss was an only child. Her mother, Florida Missouri Gaiter Brasier, was the daughter of a farm family from Valhermosa Springs, Alabama. Mrs. Brasier spent her life as a maid and, in the words of her daughter, "made it to the dean's list of preferred housekeepers; she is a maid of honor." Moss's father, Calvin Theodore Brasier of Cowan, Tennessee, was a recapper for the Cardinal Tire Company. Moss remembers her childhood as an idyllic, happy one with doting parents who catered to the needs of their precocious daughter.

Moss wrote her first short story at the age of six and her first poem ("Little Boys and Little Girls") at age seven on the back of a bulletin of the New Bethlehem Baptist Church. By the time she entered Alexander Hamilton Junior High School, she wanted to write novels.

After graduating with honors from John Adams High School, she entered Syracuse University, where she became distraught over racial tension but nevertheless remained at the school two years (1971-1973). At age sixteen she had met John Lewis Moss in church, and three years later she married him in her mother's dining room (6 July 1973). They are the parents of two sons, Dennis and Ansted. Moss cheerfully includes the names of her mother, husband, children, and relatives in her poetry and expresses unbridled joy in her fourth book. She is no longer plagued by the sometimes bitter temperament of her earlier life.

When Moss returned to college, she entered Oberlin College, where she received a B.A. in creative writing (1981). She later received her M.A. in English (1983) from the University of New Hampshire. At New Hampshire her professors encouraged her creativity but were troubled over what they sensed was a tone of anger in her poetry. She began, however, to sharpen her intellectual and creative ability and to surface from the introverted lethargy of her past.

Moss, who was always at the top of her class, has received four grants from Kenan Charitable Trust (1984-1987); an artist's fellowship from the Artists' Foundation of Massachusetts (1987); and a grant from the National Endowment for the Arts (1989). She was a winner of the Pushcart Prize (1990); the Witter Bynner Prize (1991); the Dewars Profiles Performance Artist Award (1991); and the Whiting Writer Award (1991); and she was showcased on the cable network BRAVO! (1992). She currently holds a fac-

Cover for Moss's 1990 collection, in which many of the poems are set in a mythical meeting place called Redbones

ulty position at Phillips Andover Academy in Massachusetts.

By the time Moss completed her degree at the University of New Hampshire, she was well on her way to becoming a published poet. *Hosiery Seams on a Bowlegged Woman* (1983) is the result of a request from the Cleveland State University Poetry Center. Her poetic talent had caught the attention of Alberta Turner and Leonard Trawick when she won the Academy of American Poets College Prize, sponsored by the public-library system of Cleveland. The poem "Coming of Age in Sanduski" won her the award. She was in her second year of graduate study and had never had the inclination to write a book of poetry. The poems she selected for the collection were ones she had on hand. Many of the poems included in this book were thought by her college professors to be expressions of hostility. In spite of that fact, Moss was first runner-up for the Best of the Great Lakes Prize for a first book. The poems in *Hosiery Seams* reflect introspective vision and individual experience.

Her second book, *Pyramid of Bone* (1989),

was solicited by Charles Rowell at the University Press of Virginia. Putting the book together was a deliberate effort, but Moss did not feel as much "in control" as she would like to have been. After an agreement was made about the poems to be included, Moss and the publishers reached an impasse on the title. Approximately one year elapsed before a title was selected by the publishers from a list of five titles that Moss submitted. Her stance in this book is one of interrogation about God, womanhood, and heritage. She writes in "Development of an Adult Nightmare": "As A Christian / I'm supposed to want to be this humble." Moss's tone in this book is not hostile but practical, not emotional but matter-of-fact. For *Pyramid of Bone* Moss was first runner-up for the 1989 National Book Critics Circle Award.

She calls her third book, *At Redbones* (1990), "more concept oriented, one that has an organizing principle." Redbones symbolizes a gathering place, part club, part church, but a mythical place. Moss says that the poem "Lunch Counter Freedom" and others reflect memories of the 1960s in which the struggle for personal freedom was thematic of the times.

Finally Moss feels that she has gained full "control" in the publication of *Rainbow Remnants in Rock Bottom Ghetto Sky* (1991), which has a theme of joy and reasons for jubilation. That jubilation is sparked by her reclaiming the personal happiness that she had long denied. She writes about identity, bonding, womanhood, and pregnancy—themes that are held together by the forces of joy. Hope is also a central focus in the book, a reason to survive and to find something to cheer about in a world that is not perfect. Moss says "denied joy or repressed joy is not really joy." Her main reason for celebration is her "control," which to her is ultimate empowerment and entitlement. She writes in "The Rapture of Dry Ice Burning Off Skin As the Moment of the Soul's Apotheosis":

How will we get used to joy
if we won't hold onto it?

. . . Joy
is at our tongue tips: let the great thirsts and hun-
    gers
of the world be the *marvelous* thirsts, *glorious* hun-
    gers.
Let heartbreak be alternative to coffeebreak, five
midmorning minutes devoted to emotion.

Moss's book was chosen by Charles Simic as part of the National Poetry Series.

Moss is writing a new book of poetry, scheduled for release at the end of 1992; she is also working on a children's book, another volume of poetry, a collection of tales, and an anthology of short fiction. Her readership has continually grown as her career has progressed.

Naomi Shihab Nye

(12 March 1952 -   )

Jane L. Tanner
University of North Texas

BOOKS: *Tattooed Feet* (Texas City: Texas Portfolio, 1977);
Eye-to-Eye (Texas City: Texas Portfolio, 1978);
Different Ways to Pray (Portland, Oreg.: Breitenbush, 1980);
On the Edge of the Sky (Madison, Wis.: Iguana, 1981);
Hugging the Jukebox (New York: Dutton, 1982);
Yellow Glove (Portland, Oreg.: Breitenbush, 1986);
Invisible (Denton, Tex.: Trilobite, 1987).

RECORDINGS: *Rutabaga-Roo*, San Antonio, Flying Cat, 1979;
Lullaby Raft, San Antonio, Flying Cat, 1981;
The Spoken Page, Pittsburgh, International Poetry Forum, 1988.

OTHER: "Twenty Other Worlds," in *Texas Poets in Concert: A Quartet*, edited by Richard B. Sale (Denton: University of North Texas Press, 1990), pp. 76-105.

Naomi Shihab Nye

Naomi Shihab Nye has said, "For me the primary source of poetry has always been local life, random characters met on the streets, our own ancestry sifting down to us through small essential daily tasks." Thus she announces her major themes. In poems described by Alison Heineman (*Pawn Review*, 1980-1981) as "quiet, intimate, contemplative," Nye observes the business of living and the continuity among all the world's inhabitants, whether separated by oceans or time. She lives in Texas but is regional only insofar as she has a strong sense of place wherever she happens to be; she is international in scope and internal in focus, as her poetry demonstrates. She began writing poetry when she was six and published her first poems at seven in *Wee Wisdom*, a children's magazine.

Naomi Shihab Nye was born on 12 March 1952 in St. Louis to Aziz and Miriam Naomi Allwardt Shihab, and she received her elementary and junior-high schooling in St. Louis. Her high-school years were spent in Ramallah, Jordan; Old City, Jerusalem, where the family lived for a year; and San Antonio, Texas. Her father is Palestinian, her mother American, and this dual cultural background is reflected in some of her poems. She married photographer/lawyer Michael Nye on 2 September 1978, and they live in San Antonio with their son, Madison Cloudfeather, born in 1986. In addition to her three major collections and four chapbooks, Nye has published short stories, essays, and more than one hundred individual poems in journals and anthologies. She has recorded two albums of original songs, *Rutabaga-Roo* (1979) and *Lullaby Raft* (1981), and a reading of her poetry, *The Spoken Page* (1988).

Since earning her B.A. in English and world religions from Trinity University in 1974, Nye has worked as writer in residence in Texas, Wyoming, Maine, California, Hawaii and Oregon; as a teacher at the University of California, Berkeley, the University of Texas at San Antonio, and Our Lady of the Lake in San Antonio; and as poetry therapist at Horizon House in San Antonio. She has traveled to the Middle East and Asia for the United States Information Agency, promoting international goodwill through the arts. She has twice been awarded the Voertman Poetry Prize by the Texas Institute of Letters, in 1980 for *Different Ways to Pray* and in 1982 for *Hugging the Jukebox*. Nye was selected for the Pushcart Prize in 1982 and 1984. In 1988 she was chosen by W. S. Merwin to receive the Academy of American Poets' Lavan Award. In the same year she was also a cowinner, with Galway Kinnell, of the Charity Randall Citation for Spoken Poetry from the International Poetry Forum.

The chapbook *Tattooed Feet*, a gathering of twenty-one poems, was published in 1977, followed shortly by *Eye-to-Eye* in 1978. Heineman is among the critics who note that the "quest for understanding, often symbolized by the journey, is a current motif " in Nye's work. All of her poetry is free verse, although these two first collections show some early experimentation with patterning and punctuation. What is remarkable is Nye's ability to draw clear parallels between the ordinary and the sublime. For example, in the opening poem of *Tattooed Feet*, "Pilgrimage," a street scene—laundry hanging "from windows /. . . cabbage rolls / simmering in pots"—and the braids in a child's hair take on new significance because of the symbolic nature of the street itself: the Via Dolorosa in Jerusalem. Nye finds grandeur in the mundane, even in minutiae, from the West Bank to Mexico to a car wash in Paris, Texas, "perfectly ordered images / sophisticated enough to be called poetry." Experience is treated with wry humor in a poem about her dealings with unscrupulous car salesmen, and "Home" is seen as a structure of the mind, a conglomerate of memories: "The floor is only half-formed. / In places your foot goes through // and touches loose soil under the house. / You are afraid of what lives there." Memories are treated as living things, and "voiceless, they rise like pigeons, / startled by your shoe."

Different Ways to Pray, Nye's first full-length collection, was published in 1980, and contains what poet Edward Field called (on the cover of the book) "the voice of one of the most exciting young poets in America—tender, emotional, and above all, interesting . . . a brilliant debut." Nye continues her journey motif, speaking from specific geographies—Texas, California, South America, and Mexico—calmly observing their peculiarities and their people, noting the externals, and using them to define internals. As the title suggests, the work achieves what Heineman calls an "underlying unity [that] derives from the poetry's concern with the variety of private as well as shared acts that connect the human and the divine, the finite and the infinite."

Even as Nye writes of the differences in cultures in something so homely as bread—"The Colombians eat salty bread with their coffee, / they buy it at a bakery foreigners can't find"—there is an awareness that the core of being is the center of concentric circles of outside influence. David Ignatow was impressed with Nye's "vividly drawn" people and "tactile" language: "the power of an artist who is first and foremost one of the people" (book cover). Heineman says that Nye "goes beyond cultural and ethnic distinctions to explore essence." For example, from "Madison Street," somewhere in America, the poet says, "I was not here when all this started / still there is some larger belonging." Then somewhere "north of Jerusalem": "My grandmother's eyes say Allah is everywhere."

With her acceptance of different "ways to pray" is also Nye's growing awareness that living in the world can sometimes be difficult. In "Remembered," a prose poem, is the acknowledgment that gratitude toward even the most generous person can turn sour if called for too often. "Missing the Boat" is about not recognizing the obvious, not grasping the connection between talent and wish, between opportunity and preference. And in "Grandfather's Heaven" the complexity of cultural bias is made more powerful by the simple language of a child: "Grandma liked me even though my daddy was a Moslem."

On the Edge of the Sky, published in 1981, is a small book printed on handmade paper. In these eleven poems Jeanette Burney (*Pawn Review*, 1981-1982) found a "refining of an already productive style." Again, in the description of the simplest action, such as dropping her favorite bowl and watching it break, Nye compares it to a subtler internal moment: "The unannounced blur / of something passing / out of a life."

Josephine Miles selected Nye's second full-length collection, *Hugging the Jukebox*, for the 1982 National Poetry Series. Miles subsequently invited Nye to be Holloway Lecturer at the University of California, Berkeley. In *Hugging the Jukebox* Nye continues to comment on the essential brotherhood of man, as poems from the perspective of Kansas, Texas, Mexico, Bolivia, California, Columbia, and Jerusalem illustrate, beginning with the line "we move forward, / confident we were born into a large family, / our brothers cover the earth." This collection includes humanist poetry celebrating the daily growth of the heart and embracing with childlike joy all nature and its idiosyncrasies. To reviewer David Kirby, Nye "seems to be in good, easy relation with the earth and its peoples" (*Library Journal*, August 1982).

In yards with children, she writes (in "Where Children Live"), "ants have more hope. Squirrels dance as well as hide." Paul Christensen (*Texas Books in Review*, 1983) wrote that, in this "travel book," Nye "has emerged as the voice of girlhood, sentimentalized in places, pollyanna, nostalgic, but sure enough at what she does to hit some very good lines in a poem, until you are convinced of her serious intentions." Christensen found "unexpected flashes of power" in poems such as "The Trashpickers of San Antonio," in which the phrase "murmuring in a language soft as rags" is "a beautiful perception, exactly right."

On the other hand, Paul Foreman (*Pawn Review*, 1983) criticized the "naive, almost schoolgirl, quality of the writing" in *Hugging the Jukebox*, especially what he deems Nye's misuse of the simile—an overuse of "like" without precise comparison. Why, for example, are "a billion other lives . . . like stars"?

In *Yellow Glove* (1986) Nye recognizes the obverse of her shining world. The title piece, a prose poem, holds the essence of the collection in the opening and closing questions: "What can a yellow glove mean in a world of motorcars and governments?" and "A thousand miles later, what can a yellow glove mean in a world of bankbooks and stereos?" The answer is: "Part of the difference between floating and going down."

In this journey, Nye acknowledges the shared sorrows of the world as well as its joys. In contrast to earlier collections, she uses darker, harsher language and some unpleasant images, as in "Hello": the "rat with pointed teeth," on the dining table at night where there is a bowl of peaches, is "sinking his tooth / drinking the pulp / . . . knowing you will read this message and scream." She addresses the pain of unfulfilled longing: "Any lack / carried / too close to the heart / grows teeth, nibbles off / corners." And compare this passage from the earlier "Nelle": "your hands were earth, / whatever you touched was sifted, / made pure," with the hopelessness of "The Gardener": "Everything she planted gave up under the ground."

Philip Booth (*Georgia Review*, Spring 1989) says that Nye "knows more than most of us how many people(s) live; and she does justice to them, and to the need for change, by bringing home to readers both how variously and how similarly all people live." She addresses the anguish of the Palestinian question head-on in "Blood," first printed in a Washington, D.C., anthology dealing with the Middle East and its problems, *And Not Surrender* (1982).

Many of the poems in *Yellow Glove* contain a bitterness, a world-weariness not in her earlier work. She speaks of tears; a café in war-torn Beirut; one of Mother Teresa's orphans in Calcutta; an uncle killed by a car in Mecca; and "a world where no one saves anyone." In "The White Road" Nye is "researching sadness, / finding out how it adheres to the world, / bubbling and thickening flour in broth." Still there arises out of these tragic phrases a message of hope, a realization that strength comes from facing adversity and that joy won from sorrow is priceless.

In November 1988 Nye was invited to read at the University of North Texas Poets in Concert Series with three other Texas poets. Works by these four were published in 1990 as *Texas Poets in Concert: A Quartet*. Nye entitled her nineteen selections "Twenty Other Worlds," a reflection of her continuing exploration of the places outside and their relationships with the places in the heart. She reveals a more fully realized sense of urgency, beginning with her question in "The Sail Made of Rags": "each time someone mentions 'the third world'—where / is the second world, and why are we the first?" In this latest collection Nye's voice has an even sharper edge as she again probes the Palestinian question, showing controlled anger with Israeli border guards in "Olive Jar" and quiet irony in "Even at War (for My Uncle, the Mayor)" and "How Palestinians Keep Warm": "But I know we need to keep warm here on earth / and when your shawl is as thin as mine is, you tell stories."

Lisa Russ Spaar says that these poems are "as numinous and revealing as consciousness itself." "Sleep's Little House," in which the bear in the bedtime story "recognizes the difference in his spoon / when it has been used by someone / he doesn't know," and "Password"—with the agonized question, "How can we help / someone else want to live?"—demonstrate the continuity of humanity in time and space. Naomi Shihab Nye's poems in this anthology reveal the deepest awareness that this quiet observer of the human condi-

tion has yet shown; they bespeak exciting potential for her future work.

References:

Louis McKee, "Ranting and Raving about Naomi Shihab Nye," *Swamp Root* (Spring 1989): 83-93;

Lisa Russ Spaar, Introduction to *Texas Poets in Concert: A Quartet* (Denton: University of North Texas Press, 1990), p. 2.

Sharon Olds
(19 November 1942 -   )

Carole Stone
Montclair State College

BOOKS: *Satan Says* (Pittsburgh: University of Pittsburgh Press / London: Feffer & Simons, 1980);
The Dead and the Living (New York: Knopf, 1984);
The Gold Cell (New York: Knopf, 1987).

OTHER: *Four Contemporary Poets*, includes poems by Olds (Flushing, N.Y.: La Vida, 1984).

Sharon Olds has established herself as a major American poet whose themes of sexuality and power as daughter, wife, and mother are of particular importance to women. Besides depicting family life, she describes global and political events with sensitivity toward the victims of oppression. Her family poems feature striking comparisons between her family and larger institutions of nations. Olds's strength as a poet lies in her persistent and frank use of erotic imagery in writing about the body as she describes puberty, menstruation, sexual love, childbirth, aging, and dying. She connects these life stages to her own and her children's coming-of-age and to her parents', and records the physical directly and affirmatively. In doing so she has founded a tradition of writing about the body for women poets who have followed her.

Sharon Olds was born in San Francisco on 19 November 1942 and educated at Stanford Uni-

versity (B.A., 1964) and Columbia University (Ph.D., 1972). She is married, and has two children, a boy and a girl, and lives on the Upper West Side of Manhattan. Olds is the director of the Creative Writing Program at New York University and the founding chair of the Writing Program at Goldwater Hospital for the severely physically disabled. She has also taught at writing conferences throughout the country, among them the Nathan Mayhew Seminar at Martha's Vineyard and the Squaw Valley Writer's Conference. She held the Fanny Hurst Chair at Brandeis in 1986.

Olds's poetry is intensely personal; she writes about pain, anger, violence, death, and love. Her poems are highly imagistic and build through a series of charged similes and metaphors toward an explosive closure. She writes in the first person. However, many of her poems may not be autobiographical; she presents them in an autobiographical voice to give them a sense of immediacy. Some critics compare her to Sylvia Plath because of the emphasis on the family and its connection to collective suffering. Richard Tillinghast, for example, wrote, "Olds has without a doubt been influenced deeply by Plath's poetry. Love and hatred of the father are major preoccupations for both writers, and both equate violence within the family with violence within

Sharon Olds (photograph copyright by Thomas Victor)

the state and nations" (*Nation*, 13 October 1984). The difference Tillinghast sees between the two poets is that Plath's poems are about a fantasy father, whereas Olds appears to be producing a "photographic view of a family tragedy." Olds owes much to the Plathian confessional mode, but she writes in a more narrative, earthy, sensual celebratory voice than that of Plath.

Olds's first book, *Satan Says* (1980), which received the inaugural San Francisco Poetry Center Award, is divided into sections titled "Daughter," "Woman," "Mother," and "Journeys." The fourth section includes poems about her father, mother, and husband, and a final poem about childbirth.

The first poem of the book, "Satan Says," establishes Olds's use of sexual words, which, in the context of writing about her parents, are especially shocking. She expresses her rage and hurt on a personal level, establishes herself as a poet, not a "poetess," and breaks with the tradition associated with genteel poetic foremothers. The poem, with its primal content, is one of expurgation, and Olds has said that, after writing it, she felt as if there were nothing she could not say in her work. The principal metaphor of "Satan Says" is of a cedar box "with a picture of shep-

herds pasted onto the central panel between carvings. The box stands on curved legs. / It has a gold, heart-shaped lock / and no key." The speaker says, "I am trying to write my way out of the closed box redolent of cedar." So the speaker tries to write her way out of the polite and sentimental language of the lady writer as well as out of the confinement of her family where she has been victimized.

To release herself, she accepts Satan's invitation to get her out by saying, "My father is a shit." As the box, her sexuality, begins to open, she must say, "mother is a pimp." And further Satan instructs, "*Say shit, say death, say fuck the father.*" After she utters the hitherto unutterable, "Something opens. Satan says *Don't you feel a lot better?*" Then the narrator admits her love for her parents, as Satan "sucks himself out of the keyhole." The cedar box metamorphoses into her coffin, as she discovers her knowledge of love. This complex progression of imprisonment, sexual liberation, and the acknowledgment of her love for her parents has a terrible price, namely the speaker's realization that freedom includes her own entombment. The poem suggests that while she may defy and rebel against an alcoholic father and a mother who failed to defend her from his cruelty, ultimately she will always be tied to them, both emotionally and imaginatively.

In this first book Olds begins her depiction of the father as a cruel, depriving alcoholic who inherited his drinking from his own father. In "Love Fossil," for example, the father is a man who "drank his supper," while the speaker "went hungry." The theme of being deprived of love is consistent in Olds's work, as is the depiction of father and grandfather through the recurrent image of their eyes: in "Love Fossil" the father's eyes are "Dark as massy coal deposits."

However, Olds acknowledges the nurturant father she seeks in the poem "Nurse Whitman," in which a male poet (Walt Whitman) can "move between the soldiers' cots" and "bathe the forehead, / . . . bathe the lip, the cock, as I touch my father, as if the language were a form of life." In the last stanza Olds pays homage to Whitman, the androgynous poet who bravely expressed eroticism as she does and who represents her ideal father-poet, with whom she aligns herself:

> We lean down, our pointed breasts
> heavy as plummets with fresh spermy milk—
> we conceive. Walt, with the men we love, thus,
> now, we bring to fruit.

The "Woman" section in *Satan Says* explores sexuality and marriage with startling images, as in the poem "Monarchs," where Olds compares a lover's touch to that of the butterfly, a metaphor undercut with an extended simile of cruelty: "Their wings the dark red of your hands like butcher's hands, the raised / veins of their wings like your scars." Olds juxtaposes cruelty and tenderness in sex to undercut the false bathos of women's love poems. With this extreme sexual darkness Olds places herself in the tradition of Plath and Anne Sexton by emphasizing that love, pain, gentleness, and sexual pleasure are mixed together.

The last poem of *Satan Says*, "Prayer," creates, as reviewer Joyce Peseroff puts it, "a standard of heroism" (*American Book Review*, January-February 1982), which is conveyed through the theme of childbirth. Olds affirmatively commits herself to the power of her body and to the body's language as she writes about the birth of her son and prays that she will be "faithful to the central meanings":

> the waters breaking in the birth-room which suddenly

> smelled like the sea;
> . . . .
> the terrible fear
> as the child's head moves down the vagina:
> there is no stopping it. . . .

The poem and the volume end with a prayer: "let me not forget: / each action, each word / taking its beginnings from these." Thus she combines the major themes of the book: love, which is both beautiful and violent; creativity, which stems from the body; and the power of the woman to create.

In *The Dead and the Living* (1984), which won the Lamont Poetry Prize and the National Book Critics Circle Award, Olds continues the narrative of her traumatic childhood with graphic physical and emotional detail. In this volume the cast of characters includes a cruel grandfather, drunken and violent father, bitter and passive mother, and sadistic sister. The book also contains poems about Olds's children and about motherhood, so that in this book the child victim becomes the mature survivor. In addition Olds breaks out of the family circle to encompass a wider global family by writing about sufferings and victimization in the public world. Thus, her own family becomes analogous to the oppressed of other times and other places, making her poems argue for the universality of human suffering. As critic Paula Bonnell pointed out, "Sharon Olds writes about a woman's life as women have always known their lives—in relation to other lives. . . . The central truth around which the poems collect is that to be human is to hurt and be hurt, whether in the public way by war and political violence, or in the dark private stairwells and dully flowing firesides of the family" (*Poetry*, October 1984).

This second volume is more tightly structured than her first, and Olds achieves control over the violent, erotic, disturbing material that some critics felt she had not yet mastered in her first book. This control is also evident in the extension of consciousness from private to political. Her compassion extends, in the poem "Ideographs," to a Chinese man who is about to be executed; to a starving Russian girl in "Photograph of a Girl"; and in "Portrait of a Child," to a child dead of hunger during the Turkish massacre of the Armenians. Her poems are also about public figures such as Marilyn Monroe, whose death disturbs those men who carry her into the ambulance, and the Shah of Iran, whose cruelty Olds depicts in "The Aesthetics of the Shah."

Several of Olds's private death poems concern a grandfather who passed on a legacy of alcoholism to his son. In "The Guild" Olds dramatizes, in a fireside scene, the "liquor like fire" in the grandfather's hand. She conflates the fireside metaphor with the image of coal as the liquor glasses of the grandfather and the young father become "glasses of coals." The poem's title, "The Guild," presents the notion of the inheritance of violence and anger, which becomes Olds's family curse. The inheriting of the obsessiveness of drinking can be seen in Olds's obsession with writing about it.

Olds also records the death of a best friend, a miscarriage, and the aging of a grandmother, whom she finally comes to love. In an especially moving poem about the illness of the poet Muriel Rukeyser, Olds pays another poetic debt to a benevolent, creative forebear, characterizing Rukeyser as a "flowering branch suspended over her life."

The second part of *The Dead and the Living*, a cycle of poems about marriage and Olds's children, moves toward a celebration of both erotic and family love. She delights in male and female differences in observations of her children, as she carefully records the terror and pain as well as the joyful rites of passage. She does not flinch from physical description, describing her young son's erection in the back seat of the car and imagining her daughter's first sexual experience. Olds uses direct language in her affirmation of the human body, both in erotic descriptions of her children and in her treatment of sexual love. Mixing the terror of the flesh with its joys, she writes in "Poem to My First Lover":

> I am in love with the girl who went
> offering, came to you and
> laid it like a feast on a platter, the
> delicate flesh-yes, yes,
> I accept the gift.

Listening to Olds readers hear a voice that understands the sensual.

The poems in *The Gold Cell* (1987) resemble the family, public, and sexual narratives of her earlier books and continue to depict urban life. In "On the Subway" she writes about the fears and misunderstandings between blacks and whites; in "The Abandoned Newborn," of the city's cruelty; and in "Outside the Operating Room of the Sex-Change Doctor" and "The Solution," about the

sexual confusions of contemporary society. Once more Olds makes the body her credo, using anatomical imagery to demystify relationships that have been held sacred. The best example of such iconoclasm is in her short poem "The Pope's Penis":

> It hangs deep in his robes, a delicate
> clapper at the center of a bell
> . . . .
> and at night,
> while his eyes sleep, it stands up
> in praise of God.

Olds's humanism leads her to present the pope as a man, and her eroticism presents a non-public, flesh-and-blood pope who worships God with his body. Thus she unites eros with public and private worlds.

The Gold Cell is fuller in its descriptions of a harrowing childhood. Yet Olds consistently affirms life, which is precious to her in spite of her family history. In "I Go Back to May 1937," she recreates the courtship of her parents at college age, the speaker wanting to prevent their misalliance:

> I want to go up to them and say Stop,
> don't do it—she's the wrong woman,
> he's the wrong man, you are going to do things
> you cannot imagine you would ever do,
> you are going to do bad things to children. . . .

Ultimately the speaker celebrates their union because, in spite of its failure, it gave her life:

> I want to live. I
> take them up like male and female
> paper dolls and bang them together
> at the hips like chips of flint as if to
> strike sparks from them, I say
> Do what you are going to do, and I will tell about it.

Olds thus declares herself poet and witness, appreciative of the gift of speech through which she affirms life.

In other mother-and-father poems, Olds sexualizes the parents and describes "the delicacies of the genitals" as the father is shown as Saturn devouring his children. In "What If God" she delivers a hyperbolic version of what every child needs, the father as deliverer. She asks, "Is there a God in the house?" as she sees her father washing his hands of her.

The consistent sexualizing of the parents expresses both her rage against them and her helplessness; though these poems may leave readers emotionally drained and shocked, Olds's catharsis is as graphic a case study of the oedipal triangle as one can find in contemporary poetry. Furthermore she redeems the anger and the darkness of her books through the poems about her own children, as she tries to keep them safe from public and private cruelty.

The title *The Gold Cell* is a metaphor for the power and beauty of the body. In her poem "In the Cell" Olds describes, for example, a youth torturing a man by taking off his genitals. In "The Quest" a mother exalts the beauty of her daughter's body, after the girl has been lost for an hour, and the mother buys orange juice for "every gold cell of her body." Olds sympathizes with innocence even as she depicts evil; even though some critics have been taken aback by her graphic sexual language, violent portraits, and obsessive catharsis, her poems ultimately succeed in moving readers because of her search for the source of human evil. As she writes in "The Quest," "This is my quest, to know where it is, the evil in the human heart."

Although some critics think the connections Olds makes between public and private cruelty and violence are forced, others see her as writing a badly needed political poetry. Most critics see her family poems as the most evocative in her work and especially praise the poems about her children for the humor with which she writes them.

Olds's poems are particularly important to women. They respond to her journey, to her daring to present the familiar details of a woman's life using frank language traditionally taboo to female writers. Many critics see her books as documentaries of a family tragedy and praise her for extending her humanity to those who engendered the darkness of her work. Indeed, redemption and forgiveness appear to be the future trend of Olds's poems, judging by a group of them about her father's dying published in the *American Poetry Review* in 1989. Her treatment of him, even in his dying moments in the hospital, continues to be graphically physical but with a new spirit of warmth, understanding, and love. Olds's voice continues to be one of the most direct among contemporary American poets, and her embrace of the sexual is an affirming force in what she sees as an essentially evil world.

Simon Ortiz
(27 May 1941 -)

Marie M. Schein
University of North Texas

BOOKS: *Going for the Rain* (New York: Harper & Row, 1976);

A Good Journey (Berkeley, Cal.: Turtle Island, 1977);

Howbah Indians (Tucson: Blue Moon, 1978);

The People Shall Continue, by Ortiz and Sharol Graves (San Francisco: Children's Book Press, 1978; revised, 1988);

Song, Poetry, Language: Expression and Perception (Tsaile, Ariz.: Navaho Community College Press, 1978);

Fight Back: For the Sake of the People, for the Sake of the Land (Albuquerque: University of New Mexico, 1980);

From Sand Creek (New York: Thunder's Mouth, 1981);

A Poem Is A Journey (Bourbonnais, Ill.: Pternandon, 1981);

Blue and Red (Acoma, N.Mex.: Pueblo of Acoma, 1982);

The Importance of Childhood (Acoma, N.Mex.: Pueblo of Acoma, 1982);

Fightin': New and Collected Short Stories (New York: Thunder's Mouth Press, 1983);

Woven Stone (Tucson: University of Arizona Press, 1991).

OTHER: *Earth Power Coming: Short Stories in Native American Literature*, edited by Ortiz (Tsaile, Ariz.: Navajo Community College Press, 1983).

Simon Ortiz is a poet, short-story writer, essayist, and editor. When asked to explain why he writes, Ortiz replies: "Because Indians always tell a story. The only way to continue is to tell a story." This statement informs Ortiz's works, the purpose of which is to paint a picture of what he calls "the real America." In an interview with Laura Coltelli he explained this phrase: "The real America is the Native America of indigenous people and the indigenous principle they represent." His poems and short stories, a collage of "postcards" from America, reveal a profound concern for the land and the native people. But Ortiz's message transcends ethnicity and is a universal plea for respect toward individuals and what the land offers them.

Simon Joseph Ortiz was born on 27 May 1941 at the Pueblo of Acoma, near Albuquerque, New Mexico, to Joe L. and Mamie Toribio Ortiz. After finishing high school, he worked for a year in the uranium mines and processing plants of the Grants Ambrosia Lake area. He then enlisted in the U.S. Army and after the end of his service enrolled at the University of New Mexico in Albuquerque in 1966. He also attended the University of Iowa, where he received an M.F.A. in 1969. He has taught creative writing and American Indian literature at San Diego State University; the University of New Mexico; and Sinte Gleska College in Rosebud, South Dakota. In December 1981 he married Marlene Foster and they had three children: Raho, Rainy, and Sara. The couple divorced in 1984. Since 1982 Ortiz has been the consulting editor of the Pueblo of Acoma Press. He currently lives in Acoma, where he is serving his people as lieutenant governor of the pueblo. Ortiz received a Discovery Award from the National Endowment for the Arts in 1969, an NEA Fellowship in 1981, and the Pushcart Prize for Poetry that same year for his collection of poems *From Sand Creek*.

His first important work, *Going for the Rain* (1976), is a collection of poems divided into four sections: "Preparation," "Leaving," "Returning," and "The Rain Falls." In the first section the narrator prepares for a journey. The first poem, "The Creation, According to Coyote," establishes the earth as the source of all life. Coyote says: "You were born when you came from that body, the earth." The respect for the earth is then passed on to a child who will gain a sense of his own place as well as the place marked by his ancestors. The other poems in the first section present the essential values that constitute the foundation of Ortiz's poetry: the belief in transmitting the gift of culture to the children, the importance of

Simon Ortiz circa 1978 (photograph by LaVerne H. Clark)

language and words, the respect for nature and for elders, and the harmony of the botanic, animal, and human worlds.

In "Leaving" Ortiz explains that "the main theme" of his poetry is "to recognize / the relationship I share with everything." The poems capture moments, such as a tête-à-tête with a bird and an encounter with a derelict in a bus depot, and represent the malaise of city life. But there is a sense of displacement and longing for home: "I am lonely for the hills," says the narrator, "I am lonely for myself."

"Returning" traces the narrator's trip back to his home and offers a disturbing panorama of what America is about. The comfort of going home results from the separation from industrial America, because it is a dehumanizing and lifeless realm, and the return to the mountains. "Washyuma Motor Hotel," for example, points up the automation of everyday life that robs the individual of his dreams: "The American passersby / get out of their hot, stuffy cars / at evening, pay their money wordlessly, / and fall asleep without benefit of dreams. / The next morning, they get up, dress automatically, brush their teeth, /

get in their cars and drive away." Ortiz also scrutinizes the destructive tendencies of American industry, the exploitation of the land, and the insatiable desire to expand and build. His advice is unequivocal: "Keep to the hills / and avoid America / if you can." The poems underline a fundamental lack of communication, among people and also between them and nature.

The fourth section of this collection, "The Rain Falls," places the narrator once more in his familiar setting. The poems describe the land and the people, illustrating the relationship between the two: "always see the wholeness of what is around you, / exult in your presence / with the humility / that true knowledge imparts, / that you are one part / among many and all parts." Respect for the land is anchored in the belief that the earth is mother and that she offers gifts for which one must be grateful.

In the preface to his second collection of poems, *A Good Journey* (1977), Ortiz explains his intentions: "I wanted to show that the narrative style and technique of oral tradition could be expressed as written narrative and that it would have the same participatory force and validity as words spoken and listened to." Ortiz succeeds in this goal through the choice of striking images.

A Good Journey is a celebration of life—new life, as in the birth of a child, and the life of the land—and a powerful reminder that humankind is inseparable from the earth. The poems also celebrate the endurance of a people and a culture and the struggle to protect the land. Ortiz's words stress the necessity for the present generation to ensure the continuance of the native people and their survival, while a dominant culture closes in on them. His sense of alienation is rendered through irony. He writes in "A Designated National Park": "Fee area / This morning, / I had to buy a permit to get back home." Also revealing are these lines from "Grand Canyon Christmas Eve 1969": "Kaibab National Forest / Deposit 85 cents for wood / This is ridiculous. / You gotta be kidding. / Dammit, my grandfathers used to run this place with bears and wolves / And I got some firewood / anyway from the forest, / mumbling, Sue me."

The most powerful poems in this collection are those depicting the development of Indian lands by the government and the arrival of modernity with the railroad, electricity, gas, highways, phones, and televisions. The result is a country gutted and permanently changed. Throughout these poems, Ortiz's black humor—a type of survival humor often present in American Indian literature—is heard. Of the installation of the telephone for example, Ortiz says: "I didn't know / whether or not you could talk in Acoma / into the telephone and even after I found / that you could I wasn't convinced / that the translation was coming correctly."

Ortiz fulfills the promise he makes in the preface: the stories he tells are thought-provoking and compel the non-Indian reader to listen. The strength of the words echoes in the reader's mind long after the poems are read and generates the understanding that telling the stories of the people is "the only way" to continue.

The preface to his *Fight Back: For the Sake of the People, for the Sake of the Land* (1980) reveals a shocking reality: "Indian reservations in the U.S. were conceived as convenient surplus labor pools." This statement underscores the purpose of the poet in this collection. Ortiz presents Indians under a different light; *Fight Back* is not concerned with Indians as artists, singers, dancers, or healers but with Indians as blue-collar workers. It is a proletarian manifesto whose creed is presented bluntly: "The land shall endure. /

There will be victory. / The people shall go on. / We shall have victory." Ortiz speaks of the Laguna area and of the changes that occurred there after the discovery of uranium. The nuclear theme, in Ortiz's poetry, as well as in the works of other American Indian writers such as Leslie Marmon Silko, underlines the question of identity and reveals the bleak irony of the conditions of the Indians in the area at the time. The quest for significance is jeopardized by the potential danger of total annihilation. The power of the words in these poems comes from the affirmation of existence, spiritual and physical, in a universe enshrouded by death. But suddenly life springs back from the written words, and it is the sound of one's heart beat that is amplified:

> Life beating
> Earth beating
> All beating
>   beating
>   beating
>   beating
>   beating. . . .

The references to the relationship between the land and the people occur many times as a refrain that emphasizes the need to overcome and continue. The collection closes with a humorous stab at stereotypes: the narrator of "A New Story" is phoned by a woman who is preparing a parade and who "wants an Indian, a real Indian with feathers and paint."

An intentionally didactic collection of poems, *From Sand Creek* defines Indianness. This collection juxtaposes historical evidence about the fate of the American Indians, which appears on the left-hand page, with poems that illustrate the history, on the right-hand page. The stories point to a forgotten people, a culture made invisible and pushed aside by the necessity for the colonists to expand a rich territory. The repetition of the word *shadows* emphasizes the invisibility of a people who strive for significance. Prominent in these poems is the notion that the conflicts between the settlers and the Indians—the bloodshed, agony, and destruction—could have been avoided if the settlers had been willing to compromise. The equally recurrent reference to Indian veterans and patriotism emphasizes the irony of the search for identity. The Indian veteran has fought to defend a land no longer his own. Anger and bitterness prevail in these poems, but the motivation is not revenge. The message is, again, one of rebirth and continuance.

The power of Ortiz's poems has established him as one of the best contemporary American Indian poets. But he is also the writer of many short stories. His first story collection, *Howbah Indians*, was published in 1978 and a more elaborate collection, *Fightin': New and Collected Short Stories*, was published in 1983. Ortiz chooses such subjects as marriage, abuse, grief, belonging, divorce, alcoholism, and religious beliefs. The stories present these subjects from the perspective of American Indian characters, but the first story in *Fightin'*, "To Change in a Good Way," advocates the rapprochement of Indians and non-Indians. The story describes the friendship between an Indian couple and a white couple, and reveals the necessity to accept the differences between the Indian and the non-Indian worlds.

In addition to writing poetry and short fiction, Ortiz also dedicates his time to writing about and for children. His first children's book, *The People Shall Continue* (1978), offers colorful drawings to accompany the story, a panorama of the history of American Indians from before the arrival of the first settlers to the present. *The People Shall Continue* teaches a lesson from which all children, regardless of their ethnic background, can benefit.

The message in the poetry and fiction of Simon Ortiz is twofold: it aspires to define Indian America and to make a plea for its survival by pointing to the truth that some Americans have denied but that Indians have always revered—the land must be saved. The poems warn that the abuse and exploitation of the land ultimately lead to the destruction of all life, including human life.

Interviews:

Joseph Bruchac, *Survival This Way: Interviews with American Indian Poets* (Tucson: University of Arizona Press, 1987), pp. 214-229;

Laura Coltelli, *Winged Words: American Indian Writers Speak* (Lincoln: University of Nebraska Press, 1990), pp. 103-119.

References:

Willard Gingerich, "The Old Voices of Acoma: Simon Ortiz's Mythic Indigenism," *Southwest Review*, 64 (Winter 1979): 19-30;

Patricia Clark Smith, "*Canin latrans latrans* in the Poetry of Simon Ortiz," *Minority Voices*, 3 (Fall 1979): 1-18.

Brenda Marie Osbey

(12 December 1957 -   )

Jacqueline Brice-Finch
James Madison University

BOOKS: *Ceremony for Minneconjoux* (Lexington: University Press of Kentucky, 1983);
In These Houses (Middletown, Conn.: Wesleyan University Press, 1988);
Desperate Circumstance, Dangerous Woman (Brownsville, Oreg.: Story Line, 1991).

Interviewer Violet Harrington-Bryan asked Brenda Marie Osbey about the chief subject of her poetry, the women of New Orleans and the bayou country. Osbey responded candidly: "See, the women in my poems are women who 'take no shit.' When you're living in a constant state of oppression, you can snap at any time." Osbey's poems detail the strength and resilience, as well as the psychic disorientation, of the colorful characters who inhabit this district. She describes her creative and historical study of Louisiana folklore as "a kind of cultural biography, a cultural geography." Her poems capture the essence of Afro-Louisianan culture and language.

Born on 12 December 1957 to Lawrence C. Osbey (a boxer) and his wife, Lois Emelda Hamilton, Osbey grew up in the Seventh Ward of New Orleans. An honor student, she skipped her senior year in high school (1973-1974) to participate in the Early Admissions Program at Dillard University. Following her graduation from high school in 1974, she continued her education at Dillard. Her studies in French included a year abroad as a Council for the Development of French in Louisiana (CODOFIL) scholar. During 1976 and 1977 she attended the Université Paul Valéry in Montpellier, France, where she took classes in French literature and language. She received a B.A. in French and English from Dillard University in 1978.

Along with her interest in languages, Osbey had also been developing her talent as a poet, continuing the family tradition of writing begun by her maternal grandfather and her mother. In 1980 Osbey was awarded the International Communications Agency Research Award at Dillard and the Academy of American Poets Loring-

Williams Prize. That year Osbey also embarked on her teaching career, as an instructor of French and English at her alma mater. During 1982 and 1983 she was the assistant director of the Foreign Language Division of the New Orleans Public Library. In 1984 she received the Associated Writing Programs Poetry Award and, as the Bernadine Scherman fellow, attended the MacDowell Colony in Peterborough, New Hampshire.

During 1985 Osbey was the director of public and community relations for the Arts Council of New Orleans and gave several poetry readings in Boston and Cambridge, Massachusetts, as well as in Lexington, Kentucky. She was selected as a Bunting fellow at the Mary Ingraham Bunting Institute for 1985-1986, with a concurrent appointment as Resident Scholar in Creative Writing at Currier House, both at Radcliffe College of Harvard University. She was also a resident fellow in 1986 at the Millay Colony for the Arts in Austerlitz, New York, and the Virginia Center for the Creative Arts. Osbey earned an M.A. in English and Afro-American literature from the University of Kentucky in 1986. A fellowship that same year from the Kentucky Foundation for Women and a stint as writer in residence for Marion County, Kentucky (1986-1987), gave her the opportunity to read for audiences in Kentucky, Virginia, and Massachusetts. The Fine Arts Work Center in Provincetown, Massachusetts, selected her as a fellow for 1987-1988.

She returned to Dillard University in the summer of 1988 as an assistant professor before accepting a position as a visiting assistant professor of African-American Literature at UCLA from 1988 to 1990. Since 1990 she has been an assistant professor in the Department of English at Loyola University. Her works in progress include several articles regarding Afro-Louisianian history, culture, and language; and translations of Afro-Brazilian, Francophone-African, and Caribbean poets. She is also a reader for the Callaloo Poetry Series and the Wesleyan Poets and Wesleyan New Poets series.

A collection of narrative poems about the people of New Orleans and the bayous, *Ceremony for Minneconjoux* (1983), Osbey's first book, is divided into three sections: "My Name Is Felicity," "My Voice Is an Okono Drum," and "They Will Witness the History." In each section individuals relate stories about lives thwarted by the malevolent behavior of lovers or loved ones. The various narrators do not give full details about themselves or the ceremonies that shape their lives. They force the reader to put together clues in much the same way a historian pieces together information about past events. Thus the historicity and verisimilitude of the characters is firmly established.

When Harrington-Bryan asked Osbey about the background of her women characters, she responded that these women were real Louisiana folk, "a group of black women who believe they are called upon by the Spirit to search out evil wherever it may be hiding. . . . They symbolize all that is dark and protected and sheltered about the culture, about women, about life in New Orleans."

In the title poem, "Ceremony for Minneconjoux," three generations of women are adversely affected by one man, a Native American of the Choctaw nation. The various narrators piece together the family history of Minneconjoux, a woman so named by her mother to establish the daughter's Choctaw heritage. The word *Minneconjoux* is the name of the Native American nation that once lived in Louisiana and Arkansas. An unidentified narrator begins the tale with Mama Lou Philemon's hiring of a Choctaw to do chores around her property. Her daughter Lenazette details her own growing attraction to the older man and his seduction of her following the combing of her long hair. She later bears a daughter she names Minneconjoux. Lenazette kills the Choctaw after being forced to submit to him while Minneconjoux can observe their sexual activity, and Lenazette is incarcerated for the murder. Minneconjoux becomes mentally unbalanced. Living in the city with her grandmother Mama Lou, she picks up the narration of the story, relating how her grandmother exhibits seemingly erratic behavior when she cuts off the girl's hair after a young boy is attracted to the girl's braids. Later Minneconjoux understands that the grandmother perceived the boy's attraction as a prelude to another disastrous seduction.

As an adult, Minneconjoux visits the bayou shack where her parents lived before the murder. There she finds a crone who talks about "child-having and other ceremonies." The old hag is Minneconjoux's mother, debilitated as a result of her incarceration.

In the second section the poems "Living in a Tan House," "Eileen," and "Ramona Veagis" feature protagonists who are all New Orleans women who cannot live prescribed existences. Lavinia Thierfield, who chafes at marital life in her tan house, seeks solace in singing with a voice like "an okono drum." Eileen on Onzaga Street wakes up one morning feeling like she "could kill someone" and proceeds to murder several family members. Ramona Veagis suffers a nervous breakdown after "she had fallen off the world / and could not climb back on." The portraiture of these women is deliberately incomplete, so the reader must conjecture about the rest of each story.

The third section addresses how other women handle their lives, which verge on "madness," and how the legacy of strength and endurance is transmitted among the womenfolk. In "Chifalta" a mother and daughter converse. The mother is able somewhat to control her mania. However, she tells her daughter, "go . . . / i can not bear your madness / and my own as well." A poet/narrator in "Writing the Words" vows to record "the history of migrations" of Sally and others; another persona acknowledges the *fefe* women whose feet are telling of "all the lives."

Osbey's second book, *In These Houses* (1988), continues the themes of the first by focusing on the "swift easy women," the conjure women, their female neighbors and clients who live on Onzaga Street. Again Osbey divides the book into three sections, which correspond to three principal categories: the women, the place, and the legacy. In part 1, "In These Houses of Swift Easy Women," Thelma V. Picou is a woman who "was so loose / she couldn't even hold onto herself " until, as her husband, Henry, says, "thelma came unstopped one day":

> i saw her heading out the front door
> naked as she come into the world
> and before i could say a word
> thelma was out in the middle of the neutral ground
> dancing and screaming
> eating the black dirt
> calling freedom
> freedom.

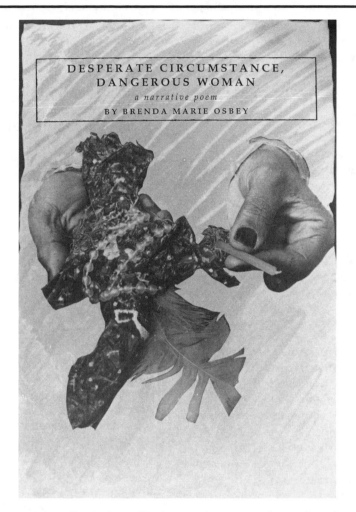

Cover for the 1991 book in which Osbey tells of a love affair between a young Creole woman and a married man in New Orleans

Although Henry appears rational, he does not understand the sexual oppression that Thelma sheds by seeking "freedom" through her madness. Other men who court and marry these women are equally baffled by their nonconformist behavior. Another woman, Eugenia, is murdered in "Little Eugenia's Lover" when her Hispanic lover bludgeons her to death one morning, apparently unable to accept her brown skin.

Parts 2 and 3 of *In These Houses* center respectively on the location of the characters and the historicity of the location. The houses, such as in "The House" and "Portrait," hold evidence of the tragic lives of past residents. Conjurer or hoodoo women who can give solace to the demented are the repositories of the events in the community. In "Consuela" they appear suddenly and break up a seemingly innocent girl's ring game. They know that the child who plays the game best can become a victim of her own vanity. These women

also give succor to "collapsible women."

Osbey suggests in "Geography" that the legacy of a community can be deciphered:

> the geography i am learning
> has me place myself
> at simultaneous points
> of celebration. . . .
>
> this place no one chooses
> is the land i tarry in.
> this ritual i go through
> is as old as its name
> and the prophet-women who dance it. . . .

Family histories, "the scraps of living," reside within the soul of every citizen, Osbey concludes in the last poem of the book, "House of Bones."

In *Desperate Circumstance, Dangerous Woman* (1991) the reader is aided in understanding Afro-Louisianan culture by a detailed glossary of Louisiana and New Orleans ethnic expressions and place names, more extensive than the list offered in *In These Houses*. Many of the character types familiar in Osbey's first two collections reappear in the twelve sections of the 1991 book, a long narrative poem that tells of an illicit love affair between a young woman, Marie Crying Eagle, and her married lover, Percy. Percy and his wife seek the aid of Ms. Regina, a conjurer to break the spell of his mistress. Yet Ms. Regina is powerless to help. In a candid revelation, the secular priestess tells him,

> i'm old
> and i'm black
> but i'm an honest woman.
> and that's why i have to tell you
> there is nothing i can do for you son.
> it's as you say.
> she's in your blood.

All sectors of the Afro-Louisianan community in the New Orleans district are affected by the mysterious blood ties that bind the inhabitants to their ancestral families, their communities, and their lovers. Percy returns to Marie once again at the poem's end.

Critic Calvin Hernton gave a description of the women of Osbey's *Ceremony for Minneconjoux* that is appropriate for characters in all three of her published books: "All of Osbey's women are 'crazy,' salt-of-the-earth women whose personas and voices are flavored by the 'quaint' heritage of the cultural melting pot of New Orleans. In addition to influences from the American Indian and French and Spanish cultures, the styles of speech and the general aura of the women reflect a certain African mystique ('primitive' ways and 'superstitions') carried over into the New World and blended with the indigenously developed folkness of southern black women" (*Parnassus*, 1985). In *Desperate Circumstance, Dangerous Woman*, the men claim the same heritage.

Osbey presents the ceremonies of living, albeit dangerously, among the black folk. While she assumes that her readers do have some knowledge of Louisiana culture, her interlacing of fact, fiction, mystery, and folklore entices her audiences to learn more.

Interview:

Violet Harrington-Bryan, "An Interview with Brenda Marie Osbey," *Mississippi Quarterly*, 40 (Winter 1986-1987): 33-45.

References:

Violet Harrington-Bryan, "Evocations of Place and Culture in the Works of Four Contemporary Black Louisiana Writers," *Louisiana Literature*, 4 (Fall 1987): 49-60;

Calvin Hernton, "The Tradition," *Parnassus*, 12-13 (Spring/Summer/Fall/Winter 1985): 518-550.

Alicia Ostriker
(11 November 1937 -   )

Amy Williams
University of Texas at San Antonio

BOOKS: *Vision and Verse in William Blake* (Madison & Milwaukee: University of Wisconsin Press, 1965);

Songs (New York: Holt, Rinehart & Winston, 1969);

Once More Out of Darkness (New York: Smith/Horizon, 1971; enlarged edition, Berkeley, Cal.: Berkeley Poets' Cooperative, 1974);

A Dream of Springtime (New York: Smith/Horizon, 1979);

The Mother/Child Papers (Santa Monica, Cal.: Momentum, 1980);

A Woman Under the Surface (Princeton, N.J. & Guildford, U.K.: Princeton University Press, 1982);

Writing Like a Woman (Ann Arbor: University of Michigan Press, 1983);

Stealing the Language: The Emergence of Women Poets in America (Boston: Beacon, 1986);

The Imaginary Lover (Pittsburgh: University of Pittsburgh Press, 1986);

Green Age (Pittsburgh: University of Pittsburgh Press, 1989);

Unwritten Volume: Re-Thinking the Bible (Oxford, U.K. & Cambridge, Mass.: Blackwell, 1992).

OTHER: *William Blake: The Complete Poems*, edited and annotated by Ostriker (Harmondsworth, U.K. & New York: Penguin, 1977).

Alicia Ostriker (photograph by Jeremiah P. Ostriker)

Like several women poets in her generation, including Sandra Gilbert, Adrienne Rich, Audre Lorde, and Alice Walker, Alicia Ostriker also writes as a literary critic. Clear and lyrical, her poetry combines intelligence and passion. Speaking in the tradition of Walt Whitman, she re-creates the American experience in each of her volumes. Her voice is personal, honest, and strong; her poetry incorporates family experiences, social and political views, and a driving spirit that speaks for growth and, at times, with rage.

Ostriker's urban background contributes to the forcefulness of her work. Born in Brooklyn on 11 November 1937, she was a "Depression baby" and grew up in Manhattan housing projects. Her parents, David and Beatrice Linnick Suskin, both earned degrees in English from Brooklyn College. Her father worked for the New York City Department of Parks; her mother, who wrote poetry and read William Shakespeare and Robert Browning to her daughter, tutored students in English and math and later became a folk-dance teacher. Alicia began writing poetry in childhood and enjoyed drawing as well. Her earliest hope was to be an artist: she studied art as a teenager and young adult and continues to carry a sketchbook on her travels. Two of her books—*Songs* (1969) and *A Dream of Springtime* (1979)—feature her graphics in the cover designs.

Ostriker received her B.A. in English from Brandeis University in 1959, and her M.A. and Ph.D. from the University of Wisconsin (1961, 1964). Her dissertation, on William Blake, became her first critical book, *Vision and Verse in William Blake* (1965); she later edited and annotated Blake's complete poems for Penguin (1977). Blake has continued to influence Ostriker as a person and poet. Ostriker began teaching at Rutgers University in 1965 and now holds the rank of full professor.

Much of the work in her first collection, *Songs*, was written during her student years. The voice is relatively formal, reflecting the influences of John Keats, Gerard Manley Hopkins, and W. H. Auden, as well as Whitman and Blake. Imagist and free-verse poems mingle somewhat tentatively with traditional, metrical poetry.

In Ostriker's second and third volumes of poetry—the chapbook *Once More Out of Darkness* (1971) and *A Dream of Springtime*—a more personal voice emerges, which captures the mind of the reader more readily. For these books, Ostriker composed consistently in free verse. The title poem of *Once More Out of Darkness* is a meditation on pregnancy and childbirth. *A Dream of Springtime* begins with a sequence of autobiographical poems designed to enable her to exorcise her childhood and become "freed from it." The organization of the book moves concentrically from the self, to the family, to teaching experiences, to the larger world of politics and history. Reviewer Valerie Trueblood calls Ostriker "one of the most intelligent and lyrical of American poets," who has given herself the "difficult assignment" of creating "an intellectually bearable picture of domestic security" while at the same time assigning herself "the equally ticklish (for poetry) job of publicizing national folly and soft spots of the culture" (*Iowa Review*, Spring 1982).

By the end of the book Ostriker emerges from the confined walls of her past and finds herself in the spring of her life. The title poem "A Dream of Springtime" reflects her movement into spring and its cold, watery vigor that wakes her senses: "The creek, swollen and excited from the melting / Freshets that are trickling into it everywhere / Like a beautiful woman unafraid is dashing / Over the stones." Nonetheless, Ostriker calls her attempt to reconcile herself to her childhood only "partially successful" but an important step in her development as a poet.

Not until *The Mother/Child Papers* (1980) did Ostriker fully reach her medium. In this book she contrasts the events of her own life with the Vietnam War. The book begins after the birth of her son, Gabriel, in 1970, but also focuses on the other members of her family: her husband, Jeremiah P. Ostriker, an astrophysicist, to whom she was married in December 1958; and her daughters, Rebecca and Eve, born in 1963 and 1965. Mary Kinzie in the *American Poetry Review* commends Ostriker on how her "work details the achievement of a connection between personal history and public fact" (July/August 1981). James McGowan in the *Hiram Poetry Review* (Fall/Winter 1982) calls the book "a product of a whole person, which is not to say a perfect person, but one alive to present, past, future, to the body and its mystifying requirements and capacities." Confronting her roles as mother, wife, and professor, Ostriker explores her identity as a woman. As she points out in the essay "A Wild Surmise: Motherhood and Poetry" in her book *Writing Like a Woman* (1983), "the advantage of motherhood for a woman artist is that it puts her in immediate and inescapable contact with the sources of life, death, beauty, growth and corruption."

The Mother/Child Papers was a ten-year project. At its inception, Ostriker had only a vague idea of what she wanted to accomplish; she struggled intermittently with it while teaching and raising her family. The offer of the Los Angeles poet and editor of Momentum Press, Bill Mohr, to publish the manuscript if she could finish it, enabled her to define its ultimate shape. The book is experimental, divided into four sections, all of which build on the artist's experience as mother.

The first section, written in prose, juxtaposes the impact of the Cambodian invasion and the shooting of student protestors at Kent State University with the birth of Ostriker's son in the sterile environment of an American hospital, where, during labor, she was given an unwanted spinal injection that deprived her of the ability to "give birth to my child, myself." Ostriker recreates the personal world of mother and infant in section 2, alternating their voices and molding them together in their own private sphere, separate from the rest of the world yet vulnerable to its incursions: "We open all the windows / the sunlight wraps us like gauze."

Part 3 of *The Mother/Child Papers* consists of a series of poems, written over a ten-year span, that captures the environment of the family and confronts the issue of "devouring Time, an enemy familiar to all mothers" (*Writing Like a Woman*). In "The Spaces" time is stressed, and the chaos of the outside world seems to threaten the secure nucleus of the family. The speaker overhears her husband discussing "the mass of the universe" and the possibility that it might "implode . . . back to the original fireball" it once was. As this discussion continues, her mind closes in on her own universe and her family's private world: "Gabriel runs upstairs. Rebecca is reading. Eve takes the hat back, . . . / Outside my window, the whole street dark and snowy."

Ostriker ties the work together in part 4 by stressing the connection between motherhood and art. In the final poem of the book, she recreates the experience of a woman in labor who enjoys her pain and is "comfortable" as she "rides with this work / for hours, for days / for the duration of this / dream." The mother is seen as the source of life's energy and of the universe beginning its never-ending process.

Ostriker continues to confront her role as a woman in her next collection of poems, *A Woman Under the Surface* (1982). X. J. Kennedy commended her "wit, verve and energy" (*Poetry*, March 1983). Lynda Koolish called the book "Cool, cerebral, studied. Passionate visceral, immediate . . . cold and fiery at the same time . . . the central metaphor of *A Woman Under the Surface* is a surfacing, emerging woman" (*San Francisco Chronicle*, 6 September 1983).

Written while Ostriker was working on her critical book *Writing Like a Woman*, this 1982 collection clearly reflects the world of women's poetry and Ostriker's indebtedness to it. The first poem, "The Waiting Room," suggests the bond of fear many women share: "We think of our breasts and cervixes. / We glance, shading our eyelids, at each other." Ostriker imagines a female ritual: "Perhaps we should sit on the floor. / They might have music for us. A woman dancer / Might perform, in the center of the circle." But the ritual is not pleasant: "What would she do? / Would she pretend to rip the breasts from her body?" Even this vision of unity is punctured as a woman's scream permeates the room from inside the office; the scream suggests the need these women have to express themselves and the satisfaction of a release that is sometimes denied them.

In "The Exchange" a mysteriously powerful woman emerges from underwater to murder the speaker's children and husband. In "The Diver," on the other hand, as in Adrienne Rich's poem "Diving into the Wreck," the female diver's body "is saying a kind of prayer." Ostriker's diver feels safe: "Nobody laughs, under the surface. / No-

body says the diver is a fool." Losing her name yet finding her space and her identity, "she extends her arms and kicks her feet," escaped from "the heat" and confinement of a surface world. Other poems in this volume touch on art—as in the poems to Henri Matisse, Vincent van Gogh, and Claude Monet—and myth, as in Ostriker's rewritten versions of the stories of Eros and Psyche, Orpheus and Euridice, and Odysseus and Penelope.

Ostriker continues to speak in her feminist voice in *The Imaginary Lover* (1986) and goes one step further. In an anonymous review in *Publisher's Weekly*, her poetry was described as "a poetry of commitment, not so much to womankind as to humankind. . . . When the voice of this rational, scholarly woman rises to crescendo, a tide of sweet human emotion lifts the poem into the realm of true experience with Keatsian intensity" (24 October 1984).

Written while Ostriker was researching her second feminist book of criticism, *Stealing the Language: the Emergence of Women Poets in America* (1986), the collection reflects the influences of Rich and H. D. In *The Imaginary Lover* Ostriker confronts the fantasies, both beautiful and horrible, that accompany womanhood. A long poem, "The War of Men and Women" explores the difficulty of male-female relations as "an archeology of pain." Several poems look at mother-daughter relationships from the perspective of the mother and that of the daughter; several are portraits of marriage. In the final poem of this book, Ostriker creates a woman's imaginary lover. Like the lovers in H. D.'s poetry, he is androgynous: "Oh imaginary lover, oh father-mother." He is not, however, the speaker's male counterpart, but rather the "form in the mind / On whom, as on a screen, I project designs." It is through this projected perception that the speaker becomes "the flock of puffy doves / . . . in a magician's hat" capable of the liberty of flight.

Green Age (1989) is Ostriker's most visionary and most successful collection. As Gail Mazur wrote in *Poetry*, "The poems are expressions of the hungry search for her real and spiritual place in the world. . . . A tough empathy informs the poems—she is no softer on others than she is on herself" (July 1990).

The three sections of the book confront personal time, history and politics, and inner spirituality. The speaker's voice in many of these poems is full of an anger that requires healing transformation. The energy for survival is reflected through the female character of "A Young Woman, a Tree," who has withstood her harsh surroundings and has developed a "Mutant appetite for pollutants." She is that city tree that can "feel its thousand orgasms each spring" and "stretch its limbs during the windy days." This woman takes a hungry bite of the world and experiences its pleasures, despite the pain of encroaching time. Another theme is the need for feminist spirituality in the face of traditional religion. Ostriker suffers in her Jewish heritage, for as a woman she is both the "vessel" of religious lineage and deprived of spiritual participation in male-dominated Jewish ritual and intellectual life. "A Meditation in Seven Days" considers and challenges the roles of women and femaleness within Judaism, concluding with a vision of potential change: "Fearful, I see my hand is on the latch / I am the woman, and about to enter." The final poem of *Green Age*, "Move," captures the mood of Ostriker's continuing quest for identity as woman and poet:

> When we reach the place we'll know
>
> We are in the right spot, somehow, like a breath
> Entering a singer's chest, that shapes itself
> For the song that is to follow.

The poetry of Alicia Ostriker consistently challenges limitations. For discovery to take place there must be movement, and Ostriker refuses to stand still; each volume tries to uncover anew what must be learned in order to gain wisdom, experience, and identity. She is a poet who breaks down walls.

Molly Peacock

(30 June 1947 -   )

Annette Allen
Salem College, Winston-Salem, North Carolina

BOOKS: *And Live Apart* (Columbia & London: University of Missouri Press, 1980);
Raw Heaven (New York: Vintage/Random House, 1984);
Take Heart (New York: Vintage/Random House, 1989).

SELECTED PERIODICAL PUBLICATION—
UNCOLLECTED: "What the Mockingbird Said," *Poetry East*, 20-21 (Fall 1986).

Molly Peacock's vital and intimate poetry stakes its imaginative reach on what she calls "the drive for what is real, deeper than the brain's detail: the drive to feel" ("Desire," *Raw Heaven*, 1984). In three volumes where the play of predictability and surprise provide a framework for sensuous details, Peacock's skillful wielding of form ensures a continuous dialectic between the inner world of memory and feeling and the external world. She accomplishes this dynamic, the balance between inner and outer worlds, by employing sound patterns that keep the poem close to unconscious rhythms and by using images or metaphors from the civilized and the natural worlds. Her work is both a play of form and a form of play. The lyrics, often couched in traditional forms such as the sonnet, set up expectations while the conversational tone, the rhetorical gestures of the language, and the verbal wit in the rhyming are set against the dark streak in her vision, compounded with the prevailing themes of family, pain, loneliness, and loss of order or control.

In her choice of the sonnet and other closed forms, Peacock was influenced by William Wordsworth, who compared a poet's formal constraints to a nun's containment: "Nuns fret not at their convent's narrow room." Because Peacock's childhood in an alcoholic household was chaotic and disturbing, she, like the nuns, sought order and restraint. But her search for order is challenging, as her article "What the Mockingbird Said" reveals: "Somehow, if I order *the expression*, I shall find order in the world it expresses. I shall find the pattern and from the pattern, I will be able to discover meaning." Her discussion resembles a primary belief of Virginia Woolf, who also saw a pattern of connectedness in all things, a theme that Peacock's poetry conveys. Discovering hidden aspects of life and poetry through engagement with pattern and its play has enabled Peacock to pursue painful memories, the raw world, and the task of re-creating the self in the texture of language, in words that made experience whole.

Born on 30 June 1947 in Buffalo, Molly Peacock grew up in an Anglo-Irish working-class family as the firstborn, a circumstance that contributed to opposite impulses in her early development: the need to be responsible and the desire for freedom. The home created by a solitary, teetotaling Baptist mother (Pauline Wright Peacock) and a wild, charming, often drunk father (Edward Frank Peacock) had its hazards. The alcoholism of her father and the consequent depression in her mother lent psychological chaos to daily activity and pushed Molly into assuming responsibility for the household and her younger sister. Imperiled family life is a thread running through Peacock's poetry. Only in the summers, when she lived with her grandmother in the country, did she find escape from the constant state of mortification her father created. Not only did these stays in the country provide her with a haven but they offered her structure—in the local Bible schools with their predictability, order, and verses. It was to this same grandmother she sent her first piece of writing, a letter penciled at four years old, and later she sent her beginning poems.

In her first poems, written under the direction of Milton Kessler in her undergraduate years at the State University of New York at Binghamton, Peacock discovered that in writing about her chaotic family she could create order. The architecture of the poem embraced and structured the content. In 1975, when she was a fellow at Mac-

Molly Peacock (photograph by Raymond Kopoho)

Dowell Colony and later a graduate student at Johns Hopkins, forms became intrinsic to the expression of feeling in her poetry.

After graduation from the State University of New York at Binghamton (B.A., 1969) and prior to becoming a Danforth fellow at Johns Hopkins, where she earned her M.A. with honors in 1977, Peacock worked as an administrator of several programs, coordinating for three years the New York State Poets-in-the-Schools program in Binghamton. At Johns Hopkins she studied with Cynthia MacDonald and later with Richard Howard, who made two important suggestions: that she think about what she was going to do when her emotion failed her in the writing of poems and that she begin to count syllables. Writing with the syllable count in mind ultimately enabled Peacock to take imaginative leaps in order to get to the end of the line and to set up in her poetry the characteristic tension between order and freedom. Peacock was able to generate and write a poem in her mind long before it moved to the page. Often she would ask herself what she would do if she were thrown in prison and deprived of any paper and pen for expression. How would she write her poem? She concluded that it was necessary for the poem's survival, just

as it had been necessary in childhood for her own survival when so much was taken away, to place everything in order in her mind so it might be preserved.

After two years as the writer in residence for the Delaware State Council on the Arts, in 1980 Peacock moved to New York City, where she taught at Hofstra University, Columbia University, the 92nd St. Y. Poetry Center, and Friends Seminary. She has received two fellowships from the Ingram Merrill Foundation and two grants from the New York Foundation for the Arts, and has been a resident at Yaddo, the MacDowell Colony, and the Virginia Center for the Arts. She has also served as president of the Poetry Society of America.

Peacock's first volume, *And Live Apart* (1980), announces a major theme in its epigraph from George Herbert: "Surely if each one saw another's heart, / There would be no commerce, / No sale or bargain passe; all would disperse, / And live apart." Many of Peacock's poems voice a desire to connect, to see "another's heart" and the fear of doing so, with the implied consequences that "all would disperse." This theme and others are braided together in narrative thrusts that demonstrate Peacock's formal interest. She says of the poems in her first collection that she did not know what she was feeling when she was writing, but technique gave her an entrance to her emotions and a way to express them with clarity. Using some rhyme and verse forms such as the villanelle, Peacock structures her struggle to become a recognizable self in poems that are skillful but sometimes too long. *And Live Apart* collects poems beginning with a very early one, "At the Memorial Park," and reveals a poet ordering her perceptions and grounding emotional experiences in her craft.

What makes *Raw Heaven* more successful is the unity that was not apparent in her first book. The poems in *Raw Heaven*, written over a two-and-a-half-year period, move like a symphony of interlocking sounds, connected largely by the sonnet form and by raw, sensual imagery. Full of energy and daring, the fifty-two poems transform childhood trauma, loneliness, pain, and desire through inventive rhyme and technical brilliance. The originality that blossoms so fully in this collection rests in Peacock's desire to follow Georgia O'Keefe's method in her flower paintings, to paint what was in her own head. Peacock combines this method with the form and impulse of the Romantic predecessors she admires, particularly John Keats, and the combination is startling, as in her poem "Desire":

> Like a paw
> it is blunt; like a pet who knows you
> and nudges your knee with its snout—but
>   more raw
> and blinder and younger and more divine, too,
> than the tamed wild—it's the drive for
>   what is real,
> deeper than the brain's detail: the drive to feel.

The heaven in Peacock's poetry is raw, untamed, the natural world of flesh and animals. In many of her poems, she develops an extended sensual image and uses it as a lens to reveal an emotional state or an aspect of the human condition. In "Cutting Tall Grass," for example, the imagery draws the reader close to the imaginative margin between death and new life: "the old grass spewn in the bleak shadows, / the new grass smelling of wet and slight rot, / to love to live between what is and is not." Peter Stitt has compared Peacock's method of revealing an inner state through the description of the outside world to T. S. Eliot's objective correlative (*Georgia Review*, 1984). The technique also resembles the approach of the metaphysical poets in its emo-

tional intensity. In Peacock's "Old Roadside Resorts" meaning unfolds through the imagery of chartreuse mountains. The tangle and veil of history and pain in a relationship is likened to the lush "veils of green washing over the mountain spines." The opening line provokes readers to enter and understand the poem: "Summer is a chartreuse hell in the mountains / green after green after green, the wet smell / of possibility in everything."

The imagery of smell and touch also permeates Peacock's poems that disclose a distinctly female sexual realm, the poem "Smell" taking menstruation as its focus: "The smoky smell of menses—Ma always / left the bathroom door open—smote the hall." "She Lays" is a candid poem about masturbation:

> This is self-love, assured, and this is lost time.
> This is knowing, knowing, known
> since growing, growing, grown;
> revelation without astonishment,
> understanding what is meant.
> This is world-love. This is lost I'm.

In a 1988 personal interview Peacock indicated the necessity of form as an underpinning, as a way of imposing limits, in order to be liberated in a poem with such highly charged emotional content.

Peacock's poetics, where form is handmaiden to the imagination, provide a mode of discovery that often shocks the reader with recognition. Another sonnet, "The Lull," begins with this line: "The possum lay on the tracks fully dead." Then the poem builds through images of the dead animal, the "healthy, hairless tail," "head smashed," "the corpse, the flies," to the last pulsing lines and the central insight that people are also animals:

> "That's disgusting." You said that. Dreams,
>   brains, fur
> and guts: what we are. That's my bargain, the Pax
> Peacock, with the world. Look hard, life's soft.
>   Life's cache
> is flesh, flesh, and flesh.

Peacock cherishes the fact of flesh and realizes that it connects people to other life forms. In several poems flesh becomes the repository of the past and of grief. This theme emerges in "There's No Earthly Reason," a double sonnet that explores bodily gestures and emotions of parents: "we tie about / our bodies their lovely or

Dust jacket for Peacock's 1989 book, in which she explores the notion of choice

The theme of freedom surfaces again, but it is devastation that lends emotional power to the book. The first poem, "How I Come to You," written in tightly wrought four-line stanzas, similar in form and spirit to some of William Blake's poetry, compares a broken rock to a smashed self and ends with lines that meet, according to Harold Bloom, the true test of poetry—memorability:

> I smashed myself
> and found my heart
> a cave ready to be
> lived in. A start,

> veined, unmined.
> This is how I come to you:
> broken,
> not what I knew.

Early in the volume, using the apt metaphor of "Blank Paper," Peacock writes out in rhyming, enjambed lines the struggle to reconstruct the disinherited self, supplying an analogue for her own life: "For him to give / me my life long ago was what I needed / thus what I write both re-blankens my life / and fills it in with a right to live."

This re-creation of the self, regardless of the unknown future, forms the physical and metaphorical bedrock in two other poems. Rhymed couplets echo through "The Valley of the Monsters," a place where rocks are shaped like members of her chaotic family. The careful control imposed by the repeated rhymes fosters the raising of unconscious, difficult material into art, a process to which Peacock lays claim: "Thus it is healthy / to speak, even in rhymes, about where we see / we're going, even if we haven't been there to find / our answer yet." A similar self-revelation occurs under the shade of a rock temple in "A Hot Day in Agrigento," though the formal structure plays off the unusual narrative while sustaining a conversational tone: "where else could you get / relief with no toilets?"

In *Take Heart* Peacock's range and control in the female world she creates, with all its embracing and bracing dilemmas, are impressive. Two poems, "Merely by Wilderness" and "Dilation, Termination, and Curettage," taken together, tell the story of an abortion. Peacock conveys the complex, private emotions of the situation. After setting up expectations of rhyme in the previous

ugly trappings. / These are our parents' unwrappings, / still warm and still smelling of another's body." In "Those Paperweights with the Snow Inside" Peacock details disturbing scenes from the past and concludes that one cannot escape past sorrow: "Not to carry / all this in the body's frame is not to see / how the heart and arms were formed on its behalf."

An individual moment or idea serves as the matrix for many of the poems in *Raw Heaven*, but in her third collection, *Take Heart* (1989), Peacock returns to the narrative thread begun in *And Live Apart*. Though the poems in *Take Heart* are plain at times, the central questions of the book—What is important? How shall one live? Given what happens, what are the choices?—draw the reader in. The emotional jeopardy that Peacock faced with the death of her father was not unlike that of other women writers of the past, and it is this feeling of fundamental loss and newfound freedom that accounts for the new direction in her poetry.

lines, Peacock stuns readers with absence of rhyme at the end:

> I can't do this alone, yet I am so alone
> no one, not even this child inside me, even
> the me I was, can feel the wild cold buzz
> that presses me into this place, bleakness
> that will break me, except I cannot be
> broken merely by wilderness, I can only
> be lost.

The joys and failures of flesh and the senses still prevail as themes in *Take Heart*, but there is a spiritualization and a deeper connection of the senses with all things, as in the works of Dylan Thomas. The titles of some of Peacock's poems demonstrate this religious impulse: "ChrisEaster," "The Smell of a God," and "Prayer," which she ends by stating, "flesh is still the church." The impulse is strongly tied to Peacock's notion of choice, which imposes limitation yet opens up possibility, just as form does in her writing. She can surprise with a statement that she *chose* to be happy after making the bed one day when she was thirty-two, but her life and her poetry bear her out. "Altruism" ends with a proclamation of choice: "Love became a decision." Choosing rhymes, stressed syllables, the number of lines in a stanza, and choosing how *to be* in the world are all ways of seeking limits or discovering patterns. They tap, according to Peacock, "an interior impulse," giving "rise to invention, like a channel to a god within."

Some critics have commented on Molly Peacock's dependency on form, particularly the sonnet, suggesting it limits her range and leads to repetition. However, with *Take Heart* she answers this criticism by broadening the scope and varying the forms. Caressing the physical world with subtle verbal magic, as her poetry does, obviously wins readers: the first edition sold out within a month of publication. The intelligence and music of her work, the belief in exploring consciousness with honesty, the sheer beauty of the language—all contribute to the "pleasure of the text." Because all the pain and joy of living are in her poetry, people will continue to turn to her poems.

Marge Piercy

(31 March 1936 -   )

Felicia Mitchell
Emory and Henry College

BOOKS: *Breaking Camp* (Middletown, Conn.: Wesleyan University Press, 1968);

Hard Loving (Middletown, Conn.: Wesleyan University Press, 1969);

Going Down Fast (New York: Trident, 1969);

Dance the Eagle to Sleep (Garden City, N.Y.: Doubleday, 1970; London: Allen, 1971);

4-Telling, by Piercy, Bob Herson, Emmet Jarrett, and Dick Lourie (Trumansburg, N.Y.: New Books/Crossing, 1971);

To Be of Use (Garden City, N.Y.: Doubleday, 1973);

Small Changes (Garden City, N.Y.: Doubleday, 1973);

Woman on the Edge of Time (New York: Knopf, 1976; London: Women's Press, 1979);

Living in the Open (New York: Knopf, 1976);

The Twelve-Spoked Wheel Flashing (New York: Knopf, 1978);

The High Cost of Living (New York: Harper & Row, 1978; London: Women's Press, 1979);

Vida (New York: Summit, 1979 [i.e., 1980]; London: Women's Press, 1980);

The Last White Class: A Play About Neighborhood Terror, by Piercy and Ira Wood (Trumansburg, N.Y.: Crossings, 1980);

The Moon Is Always Female (New York: Knopf, 1980);

Circles on the Water: Selected Poems (New York: Knopf, 1982);

Braided Lives (New York: Summit, 1982; London: Lane, 1982);

Parti-colored Blocks for a Quilt (Ann Arbor: University of Michigan Press, 1982);

Stone, Paper, Knife (New York: Knopf, 1983; London: Pandora, 1983);

Fly Away Home (New York: Summit, 1984; London: Chatto & Windus, 1984);

My Mother's Body (New York: Knopf, 1985);

Gone to Soldiers (New York: Summit, 1987);

Available Light (New York: Knopf, 1988);

Summer People (New York: Summit, 1989);

Marge Piercy with her cat (photograph copyright 1984 by Thomas Victor)

The Earth Shines Secretly: A Book of Days (Cambridge, Mass.: Zoland, 1990);

He, She, & It (New York: Knopf, 1991);

Mars and Her Children (New York: Knopf, 1992).

RECORDINGS: *Marge Piercy: Poems*, New York, Radio Free People, 1969;

"Laying Down the Tower," in *Black Box 1*, New York, Radio Free People, 1972;

Reclaiming Ourselves, by Piercy, the Painted Women's Ritual Theater, and Jeriann Hilderly, New York, Radio Free People, 1974;

Reading and Thoughts, Deland, Fla., Everett/Edwards, 1976;

At the Core, Washington, D.C., Watershed Tapes, 1976.

OTHER: "Mirror Images," in *Women's Culture: The Women's Renaissance of the Seventies*, edited by Gayle Kimball (Metuchen, N.J. & London: Scarecrow, 1980), pp. 187-194;

"Starting Support Groups for Writers," in *Words in Our Pockets: The Feminist Writers Guild Handbook*, edited by Celeste West (San Francisco: Bootlegger, 1981);

Ellen Messer and Kathryn E. May, *Back Rooms: Voices from the Illegal Abortion Era*, foreword by Piercy (New York: St. Martin's Press, 1988), pp. xi-xiii;

Early Ripening: American Women's Poetry Now, edited by Piercy (New York: Unwin Hyman, 1988);

"Active in Time and History," in *Paths of Resistance: The Art and Craft of the Political Novel*, edited by William Zinsser (New York: Houghton Mifflin, 1989), pp. 89-123;

"Simone de Beauvoir," in *Daughters of De Beauvoir*, edited by Penny Forster and Imogen Sutten (London: Women's Press, 1989), pp. 112-123;

"The Dark Thread in the Weave," in *Testimony: Contemporary Writers Make the Holocaust Personal*, edited by David Rosenberg (New York: Random House, 1989), pp. 171-191.

SELECTED PERIODICAL PUBLICATIONS—
UNCOLLECTED: "Through the Cracks: Growing Up in the Fifties," *Partisan Review*, 41 (July 1974): 202-216;

"Inviting the Muse," *Negative Capability*, 2 (Winter 1981): 5-15;

"On Being a Jewish Feminist," *Women's Review of Books*, 1, no. 5 (1984): 5-6;

"The Turn-on of Intimacy," *Ms.*, 12 (February 1984): 46-68;

"Poets on Poetry," *Literary Cavalcade*, 37 (October 1984): 24-25;

"What I Do When I Write," *Women's Review of Books*, 6 (July 1989): 25-26;

"What Are We Leaving the Children?," *Woman's Day*, 52 (24 October 1989): 57-58;

Autobiographical essay, *Cream City Review*, 15 (Spring 1990): 3-5.

Marge Piercy epitomizes a feminist maxim: "The personal is political." In the essay "Mirror Images" (1980) Piercy writes, "My poetry appears to me at once more personal and universal than my fiction. My poetry is of a continuity with itself and with the work of other women." Just as her novels have been acclaimed and have received widespread critical attention for their realism or utopian vision, her poetry has gained a place in contemporary literature for its strikingly fresh images, powerful language, and evocation of social and sexual feelings. Although Piercy is usually cited as a major representative of a revolution in literature that has grown out of and fed the feminist movement, she has also gained a strong reputation as a nature poet, urban spokesperson, and Jewish mystic.

The daughter of Robert and Bert Bedonya Bunnin Piercy, Marge Piercy was born on 31 March 1936 in Detroit and grew up in a working-class environment. Her roots are Jewish and Welsh. Piercy has written much about the significance of her Jewish roots, and her work is that of someone familiar with an intrinsically rich poetic tradition. The first person in her family to attend college, she was awarded a scholarship and received her A.B. in 1957 from the University of Michigan, where she won Hopwood Awards for poetry and fiction. She earned her M.A. from Northwestern University in 1958. Piercy received the Carolyn Kizer Poetry Prize in 1986 and 1990, the Golden Rose Poetry Prize in 1990, and the May Sarton Award in 1991. Other awards include a literature award from the Governor's Commission on the Status of Women (Massachusetts), two Borestone Mountain Poetry Awards, the Orion Scott Award in the Humanities, and a National Endowment for the Arts award in 1978. On 2 June 1982 she married the author Ira Wood, her third husband, with whom she makes her home in Wellfleet, Massachusetts.

Piercy's poetry collections show her idiosyncratic style, mature from the beginning of her publishing career, and the evolution of an original, strong voice. Because of the personal content, some readers might see the poems as autobiographical. They are, however, only autobiographical in the sense that Piercy takes incidents from her life and other lives that she observes, then infuses her personal voice. Topics range from politics to the garden, but for Piercy it is all one vision. For critic Victor Contoski, it may be a "stubborn utopian vision," but for other critics, such as Margaret Atwood, it is a conscientious vision. In response to critical remarks about her politics, Piercy commented in an interview with Richard Jackson, "Art which contains ideas which threaten the position of the ruling class is silenced by critics: it is political, they say, and not art." By publishing and publicly reading her work, Piercy has confronted that attempt at silencing.

Stylistically, Piercy writes all kinds of poems; the voice unifies them. Many see Piercy's literary ancestor as Walt Whitman, while others cite poets such as Muriel Rukeyser. Piercy herself, looking at the interrelation of her message and medium, has stated that her poems are in the company of other socially conscious poets, including Whitman, John Dryden, William Wordsworth, Percy Bysshe Shelley, and Johann Wolfgang von Goethe.

Breaking Camp (1968), her first collection, illustrates what critic Edith Wynn has observed as a major convention in Piercy's poems in general: dramatic narratives with contemplative observations link past, present, and future. The title poem, for example, begins with an image of "forsythia against wet brick" and moves to thoughts about love and commerce:

I will not abandon you. I come shuddering
from the warm tangles of winter sleep
choosing you compulsively, repetitiously, dumb as
    breath.
You will never subside into rest. But how
can we build a city of love on a garbage dump?

For Piercy, it is all connected. Her poems show how people cannot separate love from where they live, or happiness from awareness.

The earlier poems also introduce Piercy's ability to juxtapose political rhetoric with imaginative language, to personify buildings and institutions, to draw on the animal—especially the cat—world for images, to fashion worthwhile comparisons, and to criticize. While Contoski has observed that Piercy exhibits "a rather strange mixture of styles," her type of writing is representative of poets who are breaking rules about how poetry should be crafted. The experiences about which she writes in *Hard Loving* (1969) also show her connecting something as ordinary as a noisy upstairs neighbor with a childlike fantasy spun in the dark (in "The Neighbor"). "Learning Experience" depicts a college boy compelled to learn

about dangling participles; he is bored by that but less eager to "fail his license to live" and be drafted.

To Be of Use (1973), according to reviewer Marie Harris, reads like a manual on why and how to confront certain social issues. Harris, however, does not make the mistake of likening the poetry to polemics, though she does admit that "if what she [Piercy] writes about isn't important to the reader, she'll be called rhetorical" (*Parnassus*, 1974). The poem "The Best Defense Is Offensive" playfully addresses her role with an analogy based on the turkey vulture, which has an innate mechanism to ward off enemies when they attack: vomit. Piercy writes,

Sometimes only the stark
will to disgust
prevents our being consumed:
there are clearly times
when we must make a stink
to survive.

While some readers have found it easy to focus on the "will to disgust" and neglect some of Piercy's other tactics and voices, she does write of other realms.

Jean Rosenbaum remarked in *Modern Poetry Studies* (Winter 1977) that "Piercy strikes out at the attitudes, institutions, and structures which impede natural growth and development and thus destroy wholeness; she also celebrates the moments when life is consummate and joyful." Sometimes she does both simultaneously, as in "Homesick" in *Living in the Open* (1976). Starting with a celebration of having a house to return to, she then twists the traditional meaning of *homesick* to mean a sickness of heart over the slaughter of whales and seals, over oil slicks, and over cranberry bogs ruined by dirt bikes. This poem represents Piercy's ability to criticize and celebrate simultaneously as she moves swiftly from the personal to the political. This ability is what separates her poems from the purely polemical. Eleanor Bender sees *Living in the Open* as marking "an important shift in the development of Piercy's poetry," as the book reflects "the spiritual and physical renewal made possible through feminism and her success at earning a living as a writer" ("Visions of a Better World," in *Ways of Knowing*, 1991).

After the publication of *The Twelve-Spoked Wheel Flashing* (1978) more critics began to express a deeper awareness of Piercy's plan as a poet and to accept her style. Bender says the

Dust jacket for Piercy's 1988 collection, which reveals her deep regard for and connection to nature

book is about "what it means to love and work together in day-to-day mature relationships." Charles Molesworth commented in the *New York Review of Books* (26 November 1978), "Politics, domestic tranquility and discord, supportive nature and nurturing art: all are plain-spokenly addressed with an almost casual sense of form." As the poem "Athena in the Front Lines" concludes:

> Making is an act, but survival
> is luck, caught in history
> like a moth trapped in the subway.
> There is nothing to do but make well,
> finish, and let go. Words
> live, words die
> in the mouths of everybody.

E. M. Broner's review of the collection points to Piercy's connection with other women through her writing: "She reviews our legends and ballads and sings them back at us with a different voice" (*New Women's Times Feminist Review*, November 1978).

The Moon Is Always Female (1980) moves from domestic life to prophetic visions as Piercy intertwines life cycles in the various poems. A complex work, it led Ron Schreiber (*American Book Review*, March-April 1982) to classify Piercy's contributions to American poetic style: "She is the American master of the simile," and "she repeats phrases until they become litanies, but the phrases are colloquial, grounded in American speech." "To Have Without Holding" is an example of an artful poem, rich with rhythm, images, analogies, paradox, personification, and metaphor. The poem is about the paradoxical "unbound bonding" found in new human relationships. The new way of loving, the poem suggests, is as natural as the heart pumping yet as painful as a rubber band thwacking on an open palm.

Structure and sequencing are important elements in Piercy's collections, which she usually compiles just after she has finished a novel. She has commented on how she compiles books in several interviews and in her introduction to *Circles on the Water: Selected Poems* (1982): "Each book is an artifact and the poems in it are placed in a particular order to work as a whole as well as individually." Subtitles help to reinforce that order. Consequently in *Circles in the Water* the integrity is maintained even as poems are presented as excerpts from specific collections. This publication of more than 150 poems led to even more critical attention, and in 1985 Edith Wynn published a significant critical analysis tying Piercy's poems to the metaphysical: "Piercy's collected poems contain a startling array of images which, in their variety and number, in their apparently haphazard distribution, in their wide-ranging sensuousness, and in their seemingly antithetical juxtaposition of thought and feeling, create that kind of *discordia concors* so often associated with the metaphysical tradition."

Stone, Paper, Knife (1983) continued to exemplify Piercy's commitment to writing about how women have suffered, about love, about identity with nature, and about the problems of survival in modern times. Readers see again how feminism cannot be separated from ecological awareness, personal relationships, or even one's sense of humor. According to Jeanne Lebow, the book "marks Piercy's full evolution into a doer, a user of tools, a woman who has created her own vision of the world on paper" ("Bearing Hope Back into the World," in *Ways of Knowing*). The poem "A Private Bestiary" connects love, politics, and nature and illustrates a peacefulness that comes from hope. The images are less competitive with one another, separate yet interrelated:

On your skin I read bestiaries
by braille. In our bed we curl, stones
sleeping in our mountainside, fossils
locked inside; we open scarlet fragrant
petal by petal from the gold stamened center;
lion meets lion while lamb greets lamb.

The metaphor of these lines, exemplary of the sensuality and sensuousness of Piercy's voice, connects the human more closely with the natural. The poem also contrasts with the structure of earlier poems such as "Breaking Camp," which uses the natural image as a point of departure rather than as deep structure or part of the self.

My Mother's Body (1985), perhaps to some a more introspective collection, did not receive as much critical attention as the other collections though it does contain Piercy's usual themes and powerful language. In this case, personal relationships are a focus: mother-daughter, father-daughter, and husband-wife. The section titled "The Chuppah," for example, contains poems from Piercy's wedding ceremony with Ira Wood, including poems by Wood. The reader is struck by the cohesiveness of Piercy's marriage and may intuitively sense a comparison in poems about her parents. Yet there is no self-congratulation or editorial commentary in those poems, only facts conveyed in poetic terms. For example, her father's separation from her mother, because of her mother's death, in "Does the Light Fail Us, or Do We Fail the Light?" contrasts with Piercy's celebration of love, and it also offers a poignant and pungent image of old age that reminds readers of how marriage can cripple:

You hid alone in your room fighting
with the cleaning woman who came
each week but didn't do it right,

then finally one midnight wandered out naked
finally to the world among rustling
palms demanding someone make you lunch.

The poems about her parents are remarkable in their synthesis of respect and disdain, which evokes a bitter love.

Available Light (1988) led Diane Wakokski to comment that Piercy is "one of the pioneers of twentieth-century earth poetry," who also uses biblical imagery and allusion to enhance her natural imagery (*Women's Review of Books*, July 1988). In the poem "The Garden as Synagogue" Piercy talks about oneness with the earth in response to the sorrow of vegetarians who see cows as more sacred than vegetables. This poem suggests that political movements such as vegetarianism are not part of Piercy's commitment. She connects her references to nature with the symbolic seder: "At the seder I eat the lamb, the egg, the bitter / herbs, the apples and almonds and I am healed / to the sprouting earth that bears them all in me."

There is a deep connection with nature in Piercy's later poetry, a reconciliation that may not have seemed possible in the earlier, angrier poems, which cite a schism between nature and humanity. From this connection comes a peacefulness that seems inevitable. The fact that Piercy's liturgical poems follow the Jewish mystical tradition for some readers and appeal to others on a different level affirms her appeal to an audience as diverse as her poems.

Interviews:

The Ordeal of the Woman Writer [recording: panel discussion with Toni Morrison and Erica Jong], New York, Norton, 1974;

"An Interview With Marge Piercy," *Kalliope*, 4 (Winter 1982): 37-45;

"Interview with Ira Wood and Marge Piercy," *Pulp*, 8, no. 1 (1982);

Richard Jackson, "Shaping Our Choices," in his *Acts of Mind: Conversations with Contemporary Poets* (University: University of Alabama Press, 1983);

Interview [recording], American Audio Prose Library, 1986;

Interview and Poetry Reading [recording], University of Missouri—Kansas City, New Letters on the Air, 1989;

Kathy Shorr, "Marge Piercy," *Provinceton Arts Magazine* (1990): 90;

Mickey Pearlman and Katherine Usher Henderson, *Inter/View: Talks With America's Writing Women* (Lexington: University Press of Kentucky, 1990), p. 65.

References:

Margaret Atwood, "An Unfashionable Sensibility," *Nation*, 223, no. 19 (1976): 601-602;

Victor Contoski, "Marge Piercy: A Vision of the Peaceable Kingdom," *Modern Poetry Studies*, 8 (Winter 1977): 205-216;

Judson Jerome, "Grabbing the Gusto," *Writer's Digest*, 61 (July 1981): 56, 58-59, 61;

June Jordan, "The Black Poet Speaks of Poetry," *American Poetry Review* (July/August 1974): 62-63;

Judson Mazzaro, "At the Start of the Eighties," *Hudson Review*, 33 (Autumn 1980): 445-468;

Felicia Mitchell, "Marge Piercy's *The Moon is Always Female*: Feminist Text/Great Books Context," *Virginia English Bulletin*, 40 (Fall 1990): 34-35;

Jean Rosenbaum, "You Are You Own Magician: A Vision of the Integrity in the Poetry of Marge Piercy," *Modern Poetry Studies*, 8 (Winter 1977): 198-205;

Sue Walker and Eugenie Hamner, eds., *Ways of Knowing: Essays on Marge Piercy* (Mobile, Ala.: Negative Capability Press, 1991);

Edith Wynn, "Imagery of Association in the Poetry of Marge Piercy," *Publications of the Missouri Philological Association*, 10 (1985): 57-73.

Papers:

The University of Michigan Harlan Hatcher Graduate Library holds a collection of Piercy's manuscripts.

Bin Ramke
(19 February 1947 -   )

Amber Ahlstrom
University of New Hampshire

BOOKS: *Any Brass Ring* (Athens: Ohio Review, 1977);

The Difference Between Night and Day (New Haven & London: Yale University Press, 1978);

White Monkeys (Athens: University of Georgia Press, 1981);

The Language Student (Baton Rouge: Louisiana State University Press, 1986);

The Erotic Light of Gardens (Middletown, Conn.: Wesleyan University Press, 1989).

SELECTED PERIODICAL PUBLICATIONS—
UNCOLLECTED: "Communications," *Wallace Stevens Journal*, 3, nos. 3-4 (1979): 133-135;

"Mattie Lou O'Kelley: American Folk Artist," by Ramke and Linda Ramke, *Georgia Review*, 33, no. 4 (1979): 806-816;

"Verse and Reverse," *Ohio Review*, 28 (1982): 19-24;

" 'And shape is constant in the moving blade': The Poetry of John Williams," *Denver Quarterly*, 20, no. 3 (1986): 118-122;

" 'The Line' in American Poetry," *Ohio Review*, 39 (1987): 11-16;

" 'Your words is English, is a different tree': On Derek Walcott," *Denver Quarterly*, 23, no. 2 (1988): 90-99;

"Elegy as Origin," *Denver Quarterly*, 23, nos. 3-4 (1989): 33-39.

Bin Ramke (photograph by Karen Keeney)

The poetry of Bin Ramke might best be described as *unsettling* because of its disturbing themes. Ramke's poems offer a vision of a world characterized by empty relationships, doubt, and disillusionment, but the vision is put in perspective by his humor and sheer joy in language. Ramke evokes many questions and provides small comfort. If an examination of his work is unsettling, however, it is also rewarding.

Lloyd Binford Ramke was born in Port Neches, Texas, on 19 February 1947. His parents, Lloyd Binford Ramke (an engineer) and Melba Guidry Ramke, were born in Abbeville, Louisiana, and the young Ramke grew up in a

strongly Cajun atmosphere. His mother spoke Cajun French, a language Ramke never learned but which attuned him to the politics of language. In his 1988 *Denver Quarterly* article on poet Derek Walcott, he writes, "We are victims of the history of the language we use, and the richer the history, the less porous the language is to our own current experience."

Ramke and his wife, the former Linda Keating (a teacher), were married on 31 May 1967. They have a son, Nicolas, born in 1979. Ramke received his B.A. from Louisiana State University in 1970 and his M.A. from the University of New Orleans in 1971. In 1975 he earned a Ph.D. from Ohio University.

The Difference Between Night and Day (1978), Ramke's first full-length book, was selected as the winner in the Yale Series of Younger Poets competition in 1977. The book contains thirty-seven free-verse poems which are generally brief and often narrative ("Summer 1956: Louisiana") or occasional ("To Bury a Horse in Texas" and "Anniversary Waltz"). The poems move from seemingly autobiographical reminiscences such as "The Feast of the Body of Christ in Texas" to the universal "you" in "Guilt and the Long Ride Home":

> You wish your bed were already
> warm, your pillow
> damp with the tears
> you know she will give you[.]

Richard Hugo writes in his introduction to the book that Ramke's poems "are so honestly rooted in isolation that they suggest a man with no way of reaching others except through his writing." The subject matter of the poems is so intensely personal that it is difficult to conceive that Ramke is *not* describing himself. Paul Breslin noted, "Whether out of reticence or out of esthetic conviction, he doesn't care to give us detailed autobiography. . . . And yet, he has trouble conceiving of any poetic subjects other than the self " (*Poetry*, May 1979). It is therefore tempting to assume that Ramke is revealing himself more than he is. In "Picnic on the Beach," for example, the father, melancholy at his daughter's growing up, could easily be Ramke—except that he has no daughter. The reader must be careful, then, not to make assumptions about the autobiographical aspects of the poetry.

Some of the poems are clearly characterizations, ranging from portraits of a stranger, to a fundamentalist, to an old woman dancing. Ramke has a deft touch and generous empathy, as in "Poems for a Tall, Sad Lady":

> In Vienna there is a small house with blue shutters
> under the evening shadow of a Lutheran church.
> In the house you may be served a dish
> named for a saint: *Gateau Saint-Honoré*.
> It is made of dozens of eggs, spun sugar,
> *pâte sucrée, crème chantilly*.
> Served with coffee, black.
> She was never in Vienna.
> Such sweet disappointments and hunger
> make her thin and round-eyed.

As Peter Stitt has written, "Ramke's characters, the things they do, are generally just a bit odd, offbeat, not quite grotesque but existing at the fringes of what is considered ordinary" (*Georgia Review*, Fall 1978).

The major theme of the book is emptiness. Dreams, stars, and women are ultimately unattainable. Relationships are unhappy and fraught with tension, regrets, and words unsaid. Disillusionment and betrayal are the outcomes of living. In "Entropy," which Hugo identified as a microcosm of the book, the narrator describes a town consumed by heat and fear:

> And we fear such things as great success
> or obvious failure. We know ourselves.
> Each house in our terrible town has a garden,
> a wall, and a secret. We breed garish flowers
> to tend with cruel care.
> We are small and all very much alike.

Despite occasional moments of humor or love, the vision in "Entropy" reflects the pervasive theme of the book: life is never as one dreamed it would be.

Critical reception of Ramke's work has always been mixed. *The Difference Between Night and Day* was described by Stitt as "one of the best first books produced by an American poet in many years." But Breslin stated bluntly, "it's hard to believe that this was the best manuscript submitted" for the Yale prize.

White Monkeys (1981) demonstrates greater versatility and a wider field of vision. The poems in the first section ask a variety of questions, as in "The Concert for Bangladesh":

> What *is* the burden? To give
> at the office? To weave a coat,
> motley as Joseph's, of guilt?
> To drive an old car?

And the title poem sets up a paradigm for understanding the rest of the book:

> But if we are asked what purpose the *history*
> *of a monstrous nature can serve*, we will answer:
> to pass from the prodigies of nature's *deviations*
> to the marvels of *art*.

Thus, the transformation of "deviations" into "art" is a major theme of the book. White monkeys and rare albino snakes are among the oddities Ramke remembers from his travels and transforms into art. Likewise, the narrative portraits that make up the second section of the book are more than adept recordings of quirky people and places. "Sex Therapy," for example, is a masterful series of modern situations with classical references, revolving around Odysseus's adventures. In the first poem of the series, a wife waits, watches television, and weaves garish pictures: "Some husband is always late / for something, or something grows cold / as dinner in any woman's life." The story of Polyphemus prompts this observation: "these cook in the domestic kitchen: jealousy, lust, / anger and dissension, violence of flesh against / progenitive flesh."

Other poems in the section follow a similar form. Each of the twelve stanzas of "Circus" offers a different view of circles, from hawks circling, to the mouths of children singing, to a snake eating eggs, "digesting one / entire generation."

"Rose Hill Shopping Center" offers a series of "southern grotesque" portraits. Estelle's Piano Studio, Bubba's Flowers and Gifts, Big Ed's Hair Stylist—these are the settings for disturbing portrayals, both peculiar and familiar, in the tradition of Flannery O'Connor and William Faulkner. The voices are resonant and include that of the "large lewd man" describing his daughter's birth:

> She lay in a kind of nest they made
>   on Lou's belly (slack
> And still disappointing) and stared
>   at me. We'd never get on
> With this start, I said to myself,
>   this is no way to begin.
> That night I kissed Lou, left
>   for home with a nurse who tore
>
> The bed to shreds—she knew her stuff—
>   and cried to think I did
> Such things, me a family man.
>   Get out while you can.

Of his southern background Ramke has said, "I never wanted to be a southerner, but the South was also a tremendous source of energy, particularly literary." His work transcends purely regional portraits. He captures the linguistic diversity and complexity of southern dialects, but his concern for language itself remains paramount— as a personal, regional, and reality-shaping force.

The poems in the third section of *White Monkeys* echo Ramke's 1978 book: men and women are isolated, and communication is rare, as shown in "Foreign Language" and "What We Learned to Do to Each Other." In "Widow" the husband/wife relationship is ominous:

> She was twelve years married
> to the hunter who at night
> paralyzed small game
> with a bright light
>
> and shot them as they stared,
> shot while the pupils shrank
> to a point of black.
>
> In her humming house at night
> she sleeps with a light burning.

Also evident in this final section is a return to the idea of escape. In *The Difference Between Night and Day* fantasy offers escape from the emptiness of life, a theme that surfaces again in "The Desire for a Mediterranean Sea" and "Travelogue."

Critical disagreement also surfaced again. Roger Mitchell wrote of the book, "I haven't read a more assured and promising book than *White Monkeys* in the past several years." Stitt, however, wrote that the book "does not quite live up to the promise—and achievement—of *The Difference Between Night and Day*." The critical pattern continued after *The Language Student* (1986) was published. *Publishers Weekly* noted, "His successes are limited, but his promise still holds," while Stitt called the volume Ramke's "finest book" (*Georgia Review*, Summer 1987).

The Language Student reflects his continuing growth as a poet and his deepening concern with language itself. The poems are longer and denser, but places, subjects, and characters are as varied as in his previous collections.

The book opens with a familiar theme, the futility of human life, and a familiar response:

> What can one do with a body
> that will die? Nothing
> in this wily world but spend
>
> lubricious nights like
> *eternity*—a lie, true;
> small comfort, but comfort.

The Language Student moves toward philosophy, most notably in "The Last Cajun," "Hope, Which Comes with Cool Weather," "Hospital Food," and "Another Small Town in Georgia." In "The Last Cajun" a man laments his empty existence: "who doesn't feel the cruelest / fate is to get what you pay for? It's a world / full of love, when what you want is pity."

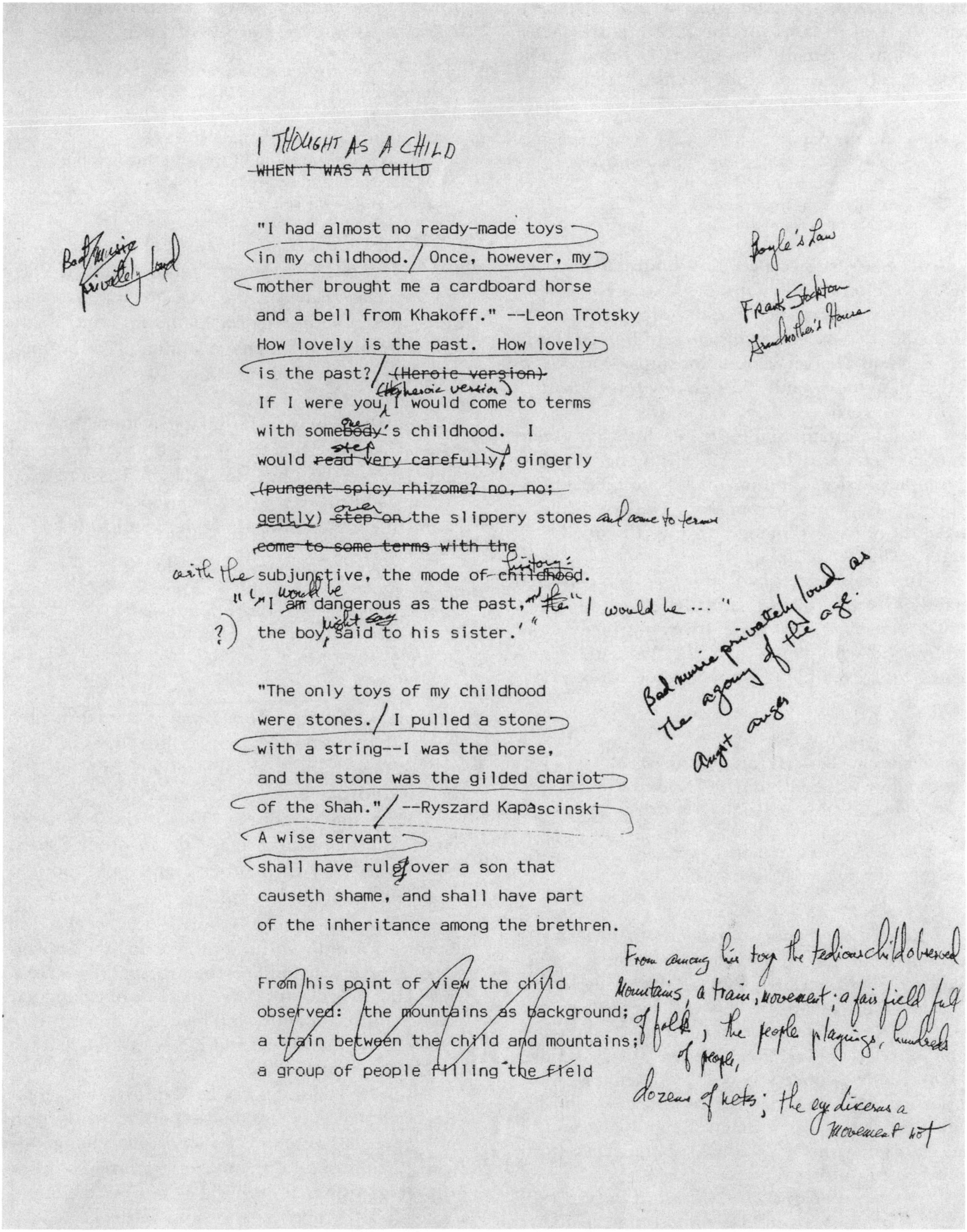

I THOUGHT AS A CHILD
~~WHEN I WAS A CHILD~~

Bad music privately loud

"I had almost no ready-made toys
in my childhood. / Once, however, my
mother brought me a cardboard horse
and a bell from Khakoff." --Leon Trotsky
How lovely is the past. How lovely
is the past? / ~~(Heroic version)~~
(the heroic version)
If I were you, I would come to terms
with some~~body~~*one*'s childhood. I
would ~~read~~ *step* very carefully, gingerly
~~(pungent spicy rhizome? no, no;~~
gently) *over* ~~step on~~ the slippery stones *and come to terms*
~~come to some terms with the~~
with the subjun*g*tive, the mode of ~~childhood.~~ *history:*
" '*I would be* ~~I am~~ dangerous as the past,' ~~then~~ ' I would be ... '
?) the boy, *might say* said to his sister.' "

Boyle's Law

Frank Stockton
Grandmother's House

*Bad music privately loud as
The agony of the age.*
angst anger

"The only toys of my childhood
were stones. / I pulled a stone
with a string--I was the horse,
and the stone was the gilded chariot
of the Shah." / --Ryszard Kapàscinski
A wise servant
shall have rule over a son that
causeth shame, and shall have part
of the inheritance among the brethren.

From his point of view the child
observed: the mountains as background;
a train between the child and mountains;
a group of people filling the field

*From among his toys the tedious child observed
Mountains, a train, movement; a fair field full
of folk, the people playings, hundreds
of people,
dozens of nets; the eye discerns a
movement not*

Page from a draft for a poem (by permission of Bin Ramke)

The realization that the present falls unexpectedly short of dreams for the future is the theme of "Another Small Town in Georgia." The speaker refuses to succumb to misery, though:

> Note how the dandelion's glory is a halo, a sphere
> of seed surrounding nothing, aimed only at
> its own tight, perfect circle of future.
> It is possible to be brave.

Ramke's subjects in this book range from pears to funerals to computers, and the places include his southern homeland ("How to Get Out of the South") as well as his current home ("Turning Forty in Denver"). Relationships—father/son, father/daughter, and husband/wife—remain a central concern.

Ramke again demonstrates his agility with characterizations. He describes, among others, a Cajun, a physicist, and an uncle who painted seascapes using "much expensive / Chinese white to make the waves dramatic, / to give the good gray water *color*."

In Ramke's first two books women consisted mainly of waiting wives and mysterious fantasies; in *The Language Student* he portrays women more subtly and completely. In "A Woman's Complaint," for example, a woman conjectures:

> Suppose I woke
> one morning and left this man, this bed,
> this house we lie in; suppose I walked barefoot
> into the garden to watch the iris, dew dripping,
> . . . .
> suppose it made me happy?
> Could any man's world survive?

Ramke continues to grow, both in terms of technique and in depth of vision. He was once chastised by Robert Pinsky for "slathering figurative language on as if it were just a harmless grease that could make everything move along better" (*New York Times Book Review*, 12 November 1978). Ramke's poetry is now less ebullient, more reflective. He examines his complex relationship with the South from a new vantage point, and he has moved from a regional perspective to a worldy, philosophical one.

The Erotic Light of Gardens, Ramke's 1989 book, continues to embed philosophy in luxuriant language. Aptly titled, this series of poems explores the nature of guilt and the tenuous lines between body and soul, pleasure and pain, past and present. The opening poem, "Something to Say," hearkens back to the Garden of Eden:

> Words filter from the skin, and sweat pours
> defensively down from the brow and we eat our
>   bread,
> and all this time we thought it was sex
> that saved us, we thought we were thrown out
> for pleasure, and really, all along,
> pain was its own reward.

Other poems, such as "Calculating Paradise," "Figure in Landscape," and "Harvard Classics 16, *The Thousand and One Nights*," are rich with allusions to science, painting, and myth. Ramke remains a "language student," continuing, as he writes in "Cinema Verité," on a "sojourn among meticulous dreams."

But he seems to be taking a more political stance, as several of these poems illustrate. In "On Hunger as the Hardest of Passions" he writes, "The poetry of praise is political." "The Poor Miller's Beautiful Daughter" concludes:

> The politics of innocence comes to this:
> Get a good lawyer, or practice holy terror.
> To scream the aisles clear, to throw a fit,
> is a way to get your way, after all.
> No tiny sovereign in our time has missed
> this lesson. . . .

In *The Erotic Light of Gardens* Ramke invites the reader to consider compelling questions of love, danger, body, and soul, set amidst a tangled background of beauty and history. As he writes in "Calculating Paradise": "This is the history of civilization, or of language, / or, in other words, some of us miss each other / and talk about it long into the night, hoping."

Currently Ramke is professor of English and director of the writing program at the University of Denver. In addition to participating in readings and workshops, he reads approximately seven hundred manuscripts per year for the University of Georgia Press and has selected twenty titles for its poetry series.

Ramke continues to experiment with language and to increase his expertise with form and genre. His vision of the world has changed—from calm disillusionment to a more complex grappling with philosophical issues. What Hugo wrote in 1978 may be the most accurate assessment of Ramke's future: "He can't be anticipated and his moves, no matter how unexpected, seem right."

William Pitt Root

(28 December 1941 -   )

Herbert V. Fackler
University of Southwestern Louisiana

BOOKS: *The Storm and Other Poems* (New York:
  Atheneum, 1969);
Striking the Dark Air for Music (New York: Athe-
  neum, 1973);
The Port of Galveston (Galveston: Galveston Arts
  Center, 1974);
Coot and Other Characters (Lewiston, Idaho: Conflu-
  ence, 1977);
A Journey South (Port Townsend, Wash.: Graywolf,
  1977);
In the World's Common Grasses (Santa Cruz, Cal.:
  Moving Parts, 1981);
Fireclock (Boston: Four Zoas Night House, 1981);
7 Mendocino Songs (Portland, Oreg.: Mississippi
  Mud, 1981);
Reasons for Going It on Foot (New York: Athe-
  neum, 1981);
The Unbroken Diamond (Oracle, Ariz.: Pipedream,
  1983);
Invisible Guests (Lewiston, Idaho: Confluence,
  1984);
Faultdancing (Pittsburgh: University of Pittsburgh
  Press, 1986).

TRANSLATION: *Selected Odes of Pablo Neruda*
  (Boston: Four Zoas Night House, 1984).

Of the poets of his generation, those William Heyen has called the "poets of the year
2000," William Pitt Root has best represented the
wandering bard. The son of a farmer, William,
and Bonita Hilbert Root, he was born on 28 December 1941 in Austin, Minnesota, and raised in
Florida near the Everglades. He has studied at
the University of Washington (B.A., 1964), the
University of North Carolina at Greensboro
(M.F.A., 1967), and Stanford University (Stegner
Fellow, 1968-1969) and has taught and written in
Pennsylvania, Michigan, Massachusetts, Texas, Arizona, Vermont, Idaho, Oregon, Louisiana, Montana, Oklahoma, Mississippi, Washington, Kansas,
and New York, as well as London, Cornwall, Scotland, and the northern Mediterranean. At present he is the director of the Creative Writing Pro-

William Pitt Root (photograph by Pamela Uschuk)

gram at Hunter College in New York. His wife is
the poet Pamela Uschuk, and he has a daughter,
Jennifer, from his previous marriage to Judith
Bechtold, which ended in divorce in 1970.

His poetic commitments and achievements
are as difficult to categorize as his geographical
habitat. He has written personal poems of convincing power, such as "The Storm," the title poem
of his first volume (1969), a poem that established him as a poet worth serious consideration
when it was published in the *Atlantic* in 1967. He
has written songs of the joy of nature's inelucta-
ble cycles, including "Songs of Vanity" and "Song

259

of Shaking" in *Striking the Dark Air for Music* (1973). He has created the memorable folk figure of Coot, whose wisdom is gained by prospecting for self in the western mountains, and he has provided comical-perceptive, aphoristic "Life Sentences," which focus a subject in a quick, succinct, and accurate phrase, as in "Master Teacher" from *Coot and Other Characters* (1977): "Imagine / trying to explain air / to a lung." He has written apocalyptic visions (*Fireclock*, 1981); prizewinning poetry of political content, filled with anguish over the plight of the Afghan Mujahadeen (*The Unbroken Diamond*, 1983); and poems that celebrate as expansively as Walt Whitman the experience of the people in a place (the splendid poems that accompany the photographs by Richard and Betty Tichich in *The Port of Galveston*, 1974). His subjects are myriad: motorcycles, wild animals, diamond engagement rings, the deracination of California Indians, the solitary life of a Russian strongman, the sex life of slugs, extended narrative jokes, and the endless variations in human relationships. What emerges from this welter of images, this array of voices, is a paradoxically distinctive and individual poetic voice.

In the *Yarrow* interview (1983) Root characterizes *The Storm and Other Poems* as a "backward-glance-book." The recurring familial relations—among father, mother, grandfather, wife, and daughter—provide both a recognizable milieu for the poems and a frame of common reference against which to judge the often-frightening things Root sees outside that circle. Fire, deadly spiders, graveyards, deaths, tigers, automobile wrecks, animals struck by cars, a child's fear of death, the inevitability of the death of a parent, and the final symbol of the storm and the nightmares it engenders—all hover and threaten in the dark universe Root inhabits. He may write a delicate and lovely song, "Jennifer by Moonlight," in which his infant child is beguiled by the moon and the songs of the crickets, but the respite is only momentary; the succeeding poem is "From the First and Lasting Dream," in which the crickets still sing, but the moon, mythic as Diana, is a hunter, and the speaker lies awake to worry: "What if the child wakes? / Or cannot wake? / Chilled in the silent instant, / I see the small, lit, moonstunned form." The antinomy of the commonplace and the threats to it continue into the final, title poem.

In "The Storm" Root pictures his father, a man dying and raging at it, violently seeding and farming his Everglades land, which seems to draw fertility from him as it does from the rest of the decay around it: "a pale brutal ferocity spreading its strength, / unthinking and gradual." Death is ominous over the scene, as is the storm. The extra crews, who sing as they try to salvage as much of the crop as they can, leave as the storm gathers; their trucks "cough to life." The father coughs, too, toward an imminent death. The destruction of the crops, the death and decay that follow, and the speaker's horrific nightmare of a pig slaughter—all crowd in on his youthful consciousness until his fear for his father, his fear *of* him, and his love for him fuse into a single emotion.

The final section of "The Storm" provides a link to the poems of *Striking the Dark Air for Music*, in which Root renounces the backward-looking poem for the present, in which one is free to examine and try to understand experience but not to manipulate it the way one can manipulate memories. In this last section of "The Storm" the speaker, years later, awakens in strange places with a sense of his father's presence and, in the final vision of the poem, lets go of memory: "But father, O father, / what silence."

Almost as if Root intends to terminate the concerns of *The Storm*, the first poem of *Striking the Dark Air for Music* is again about his father and is entitled "Closing the Casket." In the second section, "Reckonings," Root moves wholly into his new terrain, not a remembered one but one being discovered as a sort of freehand map drawn by an explorer who is unflinching in his honesty:

> I am empty
> given to a silence
> I despise and need
>
> I make nothing true
> When I try to speak
> without lies
> nothing comes[.]

In "Two Poems" he half-humorously characterizes what his situation has come to: "I'm the absurd chameleon, trying / to match the colors of the fire / instead of leaping out." This realization frees him to write the remarkable series of songs that conclude the volume. Though it is not the final poem included, the crux of Root's development in these poems is probably clearest in "Songs of Presence," which begins: "I wake up to this blazing coat of joys / no grief destroys."

This period in Root's career was followed by one in which he produced poetry that is most often focused outward. The subject is no longer the dark side—it is how one orders his perceptions into a coherent life. The confrontation with myth is evidence of his move toward narrative, in which he sought a principle of integration, as in the chapbook *The Port of Galveston*:

to be aware
just for an instant
of what in an instant
will be gone
to see
in a single heartbeat
of the light
the extraordinary
drama of order
underlying
the apparent chaos
of the everyday[.]

In *Coot and Other Characters* Coot is an archetype: the old western prospector whose wealth is not in gold but in the wilderness that is finally taken from him. He is cantankerous, comical, unregenerate, and charming with his hermit's life and quiet adventures:

Like noticing one night
how my old cedar dipper
was as full of stars
as water. Then I drank. . . .

The question the Coot poems propose is this: what does one prospect for now? As Root writes in "Old Prospector" (in the aphoristic "Life Sentences" section), "All gold is fool's gold / —*If you're so smart / how come you're rich?*" One must prospect for value but not material value.

The volume is varied in its contents. It is ameliorative in its cumulative effect, but it contains angry poems of failed love (such as "Estrangement"); a "Curse" on the poisoners of mind, soul, and earth; a twist on fame ("Swansong"); and a John Dos Passos-style elegy for a dead miner ("Walls: the Cave-In"). Like Walt Whitman, Root has learned the unity of vision to be found in the multiplicity of life.

In the World's Common Grasses (1981) was an almost inevitable step in Root's progress. It is a collation of poems from his first two books—with several new ones interspersed—but it is "new" in the sense that he has reordered the poems into a kind of coherence achieved with poetic maturity. He subtitled the book "Poems of a Son, Poems of a Father," and the poems are arranged to address these crucial relationships. Root has achieved an understanding of his filial debt. No less has he realized that part of the nature of fatherhood is inchoate; sitting by a window with his daughter he experiences fatherhood's ineffability: "as you turn to me / the blaze of / what we know / could blind the sun."

Marking this period, too, is the poem "Under the Umbrella of Blood," where Root begins by pondering his age—forty—which naturally leads him to consider death, and the thought of death leads to a recollection of grotesque old Turkish bets on how far a headless man can run. Root's dramatic presentation of the gory tableau and his subsequent musing (while taking a shower) on how long consciousness remained in the severed heads lead to a semicomic parallel in his similar dash against time and "losing the thought":

I wonder, and I rush off to the typewriter wiping
    my eyes clear,
knowing if I am to get it right
the images under the final downpour must be
    running
faster than the applauding coins of the world can
    fall.

In the same year (1981) two other important works by Root were published: the chapbook *Fireclock* and his volume of poems titled *Reasons for Going It on Foot*. *Fireclock* is a disturbing poem, a cathartic nightmare of a fire on a train in which children perish, and the speaker's helplessness is transformed to guilt, despair, and finally the recognition that he has changed:

I am still walking
as I burn.

I am still walking,
a flame within the fire.

As I walk
I hear the fire singing.

As I burn
I am the fire's song.

He is the dreaded object as well as the consciousness that seeks to understand it.

Reasons for Going It on Foot, nominated for both the Pulitzer Prize and the American Book Award, was greeted warmly by reviewers. In this volume, Root surprises. In "Slugs Amorous in the Air" he lyricizes on the mating of these common garden pests which are "wholly sexual as angels, / male and female brilliance twinned," and there follows a tense and witty poem on the mating of black widow spiders. In metaphors reminiscent of the metaphysical poets, he describes the pleasure of riding a motorcycle, in "Sometimes Heaven is a Mean Machine," and he transforms the culturally materialistic ritual of "Choosing a Diamond" into a sudden revelation:

Wear it proudly then
on the brief gift

of your flesh,
knowing how

at the heart of such a stone
Time must burn. . . .

"For the World's Strongest Man" celebrates the gentleness and power of Russian weightlifter Vasili Alexeev; poems dedicated to Gary Snyder, Wendell Berry, and Ed McClanahan are moments of recognition of nature's force and beauty. But Root has placed all in perspective. He knows the use of things as well as their emotional contexts, and he has the vantage point of the outsider, hungry and

eager to know
the ways of those

I beg my life from
as I pass. . . .

The Unbroken Diamond is a poem that could be considered political were it not for Root's focus on violence done to people rather than to their transitory political structures, and being done by a mechanized, Westernized culture against an essentially native people in their own land (Afghanistan). Root accepts the poet's role as teller of truths, and he assures the Mujahadeen: "I tell you your story is heard. / Your story is being heard."

In 1986 *Faultdancing* was published by the University of Pittsburgh Press. Its contents provide a generous opportunity to examine Root's work prior to that date. Featuring the poem "Fireclock" almost as a centerpiece, the book shows less the surrealism that Ray Gonzalez has suggested (*High Plains Literary Review*, Fall 1987) than a self-assured mastery of form and clarity of vision. Root begins by presenting a series of na-

ture poems that show not only predators but also a world tightly bound by interdependences. These poems are in sections titled "The Anonymous Welcome" (a journey in which the poet encounters a highway accident, the grandeur of the desert, the curious newness that new places can bring to a relationship, and, finally, the "anonymous welcome" of the laughter of children) and "Idiots of Appetite." "Magnet of the Heart" and "Feast of Light" are also remarkable poetic sequences. The first is sacramental in both tone and subject. When Christ walks upon the waters, he is aware of his body's "equivalence" (in "To Walk Across"), and that "equivalence" is concerned both with weight and with balance in matched proportion—the ideal between soul and body—which leads to a sacramental vision of reality.

The poem "Sweat," in the same section, is one of Root's most physical poems, yet its physicality is an experience in which

Bones
surrender their rigidity and brain
gives up ideas as easily as lungs
give up the air or flesh its water,
spirit its tent of flesh. . . .

The poem is exhilarating, an experience of spiritual and physical "equivalence."

"Feast of Light" is a series of song-poems, from a celebration of a sudden vision of nature's beauty (in "Song of an Eye's Opening") to a joyful vision of the speaker's eventual dissolution:

such sweet energy wraps these parts
breeding out of dreams and hunger
    all the beauty I can bear

Let all birds feast on the poet laid to rest then
    sing!"

With *Faultdancing* Root has established himself as one of the major poets of his generation, an apocalyptic poet who has found a hopeful vision.

Interviews:
"Talking of Michelangelo, Beehives, Gold Mines, Heroes, Specialization—and the Difficult Celebration Poetry Is, or Can Be," *Yarrow* (Spring 1983);
"Where Heart Is the Horse and Head the Rider, Poets Must Be Centaurs," *Cutbank* (Spring/ Summer 1984).

Gibbons Ruark

(10 December 1941 -   )

Fred Chappell
University of North Carolina at Greensboro

BOOKS: *A Program for Survival* (Charlottesville: University Press of Virginia, 1971);
Reeds (Lubbock: Texas Tech Press, 1978);
Keeping Company (Baltimore: Johns Hopkins University Press, 1983);
Small Rain (Purchase, N.Y.: Center for Edition Works, 1984);
Rescue the Perishing (Baton Rouge: Louisiana State University Press, 1991).

OTHER: *The Greensboro Reader*, edited by Ruark and Robert Watson (Chapel Hill: University of North Carolina Press, 1968);
Forms of Retrieval, special issue of *Yarrow* (Spring-Summer 1989)—includes poems by Ruark and an interview with him.

The ambition to live simply, quietly, and gently requires a vision so different from the one contemporary society encourages that one should feel privileged by the presence of a poet who can hold to this ambition, who is not persuaded by opportunities for spurious celebrity to abjure the values that have sustained him as a poet and as a private person. The quiet simplicity of Gibbons Ruark's poetry is its greatest strength. Many of the nouns that describe this kind of art—*grace, ease, poise, balance, steadiness, wholeness, patience, calmness,* and so forth—are to be found plentifully in his poetry, as if he wanted to show readers his goals and to demonstrate that these qualities can still be attained if they can be faithfully imagined.

Ruark was born on 10 December 1941 in Raleigh, North Carolina, to Henry Gibbons Ruark and Sarah Jenkins Ruark. The elder Ruark was a Methodist minister, so the poet's boyhood was spent in a series of parsonages in eastern North Carolina towns, including Red Springs, Chapel Hill, Weldon, and Laurinburg. After graduating from Laurinburg High School in 1959, the young Ruark earned his A.B. in English at the University of North Carolina at Chapel Hill, where

he met his future wife, Kay Stinson. They were married on 5 October 1963 in Amherst, Massachusetts, where Ruark pursued graduate studies resulting in an M.A. in English from the University of Massachusetts and took a writing course with the poet Joseph Langland, who encouraged his creative work. Among his fellow students was the poet Michael Heffernan, and thus began a long and valuable literary friendship.

Ruark's first poems were published in the *Massachusetts Review* in 1965, just after the birth of his daughter Jennifer and just as he was leaving for a teaching position at the University of North Carolina at Greensboro, where he was to stay until 1968, when he moved to the University of Delaware. His other daughter, Emily, was born in Wilmington that same year. All of Ruark's books have been published during his time at Delaware, where he remains as a professor of English; he has taken leaves of absence in Italy and Ireland, about which he has written a great deal, and served a year as visiting poet in residence at UNC—Greensboro. His first book of poetry, *A Program for Survival*, was a National Arts Council selection in 1971. *Reeds* (1978) was a finalist in the Associated Writing Programs nationwide competition. *Keeping Company*, published in 1983, was awarded the 1984 Saxifrage Prize for the best book from a small or university press during the previous two years. Ruark's fourth full-length poetry collection, *Rescue the Perishing*, was published by Louisiana State University Press in 1991. He has twice been awarded fellowships by the National Endowment for the Arts.

Ruark's insistence on the virtues of quietness and simplicity and his efforts to reassure his readers that such virtues are still attainable even in noisy and chaotic times give rise to the characteristics of much of his work. In the title poem of *A Program for Survival* a science fiction fantasy includes a visitation by a "monstrous flying thing from another / Planet that throbs and bristles with a thousand arms." How are the inhabitants

Gibbons Ruark (photograph by Kay Ruark)

of earth to assuage this stranger? By making love en masse in its presence, the poem suggests:

> Let us lie down
> With our lovers when we know them, falling on
> them
> Softly as possible, rocking with them, getting
> Up and turning to the future humming in the
> grass.
> As the salt of loving glistens on our bodies,
> Let us admire ourselves in the mirroring surface
> While the machine is gentled and admires us all.

Thus the poem is revealed as not being a fantasy. The flying machine represents the frightening mechanical civilization that one part of human nature has constructed, and controlling it will take the loving-animal aspect that can enable people to "gentle" their machines.

The narrative materials of "A Program for Survival" are humorously chosen and lie outside Ruark's usual range. His range is, in fact, deliberately a rather narrow one. Love for family members and friends is celebrated, and again and again they are elegized after their deaths; there are numerous love poems to his wife, Kay; there are travel poems and poems about works of art

and music; and there are a few portrait poems of historical figures—and that is about the whole scope. A singular devotion to a limited number of subjects is another way of achieving simplicity.

There are many poems about the poet's father, who, according to the poems, established and maintained a close, warm relationship with his son. Ruark remarked in his interview in *Yarrow* (Spring-Summer 1989) that, along with his wife, the example of his father's "sweetness and composure" stands behind his poetry. One of his earliest poems, "Night Fishing," was composed during his father's lifetime but is about the inevitability of his death. In this poem father and son travel to the shore to enjoy surf casting: "We have come again, my father and I, / To the edge of the known land, to the streak / Of sand that lips the undermining sea." The father's stalwart presence seems an unchanging stability: "My father stands like a driven piling." Yet the sea is an "undermining" force, and the pull of the tides of merciless time brings the two fishermen close together:

> Yearly we come to this familiar coast
> To wade beside each other in the shallows,

Dust jacket for Ruark's second book, in which he continued to develop his almost casual, conversational style

Reaching for bluefish in the ocean's darkness
Till our lines are tangled and our tackle lost.

The sorrow of the poem is more profound for being muted, and the sadness is all the more bitter for being a premonition rather than a fact.

When the death did take place, one of the poems that resulted is, characteristically, a reassuring gesture, an epistle addressed to Ruark's mother ("Elegy, a Letter Home"). For her he will say "these words that do not matter / Or that matter more than anything I do." Mother and son are reconciled to this death; they do not inconsolably cry out for the father's return, but they do long for him to come to tell them "how to take his leaving," to sit quietly with them, "Saying no more than I am for the sake / Of so much mildness gone out of the world."

Ruark's second book, *Reeds*, opens with "The Darkness of the Room," which retains the same steady calmness in the face of sorrow; the poem displays Ruark's talent for the easy, almost casual approach. In a nocturnal winter landscape, "Emptier than any silence," the speaker decides to go into his house and sit by the sinking fire, which he will not build higher, and he recalls

What a child says
To his sleeping father,

I came down to kiss you
Goodnight but it's so dark
I don't know where your mouth is.

His gentle approaches and quiet closures also serve Ruark well in his love poems. Here are the opening and closing passages from two such poems, the first one from *Reeds* and the second from *Keeping Company*:

Lately I think of my love for you and the rose
Growing into the house, springing up from under
   the eaves
And spiraling upward to pierce the chink in the
   corner . . .

For lately I think of my love for you and the rose
      invading the darkness,
And I long never to learn the difference.
      (from "The Rose Growing into the House")

Not knowing I was only
Awaiting all my life,

You gave your one bay leaf
Away in Sirmione.

I hid it in my shade,
That slender book where late
This gesture of leaf-light
Touches your shoulder blade.
    (from "Words to Accompany a Leaf from
      Sirmione")

The unhurried grace to be found in these poems is carried in a clear conversational tone, never muffled and never importuning. These are poems of the steady voice and the level gaze.

In a 1989 interview with Wil Gehne, Ruark spoke of clarity, remarking that his preference is for "poems which are totally accessible on one level—all the way through—the first time you read them." One of Ruark's strategic uses of clarity is to present a clear surface by means of attractive forward motion, which can postpone a reader's expectations of profound or complicated thought until the more purely aesthetic design is seen and felt as a whole. Once the whole structure of a poem is perceived and reacted to on a powerful, preliminary level, unhurried reflection reveals other levels and further implications; the total meaning of the poem becomes a delayed surprise.

"Love Letter from Clarity in Chartres," following closely on the Sirmione poem in *Keeping Company*, uses the framework of a love poem addressed to the poet's wife to encompass several seemingly unrelated subjects, one of which is the effect of luminous clarity in art. Two friends have persuaded the speaker of the poem to depart Paris in order to visit Chartres cathedral. Because he is separated from his wife and thinking about her, he encounters a quality of light in the cathedral that reminds him of the light of her eyes.

The similarity of the color of a woman's eyes and the light in the cathedral is not a metaphor many poets could have discovered or, having discovered, would have pursued, but Ruark is not constrained by its strangeness. In fact, this strangeness only leads him to a more daring trope, a comparison of the architecture of the cathedral with his wife's body, together with a contrast between the historied light of Europe and the fresh light of America and another contrast between the immortality of art and the mortality of humanity:

Here in Chartres, this solitary sun,
Radiant as it is, seems to be wandering
Longingly after its own peculiar genius,

Thinking maybe to go down once in its too long life
Behind a remarkable hill in America,
The western slope of your own left shoulder,

Happy to light just briefly before it darkens
Forever your long articulate back
Whose brave architecture dreams

It will never sleep.

This long sentence, though complex in structure, seems open in its meaning, a tender and wittily hyperbolic compliment to the loved one. When readers examine it more closely, observing the different implications of *genius, remarkable*, and *articulate*, and discovering the syntactical ambiguities in the placement of *Forever* and of the whole final clause, other levels of meaning are unveiled, some of them plangent. Yet the poem remains a tender and witty love compliment. Its essential nature has not changed, but more of its nature has been revealed.

Ruark's poems resign themselves to a world in which struggle, disharmony, sorrow, and disaster are common, but never so common as to be unremarkable. *Rescue the Perishing* takes violence as one of its themes; many of the poems are set in Ireland and deal with civil strife. The violence is not something he desires to write about, as the divorcée publican in the barroom where he sits composing one of his poems seems to know. He has shown this woman one of his love poems, and she asks, "Don't you think love makes poetry possible?" Maybe it does, but on this rainy afternoon he happens to be working on a different kind of poem, one that reflects a different kind of experience:

What can I say in Joe Nolan's quiet saloon,
The rain-streaked window momentarily whole,
About anything unshattered, poetry or love?
I ask her the spelling of *gelignite*.
She says it's no use in my peaceable poems.

These lines are from the second of two sonnets titled "North Towards Armagh," and the irony implicit in the woman's fond rejoinder—that Ruark is not the sort of poet to deal with violent subjects—underscores the more emphatic ironies of his poem "Glasnevin," in which he speaks of a tourist pilgrimage "among the gravestones at Glasnevin, / Parnell, Maud Gonne MacBride, *schoolyard dust, we prayed for nothing*

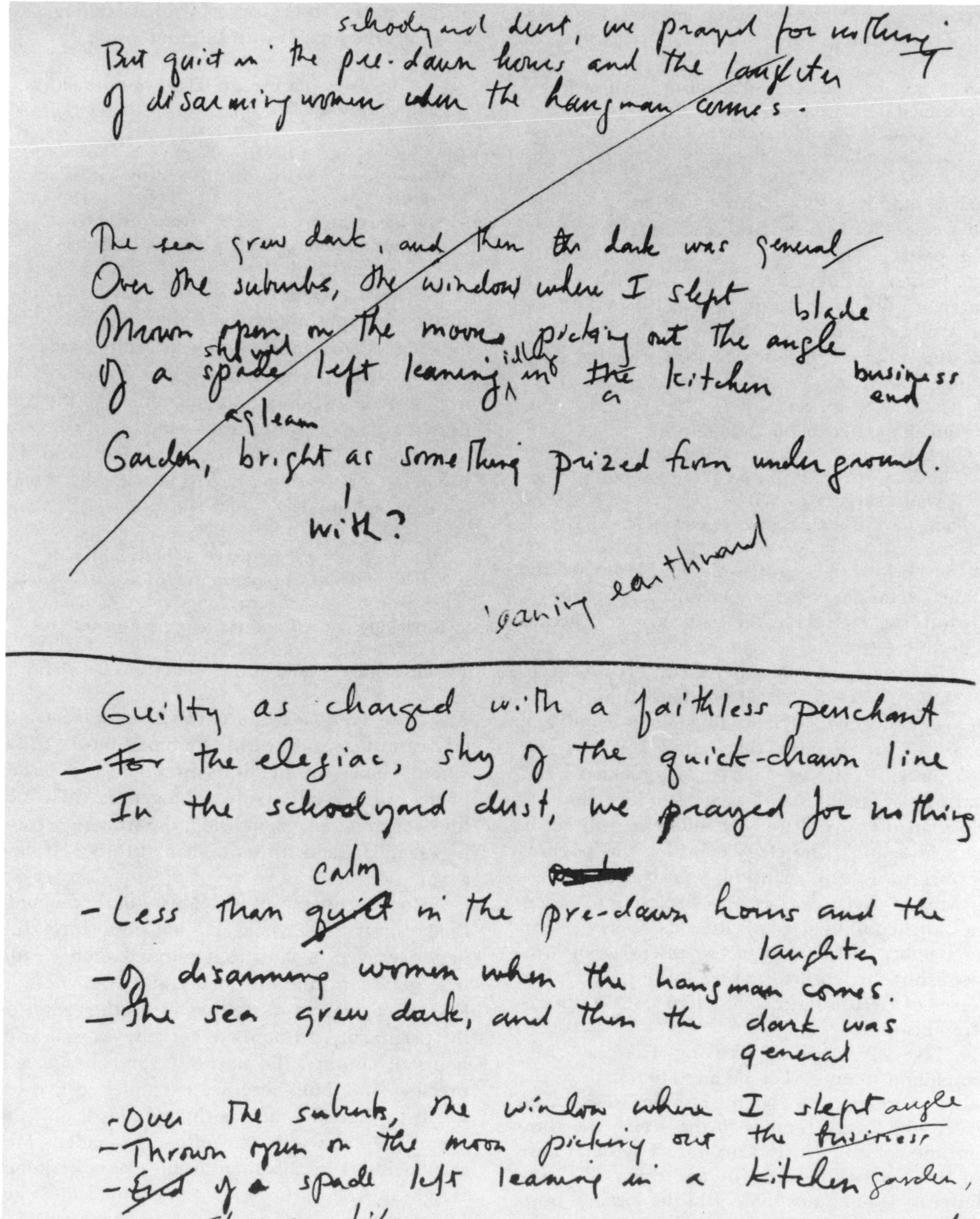

But quiet in the pre-dawn hours and the *laughter*
of disarming women when the hangman comes.

The sea grew dark, and then the dark was general
Over the suburbs, the window where I slept
blade
Thrown open on the moon, picking out the angle
shovel *idly* *a* *business*
Of a spade left leaning in the kitchen *and*
agleam
Garden, bright as something prized from underground.

with?

leaning earthward

Guilty as charged with a faithless penchant
For the elegiac, shy of the quick-drawn line
In the schoolyard dust, we prayed for nothing
calm
Less than guilt in the pre-dawn hours and the
laughter
Of disarming women when the hangman comes.
The sea grew dark, and then the dark was
general

Over the suburbs, the window where I slept *angle*
Thrown open on the moon picking out the *business*
End of a spade left leaning in a kitchen *garden*,
shining like
Garden, agleam with something prized from underground.

Page from a draft for "With Thanks for a Shard from Sandycove," collected in Rescue the Perishing *(by permission of Gibbons Ruark)*

diversi santi. . . ." The following lines explicitly depict a contrasting violent scene:

> The Sten guns roared and adamant hymn singers
> Slumped in their bloody pews, and now, rung off
> This granite, the old staunch hymns are streaming
> From the country churches of my boyhood.

Such a bloody history cannot help changing the way readers understand and react to Irish and English poetry. These are two of the most magnificent bodies of literature in the world, but even that magnificence must give way a little to the pressures of contemporary history, in the same way that the itinerary of the graveyard tour has been changed:

> With all the Republican dead so near,
> Our guide the begrudger, calling Hopkins
> "The convert," leads us first to the inventor
> Of plastic surgery, as well he might,
> These days of the gelignite ascendancy.

At the grave of Gerard Manley Hopkins the guide seems impatient. Obviously gelignite is much in the ascendant, the civilized art of poetry in decline.

Rescue the Perishing opens with "Postscript to an Elegy," a poem that shows the full burden of sorrow in losing a friend to violent death and speaks of the defenses that fail to keep the sorrow away: "Talk as I may of quickness and charm, easy laughter, / The forms of love, the sudden glint off silverware / At midnight will get in my eyes again." The elegy to which this poem is a postscript is "For a Suicide, a Little Early Morning Music," in *Keeping Company*. "Postscript" underlines the continuation of Ruark's concerns and the stability of his faith in the essentials of love, friendship, art, peace, nature, and poetry. The storms of circumstance shake him but do not destroy this faith.

Like "Postscript," "Leaving Hatteras" is a companion to an earlier poem. The death of the father, foreseen in "Night Fishing," has taken place, and Ruark returns to the scene, the summertime coast of North Carolina. The details are not the same as before; for one thing, "Leaving Hatteras" is not a nocturne. But the locale is powerfully remindful: "The surf's invisible below the dunes, / But its sound is the fallback and lift of memory." The speaker remembers his father in a different way—not fishing in the undermining surf, but safe on the porch of a beach cabin. This time it is the son who walks by the sea and in his reverie ("time forgetful of its calling") remembers the images with calm intensity:

> All I do is close my eyes. A screen door shudders
> And bangs and a boy lights out for the water
>
> And it is south of here by thirty years and more
> Where the shore curls inward and the dunes are lower
> And a boy can see his father from the water
> Cleaning and oiling his tackle in a porch chair.

"Leaving Hatteras" is one of Ruark's most adroit accomplishments and all the more adroit in being so accomplished that its skillfulness is almost invisible. The whole poem is suffused with heat, drowse, hypnotic surf-murmur, and the subtle but palpable presence of memory, in reverie so actualized that when the speaker and his brother stand ready to depart, the father is with them in the cabin:

> we breathe deep, two of us only, buttoning
> Our sleeves and zipping up the nylon duffel bags,
> Unless you count the lazybones in the doorway,
> Stretching himself and rubbing his eyes with his knuckles,
> Blinking like a child as the room turns familiar.

Any future estimate of Ruark's work will have to take careful account of his continual return to favored themes, of the ways in which the earlier poems and the later converse together, their motifs deepening and mellowing, the strange becoming familiar and the familiar turning strange again.

In the poetry of Gibbons Ruark the only final catastrophe would be oblivious forgetfulness. He avers a faith that calmness and steadiness of vision, and constancy and wholeness of love, can achieve a peace that forms the center of the personality. In hours of serenity, as well as in hours of conflict, the necessity for courage is a pressing one, but there are examples to live by, words to cherish—such as the last words and the *fact* of the last words of Wolfgang Amadeus Mozart, as Ruark recalls them in his elegy for James Wright in *Keeping Company*: "And now I must go, / When I have only just learned to live quietly."

Interview:
Wil Gehne, "Gibbons Ruark: A Conversation on Poetry," *Coraddi* (Winter 1989): 32-39.

Ira Sadoff
(7 March 1945 -)

Thomas Swiss
Drake University

BOOKS: *Settling Down* (Boston: Houghton Mifflin, 1975);
Palm Reading in Winter (Boston: Houghton Mifflin, 1978);
Maine: Nine Poems (Roslindale, Mass.: Pym-Randall, 1981);
A Northern Calendar (Boston: Godine, 1982);
Uncoupling (Boston: Houghton Mifflin, 1982);
Emotional Traffic (Boston: Godine, 1989).

SELECTED PERIODICAL PUBLICATIONS—
UNCOLLECTED:

FICTION

"Ward # 3," *Paris Review* (Spring 1976): 127-147;
"Uncoupling," *Partisan Review* (Fall 1980): 522-531;
"Please, Please Me," *Antioch Review* (Summer 1986): 355-366.

NONFICTION

"The Power of Reflection: The Reemergence of the Meditative Poem," *American Poetry Review*, 10 (November/December 1980): 18-21;
"Ben Webster," *Missouri Review*, 10 (Spring 1987): 168-172.

Ira Sadoff's initial style and approach to his subjects—his characteristic erasures and retreats—seem largely influenced by the psychological and political zeitgeist reflected in the work of many American poets in the 1970s. Shaped by the influences of the "new internationalism" in poetry, and accompanied by a renaissance of translations from Spanish, French, and East European cultures, this particular style has been called the "deep image" or "new surrealist" movement. Among the earlier practitioners of this style—those writers a generation or two older than Sadoff—were prominent and influential American poets such as James Wright, W. S. Merwin, and Mark Strand.

Ira Sadoff was born on 7 March 1945 in Brooklyn to Robert (a pianist) and Yvette Sadoff. He attended Cornell University (B.A., 1966) and did graduate work at the University of Oregon (M.

F.A., 1968). On 29 July 1968 he married Dianne Fallon, a professor. He served as an instructor of English at Hobart and William Smith Colleges in Geneva, New York, from 1968-1971, and, while teaching there, cofounded and coedited the *Seneca Review*. He continued to coedit the magazine until 1976. He became visiting assistant professor at Antioch College in Ohio in 1972. From 1974 to 1978, he was poetry editor of the *Antioch Review*. He served as writer in residence at Hampshire College in 1976, and the next year he became an assistant professor at Colby College in Maine, where he has remained.

Published when Sadoff was thirty years old, his first book, *Settling Down* (1975), was widely and positively reviewed. On the dust jacket, David Wagoner praised his "unusual gift for fresh metaphors"; Daniel Halpern admired "his wit, his imagination and intelligence, his lively evocation of the nostalgic, his pacing and sense of time"; and Sandra Hochman wrote: "I think it is one of the best books published in the past decade." The forty-seven poems in the book are spread over three sections: "Waiting for Evening," "Forgetting This World," and "Going Back to Sleep." Richard Howard called these section titles "denials," denying activity, memory, and wakeful consciousness. The major development in Sadoff's later poetry can be read as a movement *away* from denial. By being increasingly mindful of the physical and social world, and responsive to the demands of memory and self-consciousness, his work has become more accepting, assertive, and powerful.

The new surrealist movement offered Sadoff and many poets of his generation a way out of a dilemma posed by two related questions: how does a poet write about the self without duplicating the strategies used by the "confessional" poets in the 1960s? How does one write about society without imitating the strategies of the "beat" poets of the 1950s? As Sadoff wrote in his 1980 essay, "The Power of Reflection: The Reemer-

Ira Sadoff (photograph by Stephen Collins)

gence of the Meditative Poem," the new surrealism offered a strategy that encouraged "an unbridled belief in the power of the imagination, the world of the dream, the id, the unconscious, the romanticization of the body." In encouraging these beliefs, the new surrealism offered a poetry that attempted to encounter both the self and others beyond or beneath the historically entangled "I."

As in much of the work by the original surrealist writers, visual images became the principal means by which these new poets represented their private dreams and public responses. Sadoff's early poems (as seen in *Settling Down*) feature irrational juxtapositions of images ("The kapellmeister sleeps with the sausage / A man buried too deeply in thought will lose his hair") to suggest the "voice" of the unconscious. His images are transcendent: they move outward into space or spiral downward into the body and the earth. In "Role Reversal," a poem about domestic life, the movement is outward: "you fly out the

window / with my younger sister." But in the title poem, also about domestic life, Sadoff describes "settling down" as "a kind / of rest that settles onto the skin / like dust, it is the kind of dust / that comes out of the body after death."

Family life, the frailty and complexity of family roles and relationships, has always been among Sadoff's most prominent subjects and themes. His other principal subject has been American politics. Sadoff believes in the political witness of poetry; he rages against class structure and especially against those who are socially privileged but unwilling to defend the rights of those at the margins of society: minority groups, the disenfranchised, and the powerless. His later work in particular explores his own complex feelings about being a Jew in a Christian culture.

A low-key discouragement permeates Sadoff's poems, a tone that distinguishes itself from the passionate despair found in some confessional poems and the angry proclamations of beat poems. Sadoff's surrealist poems tend to blur experiences in the speaker's life. Days become interchangeable. Discouraged, resigned, the speaker views life with mild interest, as in "Disease of the Eye" (in *Settling Down*): "A film / covers the eye, and I can only recount events / Out of sequence, in a haze."

In Sadoff's early poems he is on the brink of arguing that silence is superior to expression because expression is not possible without carrying with it the taint of cultural bias, a bias that tends to exclude or oppress others. Sadoff's early work is antiverbal, denying the possibility of true or liberating speech in a world in which all language is a tool for acculturation. Let the unconscious speak for itself, Sadoff argues, in its pure unacculturated state. But to speak, the unconscious must use language. So then how does the poet represent the self except through silence? In "A Search for the Voice," an *ars poetica*, Sadoff's quest for an authentic voice leads him to muteness and the assertion that any voice rising above this silence must be repressed: "I will not allow it / to appear in my poems. / It never obeys me. / Sometimes I keep it under the paper: these poems / I send to you like a record / without grooves, a documentary / of my silence."

Following the publication of his first book Sadoff seems to have come to the conclusion that dreaming alone would not allow him much room for development or growth. After all, the interpretation of dreams undoes repression; the dream itself may simply replicate it. His next poems, then, collected in *Palm Reading in Winter* (1978), include the intellectual, the rational, the discursive, and the meditative. They are less about avoidance and denial and more about confrontation and admission. They are also less about dreaming and more about wakefulness, especially about waking, as an adolescent, into self-consciousness.

Sadoff did not quit writing surreal poems entirely. Some poems, such as "Alienation from Nature" and "Someone Plays a Piano," would not be out of place in his first book. But by the time he published *Palm Reading in Winter*, Sadoff was reconsidering his approach to poetry and developing an interest in the meditative poem. As he writes in "The Power of Reflection," "the meditative poem reintroduces time, or history, as an essential element of the poem. Gone is the naive and romantic belief that we can or should live entirely in the moment and in the body."

Sadoff's renewed interest in the past leads directly to some of the best poems in his second book. While his first book contains poems that hint at estrangement from family and loved ones, his new poems give a context for those feelings. Sadoff's father abandoned the family when Sadoff was thirteen years old. In "Meditation" he writes poignantly: "One event stands out from childhood: / the day someone left." The poem concludes: "The world was not changed / as I was, but the house I lived in / was left by itself, a thin frame standing / against the past and parting of events."

Against the seemingly untested allegorical visions of life Sadoff offered in his first book, he places poems set clearly in the biographical moment. There is no more withholding of personality. The new poems are dramatically personal, contextual, and social.

The family is, of course, one's first society. Family stories persist in most lives, continuing to matter, and people are always in conversation with them. In his second book, Sadoff begins to claim his particular family stories, asserting authority over them by exploring and meditating on them. Yet his tone is still melancholy, for reasons he explains in "Depression Beginning in 1956": "though we choose sometimes / the pastoral and lovely, it is never quite enough / to leave the melancholy we've come to know."

In 1982 Sadoff published two books: *Uncoupling*, a novel, and *A Northern Calendar*, a chapbook of poems. *Uncoupling* takes up a man's search for his father, who had deserted the family when the main character, Michael Jarriman, was a young boy. Jarriman is a marriage counselor whose own marriage is breaking apart. The novel—a dark comedy—follows both his search for his father and his quest for reconciliation with his spouse.

A Northern Calendar is transitional, collecting some of Sadoff's slighter poems with new work that approaches his obsessive subjects with renewed power. Three poems not reprinted in his next book, *Emotional Traffic* (1989), are political: "Please," "Villains," and "My Old German Girl Friends." What is striking about these poems is the increasingly complicated, self-implicating viewpoint that Sadoff will develop in his next collection.

Emotional Traffic represents Sadoff's most powerful work to date. The first section, building on the themes and strengths of *Palm Reading in Winter*, explores the complex and troubled relationship of a son to his mother in the wake of his father's departure. The poems, in part, attempt to name and accept the confusing and sometimes competing emotions both mother and son experience in light of this altered and unfamiliar family structure.

The father in these poems has become a ghost figure: menacing at times, but often just mysterious. He is first represented as a "stranger" who has come, inexplicably, to interfere with the lives of both mother and son. His subsequent departure brings confusion, guilt, anger, a sense of betrayal, and a sense of unworthiness—all of these feelings to be sorted out by the "survivors."

The family story occasionally focuses on a traditional scene of comfort, as in "Memorial Days," which presents a suffering son and a ministering mother ("I'd wake her from my nightmare / until she'd soothe me back to sleep / with a washcloth and a kiss"). But this *Pieta*-like scene is embedded in a text of greater complexity and less comforting psychological overtones: "I thought I heard my mother's heart / beating like a bat beneath an eave. Covered by a sheet / she scared me into thinking she was dead. / My hand startled her awake. She called me / by my father's name, on a day I can't forget. / Memorial Day. The day we're called on / to recall the living and the living dead."

The poems in the other two sections of *Emotional Traffic* are less frequently situated in the speaker's past. In section 2 the emphasis shifts to his present relationship with his wife and to poems of meditation. The third section contains new political poems, some of them satires, and a handful of poems about jazz.

Sadoff's new work extends the promise of his early work that was so highly praised by the critics. He has moved from denial to acceptance, from the epiphanies of his youth to the hard-earned patience of middle age.

Mary Jo Salter

(15 August 1954 -   )

Robert Darling
Keuka College

BOOKS: *Henry Purcell in Japan* (New York: Knopf, 1985);

Unfinished Painting (New York: Knopf, 1989);

The Moon Comes Home (New York: Knopf, 1989).

SELECTED PERIODICAL PUBLICATIONS—
UNCOLLECTED: "Puns and Accordions," *Yale Review*, 79 (Winter 1990): 188-221;

"A Poem of One's Own," *New Republic*, 204 (4 March 1991): 30-34.

From its first appearance in print, the poetry of Mary Jo Salter has displayed a technical virtuosity and a fineness of perception unusual in a young poet. While much of her poetry deals with domestic concerns, she is also frequently successful with larger themes, such as time, mortality, and war.

Mary Jo Salter was born in Grand Rapids, Michigan, on 15 August 1954. Her father, Albert Gregory Salter, was an advertising executive and has yet to appear frequently in her poems. Such is not the case, however, with the poet's mother; an artist, Lorima Paradise Salter plays a substantial role, especially in her daughter's second book, *Unfinished Painting* (1989). The title of the volume refers to one of Lorima Salter's paintings.

After a childhood and youth spent primarily in Detroit and Baltimore, Mary Jo Salter earned her B.A. at Harvard, from which she graduated cum laude in 1976 and where she was elected a member of Phi Beta Kappa. She continued her study at New Hall, Cambridge University, earning her M.A. with first-class honors in 1978.

Salter returned to the United States and accepted a Harvard instructorship, which she held through 1979. Her return from England once again placed her in proximity to the poet Brad Leithauser, who had earned his Harvard undergraduate degree a year earlier than Salter and in 1980 received his J.D. there. On 2 August of that year she and Leithauser were married. Shortly

Mary Jo Salter (photograph copyright Jerry Bauer)

thereafter, they set off for Japan, Leithauser having a three-year residency as a research fellow in the Kyoto Comparative Law Center. Salter found employment as an instructor in English conversation.

This first stay overseas set the pattern the couple followed for the ensuing decade. Residences in foreign lands interspersed with periods of teaching at Mount Holyoke College in Massachusetts have provided both poets with material for much of their work. Salter interrupted her stay in Japan to return to the United States to serve as poet in residence at Robert Frost Place in 1981. She won the Discovery Prize from the *Nation* (1983) and a National Endowment for the Arts Fellowship for 1983-1984. These awards, coupled with the appearance of individual poems in leading periodicals such as the *Atlantic Monthly* and the *New Yorker*, led to the publication of Salter's first book, *Henry Purcell in Japan* (1985).

Alfred Corn, writing in the *New Republic*, noted that "in the Japanese poems . . . Salter steps outside what might be considered reasonable expectations for a first book. . . . These brilliant and searching poems are the best in the volume" (8 April 1985). In the *New York Times Book Review* (7 April 1985) L. M. Rosenberg had more reservations, writing that Salter was "very successful, I'm afraid, in her imitations." Rosenberg stated further that Salter's poems are "playful, chilly, convoluted and always slightly too long for their subject." Yet Rosenberg also said, "I believe she has more fire and originality than her imitations suggest." Grace Schulman, in *Poetry* (November 1985), noted the paradox of Salter's work. Schulman referred to Salter as being "tactful, graceful, skillful, and exquisitely keen," but then went on to add that Salter's "vision is essentially apocalyptic."

This unusual blend of the domestic world with the larger themes of both personal and general history distinguishes Salter's work. "The Season of Metaphor," which begins with hearing the stirrings in the house when the heat is first turned on with the advent of cold weather, never really ascends the heights its title promises; "Inch by Inch" provides an interesting description of a snowfall ("an open-mouthed mailbox / begins to fatten") but little more. A poem about Salter's grandmother, "Mary Cazzato, 1921," ends a bit too expectedly: "There's never time to call her back— / to ask her what she meant." Yet even the poems that are disappointing are, at the worst, skillful exercises and are generally worthy of their space in the collection because of some striking line or image.

Other poems open out from the cozy domesticity of family and home in striking ways. The first in the collection, "For an Italian Cousin," begins simply enough as a consideration of the cultural and religious differences that become apparent when the speaker visits Italy and is given a tour of her cousin's church. However, by the end of the poem the speaker considers her own "world I've pieced / together with a kind of faith" and offers a view of Venice's San Marco, where a "puzzle of figures floats on the walls / and in golden domes, and you have the feeling / this heavenly gold is not a ceiling— / but space itself, from which no one falls."

In considering the poems from Japan, one finds the opposite movement in "Welcome to Hiroshima." The speaker visits Hiroshima, sees the city, tours the memorial museum, and notes how "all commemoration's swallowed up // in questions of bad taste, how re-created / horror mocks the grim original." But then she sees a child's wristwatch, "resolute / to communicate some message, although mute, / it gestures with its hands at eight-fifteen / and eight-fifteen and eight-fifteen again." The horror of the general is brought home with the particular. "Welcome to Hiroshima" then concludes with the image of a piece of glass the explosion imbedded in a woman's arm; after thirty years ("as if to make it plain / hope's only as renewable as pain") the shard rose to the skin and "worked its filthy way out like a tongue." Both the pain and the language are fresh, in no way trivializing the horror of the event.

In 1985 Salter was appointed a visiting artist at the American Academy in Rome, and the family again packed up and moved overseas. Their stay was abbreviated, however, as they returned home early because of concern over the fallout from the nuclear meltdown at Chernobyl. They did remain for some time after the accident, but eventually feared for the safety of their daughter Emily. (They later had another daughter, Hilary.)

After returning to Mount Holyoke for the 1987-1988 academic year, Salter was awarded the 1988 Lamont Poetry Prize of the Academy of American Poets for her manuscript of *Unfinished Painting*, which was published by Knopf in 1989. One of the judges was Corn, who had favorably reviewed her first volume. She was also awarded the Witter Bynner Foundation Poetry Prize in 1989, awarded by the American Academy and Institute of Arts and Letters.

Unfinished Painting received generally better reviews than *Henry Purcell in Japan*. Phoebe Pettingell remarked that whereas in the first volume Salter was only saved from seeming a "throwback" because of the poems written about the Orient, the present volume "embodies the imperfect, the dilemma of loss, the fragility of accomplishment" (*New Leader*, July 1989). Writing in the *Hudson Review* (Autumn 1989), James Finn Cotter stated that *Unfinished Painting* "reveals someone who has her eyes wide open to the world around her and is well able to describe what she sees." Christopher Benfey claimed in the *New Republic* (17 July 1989) that "Salter's world is reliably domestic," but Henri Cole, in *Poetry* (April 1980), pointed out that "she is subverting elements we count on most as 'safe and innocent': home, family, and even art."

The collection begins with "The Rebirth of Venus," about an artist copying the Sandro Botticelli painting the *Birth of Venus* but using chalk on a sidewalk, creating an imitation of the goddess done in a medium "the rain / will swamp . . . like a tide." Yet the artist will "set off, black umbrella sprung again, / envisioning faces where the streets have parted." The moment of near epiphany arising from ordinary circumstance is Salter at her strongest. In "Reading Room" a reader in the library at Mount Holyoke moves from the commonplace—"Oh, what I haven't read!"—to the awareness that "the room, importunate / as a church, leans as if reading *me*," and the poem develops into a striking meditation on time.

Much of *Unfinished Painting* is elegiac in tone and often in subject. The second section, "Elegies for Etsuko," deals with the suicide of one of Salter's Japanese friends. Most of the sequence is well achieved, though the fifth part, in slightly altered villanelle form, is not up to standard. The two repeated lines—"I know you're gone for good. And this is how: / were you alive, you would have called by now"—are simply not strong enough to bear the weight of repetition.

Probably what best conveys the range of Salter's concerns is a consideration of the titles of three successive poems in the third section of the book. "Emily Wants to Play," a poem about Salter's daughter wanting attention at 3 A.M., is fol-

lowed by "Aubade for Brad," another well-done but thoroughly domestic poem. These are followed by "Chernobyl." The leap is somewhat unsettling, but the poem begins with the "Once upon a time" of children's stories. The general becomes domesticated in a haunting way.

In 1989 Salter also published a children's book, *The Moon Comes Home*, a long poem about the moon following a young girl. After its publication Salter and her family again went overseas; Leithauser was awarded a Fulbright Fellowship to teach at the University of Iceland in Reykjavík. Their experiences there included being loaned a shovel by the president of Iceland, Vigdis Finnbogadottir, when they became stuck in the snow; another time their car was stolen—the police found it abandoned a few hours later—and they had a phone call from the worried thief. These and other adventures were recounted in columns Salter regularly wrote for the *Scandinavian Review* and the *New Republic* during their year in Iceland. In 1990 Mary Jo Salter and Brad Leithauser returned to their teaching appointments at Mount Holyoke College. Salter became the poetry editor for the *New Republic* in 1992.

She is at her best as a poet when exposure to other cultures provides a freshness that is not as evident in her domestic poems. If she continues to explore larger and riskier themes, her contribution to the poetry of her generation will be even more significant.

Gjertrud Schnackenberg

(27 August 1953 -   )

Robert McPhillips
Iona College

BOOKS: *Portraits and Elegies* (Boston: Godine, 1982; revised edition, New York: Farrar, Straus & Giroux, 1986; London: Century Hutchison, 1986);

The Lamplit Answer (New York: Farrar, Straus & Giroux, 1985; London: Century Hutchison, 1986).

OTHER: "Prefaces: Five Poets on Poems by T. S. Eliot: Gjertrud Schnackenberg: 'Marina,'" *Yale Review*, 78 (Winter 1989): 210-215;

"The Epistle of Paul the Apostle to the Colossians," in *Incarnation: Contemporary Writers on the New Testament*, edited by Alfred Corn (New York: Viking Penguin, 1990), pp. 189-211.

Gjertrud Schnackenberg, with the publication of her first chapbook, *Portraits and Elegies* (1982), established her reputation as a poet. Hers was one of the most notable and enthusiastically received debuts by a young American poet in the 1980s. The most memorable poems in the collection are found in its opening sequence, "Laughing with One Eye," a series of elegies written in 1977 in memory of her father, Walter Charles Schnackenberg, a professor who died in 1973. Poems on her shared past with her father and her profound feeling of loss after his death remain the thematic core of her work. In *Portraits and Elegies* the graceful, formal style is often enhanced by rhymed quatrains (though her rhymed and metered verse paragraphs sometimes extend as long as twenty-four lines), and their quiet musical and linguistic fluency distinguish Schnackenberg's autobiographical lyrics from the shrillness of emotion and the harsh cadences of Sylvia Plath and some other confessional poets. Schnackenberg's use of meter, rhyme, and relaxed diction to control her strongest emotions places her, along with such other poets of her generation as Dana Gioia and Timothy Steele, at the front of probably the most significant poetic movement to emerge in the United States in the

1980s, the New Formalism. Her second collection, *The Lamplit Answer* (1985), was more ambitious and uneven than her first. Nevertheless, it prompted John Hollander (*Yale Review*, Summer 1985) to call Schnackenberg "a poet of more than promise, just as she is more than skilled," and Geoffrey Stokes declared her "a major poetic voice—at this point, the most gifted American of her generation" (*Voice Literary Supplement*, 7 May 1985).

Gjertrud Cecelia Schnackenberg was born on 27 August 1953 in Tacoma, Washington, to Walter Charles and Doris Strom Schnackenberg. The poet is of Norwegian descent and was raised a Lutheran. Her father, who graduated from Saint Olaf College in Northfield, Minnesota, taught Russian and medieval history at Pacific Lutheran University, a college founded by Norwegian immigrants in Tacoma.

At nineteen, as a student at Mount Holyoke College, from which she graduated summa cum laude in 1975, Schnackenberg began to write poetry. In 1973 and 1974 she won prestigious Glascock awards for poetry, earlier won by such poets as Plath, Robert Lowell, and James Merrill. Schnackenberg's early work attracted the attention of many, including Robert Fitzgerald, the classicist and poet who influenced many younger poets at Harvard in the 1970s. Though Schnackenberg was not among his students, Fitzgerald was the judge when she received the Lavan Younger Poets Award from the Academy of American Poets in 1983. She was also the recipient of the Rome Prize in Literature for 1983-1984 from the American Academy and Institute of Arts and Letters, and an Amy Lowell Traveling Prize for 1984-1985, enabling her to spend two years in Italy. Her other awards include poetry fellowships from the Bunting Institute at Radcliffe College and from the Ingram Merrill Foundation. For 1986-1987 Schnackenberg received a grant from the National Endowment for the Arts and for 1987-1988 a Guggenheim Fellowship. Since graduating from Mount Holyoke—which awarded her

Gjertrud Schnackenberg circa 1985 (photograph copyright Shyla Irving)

an honorary doctorate in 1985—she has lived in Italy, Tacoma, and Cambridge, Massachusetts. She currently resides in Boston with her husband, Robert Nozick, the eminent Harvard philosophy professor whom she married on 5 October 1987.

Portraits and Elegies is divided into three parts. All three panels of this poetic triptych are concerned with history; hence all, in varying degrees, are connected with her father's field of academic endeavor. The first and third of these are poetic sequences, the former comprising elegies to her father and the latter focusing on the history of a Massachusetts house from the present back to the early eighteenth century. The middle panel is a narrative poem examining the life of Charles Darwin a year before his death. Combined, they present a mature and unified meditation on mortality and the human capacity to impose order on and adduce meaning from life through science, history, family, and poetry.

"Laughing with One Eye," the book's first sequence, fully displays Schnackenberg's poetic strengths. Her concern with form and memory is directly related to the death of her father and with the profound feeling of loss that this death generates. Memory, meter, and form help her compensate for the loss even as they help to recreate her shared life with him and to recall those incidents when the shadow of death, in retrospect, can be perceived to have been present. Indeed, the connection between Schnackenberg's subject matter and her aesthetic is stated in the final poem in this twelve-poem sequence, "There Are No Dead," where Schnackenberg's meditation on a detail from a Bayeux tapestry leads her to the conclusion that "death alone makes life a masterpiece."

Like Edmund Spenser, then, who through his "verse [his beloved's] vertues rare shall eternize, / And in the heavens wryte [her] glorious name" ("Sonnet 75," *Amoretti*, 1595), Schnackenberg in "Laughing with One Eye" attempts to render her father immortal through the "eternal" art of poetry, thus transforming his life into a "masterpiece." Part of this effort is accomplished by poems that revive some of her strongest memories of her father. Such is the case with the sequence's opening poem, "Nightfishing." Schnackenberg juxtaposes the security she feels with her father with the first recognition of his mortality. In "the small rowboat," where the young Schnackenberg is fishing with her father, the latter "sit[s] still, like a monument in a hall, / Watching for trout." The security that this "monument" instills in the speaker is made clear a moment later:

> A bat slices the air
> Near us, I shriek, you look at me, that's all,
> One long sobering look, a smile everywhere
> But on your mouth.

Yet the security bred by the father's smile is shortly replaced by this darker recognition:

> Something moves on your thoughtful face, recedes.
> Here, for the first time ever, I see how,
> Just as a fish lurks deep in water weeds,
> A thought of death will lurk deep down, will show
> One eye, then quietly disappear in you.

This recollection occurs shortly after her father's death; the speaker stares at the familiar face of "the kitchen's old-fashioned planter's clock" and feels psychologically unmoored:

> I'm in the kitchen. You are three days dead.
> A smiling moon rises on fertile ground,
> White stars and vegetables. The sky is blue.
> Clock hands sweep by it all, they twirl around,
> Pushing me, oarless, from the shores of you.

Even as this poem poignantly evokes the poet's sense of loss, it illustrates the ease with which Schnackenberg works in rhyme and meter to express emotion clearly, the flow of her words and meaning never coming to an artificial halt.

As the sequence progresses, Schnackenberg dramatizes other experiences shared with her father, emphasizing his role as scholar and musician, a lover of both Western culture in general and of their family in particular. In addition to fishing with him, readers see Schnackenberg visiting Europe with him.

Juxtaposed with these elegies based on her father's life are three extraordinary poems, the fourth, seventh, and eleventh poems in the sequence, each titled "Dream," presenting, in the first two instances without punctuation, Schnackenberg's haunting dream visions occasioned by her father's death:

> *Death makes of your abandoned face*
> *A secret house an empty place*
> *And I come back wanting that much*
> *To ask you to come back I touch*
>
> *The door where are you it's so black*[.]

Schnackenberg's father eerily haunts her dreams and is given the kind of eternal life in his daughter's poetry that she perceives in the Bayeux Tapestry (in "There Are No Dead"):

> There William of Normandy remounts his horse
> A fourth time, four times desperate to drive
> Off rumors of his death. His sword is drawn.
> He swivels and lifts his visor up and roars,
> *Look at me well! For I am still alive!*
> Your glasses, lying on the desk, look on.

His glasses on the table in his study, where he read history and met his students, become an appropriate image of closure for a man who passed his humane vision on to his poet daughter.

The second section of *Portraits and Elegies*, "Darwin in 1881," a narrative poem reprinted in her second volume, presents, in its portrait of Charles Darwin a year before his death, an analogue of her father. His explorations and great writings behind him, Darwin has retired permanently to his English estate with his wife, Emma, to live out his final days and is likened to Prospero in William Shakespeare's *The Tempest* as he abdicates his powers.

The final section of *Portraits and Elegies*, "19 Hadley Street," is a sequence similar in structure to the first. Schnackenberg effectively uses short lyrics to create a composite narrative portrait of a house in South Hadley, Massachusetts, tracing its history and in the process combining her father's academic discipline with her own poetic art. Her focus on quotidian details—including a man's death by cancer, counterpointed by a poem describing the earlier days of his marriage—places the sequence's historical concerns (witchcraft and the Civil War) within a more accessible context.

This technique of combining short lyrics into narrative sequences does not serve Schnackenberg quite so well in "Kremlin of Smoke," the long poem that begins *The Lamplit Answer*, a volume that breaks new ground, takes significant risks, and, when it triumphs, does so at such a high level as to make caviling seem churlish. Nevertheless, it should be admitted that the historical and cultural material to which Schnackenberg brought so deft a touch in her first volume finally weighs down such longer efforts as "Kremlin of Smoke" and "Imaginary Prisons," a sometimes ingenious version of "Sleeping Beauty" that, despite some exquisite writing and well-developed individual episodes, on the whole falters because of an absence of narrative impetus. Similarly a piece of light verse that represents a distinct change in tone in Schnackenberg's work, "Two Tales of Clumsy," is decidedly witty yet jarringly discordant when compared to her achievements both in her first book and in the final three poems of this second volume.

Preceding those final poems is another problematic but compellingly human sequence of love poems chronicling an emotionally turbulent love affair. Once again, though Schnackenberg's style is more graceful, one is reminded of the extremity of emotion in some of Plath's poems. Schnackenberg's celebration of eroticism, despite her emotional suffering, is quite distinct from Plath's work. Still, the tone and intimate subject matter of the five love poems addressed to an absent love—himself a poet "whose accent thrills my ear— / Last night you said not 'sever' but 'severe' "—that make up the fourth section of *The Lamplit Answer* invite comment both because they expand Schnackenberg's voice in an unanticipated way and because she herself, in the first of these, "Love Letter," asserts: "Two things are clear: these quatrains should be burned, / And love is awful, but it leads us to / Our places in the human comedy. . . ." Indeed these poems are extremely personal, in a sense private love letters made public. "Love Letter," for instance, concludes with the poet's personal signature as she addresses her lover who is currently in Rome: "May you sit in the company of saints / And intellectuals and fabulous beauties, / And not forget this constant love of Trude's."

But while the reader may initially feel both somewhat uncomfortable with the private circumstances that underlie these poems and put off by the self-consciousness and overindulgence of some of them, one ultimately is moved by the urgency of emotion that impels them and the formal lucidity with which Schnackenberg expresses

that urgency. Indeed, Schnackenberg tacitly legitimizes the love letter as an art form in "Paper Cities," a meditation on reading alone in her book-cluttered apartment in her lover's absence; her allusions to the correspondence between Gustave Flaubert and his mistress, Louise Colet, remind one that their letters occupy a privileged place in the literature of "Love in the Western World."

In the fourth and final section of *The Lamplit Answer*, Schnackenberg moves from meditations on the erotic to contemplations of spirituality, from natural to supernatural love. The first of these three poems, "Heavenly Feast," presents a portrait of Simone Weil, who during World War II died of starvation in England, where she fasted, while separated from her homeland, France, with more and more fanatic religious rigor:

> From summer into fall
> You cut your ration back
> To send your part to them,
>
> Your part diminishing
> To rations cut in half
> And cut in half again,
> And then nothing at all. . . .

Schnackenberg's triumph in such deliberately emaciated meters is in her ability to find language adequate to celebrate the spiritual significance of Weil's fast. Schnackenberg has written what amounts to a contemporary prayer, which ends on an image of "the little height of the grass" grasping the soil to render Weil's actions intelligible:

> It grips with a shocking might
> What matters to the last,
>
> As if the soil itself
> Were all that's left on earth,
> And all the earth were held
> Within its famished grasp.

The final two poems are also religious, though more personally so. The first of these, "Advent Calendar," explores the childlike sense of religious wonder as the speaker opens the various windows and doors of a German advent calendar. This peering triggers a meditation on time and faith, and a yearning for deeper understanding, taking the form of her desire for "entrance to the village / From my childhood where the doorways / Open pictures in the skies." But,

>   when all the doors are open,
> No one sees that I've returned.
> When I cry to be admitted,
> No one answers, no one comes.
> Clinging to my fingers only
> Pain, like glitter bits adhering,
> When I touch the shining crumbs.

The sacred and the secular search for knowledge are brought to a transcendent conclusion in the final poem, "Supernatural Love," a meditation on the transformative power of language to capture the "supernatural love" that unites Schnackenberg with her childhood self and, in so doing, resurrects once again her dead father, translating him into the realm of the eternal. She recalls in the poem a childhood scene in her father's study. Her father is poring over a dictionary, searching for "the lamplit answer" to the meaning of the word *carnation*, while his four-year-old daughter works on a needlepoint of the word *beloved*, though she is yet unable to read it. Confusing the word *carnation* for *incarnation*, the young girl believes carnations to be "Christ's flowers." The dictionary definitions the father discovers—"A pink variety of Clove, / *Carnatio*, the Latin, meaning flesh"—lead him to a deeper understanding of the word, affirming his daughter's understanding; for buried within the word *carnation* is the word for flesh, connecting it with Christ's Incarnation. Further, looking up the word *clove*, he discovers its root in the French word "*clou*, meaning a nail," connecting the word with the Crucifixion. Thus when the young poet pricks her finger with her needle, the conclusion of the poem translates the domestic scene into a symbol of both Christ's Incarnation and Crucifixion:

> I lift my hand in startled agony
> And call upon his name, "Daddy, daddy"—
> My father's hand touches the injury
>
> As lightly as he touched the page before,
> Where incarnation bloomed from roots that bore
> The flowers I called Christ's when I was four.

In these elegantly rhymed tercets Schnackenberg

does more than illustrate poetry's ability to reunite past and present, to return the child to the lost father and to the scene of her poetic origins. She reenacts the "supernatural love" between Christ on the cross—the cry "Daddy, daddy" an echo of Jesus' cry "Abba! Abba!"—and God the Father, a love that generates new life.

Since the publication of *The Lamplit Answer* Schnackenberg has maintained a low literary profile. Yet she has been recognized as one of the foremost poets of her generation and proclaimed a leading figure of the New Formalist movement—her "Supernatural Love" is included in Robert Richman's *The Direction of Poetry* (1988), an influential and controversial anthology of rhymed and metered poems written in English since 1975. Her silence has been broken only by her brief 1989 essay on T. S. Eliot in the *Yale Review* and an essay on Paul's Epistle to the Colossians for a volume of essays by poets on the New Testament, edited by Alfred Corn (1990). Schnackenberg has spent most of her time since 1985 working on a book-length poetry manuscript, whose ultimate form has yet fully to take shape. Her first published poem since the publication of *The Lamplit Answer*, "A Gilded Lapse of Time," appeared in the *New Yorker* on 15 June 1992. The publication of her third book will be of enormous interest to the poetry world, for Schnackenberg has already established herself as one of the most distinctive voices to have emerged in the last decade, a voice of such astonishing maturity, grace, and authority that one fully expects her to develop into one of the strongest American poets of the latter portion of this century and the beginning of the next.

References:

Paul Lake, "Return to Metaphor: From Deep Imagist to New Formalist," *Southwest Review*, 74 (Fall 1989): 515-529;

Lake, "Toward a Liberal Poetics," *Threepenny Review*, 8 (Winter 1988): 12-14;

Robert McPhillips, "Reading the New Formalists," *Sewanee Review*, 97 (Winter 1989): 73-96;

Peter Viereck, "Strict Wildness: The Biology of Poetry," *Poets & Writers*, 16 (May/June 1988): 7-12.

Vikram Seth

(20 June 1952 -   )

Brian Abel Ragen
Southern Illinois University at Edwardsville

BOOKS: *Mappings* (Calcutta: Lal/Writers Work-
shop, 1981);
*From Heaven Lake: Travels Through Sinkiang and
Tibet* (London: Chatto & Windus/Hogarth,
1983; London & Boston: Faber & Faber,
1986);
The Humble Administrator's Garden (Manchester,
U.K.: Carcanet, 1985);
The Golden Gate: A Novel in Verse (New York: Ran-
dom House, 1986; London & Boston: Faber
& Faber, 1986);
All You Who Sleep Tonight (New York: Knopf,
1990; London: Faber, 1990).

SELECTED PERIODICAL PUBLICATION—
UNCOLLECTED: "Forms and Inspirations," *London Review of Books*, 10 (29 September
1988): 18-20.

Vikram Seth's novel in verse, *The Golden
Gate* (1986), won wide acclaim. Its verse is sometimes playful and sometimes exquisite, and its narrative is involving, often funny, and sometimes
profoundly touching. The long narrative poem
had been making a resurgence after long years
of dormancy, but with Seth's work it seemed to
have regained not only respect but popularity:
The Golden Gate drew not just the attention of the
New York Times and the *New Republic* but also of *People* magazine and the Book-of-the-Month Club.
And it attracted the intense devotion of many
readers, who read passages aloud to whoever
would listen. What made the book all the more surprising was the range of cultures encompassed: a
novel in English about young professionals and
computer programmers in San Francisco, cast in
the fourteen-line stanza form of Aleksandr
Pushkin's *Eugene Onegin* (1833), and written by
an Indian educated at Oxford, who was a student of the economic demography of China and
whose earlier works were an entertaining travel
book about hitchhiking across Tibet and two
books of short poems.

Vikram Seth

Seth was born into a Hindu family in Calcutta on 20 June 1952. His mother is Justice
Leila Seth, a judge of the Delhi High Court; his father, Premnath Seth, is a consultant to the
leather industry. Vikram Seth received an English-
style education in India at the Doon School. He
then went to Corpus Christi College, Oxford,
where he read philosophy, politics, and economics.

After receiving his B.A., Seth went to Stanford University to study economics. Seth's academic specialty became the economic demography of Chinese villages, but while at Stanford he
also studied poetry. He balanced courses in macro-

economics with tutorials in poetry, but he later devoted one year to work in Stanford's creative-writing program. He singles out the influence of two poets with whom he studied at Stanford: Donald Davie and Timothy Steele. Both use traditional forms and craftsmanlike precision. In his 1988 essay "Forms and Inspirations" Seth describes how both those teachers molded his thinking about verse. Steele, with whom he first studied, emphasized the formal aspects of verse and introduced Seth to the work of other poets, such as Philip Larkin, who use traditional forms. Davie stressed "the crucial oral element in poetry," demanding that the poem be heard, and that the form, however exquisite, convey something to the reader beyond the poet's mastery of his craft.

Seth received his M.A. in economics from Stanford in 1979, and in 1981 his first volume of poetry was published. Seth began study in China at Nanjing University. His research there has not yet produced his projected dissertation, "Seven Chinese Villages: An Economic and Demographic Portrait," but the stay in China did bring forth other important works. In summer 1981 Seth returned home to his parents in Delhi through Tibet and Nepal, not a usual or convenient route but an appealing one for the adventurous. Seth describes his journey in *From Heaven Lake* (1983). This travel book gives a fascinating portrait of China in the years of relaxation after the upheavals of the cultural revolution. *From Heaven Lake* also shows Seth's abiding interest in different cultures: he discusses the influence of Islam in Sinkiang, the interaction of Tibetans and Han Chinese, and the contrast between Indian and Chinese life. The book makes vivid the hardships as well as the pleasures of travel, both of which are occasionally described in verse:

Cold in the mudlogged truck
I watch the southern sky:
A shooting star brings luck;
A satellite swims by.

Seth won the Thomas Cook Travel Book Award for *From Heaven Lake* in 1983, the Commonwealth Poetry Prize in 1986, and the Sahitya Akademi Award in 1988. He held a Guggenheim Fellowship for 1986-1987.

From Heaven Lake was written during Seth's second year in China. The poems in the first section of his next book, *The Humble Administrator's Garden* (1985), also date from his time as a stu-

dent at Nanjing, and some of them revisit places described in the travel book. Some poems, including "The Accountant's House" and "Research in Jiangsu Province," describe the tension between studying people as subjects of research and encountering them as human beings. Others evoke places—the ruined Confucian temple in Suzhou, Nanjing at the end of the school year, the garden described in the title poem—or moments of unexpected feeling, as in "A Little Night Music":

White walls. Moonlight. I wander through
The alleys, skein-drawn by the sound
Of someone playing the erhu.
A courtyard; two chairs on the ground.

As if he knew I'd come tonight
He gestures, only half-surprised.
The old hands poise. The bow takes flight
And unwished tears come to my eyes.

The poems written in China take many forms—there are Shakespearean sonnets, poems in ballad stanzas, and several unrhymed poems—and encompass many tones, from flippant to sober.

The poems in the two remaining sections of *The Humble Administrator's Garden* were written in India and California and reflect those locations. In many of the poems throughout the collection, Seth's attention is focused on human activity in the natural world, and images of trees and animals are juxtaposed with descriptions of human joys and sorrows. Mr. Wang, the humble administrator, and the comfortable social classes in one of the Indian poems, inhabit carefully tended gardens, which Seth renders as attractive while at the same time hinting that these preserves full of squirrels and carp are built on something dubious. In some of the California poems there is a sense of communication between a man and a wild creature. In "Curious Mishaps" the speaker sees a squirrel, which has seemed to salute him, carried away by an owl. In "Ceasing Upon Midnight," a man contemplating suicide walks out of his dreary house and finds himself not alone:

The breeze comforts him where he sprawls.
Raccoons' eyes shine. A grey owl calls.
    He imitates its cries,
    Chants shreds, invents replies.

The alcohol, his molecules,
The clear and intimate air, the rules
    Of metre, shield him from
    Himself. . . .

(That the rules of meter are as protective as the natural world is not surprising in a poem by Seth.) This concern with the interplay of the human and the natural continues in *The Golden Gate*, amusingly in the many cats that prowl through the book, more seriously in the contrast between the cultivated nature of the vineyards and the potential destruction embodied by the armaments factory.

The Humble Administrator's Garden contains confessional poems about lost or absent love, such as "From a Traveler," and "From California," as well as one fairly long narrative poem, "From the Babur-Nama, Memoirs of Babur, First Moghul Emperor of India." All are tightly structured, many are amusing, and some are deeply touching. But for all its craft and variety, *The Humble Administrator's Garden* gives only hints of the breadth of skill that Seth would display in his next work.

Most of *The Golden Gate* was written at Stanford—Seth was a senior editor at Stanford University Press from 1985 to 1986—though parts were composed during visits to England and India. Seth's immediate model was Charles Johnston's 1977 translation of *Eugene Onegin*, which accomplishes the difficult task of making Pushkin's stanza effective in English. One of the delights of *The Golden Gate* is seeing Seth work in that complicated stanza, with its alternation of feminine and masculine rhymes. From the acknowledgements and table of contents at the beginning to the note on the author at the end, everything is in the Onegin stanza. There are many echoes of Johnston, Pushkin, and Lord Byron—as in the opening "To make a start more swift than weighty / Hail Muse"—but Seth is firmly in control of his form and can adapt it to everything from comic descriptions of cats to an extended speech at an antinuclear rally.

The Golden Gate is not just a bravura technical performance. It is also an involving narrative. John, a computer programmer in a defense plant, meets Liz, a lawyer and the daughter of an old wine-making family, through a personal ad placed for him by his former lover Jan, and the novel follows these three and their friends. The plot complications are characteristic of the 1980s: John is estranged from his best friend, Phil, and later from his other friends, over the question of a freeze on nuclear arms production; Phil has a brief affair with Liz's brother Ed, a devout man who feels guilty about his homosexuality. Though some of the trappings are trendy—the personal ads, the telephone in the shape of Mickey Mouse—the central action is that of the traditional novel: a courtship leading to marriage and birth. Some of the characters become very vivid, especially as Seth describes their reaction to loss. Though *The Golden Gate* is often funny and has the overall shape of a comedy, it often describes grief in one form or other: John drives his lover Liz away, and she marries his friend Phil; as John realizes he loves Jan, she is killed on the highway.

Indeed, though *The Golden Gate* seems akin to light verse at the beginning, it is often surprisingly touching, as when Paul, a small boy, is reminded at a concert of his mother, who has divorced his father and moved away:

> The lights have dimmed. Now they're returning.
> Throats clear. Brahms' A Minor begins.
> The brisk allegro. Then a yearning
> Warm ductile length of lyric spins
> Its lovely glimmering thread at leisure
> Inveiglingly from measure to measure
> With a continuous tenderness
> So deep it smooths out all distress,
> All sorrow; ravishing, beguiling . . .
> And on and on till silence comes.
> Paul whispers, "That's the tune Mom hums!"
> Phil's eyes are closed, but Paul is smiling,
> Floating on a slow tide of Brahms,
> Back in his absent mother's arms.

One of Seth's achievements in *The Golden Gate* is making his characters speak in lively colloquial English while he follows Pushkin's form. As the novel proceeds, the characters debate many issues, such as nuclear weapons, religion, and sex. Some critics have found these discussions a distraction from the story, but most of the debates in the novel are lively.

The story ends on a note of grand reconciliation. After many deaths, the marriage of Liz and Phil, and the birth of their baby, there is only one figure left estranged: John, mourning the dead Jan and angry at Liz and Phil. In the final stanzas, Liz writes to invite John to be the godfather of the child, and John can almost hear Jan telling him how to reply:

> "I'm with you John. You're not alone.
> Trust me, my friend; there is the phone.
> It isn't me you are obeying.
> Pay what are your own heart's arrears.
> Now clear your throat; and dry these tears."

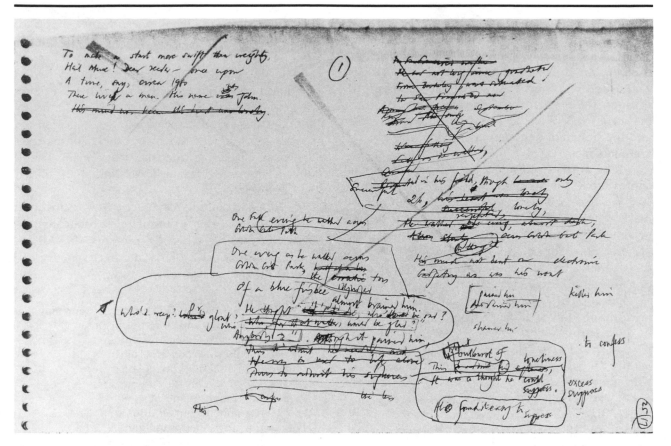

Page from an early draft for The Golden Gate: A Novel in Verse *(by permission of Vikram Seth)*

The novel comes to an almost Victorian conclusion.

The critical reaction to *The Golden Gate* was, overall, very positive. Most critics were surprised a novel in verse was attempted and were delighted that it succeeded so well. John Hollander wrote, "The use of expertly controlled verse to give moral substance and extraordinary wit and plangency to a far from extraordinary tale is an astonishing achievement in its own right (*New Republic*, 16 April 1986). X. J. Kennedy noted the involving story: "A splendid tour de force, *The Golden Gate* finally hooks us into caring less about its author's skill than in caring how its sad and wistful comedy will turn out. For pages, we forget Seth's incredible dexterity. Mesmerized, we watch, as in a kaleidoscope, the shifting and resettling pattern of five lives" (*Los Angeles Times Book Review*, 6 April 1986). Adverse commentary tended to focus on the politics and the accepting treatment of homosexuals. In a review in *Commentary* Carol Iannone objected, "The ideas and themes of *The Golden Gate* derive wholly from the arsenal of contemporary liberal orthodoxies" (3 September 1986). Iannone complained that the characters

with liberal politics win all the arguments and that "The ability to accept homosexuality in oneself or in others becomes one of those measures of a character's entitlement to emotional rewards." But most readers, even those with more conservative views, did not find that the ideology in the book reduced their pleasure in Seth's verbal skill and narrative force.

In 1990 he published another book of short poems, *All You Who Sleep Tonight*, in which many of the themes of *The Golden Gate* reappear. (There is even a meditative poem written to celebrate the fiftieth anniversary of the bridge for which the novel is named.) Once again Seth displays his mastery of a wide variety of forms. The first group of poems, "Romantic Residues," is made up of reflections on lost love—or love never quite grasped. They do not describe the grand moments of romantic drama but rather the more mundane moments that continue to agitate the heart. In "Round and Round" the speaker sees a familiar suitcase on a baggage carousel:

I knew that bag. It must be hers.
We hadn't met in seven years!

And as the steel plates squealed and clattered
My happy memories chimed and chattered.
An old man pulled it off the Claim.
My bags appeared: I did the same.

In all these poems, feeling is genuine and not overstated.

The second section, "In Other Voices," comprises dramatic monologues on historical subjects. A translation from the Chinese of Du Fu, "To Wei Ba, Who Has Lived Away from the Court," is especially good. With its delight in friendship, food, and rhyme, this address to an old friend is reminiscent of some of Ben Jonson's poetry. The remaining poems in the section are on grimmer subjects: the Holocaust, the bombing of Hiroshima, and the aftermath of the Indian mutiny. The final poem, "Soon," is the monologue of a dying AIDS patient. Like "From the Babur-Nama," these poems show a novelist's interest in capturing the voice of another.

The third group of poems, "In Other Places," continues the series of poems on China and Northern California from *The Humble Administrator's Garden*, and some of them, especially "Hill Dawn" and "Suzhou Park," are exquisite. This section is followed by a series of epigrammatic quatrains reminiscent of another Stanford poet, J. V. Cunningham. A final group of poems, "Meditations of the Heart," deal mostly with the isolation of each person. *The Golden Gate*, with its concluding vision of community, is largely about overcoming that isolation. These poems are more about the fact of isolation—which is, at least, shared:

All you who sleep tonight
Far from the ones you love,
No hand to left or right,
And emptiness above—

Know that you aren't alone.
The whole world shares your tears,
Some for two nights or one,
And some for all their years.

The Golden Gate established Vikram Seth as an important figure in American literature, and his career may take new directions. Since the publication of the novel in verse, he has written, besides the poems in *All You Who Sleep Tonight*, a verse play set in an English publishing house and a book of translations from Chinese poets of the Tang Dynasty, and he has begun a prose novel set in India. (In part because of the novel, he has recently been spending more time in his native land.) But he will remain important for more than his daring exploration of forms. The voice that speaks through his works, especially *The Golden Gate*, is unusual in modern American verse, and that, together with his great verbal skill, makes Seth a poet of interest.

Robert B. Shaw
(16 July 1947 -   )

Robert McPhillips
Iona College

BOOKS: *Curious Questions* (Oxford, U.K.: Carcanet, 1970);
In Witness (London: Anvil, 1972);
Comforting the Wilderness (Middletown, Conn.: Wesleyan University Press, 1977; Manchester, U.K.: Carcanet, 1978);
The Call of God: The Theme of Vocation in the Poetry of Donne and Herbert (Cambridge, Mass.: Cowley, 1981);
The Wonder of Seeing Double (Amherst: University of Massachusetts Press, 1988).

PLAY PRODUCTION: *Bontshe the Silent* [opera based on a story by I. L. Peretz], libretto by Shaw, music by Robert Sirota, Cambridge, Mass., Agassiz Theater, May 1982.

OTHER: *American Poetry Since 1960: Some Critical Perspectives*, edited by Shaw (Cheadle, U.K.: Carcanet, 1973; Chester Springs, Pa.: Dufour, 1974);
Henry Vaughan: A Selection of His Poems, edited by Shaw (Cheadle, U.K.: Carcanet, 1976);
"George Herbert: The Word of God and the Words of Man," in *Ineffability: Naming the Unnameable from Dante to Beckett*, edited by Peter S. Hawkins and Anne H. Schotter (New York: AMS, 1984), pp. 81-93;
"The Epistle of Paul the Apostle to the Hebrews," in *Incarnation: Contemporary Writers on the New Testament*, edited by Alfred Corn (New York: Viking, 1990), pp. 265-280.

SELECTED PERIODICAL PUBLICATIONS—
UNCOLLECTED: "Philip Larkin: A Stateside View," *Poetry/Nation*, 6 (Spring 1976): 100-109;
"Reconsideration: Edwin Muir," *New Republic*, 176 (18 June 1977): 39-41;
"Richard Wilbur's World," *Parnassus*, 5 (Spring/Summer 1977): 175-185;
"Farewells to Poetry," *Yale Review*, 70 (Winter 1981): 187-205;

Robert B. Shaw (photograph by Fred LeBlanc)

"Heaney's Purgatory," *Yale Review*, 74 (Summer 1985): 581-588;
"Is There a New Formalism?," *Cream City Review*, 12 (Summer 1988): 1-3;
Contribution to "Symposium on the New Formalism and the New Narrative," *Crosscurrents*, 8 (January 1989): 99-102;
"Robert Fitzgerald: A Tribute and Some Later Thoughts," *Verse*, 7 (Winter 1990): 28-32;
"Rereading Randall Jarrell," *Poetry*, 158 (May 1991): 100-113.

Robert B. Shaw is a poet, critic, and professor who has the unusual distinction of having spent virtually all his adult life within Ivy League universities before his move to Mount Holyoke College, where he is currently a professor of English. As an undergraduate at Harvard in the late 1960s, Shaw studied poetry with Robert Fitzgerald and Robert Lowell, from whom he learned his mastery of traditional poetic meter and forms. As it turns out, Shaw was to emerge from this atmosphere as one of the first poets among his generation to eschew the "radical" poetics of the sort promulgated in the manifestos eventually collected in 1973 by Donald Allen and Warren Tallman in *The Poetics of the New American Poetry*. Shaw's first book-length collection of poems, *Comforting the Wilderness* (1977), was pointed to by Dana Gioia, in his essay "Notes on the New Formalism" in the *Hudson Review* (Autumn 1987), as one of the first volumes—along with the first books of Timothy Steele and Charles Martin—to herald the arrival of what would be touted as the New Formalism, a movement that flourished amid controversy in the 1980s. Among its contingent were many poets similarly educated at Harvard, including Gioia, Katha Pollitt, Rachel Hadas, Brad Leithauser, and Mary Jo Salter. When Shaw's *The Wonder of Seeing Double* was published in 1988, Richard Wilbur, impressed by Shaw's "remarkable range of themes, tones, and forms [that come] natural to him," called him "certainly one of the best poets of his generation."

Robert Burns Shaw was born on 16 July 1947 in Philadelphia and was the second of four children of Gordon Walter Shaw, an advertising copywriter, and Elizabeth Anne Shaw, an artist (his parents were cousins, so his mother maintained her original name when married). The poet Robert Burns is a collateral ancestor. The young Shaw spent the first four years of his life living with his parents at the home of his maternal grandparents next door to the Presbyterian church where his grandfather was a minister. Though Shaw would later convert to the Episcopal faith and study for the priesthood, the importance of these early years in the development of his religious beliefs is shown in the essay he wrote on the Epistle of Paul to the Hebrews for *Incarnation*, Alfred Corn's 1990 anthology of essays by contemporary writers on the New Testament.

The example of Shaw's grandfather "at the center of things, which is to say, in the pulpit," influenced him as a poet: "Something new came

into his voice when he quoted Scripture, and as I listened something came into me which had little to do with intellectual understanding. There was nothing put on or actorish about his voice at such times, but it had a ritual deliberateness which stemmed, I would suppose, from due reverence.... There was a sense in all this which I could not have articulated then, of an order of being different from mine: an invisible world which interpenetrated the one I saw (or at these moments, did not see)." Shaw orchestrates sounds fluently and reverently in his poems, often trying to penetrate to the "invisible world" that underlies the ordinary details of domestic life, on which he meditates in the manner of a contemporary George Herbert. (Shaw wrote his doctoral thesis at Yale on Herbert and John Donne.)

At age four Shaw moved with his family to suburban Levittown and later to Smithtown, both on Long Island. Shaw first began reading and writing poetry in his suburban high school, influenced initially by Robert Frost and many of the poets in the Louis Untermeyer anthologies. Later influences included the more difficult poetry of W. B. Yeats, T. S. Eliot, Robert Lowell, and John Berryman. He also drew on this suburban landscape—which includes various beaches—as well as relatives' farms in Ohio and in upstate New York, which he often visited during summers, in many of his narrative poems, such as "Birth of a Critical Spirit" in *Comforting the Wilderness* and "Early Natural History" in *The Wonder of Seeing Double*.

Shaw entered Harvard University in the fall of 1965. There, in addition to studying with Lowell and Fitzgerald—who became his mentor and close friend—Shaw was also heavily involved in undergraduate literary life. He was friends with Michael Schmidt, who transferred to Oxford and eventually founded Carcanet Press. Schmidt was responsible for the publication of the first two chapbooks of Shaw's poems in England. With his roommate John Plotz, Shaw launched the literary magazine the *Island* when both were freshmen. Although printed by mimeograph and mostly consisting of students' poetry, it also featured several *Paris Review*-type interviews with W. H. Auden, Jorge Luis Borges, Howard Nemerov, and Adrienne Rich. As a sophomore he joined the *Harvard Advocate* and served as its president in his junior year, with Hadas as his poetry editor. Among his major accomplishments at the *Advocate* was helping to publish a special issue on Berryman, which appeared in 1969. That year Shaw

graduated from Harvard and delivered the class
ode at the commencement ceremony, a poem necessarily written to the tune of "Fair Harvard."

In 1969 Shaw married Nancy Anne
Olenchuk (called Hilary), whom he met when
she was attending Wellesley, where she received a
B.A. in art history. She is currently assistant to
the dean of studies at Mount Holyoke. The
Shaws have two children, Catherine Frances,
born in 1978, and Anthony Peter Gordon, born
in 1982, to each of whom Shaw dedicated a
poem in *The Wonder of Seeing Double*.

During the 1969-1970 academic year Shaw
shifted his focus from literature, attending Harvard Divinity School. In 1970 he converted to the
Episcopal church and considered becoming a
priest. Though he decided that his vocation lay
elsewhere and entered the doctoral program in
English at Yale—poor eyesight had disqualified
him from service in the army during the Vietnam War—his religious conversion and study influenced his dissertation on Donne and Herbert
(a revised version of which, *The Call of God: The
Theme of Vocation in the Poetry of Donne and Herbert*,
was published in 1981), as well as some of his poetry. Indeed, one of the strongest poems in *Comforting the Wilderness* is "On Becoming an Altar Boy,"
which contrasts the physical awkwardness of a
man in his twenties trying to perform the services of an altar boy with the redeeming value of
grace:

> So every week an hour or less
> shows me a hope that, after all,
> a Grace engaging clumsiness
> will lift what trembling hands let fall.

The modesty of this lyric voice is characteristic of
Shaw.

Shaw received his Ph.D. from Yale in 1974
and for the next two years returned to Harvard
as a Briggs-Copeland lecturer in English, teaching both creative writing and literature. In addition to Gioia, his students at this time included
the poets Julie Agoos, Judith Baumel, April Bernard, and Jacqueline Osherow. In 1976 Shaw
returned to Yale where, until 1983, he taught poetry writing and courses ranging from seventeenth-
century literature to modern poetry. Since 1983
Shaw has taught at Mount Holyoke, where he
was promoted to full professor in 1991.

Shaw's *Curious Questions* (1970) and *In Witness* (1972), as well as the anthology of essays on
contemporary poetry that he edited and contrib-

*Cover for the book that prompted Richard Wilbur to call
Shaw "one of the best poets of his generation"*

uted to, *American Poetry Since 1960* (1973), contain-
ing essays by Harold Bloom, Edward Mendelson,
J. D. McClatchy, James Atlas, Albert Gelpi, and
Alan Williamson, were published in England by
or upon the recommendation of Schmidt. During
the 1970s, while writing the poems that would
ultimately be in his first book-length collection,
Shaw was also active as a critic. Among the poets
he has written on are Lowell, Berryman, Wilbur,
W. H. Auden, Edwin Muir, Randall Jarrell,
Philip Larkin, Howard Nemerov, James Merrill,
Seamus Heaney, Charles Simic, and Amy Clampitt. He has also written frequently on southern
fiction, particularly the short story.

If generally subdued in tone, *Comforting the
Wilderness* is notable for its graceful mastery of
meter and stanzaic forms, ranging from unrhymed couplets and rhymed quatrains to more intricately rhymed longer stanzas and free verse,
and for the diversity of its subject matter, ranging from personal lyrics to a long dramatic monologue spoken by a Russian émigré in Paris. In addi-

tion to "Birth of a Critical Spirit" and "On Becoming an Altar Boy," other successful poems that could be construed as autobiographical include "Boston Sunday Dinner," "In the Attic," "A Man and His Watch," "Mid-July," "Morning Message," "Renovations," "The Pause," "Heat Wave," "Climb and Cloudburst," and "Old Photograph"—which presents "a portrait of The Poet Under Twenty" (in the form of a meditation on a photograph taken at Harvard):

> I shake my head in reminiscent judgment:
> All he was good at, now and then, was writing.
> A bit severe? A bit too baldly stated. . . .
> I wouldn't trust him, then or now or ever,
> with anything more serious than words,
> but feel he meant well, as I hope I do.

Many of the lyrics in *Comforting the Wilderness* are love poems, and among the most successful of them is "Morning Message," an aubade written to an absent lover "a hundred miles away in Maine" (reminiscent, in its focus on separation, of Donne's "A Valediction: Forbidding Mourning"):

> Is there an ether of attracted souls
> to kite their stirrings over unhappy gaps?
> Or do our minds, like magnets, reverse poles
> in a rich trade of dreams? . . .

In this first full-length volume Shaw demonstrates his interest in poetic conceits and tropes as the subject matter for poetry. While in some similar poems in his more recent work these efforts can be read as elegant exercises lacking an informing emotion, the best of these early poems, such as "Simile," perfectly match content with trope:

> Like a drunk after a knock-down, drag-out night,
> steering a weird course through a city square
> . . . .
> a poet wanders prey to his own mad dare,
> wobbles amid words, startles them into flight.

On the other hand, one of the disappointments in the volume is Shaw's longest narrative, "Safe on Friendly Soil," which comprises the third of the four sections. While this poem about an Eastern European aristocrat forced into exile in Paris after the Communist Revolution is an accomplished character sketch fleshed out with convincing details and emotions, it fails as a narrative because it lacks a sense of drama, leading neither to catharsis nor an illuminating epiph-

any. Shaw's shorter narratives are more successful. These include "Birth of a Critical Spirit" and "Boston Sunday Dinner." The latter describes the speaker's formal dinner with a wealthy older woman, an aging Boston Brahmin who reminisces about days when poets were more prominent in society that they are today, days when James Russell Lowell "was our Ambassador."

In *The Wonder of Seeing Double* Shaw remains interested in poems whose structures reflect their subjects—as in the thematically related poems "Narcissus" and "Echo"—as well as in celebrating domestic life in poems on Shaw's childhood, such as "Early Natural History" and "Homework," and on his current role as husband and father. Some poems reflect more of a sense of diminishment than the earlier poems, the middle-aged poet contemplating time and habit robbing the world of some luminosity.

Time, as it affects both the poet as observer and the objects observed, is central to many of Shaw's strongest poems. In a sequence of six brief, formal lyrics, "Chronometrics," he writes about clocks and the measurement of time. In "Turning Back the Clock," for example, he explores the Marvellian theme of trying to outrace the sun and block out full consciousness of impending winter and, subsequently, death, as seen in the setting of the clocks back an hour each fall—to "win an extra hour of sleep tonight / and make each winter morn a shade more bright," recognizing that "nothing will draw short or slow the arc / the planet orbits through an ordered dark / whose clock but once was set," while still registering the human wish to conquer time.

Time and diminishment also animate two of the most successful narrative poems in the volume. In the longer of these, "Note Found in a Room in a Summer Hotel," the speaker fancifully believes that sleeping in a bed in this same hotel he used to stay in with his parents is causing him to dream of his childhood, as in this memory of his father:

> By main force my father yanks me blubbering
> under and through each cold, concussive wave,
> trying to teach me something in his way,
> suddenly parted from me with
> a wave of his vanishing hand,
> terror breaking to empty strangeness when
> the sea I fight alone turns into sand.

"Homework," on the other hand, presents a young boy doing his homework in the presence of a grandmother who "sewed mostly by feel," pausing periodically to rethread her needle, the only thing that, owing to her failing eyesight, "she needed help with." Two lyrics dedicated to Shaw's daughter and son toward the end of the volume, "A Time Piece" and "Morning Exercise," reverse this perspective. The latter shows the speaker shaving at a mirror with his son, his biological mirror, watching:

> I notice, bending nearer,
> the decades' detriments,
> then try the kindlier mirror
> his upturned face presents.

Among Shaw's many poems on writing, "Circumlocution" is representative. There is a comparison between generations, the poet at his desk recalling the sound of an older man—his grandfather? Robert Fitzgerald?—in his office above him, "Writing? Walking. / Thinking on foot, one old man's way / of not wasting paper," keeping "the circular file" of the wastebasket enviably unfilled. This image contrasts with a final portrait of the speaker in middle age:

> As for me, what I wanted
> was a desk like this someday,
> which now I have and at which now I sit,
> saving a little paper, throwing out more,
> seeing and hearing things, not writing, waiting,
> writing again, waiting for the right sounds.

Shaw has completed a third book-length manuscript, tentatively titled "American Studies and Other Poems." The contents of this volume alternate, as in his others, between short, formal lyrics, characterized in the manuscript as "Episodes" and "Emblems," and a title sequence, which diverges from Shaw's previous books by containing more and longer narratives on historical subjects. The longest of these, "The Post Office Murals Restored," a meditation on murals painted in public buildings during the Depression, has appeared in the *Yale Review* (Spring 1989), and his narrative on Walt Whitman, "Last Days in Camden," in *Poetry* (March 1992). Shaw also intends to write further on Lowell's generation, in particular an essay on Elizabeth Bishop, and to gather his uncollected essays on contemporary poetry into a volume.

Primarily concerned with craftsmanship and artistic integrity, he has shunned both self-promotion and sensational or topical subject matter; as a result, despite his mastery of form and the polish of his erudite yet accessible language, he has yet to receive the full recognition he deserves. However, given the high quality of much of his work, Robert B. Shaw will likely find a larger audience, and his best poems will endure.

References:

Alfred Corn, "Hindsight, Insight, Foresight," *Poetry*, 153 (January 1989): 229-240;

Dana Gioia, "The Poetry of Robert B. Shaw," *Generation* (January/February 1978): 43-47;

Robert McPhillips, "Reading the New Formalists," in *Poetry After Modernism*, edited by Robert McDowell (Brownsville, Oreg.: Story Line, 1991), pp. 300-328.

Elizabeth Spires

(28 May 1952 -   )

William V. Davis
Baylor University

BOOKS: *Boardwalk* (Cleveland, Ohio: Bits, 1980);
Globe (Middletown, Conn.: Wesleyan University Press, 1981);
Swan's Island (New York: Holt, Rinehart & Winston, 1985);
Annonciade (New York: Viking/Penguin, 1989).

Elizabeth Spires's themes, she says, "draw on many sources: childhood, memories, places, and visual images such as paintings and photographs, illuminated manuscripts, and medieval books of hours." The poet she most admires, and with whom she shares themes and forms, is Elizabeth Bishop.

Spires was born in Lancaster, Ohio, on 28 May 1952 to Richard C. and Sue Wagner Spires. Her father worked in grounds maintenance; her mother was a real-estate broker. Elizabeth Spires was educated at Vassar College (B.A., 1974) and Johns Hopkins University (M.A., 1979). She is married to Madison Smartt Bell, a fiction writer. Spires currently teaches creative writing at Goucher College and at Johns Hopkins.

Globe (1981), her first full-length collection, contains twenty-two poems divided into three sections, preceded by a one-poem prelude, "Tequila," which sets the direction the book will take; the speaker leaves on a road "that leads / everywhere." The three sections of the book, each one longer than the last, "lead" out from the childhood world of home and family in the first section, through a series of character sketches (most of them dealing with women in historical settings), to the tone poems at the end of the book. Both structurally and thematically *Globe* moves to increasingly wider explorations of the world.

The first six poems of the first section are the strongest poems in the book. The speaker's parents, described as somewhat shadowy or dreamlike and "dark" (the father "dark and immediate," the mother's "face in darkness"), brood over the child, who is "falling toward the future," reaching "across the dark," singing through "the

Elizabeth Spires in June 1988 (photograph by Dixie Sheridan)

nights of my childhood," even though, caught up in and revolving through her "reveries," she knows she has forgotten "what the world meant to me then," but believes, as the first, title poem, has it, that false memories are "better than forgetting."

The other two sections of *Globe* are much more objective, at times even mechanical, and suggest the inevitable movement out into a wider world than that of childhood. The character sketches are set in several early American places ("Widow's Walk," "Salem, Massachusetts: 1692"), in literary history ("Exhumation, for Elizabeth Siddall [1832-1862], wife of Dante Gabriel Rossetti"), and in other cultures ("Courtesan With Fan," "After Three Japanese Drawings"), most of them focused on women and their difficult lives. Structurally these poems seem transitional, a necessary stage Spires needed to work through. Although they are at the center of the book, they are not central to it.

The final section of *Globe* contains the most diffuse, amorphous poems, a "negative music of silence." These are self-indulgent, precious, private, "poetic" tone poems. In several of the poems ("Snowfall" and "Blue Nude," the first two in the section, are good examples) Spires weaves words and images together into a kind of fugue of meaning and emotion in which "each page [is] only / part of a larger story," even if this "story" remains at one remove.

Although the poems in *Swan's Island* (1985) are drawn from various times (the six "Storyville Portraits," for instance, are based on E. J. Bellocq's photographs of the New Orleans red-light district of 1912), places, and sources, Spires has made them her own. There is an evenness of tone to this book that *Globe* lacks, but most of these poems, although often they are more proficient than the earlier ones, are not more memorable than the best poems in *Globe*.

The most powerful, fully realized poems in *Swan's Island* are short (several are sonnet length), compact, intense, and fully under control. Spires is a lyric poet and her longer poems, those not broken down in parts, tend to get away from her at this stage of her career. The best poem in *Swan's Island* is "Two Shadows." It begins:

When we are shadows watching over shadows,
when years have passed, enough to live
two lives, when we have passed
through love and come out speechless
on the other side, I will remember
how we spent a night, walking the streets
    in August, side by side. . . .

In Spires's next book, *Annonciade* (1989), the second, central section is a prose interlude titled "Falling Away," in which she documents in a short autobiographical "history" the dominant themes of the book:

Memory: I am sitting at my desk in sixth grade at St. Joseph's Elementary in Circleville, Ohio. It is a winter morning in 1964, and we are in the mid-

dle of catechism. The classroom is old-fashioned, with high ceilings and wood floors, the crucifix above the front blackboard in a face-off with the big round clock on the back wall.

This prose meditation mixes memory, imagination, and time, the three touchstones of Spires's work from the beginning, which are brought to climax and most fully detailed in this, her most accomplished book.

The theme of time runs throughout the book. There is hardly a page without some reference to it. "My birth," Spires says, is "a tear in time's fabric." And even if this "everlasting present" in which "there will always / be, for us, a tomorrow tomorrow," is simultaneously seen and recognized as a "past preserved and persevering," a "sentimental past," it is celebrated as it is announced—it is, indeed, that which Spires's *Annonciade* is all about.

Annonciade is, therefore, Spires's most definitive exploration of the world. There are poems set throughout America and in England, France, and Switzerland. There are poems focusing on earlier ages, on Spires's obsession with travel, and on her exploration of the psyche (particularly the female psyche).

There is an apocalyptic theme running through *Annonciade*. In "Sunday Afternoon at Fulham Palace" one reads, "It is easy, too easy, to imagine the world ending / on a day like today. . . ." In "Thanksgiving Night: St. Michael's" Spires writes: "we walk out, out on a finger of land / that points like a sign to World's End," where "the dead, living, and not-yet-born" are "gathered / around the great table." Even with this apocalyptic mood, Spires's title poem ends with "strange intimations of happiness," reminding one of William Wordsworth's "Intimations Ode" (1807), but Spires's poem, which combines allusions to Thomas Mann as well as to Wordsworth, is firmly contemporary, as she finds "intimations of happiness" even in the face of possible annihilation. An *annonciade* is an acknowledgment, like poetry itself, of the possibility of life in the face of death. In "The Celestial," the last poem in the book, fish in a Buddhist temple pond gaze "upward and forever."

Elizabeth Spires is one of the most important young poets in America. The auspicious beginning represented by her first books suggests that she will find a secure place in the world of contemporary poetry.

Maura Stanton
(9 September 1946 -   )

Sidney Burris
University of Arkansas

BOOKS: *Snow on Snow* (New Haven & London: Yale University Press, 1975);

Molly Companion (Indianapolis: Bobbs-Merrill, 1977);

Cries of Swimmers (Salt Lake City: University of Utah Press, 1984);

Tales of the Supernatural (Boston: Godine, 1988);

The Country I Come From (Minneapolis: Milkweed, 1988).

Maura Stanton's first book of poems, *Snow on Snow*, was published in 1975 as the seventieth installment of the Yale Series of Younger Poets; Stanley Kunitz presided as judge and wrote the introduction to the book. Michael Ryan preceded Stanton as a winner, and Carolyn Forché followed her. Although these three poets have since developed along different lines, their first books epitomize one of the prominent strains of American poetry written during the 1970s. Typically these poems depend on free verse as the dominant measure, deploy flexible stanza forms, and draw on a fund of images best and most often described as surrealistic, a hybrid poetics that Kunitz mastered in his own work.

Maura Stanton was born to Joseph Stanton, a salesman, and Wanda Haggard Stanton, a nurse, in Evanston, Illinois, on 9 September 1946; she received her B.A. from the University of Minnesota in 1969 and her M.F.A. in 1971 from the University of Iowa. She married Richard Cecil in 1972. Like many writers who make their living by working for colleges and universities, Stanton has traveled; she has taught at the State University of New York at Cortland (1972-1973), the University of Richmond (1973-1977), Humboldt State University (1977-1978), the University of Arizona (1978-1982), and Indiana University, where she has been employed since 1982. She won National Endowment for the Arts grants in 1974 and 1982, the Frances Steloff Fiction Prize in 1975, and the Lawrence Foundation Prize for short fiction presented by the *Michigan Quarterly Review* in 1982. She was also named as

Maura Stanton in 1977

the distinguished author in residence at Mary Washington College for the 1981-1982 academic year.

Often the poems in *Snow on Snow* resist specific regional affiliation, the kind of local detail that weds the conceptual scheme of the poem to an identifiable geography. "The Snow House" presents a nameless, cold climate; the motivating action of the poem is contained in a dream; and this tendency to rely on the mercurial yet pervasive influence of dreaming is a further hallmark of this 1970s style of verse. When poems of this sort are working efficiently, and Stanton's often do, they celebrate the mysteries of consciousness, and they often carry out their celebrations by pondering the limits of the imagination.

But in poems such as "The Conjurer," Stanton translates this traditional concern into her own fabular idiom, which although echoing the period's fascination with eccentric situations, moves beyond the period's often vague and private diction:

> In a mayonnaise jar I keep the tiny
> people I shrank with my magic; I didn't
> know they'd hold each other's hands & cry
> so sharply when I said, no the spell's
> irreversible, do you eat grass or breadcrumbs?

The poem presents an extended meditation, delivered as a monologue, on the conjurer's art, and there is a concern with the notion of imaginative responsibility.

Stanton's second poetry book, *Cries of Swimmers* (1984), identifies the strongest element of her first book because it so willfully develops it—her gift for narrative, based on her ability to move fluidly from line to line while maintaining simultaneously a sense of each line's integrity. (Of course, Stanton is also a successful story writer and novelist.) In her first poetry collection she largely avoided the sequential restrictions of plotting, but the poems of her second collection embrace those restrictions while retaining a measure of the surrealistic invention that characterizes her first book. In both collections, however, one notices the sure handling of events, the credible way in which she manages the simplest development. In "Maple Tree" (in *Cries of Swimmers*) she flirts with the sort of eccentric situation found in her first volume but grounds it within a strong narrative context:

> One day an old man turned his yellow eye
> Upon our maple tree, & climbed & climbed
> Until his grey coat shook like a squirrel's tail
> Above the black hats of the fire brigade
> & dancing children shouting, Fly! Oh, fly!

The old man apparently suffers a heart attack in the tree and is passed down to the ambulance. This bizarre incident reveals subtle but horrifying details about the crowd. The poem escapes being maudlin because of Stanton's narrative

proficiency—the reader is reminded of one of the fairy tales by the Brothers Grimm, where excruciating scenes are relayed in a disarmingly naive language.

Between her first and second collections of verse, Stanton published a novel, *Molly Companion* (1977). Particularly for a poet, novels offer rigorous exercises in plot and development, both essential to the kinds of narrative Stanton manages so deftly in her verse. Discovering the simplicity of cruelty, even the banality of evil, is certainly not new to the twentieth century, but Stanton's verse does depend on the reader's willingness to attach profound significance to the most fundamental elements of a carefully constructed situation—in other words, to enter the realm of the interpretation of dreams, the exploration of the unconscious, and the discovery of the Jungian archetype. All these were important influences on the poetry that provided Stanton her beginning, and they continue to be influences that she transforms, as in "Maple Tree," into a developing genealogy of poetic technique.

The kind of poetry that takes place in this "family" embraces what Stanton has correctly labeled "supernatural." The epigraph to her third collection, *Tales of the Supernatural* (1988), is from Samuel Taylor Coleridge's *Biographia Literaria* (1817), where he proposes, with William Wordsworth, to compose a poetry of two sorts, one of which would be supernatural. Coleridge's definition is succinct: in such poetry, "the excellence aimed at was to consist in the interesting of the affections by the dramatic truth of such emotions as would naturally accompany such situations, supposing them real." Stanton's "The Conjurer's Art" comes immediately to mind because in it she uses "incidents and agents," as Coleridge wrote, that suspend the reader's sense of the natural event and posit the supernatural event, while developing the appropriate, if incredible, emotional reaction. Stanton has effectively located in the nineteenth century one of surrealism's early forerunners, and it is an important discovery for her because it extends the tradition that she inherited in the 1970s, enriching her sense of that tradition's potential.

The school of poetry to which Stanton's early work belongs tended to avoid the kind of rational disputation found, say, in the work of W. H. Auden or Howard Nemerov, and when Stanton's poems err they do so because she loses control of their conclusions. If the remedy for this problem is the introduction of a reasonable, arguing voice, that remedy will fail because such a voice is entirely alien to the kind of poem that Stanton writes. In *Tales of the Supernatural* she avoids the sense of arbitrariness that occasionally mars her earlier work because of her newfound proficiency at choosing subject matter. At a certain point in a poet's career, it becomes evident that some subject matter will demand a tonal register foreign to the poet's most convincing scales. Stanton's previous careful attention to the neurasthenic element of human experience, when coupled with her strong gift for narrative, makes it seem inevitable that she would write a poem titled "The Headache," which begins: "I was sitting in a chair with my headache, / Wishing for something heartfelt and contagious, / To come in the mail, to telephone, or knock." Here is the barren, uncompromising simplicity of her early verse, but it is nestled within the accessible context of an event, perfectly chosen to sustain the earliest energies that gave birth to her writing but chosen as well to nourish them by removing them to other contexts, ones that demand the growth of her poetic strategies. This kind of adventurism characterizes much of *Tales of the Supernatural*.

Stanton's contemporary Ryan has recently moved toward a verse of more traditional form and acerbic tone, and Forché has insistently set her work to continuing the dialogue between the personal and political arenas. Stanton has shown a similar independence in her development and has published a collection of stories appropriately titled *The Country I Come From* (1988). Perhaps embodying more of the heralded hallmarks of her generation, she has also transformed them into a viable, distinctive idiom whose roots have been deepened and strengthened as her career has progressed. There is exhilaration in reading her latest poetic successes because they not only delight with their simple invention, but they reveal the innovative development of one dominant strain of writing that came to the forefront in America during the 1970s.

Timothy Steele

(22 January 1948 -   )

X. J. Kennedy

BOOKS: *Uncertainties and Rest* (Baton Rouge & London: Louisiana State University Press, 1979);

The Prudent Heart (Los Angeles: Symposium, 1983);

Nine Poems (Florence, Ky.: Barth, 1984);

On Harmony (Lincoln, Nebr.: Abattoir, 1984);

Short Subjects (Florence, Ky.: Barth, 1985);

Sapphics Against Anger and Other Poems (New York: Random House, 1986);

Beatitudes (Child Okeford, U.K.: Words, 1988);

Missing Measures: Modern Poetry and the Revolt Against Meter (Fayetteville: University of Arkansas Press, 1990).

OTHER: *The Music of His History: Poems for Charles Gullans on His Sixtieth Birthday*, edited by Steele (Florence, Ky.: Barth, 1989).

SELECTED PERIODICAL PUBLICATIONS— UNCOLLECTED:

POETRY

"Three Poems," *Numbers*, 1 (Autumn 1986): 35-38;

"Aurora," "Youth," "Dependent Nature," and "Pacific Rim," *New Criterion*, 6 (October 1987): 45-48;

"Decisions, Decisions" and "Practice," *Crosscurrents*, special issue, *Expansionist Poetry: The New Formalism and the New Narrative*, 8 (1989): 15-16.

NONFICTION

"The Structure of the Detective Story: Classical or Modern?," *Modern Fiction Studies*, 27 (Winter 1981-1982): 555-570;

"Matter and Mystery: Neglected Works and Background Materials of Detective Fiction," *Modern Fiction Studies*, 29 (Autumn 1983): 435-450;

"The Dissociation of Sensibility: Mannered Muses, Ancient and Modern," *Southern Review*, 19 (Winter 1983): 57-72;

Memoir of J. V. Cunningham, *Sequoia*, 29 (Spring 1985): 104-108;

"Tradition and Revolution: The Modern Move-

Timothy Steele (photograph by Julie Kwan)

ment and Free Verse," *Southwest Review*, 70 (Summer 1985): 294-319;

"An Interview with J. V. Cunningham," *Iowa Review*, 15 (Fall 1985): 1-24;

Statement in "Symposium," *Crosscurrents*, special issue, *Expansionist Poetry: The New Formalism and the New Narrative*, 8 (1989): 101-104.

Of poets born since World War II who continue to work in meter, Timothy Steele is among the most highly regarded. In recent years he has further emerged as a leading critic and theoretician of that casually organized movement in recent American poetry sometimes called New Formalism.

The son of Edward William Steele, a

teacher, and Ruth Reid Steele, a nurse, Timothy Reid Steele was born in Burlington, Vermont, on 22 January 1948. His boyhood in a part of New England remote from Boston might seem to place him in the shadow of Robert Frost, whose poems he encountered in grade school. But, although his poems recall Frost's in their fondness for synecdoche and understatement and in their devotion to traditional form, the comparison soon flags. It is difficult to imagine the modest Steele as a media figure and a performing poet-philosopher. His poetry, even when it seems to arise from his own life, does not deliberately reach out to enfold its audience; in person Steele eschews self-dramatization.

For most of his career Steele has been engaged in learning and teaching. Long before the powerful, lingering influence of formalist poet and teacher Yvor Winters had waned at Stanford University, Steele studied there, taking his B.A. in 1970. In 1975 he returned to Stanford as Jones Lecturer in Poetry, and since 1977 he has taught English on other California campuses, principally at UCLA and (at present) California State University, Los Angeles. His Ph.D. is from Brandeis University (1977).

During a sojourn back in New England as a graduate student in the early 1970s, Steele came under the sway of another eminent formalist poet and critic, J. V. Cunningham, whose emotionally intense poems are laconic and strictly fashioned. At Brandeis, Cunningham directed Steele's doctoral dissertation on the history and conventions of detective fiction. Perhaps more significantly for the younger man's poetry, Cunningham read some of Steele's work and commented (Steele recalls) "with his characteristic and supportive brevity."

Steele's first book, *Uncertainties and Rest* (1979), whose title hints at a thumbnail definition of meter, shows a younger poet still practicing an art that for two decades had been unfashionable in America. Containing sonnets, epigrams, quatrains, and ingenious stanzas, the collection is almost entirely in rhyme, its various forms managed with unusual competence. In "Jogging in the Presidio" Steele calls his favorite sport, running, "A laughable and solitary art," while displaying rare skill in placing one poetic foot after another:

Though wayside skeptics eye me, I pursue
Nothing particular, nothing that's mine,

But merely leaves brought down by a hard rain
Last evening, the clear wind the swallows ride,
And the grass over which my shadow bends
Evenly uphill as I hit my stride.

The central persona in the book struck one critic, John M. Miller (*Chowder Review*, Spring-Summer 1980), as making a certain "genteel withdrawal into elegant, decorous sensations," yet a strong, controlled intensity is everywhere. It is as if, rather than blindly courting sensation, the young poet sorts out his sensations critically. Readers glimpse contemporary America from the point of view of a young city dweller who stops to observe wryly a Florida dive, where the jukebox plays Merle Haggard and Kitty Wells, and of a slightly self-deprecating air traveler who feels "Strung out on distance and cocaine." The book harks back to Vermont and family, and it heralds, among other themes that endure in Steele's work, a devotion to love. "Last Night As You Slept" ends with a startling image:

Distance as chill as the light on the shades,
Was so uncertain, love, of our rest
That I woke you almost as I drew my chest
Against the warm wings of your shoulder blades.

The critic who works through such a poem for its subtle congeries of vowels and consonants realizes that Steele is a musician of words.

A strong debut, *Uncertainties and Rest* nevertheless took years to attract notice. Here and there, critics were impressed: in 1980 in the *Partisan Review*, J. D. McClatchy proclaimed, "It has given me . . . more pleasure than any other first book I have read this year." But the collection did not gain Steele immediate entry into many anthologies. In 1986 he was to receive much wider attention when Random House published the second of his two full-length collections, *Sapphics Against Anger and Other Poems*. Incorporating most of those poems he had printed in small and limited editions, the book seems more various and ambitious than its predecessor. It shows a more explicit and sympathetic concern for people: in "Near Olympic" the poet observes with keen-eyed sympathy the residents of a Japanese-Chicano neighborhood in Los Angeles, and "At Will Rogers Beach" has sketches of surfers and roller skaters. Steele's marriage (on 14 January 1979) to Victoria Lee Erpelding, a librarian, appears to have inspired new love lyrics. The beautifully crafted "Aubade" portrays a woman rising in the morning while her lover lingers in bed. In other engaging poems echoes of Vermont linger: in "Timothy," about new-mown hay, Steele appears to recall his boyhood through mature eyes.

> Pumping a handpump's iron arm,
> I washed myself as best I could,
> Then watched the acres of the farm
> Draw lengthening shadows from the wood
>
> Across the grass, which seemed a thing
> In which the lonely and concealed
> Had risen from its sorrowing
> And flourished in the open field.

Sapphics Against Anger shows Steele, without surpassing his mentor Cunningham in concision or intensity, going considerably beyond him in depth and range. In poem after poem Steele quietly relishes the wonders of ordinary experience: "Summer" declares its subject to be "voluptuous in plenty" and depicts a country road where a boy "initials soft tar with a stick." Physical sensations, which strike readers only occasionally in *Uncertainties and Rest*, are noticeable even in the brief, flawless poem "Waiting for the Storm." It conveys at least four sensory experiences: the sight of a "wrinkling" bay, the sensations of dampness and cold, and the sound of beginning rain. "The Sheets," about taking crisp laundry down from a clothesline, is another successful poem that apparently draws on childhood memories. Sensation in itself is never for long his object of concern, for as the more abstract "Chanson Philosophique" suggests, the nature of everyday experience invites thoughtful labeling. Steele's view of life, a classically tempered view, is made explicit in the title poem:

> For what is, after all, the good life save that
> Conducted thoughtfully, and what is passion
> If not the holiest of powers, sustaining
>   Only if mastered.

Living and working in Southern California, Steele has made himself prominent in a community of traditionalist poets, including the distinguished writer Janet Lewis, widow of Winters; the poet and fine-press publisher Charles Gullans; the English-born formalist Thom Gunn; and (at the University of California, Santa Barbara, where Steele in 1986 was visiting lecturer) poets Edgar Bowers, Alan Stephens, Dick

Davis, and John Ridland. Vikram Seth, who credits Steele with improving his metrical writing, dedicated to him the remarkable novel in verse *The Golden Gate* (1986).

In his most recent poems Steele has continued to express appreciation both for the life of the mind and for the sensuous world. These attitudes blend in "Aurora," from the chapbook *Beatitudes* (1988), in which a sleeping woman is invoked:

> Goddess, it's you in whom
> Our clear hearts joy and chafe.
> Awaken, then. Vouchsafe
> Ideas to resume.
> Draw back the drapes: let this
> Quick muffled emphasis
> Flood light across the room.

Whether or not he feels desolate before the gap between the ideal and reality, he understands the nature of pain. In "Dependent Nature," published in October 1987 in the *New Criterion*, he maintains that flowers climbing a trellis are spared

>   the sad mirth serving those who gauge
>
> The gap between the longed-for and the real,
> Who grasp provisional joy, who must not be
> Desolate, however desolate they feel.

But such desolation seems continually interrupted by moments of joy and glimpses of beauty. As Steele observes in "Eros," a poem published in *Numbers* (Autumn 1986),

> Gently to brush hair from the sleeping face,
> To feel breath on the fingers, and to try
> To check joy in that intimate, small place
> Where joy's own joyousness can't satisfy—
> This is pain. This is power that comes and goes.

Evidently, in the current poetic wars, Steele has enlisted on the side of meter. As he declared in his contribution to a 1989 symposium in *Crosscurrents*, "My keenest pleasure in reading poetry has from the beginning been bound up with the metrical experience; and I write in meter because only by doing so can I hope to give someone else the same degree of pleasure that the poetry I most love has given me." Robert McPhillips, a poet-critic sympathetic with New Formalism, has found Steele's work indebted to earlier academic formalists while containing "little of the ornateness of diction or heaviness of wit" characteristic of much American formal poetry of the 1950s. An influential judgment of Steele's poems has been that of Richard Wilbur, who calls Steele "one of the very best young poets now writing," praising him for his "easy, unforced mastery of form [and] that truth and warmth of feeling which is sometimes denied to the formalist." Gunn has also found in Steele's work a compelling synthesis of form and matter: "I never feel he has chosen to [write] in meter for any other reason than that by doing so he can make his speech more forceful."

The growing audience of those who care for Steele's poetry will find further insights in his critical book, *Missing Measures* (1990). With lightly wielded learning, Steele revises accepted histories of modern poetry, seeking to explain how meter, formerly the dominant force of English and classical poetry, can have become so widely neglected by most poets today. The revolution of Ezra Pound and T. S. Eliot, he believes, has resulted in generations of free-verse poets "merely following, by rote and habit, a procedure of writing, and breaking up into lines, predictably mannered prose."

So far, Steele's career, like Wilbur's, has been characterized not by grand gestures and epic aspirations but by the slow accumulation of unpretentious and resounding victories. The reader who appreciates fine formal poetry will watch Steele's development with keen attention. Whatever he has yet to do, Steele has already left his mark. If those critics who have celebrated him are right, then in whatever anthology future readers may distill out of late-twentieth-century American poetry, Timothy Steele must already have lodged contributions likely to prove indispensable.

References:

R. S. Gwynn, "Second Gear," *New England Review and Bread Loaf Quarterly*, 9 (Autumn 1986): 111-121;

Gordon Harvey, "Illusions Not Illusions Any Longer," *Sequoia*, 28 (Spring 1984): 91-98;

Mary Kinzie, "The Overdefinition of the Now," *American Poetry Review*, 11 (March-April 1982): 13-17;

Paul Lake, "Toward a Liberal Poetics," *Threepenny Review*, 8 (Winter 1988): 12-14;

Robert McPhillips, "What's New about the New Formalism," *Crosscurrents*, 8 (1989): 64-75.

Leon Stokesbury
(5 December 1945 -   )

R. S. Gwynn
Lamar University

BOOKS: *Often in Different Landscapes* (Austin & London: University of Texas Press, 1976);
The Drifting Away of All We Once Held Essential (Denton, Tex.: Trilobite, 1979);
The Royal Nonesuch (Tallahassee: Anhinga, 1984);
The Drifting Away (Fayetteville: University of Arkansas Press, 1986).

OTHER: *The Made Thing: An Anthology of Contemporary Southern Poetry*, edited by Stokesbury (Fayetteville: University of Arkansas Press, 1987);
Articles of War: A Collection of American Poetry About World War II, edited by Stokesbury (Fayetteville: University of Arkansas Press, 1990);
The Light the Dead See: The Selected Poems of Frank Stanford, edited by Stokesbury (Fayetteville: University of Arkansas Press, 1991).

SELECTED PERIODICAL PUBLICATIONS—
UNCOLLECTED: "Señor Wences and the Man in the Box," *New England Review*, 12 (Fall 1989): 82-83;
"The Royal Nonesuch," *Kenyon Review*, 12 (Winter 1990): 78-79.

Leon Stokesbury in 1990

Among the poets of the generation born between 1940 and 1955, those whose work was included in *The Morrow Anthology of Younger American Poets* (1985), Leon Stokesbury has perhaps been the most selective about the number of poems he has allowed into print, having published only two collections and two chapbooks in a career that spans four decades. In an age when many poets have seemingly confused quantity with quality, Stokesbury remains a scrupulous craftsman, often revising poems up to the moment of publication. A public performer of great skill, he has increasingly tailored his poems over the years to the cadences and range of idioms of his speaking voice, and as remarkable as his poems may appear on the page they gain immeasurably when the poet presents them in one of his frequent readings. However, Stokesbury's work possesses depths beyond the poems' surface humor and pathos; a serious student of traditional techniques, Stokesbury has also written formal poems, some of which have been included in the anthology *Strong Measures: Contemporary American Poetry in Traditional Forms* and in the reference book *Patterns of Poetry* (both 1986). His successes as a maker of poems, as a memorable reader of his own work, and, in recent years, as an editor of anthologies and collections mark him as a leading figure among his contemporaries.

Leon Stokesbury, the son of Leon B. and Jennie Smith Stokesbury, was born on 5 December

1945 in Oklahoma City. During his childhood his father held various jobs in the petroleum industry. When the poet was four he was stricken with polio of the stomach muscles, from which he fully recovered, and when he was eight, the family moved to Texas, living in Conroe and Houston before settling in 1959 in Silsbee, a small town at the edge of the East Texas pine forests, where Stokesbury would spend the rest of his childhood. In 1964 Stokesbury entered Lamar State College of Technology (now Lamar University) in Beaumont, commuting approximately one-hundred miles daily for the next four years. Lamar Tech, as the name indicates, was primarily a training ground for scientists and engineers but had a strong English department, which sponsored a variety of literary activities and undergraduate writing awards. Stokesbury published his first poems in *Pulse*, the student magazine, and several times won the Eleanor P. Weinbaum Award for poetry, going on to edit the magazine himself during his senior year.

A visit to Beaumont by poet Alistair Reid proved lucky for the young poet. Impressed by Stokesbury's poetry, Reid suggested that he submit to the *New Yorker*; Stokesbury's "The Lamar Tech Football Team Has Won Its Game" was accepted and appeared in a 1967 issue. This and several other undergraduate poems reveal a remarkable early talent and hold up well when compared with the more mature work collected with them in his first book. These successes strengthened Stokesbury's determination to follow a career in writing, and he began graduate work in the creative-writing program at the University of Arkansas in the fall of 1968. During his years there he studied with James Whitehead and Miller Williams and formed close associations with other young poets in the poetry workshop, among them Frank Stanford, whose selected poems Stokesbury was to edit two decades later. In 1969 he attended the Bread Loaf Writers Conference on a scholarship (he returned there as a fellow in 1990).

In the summer of 1970, following his parents' move to Fairbanks, Alaska, where his father was employed by Atlantic Richfield Corporation, Stokesbury found three months' employment in the North Slope oil fields, an experience that would provide material for several poems. Following his graduation from Arkansas with an M.A. and M.F.A. in 1972, Stokesbury returned to Lamar as an instructor, serving there until 1975, when he entered the Ph.D. program in oral inter-

pretation at the University of Texas. His first book, *Often in Different Landscapes* (1976), was co-winner of the Associated Writing Programs' poetry competition and the first selection of the University of Texas Press poetry series.

As the title makes clear, many of the poems in this collection take their direction from a literal sense of locale. "East Texas," an unmetered sonnet, opens with a description of the surroundings of the poet's childhood:

> The taste in my mouth
> Was the taste of blood or rust on backdoor thermom-
>   eters
> Unread for twenty years. With my cheesecloth
> Net I waited in the woods. Then the flutters
> Of the giant swallowtails could be heard far away.

"To All Those Considering Coming to Fayetteville" speaks of the Ozarks: "small mountains, almost / not mountains at all, but rather, with trees / sticking up, they seem more like / the white hairy bellies of fat old men / who have lain down here." "California" describes an apocalyptic coastal scene that seems like the reverse side of Robert Frost's "Once by the Pacific" (1928): "The leaves, the leaves keep on falling. / The black leaves have covered the beaches. / And why do we still only stand here?"

Most interesting perhaps are the poems that draw on Stokesbury's Alaskan experiences. The subject of "Summer in Fairbanks" is the psychological dislocations of those who must adapt to the endless daytime of an Arctic summer:

> Strange, not to tell
> the end of days by any other way
> than clocks, and meals; televisions turning off.
> Different, for things to seem
> to the eyes like one day, that somehow
> has slowed down to months, years, icebergs
> of minutes. . . .

"The North Slope," a stream-of-consciousness meditation, connects the absolute blankness of the frozen tundra with the speaker's own emotional numbness—trapped as he is for three months in the remote oilfields ("the un-deodorized the raw / twelve hours a day seven days a week")—and merges both with Herman Melville's white whale, the ultimate literary sign of a man in collision with the indifference of nature:

> here where you aim
> the harpoon sailor see it surface see it wallow

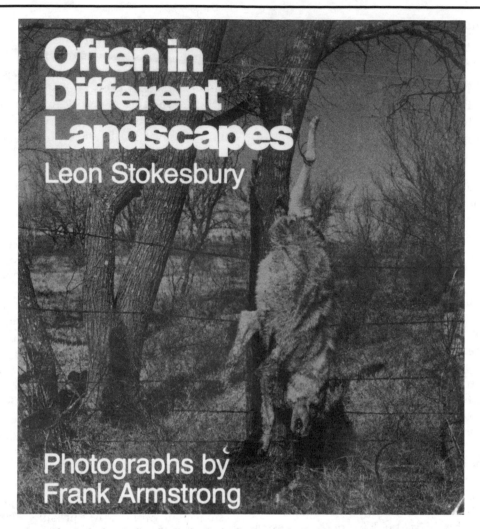

Cover for Stokesbury's first book, the first selection of the University of Texas poetry series

unrelieved see it dive here where the wait is
the ache for anything anything not dropping away
she breaches she breaches they cried and that
image charging my head all the white reaching
up that vacuum revealed unrelieved[.]

Like many poets of his generation who began writing during the unsettled 1960s, Stokesbury found surrealism appealing, and many of the "landscapes" of other poems in his first collection are dreamlike in their blend of incongruous details. The title character in "The Man Who Distributes the Fever Blister Ointment" possesses a "company map / Showing which dark country, or steaming zone / Is the place where skins swell fevered with pulp." "Back Behind the Eyes" opens with a cartoonlike image of the poet "fast asleep in bed":

Over my head, there floats
a large and white oval bubble, in which

can be seen, not a log being sawed
by a saw, but instead, two people
familiar to me.

The bubble also contains a sleeping child: "The bubble over his [the child's] head contains / a tiny chain saw that whines softly and whirrs." A poem about a love affair gone sour, "Gifts," turns on a similar visual conceit, in this case "our big painting / exchange." The speaker wishes to put the former lover as far away in both literal and emotional distance as he can, "way out in those dark, waist-high / weeds . . . and a little / nearer the vanishing point, thank you." Analogies with the visual arts—cartoons, paintings, and, most important, motion pictures—play an increasingly important part in Stokesbury's later work. *Landscapes* contains three poems that allude directly to the cinematic mythos: "The Gold Rush," "The

Death of Harpo Marx," and "Footlight Parade," the last a dramatic monologue in which a hopelessly naive speaker tries to deliver a plot synopsis of a typically bizarre Busby Berkeley musical:

> Then they put on another show. The man
> and woman sang again. Then a lot of women swam.
> They were happy. They swam. They were pretty.
> Then
> that was the end of that show. Then they went
> and put on another show.

Landscapes remains a remarkable first book. Stokesbury's influences are as diverse as T. S. Eliot, W. H. Auden, Weldon Kees, Alan Dugan, and James Tate, but he manages to incorporate them into his own subject matter and voice without their presence being obvious; what one primarily senses, instead of a single dominant influence, is an easy familiarity with the whole tradition of English and American poetry. One poem ("Aesthetic Distances") refers directly to Hamlet, seen from a balcony seat as "a black stumbling ant / or mote of dust swirled in white / footlights"; another alludes in its title ("The Murder of Gonzago and His Friends") to the famous play-within-a-play. "To His Book," the last poem in the collection, is an example of the rare curtal sonnet and conflates the theme of Ezra Pound's "Envoi" (1919) and the form and cataloging technique of Gerard Manley Hopkins's "Pied Beauty" (written in 1877), as Stokesbury writes:

> Dreams, the nightmares, shadows, red flames high
>   High up on mountains; wilted zinnias, rain
>   On dust, and great weight, the dead dog, and
>   wild
> Onions; mastodonic woman who knows how....

Perhaps the most remarkable achievement in *Landscapes* is the elegiac poem "To Laura Phelan: 1880-1906," which won the *Southern Poetry Review* National Collegiate Poetry Competition in 1971 and was collected in *Best Poems of 1971: Borestone Mountain Poetry Awards*. In an autobiographical essay published in the 1973 anthology *New Voices in American Poetry*, Stokesbury speaks of the poem's genesis in a practical joke: "It seemed the right thing to do at the time. And we were really drunk. So we took the tombstone [of Laura Phelan], which must have weighed about 250 pounds, and set it up in [Arkansas professor and poet] Jim Whitehead's front yard. This was about one in the morning." Later Stokesbury and his companions attempted to re-

turn the stone to its proper place in the graveyard but could not find its original location: "Not really feeling much inclination to hunt for the gravesite, we just set the stone in a vacant spot and I picked up some plastic flowers from one of the graves nearby and dropped them down in the front of Laura's new place...." The poem stays close to these black-comedy details, which recall the famous scene between Hamlet and the gravediggers, yet it becomes Stokesbury's most serious meditation on temporality:

> This is not you. Drunk
> I have been. Across this graveyard, that
> is where you are. Yet I stand here. Would ask
> things of your name. Would wish. Would not be
> told
> of the stink in the skull, the eye's collapse.
> Would be told something new, something unknown.

Stokesbury's first book did not attract a great deal of critical attention, though it was widely discussed in regional publications such as *Cedar Rock*. Stokesbury's ties to Texas remain tenuous at best. His work is included in *The New Breed* (1973) and *Washing the Cow's Skull* (1981), two ambitious anthologies of Texas poetry edited by Dave Oliphant; Stokesbury has taught at three Texas colleges; and he is a member of the Texas Institute of Letters; but his poems do not often bespeak traditional regional concerns. Thus his first book was in a paradoxical situation. On the one hand, coming from a university press with no background in publishing poetry, it would not immediately attract critical notice in the way that a first book from the University of Pittsburgh Press or Wesleyan University Press would. On the other, the purists of Texas literature could find fault with the book's sophistication and the poet's obvious desire to speak to a national audience. Though the edition sold out quickly, the University of Texas Press soon discontinued its poetry series. A decade was to pass before Stokesbury published another full-length collection.

He held various academic appointments in the meantime, serving as poet in residence at North Texas State University (now the University of North Texas), where he met his future wife, Susan Thurman, in 1978, and at Hollins College from 1980 to 1981. (The couple married in 1980 and have a daughter, Erin Elizabeth, born in 1985.) Stokesbury entered the Ph.D. program at Florida State University in the fall of 1981, and his fellow students included poets David Bottoms and John Bensko. Completing his degree in

1984, he served as visiting writer in residence at the University of Southwestern Louisiana for one semester before accepting a position at McNeese State University in Lake Charles, Louisiana, in 1985. Since the fall of 1987 he has taught at Georgia State University, where he is director of creative writing.

Two chapbooks by Stokesbury were published during the late 1970s and early 1980s. The first, *The Drifting Away of All We Once Held Essential* (1979), was published while he was teaching at North Texas State. The second, *The Royal Nonesuch* (1984), was the winner of Tallahassee's Anhinga Press competition and was published while Stokesbury was a graduate student at Florida State. The contents of these form the main portion of *The Drifting Away* (1986), which also contains poems from his out-of-print first book. Critic David Baker praised the collection highly: "though his production of poems may be painfully deliberate, Stokesbury's new book is outstanding. His new readers have a chance here to see his full talent, and the rest of us have a generous-enough selection of new poems to warrant our interest and excitement. Stokesbury's apparently small output does pay off; his poems are finished, full, original, powerful, and these poems work awfully well together."

The eponymous poem of the collection provides yet another example of what W. D. Snodgrass has noted as a "way of making opposed tones of voice collide that is uniquely his own. He has a genuine grasp of the loneliness and horror of this world, but he is never so tragic as when he is hilariously clowning. These opposed qualities, like the opposed tones of voice, give his work an astonishing tension and breadth." At the heart of "The Drifting Away of All We Once Held Essential" is an unpleasant memory of a childhood incident in which "the young stylist" takes "the whole fourteen dollars / he had made from selling Boy Scout peanut brittle" and spends it on toys, candy, and movies. After confessing tearfully to his father, the child is forgiven and loaned the missing money. But the poem turns suddenly upon itself—"Look at them there: father and son, driving / along. So close. Real pals. My / God! What a load of crap!"—ending with a raging threat from *King Lear*: "I will do such things! I will steal / such things! What they are I know not." In this final paroxysm of verbal violence, the poem attempts to exorcise both the guilt-ridden memory of the childhood transgression and the sentimentality of its

own conventionally happy resolution. In essence it is a critique, like many of Stokesbury's other poems, of the mythos of American family life that is forced on the public by advertising, television programs, and the other media of popular culture. This critical stance, satirical here, becomes more bitter in subsequent poems dealing with Stokesbury's family.

In "A Funny Joke" Stokesbury describes his father's incapacitating stroke, suffered while working in Alaska:

> My brother said
> his mouth was twisted
>
> into a permanent ghastly grin.
> It looked always as if
>
> his was the only smile around,
> as if someone had told
>
> the funniest joke finally,
> but only he had heard. . . .

Stokesbury addresses another troubled family member in "Unsent Message to My Brother in His Pain," which has the urgency of one man talking another down from a ledge. Like Snodgrass, Baker notes Stokesbury's tonal variety, first citing this poem's conclusion:

> If you come to see me, I shit you not,
> we will cook with wine. Listen
> to me. Listen to me, my brother,
> please don't go. Take a later flight,
> a later train. Another look around.

As Baker has noted, "Stokesbury takes us to, and teases us back from, the brink of calamity and despair. It's as if trapped animals, turning desperately on their attackers, suddenly stand up and break into song-and-dance routines to postpone, even prevent, disaster." Stokesbury's early poetry may have been marked by solipsism; as his work has matured, he has increasingly embraced otherness—people and subjects—with humane concern.

But even the strongest powers of sympathy failed, or came too late, to rescue Frank Stanford, the brilliant young poet who killed himself in 1978 in what Stokesbury's elegy "A Few Words for Frank Stanford: 1948-1978" terms a "ragged, barren, / ignorant, excessive end." Stokesbury sees Stanford's death as a possible validation of a poetic life of extremes, but ultimately he draws back in dismay. The ability to write "about moon-

Señor Wences & the Man in the Box
~ L. B. Stokesbury 1924-1987

Jokester, prankster, son,
Let me see you laugh your way out of this one.
No one ought to know better than you,
except maybe now me,
that there is no word, no chain of words,
not this one An I not this one
No scratch the silent blankness that can capture,
ever for an instant, what we are was at any time
And certainly not what I am now.
And so, & even so Mr. Futility, Sysyphus laddybuck
son, I lie herenow, blessed
to watch your scared frown
STARING DOWN

And what did you expect? Some
hideous blaming rictus glaring back? What
you deserved for the thousand times
you flashed that crappy gaze of yours, that said
I owed you something obligatory,
A gift I never gave? Oh no. Not me.
And not here assuredly. No
in faith
But if I do owe you something, if there is
A Remembrance that you might require, some helpful sachet
to hold before the nose in future years,

Page from the first draft for a poem by Stokesbury that was published in fall 1989 in the New England Review *(by permission of Leon Stokesbury)*

light, ... / about swine ... / about starfish, / lunchmeat, Memphis, / minnows and bay rum, / [and] Robert Desnos" sustained Stanford for a time and justified his existence, even attracted "devoted disciples not / to be denied." But genius alone, as the deaths of many modern poets have made clear, provides no sure salvation. Stanford's tragedy, Stokesbury seems to say, lay in equating his talent, which was considerable, with an increasing sense of superiority that finally led him to believe "he was immortal, / . . . had arrived at a country where / others could scream and / call and he could not / hear." Death may be the mother of beauty, but the infant who survives to adulthood must find nourishment elsewhere. Stanford did not. His last book was titled *Crib Death* (1979).

In other poems in *The Drifting Away* Stokesbury ranges far and wide, taking on such subjects as the suburban shopping mall (in "Day Begins at Governor's Square Mall"), which has become as genuine an emblem of American culture as a different type of structure was for an earlier one:

> O bright communion! O new cathedral!
> where the appetitious, the impure, the old, the
>   young,
> the bored, the lost, the dumb, with wide dilated
>   eyes
> advance with offerings to be absolved and be made
>   clean.

In another poem, "Airport Bars," he recalls childhood memories of "one of those / 'Golden Age' TV variety hours" starring Jimmy Durante, in which "a glimpse of the Essence / was portioned out / for the boy to see: / a loud old man, a total ass."

In all of these sardonic observations the artist, in his various guises, becomes the filter of experience. In the title poem it is the "stylist" who tries to make sense of things; in another, "Lonzo, / a recent twinkle in the art world sky," presents work that fails to please the critical establishment. Even if the artist must stand at a distance, fitting in about as well as "a platterful of pope's noses at a White House dinner," Stokesbury, in the true tradition of the belated romantic, sees him as a hero, society's best hope of making sense of itself. "Renoir," one of the most ambitious poems Stokesbury has produced, is a reading of the painting *The Luncheon of the Boating Party* (1881) and is a revelation of a secret that poet and painter share. After a careful examination of Pierre-Auguste Renoir's nuances of pos-

ture and expression, Stokesbury concludes with what could stand as a definition of what John Keats called "negative capability":

> But the artist sees it. And this is his gift,
> this warm afternoon, his funny story to tell again
> and again: a day of blue grapes and black wine,
>   of tricks
> of the eye, of the flow and lulls of time, and
>   everything,
> everything soaked in the light of sex and love and
>   the sun.

Since the publication of *The Drifting Away* Stokesbury has continued to publish new work in distinguished journals such as the *New England Review* and the *Kenyon Review*. In particular, two elegies, "The Royal Nonesuch" and "Señor Wences and the Man in the Box," stand out as bearing the seriocomic signature of Stokesbury's best work. "The Royal Nonesuch," written for the New Orleans poet Everette Maddox, explains how Stokesbury came to title one of his chapbooks. In the poem Maddox, a self-destructive alcoholic, presents Stokesbury with a manuscript of his (Maddox's) poems:

> you raised it
> at last, dog-eared
> and dirty, on high
> for me to read. And
> I was so smitten, so
> enamored, by the
> incredible original
> aptness of the title
> ... I exclaimed, "Damn!
> I'll swap you one
> fifth of Chivas for
> the use of this!"

After the death of Maddox (thinnest person I / had seen: only man / to match poem and / body to perfection") Stokesbury ruefully wishes that instead he "had offered a big / beef filet."

"Señor Wences and the Man in the Box" takes its title from a comic ventriloquism routine ("S'all right?" "S'all right!") from the Ed Sullivan television show, popular during Stokesbury's childhood. The poem itself, as the epigraph makes clear, is an elegy for the poet's father, and it is characteristically original in its dramatic situation in that Stokesbury makes the father's corpse ("the man in the box") speak a message of consolation. Poetry, as Stokesbury makes abundantly clear through the many personae who speak in his poems, is the ultimate method of throwing one's voice:

> Ah, laddybuck, if we could have found
> Some demilitarized zone, which we could not;
> If I could for once
> Have raised you up out of your maze of corridors,
> Which I could not; you
> With your boxcars of words words words:
> Little links of ink lined up, all in a row, chugging
> Off toward the horizon; maybe then
> I could have told you what you wanted to hear.

But the only words worth hearing, according to Stokesbury, the only words one truly desires from the dead, are the same as the comic punchline—a cosmic affirmation in the face of darkness: "It's all right." In his most recent work Stokesbury continues to exhibit the originality of treatment and the emotional depth that mark him as one of the best poets of his generation.

References:

David Baker, "Two Young Poets," *Crazy Horse*, 33 (Winter 1988): 124-130;

R. S. Gwynn, "Second Gear," *New England Review and Bread Loaf Quarterly*, 9 (Autumn 1986): 111-121.

Ellen Bryant Voigt
(9 May 1943 -   )

Laura B. Kennelly
University of North Texas

BOOKS: *Claiming Kin* (Middletown, Conn.: Wesleyan University Press, 1976);

The Forces of Plenty (New York & London: Norton, 1983);

The Lotus Flowers (New York & London: Norton, 1987);

Two Trees (New York & London: Norton, 1992).

SELECTED PERIODICAL PUBLICATIONS— UNCOLLECTED: "Poetry and Gender," *Kenyon Review*, 9 (Summer 1987): 127-140;

"On Tone," *New England Review*, 12 (Spring 1990): 249-266.

Ellen Bryant Voigt draws from her childhood in rural Virginia and her life as a wife, mother, and teacher in New England to write poetry, grounded in regional, domestic experiences, which shows the possibilities of transcendence. She has been recognized, primarily by East Coast critics such as Edward Hirsch, as one of the most highly skilled, sensitive poets of her generation.

She was born in Danville, Virginia, on 9 May 1943. Her father, Lloyd Gilmore Bryant, was a farmer; her mother, Missouri (Zue) Yeatts Bryant, was an elementary-school teacher. After graduating from Converse College in South Carolina with a B.A. in 1964, Ellen Bryant married Francis George Wilhelm Voigt, a college dean, on 5 September 1965. A concert pianist, she then earned her M.F.A. (in music and literature) from the University of Iowa in 1966. The Voigts later had two children, Jula and William.

Ellen Bryant Voigt taught English at Iowa Wesleyan College from 1966 to 1969. In 1970 she moved to Vermont and began teaching at Goddard College in Plainfield. While teaching there and directing the writing program, she received a grant from the Vermont Council on the Arts that allowed her to complete her first collection of poetry, *Claiming Kin* (1976).

It received immediate recognition as a "stunning first collection," to cite Hirsch's review (*Nation*, August 1977). Critics noted with approval her ability to combine fidelity to the physical world with precise diction and lush verbal patterns. Correspondences between nature and human life serve as a leitmotiv for the first section of the book. A woman wakes (in "Tropics") and turns to her lover while dreaming of "an island where long-stemmed cranes" stand; then the lovers move together in "the ripe air of summer." More sensual, and violent, analogies are sug-

father who dives into "that dark closet of water" to try to find the already dead child. The wife, who must wait and watch,

> turned away from the lost child,
> chose the two live children rooted behind her
> receiving the permanent visions of their sleep,
> chose life,
> chose to live with ice at the heart.

Although *Claiming Kin* was widely reviewed and praised for its pastoral scenes, intensity, and verbal richness, some critics, such as Helen Vendler (*Yale Review*, Spring 1977), felt that Voigt's interest in the lurid and her occasional banal statements made her work uneven. Overall, however, she was praised as a promising new poet whose southern family roots gave her work strength and power.

After this first publication, Voigt's career accelerated. She received the Discovery Award from the 92nd Street YMCA/*The Nation* in 1976 and, more important financially, a grant from the National Endowment for the Arts for 1976-1977. For 1978-1979 she received a Guggenheim Foundation grant and in 1980, by then an associate professor at M.I.T., she received a fellowship there. Voigt's work also began to be anthologized.

Her second volume of poetry, *The Forces of Plenty*, was published in 1983. This collection, again arranged in three parts, but with less distinction between the sections than in her first book, is rich with images centered in the Vermont landscape where Voigt makes her home. She deals again with the problem of pain found in everyday life and whether or not it is balanced by joy. In the first poem, "The Spire," two mechanical figures emerge from a large clock to mark each hour. They seem to represent "summer and winter, youth and age, / as though the forces of plenty and of loss / played equally on the human soul."

These forces are seen at work primarily in domestic struggles to maintain a marriage, nurse children through illness, and deal with the aging and death of parents—problems common to the middle-aged. Nature is still a force, but animals play a less important part in these poems than they did in *Claiming Kin*. More important is what reviewer Penelope Mesic calls the "drama" of Voigt's narratives, which are "so quietly various, so intense yet decorous, so aloof from common impatience and fully fledged with wit that Voigt's

Ellen Bryant Voigt (photograph by Thomas Victor)

gested in "Black Widow." The spider waits for her mate (who will later serve as her dinner):

> Heavy in her hammock, she makes
> ready for mating. All black,
> black love in the pit of her
> eye, she lolls at the center,
> a soft black flower.

In part 2 of *Claiming Kin* Voigt explores family relationships, with poems about her family and imagined families. The title poem of the book is addressed to her mother, "rising at night to wander the dark house." Another poem, "Sister," ironically reveals the ambiguity inherent in loving a sibling rival.

Violence surfaces in the last section with poems about infant death, sterility, accidental shootings, the problem of pain, and the meaning of life. "The Drowned Man," for example, shows the terrible beauty in a father and mother's selfless actions in the face of tragedy: "How I love you in your hopeless act," the speaker says to the

early draft,
"Sweet Everlasting"

THE FELLED TREE

Swarming over the hard ground with pocket lenses
that discover and distort like an insect's
compound eye, the second grade
slows at the barrier on the path.
They straddle the horizontal trunk to rub
the rough track of the saw; then focus
on the pallid green at the other end.
Down for months // but still enjoined
by seasonal memory, the tree responds
with new leaves and branches--what can we make
of this residual life? Each night,
as the intervening brilliance of the sun
subsides, and we are turned
away / the logic of earth, the stars appear
to substantiate what we could not see.
Even now, in the vast sky
darkened / by grief, the constellations
form / their faint pulsing inconclusive shapes,
bodies both active and extinguished,
and I must sustain my father there
with any evidence
the amplifying heart provides.

Early draft for a poem (by permission of Ellen Bryant Voigt)

voice could never be confused with another's" (*Poetry*, February 1984).

Voigt casts a sober, unsentimental eye on life, a view perhaps best exemplified in "Year's End," which describes parents who, while at the sickbed of their child, hear of the death of a neighbor's child. The parents, "rubbing the window clear of steam" that is in the room to keep their own child alive, look out onto the snowy hillside where the dead child had just played and had

> plunged the sled up and down the hill,
> we could still see the holes his feet made,
> a staggered row of graves
> extracting darkness from the snow.

Critic Carolyne Wright believes Voigt's strengths "reside in cultivation of the longer line, the denser linguistic texture, the accumulation of sensory experience played off against abstractions demanded by their imagistic occasions— prosodic devices, in short, that can mirror the fullness and subtlety of nuance she is drawn to in the world" (*Literary Review*, Fall 1986). Wright also noted, however, that Voigt's work is weaker when she attempts a sparer style, when she uses "description to build up a suspense for which there is not always a dramatic payoff," and when she inserts "weighty and abstract pronouncements." But Wright, like the other reviewers of this collection, generally admired Voigt's work.

Voigt published *The Lotus Flowers* in 1987. In this collection, which is also divided into three parts, Voigt writes with richness and maturity of her familiar concerns: the rural Virginia of her childhood home, the paradox of good and evil, and the relationships between mortal creatures who know they must die. She chose W. B. Yeats's line "Man is in love and loves what vanishes" as the epigraph for the volume, and each poem in it, in distinct ways, echoes that theme.

The home of her memory is, as reviewer Peter Harris wrote, "a place . . . partly idyllic and partly a vale of tears." He also said that she "explores her origins from the complex perspective of someone who finds home a place that's necessary to leave and to return to" (*Virginia Quarterly Review*, Spring 1988). Voigt relies heavily on memories moving into her present life. "The Photograph," which begins by describing a photograph of her black-haired mother, ends by showing how the pain of one generation invariably affects the next:

> The horseshoe hung in the neck of the tree sinks
> deeper into the heartwood every season.

> Sometimes I hear the past
> hum in my ear, its cruel perfected music,
> as I turn from the stove
> or stop to braid my daughter's thick black hair.

As James Finn Cotter (*Hudson Review*, Spring 1988) noted, Voigt's *The Lotus Flowers* shows her power as a storyteller: "Many of the tales deal with family and neighbors. . . . Even a dog secretly killing sheep at night while faithfully guarding his own flock by day offers a subject for compactly staged narrative that reflects on the animal instinct to kill and the human need to tame." This poem, "The Trust," also illustrates Voigt's awareness of the uselessness of hypocrisy in the face of evidence, and it offers an unsentimental view of the consequences of wrong action when the farmer, confronted with the beloved dog's unmistakable guilt, matter-of-factly shoots the beloved animal and buries him.

Stylistically Voigt's poems are traditional in that she describes a scene or an image in musical phrases and lines. As critic Reginald Gibbons observed, she is "mainstream" in the sense that Robert Frost and Yeats are, and she works well in an inherited tradition of "poetics of images set like ornaments in free verse, as opposed to metrical manipulation of sound and syntax" (*TriQuarterly*, Winter 1988). But fashioning the questions she asks in her poetry seems more important to her than achieving new heights of technical virtuosity. Often the endings of Voigt's poems emphasize experience's duality and carry a sting, what reviewer Peter Stitt called operating on the reader "with a velvet ice pick" (*Poetry*, June 1988).

One striking aspect of Voigt's poems is her method of direct address, especially as seen in the opening and closing poems in *The Lotus Flowers*. In the first poem, "The Last Class," the speaker orders: "Put this in your notebooks: / All verse is occasional verse." Then, "leaving the city, leaving our sullen classroom," she wonders, "who am I to teach the young, / having come so far from honest love of the world." She concludes with lines that suggest Holden Caulfield's passionate desire to be the "catcher in the rye" who saves and protects:

> I wanted to salvage
> something from my life, to fix
> some truth beyond all change, the way
> photographers of war, miles from the front,
> lift print after print into the light. . . .

In the last poem in *The Lotus Flowers*, "Dancing with Poets," Voigt directly addresses, in long, tightly packed lines, her vision of a communion between all true poets. What begins as a dance with an awkward poet who was permanently injured when "he threw himself from a window four floors up," turns into a festival of dead poets dancing alongside them: "[John] Berryman back from the bridge, and Frost, relieved / of grievances, [Emily] Dickinson waltzing there with lavish [John] Keats. . . ." Voigt concludes:

and now we are one body, sweating and foolish,
one body with its clear pathetic grace, not
lifted out of grief but dancing it, transforming
for one night this local bar, before we're turned
    back out
to our separate selves, to the dangerous streets and
    houses,
to the overwhelming drone of the living world.

These two poems suggest the place Voigt sees for herself as an artist. Her concern as a poet is to describe the world faithfully, the horror as well as the beauty, not as a "Southern Gothic" writer, a sentimentalist, or a partisan of any school, but as she sees it. In her 1987 essay in the *Kenyon Review* ("Poetry and Gender") she wrote that "what is best for poetry . . . is fidelity to the most rigorous standards possible." Women, in particular, should see themselves as free to write in any tradition, feminist or not, that "discipline, courage and talent will support." The positive critical reception of *The Lotus Flowers* suggests that Voigt has taken advantage of such freedom.

Marilyn Nelson Waniek

(26 April 1946 -)

Kirkland C. Jones
Lamar University

BOOKS: *For the Body* (Baton Rouge & London: Louisiana State University Press, 1978);
The Cat Walked Through the Casserole and Other Poems for Children, by Waniek and Pamela Espeland (Minneapolis: Carolrhoda, 1984);
Mama's Promises (Baton Rouge & London: Louisiana State University Press, 1985);
The Homeplace (Baton Rouge & London: Louisiana State University Press, 1990).

OTHER: Phil Dahlerup, *Literary Sex Roles*, translated by Waniek (Minneapolis: Minnesota Women in Higher Education, 1975);
"The Space Where Sex Should Be: Toward a Definition of the Black American Literary Tradition," *Studies in Black Literature*, 6 (Fall 1975): 7-13;
Halfdan Rasmussen, *Hundreds of Hens and Other Poems for Children*, translated by Waniek and Pamela Espeland (Minneapolis: Black Willow, 1982);
"A Black Rainbow: Modern Afro-American Poetry," by Waniek and Rita Dove, in *Poetry After*

Modernism, edited by Robert McDowell (Brownsville, Oreg.: Story Line, 1990), pp. 171-217.

Marilyn Nelson Waniek (pronounced Vonyek) has established herself as a writer for children and juveniles. In this respect she is much like Arna Bontemps and Langston Hughes, who, early on, learned that writing for children would keep bread on the table while they pursued adult topics. Waniek's publications include *Hundreds of Hens and Other Poems for Children* (1982)—her translations (with Pamela Espeland) from the humorous works of Danish poet Halfdan Rasmussen—and *The Cat Walked Through the Casserole and Other Poems for Children* (1984), another collaboration with Espeland. Waniek's books for adults are the poetry collections *For the Body* (1978), *Mama's Promises* (1985), and *The Homeplace* (1990), for which she made the National Book Award list of finalists for 1991. All five of these collections show a skillful handling of narrative and lyric, as well as a vision that is at once simple and complex, traits

Marilyn Nelson Waniek (photograph by Frank Funk)

that have begun to earn for Waniek a place among the best contemporary poets. She has two collections in progress, "Lost and Found" and "Poems for Children." Waniek is an unapologetic traditionalist and has had success with a variety of traditional and free-verse forms.

She was born in Cleveland, Ohio, on 26 April 1946 to Melvin M. Nelson, a U.S. serviceman in the air force, and Johnnie Mitchell Nelson, a teacher. The poet's first marriage was to Erdmann F. Waniek (September 1970). On 22 November 1979, after her divorce from Waniek, she married Roger R. Wilkenfield, a university professor with whom she has a son, Jacob, and a daughter, Dora.

Brought up on first one military base and then another, Marilyn Nelson Waniek started writing while still in elementary school. She credits her sixth-grade teacher, a Mrs. Gray of Kittery Point, Maine, for the discovery of her literary talents. Waniek received her B.A. degree in 1968 from the University of California, Davis, and her M.A. in 1970 from the University of Pennsylvania. In 1979 she earned a Ph.D. from the University of Minnesota; her doctoral thesis was "The Schizoid Nature of the Implied Author in Twentieth-Century American Ethnic Novels."

Waniek is also a seminary-trained Lutheran. Her career accomplishments include a position as lay associate in the National Lutheran Campus Ministry program, 1969-1970, at Lane Community College of Eugene, Oregon. She held an assistant professorship in English (1970-1972) at that college and the Norre Nissum Seminary Fellowship in Denmark (1972-1973). From 1973 to 1978 she taught English at Saint Olaf College in Northfield, Minnesota, and since 1978 she has taught English at the University of Connecticut at Storrs, where in 1988 she was promoted to full professor. In 1982 she was granted a National Endowment for the Arts Fellowship.

Waniek reports that her interest in writing poems for children began when she started translating the "wonderfully funny" work of Rasmussen. During the 1980s she experimented with children's verse and learned how to make children laugh.

While still a graduate student in her twenties, Waniek joined the debate over an African-American aesthetic. Her article "The Space Where Sex Should Be: Toward a Definition of the Black Literary Tradition" (1975) examines the dispute between James Baldwin and Richard Wright, and explores what Ralph Ellison and

Amiri Baraka have contributed toward a definition of "a Black-American literary tradition." As she offers her own definition of that concept, she asserts: "it is the fact of oppression that distinguishes this literature from all others." In the process of examining this topic, she embraces her own Africanness, believing that African-American authors have portrayed this literature as one of "construction" and "creation," one that affirms instead of opposing. Waniek sees the African-American literary tradition as one that makes something positive out of a negative condition. She believes that virtually every African-American writer has struggled to reconcile the two warring aspects of his identity: "the Black American writer strives to demonstrate to white America that his Negro individuality is as much a kind of personhood as any colorless [white] individuality." In other words, she defends the sociopolitical nature of African-American literature.

Waniek also believes that, because of hypocrisy, black male-female relationships cannot flourish. Like Baldwin, she believes that the most completely developed relationships in African-American writing are those "between the Black protagonists and their white male friends who, as a rule, are older." She sums up her argument: "in the space where sex should be is instead the awful confrontation of Black self with white self, and the Black self with white society."

Waniek's first book, *For the Body*, received little attention from critics. The dedicatory page reads: "For my people: You know who you are." The book contains some forty-eight poems divided into three unequal sequences, the first titled "Driving Home," and the remaining two labeled, respectively, "The Ice Cream Woman" and "The Language We Speak Is Not the One We Dream."

Most of the poems are in free verse, some merging into stanzaless collages, others divided into arbitrary groupings. Some lines consist of only one word, as in "Neighbors" and "Venezuela: Three Places," or two words, as in "Mrs. Hong's House," "Emily Dickinson's Defunct," and "The Professor Falls." In "Baptizing the Penguins" the longest lines are of five words with some variations of one-word or two-word lines. This breaking up of thought creates a meter both emphatic and arresting:

the formal penguins
bowing

as they bless the saint . . .
they are white
they are
an army of saints . . .
accepting his blessings
with no words.

Many of the poems in the volume come to halting conclusions, as seen in "Woodcut by a Friend" (concerning a picture of flowers): "They are scented like women, / their petals are as soft as / I think / your mouth."

The *body* of the title becomes a metaphor for the individual, the family, and the extended family. This metaphor is rich in its meanings and, using it, Waniek sometimes sings, sometimes narrates. She also uses, from time to time, well-chosen biblical allusions. Her themes are domestic and childhood memories: sitting between Mother's knees getting her hair combed and braided; Grandfather's winter walks and his communion with nature; the frequent moves from one base to another with a mother who wants to cry but will not; the stoic, child and adult, who suffers in silence; matrons who cover their furniture with doilies; childhood friendships; loneliness and remorse; death; creation and procreation.

One of the most outstanding poems in the volume is "Grass Turned Out Green," where things happen in sevens, and where human plans become "mouse tracks in a field of snow." The most powerful poem is narrated in an African-American idiom and is about the black church experience: "Churchgoing with Philip Larkin." The speaker laments the loss of African values in the effort to conform to the customs of white Christianity: "The Lutherans sit stolidly in pews / only their children feel the holy ghost that makes them jerk and hobble and almost / destroys the prim atmosphere. . . . / We sing a spiritual as the last song / and we are moved by a peculiar grace / that settles a new aura on the place."

The Cat Walked Through the Casserole is indicative of Waniek's ability to communicate with young readers. The title poem presents the family dog "doing his business" always in the neighbors' yards and the family cat, who walks through a warm casserole, plastering it on the floor. Both dog and cat "have to go." Laughs come when little brother breaks Mom's best crystal vase: "It sure will be a big relief / Not to ever see his face / Around here again." The range of subject matter is broad and always appealing: "When I Grow Up," "Father Fitzgerald," "Grampa's Whiskers," "I Used to Have a Dinosaur," and "Queen of the Rainbow" are representative titles.

In *Mama's Promises* Waniek returns, for the most part, to adult topics. On one of the dedicatory pages the tone is set: "Life is good / Knock on wood / Mama." The more than twenty poems appeal to both adult and adolescent readers. Waniek remembers her mother in the brief lyric "A Strange Beautiful Woman." "My Second Birth" shows the narrator telling of her infanthood to her own child: "Mama / was my first image of God / I will remember how she leaned over my crib / her eyes full of sky." The titles suggest the unity of subject matter that characterizes the volume: "Mama's Promise," "The Lost Daughter," "The Marriage Nightmare," "Women's Locker Room," and so on. In "Levitation with Baby" the narrator shares the conflict of needing simultaneously to write poems and nurture a small child: "The Muse bumped / against my window this morning / No one was at home but me / and the baby. The Muse said / there was room on her back for two / Okay, I said, but first. . . . "

In this volume Waniek is still experimenting with forms but favors stanzas more than in earlier works. She leans toward the ballad stanza, which is used most successfully in "Cover Photograph." The volume ends with a narrative poem in five brief sequences: "I Dream the Book of Jonah." The frame for the poem is a catnap on the living-room couch. Waniek opens with a six-line blues poem, followed by a sermonette spawned by God, who arouses the dreamer. Then Jonah sings a song, accompanying himself on his guitar, which needs tuning; he stops to tune it and then strokes out a "tentative rhythm." At last his fingers find the melody, and Jonah ends with a blues song, the same song with which the dreamer has opened the poem:

Lord, Lord, sweet Mama,
Trouble on my mind.
Lord, sweet Mama,
Trouble on my mind.
If you love me like you tell me,
Please, Mama, give a sign.

In her 1990 book of poems, *The Homeplace*, Waniek tackles the difficult subject of miscegenation and the so-called cultural bastardy that results from mingling the blood of white slave owners with the blood of the slaves. She writes of a passion that neither engendered rape nor love but which bred relationships of a peculiar sort.

The Homeplace, like Rita Dove's *Thomas and Beulah* (1986), is an intergenerational work, starting with a re-creation of Waniek's great-great-grandmother Diverne, whose son was sired by her white master. Diverne sends her powerful spirit through the generations. In the second half of the book, she brings to light an often-overlooked aspect of the history of African-Americans, the role black males played as American troops in the World Wars. Waniek commemorates her own father's role and that of his "extended family," those World War II aviators who were also African-American and who are remembered as the "Tuskegee Airmen."

In re-creating generations from before the Civil War to the present, Waniek appropriately uses traditional forms—the sonnet, the villanelle, and the ballad—achieving success with them all, but her sonnets are more polished than the others. She begins the first part of the book with a ballad in five stanzas titled "Diverne's Waltz." Diverne is a cook in the big house, who watches from the kitchen the "laughing and flirting" of the master's children "on the bare parlor floor" during a party for the younger set. Mister Tyler, the master, drunk on rye, foolishly grabs Diverne and waltzes with her, to the utter embarrassment of some and the amusement of others. "Annunciation," an unrhymed sonnet, dreams of "Up North," where "night don't mean nothing, just like day." But one night Posterity (a composite of various forebears) appears to the dreamer. When these relatives—long dead—see the dreamer's children, the relatives scream in black dialect: "Lord, they daddy WHITE?"

Desire and courtship are frequent themes, and in "Balance," a Petrarchan sonnet, black dialect sparkles: "He watch her like a coonhound watch a tree / . . . She thinks she something, stuck-up island bitch / . . . That hoe Diverne think she Marse Tyler's wife." In "Chosen," a sonnet in four tercets and an unrhymed couplet, Waniek reflects on how "Diverne wanted to die, that August night," when Tyler took her, killing "part of her heart," the act that created Pomp Atwood, her only son, born with a double race. Tyler had run out of his twelve-room house to her shack close by "to leap onto her cornshuck pallet." Pomp was their "share of the future / And it wasn't rape. / In spite of her raw terror / and his whip." The voices of Waniek's characters, most in dramatic monologues, come out clear and true, and the experiences she re-creates are vivid.

"Daughters, 1900" is a villanelle. The best feature of this poem is that Waniek makes the closing quatrain a dialogue:

The eldest sniffs, "A Lady doesn't scratch."
The third snorts back "knock knock: nobody home."
The fourth concedes, "Well, maybe not in church. . . . "
Five daughters in the slant light on the porch.

Waniek's apprenticeship has lasted longer than that of some of her contemporaries, partially because of underexposure. Her friend Dove had her apprenticeship terminated by receiving the Pulitzer Prize in 1987 for her 1986 narrative sequence *Thomas and Beulah*. An equally talented Waniek has taken a slower route toward Dove's status, but Waniek has been encouraged by her acquaintances with writers in the United States and abroad, and she has lately gained recognition as one of the major voices of a younger generation of black poets.

Papers:
The Kerlan Collection at the University of Minnesota holds manuscripts by Waniek and other archives relevant to her writing career.

Michael Waters
(23 November 1949 -   )

Jack Turner
University of South Carolina

BOOKS: *A Rare Breed of Antelope* (Nottingham, U.K.: Byron, 1972);
Fish Light (Ithaca, N.Y.: Ithaca House, 1975);
The Scent of Apples (Athens, Ohio: Croissant, 1977);
In Memory of Smoke (Derry, Pa.: Rook, 1977);
Instinct (Athens, Ohio: Croissant, 1978);
Among Blackberries (N.p.: Service-berry, 1979);
Not Just Any Death (Brockport, N.Y.: BOA, 1979);
Air Touched by the Axe (Tempe, Ariz.: Inland Boat/ Porch, 1980);
Dogs in the Storm (Portland, Oreg.: Breakwater, 1981);
The Stories in the Light (Birmingham, Ala.: Thunder City, 1983);
The Faithful (Memphis: Raccoon, 1984);
Anniversary of the Air (Pittsburgh: Carnegie-Mellon University Press, 1985);
The Barn in the Air (Livingston, Ala.: Livingston University Press, 1987);
The Burden Lifters (Pittsburgh: Carnegie-Mellon University Press, 1989);
Bountiful (Pittsburgh: Carnegie-Mellon University Press, 1992).

OTHER: "Gentleman Bear," *Southern Poetry Review*, 15 (Spring 1975): 42;
Dissolve to Island: On the Poetry of John Logan, edited, with an introduction, by Waters (Houston: Ford-Brown, 1984).

"I have been following the poetry of Michael Waters for many years," fellow poet Ted Kooser wrote, "and have never been disappointed by his books. His poems can be counted on to be warm, open, friendly, original, and sometimes deceptively simple" (*Georgia Review*, Fall 1990). Beyond such general terms, though, Waters's poetry is difficult to classify. He is a virtuoso of variety; there is no "typical" Waters poem. In *Poetry* (May 1990) Steven Cramer called attention to Waters's "dizzying variety of stylistic selves and verbal registers." Roger Mitchell, also writing for *Poetry* (January 1986), referred to Waters as "a confessional poet writing at a time when confessionalism has been discredited—wrongfully discredited, I would say. . . . " Yet the most extensive interview with Waters is included in a book titled *The Post-Confessionals* (1989), and his poems are rarely personal in any solipsistic way—most

Michael Waters (photograph by Rick Maloof)

of them centering on subjects outside himself. Neither are Waters's poems coldly objective or cynical. They exhibit a generous, energetic humanity; a strong talent for sensual description—especially in the limning of visual details; a deep, keen intelligence; and a sharp, sometimes self-deprecating wit. Waters does not simply observe and present widely varied characters and subjects; he penetrates them, becomes a part of them, and speaks from within them. As William Butler Yeats said, "The poet will play with all masks." For Waters, as it was for Yeats, this type of play is serious: Waters works "on only one poem at a time," as he told Stan Sanvel Rubin and Gregory Fitz Gerald in the interview in *The Post-Confessionals*; sometimes he goes through "120 drafts, and what a wonderful feeling it is when it's finally finished, Yeats's box clicking shut."

Born in Brooklyn on 23 November 1949, Waters was an only child. His father, Raymond, was a New York City fire marshal who moonlighted as a bartender, and his mother, Dorothy Smith Waters, worked as a secretary. While his parents were at their jobs, Waters stayed with his grandparents ("who weren't very talkative") and became an enthusiastic reader and writer. His poems

often allude, indirectly or directly, to well-known authors. "Reading Dickens" (in *The Burden Lifters*, 1989) relates great literature to daily life. The speaker's father, after reading from a Charles Dickens novel, is "happy not to be / living some great adventure, // happy to close the book / before my mother slept, / saving the ending for tomorrow."

Prior to earning a B.A. (1971) and M.A. (1972) in English at the State University of New York College at Brockport, Waters spent the 1970-1971 school year studying at the University of Nottingham in England, where he was a winner in the National Young Poets Competition, leading to the publication of his chapbook *A Rare Breed of Antelope* in 1972. The best poems in this pamphlet were republished in *Fish Light* (1975), which was his M.F.A. thesis at the University of Iowa. After graduating from there in 1974, Waters attended Ohio University, earning his Ph.D. in 1977. He married Robin Irwin on 13 May 1972; the marriage ended in divorce in 1992. A daughter, Kiernan, was born in 1988. Since 1978 Waters has taught English and creative writing at Salisbury State University on the Eastern Shore of Maryland.

Having won a National Endowment for the Arts Fellowship (1984), two Pushcart Prizes (1984 and 1990), and six Yaddo Fellowships (between 1978 and 1992), Waters is a popular lecturer and reader. He has attended conferences, taught workshops and classes, and presented his poetry all over the United States and in England, Iraq, and Greece. "I've always been one . . . whose heart is touched by strangers," he says, and one reason he became a writer "is the desire simply to talk to people." His main concerns both personally and professionally are clear communication and accessibility. Since 1972 he has published ten chapbooks and five full-length poetry collections: *Fish Light, Not Just Any Death* (1979), *Anniversary of the Air* (1985), *The Burden Lifters* (1989), and *Bountiful* (1992). In 1984 he edited a book of essays on John Logan, one of his favorite poets.

Pointing out that *Fish Light* was published when he was only twenty-five, Waters seems mildly embarrassed by this early work: "I was thinking not in terms of the poetic line, but the sentence, the image, something flashy. Having gotten that out of my system, I began writing poems with a calm voice. . . . " Among other influences Waters mentions Robert Bly, "particularly his short poems." Only after Waters wrote his first poems did he realize that Bly had spent a great deal of time revising his brief lyrics, not relying solely on "the white heat of inspiration." *Fish Light* does show the marks of youthful exuberance, experimentation, and angst for the sake of angst—with many of the poems focusing on death and despair. Nevertheless, in fall 1990 Robert Crist, reviewing *The Burden Lifters* for *Carolina Quarterly*, still remembered the "arresting honesty" and "pristine imagery" in *Fish Light*.

The book is important to an understanding of Waters's oeuvre because it shows his basic style and vision while introducing his most important themes: the need for compassion and attention to people and other creatures; the Wordsworthian idea that the full appreciation of nature can act as a balm for emotional pain (as in "Winter Return," in which Waters mentions Theodore Roethke); the concomitant danger that the closer one gets to nature and natural instincts the more one may become animalistic; and, most important, the concept that literature is one of the most effective means of dealing with and preparing for death—confronting it, rehearsing it, and, perhaps, transcending it, or at least the fear of it. Yet Waters rarely ventures into the metaphysical. His ideas are more in the existential-humanist

vein of Roethke and Logan, two of his main influences. In "Behind the House" Waters writes:

There are many ways to prepare
for death:
tattoo bones on the skin,
chant Indian mantras,
invoke every god we know.

Implicitly, in almost every poem in *Fish Light*, Waters is contemplating and preparing for death, invoking the names of Logan, Roethke, and Henry David Thoreau—secular priests in the house of literature.

Waters occasionally blends animal imagery with human feelings not only to show our natural ancestry but also to warn of the pitfalls of emulating animal tendencies. He rarely focuses on the grotesque, but when he does, the results can be especially powerful. His most explicit blending of animals and humans—a basic technique of writers working with the grotesque—occurs in the uncollected poem "Gentleman Bear" (1975), in which wrestling a bear symbolizes crude sexuality ("shagging the dreary fur with knives, / . . . imagining an angel / who will . . . drag you into her wetness"). At the end of the poem, the bear is within the human body: "that whatever in your body taking shape: // one awful American grizzly. . . ." The threatening-bear imagery is repeated in "Harvest," which Waters included in his 1975 collection: "the nuzzle of bear / breathing its death in my face. . . . "

The title of Waters's next full-length collection, *Not Just Any Death*, indicates that he is still emphasizing the end of life, but many poems in the book also celebrate life. It is a clear progression from *Fish Light*: the voice in the poems is more assured, the outlook is brighter and more realistic, and the focus is more outside the self. Ralph J. Mills, Jr., writing in *Tar River Poetry* (Fall 1980), praised the "substance and imaginative strength" in the book and said that the "themes, imagery, objects, persons and experiences are inextricably woven together to form a whole." The overarching theme is the temporality of life, and again Waters finds solace in literature as a means of assuaging the pain of inevitable loss. Writing of the poem "Preserves," Rachel Hadas said, "The sequence of thought—preserved fruit, *temps retrouvé*—is none the less valid for its failure to surprise" (*Parnassus*, 1980). Waters hints of the ephemeral nature of such preservation, however, in the last few lines:

> the slow spirals of dust
>
> still resist sweeping,
> having been written in the journal
> of the lost, to keep track
> of what passes, what preserves.

The poem is also a good example of his increasing skill in using tightly controlled four-line stanzas, which gradually became the preferred building blocks for his poetry: "I've become very comfortable with unrhymed quatrains," he told Rubin and Fitz Gerald, although he employs many other forms, especially in his later books.

Two of the best poems in *Not Just Any Death* are written in quatrains: "Apples," dedicated to his father, and "In Memory of Smoke," written for his mother. The first one demonstrates how Waters can take a mundane symbol and give it new and refreshing life. Standing for the color, vivacity, and rejuvenative quality of nature, apples are part of a recurrent image pattern in Waters's early poetry. Opposed to them are images of death and decay, primarily frost, snow, and rotting, green mushrooms—green being the complementary color to red. Thus Waters presents death and life as integral parts of the same essential spectrum. In "Apples" he writes to his father:

> I was the clumsy child
> who stole apples
> from your favorite tree
> to toss them into the lake.

But the apples are not all lost. While the father sleeps, the speaker takes an apple that has washed ashore and symbolically gives it back: "Sometimes I remember that desire // to take whatever belongs to you / so I can return it." Waters's love for his often-absent father shows in many of his poems, as does his need to replace such a father, at least temporarily, with certain literary priests who are always available.

His love for his mother is less ambivalent, but it appears less often in his poetry. "In Memory of Smoke" touches on her Jewish ancestry:

> I found her again this morning,
> my mother, sleeping
> with her head in the oven,
> on a pillow of human hair.
>
> On her knees, exhausted,
> wanting the oven forever clean,
> she might have been praying
> in memory of smoke.

The speaker leaves his mother alone and allows her to continue sleeping; he imagines that, before she went to sleep, she said "a prayer for her family, // . . . / in memory of smoke, / in fear of the coming snow."

In "Frogs" death is seen as sometimes creeping up "on little frog legs" (an allusion to Carl Sandburg's "Fog," in which "the fog comes / on little cat feet"). Frogs are compared to "green, / almost shapeless, bits of rotten mushroom." In *Fish Light* the green-death imagery appears in "The Dead" ("the sad green odor of mushrooms") and in "Harvest" ("the sad green light of mushrooms"). "The Rehearsal" (in *Not Just Any Death*) is explicitly about rehearsing for death:

> I imagine the dead sweating
> prayer into their clasped hands,
>
> waiting for the earth to open.
> I rehearse their great patience.

Waters, though raised a Catholic, is speaking, like Thomas Hardy in his 1917 poem "The Oxen" ("Hoping it might be so"), with more of a sense of evocative imagination than a sense of religion. As Waters says in "Our Lady of the Valkyries" (in *Fish Light*), "The power / of the Lord is in its last bloom."

Anniversary of the Air represents a turning point in Waters's career. It was his best-received work to date and the first of his books published by a major university press (Carnegie-Mellon). It also continued his gradual turning away from the self. Many of the poems are focused on, and sometimes "spoken" by, other people, "characters . . . I've seen on the streets of New York and whose lives I imagine," as he said in his interview with Rubin and Fitz Gerald. Even though poems about Waters's boyhood are also featured, the boy in the poems is seen from as great a distance as the other characters are. Moreover, the thrust of the collection is the need for calm, emotional distance, for perspective, and for clarity of vision. "The Story of the Caul" is about Waters's grandmother: "She knows, she tells me now, / how the world begins to come true / if we stare long enough, / if we stare hard."

The epigraph to the collection is from Ernest Hemingway's story "Ten Indians" (1927): "In the morning there was a big wind blowing and the waves were running high up on the beach and he was awake for a long time before he remembered that his heart was broken." This biblical-sounding statement again points up the

Cover for Waters's 1985 book, which, according to critic Joseph Parisi, reveals "the elusive, sustaining will to connect and make some meaning from the entanglements of human relations" (Booklist, July 1985)

possibilities that nature offers for cleansing the mind and easing pain, and Waters's work resembles Hemingway's in its stark, natural imagery and its immediate closeness to feelings.

In his January 1986 review of *Anniversary of the Air* in *Poetry*, Roger Mitchell wrote that "The Mystery of the Caves," the first poem in the book, "is the best poem in it and one of the best I've read in some time." Often anthologized, the poem succeeds because of a seductive power based on the innate appeal of narratives. The reader is drawn into a story that gradually becomes more and more personal until the speaker becomes the boy in the story (and any child in an analogous situation: a violent argument between parents). Waters forcefully presents the feelings of drowning in a sea of uncontrollable emotions:

> The boy wasn't able to breathe.
> I think he wanted me to help,
>
> but I was small, and it was late.
> And my mother was sobbing now,
> no longer cursing her life,
> repeating my father's name

> among bright islands of skirts
> circling the rim of the bed.
> I can't recall the whole story,
> what happened at the end. . . [.]

The safe cave of literature fails the speaker when it fills with the water of tears: emotions overwhelm any possible escape or consolation. It is not loneliness or death that threatens him but the very real possibility of violence and the disruption of his warm, orderly life. As an ironic contrast to the swirling chaos, Waters's carefully structured and firmly controlled presentation of the scene doubles its built-in strength.

Occasionally Waters has female characters narrate poems, and such is the case in "Bonwit Teller," one of the longest poems in *Anniversary of the Air*. In this narrative about a middle-aged woman who stops before a department-store window, fantasy women, represented by bikini-clad mannequins, are seen as "more eloquent" and more desirable than the ordinary woman whose reflection stares back at her from the window:

> plump
> ghost in a wet, woolen coat,

foolishly brushing my dampening hair.
....

Their world remains, and remains
more eloquent than mine.

Such a juxtaposition might verge on the mundane were it not for Waters's implicit condemnation of the brutalizing force of American superficiality and consumerism. The woman in the poem briefly imagines herself becoming what to her seems the ideal creature in such a society: "a speechless mannequin."

Writing for *Booklist* (July 1985), Joseph Parisi noted the "mature understanding" evident in *Anniversary of the Air* and also called attention to Waters's use of the motif of hair as a symbol for life and humanity, as especially seen in the poem titled "Hair." No matter how much the narrator tries to escape into literature or use it as a religion ("I browse through the dust- / laden volumes along the wall, / searching for some passage / that might affirm"), he is finally forced to recognize and admit the resemblance of his cut hair on a barbershop floor to that of his neighbor who has just died, as the barber grabs "the dust- // pan and whisk broom, / to sweep away the dead / bristles of my beard. . . ." Waters's manipulation of line breaks in the poem reinforces the theme of facing death without walls behind which one can hide: the word *dust* is doubly emphasized, for example. Literature should be a means of understanding, coping with, and preparing for death, he implies, not a route of escape.

The Burden Lifters is, appropriately with such a title, lighter in tone than Waters's previous collections, and the focus is usually even more at a distance from the self of the poet. Though there are some personal poems, they include characters who, while ostensibly based on Waters, are also clearly literary creations; sometimes the poems employ the sort of tongue-in-cheek humor that Paul Zimmer uses in his poems with the character called "Zimmer." Waters, in the lyrical "The Conversion of Saint Paul," remembers himself as a child in religious pageants: "O little, wild-eyed prophet of Brooklyn!" Unusual for Waters, the poem is written in couplets and often includes rhyme, as in these lines that show his adult perspective: "Funny enough today, I guess, / but then I pleaded for forgiveness."

The Burden Lifters also includes serious, Proustian poems about the loss of joy and innocence. Even "The Conversion of Saint Paul" has resonances of the terror inherent in a religious ed-

ucation by strict nuns. "Horse," the first poem in the collection, shows an education of another kind. Waters sensually links the symbolic (the signifying word or image) with the real (the thing signified) when he shows a four-year-old boy touching a workhorse on Knickerbocker Avenue in Brooklyn:

I worked behind his triangular head
    to touch his foreleg above the knee,
        the muscle jerking the mat of hair.
Horse, I remember thinking,
....
        while the power gathered in his thigh
surged like language into my thumb.

Such sensual knowledge stands in direct opposition to the vague but frightening superstitions whispered into the child's ear in "The Conversion of Saint Paul."

In "Deadly Nightshade" it is not nuns who terrify a young boy but teenage girls in a bowling alley. They drag him into "their bathroom" and undo "the buttons of their blouses / to taunt me with black bras / . . . / no giggling, the moment serious / —especially for breathless Michael! . . . " Waters looks back with warmth and affection at his bewildered younger self, in this first of the four parts of the book.

Part 2 is made up of a single poem, "The Lighthouse Keeper at Sparrow Point," the longest Waters has included in a book. It seems a poetic, workingman's version of T. S. Eliot's essay "Tradition and the Individual Talent" (1920). The lighthouse keeper in the poem is reading a journal kept by the earlier, now-deceased masters of "the last of the manned screwpile-design lighthouses," as the structure is called in the Sunday paper that he also reads: "*I'm human interest*, / he thinks, coffee steaming / the lenses of binoculars. . . . " Thus, as soon as he thinks of his own ego, a means of vision begins to blur. He judges some of the entries in the old journal to be "the labor of an inarticulate man / hoping to explain. . . . " But then he himself begins to write in the journal:

At dusk the water is gray, metallic, fringed with rust.
The dissolving light . . .
                        he pauses.

What does he have to say about light
....
that hasn't already been spoken?

In the deceptive simplicity of this poem is the crux of the whole artistic enterprise: how does one add anything significant to the work that has gone before, while at the same time steering clear of egotism and the resultant distortion? The means of avoiding such a pitfall, Waters implies, is to shun mirrors and favor such aids to vision as clear binoculars.

In part 3 of *The Burden Lifters* Waters's scope expands to include raw nature—in "Snakes" (where he says "nothing should be ignored"), "Mosquitoes," and "Monsoon"—as well as literary ancestors ("Keats' Lips") and the grotesque ("Morpho"). In "Mosquitoes," as in many of his nature poems, Waters gives importance to small, almost inconsequential creatures and shows how they have a significant place in human lives. The poem is the compressed story of a troubled marriage and a sleepless night in which the husband spends time thinking of and smashing mosquitoes: *"Clap!*—then another." Toward dawn he learns "to bear our bitterness, // to applaud our flawed / selves, to praise / the words we withheld, / blood staining my hands." The killing of the mosquitoes leads to a celebration of life, including its irritations. "Keats' Lips" shows Waters at his meditative best, as he reports his feelings after seeing a death mask of Keats:

the lips remain swollen,
almost pursed, what's left
of Keats' tumultuous spirit
struggling to forsake the mouth.

Keats might have been his own
best poem, transmutable as smoke[.]

Perhaps the most memorable poem in the book is "Morpho." Certainly its images are the most striking, as Waters tries to subvert the conventional view of beauty by including in the concept what would normally be viewed as ugliness. The poem is Rabelaisian in that Waters uses the grotesque to question and undermine socially sanctioned norms and mores. Two grotesque images are described in detail: the first is that of a raped and murdered Kenyan girl who is discovered with "two large, blue-green, rarely seen butterflies / trembling upon her glazed, staring eyes, / opening and closing their wings / . . . / . . . probably / the *Morpho* butterfly, / each lulled in the mirror of her dissolving eye." The second image, reminiscent of Hemingway's obese character Alice in the story "The Light of the World" (1933), shows the perverse attractiveness of the grotesque, as

Waters with his daughter, Kiernan, in 1991

seen by a traveler in an Amsterdam bar. The owner of the bar had instructed that, at her wake, her body should be displayed at the establishment in a bizarre way, and the narrator of the poem has walked in during the wake:

a three-hundred pound, nude, quite dead
    woman
shaded the jungle of a back-room pool table.
. . . .
and there, between her enormous thighs,
one silver-blue, scratchless, polished and buffed
        billiard ball
was blazing!

Such juxtapositions of the repulsive and the attractive were favored by Cesare Pavese, an Italian writer whose work influenced Waters significantly. The narrator in "Morpho" labels the combinations "beautiful, / or . . . near to what we think of as beauty," thus calling attention to the arbitrary lines society draws between beauty and ugliness, and, by extension, the boundaries erected between art and nonart, between poetry and prose.

321

Waters's use of the grotesque to make this point seems natural and is highly effective, but he rarely uses this tool in his poetry. He realizes that such poems are best presented in small doses, lest the reader reach a point of over-stimulation and resultant numbness.

Also rare in Waters's collections are romantic poems, which can sometimes be weak spots for him. The title poem of *The Burden Lifters* may be the most personal and romantic in the book. It presents a bored, miserable, rejected lover, speaking from a first-person point of view. He listens to talk shows on all-night radio stations until he tunes in "the gospel / station, letting Willis Pittman / and his Burden Lifters / undo the damage of too // much talk. . . . " There seems too much talk in the poem itself, and it ends with the trite citing of the speaker's "burden" and his "godforsaken shoulders."

In part 4 of the book Waters includes only a few personal poems. One of the best poems, "Romance in the Old Folks' Home," is about an emotional connection, but one that is at a distance from the poet. The main character is an old woman named Anna, who is reluctantly being wooed by a fellow resident of a nursing home. He "speaks" to her by taping nostalgic cut-out pictures to her door: "She knew she was being spoken to / in a language long forgotten, / like Latin lost after school." She finally gives in, allowing her suitor to read to her from Nathaniel Hawthorne's novel *The Marble Faun* (1860). Such a narrative poem is artistically dangerous in that it skirts the edge of sentimentality, but it is to Waters's credit that he writes of such situations rather than refusing to take chances with them. Such events do happen, and he presents them realistically in his poetry.

The Burden Lifters generally demonstrates Waters's ability to rise above the personal to embrace a wide, compassionate view of humanity and to produce carefully drawn word paintings of the world of nature; the book received favorable reviews. Writing in the *Gettysburg Review* (Winter 1990), Floyd Collins praised Waters's "careful scrutiny and charged diction." The anonymous critic for the *North American Review* (December 1989), noting the plaintive epigraph from Logan that Waters used for the book, felt that the collection was "orchestrated with that poet's sense of euphony and—yes, say it, style—so largely missing from Waters' contemporaries."

Waters surpasses that achievement, though, with *Bountiful*, which is his best book to date, pub-

lished when he was forty-two. It shows in full fruition the aesthetic benefits of his steady craft, outward focus, and artistic maturity. He is a sharp-eyed traveler who ventures deeply into both the unfamiliar and the everyday and reports back with original perspectives. "My poems are always triggered by something I've seen," he says. "I'm a poet of eyesight rather than a poet of vision." The visions and the ideas are imbedded in and conveyed by the sensuality of the descriptions. Even the more personal poems are driven by images that remain in the mind's eye long after one has finished reading. (In many ways the poems are imagistic, though not as stark or terse as those of Ezra Pound or William Carlos Williams, and Waters does not buy into such rigid dogma as "No ideas but in things.") The reader of Waters's books could easily come away with a newly sharpened awareness and a freshened appreciation for the senses.

Waters includes two epigraphs in *Bountiful*: the first, from Italo Svevo, is a statement of the unquenchable desire for ideal love and beauty; the second, spoken by Brett Ashley in Hemingway's *The Sun Also Rises* (1926), undercuts the first: "What are these outbursts of affection, Michael?" Waters again features his first name in a humorous, self-deprecatory way, but the contrast between the two epigraphs points to a serious concern in the book: the sometimes startling difference between expectations and reality, between dreams and daily life. Some of the poems center on disillusionment, emptiness, and the transiency of human endeavor. Any nihilistic tendencies, however, are lightened and leavened by Waters's overt joy and optimism, and his sense of simple wonder. In *Bountiful* Waters again shows that nothing should be ignored and that one should stare hard at the whole available spectrum of existence, not just at selected parts.

There is bitterness and sarcasm in the book, though. Such feelings are probably related to the fact that Waters's marriage ended between the time *The Burden Lifters* was published and the publication of *Bountiful*. His pain and disappointment extend out into the cosmos in the first poem, "Creation": "Imagine God's exhaustion once the earth / neared completion, before man was abandoned / to video arcades and two-story malls. . . ." The title poem mentions sorrow "remaining in cookbooks / bought by husbands roaming malls after the divorce." But the rest of "Bountiful" focuses on the multifaceted feast of life, as Waters mixes detailed food imagery with that of sex and religion. All three can satisfy existential hunger—at least momentarily.

Some of the best poems in the collection center on childhood and the sense that the world is just beginning fresh and unspoiled. "Covert Street," the first of these poems, again shows Waters's indebtedness to literature and his literary fathers. The setting and scenario of the poem recall a story by Jorges Luis Borges: "The Library of Babel" (1944; translated, 1962), in which the narrator lives permanently in a library. Borges's writing style and Waters's poetry sometimes resemble each other, as when Borges writes, "I am preparing to die a few leagues from the hexagon in which I was born. Once dead, there will not lack pious hands to hurl me over the banister; my sepulchre shall be the unfathomable air: my body will sink lengthily and will corrupt and dissolve in the wind engendered by the fall, which is infinite. I affirm that the Library is interminable." In Waters's poem, "The boy who lived in the library / . . . / could leave the library," but the streets are like the aisles of Borges's library, as Waters writes of "those eternal, / Brooklyn blocks he'd never forget." He has encased his childhood and his first neighborhood in poetry and thereby placed them in the universal library; he has preserved them in literature.

Another of Waters's poems on childhood, "Shadow Boxes," dedicated to artist Joseph Cornell, shows a little boy visiting a collage artist who lives underground. It is a surreal poem that relates the world of art to the world of dreams,

> . . . the blue that blazed
>   below the earth, in darkness,
>
> in a world where nothing would be lost,
>   where everything was given purpose,
>   if only it could remain patient.

Once again, in *Bountiful*, one sees Waters's careful attention to nature, in poems such as "Hummingbirds," "Ticks," and "Scorpions" (Consider their power: to make a man / meditate, ignore the sun / to gaze into the shadows in his shoes"). And there are visceral poems that explore the grotesque, the best example of which is "River Wife," a startling, dark-visioned narrative that symbolically links a rat caught in a barrel with a wife trapped in a loveless marriage. Shocking images abound, as when the wife first sees the rat: "larger / than a rat, nightmare of teeth and hair, berserk / with thirst and singular in-

tent, leaping again and again / against the curved walls toward the impossible hatch."

Possibly the most powerful poem in the book is "Village Dogs," which follows "River Wife" and juxtaposes a vicious battle between two dogs with the end of a marriage. "Village Dogs" is reminiscent of "The Mystery of the Caves" in that only gradually does the story become personal and highly emotional. The poem begins as simply a description of a desultory New Year's Eve, as a feuding couple watch the celebrations on television. When the husband takes their dog for a walk, a pit bull springs "through a hedge-wall with a primal / snarl. . . . " The attacker injures both the couple's dog and the husband before the man fights back with all the pent-up rage inside him, nearly killing the pit bull with a tree branch and a brick. Finally the man's wife, "pale on the porch," cries out: "Don't. Haven't you done enough harm?" As the husband, "bruised and sober," returns home, he thinks, "who / could deny that the marriage was over?"

The people in Waters's poetry traverse the same emotional territory that almost all humans do: from being fascinated by the initiation into the symbolic order, language entering one's system like a welcome invasion; to facing and coming to terms with death, the ultimate end of language; to embracing life and love; to experiencing a bitterness that can make one wish to be "a speechless mannequin"; to coping with words that mean the end of something, words that choke off love and marriage; then, finally, if fortunate, to an emotional rebirth. Between and during such stages, though, as Waters's poems show, the beauty of life, love, and nature still pulsates, and the way to rejuvenate the spirit is to be open to such beauty, to stare hard at the world, unblinkingly whenever possible.

Waters's work demonstrates the possibilities of using one's senses and abilities unafraid. "I love the possibilities and promise inherent in using our language," he says, "to express an emotion with some precision." In the final poem in *Bountiful*, "At Homer's Tomb," Waters explores disillusionment and the commercialization of literature, calling attention to the fact that the "tomb" of the great Greek poet is merely an invention of the tourist bureau. In Waters's poem such exploitation is linked with the petty human jealousies that can disrupt serenity: greed and selfishness are shown as the primary destructors of genuine affection and peace of mind. But the calm, knowledgeable narrator is not immune to the corrosive effects of such forces. At the end of the poem he questions whether "the romantic ideals we once placed faith in" are "nothing more than a gorgeous sham."

Though the book ends on this emotional low point, *Bountiful*—like most of Waters's poetry—more often affirms the inherent appeal of life and truth by showing lucidly, without prejudice, all the aspects of living. "Let those who want to save the world," Hemingway wrote, "if you can get to see it clear and as a whole. Then any part you make will represent the whole if it's made truly" (*Death in the Afternoon*, 1932). Michael Waters will be remembered for his ability

to capture significant features of people, nature, and emotions in sharp, aesthetically effective delineations that show the world the way it is rather than the way one might wish it to be.

Interview:

Stan Sanvel Rubin and Gregory Fitz Gerald, "A Poet of Eyesight: A Conversation with Michael Waters," in *The Post-Confessionals*, edited by Rubin, Earl G. Ingersoll, and Judith Kitchen (Rutherford, N.J.: Fairleigh Dickinson University Press / London & Toronto: Associated University Presses, 1989), pp. 235-248.

Bruce Weigl

(27 January 1949 -   )

Roger D. Jones
Southwest Texas State University

BOOKS: *A Sack Full of Old Quarrels* (Cleveland, Ohio: Cleveland State University Poetry Center, 1976);

Executioner (Tucson, Ariz.: Ironwood, 1976);

A Romance (Pittsburgh: University of Pittsburgh Press, 1979; London: Feffer & Simons, 1979);

The Monkey Wars (Athens: University of Georgia Press, 1985);

Song of Napalm (New York: Atlantic Monthly, 1988).

OTHER: *The Giver of Morning*, edited by Weigl (Birmingham, Ala.: Thunder City, 1982);

"Welcome Home" [essay], *Nation*, 249 (27 November 1982): 549;

The Imagination as Glory: Essays on the Poetry of James Dickey, edited by Weigl and T. R. Hummer (Urbana: University of Illinois Press, 1984).

"To be a writer," Bruce Weigl told *Contemporary Authors* (1984), "is to accept who you are, your background, the ruckus of your family life,

the whole landscape of your past. For me it was steel mills and industrial waste. That's who I was and what I have to go on. If I'm lucky and work hard enough, I can turn the gritty language of an industrial city into poetry." While the urban landscape and family life certainly figure in Weigl's work, he is better known as one of the most eloquent poets to emerge from America's involvement in the Vietnam War. These subjects—Vietnam and family life in the industrial part of the United States—mirror and complement each other, giving Weigl's poetry its particular distinction and power.

Bruce Weigl was born on 27 January 1949 in Lorain, Ohio, to Albert Louis Weigl and Zora Grasa Weigl. He received his B.A. in English from Oberlin College in 1974, his M.A. in 1975 from the University of New Hampshire, and his Ph.D. in 1979 from the University of Utah, where he studied with poet Dave Smith. Weigl taught from 1975 to 1976 at Lorain County Community College in Elyria, Ohio, from 1979 to 1981 at the University of Arkansas at Little Rock, from 1981 to 1986 at Old Dominion University

Bruce Weigl (photograph by Brenda Wright)

in Norfolk, Virginia (where he served as director of the Associated Writing Program), and after 1986 at Pennsylvania State University. From 1967 to 1970 Weigl served in the U.S. Army in Vietnam, and he received the Bronze Star. He has won some major literary prizes, including the Academy of American Poets Prize in 1979, Pushcart Prizes in 1980 and 1985, and a fellowship from the Bread Loaf Writers' Conference in 1981.

As an Ohio native, Weigl could not easily have escaped the influence of fellow Ohioan James Wright, and Wright's influence is evident throughout Weigl's work—particularly in the short, terse lines Weigl employs and in Weigl's emphasis on downtrodden characters and somber situations. The ironic title of Weigl's first full-length collection, *A Romance* (1979)—a book that includes work from his two previous chapbooks, *A Sack Full of Old Quarrels* (1976) and *Executioner* (1976)—is particularly fitting, since in literary tradition *romance* refers variously to medieval adventures of knights and heroes, to literature in

which the emphases are on love and romance, and to the type of romance—such as some works of Nathaniel Hawthorne—in which atmosphere, chiaroscuro, and imagination are of particular importance. Such applications are ironic in Weigl's book, however, since the "knights" are Vietnam soldiers, the love is often the grim love between family members, and the imagination is used to create a disturbing, surreal atmosphere, a juxtaposition of Weigl's Vietnam experience with the world back home, each of which is a form of nightmare.

Americans are accustomed to works about Vietnam that present that country and its culture as strange, exotic, and forbidding. In Weigl's hands, both Vietnamese and American cultures contain their own individual elements of shock, heartbreak, and peculiarity, as in "The Sharing":

> I have not ridden a horse much,
> two, maybe three times,
> . . . .
> but I watched two Chinese tanks
> roll out of the jungle side by side,
> their turret guns feeling before them
> like a man walking through his dream,
> their tracks slapping the bamboo like hooves.

Readers are lulled by the matter-of-fact diction and the commonness of the experience, so that the appearance of the tanks thrusts readers as suddenly into the situation as the speaker found himself thrust into it as it was happening.

In his discussion of *A Romance* (in *American Literature and the Experience of Vietnam*, 1982), Philip Beidler traces the conventions of the romance genre: "there is the dream vision, the wounded warrior arising from his infirmity, the voyage, the new epic quest, the siren call of the faraway remembered land, the place half sinister hallucination and half magical realism." In a review of *A Romance* T. R. Hummer (*New England Review*, Winter 1980) emphasized the importance of the theme of love. The book presents a speaker who could be any American seeking wholeness in a world where violence and desperation seem the primary laws of life. In the title poem, for instance, he describes a scene in a honky-tonk bar: "it is always like this with me . . . / wanting women I know / I'll have to get my face punched bloody to love."

Though Weigl writes compellingly about Vietnam in such poems as "Mines," "Him, On the Bicycle," "When Saigon Was French," and "Convoy," he is always mindful of home and its terrible realities as well. Indeed, in much of the literature and many of the films about Vietnam, characters find themselves trapped in an absurd world where problems at home are distorted by the war's horrors and the profound moral ambiguities that accompany it. Weigl focuses these anxieties into poems about the relationship between the speaker and his family (notably, the father). Reading through such poems as "Fourth of July: Toledo, Ohio" and "The Harp," one senses the same aching need for meaning that characterizes Weigl's Vietnam poems. In "The Harp" the father has shaped "a wire piece of steel / with many small and beautiful welds / ground so smooth they resembled / rows of pearls." "He went broke with whatever it was," the speaker says. "I think it was his harp." The speaker finds it later, cleans it, and tries "to make it work." The son's desperate desire to rectify the father's failure repeats an underlying emphasis that runs through the book. *A Romance* is populated by sad, lonely, and often heroic characters seeking fulfillment in an American landscape where conflicting ideals and realities are made more painful by involvement in the Vietnam War.

A Romance was generally praised. Though Peter Stitt complained about the "flaccid and uninteresting" writing in "Fourth of July: Toledo, Ohio," he noted the imaginative qualities of "Sailing to Bien Hoa" and concluded, "it is this element of the imagination that will have to come to dominate if Weigl . . . is to have a second book to follow this first" (*Georgia Review*, Winter 1980). Emily Grosholz, in her *Hudson Review* essay (Summer 1980), disapproved of the book, which she cited as exemplifying the clipped, present-tense diction fashionable in contemporary poetry. Such criticism might raise good and even necessary points, but Grosholz's complaints seem shortsighted against a work such as Weigl's, whose grim subjects and tone suit completely the terse diction he employs.

The war and its terrible consequences figure more heavily in Weigl's *The Monkey Wars* (1985) and *Song of Napalm* (1988). The images are more shocking and the sense of tragedy more intense than in *A Romance*. In *The Monkey Wars* the poem "The Ghost Inside" depicts a war veteran who is a cocaine addict: "Like Ezekiel," the speaker says, "Unless the ghost is inside you / Your tongue is tied . . . / And in your eyes you look a hundred years old." In "For the Wife Beater's Wife," a veteran is an abusive husband who "sleeps it off next door"; the speaker of "Debris"

shoots seagulls "to get my fill of blood"; the main character, Joe, in "Hope" is a pipe mill worker who is both tender and violent and who strangles a dog he's found hit by the highway because it "didn't have no hope."

Throughout the poems of *The Monkey Wars*, Weigl records characters and situations directly, objectively. The world he presents reflects both tenderness and violence, which Weigl sees as the two poles of human action and motive. One is reminded of T. S. Eliot's lines in "The Love Song of J. Alfred Prufrock" (1915) that "there will be a time to murder and create." In Weigl's world the two urges coexist, like opposite sides of a coin. As Hummer pointed out in a review of the book, Weigl "presents war . . . and peace as a moral spectrum, not as separate worlds; violence, and beauty interpenetrate both, in unexpected and often shocking ways" (*Western Humanities Review*, Spring 1986). Critic James Kirkland (*Tar River Poetry*, Fall 1985) described the speakers' attempts "to open new lines of communication with . . . fellow human beings or restore those which have been broken—a process that Weigl conveys through subtle manipulations of speaker-audience relationships." With Vietnam as a constant backdrop, we are always aware of the profoundly violent, disorienting effect of warfare on human interaction and on the psyche of the individual, no matter how far removed he or she is from the actual combat.

That it took until the mid 1980s for Vietnam veterans to receive their first official welcome-home parade illustrates the deep split between the war as a political issue and the war as reality for those who fought it. Weigl's characters never lose sight of both the irony and the injustice of this split. Often they react with rage (frequently enacted on those around them), as does the soldier in "The Last Lie" who rides on the back of a convoy truck, grips a can of C rations as though "it were the seam of a baseball," and hurls it at children in the road, "his rage ripped / Again into the faces of children / Who called to us for food." In such moments, the political and personal interact. In "Dream of Santiago, 1973" Weigl draws upon the political assassinations in Chile following Pinochet's overthrow of Salvador Allende, to underscore not only the political nature of personal action but also the political nature of art, since many artists and poets were among those assassinated in Santiago. The speaker of the poem (apparently a veteran, since he awakens "sweating, at attention") rises from a nightmare in which children are being murdered—an allusion to the children who died during the Vietnam War—to check on his own sleeping child, while birds make noises outside. "One point which *The Monkey Wars* wants to make," Hummer has written, "is that the world is a war and the persona is in a perpetual state of shellshock. . . . In Weigl's vision, there is something in the world . . . which carries out an inexorable program of punishment."

Perhaps the most powerful poem in the volume is "Burning Shit at An Khe," a long monologue by a speaker who has been assigned to burn servicemen's excrement. Helicopters circle nearby, and as he tries to light the fire, his match goes out repeatedly:

> And it all came down on me, the stink
> > And the heat and the worthlessness
> Until I slipped and climbed
> > Out of that hole and ran
> Past the olive drab
> > Tents and trucks and clothes and everything
> Green as far from the shit
> > As the fading light allowed.
> Only now I can't fly.
> > I lay down in it
> And finger paint the words of who I am
> > Across my chest
> Until I'm covered and there's only one smell,
> > One word.

Weigl's metaphor of excrement operates like the Russian-roulette metaphor in Michael Cimino's film *The Deer Hunter*: to signify the futility and self-obliteration that the war enacts and represents. However, in *The Masks of God: Primitive Mythology* (1968) Joseph Campbell points out that the origins of the modern-day clown come from primitive man's practice of smearing himself with feces for both comical and magical effects. Hence in Weigl's poem the action is both purgative and self-damning.

Perhaps Weigl's greatest triumph in *The Monkey Wars* is the successful psychic linkage he makes between Vietnam and the private world of the American individual. Drawn out in taut, resonant lines, the poems of the volume capture the trauma and embattled soul of the American veteran-turned-civilian. *The Monkey Wars* received critical praise, reflected in James Kirkland's citing it as a "bold and imaginative new book, deserving of study and recognition in its own right, both for its technical excellence and for its emo-

tional range and power" (*Tar River Poetry*, Fall 1985).

All but eleven of the thirty-three poems in Weigl's pointedly titled *Song of Napalm* were published earlier in *A Romance* and *The Monkey Wars*, and the volume seems intended as a deliberately focused "Vietnam book." As Robert Stone points out in his introduction,

> Weigl's poetry is a refusal to forget. It is an angry assertion of the youth and life . . . spent in Vietnam with such vast prodigality, as though youth and life were infinite. Through his honesty and toughmindedness, he undertakes the traditional duty of the poet: in the face of randomness and terror to subject things themselves to the power of art and thus bring them within the compass of moral comprehension.

In one of the best of the new poems, "A Soldier's Brief Epistle," a veteran, whose defensiveness about his killings during the war illustrates the moral quandary Americans have faced about the war and its perpetrators since it ended, unwittingly depicts the war as, among other things, repressed sexuality, suggesting the link between America's puritanical background and its propensity for violence: "You think you're far away from me," he says, "but you're right here in my pants / and I can grab your throat // like a cock and squeeze."

In the title poem (which originally appeared in *The Monkey Wars*) the speaker remembers a napalm attack and a girl running from a village, "napalm / stuck to her dress like jelly":

> I try to imagine she runs down the road and wings
> beat inside her until she rises
> above the stinking jungle and her pain
> eases, and your pain, and mine.
>
> But the lie swings back again. . . .
> > Nothing
> can change that, she is burned behind my eyes
> and not your good love and not the rain-swept air
> and not the jungle-green
> pasture unfolding before us can deny it.

In "Elegy," Weigl describes an attack on an unspecified army unit. "The bullets sliced through the razor grass," he writes. "Some of them died. / Some of them were not allowed to." This last statement is, in many respects, the unifying idea behind most of Weigl's Vietnam poetry. Phrased in the passive voice, the last sentence illustrates the final indignity of the war—that its veterans, on both sides, were the victims of larger political and death-delivering forces. One of the most persistent themes in postmodern war literature such as Kurt Vonnegut's *Slaughterhouse Five* and Joseph Heller's *Catch-22* is the horror that the coming world, more and more, is a world of impersonal forces whose final triumph will be the extinguishing of the individual soul.

Reviewing *Song of Napalm* for the *Hudson Review* (Spring 1989), Robert Schultz asserted that "we need books like this which tell us, with accuracy, what war is like. . . . Weigl renders the terrible beauty of a sensibility which denies nothing, forgets nothing, and refuses to cease being human."

While Weigl has spent much of his time exorcizing the demons of Vietnam, his technical skill, voice, and sense of the universality of suffering indicate that he will be capable of rendering a broad, compelling body of poetry on other subjects. In the meantime, however, he has already contributed a distinguished service to American literature by giving voice to a war whose haunting images and memory refuse to go away. Since the end of the Vietnam War, the task of American his-

torians, philosophers, writers, and artists has been to break down the war experience, to give it some sense of meaning in the overall context of national history. Weigl's poetry has been an important part of this process. As Walt Whitman expressed concepts of the Civil War, Wilfred Owen of World War I, and Randall Jarrell of World War II, so Weigl may be remembered as the voice of the Vietnam War. Like Owen's World War I soldiers, Weigl's Vietnam fighter is the prototypical modernist hero—who is trapped in a technological world, who is not quite an individual—fulfilling a role prescribed by larger powers that he neither understands nor has any control over, a role that only the longer scheme of history can place in its accurate context.

References:

Philip Beidler, *American Literature and the Experience of Vietnam* (Athens: University of Georgia Press, 1982), pp. 182-191;

Robert Stone, Introduction to Weigl's *Song of Napalm* (New York: Atlantic Monthly, 1988).

C. D. Wright

(6 January 1949 -)

Jenny Goodman
University of Massachusetts—Amherst

BOOKS: *Alla Breve Loving* (Seattle: Mill Mountain, 1976);

Room Rented by a Single Woman (Fayetteville, Ark.: Lost Roads, 1977);

Terrorism (Fayetteville, Ark.: Lost Roads, 1979);

Translations of the Gospel Back into Tongues (Albany: State University of New York Press, 1982);

Further Adventures with You (Pittsburgh: Carnegie-Mellon University Press, 1986);

String Light (Athens: University of Georgia Press, 1991);

Just Whistle (Berkeley, Cal.: Kelsey Street, 1992).

SELECTED PERIODICAL PUBLICATIONS—
UNCOLLECTED: "A Note on The Battlefield Where the Moon Says I Love You," *Ironwood*, 17 (Spring 1981): 157-164;

"Argument with the Gestapo Continued: Literary Resistance," *Five Fingers Review*, 1 (1984): 30-34;

"Argument with the Gestapo Continued: II," *Five Fingers Review*, 5 (1987): 79-89;

"The Adamantine Practice of Poetry," *Brick*, 35 (Spring 1989): 55-59;

"A Taxable Matter," *Field*, 40 (Spring 1989): 24-26;

"The New American Ode," *Antioch Review*, 47 (Summer 1989): 287-296;

"Infamous Liberties and Uncommon Restraints," *AWP Chronicle*, 23 (May 1991): 1 + .

C. D. Wright (photograph by Kay Duvernet)

C. D. Wright has published seven collections of poetry, the first in 1976 and the most recent in 1992. Her poems have appeared in *Field, Ironwood*, the *New Yorker*, the *Paris Review*, and *TriQuarterly*, among many other magazines and journals. Her work has also appeared in several anthologies. Her awards include two National Endowment for the Arts Fellowships (1981 and 1988), the Witter Bynner Prize for Poetry from the American Academy and Institute of Arts and Letters (1986), a Guggenheim Fellowship (1987), a fellowship from the Mary Ingraham Bunting Institute (1987), a General Electric Award for Younger Writers (1988), a Whiting Writers Award (1989), and a Rhode Island Governor's Award for the Arts (1990).

Wright's given name is Carolyn, but she began using her initials to distinguish herself from the poet Carolyne Wright, who started publishing at approximately the same time as she did. Wright was born on 6 January 1949 in the Ozark town of Mountain Home, Arkansas. Her mother, Alyce E. Wright, was a chancery-court reporter, and Carolyn's father, Ernie E. Wright, a chancery and probate judge, also served as chief judge on the State Court of Appeals. Wright has an older brother, Warren, who is a psychologist. Wright received her B.A. in French from Memphis State University in 1971 and entered the graduate creative-writing program at the University of Arkansas, Fayetteville, in 1973, receiving her M.F.A. in 1976. In 1979 she moved to San Francisco, where she worked at the Poetry Center at San Francisco State University and met poet Forrest Gander, whom she married in 1983. After she received her first NEA Fellowship in 1981, she and Gander lived in the town of Dolores Hidalgo in Mexico and in Eureka Springs, Arkansas, before moving to Providence, Rhode Island, in 1983, when Wright was hired to teach in the Department of English at Brown University, where she is an associate professor. She and Gander run Lost Roads Publishers, a small, nonprofit literary press. Their son, Brecht Wright Gander, was born in the fall of 1986.

Wright brings to contemporary American poetry a political vision rooted in her generation's experience in the civil-rights and antiwar movements, along with an uncompromising commitment to what she refers to as "the word." Her poems are known for their startling images and their jarring juxtapositions. The details and colloquial speech of her native Ozarks permeate the poems, but it is Wright's rich imagination, finally, that brings them to life.

While a graduate student in Fayetteville, Wright met her close friend and mentor the poet Frank Stanford. Stanford was the primary influence on her first three collections of poems, all chapbooks, the first published by Mill Mountain Press in Seattle and the second and third by Lost Roads Publishers, the small press Stanford had started to meet the need for a literary press in the region. The first two chapbooks, *Alla Breve Loving* (1976) and *Room Rented by a Single Woman* (1977), were completed while Wright was in the M.F.A. program at Fayetteville. The third, *Terrorism* (1979), was completed in Fayetteville after Wright had finished her M.F.A., and it was published after Stanford's suicide at age twenty-nine. (Wright, with Stanford's wife, Ginny, took over Lost Roads after Stanford's death.) The chapbooks show Stanford's influence in their themes: desire, loneliness, dreams, madness, violence, and especially injustice. The speaker of the first poem in *Room Rented by a Single Woman*, "Alibi of the Woman Lacing Her Boots in Hell," begins her soliloquy with these lines: "As long as my butt's still behind me / I might as well / sing

about the slaughter of innocents." The hard-bitten attitude, colloquial speech, and biblical frame of reference are typical of Wright's early work.

Wright's first full-length book, *Translations of the Gospel Back into Tongues* (1982), includes poems that are more terse and polished than those in the chapbooks. Seven poems are revised from *Terrorism*; the ones with more than minor revisions have been shortened, reflecting Wright's move toward concision. Each of the poems in *Translations* fits on one page, and more than a few consist of fifteen lines or less. Written in the Ozarks and in San Francisco, with final editing completed in Mexico, the book was published as part of the now-defunct SUNY Poetry Series, whose editor was the late Paul Zweig. *Translations* includes many of the same themes of the chapbooks: injustice, lost or stolen innocence, violence of many kinds, music, and desire. In "Hills," the prose introduction to her 1986 book of poems, *Further Adventures with You*, Wright calls *Translations* "a lamentation for the late Frank Stanford . . . and a tribute to the great American experience of jazz." William Faulkner and Flannery O'Connor are also in the background of the 1982 book. Blues and jazz provide subject matter, diction, and phrasing, as does the gospel of the title. (While growing up, Wright was thrilled by language and music of the radio *Gospel Hour*.)

The book is divided into three sections: "True Accounts from the Imaginary War," "The Secret Life of Musical Instruments," and "Livelihoods of Freaks and Poets of the Western World." The section titles not only suggest thematic concerns but also point to the way in which Wright's language intensifies the stories she tells so that they achieve the quality of myth or folk legend. Wright's voice in *Translations* is tough and unflinching. The speaker is someone who has lived, who can take a hard look at an often gritty and painful, and sometimes funny, reality. In "Bent Tones," describing a town on a stiflingly hot day, she tells the reader, "The sun drove a man in the ground like a stake."

Wright's description (in "Hills") of her poems seems particularly applicable to *Translations*: "They are succinct but otherwise orthodox novels in which the necessary characters are brought out, made intimate . . . , engage in dramatic action and leave the scene forever with or without a resolution in hand or sight." The narrative element of the poems makes them intriguing and accessible, but the reader must make the imaginative leaps necessary to give meaning to stories intentionally left ambiguous or unresolved. Hence some reviewers have pointed to the difficulty of Wright's poetry, while acknowledging the recompense the poems provide in exchange for the reader's imaginative work.

In "Tours," one of the more accessible narrative poems in the book, "A girl on the stairs listens to her father / Beat up her mother." Wright refuses sentimentality; it is her spare presentation of the scene that gives the poem its force. Without any overt commentary, readers know where her sympathy lies. Characteristically she finds an evocative metaphor to end the poem. As the girl plays the piano in the dark, "The last black key / She presses stays down, makes no sound, / Someone putting their tongue where their tooth had been." The ending suggests images of the mother who has been hit (perhaps in the mouth), the girl's youth (her first set of teeth falling out), and, of course, the loneliness and missing love that characterize the girl's life.

"Fields," another poem in *Translations*, shows a different narrative strategy. Dedicated to the poet and Vietnam veteran Bruce Weigl, "Fields" deals explicitly with Wright's generation and with the Vietnam War, both of which emerge more subtly in other poems. Two different times and places are intertwined (the plowed fields of an American town and the battlefields of Vietnam); through their association, the poem resonates with the losses of those at home and those at war. As in other poems, the narrator's matter-of-fact pronouncements allow readers to experience for themselves the random violence and destroyed innocence: "It was their reunion. Those who didn't attend / Lived too far, lost their invitation / Or their life in the meantime." The poem ends with the words, "Through the smoke in the corridor / He hears the sargeant [*sic*] yelling Haul ass." The character is in his hometown and in the war—simultaneously. The juxtaposition speaks of the incongruity of experience with which the young man must live.

Further Adventures with You, published four years after *Translations*, departs from Wright's earlier work most noticeably in its personal tone. She has remarked on the decreased distance between poet and speaker in many of the poems. The book was written while she was living in San Francisco and Providence, and Wright's experiences in these places helped shape the poems. The voice in many poems is familiar to readers who know her earlier work; the Ozark colloquial-

isms are present, but they are only one strain in a wide-ranging, sometimes esoteric or even made-up vocabulary. The book also shows a variety of forms, from narratives like those in earlier work to strategies clearly influenced by the experimental writers Wright encountered in San Francisco, most notably the self-identified $L = A = N = G = U = A = G = E$ writers. Some readers might find certain poems, particularly her prose poems, difficult to penetrate. There are poems in the collection that fail, intentionally, to conform to a mimetic theory of art; they are chiefly concerned with the reflexivity of language. There is no question that this is an intellectually challenging book; still, it is in no way devoid of emotional and sensual appeal.

In "Argument with the Gestapo Continued: II" (*Five Fingers Review*, 1987), Wright discusses her view on certain debates over poetics: "I appreciate the return of reflexivity to the imaginative writer's linguistic province, but does that mean, the province of the writer is language period. What about us. What about what [James] Agee named 'the sorrow, the effort and the ugliness of the beautiful world.' What about EVIL." Like Agee, Wright pays close attention to daily lives. Identifying with the commitments of her generation, and of the women of her generation in particular, she merges the personal and the political. In *Further Adventures* preparing dinner and facing nuclear holocaust are equally a part of consciousness. Wright makes mundane occurrences fresh and strange. Though she is more explicit in this book about her deeply felt political concerns, it is more hopeful than earlier books. Humor, often grotesque, is in abundance (the cover photograph is of a three-legged dog), and love poems are included as well.

"Nothing to Declare," written before the birth of her son, seems to emerge from musings over what to pass on to the next generation, in personal history and in values. A poem in one long stanza, it contains these lines:

> If I had a daughter I'd tell her
> Go far, travel lightly.
> If I had a son he'd go to war
> over my hard body.

The poem ends on a note of solidarity with those, like Wright, who dare to defy the government or societal norms:

> If the hunter turns his dogs loose
> on your dreams

Start early, tell no one
get rid of the scent.

"Scratch Music," a prose poem addressed to Frank Stanford, is written in a highly personal yet self-conscious manner. The poem, by free association, evokes the landscape of Wright's past. More than halfway through the poem, the speaker says, "But I wanted to show you how I've grown, what I know." Though this statement, in context, refers to the wisdom of six years' experience of daily living, it applies as well to Wright's new explorations in her work, evident in the form of the poem.

"The Legend of Hell," as do other poems, invokes the nuclear threat. In the first two strophes, the speaker presents images (a ringing telephone, a white dog on a chain) as though she were a tour guide in a peculiarly familiar time and place. Though the four- to six-line strophes that accumulate seem to present random events, the voice and the repetition of verbs and phrases suggest more than mere randomness. The poem, which becomes increasingly dark in tone, is replete with grotesque humor. In the same strophe in which the dog's chain catches on a shopping cart, "Someone saunter[s] through an orchard / with murdering the whole family on his mind." Two stanzas later these lines appear: "In the cities you had your braille libraries; / couples dining on crustacean / with precious instruments. . . ." By the end readers understand that this poem is about the postmodern era, in particular the nuclear threat that many have taken for granted but that Wright cannot.

In *String Light* (1991) Wright intensifies her experiments with autobiography and poetic structure. As in *Further Adventures*, she incorporates a variety of innovative forms, including unconventional narratives, lists, and prose poems. "The Night I Met Little Floyd" and "The Next Time I Crossed the Line into Oklahoma" serve as twin narratives evoking the wildness of her young adulthood. Both appear as prose blocks punctuated solely with dashes; their vivid and unusual imagery is evident in the following passage from the first narrative: "Oklahoma was a stand of trees without leaves—brown grass brown sky—weathervanes sharp and thin as women blown this away and that—. . . Arkansas—a pot of lentils and bad coffee—rocking chairs—three-way lamps—night running down our face like mascara. . . ." Another poem, "Remarks on Colour," consists of a list of forty-one numbered sentences

Cover for Wright's experimental 1991 collection, which includes narratives, lists, and prose poems

and phrases juxtaposed without transition yet organized along the theme of various associations with "colour," including race. The poem depends on readers to make connections among the numbered items. Images and language from Wright's Ozark home are a strong presence in *String Light*, too. For example, five pages are devoted to "The Ozark Odes," a series of sixteen brief sections, the first of which, "Lake Return," also serves as a prefatory poem to the book.

Two poems in *String Light* dwell extensively on Wright's poetics. The first, "Our Dust," is addressed to future descendants. In it she presents her poetic vision, which is intimately connected with her politics and the daily events of her life:

I never raised your rent. Or anyone else's by God.
Never said I loved you. The future gave me chills.
I used the medium to say: Arise arise and
come together.

Free your children. Come on everybody. Let's start with Baltimore.

The sermon or oration embedded in this strophe is funny in its incongruity with most current political rhetoric and most aesthetics, but it also recalls something serious: the lived history of the civil-rights movement that emerges elsewhere in the book. The final piece in the book, probably its most ambitious, is called "The box this comes in (*a deviation on poetry*)." It defies generic classification. This four-page *ars poetica* could easily be described as poetic prose or as a memoir. Wright uses the metaphor of a box containing personal effects to articulate her poetics more fully than in "Our Dust." "The box this comes in" ends with these lines: "Of a morning and an evening, I face myself, a poet of forty. Within the limits of this di-

minutive wooden world, I have made do with the cracks of light and tokens of loss and recovery that came my way. I can offer no more explicit demonstration as to what my poetry is. The box this comes in is mine; I remain faithfully, CD."

In an especially perceptive review of *Further Adventures* in the Fall/ Winter 1987 *Pennsylvania Review*, Judith Vollmer describes Wright as "a poet of change and the necessity for it, a poet whose political anthem seamlessly matches her forms and voices." No attempt to identify Wright with a particular poetic movement, regional, experimental, political, or any other, can adequately account for the range, vitality, and development of her work. As Philip Booth states in the *Georgia Review* (Spring 1989), "C. D. Wright has language, she has voice, her work is nobody else's."

Lisa Zeidner
(27 March 1955 -   )

Brenda L. Herbel

BOOKS: *Customs* (New York: Knopf, 1981; London: Cape, 1981);
Talking Cure (Lubbock: Texas Tech Press, 1982);
Alexandra Freed (New York: Knopf, 1983; London: Cape, 1983);
Pocket Sundial (Madison: University of Wisconsin Press, 1988);
Limited Partnerships (San Francisco: North Point, 1989).

In the foreword to *Talking Cure* (1982) Cynthia McDonald calls Lisa Zeidner's poetry "fugal": "The new lines enter, extending the work past the natural stopping point of each phase so the poems continually re-engage." Zeidner's repetition and interweaving of ideas exist in each poem as well as in the cumulative scheme of the collections. Her major themes—time, love, sex, birth, death, individual personal worth, and God—continually reappear with an adequate amount of tension and humor to prevent these familiar poetic subjects from becoming hackneyed.

Lisa Zeidner was born on 27 March 1955 in Washington, D.C., to Joseph and Dorothy

Zeidner. In 1976 she received her B.A. in English from Carnegie-Mellon. She earned her M.A. from Johns Hopkins in 1977, and though she entered the doctoral program at Washington University in Saint Louis, she did not complete the degree. Zeidner's poetry has appeared in many magazines and journals, including the *Antioch Review*, *Poetry*, and *Three Rivers Poetry Journal*. She is currently an assistant professor of English at Camden College of Arts and Sciences at Rutgers and lives in Philadelphia with her husband and their child. Zeidner also reviews contemporary fiction for the *New York Times Book Review* on a fairly regular basis. *Talking Cure*, Zeidner's first book of poems, was an Associated Writing Programs Award Series Selection. Her second book of poems, *Pocket Sundial* (1988), was the winner of the Brittingham Prize in Poetry. She has also published three novels.

Several of the poems in *Talking Cure* share a theme of self-judgment: the speakers question their importance to themselves and to others. In "Light" the child-speaker faces the fear of being

Lisa Zeidner circa 1988

unimportant in a world full of so many frightening, adult traumas:

> My mother left three fingers of light
> between me and outside
> when she closed my door at bedtime,
>
> because the man with a thousand eyes
> could walk in if my door were open
> and kick in my door if it were closed,
>
> but if it were ajar he got confused
> and had to enter some other child's nightmare.
> He was scared of half-light; me, of half-life.

A party going on downstairs, with its clinking of glasses and charm bracelets, soothes the child's fears. When she tiptoes from her anxiety-ridden bed toward the staircase to see the party, the child wonders when her time will come, when her infinite battle with growing up will end and place her among the adults, laughing heartily and seeming important.

But youth and age, according to Zeidner, have nothing to do with worthiness. In "The Sadness of Men" she writes: "men are born with erections and die with them," as if their entire purpose is satisfied simply by being male. In the companion poem, "The Sadness of Women," she imag-

ines "sad women [who] trim the hedges, / dreaming of roses they'll be sent / when they suffer mastectomies." Zeidner's attention to the physical and emotional characteristics of the sexes is not so much to separate the genders as to serve as a reminder that the human animal is often insecure and vulnerable; while intellect might guard against physical and emotional damages, the primary worth, Zeidner implies, is ultimately not in individuality but in the capacity and responsibility to perpetuate the species.

"Make-Up," the longest poem in *Talking Cure*, deals with the pressures and anxieties of those who grew up in the 1960s and 1970s. Zeidner writes convincingly of a multitude of difficulties, from the drug scene and cover-ups of government scandals to feminism and hypocrisy, technology and ideology, and much more bitterness and unrest: "sugar lobotomizes"; "our leaders are thugs,"; "ozone [is] already poisoned by our deodorants"; and "the truth is never plain." But if these hurts cannot be healed, perhaps they can be relieved or at least disguised:

> We're even allowed to put on make-up
> and improve upon what nature gave us—

it's not just a privilege to do so,
but a responsibility, our social conscience
bidding us once more to do our best.

As the search for truth, knowledge, and information accelerates, so does the creation of new technological processes, chemicals, and scientific miracles; but with them come new obstacles, so that the old problems are not conquered but merely masked. Thus the societal quagmire humans have carelessly created must remain; nevertheless, Zeidner's conclusion is one of hope:

That our fashions will soon be obsolete
as bustles and powdered wigs
doesn't trouble me—by then
I'll be too old to look good anyway,
and will hopefully be able to rest
on whatever laurels I've accumulated
by virtue of hard work and experience.
Besides, thinking about the appearance
not only kills some time, but provides
a useful model of what it would be like
to lift the face of the entire planet,
and presently, alas, we must
be content to start small.

All of the poems in *Talking Cure* include Zeidner's nimble witticisms, but the purpose is always meaningful, as in "Audience," where "God wracked His brain inventing forests / so we could hear the lone tree falling there," or in "Etiquette for Automatic Writing," where Zeidner laments, "my next birthday is a whole year away. / What will I do in between?" Of the thirty-nine poems in the collection, one is a loose sonnet ("God's Jukebox"), one is in rough heroic couplets ("Still"), and the rest are in what Zeidner herself calls a "shaggy dog" form.

Pocket Sundial, her next poetry collection, includes a long poem titled "The Collector's Fire," in which Zeidner again examines the question of worth, but this time she also ponders possessiveness and selfishness. She loves to play with language, and she is at her best when creating dual meanings for words and making unexpected comparisons. In "The Collector's Fire" a house burns down, all is destroyed, and a man is left with nothing, but a second meaning comes to light. The poem is also about the collector's passion, the "fire" that causes him to accumulate valuables, and about what it must be like to be stripped of a lifetime's work:

Losing music hurt the most.
He had every composer's every piece

in almost every performance,
often in multiple copies in case of—
not fire but scratches, dust,
all matter's gravitation to decay.
Most albums he would never
have listened to anyway,
but the best and worst rarities
are the 1% he could never replace.

To a man whose attention was focused on the collection of various recordings, everything is lost, "as if timbre died when timber did."

Many other things have been burned, too. The dictionary, where the man spent hours reading and learning—for this was "the kind of thing / the collector liked to do / before the fire, before the fire"—is destroyed, along with chairs, rugs, paintings, and artifacts. Soon the poem begins to sound as if it is a treatise on possessiveness and selfishness, but Zeidner saves the poem by shifting her attention from the physical to the metaphysical:

Life is what's supposed to count,
not the shirt on your back.
God, the television fires!
One minute of tragedy like a commercial,
. . . .
though the point is let us pause now
and be glad it happened to someone else,
the superstition being that each fire
reduces the odds of another—

like lighting or chicken pox
we assume one per customer.

"The Collector's Fire," divided into sixteen stanzas, has the perfect topic to complement Zeidner's usual pace—fast. The lines clip along, giving a light tone to even the most disastrous of events. Her quickness shows that she has a fascination for combining tragedy and comedy.

A good joke, however, can go too far. "Dementia Colander" is twenty pages of what should be knee-slapping quips aimed at a king who suffers from the mental disability suggested by the poem's title. The discoverer of the disease, "Ranier Colanderi," loans his last name to the disease, thus causing the hilarity of the entire situation:

The accidental metaphor of the colander

misled the scientists after Colanderi
to portray the brain as a massive rock
in a colander which is the skull.

Also in the colander are flowerlets
from a head of broccoli—the ideas
which the victim tries to flush
through the colander into his mouth

as speech, or into his limbs
as movement (for even stabbing a pea
with a fork is an idea,
loosely translated).
Usually there is no problem:
the colander is not air tight
and like ideas, broccoli is malleable.

The jocular, slapstick tone continues for the duration of the poem, only to become tiresome.

Though her intent is clever and well-reasoned, Zeidner's nimbleness with language is lost in the shuffle.

All in all, though, Zeidner's poems are endearing because of their autobiographical tone. Her closeness of point of view makes her poetry readable and entertaining; she earns the reader's trust.

Reference:
Cynthia McDonald, Foreword to Zeidner's *Talking Cure* (Lubbock: Texas Tech Press, 1982).

Checklist of Further Resources

Allen, Dick, ed. *Expansionist Poetry: The New Formalism and the New Narrative. Crosscurrents*, special issue, 8 (January 1989).

Allen, Donald M., ed. *The New American Poetry: 1945-1960*. New York: Grove, 1960.

Allen and Warren Tallman, eds. *Poetics of the New American Poetry*. New York: Grove, 1974.

Altieri, Charles. *Enlarging the Temple: New Directions in American Poetry During the 1960s*. Lewisburg, Pa.: Bucknell University Presses / London: Associated University Presses, 1979.

Altieri. *Self and Sensibility in Contemporary American Poetry*. New York: Cambridge University Press, 1984.

Ashbery, John, ed. *The Best American Poetry 1988*. New York: Scribners, 1988.

Bawer, Bruce. *The Middle Generation: The Lives and Poetry of Delmore Schwartz, Randall Jarrell, John Berryman, and Robert Lowell*. Hamden, Conn.: Archon, 1986.

Bell, Marvin. *Old Snow Just Melting*. Ann Arbor: University of Michigan Press, 1983.

Berg, Stephen, and Robert Mezey, eds. *Naked Poetry: Recent American Poetry in Open Forms*. Indianapolis: Bobbs-Merrill, 1969.

Berg and Mezey, eds. *The New Naked Poetry: Recent American Poetry in Open Forms*. Indianapolis: Bobbs-Merrill, 1976.

Berke, Roberta Elzey. *Bounds Out of Bounds: A Compass for Recent American and British Poetry*. New York: Oxford University Press, 1981.

Biggs, Mary. *A Gift that Cannot Be Refused: The Writing and Publishing of Contemporary American Poetry*. New York: Greenwood Press, 1990.

Bigsby, C. W. E., ed. *The Black American Writer*. De Land, Fla.: Everett/Edwards, 1969.

Bloom, Harold. *Figures of Capable Imagination*. New York: Seabury Press, 1976.

Bloom, ed. *American Poetry 1915-1945*. New York: Chelsea House, 1987.

Bloom, ed. *American Poetry 1946-1965*. New York: Chelsea House, 1987.

Bloom, ed. *Contemporary Poets*. New York: Chelsea House, 1987.

Bly, Robert. *Talking All Morning*. Ann Arbor: University of Michigan Press, 1980.

Boyars, Robert, ed. *Contemporary Poetry in America*. New York: Schocken Books, 1974.

Breslin, James E. B. *From Modern to Contemporary: American Poetry: 1945-1965*. Chicago & London: University of Chicago Press, 1984.

Cambon, Glauco. *Recent American Poetry*. Minneapolis: University of Minnesota Press, 1962.

Cargas, Harry J. *Daniel Berrigan and Contemporary Protest Poetry*. New Haven, Conn.: College & University Press, 1972.

Carr, John, ed. *Kite-Flying and Other Irrational Acts: Conversations with Twelve Southern Writers*. Baton Rouge: Louisiana State University Press, 1972.

Carruth, Hayden. *Effluences from the Sacred Caves*. Ann Arbor: University of Michigan Press, 1983.

Charters, Samuel. *Some Poems/Poets: Studies in American Underground Poetry Since 1945*. Berkeley: Oyez, 1971.

Christopher, Nicholas. *Under 35: The New Generation of American Poets*. New York: Doubleday, 1989.

Clampitt, Amy. *Predecessors, Et Cetera*. Ann Arbor: University of Michigan Press, 1991.

Clark, Tom. *The Poetry Beat*. Ann Arbor: University of Michigan Press, 1990.

Conversations with Writers, 2 volumes. Detroit: Bruccoli Clark/Gale Research, 1977, 1978.

Cooke, Bruce. *The Beat Generation*. New York: Scribners, 1971.

Dacey, Philip, and David Jauss, eds. *Strong Measures: Contemporary American Poetry in Traditional Forms*. New York: Harper & Row, 1986.

David, Lloyd, and Robert Irwin, eds. *Contemporary American Poetry: A Checklist*. Metuchen, N.J.: Scarecrow, 1975.

Davison, Peter. *One of the Dangerous Trades*. Ann Arbor: University of Michigan Press, 1991.

Deodene, Frank, and William P. French, eds. *Black American Poetry Since 1944: A Preliminary Checklist*. Chatham, N.J.: Chatham Bookseller, 1971.

Dickey, James. *Babel to Byzantium: Poets & Poetry Now*. New York: Farrar, Straus & Giroux, 1968.

Dickey. *Spinning the Crystal Ball: Some Guesses at the Future of American Poetry*. Washington, D.C.: Library of Congress, 1967.

Dickey. *The Suspect in Poetry*. Madison, Minn.: Sixties Press, 1964.

DiYanni, Robert, ed. *Modern American Poets: Their Voices and Visions*. New York: Random House, 1987.

Dodsworth, Martin, ed. *The Survival of Poetry: A Contemporary Survey*. London: Faber & Faber, 1970.

Duberman, Martin. *Black Mountain: An Exploration in Community*. New York: Dutton, 1972.

Ehrhart, W. D., ed. *Carrying the Darkness: The Poetry of the Vietnam War*. Lubbock: Texas Tech University Press, 1989.

Ehrhart, ed. *Unaccustomed Mercy: Soldier-Poets of the Vietnam War.* Lubbock: Texas Tech University Press, 1989.

Ellmann, Richard, and Robert O'Clair, eds. *The Norton Anthology of Modern Poetry*, second edition. New York: Norton, 1988.

Feirstein, Frederick, ed. *Expansive Poetry: Essays on the New Narrative & the New Formalism.* Santa Cruz: Story Line Press, 1989.

Feldman, Gene, and Max Gartenberg, eds. *The Beat Generation and the Angry Young Men.* New York: Citadel, 1958.

Fifty Years of American Poetry: Anniversary Volume for the Academy of American Poets. New York: Abrams, 1984.

First Printings of American Authors, 5 volumes. Detroit: Bruccoli Clark/Gale Research, 1977-1987.

Fox, Hugh, ed. *The Living Underground: An Anthology of Contemporary American Poets.* New York: Whitsun, 1973.

Francis, Robert. *Pot Shots at Poetry.* Ann Arbor: University of Michigan Press, 1980.

French, Warren, ed. *The Fifties: Fiction, Poetry, Drama.* De Land, Fla.: Everett/Edwards, 1970.

Gallagher, Tess. *A Concert of Tenses.* Ann Arbor: University of Michigan Press, 1986.

Gayle, Addison, Jr., ed. *Black Expression: Essays by and about Black Americans in the Creative Arts.* New York: Weybright & Talley, 1969.

Gershator, Phillis, ed. *A Bibliographic Guide to the Literature of Contemporary American Poetry, 1970-1975.* Metuchen, N.J.: Scarecrow, 1976.

Gioia, Dana. *Can Poetry Matter?: Essays on Poetry and American Culture.* St. Paul: Graywolf, 1992.

Glicksberg, Charles I. *The Sexual Revolution in Modern American Literature.* New York: Humanities Press, 1972.

Gould, Joan. *Modern American Women Poets.* New York: Dodd, Mead, 1984.

Graham, Jorie, ed. *The Best American Poetry 1990.* New York: Scribners, 1990.

Guttman, Allen. *The Jewish Writer in America: Assimilation and the Crisis of Identity.* New York: Oxford University Press, 1971.

Haines, John. *Living Off the Country.* Ann Arbor: University of Michigan Press, 1981.

Hall, Donald. *Goatfoot Milktongue Twinbird.* Ann Arbor: University of Michigan Press, 1978.

Hall. *Poetry and Ambition.* Ann Arbor: University of Michigan Press, 1988.

Hall. *The Weather for Poetry.* Ann Arbor: University of Michigan Press, 1982.

Hall, ed. *The Best American Poetry 1989.* New York: Scribners, 1989.

Hall, ed. *Contemporary American Poetry*. Baltimore: Penguin, 1962.

Halpern, Daniel, ed. *The American Poetry Anthology*. New York: Avon, 1975.

Hamilton, Ian. *A Poetry Chronicle*. New York: Barnes & Noble, 1973.

Harris, Marie, and Kathleen Aguero, eds. *An Ear to the Ground: An Anthology of Contemporary American Poetry*. Athens: University of Georgia Press, 1989.

Hassan, Ihab. *Contemporary American Literature, 1945-1972: An Introduction*. New York: Ungar, 1973.

Hayden, Robert. *Collected Prose*. Ann Arbor: University of Michigan Press, 1984.

Henderson, Stephen, ed. *Understanding the New Black Poetry*. New York: Morrow, 1973.

Heyen, William, ed. *American Poets in 1976*. Indianapolis: Bobbs-Merrill, 1976.

Hill, Herbert, ed. *Anger and Beyond: The Negro Writer in the United States*. New York: Harper & Row, 1966.

Hine, Daryl, and Joseph Parisi, eds. *The "Poetry" Anthology 1912-1977*. Boston: Houghton Mifflin, 1978.

Hoffman, Daniel, ed. *American Poetry and Poetics*. Garden City, N.Y.: Doubleday, 1962.

Hoffman, ed. *Harvard Guide to Contemporary American Writing*. Cambridge & London: Belknap Press of Harvard University Press, 1979.

Hoffman, ed. *New Poets 1970*. Philadelphia: Department of English, University of Pennsylvania, 1970.

Holden, Jonathan. *The Fate of American Poetry*. Athens: University of Georgia Press, 1991.

Holden. *Style and Authenticity in Postmodern Poetry*. Columbia: University of Missouri Press, 1986.

Hollander, John, ed. *Modern Poetry: Essays in Criticism*. London, Oxford & New York: Oxford University Press, 1968.

Howard, Richard. *Alone with America: Essays on the Art of Poetry in the United States since 1950*, enlarged edition. New York: Atheneum, 1980.

Howard, ed. *Preferences: 51 American Poets Choose Poems From Their Own Work and From the Past*. New York: Viking, 1974.

Ignatow, David. *Open Between Us*. Ann Arbor: University of Michigan Press, 1980.

Ignatow, ed. *Political Poetry*. New York: Chelsea, 1960.

Ingersoll, Earl G., and others, eds. *The Post-Confessionals*. Rutherford, N.J.: Fairleigh Dickinson University Press / London & Toronto: Associated University Presses, 1989.

Juhasz, Suzanne. *Naked and Fiery Forms: Modern American Poetry by Women, A New Tradition*. New York: Harper & Row, 1976.

Justice, Donald. *Platonic Scripts*. Ann Arbor: University of Michigan Press, 1984.

Kalstone, David. *Five Temperaments*. New York: Oxford University Press, 1977.

Kazin, Alfred. *Contemporaries*. Boston: Little, Brown, 1962.

Keller, Lynn. *Remaking It New: Contemporary American Poetry and the Modern Tradition*. New York: Cambridge University Press, 1987.

Kinnell, Galway. *Walking Down the Stairs*. Ann Arbor: University of Michigan Press, 1978.

Kostelanetz, Richard. *The Old Poetries and the New*. Ann Arbor: University of Michigan Press, 1981.

Kostelanetz, ed. *The Young American Writers: Fiction, Poetry, Drama, and Criticism*. New York: Funk & Wagnalls, 1967.

Kumin, Maxine. *To Make a Prairie*. Ann Arbor: University of Michigan Press, 1979.

Lacey, Paul A. *The Inner War: Forms and Themes in Recent American Poetry*. Philadelphia: Fortress Press, 1972.

Leary, Paris, and Robert Kelly, eds. *A Controversy of Poets*. Garden City, N.Y.: Anchor, 1965.

Lee, Al, ed. *The Major Young Poets*. New York: Meridian, 1971.

Lehman, David, ed. *Ecstatic Occasions, Expedient Forms: 65 Leading Contemporary Poets Select and Comment on Their Poems*. New York: Collier, 1987.

Lensing, George S., and Ronald Moran. *Four Poets and the Emotive Imagination: Robert Bly, James Wright, Louis Simpson, and William Stafford*. Baton Rouge: Louisiana State University Press, 1976.

Lepper, Gary M. *A Bibliographical Introduction to Seventy-Five Modern American Authors*. Berkeley: Serendipity Books, 1976.

Levertov, Denise. *The Poet in the World*. New York: New Directions, 1973.

Levine, Philip. *Don't Ask*. Ann Arbor: University of Michigan Press, 1981.

Libby, Anthony. *Mythologies of Nothing: Mystical Death in American Poetry 1940-1970*. Urbana & Chicago: University of Illinois Press, 1984.

Lieberman, Laurence. *Unassigned Frequencies*. Urbana: University of Illinois Press, 1977.

Logan, John. *A Ballet for the Ear*. Ann Arbor: University of Michigan Press, 1983.

Malkoff, Karl. *Crowell's Handbook of Contemporary American Poetry*. New York: Crowell, 1973.

Malkoff. *Escape from the Self: A Study in Contemporary American Poetry and Poetics*. New York: Columbia University Press, 1977.

Margolies, Edward. *Native Sons: A Critical Study of Twentieth-Century Negro American Authors*. Philadelphia & New York: Lippincott, 1968.

Martin, Robert K. *The Homosexual Tradition in American Poetry*. Austin: University of Texas Press, 1979.

Martz, William J., ed. *The Distinctive Voice.* Glenview, Ill.: Scott, Foresman, 1966.

Matthews, William. *Curiosities.* Ann Arbor: University of Michigan Press, 1989.

Mazzaro, Jerome. *Postmodern American Poetry.* Urbana & Chicago: University of Illinois Press, 1980.

Mazzaro, ed. *Modern American Poets.* New York: McKay, 1970.

McCorkle, James. *The Still Performance: Writing, Self, and Interconnection in Five Postmodern American Poets.* Charlottesville: University Press of Virginia, 1989.

McDowell, Robert, ed. *Poetry After Modernism.* Brownsville, Oreg: Story Line Press, 1990.

McPhillips, Robert, ed. *The New Formalism in American Poetry. Verse,* special issue, 7 (Winter 1990).

Meredith, William. *Poems Are Hard to Read.* Ann Arbor: University of Michigan Press, 1991.

Mersmann, James F. *Out of the Vietnam Vortex: A Study of Poets and Poetry Against the War.* Lawrence: University Press of Kansas, 1974.

Mills, Ralph J., Jr. *Cry of the Human: Essays on Contemporary American Poetry.* Urbana & Chicago: University of Illinois Press, 1975.

Molesworth, Charles. *The Fierce Embrace: A Study of Contemporary American Poetry.* Columbia & London: University of Missouri Press, 1979.

Morse, Carl, and Joan Larkin, eds. *Gay and Lesbian Poetry in Our Time.* New York: St. Martin's Press, 1988.

Moss, Howard, ed. *The Poet's Story.* New York: Macmillan, 1973.

Myers, Carol Fairbanks. *Women in Literature: Criticism of the Seventies.* Metuchen, N.J.: Scarecrow, 1976.

Myers, Jack, and Michael Sims. *The Longman Dictionary of Poetic Terms.* New York: Longman, 1989.

Nielsen, Aldon Lynn. *Reading Race: White American Poets and the Racial Discourse in the 20th Century.* Athens: University of Georgia Press, 1988.

Nims, John Frederick. *A Local Habitation.* Ann Arbor: University of Michigan Press, 1985.

Oberg, Arthur. *Modern American Lyric.* New Brunswick: Rutgers University Press, 1977.

O'Brien, John, ed. *Interviews with Black Writers.* New York: Liveright, 1973.

Oresick, Peter, and Nicholas Coles, eds. *Working Classics: Poems on Industrial Life.* Urbana: University of Illinois Press, 1990.

Ostriker, Alicia. *Stealing the Language: The Emergence of Women's Poetry in America.* Boston: Beacon, 1986.

Ostriker. *Writing Like a Woman.* Ann Arbor: University of Michigan Press, 1983.

Packard, William, ed. *The Craft of Poetry: Interviews from the New York Quarterly.* Garden City, N.Y.: Doubleday, 1974.

Padgett, Ron, and David Shapiro, eds. *An Anthology of New York Poets*. New York: Vintage, 1970.

Paolucci, Anne, ed. *Dante's Influence on American Writers, 1776-1976*. New York: Griffon House for the Dante Society of America, 1977.

Parkinson, Thomas, ed. *A Casebook on The Beats*. New York: Crowell, 1961.

Paul, Sherman. *In Search of the Primitive: Rereading David Antin, Jerome Rothenberg, and Gary Snyder*. Baton Rouge: Louisiana State University Press, 1986.

Perkins, David. *A History of Modern Poetry*, 2 volumes. Cambridge: Belknap Press of Harvard University Press, 1987.

Perloff, Marjorie. *Frank O'Hara: Poet among Painters*. New York: Braziller, 1977.

Perloff. *The Poetics of Indeterminacy: Rimbaud to Cage*. Princeton: Princeton University Press, 1981.

Peters, Robert. *The Great American Poetry Bake-off*, 4 volumes. Metuchen, N.J.: Scarecrow, 1979-1991.

Peters. *Hunting the Snark: A Compendium of New Poetic Terminology*. New York: Paragon House, 1989.

Peters. *The Peters Black and Blue Guide to Current Literary Journals*, 3 volumes. Silver Spring, Md.: Cherry Valley Editions, 1983, 1985, 1987.

Phillips, Robert. *The Confessional Poets*. Carbondale: Southern Illinois University Press, 1973.

Piercy, Marge. *Parti-Colored Blocks for a Quilt*. Ann Arbor: University of Michigan Press, 1982.

Pinsky, Robert. *The Situation in Poetry: Contemporary Poetry and Its Tradition*. Princeton: Princeton University Press, 1976.

Pope, Deborah. *A Separate Vision: Isolation in American Women Poets*. Baton Rouge: Louisiana State University Press, 1984.

Poulin, A., Jr., ed. *Contemporary American Poetry*, fourth edition. Boston: Houghton Mifflin, 1985.

Power of the Word [television series], Bill Moyers, host. PBS, 15 September - 20 October 1989 [available on videocassette from PBS, P.O. Box 68618, Indianapolis, Ind. 46286].

Prunty, Wyatt. *"Fallen from the Symboled World": Precedents for the New Formalism*. New York: Oxford University Press, 1990.

Ramsey, Paul, ed. *Contemporary Religious Poetry*. Mahwah, N.J.: Paulist Press, 1987.

Ransom, John Crowe, Delmore Schwartz, and John Hall Wheelock. *American Poetry at Mid-Century*. Washington, D.C.: Library of Congress, 1958.

Rexroth, Kenneth. *American Poetry in the Twentieth Century*. New York: Herder & Herder, 1971.

Richman, Robert. *The Direction of Poetry: An Anthology of Rhymed and Metered Verse Written in the English Language Since 1975*. Boston: Houghton Mifflin, 1988.

Rosenthal, M. L. *The Modern Poets: A Critical Introduction*. London, Oxford & New York: Oxford University Press, 1960.

Sexton, Anne. *No Evil Star*. Ann Arbor: University of Michigan Press, 1985.

Shaw, Robert B., ed. *American Poets Since 1960: Some Critical Perspectives*. Cheadle, England: Carcanet Press, 1973.

Simic, Charles. *The Uncertain Certainty*. Ann Arbor: University of Michigan Press, 1985.

Simic. *Wonderful Words, Silent Truth*. Ann Arbor: University of Michigan Press, 1990.

Simpson, Louis. *The Character of the Poet*. Ann Arbor: University of Michigan Press, 1986.

Simpson, *Collected Prose*. New York: Paragon House, 1989.

Simpson. *A Company of Poets*. Ann Arbor: University of Michigan Press, 1981.

Slesinger, Warren, ed. *Spreading the Word: Editors on Poetry*. Columbia, S.C.: Bench Press, 1990.

Smith, Dave, and David Bottoms, eds. *The Morrow Anthology of Younger American Poets*. New York: Quill, 1985.

Spears, Monroe K. *Dionysus and the City: Modernism in Twentieth Century Poetry*. New York: Oxford University Press, 1970.

Stafford, William. *Writing the Australian Crawl*. Ann Arbor: University of Michigan Press, 1986.

Stafford. *You Must Revise Your Life*. Ann Arbor: University of Michigan Press, 1978.

Steele, Timothy. *Missing Measures: Modern Poetry and the Revolt Against Meter*. Fayetteville: University of Arkansas Press, 1990.

Steinman, Lisa Malinowski. *Made in America: Science, Technology, and American Modern Poets*. New Haven: Yale University Press, 1987.

Stepanchev, Stephen. *American Poetry Since 1945: A Critical Survey*. New York: Harper & Row, 1965.

Stokesbury, Leon, ed. *Articles of War: A Collection of American Poetry About World War II*. Fayetteville: University of Arkansas Press, 1990.

Stokesbury, ed. *The Made Thing: An Anthology of Contemporary Southern Poetry*. Fayetteville: University of Arkansas Press, 1987.

Strand, Mark, and David Lehman, eds. *The Best American Poetry 1991*. New York: Scribners, 1991.

Strand, ed. *The Contemporary American Poets: American Poetry Since 1940*. New York: World, 1969.

Taylor, Henry. *Compulsory Figures*. Baton Rouge: Louisiana State University Press, 1992.

Trawick, Leonard M., ed. *World, Self, Poem: Essays on Contemporary Poetry from the "Jubilation of Poets."* Kent, Ohio: Kent State University Press, 1990.

Turco, Lewis Putnam. *The New Book of Forms: A Handbook of Poetics.* Hanover, N.H.: University Presses of New England, 1986.

Turco. *The Public Poet: Five Lectures on the Art and Craft of Poetry.* Ashland, Ohio: Ashland Poetry Press, 1991.

Turco. *Visions and Revisions of American Poetry.* Fayetteville: University of Arkansas Press, 1986.

Turner, Alberta, ed. *50 Contemporary Poets: The Creative Process.* New York: Longman, 1977.

Turner, ed. *45 Contemporary Poets: The Creative Process.* New York: Longman, 1985.

Turner, Darwin T. *Afro-American Writers.* New York: Appleton-Century-Crofts, 1970.

Turner, Frederick. *Natural Classicism: Essays on Literature and Science.* New York: Paragon House, 1985.

Tytell, John. *Naked Angels: The Lives and Literature of the Beat Generation.* New York: McGraw-Hill, 1976.

Vendler, Helen. *Part of Nature, Part of Us: Modern American Poets.* Cambridge: Harvard University Press, 1980.

Vendler, ed. *The Harvard Book of Contemporary Poetry.* Cambridge: Belknap Press of Harvard University Press, 1985.

Vendler, ed. *Voices & Visions: The Poet in America.* New York: Random House, 1987.

Vinson, James, and D. L. Kirkpatrick, eds. *Contemporary Poets,* third edition. New York: St. Martin's Press, 1985.

Voices & Visions [television series]. Annenberg/CPB/SCETV, 1988 [available on videocassette from SCETV, 2712 Millwood Avenue, Columbia, S.C. 29205-1221].

Von Hallberg, Robert. *American Poetry and Culture 1945-1980.* Cambridge: Harvard University Press, 1985.

Waggoner, Hyatt H. *American Poets: From the Puritans to the Present,* revised edition. Baton Rouge: Louisiana State University Press, 1984.

Wakoski, Diane. *Creating a Personal Mythology.* Los Angeles: Black Sparrow Press, 1975.

Wakoski. *Toward a New Poetry.* Ann Arbor: University of Michigan Press, 1980.

Wallace, Ronald, ed. *Vital Signs: Contemporary American Poetry from the University Presses.* Madison: University of Wisconsin Press, 1989.

Williamson, Alan. *Introspection and Contemporary Poetry.* Cambridge: Harvard University Press, 1984.

Wright, Charles. *Halflife.* Ann Arbor: University of Michigan Press, 1988.

Wright, James. *Collected Prose.* Ann Arbor: University of Michigan Press, 1982.

Writers at Work: The "Paris Review" Interviews, 8 volumes. New York: Viking, 1958-1988.

Writers' Workshop [television series], William Price Fox, host. PBS/SCETV, 1982 [available on videocassette from SCETV, 2712 Millwood Avenue, Columbia, S.C. 29205-1221].

Zaranka, William, ed. *The Brand-X Anthology of Poetry*. Cambridge: Apple-Wood Books, 1981.

Contributors

Amber Ahlstrom ....*University of New Hampshire*
Julie Gleason Alford ....*Lamar University*
Annette Allen ....*Salem College, Winston-Salem, North Carolina*
Christopher Baker...*Lamar University*
Wendy Barker...*University of Texas at San Antonio*
Gerri Bates ....*Howard University*
Ronald Baughman...*University of South Carolina*
Jacqueline Brice-Finch ....*James Madison University*
Peyton Brien...*University of Toronto*
Michael Burns ....*Southwest Missouri State University*
Sidney Burris ....*University of Arkansas*
Fred Chappell ....*University of North Carolina at Greensboro*
Robert Darling ....*Keuka College*
William V. Davis...*Baylor University*
Barbara Drake...*Linfield College*
Nancy Eimers ....*Western Michigan University*
Herbert V. Fackler ....*University of Southwestern Louisiana*
C. Renee Field...*Lamar University*
Richard Flynn ....*Georgia Southern University*
Bob Gaskin ....*Lamar University*
Norman German ....*Southeastern Louisiana University*
Jenny Goodman ....*University of Massachusetts—Amherst*
R. S. Gwynn...*Lamar University*
Brenda L. Herbel...*Odessa, Texas*
Jonathan Holden...*Kansas State University*
Jane Hoogestraat...*Southwest Missouri State University*
Kirkland C. Jones...*Lamar University*
Roger D. Jones...*Southwest Texas State University*
X. J. Kennedy...*Bedford, Massachusetts*
Laura B. Kennelly...*University of North Texas*
Robin M. Latimer...*Lamar University*
Robert McPhillips ....*Iona College*
Felicia Mitchell ....*Emory and Henry College*
Richard Moore ....*New England Conservatory of Music*
Joe Nordgren ....*Lamar University*
Gary Pacernick...*Wright State University*
Joyce Pettis ....*North Carolina State University*
Brian Abel Ragen ....*Southern Illinois University at Edwardsville*
Clay Reynolds ....*Denton, Texas*
Lynn Risser ....*Texas Wesleyan University*
Marie M. Schein ....*University of North Texas*
De Villo Sloan ....*Wells College*
James David Spreckels ....*Lamar University*
David Starkey ....*Francis Marion College*
Carole Stone ....*Montclair State College*
Tim Summerlin...*Lamar University*

Thomas Swiss ....*Duke University*
Jane L. Tanner ....*University of North Texas*
Marcella Thompson ....*University of Arkansas*
Ann Townsend ....*Denison University*
Lewis Turco ....*State University of New York at Oswego*
Jack Turner...*University of South Carolina*
Gwendolyn Whitehead...*Lamar University*
Chris Willerton...*Abilene Christian University*
Amy Williams ....*University of Texas at San Antonio*
Steven M. Wilson ....*Southwest Texas State University*

Cumulative Index

Dictionary of Literary Biography, Volumes 1-120
Dictionary of Literary Biography Yearbook, 1980-1991
Dictionary of Literary Biography Documentary Series, Volumes 1-9

Cumulative Index

DLB before number: *Dictionary of Literary Biography,* Volumes 1-120
Y before number: *Dictionary of Literary Biography Yearbook,* 1980-1991
DS before number: *Dictionary of Literary Biography Documentary Series,* Volumes 1-9

A

Cumulative Index

Cumulative Index

J

K

L

M

N

P

S

ACL0392

Ref
PS
323.5
A5
1992

9/22/92
S.O,
113 –

(Continued from front endsheets)

80: *Restoration and Eighteenth-Century Dramatists,* First Series, edited by Paula R. Backscheider (1989)

81: *Austrian Fiction Writers, 1875-1913,* edited by James Hardin and Donald G. Daviau (1989)

82: *Chicano Writers,* First Series, edited by Francisco A. Lomelí and Carl R. Shirley (1989)

83: *French Novelists Since 1960,* edited by Catharine Savage Brosman (1989)

84: *Restoration and Eighteenth-Century Dramatists,* Second Series, edited by Paula R. Backscheider (1989)

85: *Austrian Fiction Writers After 1914,* edited by James Hardin and Donald G. Daviau (1989)

86: *American Short-Story Writers, 1910-1945,* First Series, edited by Bobby Ellen Kimbel (1989)

87: *British Mystery and Thriller Writers Since 1940,* First Series, edited by Bernard Benstock and Thomas F. Staley (1989)

88: *Canadian Writers, 1920-1959,* Second Series, edited by W. H. New (1989)

89: *Restoration and Eighteenth-Century Dramatists,* Third Series, edited by Paula R. Backscheider (1989)

90: *German Writers in the Age of Goethe, 1789-1832,* edited by James Hardin and Christoph E. Schweitzer (1989)

91: *American Magazine Journalists, 1900-1960,* First Series, edited by Sam G. Riley (1990)

92: *Canadian Writers, 1890-1920,* edited by W. H. New (1990)

93: *British Romantic Poets, 1789-1832,* First Series, edited by John R. Greenfield (1990)

94: *German Writers in the Age of Goethe: Sturm und Drang to Classicism,* edited by James Hardin and Christoph E. Schweitzer (1990)

95: *Eighteenth-Century British Poets,* First Series, edited by John Sitter (1990)

96: *British Romantic Poets, 1789-1832,* Second Series, edited by John R. Greenfield (1990)

97: *German Writers from the Enlightenment to Sturm und Drang, 1720-1764,* edited by James Hardin and Christoph E. Schweitzer (1990)

98: *Modern British Essayists,* First Series, edited by Robert Beum (1990)

99: *Canadian Writers Before 1890,* edited by W. H. New (1990)

100: *Modern British Essayists,* Second Series, edited by Robert Beum (1990)

101: *British Prose Writers, 1660-1800,* First Series, edited by Donald T. Siebert (1991)

102: *American Short-Story Writers, 1910-1945,* Second Series, edited by Bobby Ellen Kimbel (1991)

103: *American Literary Biographers,* First Series, edited by Steven Serafin (1991)

104: *British Prose Writers, 1660-1800,* Second Series, edited by Donald T. Siebert (1991)

105: *American Poets Since World War II,* Second Series, edited by R. S. Gwynn (1991)

106: *British Literary Publishing Houses, 1820-1880,* edited by Patricia J. Anderson and Jonathan Rose (1991)

107: *British Romantic Prose Writers, 1789-1832,* First Series, edited by John R. Greenfield (1991)

108: *Twentieth-Century Spanish Poets,* First Series, edited by Michael L. Perna (1991)

109: *Eighteenth-Century British Poets,* Second Series, edited by John Sitter (1991)

110: *British Romantic Prose Writers, 1789-1832,* Second Series, edited by John R. Greenfield (1991)

111: *American Literary Biographers,* Second Series, edited by Steven Serafin (1991)

112: *British Literary Publishing Houses, 1881-1965,* edited by Jonathan Rose and Patricia J. Anderson (1991)

113: *Modern Latin-American Fiction Writers,* First Series, edited by William Luis (1992)

114: *Twentieth-Century Italian Poets,* First Series, edited by Giovanna Wedel De Stasio, Glauco Cambon, and Antonio Illiano (1992)

115: *Medieval Philosophers,* edited by Jeremiah Hackett (1992)

116: *Bri[...] [...]dited by Bradford K. Mudge (1992)

117: *Tw[...] African Writers,* First Series, edited by Bernth Lindfors and [...]

For Reference

Not To Be Taken

From This Building

0 00 02 0549138 4
MIDDLEBURY COLLEGE

ISBN 0-8103-7597-4